American National Biography On[line]

Free subscription with purchase of a new book!

D0780925

Visit the online user's guide of *American National Biography* at www.anb.org/userguide

American National Biography Online offers **portraits of more than 18,300 women and men**—from all eras and walks of life—whose lives have shaped the nation. Originally published in 24 volumes in 1999, the *American National Biography* won instant acclaim as the new authority in American biographies. **Winner of the American Library Association's Dartmouth Medal** as the best reference work of the year, the *ANB* now serves readers in thousands of school, public, and academic libraries around the world.

The publication of the online edition makes the *ANB* even more useful as a dynamic source of information—updated semi-annually, with hundreds of new entries each year and revisions of previously published entries to enhance their accuracy and currency. The *ANB Online* features **thousands of illustrations**, more than **80,000 hyperlinked cross-references**, links to select websites, and powerful search capabilities.

- Over 18,300 biographies, including the 17,435 original biographies from the print edition
- New biographies added and others revised semi-annually—including articles on recently deceased notables as well as figures from the past who were not subjects in the print edition
- Over 900 articles from *The Oxford Companion to United States History* provide historical and social context to the biographies
- Over 2,500 illustrations with more added with each update
- Regular updates to the bibliographies

To activate your **FREE** subscription to *American National Biography Online*, go to https://ams.oup.com/order/ANBAHSSCRIP and follow the instructions for entering your activation code.

Please note that your subscription will start as soon as the activation code is entered. This code must be entered before June 15, 2014 in order to be valid. This offer is only valid in the Americas and the Caribbean.

FFPH-WE1Y-RTI0-R9JI

www.anb.org

OXFORD
UNIVERSITY PRESS

ANB Online is a dynamic, easy-to-use resource

Search

- By full text (words and phrases)
- By subject name
- By gender
- By occupation or realm of renown
- By birth date
- By birthplace
- By death date
- By contributor name

Your search results will display alphabetically. The first listing of results are biographies from the ANB Online. Some of the entries are followed by a camera and/or globe, indicating that there is a picture or online resource available. All online resources are carefully reviewed by our editors.

A Teacher's Guide to Using *ANB Online*: Make *ANB Online* work for you with a Teacher's Guide designed to help you get the most out of this valuable resource.

- How to Read a Biographical Essay
- An Introductory Lesson: *Thomas Jefferson*
- Using the Image to Learn More about the Subject: *Abigail Adams*
- Using Biography with Primary Sources: *Plessy v. Ferguson*
- Using Cross-References to do Collective Biography: *The Cuban Missile Crisis*
- A Research Lesson: *Frederick Douglass*

Jump-Start Your Research: You can now jump-start your research by browsing through pre-selected lists of articles from the *ANB Online* and *The Oxford Companion to United States History*, encyclopedia content that supports the 19,000 biographies. Selected by Oxford editors, the 12 research topics cover American Literature, Arts in America, Black History, Civil Rights Movement, Civil War, Depression and New Deal, Frontier and Western Expansion, Gilded Age, Hispanic American Heritage, Native American Heritage, Women's History, and World War II.

Special Collections: A special search feature allows you to guide your research with specially selected collections that celebrate the diversity of American history: Black History, Women's History, Asian Pacific American Heritage, American Indian Heritage, and Hispanic Heritage.

The Oxford Companion to United States History: Over 900 articles from the acclaimed *The Oxford Companion to United States History* have been incorporated into *ANB Online* to enhance and enrich the study of history through biography. As big and as varied as the nation it portrays, *The Oxford Companion to United States History* explores not only America's political, diplomatic, and military history, but also social, cultural, and intellectual trends; science, technology, and medicine; the arts; and religion. The articles selected for inclusion in *ANB Online* expand the learning experience, providing context to the biographies and further illuminating the nation's history through defining events, social movements, ideologies, and even natural disasters and iconic sites.

www.anb.org

OXFORD
UNIVERSITY PRESS

Of the People

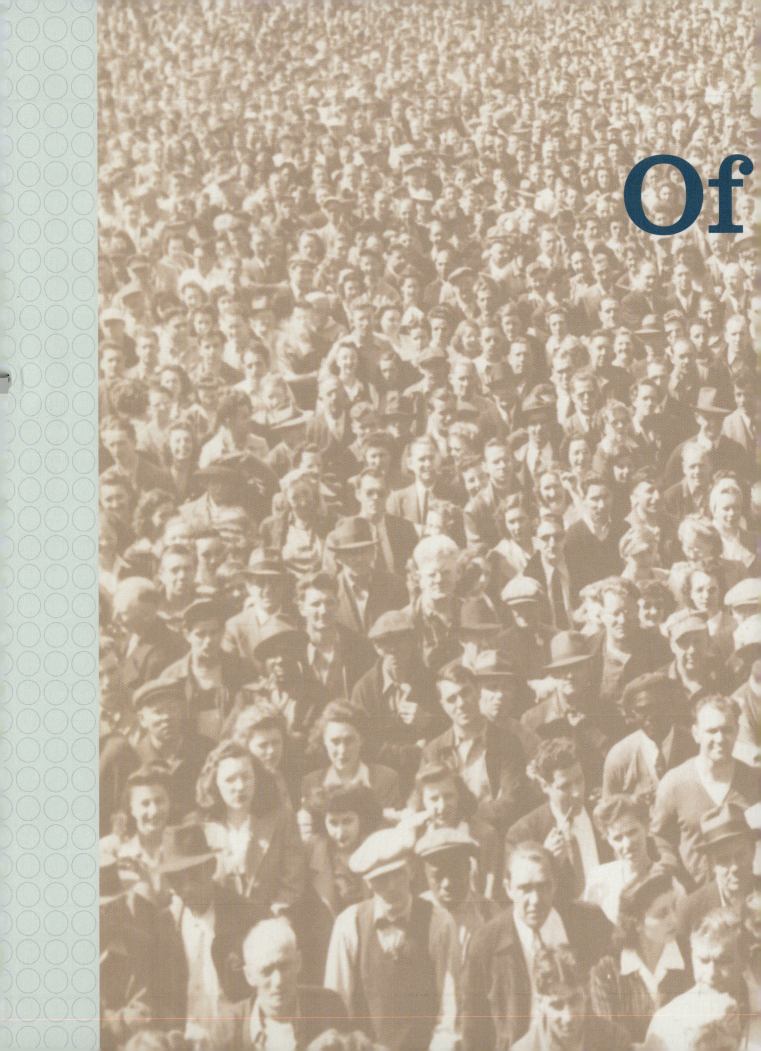

Of

the People

A HISTORY OF THE UNITED STATES

Volume II
Since 1865

James Oakes
City University of New York Graduate Center

Michael McGerr
Indiana University–Bloomington

Jan Ellen Lewis
Rutgers University, Newark

Nick Cullather
Indiana University–Bloomington

Jeanne Boydston
University of Wisconsin–Madison

New York   Oxford
Oxford University Press
2010

Jeanne Boydston
1944–2008
Historian, Teacher, Friend

Oxford University Press, Inc., publishes works that further Oxford University's
objective of excellence in research, scholarship, and education.

Oxford New York
Auckland Cape Town Dar es Salaam Hong Kong Karachi
Kuala Lumpur Madrid Melbourne Mexico City Nairobi
New Delhi Shanghai Taipei Toronto

With offices in
Argentina Austria Brazil Chile Czech Republic France Greece
Guatemala Hungary Italy Japan Poland Portugal Singapore
South Korea Switzerland Thailand Turkey Ukraine Vietnam

Published by Oxford University Press, Inc.
198 Madison Avenue, New York, New York 10016
http://www.oup.com

Oxford is a registered trademark of Oxford University Press

Library of Congress Cataloging-in-Publication Data

Of the people: a history of the United States/James Oakes . . . [et al.].—1st
    ed.
    p. cm.
    Includes index.
    ISBN 978-0-19-537103-1 (cloth)—ISBN 978-0-19-537094-2 (v. 1)—ISBN
    978-0-19-537095-9 (v. 2) 1. United States—History. 2. Democracy—United
    States—History. I. Oakes, James.
    E178.O37 2009
    973—dc22

                                                    2009021953

Printing number: 9 8 7 6 5 4 3 2 1

Printed in the United States of America
on acid-free paper

Contents

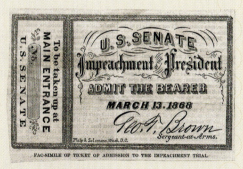

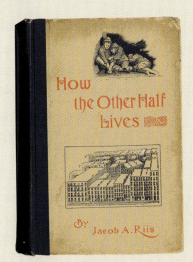

Chapter 19 ⬤⬤ The Politics of Industrial America, 1870–1892   **632**

Chapter 22 ⬤⬤⬤ A Global Power, 1914–1919   **726**

Chapter 23 ● The Modern Nation, 1920–1928   758

Chapter 26 ●●● The Cold War, 1945–1952   **858**

Chapter 27 ●●● The Consumer Society, 1945–1961   890

Chapter 28 ●●● The Rise and Fall of the New Liberalism, 1960–1968   **922**

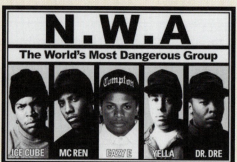

Chapter 31 ●●● "A Nation Transformed," 1989–2008   1032

Appendixes

Maps

Features

America and the World

Preface

At Gettysburg, Pennsylvania, on November 19, 1863, President Abraham Lincoln dedicated a memorial to the more than 3,000 Union soldiers who had died turning back a Confederate invasion in the first days of July. There were at least a few ways that the president could have justified the sad loss of life in the third year of a brutal war dividing North and South. He could have said it was necessary to destroy the Confederacy's cherished institution of slavery, to punish southerners for seceding from the United States, or to preserve the nation intact. Instead, at this crucial moment in American history, Lincoln gave a short, stunning speech about democracy. The president did not use the word, but he offered its essence. To honor the dead of Gettysburg, he called on northerners to ensure "that government of the people, by the people, for the people, shall not perish from the earth."

With these words, Lincoln put democracy at the center of the Civil War and at the center of American history. The authors of this book share his belief in the centrality of democracy; his words, "of the people," give our book its title and its main theme. We see American history as a story "of the people," of their struggles to shape their lives and their land.

Our choice of theme does not mean we believe that America has always been a democracy. Clearly, it has not. As Lincoln gave the Gettysburg Address, most African Americans still lived in slavery. American women, north and south, lacked rights that many men enjoyed; for all their disagreements, white southerners and northerners viewed Native Americans as enemies. Neither do we believe that there is only a single definition of democracy, either in the narrow sense of a particular form of government or in the larger one of a society whose members participate equally in its creation. Although Lincoln defined the northern cause as a struggle for democracy, southerners believed it was anything but democratic to force them to remain in the Union at gunpoint. As bloody draft riots in New York City in July 1863 made clear, many northern men thought it was anything but democratic to force them to fight in Lincoln's armies. Such disagreements have been typical of American history. For more than 500 years, people have struggled over whose vision of life in the New World would prevail.

It is precisely such struggles that offer the best angle of vision for seeing and understanding the most important developments in the nation's history. In particular, the democratic theme concentrates attention on the most fundamental concerns of history: people and power.

Lincoln's words serve as a reminder of the basic truth that history is about people. Across the 31 chapters of this book, we write extensively about complex events, such as the five-year savagery of the Civil War, and long-term transformations, such as the slow, halting evolution of democratic political institutions. But we write in the awareness that these developments are only abstractions unless they are grounded in the lives of people. The test of a historical narrative, we believe, is whether its characters are fully rounded, believable human beings.

We hope that our commitment to a history "of the people" is apparent on every page of this book. To underscore it, we open each chapter with an **"American Portrait"** feature, a story of someone whose life in one way or another embodies the basic theme of the pages to follow. So, we begin Chapter 8 on the United States in the 1790s with William Maclay, a senator from rural Pennsylvania, who feared that arrogant northeasterners and "pandering" Virginians would quickly turn the new nation into an aristocracy. In Chapter 23, we encounter 19-year-old Gertrude Ederle, whose solo swim across the English Channel and taste for cars and dancing epitomized the individualistic, consumer culture emerging in the 1920s.

The choice of Lincoln's words also reflects our belief that history is about power. To ask whether America was democratic at some point in the past is to ask whether all people had equal power to make their lives and their nation. Such questions of power necessarily take us to political processes, to the ways in which people work separately and collectively to enforce their will. We define politics quite broadly in this book. With the feminists of the 1960s, we believe that "the personal is the political," that power relations shape people's lives in private as well as in public. *Of the People* looks for democracy in the living room as well as the legislature, and in the bedroom as well as the business office.

To underscore our broad view of the political, each chapter presents an **"American Landscape"** feature, a particular place in time where issues of power appeared in especially sharp relief. So, Chapter 2 describes the sixteenth-century Native American villages of Huronia, whose social spaces and sexual relations reflected distinctive ideas about individual freedom and female power. Chapter 21 details the contrasting understandings of democracy at the heart of the early twentieth-century battle over creating a new water supply for San Francisco by building a dam in the Hetch Hetchy Valley of California.

Focusing on democracy, on people and power, we have necessarily written as wide-ranging a history as possible. In the features and in the main text, *Of the People* conveys both the unity and the great diversity of the American people across time and place. Lincoln's "people" have shared a common identity as Americans; but at the same time they have been many distinctive "peoples." So, we chronicle the racial and ethnic groups who have shaped America. We explore differences of religious and regional identity. We trace the changing nature of social classes. We examine the different ways that gender identities have been constructed and reconstructed over the centuries.

While treating different groups in their distinctiveness, we have integrated them into the broader narrative as much as possible. A true history "of the people" means not only acknowledging their individuality and diversity but also showing their interrelationships and their roles in the larger narrative.

Of the People also offers comprehensive coverage of the different spheres of human life—cultural as well as governmental, social as well as economic, environmental as well as military. This commitment to comprehensiveness is a reflection of our belief that all aspects of human existence are the stuff of history. It is also an expression of the fundamental theme of the book: the focus on democracy leads naturally to the study of people's struggles for power in every dimension of their lives. Moreover, the democratic approach emphasizes the interconnections between the different aspects of Americans' lives; we cannot understand politics and government without tracing their connection to economics, religion, culture, art, sexuality, and so on.

The economic connection is especially important. *Of the People* devotes much attention to economic life, to the ways in which Americans have worked and saved and spent. Economic power, the authors believe, is basic to democracy. Americans' power to shape their lives and their country has been greatly affected by whether they were farmers or hunters, plantation owners or slaves, wageworkers or capitalists, domestic servants or bureaucrats. The authors do not see economics as an impersonal, all-conquering force: instead, we try to show how the values and actions of ordinary people, as well as the laws and regulations of government, have made economic life.

We have also tried especially to place America in global context. The story of individual nation-states such as the United States remains a critically important kind of history. But the history of America, or any nation, cannot be adequately explained without understanding its relationship to transnational events and global developments. That is true for the first chapter of the book, which shows how America began to emerge from the collision of Native Americans, West Africans, and Europeans in the fifteenth and sixteenth centuries. It is just as true for the last chapter of the book, which demonstrates how globalization and the war on terror transformed the United States at the turn of the twenty-first century. In the chapters in between these two, the authors detail how the world has changed America and how America has changed the world. Reflecting the concerns of the rest of the book, we focus particularly on the movement of people, the evolution of power, and the attempt to spread democracy abroad.

To underscore the fundamental importance of global relationships, each chapter includes a feature on **"America and the World."** So, Chapter 15 reveals how ordinary Europeans' support for the abolition of slavery made it impossible for their governments to recognize the southern Confederacy. Chapter 20 shows how Singer, a pioneering American multinational company, began to export an economic vision of a consumer democracy along with its sewing machines in the nineteenth and early twentieth centuries.

In a sense, Singer had arrived at Abraham Lincoln's conclusion about the central importance of democracy in American life. The company wanted to sell sewing machines; the president wanted to sell a war. But both believed their audience would see democracy as quintessentially American. Whether they were right is the burden of this book.

Supplements

For Students

Oxford University Press is proud to offer a complete and authoritative supplements package for students—including print and new media resources designed for chapter review, for primary source reading, for essay writing, for test-preparation and for further research.

Student Companion Website at www.oup.com/us/ofthepeople

The open-access Online Study Center designed specifically for *Of the People: A History of the United States* helps students to review what they have learned from the

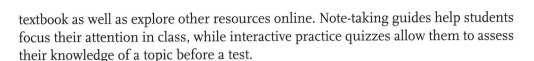

textbook as well as explore other resources online. Note-taking guides help students focus their attention in class, while interactive practice quizzes allow them to assess their knowledge of a topic before a test.

- **Online Study Guide**, including
  - ○ Note-taking outlines
  - ○ Multiple-choice and identification quizzes, (two quizzes per chapter, thirty question quizzes—*different* from those found in the Instructor's Manual/Testbank)
- **Primary Source Companion & Research Guide**, a brief online Research Primer, with a library of annotated links to primary and secondary sources in U.S. history.
- **Interactive Flashcards**, using key terms and people listed at the end of each chapter, help students remember who's who and what's what.

American National Biography Online www.anb.org

Students who purchase a **new** copy of Oakes's *Of the People: A History of the United States* will find an access code for a six-month (Volume 1 or 2) or a one-year **free subscription** to this powerful online resource published by Oxford University Press.

American National Biography Online offers **portraits of more than 17,400 women and men**—from all eras and walks of life—whose lives have shaped the nation. More than a decade in preparation, the *American National Biography* is the first biographical resource of this scope to be published in more than sixty years. Originally published in 24 volumes in 1999, the *American National Biography* won instant acclaim as the new authority in American biographies. **Winner of the American Library Association's Dartmouth Medal** as the best reference work of the year, the *ANB* now serves readers in thousands of school, public, and academic libraries around the world. The publication of the online edition makes the *ANB* even more useful as a dynamic source of information—updated semi-annually, with hundreds of new entries each year and revisions of previously published entries to enhance their accuracy and currency. The *ANB Online* features **thousands of illustrations**, more than **80,000 hyperlinked cross-references**, links to select websites, and powerful search capabilities.

ANB Online **is also a great teaching resource, since it can be actively incorporated into classroom lessons.** To assist teachers in fully utilizing *ANB Online*, we have prepared a Teacher's Guide to Using *ANB Online*. Developed with the participation of librarians and teachers, the Teacher's Guide offers six lessons that highlight the importance and value of studying biography as an end in itself and as a starting point for doing further research into the lives of those who shaped the American experience.

Writing History: A Guide for Students Third edition, by William Kelleher Storey, Associate Professor at Millsaps College.

Bringing together practical methods from both history and composition, *Writing History* provides a wealth of tips and advice to help students research and write essays for history classes. The book covers all aspects of writing about history, including **finding topics** and **researching** them, **interpreting source materials, drawing** inferences from sources, and constructing arguments. It concludes with three chapters that discuss writing effective sentences, using precise wording, and revising. Using numerous examples from the works of cultural, political, and social historians, *Writing History* serves as an ideal supplement to history courses that require students to conduct research. The third edition includes expanded sections on **peer editing** and **topic selection**, as well as new sections on searching and using the Internet. *Writing History* can be packaged for free with Oakes's *Of the People: A History of the United States*. Contact your Oxford University Press Sales Representative for more information.

The Information-Literate Historian: A Guide to Research for History Students by Jenny Presnell, *Information Services Library and History, American Studies,* and *Women's Studies Bibliographer, Miami University of Ohio*

This is the only book specifically designed to teach today's history student how to most successfully select and use sources—primary, secondary, and electronic—to carry out and present their research. Written by a college librarian, *The Information-Literate Historian* is an indispensable reference for historians, students, and other readers doing history research. *The Information-Literate Historian* can be packaged for free with Oakes's *Of the People: A History of the United States*. Contact your Oxford University Press Sales Representative for more information.

Primary Source Documents

Our Documents: 100 Milestone Documents from the National Archives brings documents to life, including facsimiles side-by-side with transcripts for students to explore, explanations, and a foreword provided by Michael Beschloss. This primary source book can be **packaged for free** with Oakes's *Of the People: A History of the United States*. Among the documents it contains are: Declaration of Independence; U.S. Constitution; Bill of Rights; Louisiana Purchase Treaty; Missouri Compromise; The Dred Scott decision; Emancipation Proclamation; Gettysburg Address; Fourteenth Amendment to the U.S. Constitution; Thomas Edison's lightbulb patent; Sherman Anti-Trust Act; Executive order for the Japanese relocation during wartime; Manhattan Project notebook; press release announcing U.S. recognition of Israel; President John F. Kennedy's inaugural address, as well as many more.

Other primary source books that can be packaged with Oakes's *Of the People: A History of the United States* include Chafe's **History of Our Time** and Bloom's **Takin' It to the Streets**, as well as **The Boisterous Sea of Liberty: A Documentary History of America from Discovery through the Civil War**; and **Documenting American Violence: A Sourcebook**.

For Professors

For decades American History professors have turned to Oxford University Press as the leading source for high quality readings and reference materials. Now, when you adopt Oakes's *Of the People: A History of the United States*, the Press will partner with you and make available its best supplemental materials and resources for your classroom. Listed here are several series of high interest, but you will want to talk with your Sales Representative to learn more about what can be made available, and about what would suit your course best.

Instructor's Manual and Testbank. This useful guide contains helpful teaching tools for experienced and first-time teachers alike. It can be made available to adopters upon request, and is also available electronically on the Instructor's Resource CD. This extensive manual and testbank contains:

- **Sample Syllabi**
- **Chapter Outlines**
- **In-Class Discussion Questions**
- **Lecture Ideas**
- **Oxford's Further Reading List**
- **Quizzes** (two per chapter, one per half of the chapter, content divided somewhat evenly down the middle of the chapter: 30 multiple choice questions each)
- **Tests** (two per chapter, each covering the entire chapter contents: each offering 10 identification/matching; 10 multiple-choice; five short-answer, two essay)

Instructor's Resource CD. This handy CD-ROM contains everything you need in an electronic format—the Instructor's Manual (PDF), PowerPoint Slides (fully customizable), Image Library with PDF versions of *all* 120 maps from the textbook, and a Computerized Testbank.

A complete **Course Management cartridge** is also available to qualified adopters. Instructor's resources are also available for download directly to your computer through a secure connection via the instructor's side of the companion website. Contact your Oxford University Press Sales Representative for more information.

Other Oxford Titles of Interest for the U.S. History Classroom

Oxford University Press publishes a vast array of titles in American history. Listed below is just a small selection of books that pair particularly well with Oakes's *Of the People: A History of the United States.* Any of the books in these series can be packaged with Oakes at a significant discount to students. Please contact your Oxford University Press Sales Representative for specific pricing information, or for additional packaging suggestions. Please visit www.oup.com/us for a full listing of Oxford titles.

NEW NARRATIVES IN AMERICAN HISTORY

At Oxford University Press, we believe that good history begins with a good story. Each volume in this series features a compelling tale that draws on a sustained narrative to illuminate a greater historical theme or controversy. Then, in a thoughtful Afterword, the authors place their narratives within larger historical contexts, discuss their sources and narrative strategies, and describe their personal involvement with the work. Intensely personal and highly relevant, these succinct texts are innovative teaching tools that provide a springboard for incisive class discussion as they immerse students in a particular historical moment.

Escaping Salem: The Other Witch Hunt of 1692, by Richard Godbeer
Sleuthing the Alamo: Davy Crockett's Last Stand and Other Mysteries of the Texas Revolution, by James E. Crisp

In Search of the Promised Land: A Slave Family in the Old South, by John Hope Franklin and Loren Schweninger

The Making of a Confederate: Walter Lenoir's Civil War, by William L. Barney

"They Say": Ida B. Wells and the Reconstruction of Race, by James West Davidson

Wild Men: Ishi and Kroeber in the Wilderness of Modern America, by Douglas Cazaux Sackman

The Gentle Subversive: Rachel Carson, Silent Spring, *and the Rise of the Environmental Movement,* by Mark Hamilton Lytle

"To Everything There is a Season": Pete Seeger and the Power of Song, by Allan Winkler

PAGES FROM HISTORY

Textbooks may interpret and recall history, but these books **are** history. Each title, compiled and edited by a prominent historian, is a collection of primary sources relating to a particular topic of historical significance. Documentary evidence includes news articles, government documents, memoirs, letters, diaries, fiction, photographs, advertisements, posters, and political cartoons. Headnotes, extended captions, sidebars, and introductory essays provide the essential context that frames the documents. All the books are amply illustrated and each includes a documentary picture essay, chronology, further reading, source notes, and index.

Encounters in the New World (Jill Lepore)
Colonial America (Edward G. Gray)
The American Revolution (Stephen C. Bullock)
The Bill of Rights (John J. Patrick)
The Struggle Against Slavery (David Waldstreicher)
The Civil War (Rachel Filene Seidman)
The Gilded Age (Janette Thomas Greenwood)
The Industrial Revolution (Laura Levine Frader)
Imperialism (Bonnie G. Smith)
World War I (Frans Coetzee and Marilyn Shevin-Coetzee)
The Depression and the New Deal (Robert McElvaine)
World War II (James H. Madison)
The Cold War (Allan M. Winkler)
The Vietnam War (Marilyn B. Young)

PIVOTAL MOMENTS IN AMERICAN HISTORY

Oxford's *Pivotal Moments in American History Series* explores the turning points that forever changed the course of American history. Each book is written by an expert on the subject and provides a fascinating narrative on a significant instance that stands out in our nation's past. For anyone interested in discovering which important junctures in U.S. history shaped our thoughts, actions, and ideals, these books are the definitive resources.

The Scratch of a Pen: 1763 and the Transformation of North America (Colin Calloway)
As if an Enemy's Country: The British Occupation of Boston and the Origins of the Revolution (Richard Archer)
Washington's Crossing (David Hackett Fischer)
James Madison and the Struggle for the Bill of Rights (Richard Labunski)
Adams vs. Jefferson: The Tumultuous Election of 1800 (John Ferling)

The Birth of Modern Politics: Andrew Jackson, John Quincy Adams, and the Election of 1828 (Lynn Parsons)
Storm over Texas: The Annexation Controversy and the Road to Civil War (Joel H. Silbey)
Crossroads of Freedom: Antietam (James M. McPherson)
The Last Indian War: The Nez Perce Story (Elliot West)
Seneca Falls and the Origins of the Women's Rights Movement (Sally McMillen)
Rainbow's End: The Crash of 1929 (Maury Klein)
Brown v. Board of Education *and the Civil Rights Movement* (Michael J. Klarman)
The Bay of Pigs (Howard Jones)
Freedom Riders: 1961 and the Struggle for Racial Justice (Raymond Arsenault)

VIEWPOINTS ON AMERICAN CULTURE

Oxford's *Viewpoints on American Culture Series* offers timely reflections for twenty-first century readers. The series targets topics where debates have flourished and brings together the voices of established and emerging writers to share their own points of view in compact and compelling format.

Votes for Women: The Struggle for Suffrage Revisited (Jean H. Baker)
Long Time Gone: Sixties America Then and Now (Alexander Bloom)
Living in the Eighties (Edited by Gil Troy and Vincent J. Cannato)
Race on Trial: Law and Justice in American History (Annette Gordon-Reed)
Sifters: Native American Women's Lives (Theda Perdue)
Latina Legacies: Identity, Biography, and Community (Vicki L. Ruiz)

OXFORD WORLD'S CLASSICS

For over 100 years Oxford World's Classics has made available a broad spectrum of literature from around the globe. With well over 600 titles available and a continuously growing list, this is the finest and most comprehensive classics series in print. Any volume in the series can be **packaged for free** with Oakes's *Of the People: A History of the United States*. Relevant titles include Benjamin Franklin's *Autobiography and Other Writings*, J. Hector St. John de Crèvecœur's *Letters from an American Farmer*, Booker T. Washington's *Up from Slavery*, and many others. **For a complete listing of Oxford World's Classics, please visit www.oup.com/us/owc.**

Acknowledgments

The authors are grateful to our families, friends, and colleagues who encouraged us during the planning and writing of this book.

Nick Cullather: To Isabel and Joey, for (occasionally) allowing me to work, and to Melanie for the 16 best years.

Jan Lewis: I want to express special thanks to Andy Achenbaum, James Grimmelmann, Warren F. Kimball, Ken Lockridge, and Peter Onuf, who either read portions of the manuscript or discussed it with me. And I am grateful to Barry Bienstock for his enormous library, his vast knowledge, and his endless patience.

The authors would like once again to thank Bruce Nichols for helping launch this book years ago. We are grateful to the editors and staff at Oxford University

Press, especially our acquisitions editor, Brian Wheel, and our development editors, Angela Kao and Frederick Speers. Brian's commitment made this edition possible; Fred's vision helped us give the book a new direction. Thanks also to our talented production team, Barbara Mathieu, senior production editor, and Paula Schlosser, art director, who helped to fulfill the book's vision. And special thanks go to Linda Sykes, who managed the photo research; to Teresa Nemeth, our copyeditor; and to Mike Powers and Martha Bostwick, cartographers, and Deane Plaister, editor, at Maps.com, who created the maps; and to the many other people behind the scenes at Oxford for helping this complex project happen.

The authors and editors would also like to thank the following people, whose time and insights have contributed to this edition:

Supplement Authors

Laura Graves,
South Plains College
Instructor's Manual

Andrew McMichael,
Western Kentucky University
Student Companion Website

Jim Jeffries,
Clemson University
PowerPoint slides

Archie McDonald,
Stephen F. Austin State
University
Test Bank

Expert Reviewers

Thomas L. Altherr
Metropolitan State College
of Denver

Luis Alvarez
University of California–
San Diego

Adam Arenson
University of Texas–El Paso

Melissa Estes Blair
University of Georgia

Susan Roth Breitzer
Fayetteville State University

Margaret Lynn Brown
Brevard College

W. Fitzhugh Brundage
University of North
Carolina–Chapel Hill

Lawrence Bowdish
Ohio State University

Gregory Bush
University of Miami

Brian Casserly
University of Washington

Ann Chirhart
Indiana State University

Bradley R. Clampitt
East Central University

Cheryll Ann Cody
Houston Community College

William W. Cobb Jr.
Utah Valley University

Sondra Cosgrove
College of Southern Nevada

Thomas H. Cox
Sam Houston State
University

Carl Creasman
Valencia Community College

Christine Daniels
Michigan State University

Brian J. Daugherity
Virginia Commonwealth
University

Mark Elliott
University of North
Carolina–Greensboro

Katherine Carté Engel
Texas A&M University

Michael Faubion
University of Texas–
Pan American

John Fea
Messiah College

Anne L. Foster
Indiana State University

Matthew Garrett
Arizona State University

Tim Garvin
California State University–
Long Beach

Lloyd Ray Gunn
University of Utah

Suzanne Cooper Guasco
Queens University of
Charlotte

Richard Hall
Columbus State University

Marsha Hamilton
University of South Alabama

Mark Hanna
University of California–
San Diego

Joseph M. Hawes
University of Memphis

Melissa Hovsepian
University of Houston–
Downtown

David K. Johnson
University of South Florida

Lloyd Johnson
Campbell University

Jorge Iber
Texas Tech University

Michael Kramer
Northwestern University

Catherine O'Donnell Kaplan
Arizona State University

Rebecca M. Kluchin
California State University–
Sacramento

Louis M. Kyriakoudes
University of Southern
Mississippi

Jason S. Lantzer
Butler University

Shelly Lemons
St. Louis Community College

Charlie Levine
Mesa Community College

Denise Lynn
University of Southern
Indiana

Lillian Marrujo-Duck
City College of San Francisco

Noeleen McIlvenna
Wright State University

Michael McCoy
Orange County Community
College

Elizabeth Brand Monroe
Indiana University–Purdue
University, Indianapolis

Kevin C. Motl
Ouachita Baptist University

Todd Moye
University of North Texas

Julie Nicoletta
University of Washington–
Tacoma

Charlotte Negrete
Mt. San Antonio College

David M. Parker
California State University–
Northridge

Jason Parker
Texas A&M University

Burton W. Peretti
Western Connecticut State
University

Jim Piecuch
Kennesaw State University

John Putman
San Diego State University

R. J. Rockefeller
Loyola College of Maryland

Herbert Sloan
Barnard College, Columbia
University

Vincent L. Toscano
Nova Southeastern University

William E. Weeks
San Diego State University

Timothy L. Wood
Southwest Baptist University

Jason Young
SUNY–Buffalo

About the Authors

James Oakes has published several books and numerous articles on slavery and antislavery in the nineteenth century, including *The Radical and the Republican: Frederick Douglass, Abraham Lincoln, and the Triumph of Antislavery Politics* (2007), winner of the Lincoln Prize in 2008. Professor Oakes has previously taught at Princeton and Northwestern Universities, and he is now Distinguished Professor of History and Graduate School Humanities Professor at the City University of New York Graduate Center. In 2008 he was a fellow at the Cullman Center at the New York Public Library. His current writing involves a history of emancipation during the Civil War.

Michael McGerr is Paul V. McNutt Professor of History in the College of Arts and Sciences at Indiana University–Bloomington. He is the author of *The Decline of Popular Politics: The American North, 1865–1928* (1986) and *A Fierce Discontent: The Rise and Fall of the Progressive Movement, 1870–1920* (2003). He is writing *"The Public Be Damned": The Vanderbilts and the Unmaking of the Ruling Class*. The recipient of a yearlong fellowship from the National Endowment for the Humanities, Professor McGerr has won numerous teaching awards at Indiana, where his courses include the U.S. Survey, Race and Gender in American Business, War in Modern American History, The Politics of American Popular Music, The Sixties, and American Pleasure Wars. He has previously taught at Yale University and the Massachusetts Institute of Technology. He received the BA, MA, and PhD from Yale.

Jan Ellen Lewis is Professor of History and Associate Dean of the Faculty of Arts and Sciences, Rutgers University, Newark. She also teaches in the history PhD program at Rutgers, New Brunswick, and was a visiting professor of history at Princeton. A specialist in colonial and early national history, she is the author of *The Pursuit of Happiness: Family and Values in Jefferson's Virginia* (1983) as well as numerous articles and reviews. She has coedited *An Emotional History of the United States* (1998), *Sally Hemings and Thomas Jefferson: History, Memory, and Civic Culture* (1999), and *The Revolution of 1800: Democracy, Race, and the New Republic* (2002). She has served on the editorial board of the *American Historical Review* and as chair of the New Jersey Historical Commission. She received her AB from Bryn Mawr College and MAs and PhD from the University of Michigan.

Nick Cullather is a historian of U.S. foreign relations at Indiana University–Bloomington. He is author of two books on nation building: *Illusions of Influence* (1994), a study of U.S.-Philippines relations, and *Secret History* (1999 and 2006), a history of the CIA's overthrow of the Guatemalan government in 1954. His current work includes *Calories and Cold War: America's Quest to Feed the World*. He received his PhD from the University of Virginia.

Jeanne Boydston was Robinson-Edwards Professor of American History at the University of Wisconsin–Madison. A specialist in the histories of gender and labor, she was the author of *Home and Work: Housework, Wages, and the Ideology of Labor in the Early American Republic* (1990); coauthor of *The Limits of Sisterhood: The Beecher Sisters on Women's Rights and Woman's Sphere* (1988), and coeditor of *Root of Bitterness: Documents in the Social History of American Women*, second edition (1996). Her most recent article is "Gender as a Category of Historical Analysis," *Gender History* (2008). She taught courses in women's and gender history, the histories of the early republic and the antebellum United States, and global and comparative history, and she was the recipient of numerous awards for teaching and mentoring. Her BA and MA were from the University of Tennessee, and her PhD was from Yale University.

Of the People

Common Threads

>> In what ways did emancipation and wartime Reconstruction overlap?

>> When did Reconstruction begin?

>> Did Reconstruction change the South? If so, how? If not, why not?

>> What brought Reconstruction to an end?

Reconstructing a Nation

1865–1877

>> John Dennett Visits a Freedmen's Bureau Court

John Richard Dennett arrived in Liberty, Virginia, on August 17, 1865, on a tour of the South during which he sent back weekly reports for publication in *The Nation*. The editors wanted accurate accounts of conditions in the recently defeated Confederate states, and Dennett was the kind of man they could trust. He graduated from Harvard, was a firm believer in the sanctity of the Union, and belonged to the class of elite Yankees who thought of themselves as the "best men" the country had to offer.

At Liberty, Dennett was accompanied by a Freedmen's Bureau agent. The Freedmen's Bureau was a branch of the U.S. Army established by Congress to assist the freed people. Dennett and the agent went to the courthouse because one of the Freedmen's Bureau's functions was to adjudicate disputes between the freed people and southern whites.

The first case was that of an old white farmer who complained that two blacks who worked on his farm were "roamin' about and refusin' to work." He wanted the agent to help find the men and bring them back. Both men had wives and children living on his farm and eating his corn, the old man complained. "Have you been paying any wages?" the Freedmen's Bureau agent asked. "Well, they get what the other niggers get," the farmer answered. "I a'n't payin' great wages this year." There was not much the agent could do. He had no horses and few men, but one of his soldiers volunteered to go back to the farm and tell the blacks that "they ought to be at home supporting their wives and children."

A well-to-do planter came in to see if he could fire the blacks who had been working on his plantation since the beginning of the year. The planter complained that his workers were unmanageable now that he could no longer punish them. The sergeant warned the planter that he could not beat his workers as if they were still slaves. In that case, the planter responded, "Will the Government take them off our hands?" The Freedmen's Bureau agent suspected that the planter was looking for an excuse to discharge his laborers at the end of the growing season, after they had finished the work but before they had been paid. "If they've worked on your crops all the year so far," the agent told the planter, "I guess they've got a claim on you to keep them a while longer."

Next came a "good-looking mulatto man" representing a number of African Americans. They were worried by rumors that they would be forced to sign five-year contracts with their employers. "No, it a'n't true," the agent said. They also wanted to know if they could rent or buy land so that they could work for themselves. "Yes, rent or buy," the agent said. But the former slaves had no horses, mules, or ploughs to work the land. So they wanted to know "if the Government would help us out after we get the land." But the agent had no help to offer. "The Government hasn't any ploughs or mules to give you," he said. In the end the blacks settled for a piece of paper from the Freedmen's Bureau authorizing them to rent or buy their own farms.

The last case involved a field hand who came to the agent to complain that his master was beating him with a stick. The agent told the field hand to go back to work. "Don't be sassy, don't be lazy when you've got work to do; and I guess he won't trouble you." The field hand left "very reluctantly," but came back a minute later and asked for a letter to his master "enjoining him to keep the peace, as he feared the man would shoot him, he having on two or three occasions threatened to do so."

Most of the cases Dennett witnessed centered on labor relations, but labor questions often spilled over into other matters including the family lives of the freed people, their civil rights, and their ability to buy land. The freed people preferred to work their own land, but they lacked the resources to rent or buy farms. Black workers and white owners who negotiated wage contracts had trouble figuring out the limits of each other's rights and responsibilities. The former masters wanted to retain as much of their old authority as possible. Freedmen wanted as much autonomy as possible, while freedwomen were forced to seek the patriarchal protection of their husbands.

continued

>> AMERICAN PORTRAIT *continued*

The Freedmen's Bureau was placed in the middle of these conflicts. Most agents tried to ensure that the freed people were paid for their labor and that they were not brutalized as they had been as slaves. Southern whites resented this intrusion, and their resentment filtered up to sympathetic politicians in Washington, DC. As a result, the Freedmen's Bureau became a lightning rod for the political conflicts of the Reconstruction period.

Conditions in the South raised several questions for lawmakers in Washington. How far should the federal government go to protect the economic well-being and civil rights of the freed people? What requirements should the federal government impose on the southern states before they could be readmitted to the Union? Politicians in Washington disagreed violently on these questions. At one extreme was Andrew Johnson, who, as president, believed in small government and a speedy readmission of the southern states and looked on the Freedmen's Bureau with suspicion. At the other extreme were radical Republicans, who believed that the federal government should redistribute confiscated land to the former slaves, guarantee their civil rights, and give African American men the vote. They viewed the Freedmen's Bureau as too small and weak to do the necessary job. Between the radicals and the president's supporters were moderate Republicans who at first tried to work with the president. But as reports of violence and the abusive treatment of the freed people made their way back to the nation's capital, Republicans shifted toward the radical position.

It went back and forth this way: policy makers in Washington responded to what went on in the South, and events in the South were shaped in turn by the policies emanating from Washington. What John Dennett saw in Liberty, Virginia, was a good example of this. The Freedmen's Bureau agent listened to the urgent requests of former masters and slaves, his responses shaped by the policies established in Washington. But those policies were, in turn, shaped by reports on conditions in the South sent back by Freedmen's Bureau agents like him and by journalists like John Dennett. From this interaction the politics of Reconstruction, and with it a "New South," slowly emerged. ●

OUTLINE

Wartime Reconstruction

For several years emancipation overlapped with Reconstruction. Emancipation began early in the war and was not completed until the very end of 1865. Experiments with Reconstruction began during the war, long before emancipation was complete. Indeed, what is known as "Presidential Reconstruction" was also the crucial phase in the completion of emancipation. Congress and the president often had very different ideas about how to reconstruct the defeated Confederacy, but on one thing they agreed from the very beginning. Until the Thirteenth Amendment was ratified in December of 1865, state emancipation was the most legally secure means of abolishing slavery. Congress and the president therefore agreed that before any southern state could be readmitted to the Union, it had to emancipate its own slaves.

After that, however, came several more contentious questions. What system of free labor would replace slavery? What civil and political rights should the freed people receive? During the war Congress and the Lincoln administration responded piecemeal to developments in regions of the South under Union control. A variety of approaches to Reconstruction emerged.

Experiments with Free Labor in the Lower Mississippi Valley

In November 1861, several of the Sea Islands off coastal South Carolina were occupied by Union troops. The slaveholders fled from the advancing Union army, leaving

Slaves Planting Sweet Potatoes Slaves in parts of coastal South Carolina were freed early in the Civil War. Here the freed people on Edisto Island in 1862 are shown planting sweet potatoes rather than cotton. In other parts of the South the former slaves returned to the cultivation of cash crops.

behind between 5,000 and 10,000 slaves. Were they free? Or merely contrabands of war? In December, responding to concerns about the status of contrabands, President Lincoln declared them "liberated." So began the first notable "rehearsal for Reconstruction." By the end of the war the abandoned plantations of the Sea Islands had been reorganized. Slave families were given small plots of their own to cultivate, and in return for their labor they would receive a "share" of the year's crop.

When the masters returned after the war to reclaim their lands, the labor system evolved swiftly into what would become known as "sharecropping."

Southern Louisiana also came under Union control early in the war. The sugar and cotton plantations around New Orleans therefore provided another major experiment in the transition from slave to free labor. Unlike the Sea Islands, however, Louisiana's planters did not abandon their plantations, and there were tens of thousands of slaves involved. This created a dilemma for Union commanders. The plantation workers were no longer slaves, but their masters were still in place, so the plantations could not be broken up. And in any case sugar plantations could not be effectively organized into small sharecropping units. The labor system that emerged was unusual in the post-emancipation South, but it played an important role in the politics of Reconstruction.

Union general Nathaniel Banks, hoping to stem the flow of blacks running to Union lines and prevent the shocking number of deaths among blacks in the refugee camps, issued stringent labor regulations designed to put the freed people back to work quickly. The Banks Plan required freed people to sign yearlong contracts to work on their former plantations, often for their former owners. Workers would be paid either 5 percent of the proceeds of the crop or three dollars per month. The former masters would provide food and shelter. African American workers were forbidden to leave the plantations without permission. So harsh were these regulations that to many critics Banks had simply replaced one form of slavery with another. But as harsh as it was, the Banks Plan was not slavery, and most of the freed people returned to work fully aware of the difference. The Banks Plan was implemented throughout the lower Mississippi Valley, especially after the fall of Vicksburg in 1863.

The Banks Plan touched off a political controversy. Established planters had the most to gain from the plan, which allowed them to preserve much of the pre-

> A few days ago, a gentleman below the city hired a new overseer, one who was. . . . in the habit of wielding the whip pretty freely, and of using abusive language to the negro women . . . [A] delegation from the field-hands waited upon the proprietor, and very respectfully stated their objections against the newcomer. . . . He dismissed them with an oath. . . . The delegation at once went to their cabins, packed up their little bundles, and started on the road to Fort Jackson. They knew, that, once there, they could get employment. They had not gone far, however, before the master came to his senses. He was no longer the owner of mere chattels. . . . He called them all back; told them they should have any overseer they wanted: upon which they unpacked their bundles, and went quietly to the field, as if nothing had happened.
>
> GEORGE HEPWORTH,
> surveying the effect of the Banks Plan in Louisiana, 1863

war labor system. Louisiana Unionists, who had remained loyal to the government in Washington, formed a Free State Association to press for more substantial changes. Lincoln publicly supported the Free State movement and issued a Proclamation of Amnesty and Reconstruction to undermine the Confederacy by cultivating the support of southern Unionists. The Proclamation contained, in outline, the first plan for reconstructing the South.

The most important thing Lincoln's plan did was to require Louisiana to abolish slavery, as the price for readmission to the Union. The precedent for such a precondition had been established earlier the same year, when West Virginia was required to emancipate its slaves as a condition for admission to statehood. Lincoln quickly applied that precedent to the seceded states, beginning with Florida and Louisiana. But the attempt to establish a loyal government in Florida foundered, so Louisiana became the first great experiment in wartime Reconstruction.

Lincoln's Ten Percent Plan Versus the Wade-Davis Bill

Beyond requiring the abolition of slavery, Lincoln's Ten Percent Plan promised full pardons and the restoration of civil rights to all those who swore loyalty to the Union, excluding only a few high-ranking Confederate military and political leaders. When the number of loyal whites in a former Confederate state reached 10 percent of the 1860 voting population, they could organize a new state constitution and government. Abiding by these conditions, Free State whites met in Louisiana in 1864 and produced a new state constitution. It provided for free public education, a minimum wage, a nine-hour day on public works projects, and a graduated income tax. However, although it abolished slavery, it also denied blacks the right to vote.

By the spring of 1864 such denials were no longer acceptable to radical Republicans, a small but vocal wing of the Republican Party. Unionists were active in many parts of the South immediately after the war, and they developed strong ties to leading radicals in Congress, such as Thaddeus Stevens of Pennsylvania and Charles Sumner of Massachusetts. Despite their differences, most radicals favored federal guarantees of the civil rights of former slaves, including the right to vote. Radicals were prepared to use the full force of the federal government to enforce congressional policy in the South. Although the radicals never formed a majority in Congress, they gradually won over the moderates to many of their positions. As a result, when Congress took control of Reconstruction after the elections in 1866, the process became known as radical Reconstruction.

The radicals were particularly strong in New Orleans, thanks to the city's large and articulate community of free blacks. In the spring of 1864 they sent a delegation to Washington to meet with President Lincoln and press the case for voting rights.

Charlotte Forten Born to a prominent African American family in Philadelphia, Charlotte Forten was one of many northern women who went to the South to become a teacher of the freed slaves. Forten helped found the Penn School on St. Helena's Island in South Carolina.

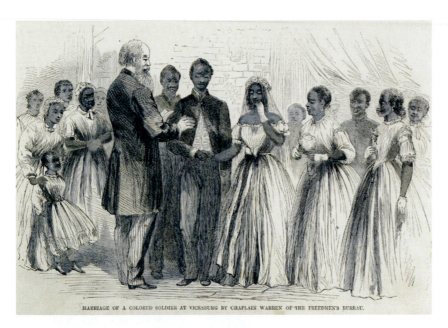

MARRIAGE OF A COLORED SOLDIER AT VICKSBURG BY CHAPLAIN WARREN OF THE FREEDMEN'S BUREAU.

Freedman Wedding Because slave marriages had no legal standing, many freed people got married as soon as they could. Pictured here is one such wedding, performed at the Freedmen's Bureau.

The next day Lincoln wrote to the acting governor of Louisiana suggesting a limited suffrage for the most intelligent blacks and for those who had served in the Union army. The delegates to Louisiana's constitutional convention ignored Lincoln's suggestion. Shortly thereafter free blacks in New Orleans and former slaves together demanded civil and political rights and the abolition of the Banks labor regulations. Radicals complained that Lincoln's Ten Percent Plan was too kind to former Confederates and that the Banks Plan was too harsh on former slaves.

Moved largely by events in Louisiana, congressional radicals rejected Lincoln's plan. In July 1864 Congressmen Benjamin F. Wade and Henry Winter Davis proposed a different Reconstruction plan. Under the Wade-Davis Bill, Reconstruction could not begin until a majority, rather than merely 10 percent, of a state's white men swore an oath of allegiance to the Union. In addition, the Wade-Davis Bill guaranteed full legal and civil rights to African Americans, but not the right to vote. Lincoln pocket vetoed the bill because it required Louisiana to emancipate its slaves as a condition for readmission to the Union. Lincoln believed that only he, as commander in chief, could emancipate slaves, as a necessity of war. He included an emancipation provision in his own plan for Louisiana Reconstruction.

The Louisiana experience made several things clear. The radical Republicans were determined to press for more civil and political rights for blacks than moderates initially supported; however, the moderates showed a willingness to move in a radical direction. Equally important, any Reconstruction policy would have to consider the wishes of southern blacks.

The Freed People's Dream of Owning Land

Freedom meant many things to the former slaves. It meant they could move about their neighborhoods without passes, that they did not have to step aside to let whites pass them on the street. Following emancipation, southern blacks withdrew from white churches and established their own congregations, and during Reconstruction the church emerged as a central institution in the southern black community. Freedom also meant literacy. Even before the war ended northern teachers poured into the South to set up schools. The American Missionary Association organized hundreds of such northern teachers. When the fighting stopped, the U.S. Army helped recruit and organize thousands more northern women as teachers. The graduates of the missionary schools sometimes became teachers themselves. As a result, hundreds of thousands of southern blacks became literate within a few years.

More importantly, the former slaves went out of their way to have their marriages secured by the law. There was more to this than sentiment, or even the privacy of the home. In 1865 marriage became an urgent necessity for many recently freed slaves, particularly women. Under slavery black women were valued in part for their labor and in part for their ability to reproduce more slaves. With emancipation black women and their offspring were no longer valuable as property to be accumulated. Hoping to avoid the expense of caring for such workers, planters in some parts of the South began expelling women and children from their plantations in late 1865. Desperate women quickly realized that their best hope for avoiding starvation was to rely on the patriarchal protection of their husbands. Once married, their husbands would demand sharecropping contracts that allowed their families to live with them on the plantations. For the first time in their lives black women across the South became what the law called "domestic dependents." Emancipation moved black women—no longer human property—out of slavery and into patriarchy.

The freed people also wanted land. Without it the former slaves saw no choice but to work for their old masters on their farms and plantations. As the war ended, many African Americans had reason to believe that the government would assist them in their quest for independent land ownership. Marching through the Carolinas in early 1865, Union general William Tecumseh Sherman discovered how important land was to the freed people on the Sea Islands. "The way we can best take care of ourselves is to have land," they declared, "and turn it out and till it by our own labor." Persuaded by their arguments, Sherman issued Special Field Order No. 15 granting captured land to the freed people. By June 1865, 400,000 acres had been distributed to 40,000 former slaves.

Congress seemed to be moving in a similar direction. In March 1865, the Republicans established the Bureau of Refugees, Freedmen and Abandoned Lands, commonly known as the Freedmen's Bureau, which quickly became involved in the politics of land redistribution. The Freedmen's Bureau controlled the disposition of 850,000 acres of confiscated and abandoned Confederate lands. In July 1865, General Oliver Otis Howard, the head of the bureau, issued Circular 13, directing his agents to rent the land to the freed people in 40-acre plots that they could eventually purchase. Many bureau agents believed that to reeducate them in the values of thrift and hard work, the freed people should be encouraged to save money and buy land for themselves. From the bureau's perspective, redistributing land was like giving it away to people who had not paid for it.

From the perspective of the former slaves, however, black workers had more than earned a right to the land. "The labor of these people had for two hundred years cleared away the forests and produced crops that brought millions of dollars annually," H. C. Bruce explained. "It does seem to me that a Christian Nation would, at least, have given them one year's support, 40 acres of land and a mule each." Even Abraham Lincoln seemed to agree. But in April 1865 Lincoln was dead and Andrew Johnson became president of the United States.

Presidential Reconstruction, 1865–1867

When Andrew Johnson took office in April 1865, it was still unclear whether Congress or the president would control Reconstruction policy, and whether that policy would be lenient or harsh. As with so many Democrats, Johnson's sympathy for the common man did not extend to African Americans. Determined to reconstruct the South in his own way and blind to the interests of the freed people, Johnson grew increasingly bitter and resentful of the Republicans who controlled Congress.

The Political Economy of Contract Labor

In the mid-nineteenth century, Congress was normally out of session from March until December. Having assumed the presidency in April 1865, Johnson hoped to take advantage of the recess to complete the Reconstruction process and present the finished product to lawmakers in December. At the end of May the president offered amnesty and the restoration of property to white southerners who swore an oath of loyalty to the Union, excluding only high-ranking Confederate military and political leaders and very rich planters. He named provisional governors to the seceded states and instructed them to organize constitutional conventions. To earn readmission to the Union, the first thing the seceded states were required to do was abolish slavery, preferably by ratifying the Thirteenth Amendment. In addition, Johnson required the states to nullify their secession ordinances and repudiate their Confederate war debts. These terms were far more lenient than those Lincoln and the congressional Republicans had contemplated. They did nothing to protect the civil rights of the former slaves.

Johnson's leniency encouraged defiance among white southerners. Secessionists had been barred from participating in the states' constitutional conventions, but they participated openly in the first elections held late in the year because Johnson issued thousands of pardons. Leading Confederates thus assumed public office in the southern states. Complying with Johnson's requirements, the former Confederate states began abolishing slavery, and in the fall of 1865 the last great wave of emancipation spread across the South. Right up to the end of the war most slaveholders hoped that they could retain their slaves, even if they were forced to rejoin the Union. When the last holdouts—and there were many thousands of them—were finally forced to accept emancipation they were furious and resentful. Consequently, as Johnson's new state governments were coming into existence a wave of violence spread across the South.

Blacks who had been freed earlier were not immune to the reaction. Restored to power, white southerners demanded the restoration of all properties confiscated or abandoned during the war. In September 1865 Johnson ordered the Freedmen's Bureau to return all confiscated and abandoned lands to their former owners. In late 1865 former slaves were being forcibly evicted from the 40-acre plots they had been given by the Union army or the Freedmen's Bureau. On Edisto Island off South Car-

---

New Orleans, La., August 2, 1866

U. S. Grant, General, Washington, D.C.

The more information I obtain about the affair of the 30th, in this city, the more revolting it becomes. It was no riot; it was an absolute massacre by the police. . . . It was a murder which the Mayor and the police of the city perpetrated without the shadow of a necessity; furthermore, I believe it was premeditated, and every indication points to this. I recommend removing this bad man. I believe it would be hailed with the sincerest gratification by two-thirds of the population of the city. There has been a feeling of insecurity on the part of the people here on account of this man, which is now so much increased that the safety of life and property does not rest with the civil authorities, but with the military.

P. H. Sheridan
Major-General Commanding

olina, for example, the freed people had carved farms out of the former plantations. But in January 1866 General Rufus Saxton restored the farms to their previous owners and encouraged the freed people to sign wage contracts with their old masters. The blacks unanimously rejected his offer, whereupon the general ordered them to evacuate their farms within two weeks.

Alongside their emancipation ordinances the Johnsonian state governments enacted a series of "Black Codes" severely restricting the civil rights of freed people. In many states the Black Codes *were* the emancipation statutes. Vagrancy statutes, for example, allowed local police to arrest and fine virtually any black man. If he could not pay the fine, the "vagrant" was put to work on a farm, often the one owned and operated by his former master. Even more disturbing to the former slaves were apprenticeship clauses that allowed white officials to remove children from their parents' homes and put them to work as "apprentices" on nearby farms.

Presidential Reconstruction left the freed people with no choice but to sign labor contracts with white landlords. The contracts restricted the personal as well as the working lives of the freed people. In one case, a South Carolina planter contractually obliged his black workers to "go by his direction the same as in slavery time." Contracts required blacks to work for wages as low as one-tenth of the crop, and cotton prices were steadily falling. It is no wonder that contract labor struck the freed people as little different from slavery.

Resistance to Presidential Reconstruction

In September 1865, blacks in Virginia issued a public appeal for assistance. They declared that they lacked the means to make and enforce legal contracts, because the Black Codes denied African Americans the right to testify in court in any case involving a white person. In many areas planters blocked the development of a free labor market by agreeing among themselves to hire only their former slaves and by fixing wages at a low level. Finally, there were numerous incidents in which black workers who had faithfully obeyed the terms of their contracts were "met by a contemptuous refusal of the stipulated compensation."

Across the South whites reported a growing number of freed people who would not abide by the humiliating conditions of the contract labor system. Some blacks refused to perform specific tasks, while others were accused of being "disrespectful" to their employers or to whites in general. Most important, thousands of freedmen declined to sign new contracts at the end of the year.

As the white backlash and black defiance spread, reports of violence flooded into Washington. A former slave named Henry Adams claimed that "over two thousand colored people" were murdered around Shreveport, Louisiana, in 1865. Near Pine Bluff, Arkansas, in 1866 a visitor arrived at a black community the morning after whites had burned it to the ground. Blacks were assaulted for not speaking to whites with the proper tone of submission, for disputing the terms of labor contracts, or for failing to work up to the standards white employers expected. Through relentless intimidation, whites prevented blacks from buying their own land or attending political meetings to press for civil rights.

Northerners read these reports as evidence that whites were resisting emancipation and that "rebel" sentiment was reviving in the South. When Congress came back into session in December 1865, moderate Republicans were already suspicious

> The Congress owes it to its own character to set the seal of reprobation upon a doctrine which is becoming too fashionable, and unless rebuked will be the recognized principle of our Government. Governor Perry and other provisional governors and orators proclaim that "this is the white man's Government." The whole copperhead party, pandering to the lowest prejudices of the ignorant, repeat the cuckoo cry, "This is the white man's Government." Demagogues of all parties, even some high in authority, gravely shout, "This is the white man's Government." What is implied by this? That one race of men are to have the exclusive right forever to rule this nation, and to exercise all acts of sovereignty, while all other races and nations and colors are to be their subjects, and have no voice in making the laws and choosing the rulers by whom they are to be governed. Wherein does this differ from slavery except in degree? Does not this contradict all the distinctive principles of the Declaration of Independence?
>
> CONGRESSMAN THADDEUS STEVENS,
> speech on Reconstruction, December 18, 1865

of presidential Reconstruction. Radicals argued that the contract system made a mockery of their party's commitment to free labor and insisted that the only way to protect the interests of the freed people was to grant them the right to vote.

Congress Clashes with the President

Increasingly distressed by events in the South, Republican moderates in Congress were radicalized. They accepted the need for a more active government in the South and they endorsed voting rights for black men. President Johnson, meanwhile, became obsessed with fears of "negro rule" in the South. When he insisted on the swift readmission of southern states that were clearly controlled by unrepentant Confederates, Congress refused. Instead, the Republicans formed a Joint Committee on Reconstruction to propose the terms for readmission. Established in December 1865, the joint committee reflected Congress's determination to follow its own course on Reconstruction.

In February 1866 Congress voted to extend the life of the Freedmen's Bureau and empowered the bureau to set up its own courts, which would supercede local jurisdictions. The bureau's record during its first year had been mixed. In the crucial area of labor relations, the bureau too often sided with the landowners and against the interests of the freed people. It emancipated thousands of slaves still being held by their owners. It provided immediate relief to thousands of individual freed people, and it assisted in the creation of schools. The bureau's effectiveness varied with the commitments of its agents. Indifferent or even hostile to the needs of the freed people, some agents sided instinctively with the former masters. The more idealistic agents often acted under difficult circumstances to protect the freed people from racist violence, unfair employers, and biased law enforcement officials. For this reason, thousands of freedmen and freedwomen looked to the bureau as their only hope for justice. For the same reason, thousands of southern whites resented the bureau, and they let Andrew Johnson know it.

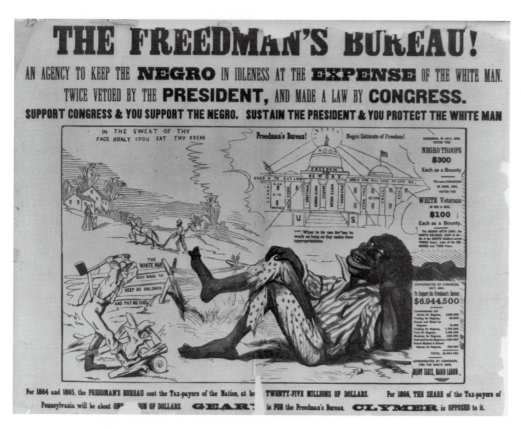

The Freedmen's Bureau Led by President Andrew Johnson, attacks on the Freedmen's Bureau became more and more openly racist in late 1865 and 1866. This Democratic Party broadside was circulated during the 1866 election.

To the amazement of moderate Republicans, Johnson vetoed the bill to extend the life of the Freedmen's Bureau. The president complained that the legislation would increase the power of the central government at the expense of the states. He invoked the Jacksonian ideal of the free market, insisting that the "laws that regulate supply and demand" were the best way to resolve the labor problem in the South. Republicans fell just short of the two-thirds vote they needed to override the veto. Johnson reacted to his narrow victory with a speech attacking the Republicans in Congress and questioning the legitimacy of the Joint Committee on Reconstruction.

Origins of the Fourteenth Amendment

In March 1866 Congress passed a landmark Civil Rights Act. It overturned the Dred Scott decision by granting United States citizenship to Americans regardless of race. This marked the first time that the federal government intervened in the states to guarantee due process and basic civil rights. But President Johnson vetoed the Civil Rights Act of 1866. In addition to the usual Jacksonian rhetoric about limited government, Johnson made an overtly racist argument to justify his veto. He doubted that blacks "possess the requisite qualifications to entitle them to all the privileges and immunities of citizens of the United States."

Johnson's actions and rhetoric forced the moderate Republicans to confront the president. The Republican Congress overrode Johnson's veto of the Civil Rights Act

>> Race Riots in Memphis and New Orleans

A few weeks after Congress passed the Civil Rights Act, white mobs in Memphis rioted for three days. In the year since the war had ended, the city's black population had multiplied four times over as former slaves fled from the countryside in hopes of better opportunities in the city. But whites in Memphis grew increasingly hostile to the presence of so many blacks. "Would to God they were back in Africa, or some other seaport town," the Memphis *Argus* complained, "anywhere but here." Under President Johnson's terms for a newly reconstructed government the old Tennessee elite had been displaced in the city by Irish politicians who proved at least as hostile to freed people as the old guard. Not surprisingly, there were numerous reports of conflict breaking out between whites and blacks on the streets of Memphis.

In this atmosphere of heightened racial tension one incident sparked a riot. On May 1, 1866, two hack drivers—one black, one white—had a traffic accident, and when the police arrived they arrested the black man. Matters soon escalated. A group of black veterans tried to prevent the arrest. A white crowd gathered and began rioting in the streets. Over the next three days white mobs burned hundreds of homes, destroyed churches, and attacked black schools. Five black women were raped and nearly fifty people, all but two of them black, were killed.

Three months later, white mobs in New Orleans rioted as well. Once again both the state and municipal governments were quickly falling into the hands of former Confederates. But the New Orleans massacre had a more explicitly political dimension. The city had a well-established community of free blacks who, by the middle of 1866, had grown disillusioned with the direction Reconstruction was taking in Louisiana and New Orleans. A group of radicals issued a call to bring the state's 1864 constitutional convention back into session. They proposed giving blacks the vote, stripping "rebels" of the franchise, and establishing an entirely new state government. The convention was scheduled to meet on July 30.

But as the delegates met, white mobs set out to stop them. Led by the city's police and firemen, many of them Confederate veterans, whites first attacked a parade of about 200 blacks who were marching to the Mechanics' Institute to support the delegates. When the mob reached the convention hall, deadly violence ensued. They attacked the hall, shooting and killing the delegates as they tried to escape through the windows, even after the victims raised the white flag of surrender. As one Union veteran who witnessed the massacre reported, "the wholesale slaughter and the little regard paid to human life" were worse than anything he had seen in battle. When the mob finally dispersed, 34 blacks and 3 white supporters had been killed, and another 100 had been injured.

The Memphis and New Orleans massacres quickly became political issues in the North, thanks in large part to Andrew Johnson's reaction to them. In late August the president undertook an unprecedented campaign tour designed to stir up voters' hostility to Congress, but his trip backfired. The president blasted congressional Republicans, blaming them for the riots. At one point he suggested that radical congressman Thaddeus Stevens should be hanged. Republicans charged in turn that

Johnson's own policies had revived the rebellious sentiments in the South that led to the massacres.

The elections of 1866 became a referendum on competing visions of what American democracy should mean at that point. For President Johnson "democracy" meant government by local majorities, which often meant white supremacy. For African Americans and a growing number of Republicans in Congress, genuine democracy could only be constructed on a firm foundation of equal civil and political rights. The results were "overwhelmingly against the President," the *New York Times* noted, "clearly, unmistakably, decisively in favor of Congress and its policy." The Republicans gained a veto-proof hold on Congress, and Republican moderates were further radicalized. Congressional Reconstruction was about to begin. ●

and passed another Freedmen's Bureau Bill. Once again Johnson vetoed it, but this time Congress overrode his veto.

To ensure the civil rights of the freed people, the Joint Committee on Reconstruction proposed a Fourteenth Amendment to the Constitution. The most powerful and controversial of all the Constitution's amendments, it guaranteed citizenship to all males born in the United States, regardless of color (see Table 16–1). Although the amendment did not guarantee blacks the right to vote, it based representation in Congress on a state's voting population. This punished southern states by reducing their representation if they did not allow blacks to vote.

By mid-1866, Congress had refused to recognize the state governments established under Johnson's plan, and it had authorized the Freedmen's Bureau to create a military justice system to override the local courts. Congress thereby guaranteed the former slaves basic rights of due process. Finally, it made ratification of the Fourteenth Amendment by the former Confederate states a requirement for their readmission to the Union. Congress and the president were now at war, and Andrew Johnson went on a rampage.

 Table 16–1 Reconstruction Amendments, 1865–1870

Amendment	Main Provisions	Congressional Passage (2/3 majority in each house required)	Ratification Process (3/4 of all states including ex-Confederate states required)
13	Slavery prohibited in United States	January 1865	December 1865 (27 states, including 8 southern states)
14	1. National citizenship for all men and women born in the U.S.	June 1866	Rejected by 12 southern and border states, February 1867
	2. State representation in Congress reduced proportionally to number of voters disfranchised		Radicals make readmission of southern states hinge on ratification
	3. Former high ranking Confederates denied right to hold office		Ratified July 1868
	4. Confederate debt repudiated		
15	Denial of franchise because of race, color, or past servitude explicitly prohibited	February 1869	Ratification required for readmission of Virginia, Texas, Mississippi, Georgia. Ratified March 1870.

Congressional Reconstruction

Johnson's outrageous behavior during the 1866 campaign, capped by a Republican sweep of the elections, ended presidential Reconstruction. Congressional Reconstruction would be far different. It was an extraordinary series of events, second only to emancipation in its impact on the history of the United States.

Origins of the Black Vote

The Congress that convened in December 1866 was far more radical than the previous one. Nothing demonstrated this as clearly as the emerging consensus among moderate Republicans that southern blacks should be allowed to vote. Radical Republicans and black leaders had been calling for such a policy for two years, but moderate Republicans initially resisted the idea. At most, moderates contemplated granting the vote to veterans and to educated blacks who had been free before the war. Not until early 1867 did the majority of Republicans conclude that the only way to avoid a lengthy military occupation of the South was to put political power into the hands of all male freedmen.

Andrew Johnson finally pushed the moderate Republicans over the line. Ignoring the results of the 1866 elections, Johnson urged the southern states to reject the Fourteenth Amendment. Frustrated Republicans finally repudiated presidential Reconstruction from top to bottom. On March 2, 1867, Congress assumed control of the process by passing the First Reconstruction Act. It reduced the southern states to the status of territories and divided the South into five military districts directly controlled by the army (see Map 16–1). Before the southern states could be readmitted to the Union they had to draw up new "republican" constitutions, ratify the Fourteenth Amendment, and allow black men to vote. The Second Reconstruction Act, passed a few weeks later, established the procedures to enforce black suffrage by placing the military in charge of voter registration. Johnson vetoed both acts, and in both cases Congress immediately overrode the president. This was congressional Reconstruction at its most radical, and for this reason it is often referred to as "radical Reconstruction."

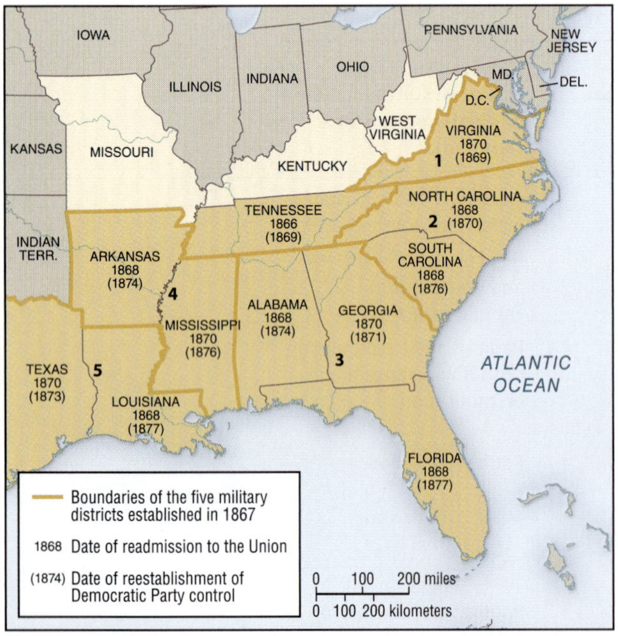

Map 16–1 Reconstruction and Redemption By 1870 Congress readmitted every southern state to the Union. In most cases the Republican Party retained control of the "reconstructed" state governments for only a few years.

Radical Reconstruction in the South

Beginning in 1867 the constitutions of the southern states were rewritten, thousands of African Americans began to vote, and hundreds of them assumed public office. Within six months 735,000 blacks and 635,000 whites had registered to vote across the South. Blacks formed electoral majorities in South Carolina, Florida, Mississippi, Alabama, and Louisiana. In the fall these new voters elected delegates to conventions that drew up progressive state constitutions that guaranteed suffrage for all men, mandated public education systems, and established progressive tax structures.

The governments elected under congressional authority were based on an unstable political coalition. Northern whites occupied a prominent place in the southern Republican Party. Stereotyped as greedy carpetbaggers, they included Union veterans who stayed in the South when the war ended, idealistic reformers, well-meaning capitalists, and opportunistic Americans on the make. More important to the Republican coalition were southern whites, or scalawags. Some of them lived in up-country regions where resistance to secession and the Confederacy had been strongest. Others had been Whigs before the war and hoped to regain some of their former influence. But new black voters were the backbone of the Republican Party in the South. Like the carpetbaggers and scalawags, black voters were a varied lot. Elite black artisans and professionals did not always share the interests of poor black farmers and farm laborers. Nevertheless, most African Americans were drawn together by a shared interest in securing civil rights.

In the long run the class and race divisions within the southern Republican coalition weakened the party, but in the late 1860s and early 1870s the southern Republicans launched an impressive experiment in interracial democracy in the South. Racist legend paints these years as a dark period of "negro rule" and military domination, but military rule rarely lasted more than a year or two, and in only one state, South Carolina, did blacks ever control a majority of seats in the legislature. Blacks who held office came largely from the ranks of the prewar free African American elite. Teachers, ministers, and small businessmen were far more common among black elected officials than were sharecroppers or farm workers. Nevertheless, these Reconstruction legislatures were more representative of their constituents than most legislatures in nineteenth-century America (see Figure 16–1).

Achievements and Failures of Radical Government

Once in office, southern Republicans had to cultivate a white constituency and at the same time serve the interests of the blacks who elected them. To strengthen this biracial coalition, Republican politicians emphasized active government support for economic development. Republican legislatures granted tax abatements for corporations and spent vast sums to encourage the construction of railroads. They preached a "gospel of prosperity" that promised to bring the benefits of economic development to ordinary white southerners.

In the long run, the gospel of prosperity did not hold the Republican coalition together. Outside investors were unwilling to risk their capital on a region marked by political instability. By the early 1870s, black politicians questioned the diversion of scarce revenues to railroads and tax breaks for corporations. Instead, they demanded public services, especially universal education. But more government services meant higher property taxes at a time of severe economic hardship. White small farmers had been devastated by the Civil War. Unaccustomed to paying

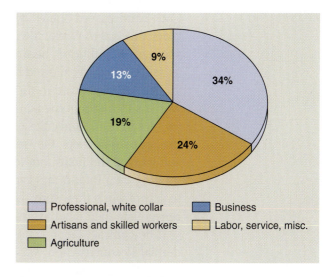

Figure 16–1 Occupations of African American Officeholders During Reconstruction Although former slaves were under-represented among black officeholders, the Reconstruction governments were among the most broadly representative legislatures in U.S. history.

"Radical Members" One of the greatest achievements of congressional Reconstruction was the election of a significant number of African Americans to public office. Only in South Carolina, however, did African Americans ever form a legislative majority.

high taxes, and believing strongly in limited government, they grew increasingly receptive to Democratic appeals for restoration of "white man's government." Thus southern Republicans were unable to develop a program that could unite the diverse interests of their party's constituents.

Despite powerful opposition at home and lukewarm support from Washington, DC, radical governments in the South boasted several important achievements. They funded the construction of hospitals, insane asylums, prisons, and roads. They introduced homestead exemptions that protected the property of poor farmers. One of their top priorities was the establishment of universal public education. Republican legislatures established public school systems that were a major improvement over their antebellum counterparts. The literacy rate among southern blacks rose steadily.

Nevertheless, public schools for southern blacks remained inadequately funded and sharply segregated. In Savannah, Georgia, for example, the school board allocated less than 5 percent of its 1873 budget to black schools, although white children were in the minority in the district. In South Carolina, fewer than one in three school-age children was being educated in 1872.

The Political Economy of Sharecropping

Congressional Reconstruction made it easier for the former slaves to negotiate the terms of their labor contracts. Republican state legislatures abolished the Black Codes and passed "lien" laws, statutes giving black workers more control over the crops they grew. Workers with grievances had a better chance of securing justice, as southern Republicans became sheriffs, justices of the peace, and county clerks, and as southern courts allowed blacks to serve as witnesses and sit on juries.

The strongest card in the hands of the freed people was a shortage of agricultural workers throughout the South. After emancipation thousands of blacks sought opportunities in towns and cities or in the North. And even though most blacks remained in the South as farmers, they reduced their working hours in several ways. Black women still worked the fields, but less often than they had as slaves. They spent more time nursing their infants and caring for their children. And the children themselves went to school when they were able. The resulting labor shortage forced white landlords to renegotiate their labor arrangements with the freed people.

The contract labor system that had developed during the war and under presidential Reconstruction was replaced with a variety of arrangements in different regions. On the sugar plantations of southern Louisiana, the freed people became wage laborers. But in tobacco and cotton regions, where the vast majority of freed people lived, a new system of labor called *sharecropping* developed. Under the sharecropping system, an agricultural worker and his family typically agreed to work for one year on a particular plot of land, the landowner providing the tools, seed, and work animals. At the end of the year the sharecropper and the landlord split the crop, perhaps one-third going to the sharecropper and two-thirds to the owner.

Sharecropping shaped the economy of the postwar South by transforming the way cash crops were produced and marketed. Most dramatically, it required landowners to break up their plantations into family-sized plots, where sharecroppers worked in family units with no direct supervision. Each sharecropping family established its own relationship with local merchants to sell crops and buy supplies. Merchants became crucial to the southern credit system because during the Civil War Congress had established nationwide banking standards that most southern banks could not meet. Therefore storekeepers were usually the only people who could extend credit to sharecroppers. They provided sharecroppers with food, fertilizer, animal feed, and other provisions over the course of the year, until the crop was harvested.

These developments had important consequences for white small farmers. As the number of merchants grew, they fanned out into up-country areas inhabited mostly by ordinary whites. Reconstruction legislatures meanwhile sponsored the construction of railroads in those districts. The combination of merchants offering credit and

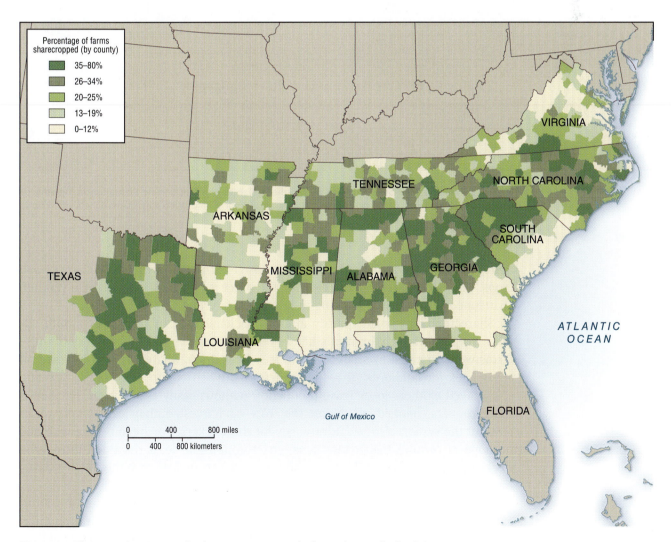

Map 16-2 Sharecropping By 1880 the sharecropping system had spread across the South. It was most common in the inland areas, where primarily cotton and tobacco plantations existed before the Civil War.

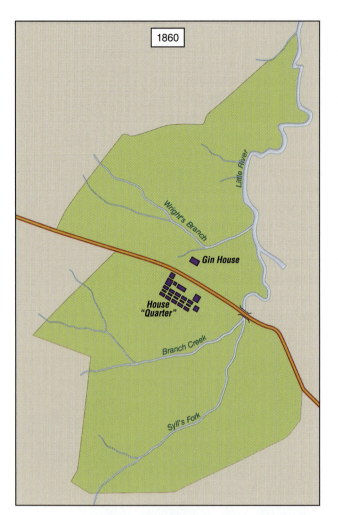
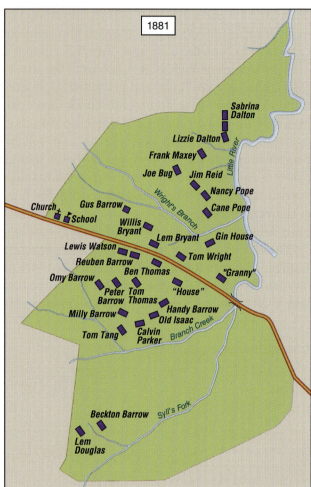

Map 16-3 The Effect of Sharecropping on Southern Plantations: The Barrow Plantation in Oglethorpe County, Georgia Sharecropping cut large estates into small landholdings worked by sharecroppers and tenants, changing the landscape of the South.

railroads offering transportation made it easier for small farmers to produce cash crops. Thus Reconstruction accelerated the process by which the southern yeomen abandoned self-sufficient farming in favor of cash crops.

Sharecropping spread quickly among black farmers in the cotton South. By 1880, 80 percent of cotton farms had fewer than 50 acres and the majority of those farms were operated by sharecroppers (see Map 16–2). Sharecropping had several advantages for landlords. It reduced their risk when cotton prices were low and encouraged workers to increase production without costly supervision. Further, if sharecroppers changed jobs before the crop was harvested, they lost a whole year's pay. But the system also had advantages for the workers. For freed people who had no hope of owning their own farms, sharecropping at least rewarded those who worked hard. The bigger the crop, the more they earned. It gave the former slaves more independence than contract labor.

Sharecropping also allowed the freed people to work in families rather than in gangs. Freedom alone had rearranged the powers of men, women, and children within the families of former slaves. Parents gained newfound control over the lives of their children. They could send sons and daughters to school; they could put them to work. Successful parents could give their children an important head start in life. Similarly, African American husbands gained new powers.

The laws of marriage in the mid-nineteenth century defined the husband as the head of the household. These laws had been irrelevant to slaves, since their marriages had no legal standing. With emancipation the patriarchal assumptions of American family law shaped the lives of freedmen and freedwomen in ways they never had before. Once married, women often found that their property belonged to their husbands. The sharecropping system further assumed that the husband was the head of the household and that he made the economic decisions for the entire family. Men signed most labor contracts, and most contracts assumed that the husband would take his family to work with him.

Sharecropping thereby shaped the social system of the postwar South: It influenced the balance of power between men and women. It established the balance of power between landowners and sharecroppers. It tied the southern economy to agriculture, in particular to cotton production, seriously impeding the region's overall economic development. Yet even as this new way of life was taking shape, the Republican Party was retreating from its commitment to the freed people.

The Retreat from Republican Radicalism

By the late 1860s the Republican coalition was splintering in ways that weakened the party's continued commitment to radical Reconstruction. By 1868 the Republicans were presenting themselves to voters as the party of moderation. The success of this appeal brought in its wake the last major achievements of Reconstruction.

The Impeachment and Trial of Andrew Johnson

Throughout 1866 and much of 1867, President Johnson waged a relentless campaign against Congress and the radicals. Inevitably, this conflict led to a struggle over control of the military in the South. The First Reconstruction Act placed the entire South under

Question: Where did you come from?

Answer: I came from Winston County.

Question: What occasioned your coming here?

Answer: I got run by the Ku-Klux. . . .

Question: What did they do to you?

Answer: . . . They surrounded me in the floor and tore my shirt off. They got me out on the floor; some had me by the legs and some by the arms and the neck and anywhere, just like dogs string out a coon, and they took me out to the big road before my gate and whipped me until I couldn't move or holler or do nothing, but just lay there like a log, and every lick they hit me I grunted just like a mule when he is stalled fast and whipped. . . .

Question: Did they tell you they whipped you because you were a radical?

Answer: They told me, "God damn you, when you meet a white man in the road lift your hat; I'll learn you, God damn you, that you are a nigger, and not to be going about like you thought yourself a white man."

CONGRESSIONAL TESTIMONY OF WILLIAM COLEMAN,
Macon, Mississippi, November 6, 1871

direct military power. The Freedmen's Bureau itself was a branch of the U.S. Army. Judicial authority was vested in the provost marshals. The military also oversaw voter registration. But the president was the commander in chief of the military, and, exercising his authority over the military, Andrew Johnson removed dozens of Freedmen's Bureau officials who enforced the Civil Rights Act of 1866. He replaced Republican provost marshals with men who were hostile to Congress and contemptuous of the former slaves. In short, Johnson went out of his way to undermine the will of Congress.

Impeachment Ticket Congressmen were besieged with requests for these tickets to the Senate gallery by constituents who wanted to observe the impeachment proceedings.

Radicals called for Johnson's impeachment, but moderates and conservatives resisted. Instead, Congress hoped to restrain the president by refining the Reconstruction Acts and by using the Tenure of Office Act of March 2, 1867. This act prohibited the president from removing officials whose appointments required Congressional approval. One purpose of the law was to prevent Johnson from firing Secretary of War Edwin M. Stanton, who was sympathetic to the Republicans. A related statute required that all presidential orders to the military pass through General Ulysses S. Grant. Republicans hoped that this would prevent the president from removing military officials who enforced the Reconstruction Acts.

Congress's actions only provoked the president. In his veto messages and public pronouncements Johnson indulged in blatant racist pandering. He played on fears of "amalgamation," "miscegenation," and racial "degeneration." He expressed fear for the safety of white women, when all the evidence suggested that it was black women who were most in danger. In the off-year elections of 1867, northern Democrats played the race card relentlessly and successfully. Democratic victories erased many of the huge Republican gains of 1866 and inspired the president to defy congressional restraints. As a deliberate provocation, Johnson asked Secretary of War Stanton to resign on August 5, 1867. Stanton refused, and the president appointed General Grant as interim secretary of war. Still Stanton would not budge, so in February 1868 Johnson fired him. For this the House of Representatives voted to impeach the president and put him on trial in the Senate.

For all the congressional animosity that Johnson had aroused by his obnoxious behavior, the senators trying him took their job seriously. Many were concerned that the Tenure of Office Act, which Johnson was accused of violating, was in fact unconstitutional. Others wondered whether his technical breach of the law was serious enough to warrant his removal from office. These and other doubts, along with Johnson's promise of good behavior in the future, led the Senate to acquit the president by a single vote.

Republicans Become the Party of Moderation

While Andrew Johnson was on trial in the Senate, voters in Michigan went to the polls and overwhelmingly rejected a new state constitution that granted blacks the right to vote. Coming on the heels of Democratic victories in 1867, the Michigan results were read by Republicans as a rejection of radical Reconstruction.

AMERICA AND THE WORLD

>> Reconstructing America's Foreign Policy

Before the Civil War, Republicans associated expansionism with the slave power and the Democratic Party. But with the triumph of nationalism, the Republicans equated American overseas expansion with the spread of liberty. They went on the offensive. In 1867 Secretary of State William Seward successfully negotiated the purchase of Alaska from Russia. The successful acquisition of Alaska ignited expansionist dreams of eventual U.S. control of all of North America, including Canada and Mexico, and "all the West Indian Islands."

The administration was equally adroit in its negotiations with Great Britain over the settlement of the so-called *Alabama* claims. In 1872 the English accepted responsibility for having helped equip the Confederate navy during the Civil War and agreed to pay over $15 million for damage to American shipping by the *Alabama* and other southern warships built in England.

Two years earlier, in 1870, a coalition of supporters with varying interests came together in support of the annexation of the island nation of Santo Domingo. The Grant administration strongly supported the treaty. Republicans who had once objected to such schemes as tainted by their association with slavery now switched sides and endorsed annexation. It would, they claimed, allow "our neighbors to join with us in the blessings of our free institutions." Thus the abolition of slavery in the United States

was said to have purified the motives for American expansion. Even Frederick Douglass endorsed the annexation of Santo Domingo. It would help the island's inhabitants rise out of their truly grinding poverty, Douglass said, by transplanting "within her tropical borders" America's "glorious institutions."

But Grant's aggressive foreign policy did not go uncontested. Grant tried to bulldoze the treaty through Congress, but he was thwarted by Senator Charles Sumner of Massachusetts, the powerful chairman of the Foreign Relations Committee. Sumner took a principled stance against imperial ventures in general, but he was particularly concerned to protect the independence of the black republic of Haiti, which shared the island with Santo Domingo. A handful of Republicans, including Carl Schurz and Oliver P. Morton, likewise opposed the treaty, but most of the party sided with the president. Yet Sumner succeeded in having the treaty rejected, by a 28–28 tie vote, thanks to the opposition of Senate Democrats. They opposed annexation for racist reasons: they objected to incorporating into the United States an island populated by dark-skinned peoples of an inferior race. Thus the prewar alignments on expansionism were largely reversed by the Civil War. The Republican Party became the spearhead of American imperialism, while Democrats largely opposed it. ●

During the 1868 elections Republicans repudiated the radicals' demand for nationwide black suffrage, arguing that the black vote was a uniquely southern solution to a uniquely southern problem. The northern states should be free to decide for themselves whether to grant African American men the vote. Congress readmitted six southern states to the Union, thereby demonstrating that Republican policies had successfully restored law and order to the South. By nominating General Ulysses Grant as their presidential candidate, the Republicans confirmed their retreat from radicalism. "Let Us Have Peace" was Grant's campaign slogan.

In sharp contrast, the Democrats nominated Horatio Seymour, who ran a vicious campaign of race-baiting. The Democratic platform denounced the Reconstruction Acts and promised to restore white rule to the South. Seymour suggested that a Democratic president might nullify the governments organized under congressional Reconstruction. Where the Republicans promised order and stability, the Democrats seemed to promise continued disruption. Northern fears were confirmed by the violence that swept the South during the election, incited by southern Democrats to keep black voters from the polls.

The Ku Klux Klan, which systematically intimidated potential black voters, was one of several secretive organizations dedicated to the violent overthrow of radical Reconstruction and the restoration of white supremacy. They included the Knights of the White Camelia, the Red Shirts, and the Night Riders. Some tried to force blacks to go back to work for white landlords. Some attacked African Americans who refused to abide by traditional codes of racial etiquette. But in the main, such organizations worked to restore the political power of the Democratic Party in the South. They intimidated white Republicans, burned homes of black families, and lynched African Americans who showed signs of political activism. It is fair to say that in 1868 the Ku Klux Klan served as the paramilitary arm of the southern Democratic Party.

As a means of restoring white supremacy, the Klan's strategy of violence backfired. A wave of disgust swept across the North, and the Republicans regained control of the White House, along with 25 of the 33 state legislatures. The victorious Republicans quickly seized the opportunity to preserve the achievements of the Reconstruction.

The Republicans reinforced their moderate image by attempting to restore law and order in the South. Congressional hearings produced vivid evidence of the Klan's violent efforts to suppress the black vote. Congress responded with a series of Enforcement Acts, designed to "enforce" the recently enacted Fifteenth Amendment (see the following section). After some initial hesitation, the Grant administration used the new laws to initiate anti-Klan prosecutions that effectively diminished political violence throughout the South. As a result the 1872 presidential elections were relatively free of disruption.

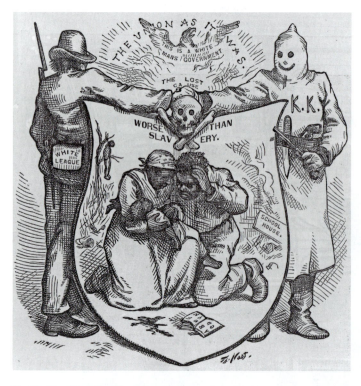

The Ku Klux Klan The Klan was one of a number of racist vigilante groups trying to restore the Democratic Party to power in the postwar South.

Reconstructing the North

Although Reconstruction was aimed primarily at the South, the North was affected as well. The struggle over the black vote spilled beyond the borders of the defeated Confederacy. Although not as dramatic as developments in the South, the transformation of the North was still an important chapter in the history of Reconstruction.

The Fifteenth Amendment and Nationwide African American Suffrage

Before the Civil War, blacks in the North were segregated in theaters, restaurants, cemeteries, hotels, streetcars, ferries, and schools. Most northern blacks could not vote, either because they were expressly denied the privilege or because of discriminatory property requirements that blacks alone were required to meet. The Civil War galvanized the northern black community to launch an assault on racial discrimination, with some success. In 1863 California removed the ban on black testimony in criminal courts. Two years later Illinois did the same. During the war, many northern cities abolished streetcar segregation. But when they considered black voting, northern whites retained their traditional racial prejudices. In 1865 voters in three northern states (Connecticut, Wisconsin, and Minnesota) rejected constitutional amendments to enfranchise African American men. In 1867, even as the Republican Congress was imposing the black vote on the South, black suffrage was defeated by voters in Ohio, Minnesota, and Kansas.

The shocking electoral violence of 1868 persuaded many northerners that, given the chance, southern whites would quickly strip blacks of the right to vote. In Iowa and Minnesota, voters finally approved black suffrage. Emboldened by their victory in the 1868 elections, the following year Republicans passed the Fifteenth Amendment to the Constitution. It prohibited the use of "race, color, or previous condition of servitude" to disqualify voters anywhere in the United States. By outlawing voter discrimination on the basis of race, the Fifteenth Amendment protected the most radical achievement of congressional Reconstruction.

The Fifteenth Amendment brought Reconstruction directly into the North by overturning the state laws that discriminated against black voters. In addition, Congress required ratification of the amendment in those southern states still to be readmitted to the Union. Virginia, Mississippi, and Texas did so and were restored to the Union in early 1870. On March 30, 1870, the Fifteenth Amendment became part of the Constitution. For the first time, racial criteria for voting were banned everywhere in the United States, North as well as South.

Women and Suffrage

The issue of black voting divided northern radicals, especially feminists and abolitionists, who had long been allies in the struggle for emancipation. Signs of trouble appeared as early as May 1863 when a dispute broke out at the convention of the Woman's National Loyal League in New York City. One of the convention's resolutions declared that "there never can be a true peace in this Republic until the civil and political rights of all citizens of African descent and all women are practically established." For some of the delegates, this went too far. The Loyal League had been organized to assist in defeating the slave South. Some delegates argued that it was inappropriate to inject the issue of women's rights into the struggle to restore the Union.

By the end of the war, radicals were pressing for black suffrage in addition to emancipation. This precipitated an increasingly rancorous debate among reformers. Abolitionists argued that, while they supported women's suffrage, the critical issue was the protection of the freed people of the South. This, abolitionist Wendell Phillips argued, was "the Negro's Hour." Phillips's position sparked a sense of betrayal among some women's rights activists. For 20 years they had pressed their claims for the right to vote. They were loyal allies of the Republican Party, and now the Republicans abandoned them. It would be better, Elizabeth Cady Stanton argued, to press for "a vote based on intelligence and education for black and white, man and woman." Voting rights based on "intelligence and education" would have excluded virtually all the freed slaves as well as the working-class Irish, Germans, and Chinese. Thus, Stanton's remarks revealed a strain of elitism that further alienated abolitionists.

Not all feminists agreed with Stanton, and as racist violence erupted in the South, abolitionists argued that black suffrage was more urgent than women's suffrage. The black vote "is with us a matter of life and death," Frederick Douglass argued. "I have always championed women's right to vote; but it will be seen that the present claim for the negro is one of the most urgent necessity."

Stanton was unmoved by such arguments. For her the Fifteenth Amendment barring racial qualifications for voting was the last straw. Supporters of women's suffrage opposed the Fifteenth Amendment on the ground that it subjected elite, educated women to the rule of base and illiterate males, especially immigrants and blacks. Abolitionists were shocked by such opinions. They favored universal suffrage, not the "educated" suffrage that Stanton was calling for. The breach between reformers weakened the coalition of radicals pushing to maintain a vigorous Reconstruction policy in the South.

The Rise and Fall of the National Labor Union

Inspired by the radicalism of the Civil War and Reconstruction, industrial workers across the North organized dozens of craft unions, Eight-Hour Leagues, and workingmen's associations. The general goal of these associations was to protect northern workers who were overworked and underpaid. They called strikes, initiated consumer boycotts, and formed consumer cooperatives. In 1867 and 1868 workers in New York and Massachusetts launched campaigns to enact laws restricting the workday to eight hours. Shortly thereafter workers began electing their own candidates to state legislatures.

Elizabeth Cady Stanton A leading advocate of women's rights, Stanton was angered when Congress gave African American men the vote without also giving it to women.

Founded in 1866, the National Labor Union (NLU) was the first significant postwar effort to organize all "working people" into a national union. William Sylvis, an iron molder, founded the NLU and became its president in 1868. He denied that there was any "harmony of interests" between workers and capitalists. On the contrary, every wage earner in America was at war with every capitalist, whose "profits" robbed working people of the fruits of their labor.

Under Sylvis's direction the NLU advocated a wide range of political reforms, not just bread-and-butter issues. Sylvis believed that through successful organization American workers could take the "first step toward competence and independence." He argued for a doubling of the average worker's wages. He supported voting rights for blacks and women. Nevertheless, after a miserable showing in the elections of 1872, the NLU fell apart. By then Reconstruction in the South was also ending.

The End of Reconstruction

National events had as much to do with the end of Reconstruction as did events in the South. A nationwide outbreak of political corruption in the late 1860s and 1870s provoked a sharp reaction. Influential northern Liberals, previously known for their support for Reconstruction, abandoned the Republican Party in disgust in 1872. The end of Reconstruction finally came after electoral violence corrupted the 1876 elections. Republican politicians in Washington, DC, responded with a sordid political bargain that came to symbolize the end of an era.

Corruption as a National Problem

Postwar Americans witnessed an extraordinary display of public dishonesty. Democrats were as prone to thievery as Republicans. Northern swindlers looted the public treasuries from Boston to San Francisco. In the South, both black and white legislators took bribes. Corruption, it seemed, was endemic to postwar American politics.

If corruption was everywhere in the late 1860s and 1870s, it was largely because there were more opportunities for it than ever before. The Civil War and Reconstruction had swollen government budgets. Never before was government so

> Within the last seven years we have passed through the most gigantic war the world ever saw. A rebellion such as no other government could have successfully combated. . . . No man in America rejoiced more than I at the downfall of negro slavery. But when the shackles fell from the limbs of those four millions of blacks, it did not make them **free** men; it simply transferred them from one condition of slavery to another; it placed them upon the platform of the white workingmen, and made all slaves together. I do not mean that freeing the negro enslaved the white; I mean that we were slaves before, always have been, and that that abolition of the right of property in man added four millions of black slaves to the white slaves of the country. We are now all one family of slaves together; and the labor reform movement is a second emancipation proclamation.
>
> SPEECH BY WILLIAM SYLVIS,
> September 16, 1868

active in collecting taxes and disbursing vast sums for the public good. Under the circumstances, many government officials traded bribes for votes, embezzled public funds, or used insider knowledge to defraud taxpayers.

The federal government set the tone. In the most notorious case, the directors of the Union Pacific Railroad set up a dummy corporation called the Credit Mobilier, awarded it phony contracts, and protected it from inquiry by bribing influential congressmen. The Grant administration was eventually smeared with scandal as well. Although personally honest, the president surrounded himself with rich nobodies and army buddies rather than respected statesmen. Grant's own private secretary was exposed as a member of the "Whiskey Ring," a cabal of distillers and revenue agents who cheated the government out of millions of tax dollars every year.

State and city governments in the North were no less corrupt. Wealthy businessmen curried favor with politicians whose votes would determine where a railroad would be built, which land would be allocated for rights of way, and how many government bonds had to be floated to pay for such projects. State officials regularly accepted gifts, received salaries, and sat on the boards of corporations directly affected by their votes. Municipalities awarded lucrative contracts for the construction of schools, parks, libraries, water and sewer systems, and mass-transportation networks, creating temptations for corruption. The Tweed Ring alone bilked New York City out of tens of millions of dollars. By these standards the corruption of the southern Reconstruction legislatures was relatively small.

But corruption in the South was real enough, and it had particular significance for Reconstruction. Southern Republicans of modest means depended heavily on the money they earned as public officials. These same men found themselves responsible for the collection of unusually high taxes and for economic development projects. As elsewhere in industrializing America, the lure of corruption proved overwhelming. The Republican governor of Louisiana grew rich while in office by "exacting tribute" from railroads seeking state favors. Corruption on a vast scale implied petty corruption as well. Individual legislators sold their votes for as little as $200.

In many cases opponents of Reconstruction used attacks on corruption to mask their contempt for Republican policies. Their strategy helped galvanize opposition, destroying Republican hopes of attracting white voters. Finally, corruption in the South helped provoke a backlash against active government nationwide, weakening northern support for

William Marcy Tweed The boss of New York's notoriously corrupt "Tweed Ring" was parodied by the great cartoonist Thomas Nast. His portrayal of the bloated public official became an enduring symbol of governmental corruption.

Reconstruction. The intellectual substance of this backlash was provided by influential liberal Republicans, many of whom had once been ardent supporters of radical Reconstruction.

Liberal Republicans Revolt

The label "liberal Republicans" embraced a loosely knit group of intellectuals, politicians, publishers, and businessmen from the northern elite who were discouraged by the failure of radical Reconstruction to bring peace to the southern states and disgusted by the corruption of postwar politics. Although small in number, liberals exercised important influence in northern politics.

At the heart of liberal philosophy was a deep suspicion of democracy. Liberals argued that any government beholden to the interests of the ignorant masses was doomed to corruption. They believed that public servants should be chosen on the basis of intelligence, as measured by civil-service examinations, rather than by patronage appointments that sustained corrupt party machines. Indeed, to liberals, party politics was the enemy of good government.

Liberals therefore grew increasingly alienated from the Republican Party and from President Grant. Above all, they resented the fact that the Republican Party had changed as its idealistic commitment to free labor waned and its radical vanguard disappeared. To the rising generation of Republican leaders, getting and holding office had become an end in itself.

As Republicans lost their identity as moral crusaders, liberal reformers proposed a new vision of their own. In 1872 they supported Horace Greeley as the Democratic presidential candidate. The liberal plank in the Democratic platform proclaimed the party's commitment to universal equality before the law, the integrity of the Union, and support for the Thirteenth, Fourteenth, and Fifteenth Amendments. At the same time, liberals demanded "the immediate and absolute removal of all disabilities" imposed on the South, as well as a "universal amnesty" for ex-Confederates. Finally, the liberals declared their belief that "local self-government" would "guard the rights of all citizens more securely than any centralized power." In effect, the liberals were demanding the end of federal efforts to protect the former slaves.

In the long run, the liberal view would prevail, but in 1872 it did not go over well with the voters. The liberals' biggest liability was their presidential candidate. Horace Greeley's erratic reputation and Republican background were too much, and Democrats refused to vote for him. Grant was easily reelected, but he and his fellow Republicans saw the returns as evidence that Reconstruction was becoming a political liability.

The 1874 elections confirmed the lesson. Democrats made sweeping gains all across the North, and an ideological stalemate developed. For a generation, neither party would clearly dominate American politics. The Republicans would take no more risks in support of Reconstruction.

During his second term, therefore, Grant did little to protect black voters from violence in the South. Not even the Civil Rights Act of 1875 undid the impression of waning Republican zeal. Ostensibly designed to prohibit racial discrimination in public places, the Civil Rights Act lacked enforcement provisions. The bill's most important clause, prohibiting segregated schools, was eliminated from the final version. Southern states ignored even this watered-down statute, and in 1883 the Supreme Court declared it unconstitutional. Thus the last significant piece of

Reconstruction legislation was an ironic testament to the Republican Party's declining commitment to equal rights.

A Depression and a Deal "Redeem" the South

Angered by corruption and high taxes, white voters across the South succumbed to the Democratic Party's appeal for restoration of white supremacy. As the number of white Republicans fell, the number of black Republicans holding office in the South increased, even as the Grant administration backed away from civil rights. But the persistence of black officeholders only reinforced the Democrats' determination to "redeem" their states from Republican rule. Democrats had taken control of Virginia in 1869. North Carolina was redeemed in 1870, Georgia in 1871, and Texas in 1873. Then panic struck.

In September 1873 America's premier financial institution, Jay Cooke, went bankrupt after overextending itself on investments in the Northern Pacific Railroad. Within weeks hundreds of banks and thousands of businesses went bankrupt as well. The country sank into a depression that lasted five years. Unemployment rose to 14 percent as corporations slashed wages. To protect their incomes, railroad workers tried to organize a nationwide union and attempted to strike several times. Their employers, however, repeatedly thwarted such efforts, and the strikes failed.

As the nation turned its attention to labor unrest and economic depression, the Republican Party's commitment to Reconstruction all but disappeared. Democrats regained control of the governments of Alabama and Arkansas in 1874. In the few southern states where black Republicans clung to political power, white "redeemers" used violence to overthrow the last remnants of Reconstruction.

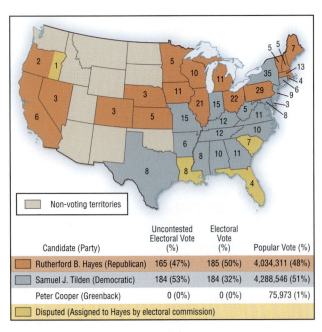

Candidate (Party)	Uncontested Electoral Vote (%)	Electoral Vote (%)	Popular Vote (%)
Rutherford B. Hayes (Republican)	165 (47%)	185 (50%)	4,034,311 (48%)
Samuel J. Tilden (Democratic)	184 (53%)	184 (32%)	4,288,546 (51%)
Peter Cooper (Greenback)	0 (0%)	0 (0%)	75,973 (1%)

Non-voting territories

Disputed (Assigned to Hayes by electoral commission)

Map 16–4 The Presidential Election, 1876 In 1876 the Democratic presidential candidate, Samuel Tilden, won the popular vote but was denied the presidency because the Republicans who controlled Congress chose to interpret voting irregularities in Louisiana, South Carolina, Oregon, and Florida in a way that gave their candidate, Rutherford B. Hayes, all of the disputed electoral votes.

Mississippi established the model in 1875, so much so that it became known as "the Mississippi Plan." Confident that authorities in Washington, DC, would no longer interfere in the South, Democrats launched an all-out campaign to regain control of the state government. The Democratic campaign was double edged. Crude appeals to white supremacy further reduced the dwindling number of scalawags. To defeat black Republicans, White Leagues organized a campaign of violence and intimidation to keep blacks away from the polls. Republicans were beaten, forced to flee the state, and in several cases murdered. Washington turned a deaf ear to African American pleas for protection. In the end enough blacks were kept from the polls and enough scalawags voted their racial prejudices to put the Democrats in power. Mississippi was "redeemed."

The tactics used in Mississippi were repeated elsewhere the following year, with dramatic consequences for the presidential election of 1876. Amidst a serious economic depression, and with an electorate tired of Reconstruction, the Democrats stood a good chance of winning the presidency. In fact, the

Democratic candidate, Samuel J. Tilden, won 250,000 more votes than the Republican, Rutherford B. Hayes (see Map 16–4). But electoral fraud in South Carolina, Louisiana, Florida, and Oregon threw the results into doubt.

If all of the electoral votes from those states went to Hayes, he would win, but if even a single electoral vote went to Tilden, he would win, the first Democrat to win the presidency in 20 years. The outcome was determined by an electoral commission with a Republican majority, and the commission awarded every disputed electoral vote to the Republican candidate. When Hayes was inaugurated on March 4, 1877, the legitimacy of his presidency was already in doubt. But what he did shortly after taking office made it appear as though he had won thanks to a sordid "compromise" with the Democrats to end Reconstruction in the South. There is no solid evidence that such a deal was ever actually made. Nevertheless, Hayes ordered the federal troops guarding the Republican statehouses in South Carolina and Louisiana to leave. This order marked the formal end of military occupation of the South and the symbolic end of Reconstruction. By late 1877, every southern state had been redeemed by the Democrats.

The following year the Supreme Court began to issue rulings that further undermined the achievements of Reconstruction. In *Hall v. DeCuir* (1878) the Supreme Court invalidated a Louisiana law that prohibited racial segregation on public transportation. In 1882, the justices declared unconstitutional a federal law that protected southern African Americans against racially motivated murders and assaults. More important, in the Civil Rights Cases of 1883, the Supreme Court declared that the Fourteenth Amendment did not pertain to discriminatory practices by private persons. The Supreme Court thus put the finishing touches on the national retreat from Reconstruction.

Conclusion

Inspired by an idealized vision of a society based on equal rights and free labor, Republicans expected emancipation to bring about a dramatic transformation of the South. Freed from the shackles of the slave power, the entire region would soon become a shining example of democracy and prosperity. If the results were less than Republicans expected, the achievements of Reconstruction were nonetheless impressive. Across the South, African American men and women carved out a space in which their families could live more freely than before. Black men by the tens of thousands elected to office some of the most democratic state legislatures of the nineteenth century. Thousands more black workers repudiated an objectionable contract-labor system in favor of an innovative compromise known as sharecropping. Furthermore, Reconstruction added three important amendments to the Constitution that transformed civil rights and electoral laws throughout the nation.

Nevertheless, the Republicans washed their hands of Reconstruction with unseemly haste. The Republicans left southern blacks unprotected in a hostile world. Sharecropping offered them a degree of personal autonomy but little hope of real economic independence. Democratic redeemers excluded blacks from the substance of power. Tired of Reconstruction, Americans turned their attention to the new and difficult problems of urban and industrial America.

Further Readings

Dan T. Carter, *When the War Was Over: The Failure of Self-Reconstruction in the West* (1985). Particularly good on the crucial year of 1865.

W. E. B. DuBois, *Black Reconstruction in America, 1860–1880* (1935). A work of passion and scholarship, with a devastating critique of the way historians of his day discussed Reconstruction.

Carol Faulkner, *Women's Radical Reconstruction* (2004). One of a number of important recent studies of women and Reconstruction.

Eric Foner, *Reconstruction: America's Unfinished Revolution, 1863–1877* (1988). A modern classic, the best one-volume treatment of the period.

Susan Eva O'Donovan, *Becoming Free in the Cotton South* (2007). A finely grained case study, especially insightful on gender.

Roger Ransom and Richard Sutch, *One Kind of Freedom* (2001, revised edition). The authors provide a clear picture of the breakup of the plantation system and the emergence of sharecropping.

John C. Rodrigue, *Reconstruction in the Cane Fields* (2001). An important study of an important part of the story.

Mark W. Summers, *The Era of Good Stealings* (1993). A lively treatment of the corruption issue.

Who, What

>> Timeline >>

▼ 1863
Lincoln's Proclamation of Amnesty and Reconstruction

▼ 1864
Wade-Davis Bill

▼ 1865
General Sherman's Special Field Order No. 15
Freedmen's Bureau established
Lincoln's second inaugural

Lincoln assassinated; Andrew Johnson becomes president
General Howard's Circular 13
President Johnson orders the Freedmen's Bureau to return confiscated lands to former owners
Joint Committee on Reconstruction established by Congress

▼ 1866
Congress renews Freedmen's Bureau; Johnson vetoes renewal bill

Civil Rights Act vetoed by Johnson
Congress overrides presidential veto of Civil Rights Act
Congress passes Fourteenth Amendment
Congress passes another Freedmen's Bureau Bill over Johnson's veto
Republicans sweep midterm elections

Review Questions

1. What were the three major phases of Reconstruction?

2. What made congressional Reconstruction "radical?"

3. How did Reconstruction change the South?

4. How did Reconstruction change the North?

5. What were the major factors that brought Reconstruction to an end?

Websites

Freedmen's Bureau Online. http://www.freedmensbureau.com/

Reconstruction: The Second Civil War. http://www.pbs.org/wgbh/amex/reconstruction/

For further review materials and resource information, please visit www.oup.com/us/ofthepeople

▼ **1867**
First and Second Reconstruction Acts
Tenure of Office Act

▼ **1868**
Johnson fires Secretary of War Stanton
House of Representatives impeaches Johnson
Senate trial of Johnson begins
Acquittal of Johnson

Fourteenth Amendment ratified
Ulysses S. Grant wins presidential election

▼ **1869**
Congress passes Fifteenth Amendment

▼ **1870**
Fifteenth Amendment ratified

▼ **1872**
"Liberal Republicans" leave their party
Grant reelected

▼ **1873**
Financial "panic" sets off depression

▼ **1875**
"Mississippi Plan" succeeds
Civil Rights Act of 1875 enacted

▼ **1876**
Disputed presidential election

▼ **1877**
Electoral commission awards presidency to
    Rutherford B. Hayes

CHAPTER

17

Common Threads

>> In what ways were the problems of Reconstruction and the problems of industrialization similar?

>> What made "big business" different from earlier enterprises?

>> Does the new social order of the late nineteenth century look more like what came before it, or more like what came later on?

The Triumph of Industrial Capitalism 1850–1890

>> Rosa Cassettari

In 1884 Rosa Cassettari left the Italian village of Cuggiono, near Milan, to meet her husband Santino, a miner in Union, Missouri. Theirs had been an arranged marriage, and Rosa was reluctant to go, especially because she had to leave behind her infant son. "It is wonderful to go to America even if you don't want to go to Santino," Rosa's friends told her at the train station in Milan. "You will get smart in America. And in America you will not be so poor." Along with millions of others, Rosa entered a stream of migrants coming from the far corners of Europe. At Le Havre, France, she embarked on a ship for America. "All us poor people had to go down through a hole to the bottom of the ship," she remembered. But she was going to "America! The country where everyone would find work! Where wages were so high that no one had to go hungry! Where all men were free and equal and where even the poor could own land!"

Rosa's first taste of America did not live up to such dreams. In New York she was cheated and forced to make the long trip to Missouri with nothing to eat. When she arrived at the town of Union she found a shabby collection of tents and shacks. Life in the mining camp lived up to her fears rather than her hopes. With no doctors or midwives available, Rosa gave birth to a premature child alone on the floor of her cabin. Santino was an abusive husband and a cruel father. Rosa had to supplement his earnings by cooking for 12 additional miners.

Yet Rosa was impressed by many things about America. Poor people did not behave humbly in the presence of the rich, for example, and even in the difficult circumstances of the mining camp Rosa became accustomed to wearing decent clothing and eating meat every day, things she could never do back in Europe.

When Rosa discovered that her husband planned to spend all their savings to open a house of prostitution, she separated from Santino. With the help of her immigrant friends from Missouri, Rosa moved to Chicago with her two children. She took a job at a place called Hull House where the social workers were so impressed by her life story that they wrote it down and published it as *Rosa Cassettari's Autobiography*.

Rosa was one of millions of men and women who were moving around the world in the late nineteenth century. They moved from the countryside to the city or from town to town. They moved from less developed regions to places where industrialization was well under way. The nerve center for all of the movement was a powerful core of industrial capitalist societies, and at the center of the core was the United States. Migrants were on a worldwide trek, but more of them came to the United States than any other nation.

Perpetual human migration, global in its extent, had become a hallmark of the political economy of industrial capitalism. Common laborers moved from place to place because jobs were unsteady. Railroads hired construction workers who moved as the track was laid and had to find other work when the line was finished. African American sharecroppers in the South moved at year's end. Over time they moved into cotton-growing districts, into towns and cities, or out of the South. White tenant farmers moved into mill towns. Native Americans were pushed off their lands throughout the trans-Mississippi West, making room for a flood of white settlers. And all across America the children of farmers abandoned the rural life: they went to mill villages and to huge cities like New York, Chicago, and Philadelphia.

They went looking for work, and for most migrants that meant working in a bureaucracy under professional managers who controlled the work process. It meant working with new and complicated machines. It meant working with polluted air, dirty rivers, or spoiled land. Most of all, industrial capitalism meant wage labor. Working people had been freed from the

continued

>> AMERICAN PORTRAIT *continued*

things that tied them to the land in other places and earlier times, such as feudal dues, slavery, and even independent farming. But wage labor released men and women to move about from community to community, from country to country, and finally from continent to continent. To watch Rosa Cassettari as she traveled from Cuggiono to Missouri and Chicago is to witness one small part of a global process set in motion by the triumph of wage labor. ●

The Political Economy of Global Capitalism

The economic history of the late nineteenth century was sandwiched between two great financial panics in 1873 and 1893. Both were followed by prolonged periods of high unemployment and led directly to tremendous labor unrest. The years between the two panics were marked by a general decline in prices that placed a terrible burden on producers. Farmers found that their crops were worth less at harvest time than they had been during planting season. Manufacturers increased production to maintain profits, but the more they produced, the lower prices for their products fell. In search of an inexpensive workforce that could produce more for less, industrialists turned to an international labor market. Amidst financial panics and nationwide strikes, depressions and deflation, Americans experienced a dramatic economic transformation. When it was over, the United States had become the leading capitalist nation on earth.

The "Great Depression" of the Late Nineteenth Century

On July 16, 1877, workers for the Baltimore and Ohio Railroad struck at Martinsburg, West Virginia. Within days the strike spread to the Pennsylvania Railroad, the New York Central, the Great Western, and the Texas Pacific. Governors issued orders for the strikers to disperse and asked for federal assistance. Federal troops were sent to major cities, but confrontations between workers and armed forces only fanned the flames of insurrection. "Other workingmen followed the example of the railroad employees," explained Henry Demarest Lloyd, a prominent social critic. "At Zanesville, Ohio, fifty manufactories stopped work. Baltimore ceased to export petroleum. The rolling mills, foundries, and refineries of Cleveland were closed. . . . Merchants could not sell, manufacturers could not work, banks could not lend. The country went to the verge of a panic." A strike in one key industry now threatened the entire nation.

The railroad strike of 1877 was fueled by an economic depression that began with the Panic of 1873 (see Chapter 16, "Reconstructing A Nation") and spread throughout the developed world. The number of immigrants who had arrived in New York—200,000 every year between 1865 and 1873—fell to less than 65,000 in 1877. Although employment recovered in the 1880s, prices and wages continued to fall. Then in 1893 another panic struck. Once again several major railroads went bankrupt and more than 500 banks and 15,000 businesses shut down. From 1873 to 1896 a "great depression" blighted much of the globe.

The world was shrinking, and most Americans knew it. In 1866 a telegraph cable was laid across the Atlantic Ocean. From that moment, Americans could read about events in Europe in the next morning's newspaper. Railroads slashed the distances that separated eastern from western Europe and the East Coast from the West Coast of the United States. Steamships brought distant ports into regular contact. Midwestern farmers sold their wheat in Russia. Chinese workers laid the tracks of the Union Pacific Railroad. Eastern Europeans worked the steel mills of Pittsburgh. The political economy of capitalism was tying the world's nations together.

The clearest sign of this linkage was the emergence of an international labor market. As economic change swept through the less developed parts of the world, men and women were freed from their traditional ties to the land

Chicago, Sunday Oct. 15, 1871

My dear Brother,

I snatch the first moment I have had since one week ago to-night. Our beautiful city is in ruins. The greatest calamity that ever befell a city is upon us. . . .

The fire broke out about eleven o'clock on Sunday night. The wind was blowing heavily from the south-west. The portion of the city where it broke out was thickly settled by the laboring people, on narrow streets and alleys—buildings all of wood—one and two stories high with barns and sheds in alleys. The wind soon increased to almost a gale and it soon became apparent to me that all efforts to stay it were fruitless. . . .

The flames were rushing most frantically, leaping from block to block—whole squares vanishing as though they were gossamer. Men, women and children rushing frantically in all directions to save their lives—some away—but others into traps and places where they were soon surrounded and no retreat left. Hundreds rushed upon the shore of the lake where they had to hug the beach and waters until the flames subsided, giving them a chance to escape. The most heart rending scenes that could be imagined were transpiring in all directions and the tales that are told are most appalling. . . .

Chicago is burned down but not despairing—she has the energy and push and will rise phoenix like from the ashes. . . .

Your affectionate brother,
William.

WILLIAM H. CARTER,
president, Chicago Board of Public Works

>> The Global Migration of Labor

Nineteenth-century migrants tended to leave areas already in the grip of social and economic change. Rosa Cassettari, for example, had worked in a silk-weaving factory in Italy. At first, the largest numbers emigrated from the most developed nations, such as Great Britain and Germany. Later in the century, as industrial or agricultural revolution spread, growing numbers of immigrants came from Scandinavia, Russia, Italy, and Hungary (see Map 17–1). As capitalism developed in these areas, small farmers were forced to produce for a highly competitive international market. The resulting upheaval sent millions of rural folk into the worldwide migratory stream.

Improvements in transportation and communication were a sign that capitalism was spreading; they also made migration easier. In 1856, more than 95 percent of immigrants came to America aboard sailing vessels. By the end of the century, more than 95 percent came in steamships. The Atlantic crossing took one to three months on a sailing ship, but only 10 days on a steamship. Beginning in the 1880s, fierce competition among steamship lines dramatically lowered the cost of a transatlantic ticket, making two-way movement easier. Many immigrants went back and forth across the Atlantic, particularly workers in seasonal trades like construction.

But the great migrations of the late nineteenth century were also related to political upheaval. In China, for example, the Taiping Rebellion of 1848 was accompanied by an economic disaster rivaling the Irish potato famine

of the same decade. This combination of economic and political disruption sent some 300,000 Chinese to the Pacific Coast of North America between 1850 and 1882. They labored in mines and panned for gold, and large numbers of Chinese workers helped build the transcontinental railroad. Desperate for employment and willing to work for low wages, the Chinese soon confronted racist hostility from American and European workers. Union organizers in San Francisco argued that the Chinese threatened the "labor interests" of white workers. In 1882 Congress responded by passing the Chinese Exclusion Act, banning further immigration from China.

A similar combination of economic and political forces lay beneath European immigration. The revival of employment in the 1880s brought with it a revival of movement. After 1890, immigration from northern and western Europe fell off sharply, as capitalist development made labor scarce in those areas. But by then agrarian crisis and political disruption had set off a wave of emigration from eastern and southern Europe. In Austria-Hungary, for example, the revolution of 1848 brought with it economic and political changes that resulted, by the 1880s, in a profound agrarian crisis. In southern Italy, citrus fruits from Florida and California arrived on the market, and protective tariffs thwarted the sale of Italian wines abroad. Desperate farmers from southern Italy started coming to the United States.

Jewish immigration was propelled by a different combination of politics and economics. The assassination of Czar Alexander II in 1881 was followed by a surge of Russian nationalism. Anti-Jewish riots (called pogroms) erupted in 1881–1882, 1891, and 1905–1906, during which countless Jews were massacred. Anti-Semitic laws forced Russian Jews to live within the so-called Pale of Settlement along Russia's western and southern borders, and the May Laws of 1882 severely restricted Russian Jews' religious and economic life. In the 1880s, Russian Jews began moving to America in significant numbers.

Most immigrants came to America looking for work. Some came with education and skills; some were illiterate. Most came with little more than their ability to work, and they usually found their jobs through families, friends, and fellow immigrants. Letters from America told of high wages and steady employment. Communities of immigrant workers provided the information and the connections that newcomers needed. Large Scandinavian communities settled the upper Midwest; the Chinese were concentrated on the West Coast. Some immigrants settled directly on farms, but the overwhelming number lived in cities. ●

and hurled into a global stream of wage laborers. Irish women went to work as domestic servants. African Americans took jobs as railroad porters. Wage laborers built and maintained the transportation network, the steel mills, and the petroleum refineries; slaughtered beef in Chicago; sewed ready-made clothing in factories; and staffed department store sales counters.

America Moves to the City

Between 1850 and 1900 the map of the United States was redrawn thanks to the appearance of dozens of new cities (see Figure 17–1). Of the 150 largest cities in the United

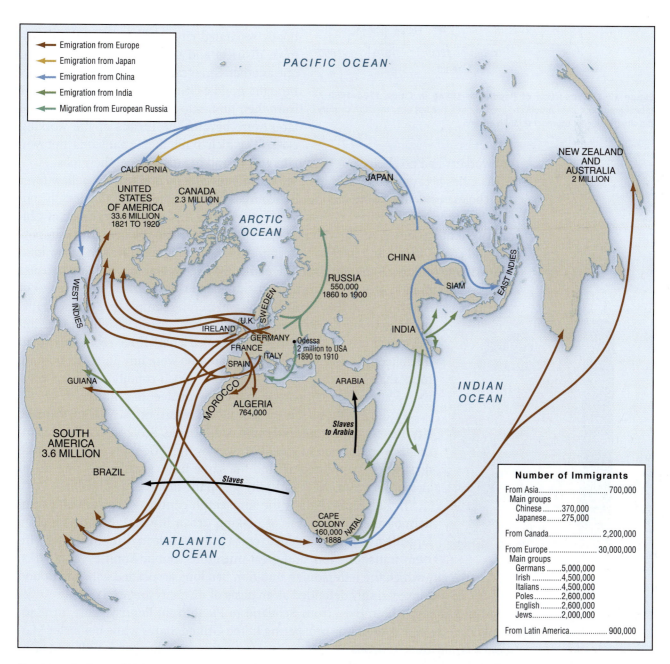

Map 17–1   Patterns of Global Migration, 1840–1900 Emigration was a global process by the late 19th century. But more immigrants went to the United States than to all other nations combined. *London Times Atlas*

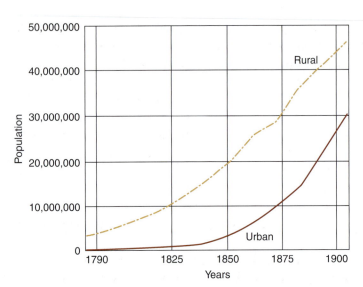

Figure 17–1 Proportion of Population Living in Cities, 1790–1900 A growing proportion of Americans lived in cities, but not until the 20th century did city dwellers outnumber rural Americans.

States in the late twentieth century, 85 were founded in the second half of the nineteenth century. In 1850 the largest city in the United States was New York, with a population of just over half a million. By 1900 New York, Philadelphia, and Chicago each had more than a million residents.

The industrial city was different from its predecessors. By the middle of the nineteenth century the modern "downtown" was born, a place where people shopped and worked but did not necessarily live. Residential neighborhoods separated city dwellers from the downtown districts and separated the classes from one another. Streetcars and commuter railroads brought middle-class clerks and professionals from their homes to their jobs and back, but the fares were beyond the means of the working class. The rich built their mansions uptown, but workers had no choice but to remain within walking distance of their jobs.

As cities became more crowded they became unsanitary and unsafe. Yellow fever and cholera epidemics were among the scourges of urban life in the nineteenth century. Fires periodically wiped out entire neighborhoods. In October 1871 much of Chicago went up in flames. Along with fires and epidemics, urban life was marred by poverty and crime. Beginning in New York in the 1880s, immigrants lived in a new kind of apartment building—the "dumbbell" tenement, a five- or six-story walk-up housing a huge concentration of people. Immigrant slums appeared in most major cities of

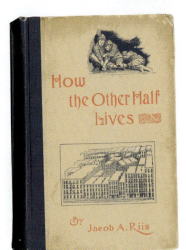

America, as well as in mill towns and mining camps. In 1890 Jacob Riis published *How the Other Half Lives,* his famous exposé of life in the immigrant slums of New York. He described a dark three-room apartment inhabited by six people. The two bedrooms were tiny, the beds nothing more than boxes filled with "foul straw." Such conditions were a common feature of urban poverty in the late nineteenth century.

Yet during these same years urban reformers set about to make city life less dangerous and more comfortable. Professional fire departments were formed in most big cities by the 1860s. Professional police departments appeared around the same time, greatly reducing urban violence. In 1866 New York City set up the first board of health.

In the second half of the nineteenth century American cities undertook the colossal task of making urban life decent and safe. To a large degree they succeeded: cities provided clean drinking water, efficient transportation, and great museums, public libraries, and parks. And so the city, which the Jeffersonian tradition had long associated with corruption and decay, was increasingly defended as an oasis of diversity and excitement.

Annie Aitken, who moved from Scotland to Pittsburgh, Pennsylvania, in 1840, would have agreed. Aitken was prospering in the United States while her sister Margaret's family back in Scotland was sinking fast. Margaret's husband, Will, had been a traditional handloom weaver whose livelihood was destroyed by the rise of textile mills. With Aitken's encouragement, in 1848 Will and Margaret Carnegie and their two sons, Tom and Andrew, left Scotland and moved to Pittsburgh. Annie Aitken let her sister's family live rent free in a small house she owned. Her nephew, Andrew, took a job in a textile mill for $1.20 a week. Fifty years later, Andrew Carnegie sold his steel mills to J. Pierpont Morgan for $480 million.

The Rise of Big Business

Before the Civil War the only enterprises in the United States that could be called "big businesses" were the railroads. Indeed, railroads became the model for a new kind of business—big business—that emerged during the 1880s. Big businesses had massive bureaucracies that were managed by professionals rather than owners and were financed through a national banking system centered on Wall Street. They marketed their goods and services across the nation and around the world and generated wealth in staggering concentrations, giving rise to a class of men whose names—Carnegie, Rockefeller, Morgan, and Vanderbilt—became synonymous with American capitalism.

The Lower East Side of Manhattan This busy street scene is from an area swollen with largely Jewish immigrants.

The Rise of Andrew Carnegie

Andrew Carnegie was an immigrant, whereas most businessmen were native born. His childhood in Scotland was marked by poverty, whereas most of America's leading men of business were raised in relative prosperity. Certainly few working families in the late nineteenth century could hope to match Carnegie's spectacular climb from rags to riches. Nevertheless, Andrew Carnegie was the perfect reflection of the rise of big business. In the course of his career, Carnegie mastered the telegraph, railroad, petroleum, iron, and steel industries and introduced modern management techniques and strict accounting procedures to American manufacturing. Other great industrialists and financiers made their mark in the last half of the nineteenth century—Henry Clay Frick, Collis P. Huntington, George M. Pullman, John D. Rockefeller, and Cornelius Vanderbilt—but none of their lives took on the mythic proportions of the Scottish lad who came to America at the age of 12 and ended up the richest man in the world.

"I have made millions since," Carnegie once wrote, "but none of these gave me so much happiness as my first week's earnings." Young Andrew might have been happy to earn a wage, but he was not content with his job in a mill. He enrolled in a night course to study accounting, and a year later got a job as a messenger boy in a telegraph

> Liberty produces wealth, and wealth destroys liberty. . . . Our bignesses—cities, factories, monopolies, fortunes, which are our empires, are the obesities of an age gluttonous beyond its powers of digestion. . . . The vision of the railroad stockholder is not far-sighted enough to see into the office of the General Manager; the people cannot reach across even a ward of a city to rule their rulers; Captains of Industry "do not know" whether the men in the ranks are dying from lack of food and shelter; we cannot clean our cities nor our politics; the locomotive has more man-power than all the ballot-boxes. . . . This era is but a passing phase in the evolution of industrial Caesars, and these Caesars will be of a new type— corporate Caesars.
>
> HENRY DEMAREST LLOYD,
> *Wealth Against Commonwealth*, 1894

office. So astute and hardworking was Andrew that by 1851 he was promoted to telegraph operator. In his dealings with the other operators, Carnegie soon displayed the leadership ability that served him throughout his career. He recruited talented, hardworking men and organized them with stunning efficiency.

The most successful businessmen in Pittsburgh, such as Tom Scott, a superintendent for the Pennsylvania Railroad, noticed Carnegie's talents. In 1853, Scott offered Carnegie a job as his secretary and personal telegrapher. Carnegie stayed with the Pennsylvania Railroad for 12 years during a time when railroad construction soared. Railroads stood at the center of the booming industrial economy. They would become the steel industry's biggest customer. Petroleum refiners shipped their kerosene by rail. Mining corporations needed railroads to ship their coal and iron. Ranchers shipped their cattle by rail to the slaughterhouses of Chicago, and meat packers distributed butchered carcasses in refrigerated railroad cars. Thus his position at the Pennsylvania Railroad gave Carnegie an unrivaled familiarity with the workings of big business.

By the mid-1850s, the largest factory in the country, the Pepperell Mills in Biddeford, Maine, employed 800 workers, while the Pennsylvania Railroad had more than 4,000 employees. If the men who maintained the track fell down on the job, if an engineer arrived late, or if a fireman came to work drunk, trains were wrecked, lives were lost, and business failed. The railroads thus borrowed the disciplinary methods and bureaucratic structure of the military to ensure that the trains ran safely and on time.

The man who introduced this organizational discipline to the Pennsylvania Railroad was Tom Scott, the man who hired Andrew Carnegie. J. Edgar Thomson, the Pennsylvania's president, was a pioneer of a different sort. He established an elaborate bookkeeping system that provided detailed knowledge of every aspect of the Pennsylvania's operations. Scott used the statistics Thomson collected to reward managers who improved the company's profits and eliminate those who failed.

Carnegie succeeded. After Scott was promoted to vice president in 1859, Carnegie took Scott's place as superintendent of the western division, where he helped make the Pennsylvania Railroad into a model of industrial efficiency. By 1865 the Pennsylvania had 30,000 employees and had expanded its line east into New York City and west to Chicago. It was the largest private company in the world.

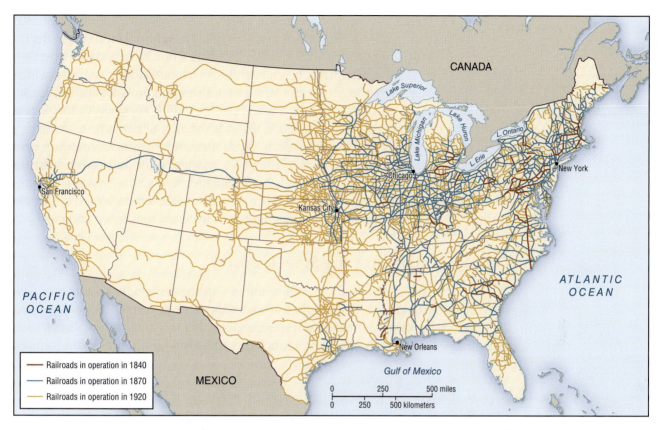

Map 17-2   The Growth of Railroads, 1850–1890 Railroads were more than a means of transportation; they were also America's first "big business." Railroad management established the model for running huge industrial corporations, and the growth of railroads sustained the initial growth of the iron and steel industries.

Carnegie's experience at the Pennsylvania Railroad gave him a keen understanding of the modern financial system. Railroads dwarfed all previous business enterprises in the amount of investment capital they required and in the complexity of their financial arrangements. Railroads were the first corporations to issue stocks through sophisticated trading mechanisms that attracted investors from around the world. To organize the market in such vast numbers of securities, the modern investment house was developed. J. Pierpont Morgan grew rich selling railroad stocks. The House of Morgan prospered greatly from its association with Andrew Carnegie, for there was no shrewder investor in all of America.

Carnegie Becomes a Financier

Carnegie began making money from money in 1856. On Tom Scott's advice Carnegie borrowed $600 and invested it in Adams Express Company stock, which soon began paying handsome dividends. Carnegie had become a successful capitalist, and for the next 15 years he made a series of financial moves that earned him several more fortunes.

Carnegie invested in the Woodruff Sleeping Car Company in the late 1850s and, a decade later, used his shares and influence to help George Pullman win near-monopoly control of the industry—and make millions in the bargain. Carnegie brokered a similar deal that created the Western Union monopoly of the telegraph industry. He invested in an oil company in western Pennsylvania and demonstrated that strict management would produce steady profits. He made shady deals on the international financial markets; he made millions selling worthless bonds to naive German investors. More substantially, he created the Keystone Bridge Company, which built the first steel arch bridge over the Mississippi River and provided the infrastructure for the Brooklyn Bridge over New York's East River. With Keystone, Carnegie perfected a model of managerial organization that was the envy of the industrial world.

By 1872 Carnegie was tired of financial speculation and ready for something new. He was 37 years old and had proven himself a master of the railroad industry, a brilliant manager, and a shrewd financial manipulator. Now Carnegie wanted to create an industry of his own. "My preference was always for manufacturing," he explained. "I wished to make something tangible." He would make iron and steel.

Carnegie Dominates the Steel Industry

In 1865 Carnegie acquired a controlling interest in the Union Iron Company. Carnegie's first goal was to speed the flow of materials to his Keystone Bridge Company. This was an important innovation. Iron manufacturing in America had always been decentralized, with each stage of production handled by a different manufacturer.

The Eads Bridge The steel arches of the Eads Bridge across the Mississippi River at St. Louis were both an engineering marvel and a triumph of Andrew Carnegie's managerial skills.

But Carnegie forced Union Iron and Keystone Bridge to coordinate their operations, thereby eliminating middlemen and making production more efficient. Carnegie also forced Union Iron to adopt the managerial techniques and accounting practices he had learned at the Pennsylvania Railroad. By keeping a strict account of all costs, Carnegie could locate the most wasteful points in the production process and reward the most efficient workers. Because he knew exactly what his costs were, Carnegie figured out that his iron mill would be more profitable if he invested in expensive new equipment. He ran his furnaces at full blast, wearing them out after only a few years and replacing them with still more modern machines. Carnegie's great achievement was his introduction of modern management techniques to American industry, but it was in steel rather than iron that Carnegie would prove the worth of those techniques.

As with so many industries, the development of steel was driven by the development of railroads. Traditional iron rails deteriorated rapidly, and as trains grew larger and heavier, iron withered under the load. J. Edgar Thomson, head of the Pennsylvania Railroad, began experimenting with steel rails in 1862. Steel was also a better material for locomotives, boilers, and railroad cars themselves. In the 1860s two developments cleared the path for the transition from iron to steel. First, Henry Bessemer's patented process for turning iron into steel became available to American manufacturers. Second, iron ore began flowing freely onto the American market from deposits in northern Michigan.

Andrew Carnegie was uniquely situated to take advantage of these developments. His experience with Union Iron taught him how to run a mill efficiently, and he

Chinese Laborers Building Railroad This 1877 picture of a Southern Pacific Railroad trestle shows the construction methods used in building the first railroad across the Sierra Nevada.

had access to investment capital. In 1872 Carnegie built a steel mill, the Thomson Works. Despite a worldwide depression, the steel mill was profitable from the start.

Big Business Consolidates

In the late nineteenth century the names of a handful of wealthy capitalists became closely associated with different industries: Gustavus Swift in meat packing, John D. Rockefeller in oil refining, Collis P. Huntington in railroads, J. P. Morgan in financing, and Andrew Carnegie in steel (see Map 17–3). These powerful individuals, sometimes called "robber barons," represented a passing phase in the history of American enterprise. Most big businesses were so big that no single individual or family could own them. They were run by professionally trained managers, and the highest profits went to companies with the most efficient bureaucracies. Because the businesses were so big and their equipment was so expensive, they had to be kept in operation continuously. An average factory could respond to an economic slowdown by closing its doors for a while, but big businesses could not afford to do that.

Beginning in the 1880s big businesses developed strategies designed to shield them from the effects of ruinous competition. The most common strategy was vertical integration, the attempt to control as many aspects of a business as possible, from the production of raw materials to the sale of the finished product. Carnegie integrated the steel industry from the point of production forward to the distribution of steel but also backward to the extraction of iron ore. He bought iron mines to produce his own ore, and railroads to ship the ore to his mills and the finished product to market. His Keystone Bridge Company then purchased the steel.

In 1882 John D. Rockefeller devised a new solution to the problem of ruinous competition by forming the Standard Oil Trust. Rockefeller had founded Standard Oil in 1867 in Cleveland, Ohio. Like Carnegie, Rockefeller surrounded himself with the best managers and financiers to build and run the most efficient modern refineries, but he was more willing than Carnegie to use ruthless tactics to wipe out his competitors. Rockefeller extracted preferential shipping rates from the railroads, giving him a critical advantage in the savagely competitive oil business. In 1872 Rockefeller began imposing on the national oil refining industry the same control that he had already achieved in Ohio. As president of the National Refiners' Association he formed cartels with the major operators in other states. But the cartels were too weak to eliminate independent refiners.

Rockefeller therefore set out to control the entire oil industry by merging all of the major companies together under Standard Oil. By 1879 the Standard Oil monopoly was largely in place, but not until 1882 was it formalized as a "trust," an elaborate legal device by which different producers came together under the umbrella of a single company that could police competition internally. In 1889 the New Jersey legislature passed a law that allowed corporations based in that state to form "holding companies" that controlled companies in other states. Thus the trust gave way to the holding company, with Standard Oil of New Jersey as its most prominent example. Within a decade many of the largest industries in America were dominated by massive holding companies.

Rockefeller's Standard Oil monopoly was a notorious example of how big business had changed the American economy. Rockefeller himself came to represent a powerful new class of extraordinarily wealthy businessmen. Their names—Carnegie, Rockefeller, Morgan, Harriman, and others—soon became associated with the upper class of the new social order of industrial America.

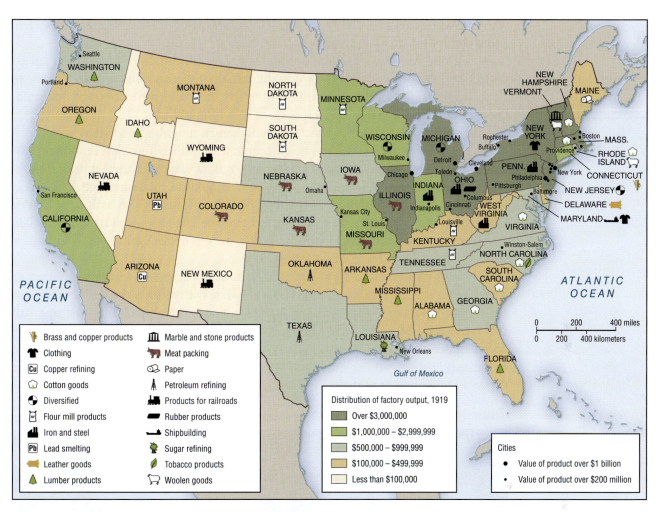

Map 17–3   Major American Industries, ca. 1890 An industrial map of late 19th-century America shows regions increasingly defined not by their crops but by their major industries.

A New Social Order

Classes were not supposed to exist in the United States the way they existed in Europe, as many Americans continued to believe in the late nineteenth century. Yet the reality of class divisions was so obvious that it had become part of public discussion. It was hard not to notice the conspicuous gap between the astonishing wealth of Andrew Carnegie and the daily struggles of Rosa Cassettari.

Lifestyles of the Very Rich

Between 1850 and 1890 the proportion of the nation's wealth owned by the 4,000 richest families nearly tripled. At the top of the social pyramid rested some 200 families worth more than $20 million each. Concentrated in the Northeast, especially in New York, these families were known throughout the world for their astonishing wealth. Spread more evenly across America were the several thousand millionaires

> The most valuable class in any community is the middle class, the men of moderate means, living at the rate of a thousand dollars a year or thereabouts.
>
> WALT WHITMAN, 1858

whose investments in cattle ranching, agricultural equipment, mining, commerce, and real estate made them wealthy capitalists.

As a group America's millionaires had a lot in common. Most traced their ancestry to Great Britain. Most were Protestant, usually Episcopalians, Presbyterians, or Congregationalists. By the standards of their day they were unusually well educated. Except in the South, America's upper class voted Republican.

The upper classes lived in spectacular houses in neighborhoods that became famous for their wealth: Fifth Avenue in Manhattan, Nob Hill in San Francisco, Rittenhouse Square in Philadelphia, and Boston's Back Bay. Wealthy suburbs (Brooklyn Heights, Philadelphia's Main Line, and Brookline, Massachusetts) acquired similar reputations as privileged retreats. The richest families also built rural estates that rivaled the country homes of England and the chateaus of France. In the late nineteenth century the richest families built a string of spectacular summer homes along the Newport, Rhode Island, shoreline.

The leading figures in New York's high society competed with one another to stage the most lavish balls and dinner parties. The competition reached a climax on March 26, 1883, when Mrs. William Vanderbilt staged a stupendous costume ball that challenged Mrs. William Astor's long-standing position as the queen of New York's upper class. The ball was a great success. All of New York society turned out at the magnificent Vanderbilt mansion, where the hostess made a grand entrance dressed as a Venetian princess.

Biltmore Estate The homes of the industrial rich were huge by comparison with those of their antebellum predecessors. Pictured here is the immense Biltmore Estate outside Asheville, North Carolina. Built by George Vanderbilt in the late 1800s, Biltmore had 255 rooms and required a railroad of its own to bring the construction materials to the building site.

It was left to the new middle class to preserve the traditional virtues of thrift and self-denial.

The Consolidation of the New Middle Class

In 1889 *The Century Dictionary* introduced the phrase "middle class" in the United States. The new term reflected a novel awareness that American society had become permanently divided in a way that earlier generations had stoutly denied.

Professionals were the backbone of the new middle class that emerged in the nineteenth century. All professions defined what it meant to be a member of their tribe, organized themselves into professional associations, and set educational standards for admission. By these means professionals could command high salaries and enjoy both prestige and a comfortable standard of living. Between 1870 and 1890 some 200 societies were formed to establish the educational requirements and maintain the credentials of their members. Even the management of corporations became a professional occupation, as business schools were created to train professionals in the science of accounting and the art of management. Some professionals succeeded in having their standards written into law. In most states, by 1900, doctors and lawyers could practice legally only when licensed under the auspices of professional associations.

Behind the new professional managers marched an expanding white-collar army of cashiers, clerks, and government employees. They were overwhelmingly men, and they earned annual incomes far beyond those of independent craftsmen and factory workers. They also enjoyed much better opportunities for upward mobility. A beginning clerk might make only $100 a year, but within five years his salary could be closer to $1,000. At a time when the average annual income of a skilled factory worker in Philadelphia was less than $600, over 80 percent of the male clerks in the Treasury Department earned over $1,200 a year.

As it developed, the middle class withdrew from the messy uncertainties of the central city. Improved roads and mass-transit systems allowed middle-class families to escape the urban extremes of great wealth and miserable poverty. Middle-class residents idealized the physical advantages of trees, lawns, and gardens, as well as the comfortable domestic life that suburbs afforded.

Only the most successful craftsmen matched the incomes and suburban lifestyles of white-collar clerks. Butchers might earn more than $1,600 annually, for example, but shoemakers averaged little more than $500. A shoemaker who owned his own tools and ran a small shop maintained the kind of independence that was long cherished among middle-class Americans, yet his income scarcely distinguished him from skilled factory workers. The manual crafts were therefore a bridge between the remnants of the independent middle class and the growing industrial working class made up of men and women like Rosa Cassettari.

The Industrial Working Class Comes of Age

"When I first went to learn the trade," John Morrison told a congressional committee in 1883, "a machinist considered himself more than the average workingman; in fact he did not like to be called a workingman. He liked to be called a mechanic." Morrison put his finger on one of the great changes in the political economy of nineteenth-century America. Before the Civil War, urban workingmen were skilled laborers who were referred to as artisans and mechanics. "Today," Morrison explained, the mechanic "is simply a laborer." Big businesses replaced mechanics with semiskilled or unskilled factory laborers. For traditional mechanics, this felt like downward mobility.

But most factory operatives and common laborers were migrants (or children of migrants) from small towns and farms. Few, therefore, experienced factory work as a degradation of their traditional skills, as John Morrison did. But most migrants did experience industrial labor as a harsh existence. Factory operatives worked long hours in difficult conditions performing repetitive tasks with little job security.

The clothing industry is a good example of the lives of urban workers. The introduction of the sewing machine in the 1850s gave rise to sweatshops where work was subdivided into simple, repetitive tasks. One group produced collars for men's shirts, another produced cuffs, and another stitched the parts together. Jobs were defined to ensure that workers could be easily replaced. Factory operatives learned this lesson quickly. They were young; often they were women or children who moved into and out of different factory jobs with astonishing frequency. But even among men, factory work was at best unsteady. The business cycle swung hard and often, leaving few factory operatives with secure, long-term employment.

At the bottom of the hierarchy of wage earners were the common laborers, whose trademark was physical exertion. Their numbers grew throughout the century until by 1900 common laborers accounted for a third of the industrial workforce. Hundreds of thousands of common laborers worked for railroads and steel companies. Before Andrew Carnegie and his competitors revolutionized their industry, for example, no more than 20 percent of iron and steel workers were common laborers. By the 1890s, 40 percent of steel workers were common laborers.

Common laborers were difficult to organize into effective unions. A large proportion were immigrants and African Americans, and ethnic differences and language barriers often frustrated the development of workers' alliances. Even the kind of work common laborers performed inhibited the growth of effective unions. It was rarely steady work. Men who laid railroad tracks or dug canals and subway tunnels generally moved on when they finished. Common labor was often seasonal; as a result, unskilled workers changed jobs frequently. Common laborers were unusually mobile and easily replaceable, and they increasingly came from parts of the world where the idea of organized labor was unknown. Even when they did organize, common laborers faced the biggest, most powerful, most effectively organized corporations in the country.

A great deal of the wage work done by women fell into the category of common labor. In 1900 women accounted for nearly one of every five gainfully employed Americans. They stood behind the counters of department stores, and young Irish women worked as domestics in northern middle-class homes. In the South, African American women worked as domestics. A smaller proportion of women held white-collar jobs, as teachers, nurses, or low-paid clerical workers and sales clerks.

The same hierarchy that favored men in the white-collar and professional labor force existed in the factories and sweatshops. In the clothing industry, for

Women Workers in a New York City Hat Factory, ca. 1900 In the hierarchy of wage laborers, women were the lowest paid and the least skilled.

example, units dominated by male workers were higher up the chain of command than those dominated by women. Indeed, as the textile industry became a big business, the proportion of women working in textile mills steadily declined. The reverse trend appeared among white-collar workers. As department stores expanded in the 1870s and 1880s, they hired low-paid women, often Irish immigrants, with none of the prospects for promotion still available to men. White-collar work was not a signal of middle-class status for women as it was for most men in the late nineteenth century.

The story was somewhat different for married women and their children. As few as 1 in 50 working-class wives and mothers took jobs outside the home. Women supplemented the family income by taking in boarders or doing laundry. Most often, however, working-class families survived by sending their children to work. Even in the families of the highest-paid industrial workers, 50 percent of the children worked. Among the poorest working-class families, three out of four children worked. Child labor was a clear sign of class distinction. The rich sent their daughters to finishing schools and their sons to elite boarding schools, middle-class parents sent their children to public schools, and working-class families sent their children to work. This was especially true in the South, where sharecropping was becoming a form of wage labor.

Sharecropping Becomes Wage Labor

As the southern economy recovered from the devastation of the Civil War, many observers predicted a bright future for the region. Optimists saw a wealth of untapped natural and human resources, a South freed from the constraints of an inefficient slave labor system ripe for investment, brimming with opportunities, and ready to go.

African American Exodus from the South "Remarkable Exodus of Negroes from Louisiana and Mississippi—Incidents of the Arrival, Support and Departure of the Refugees at St. Louis." Notice the four scenes: 1) "Procession of refugees from the steamboat landing," 2) "Embarkation for Kansas," 3) "Feeding the refugees at one of the colored churches," and 4) "St. Louis colored citizens welcoming the immigrants upon arrival."

In an age when Americans were building railroads at an exuberant clip, southerners built them faster. By 1890 nine out of ten southerners lived in a county with a railroad. By then impressive steel mills were coming to life in Birmingham, Alabama. The Piedmont Plateau (running along the eastern foothills of the Appalachian Mountains from Virginia to Georgia) was dotted with textile mills bigger and more efficient than those in New England. Southerners were migrating from the countryside to the towns, expanding the production of cotton into new areas, bringing the rich soil of the Mississippi Delta under cultivation. For ordinary southerners, however, especially African Americans, there was no great prosperity in the New South.

After the war most blacks returned to work on land they did not own (see Chapter 16). In place of the master-slave relationship emerged a new labor relationship between landlords and sharecroppers. Between the landlords and croppers, supplying the credit that kept the system alive, arose a powerful class of merchants. At the beginning it was unclear how much power the landlords, the merchants, and the sharecroppers each had. The most important question was who owned the cotton crop at the end of the year: the sharecropper who produced it, the landlord who owned the farm, or the merchant who loaned the supplies needed until the crop came in. The answer would be decided in the state legislatures and courts where the credit laws were written and interpreted.

The resolution was legally complete by the middle of the 1880s. First the courts defined a sharecropper as a wage laborer. The landlord owned the crop and paid his workers a wage in the form of a share of what was produced. Landlords also won a stronger claim on the crop than the merchant creditors. The struggle among landlords, sharecroppers, and merchants was therefore settled in favor of the landlord.

Under the circumstances, merchants were reluctant to loan money to sharecroppers. Many left the plantation districts and moved to the up-country, where they established commercial relations with white yeomen farmers. Trapped in a cycle of debt, white farmers in the 1880s began losing their land and falling into tenancy. Meanwhile, in the "black belt" (where most African Americans lived and most of the cotton was produced), successful landlords became merchants while successful merchants purchased land and hired sharecroppers of their own. By the mid-1880s, black sharecroppers worked as wage laborers for the landlord-merchant class across much of the South.

Sharecropping differed in two critical ways from the wage work of industrial America. First, sharecropping was family labor, depending on a husband and father who signed the contract and delivered the labor of his wife and children to the landlord. Second, because sharecropping contracts were yearlong, the labor market was restricted to a few weeks at the end of each year. If croppers left before the end of the year, they risked losing everything.

The political economy of sharecropping impoverished the South by binding the region to a single crop—cotton—that steadily depleted the soil even as prices fell. Yet for most southern blacks there were few alternatives. Over time a small percentage of black farmers purchased their own land, but their farms were generally tiny and the soil poor. The skilled black artisans who had worked on plantations before the Civil War moved to southern cities where they took unskilled, low-paying jobs. Industrialization was not much help for African Americans. Northern factories were segregated, as were the steel mills of Birmingham, Alabama, and the Piedmont textile mills. Black women worked as domestic servants to supplement their husbands' meager incomes. Wage labor transformed the lives of southern blacks, but it did not bring prosperity.

Hoping to escape the poverty and discrimination of southern life, a number of former slaves moved west. One group, the Exodusters, began moving to the Kansas prairie during the mid-1870s. By 1880 more than 6,000 blacks had joined them, searching for cheap land on which to build independent farms. The Exodusters became locked in the same battles with cattlemen that troubled white farmers, and blacks who settled in cow towns like Dodge City and Topeka found the same pattern of discrimination they had known in the South. Nevertheless, some of the Exodusters did manage to buy land and build farms. In this respect, the black exodus was similar to the movement of Americans headed west for relief from the constraints of urban and industrial America.

Clearing the West for Capitalism

The Homestead Act, passed by Congress during the Civil War, was designed to ensure that the West would be settled by hardworking, independent small farmers. And millions of farmers actually did settle in the West during the second half of the nineteenth century. Their movement has become the stuff of legend.

AMERICAN LANDSCAPE

>> Mining Camps in the West

Rosa Cassettari's experience in the mining camps of Missouri was not unique. But it is overshadowed by the more famous mining camps of California and the Far West. Mining fever began in 1848 when James Marshall discovered gold close to John Sutter's mill on the American River near what is now Sacramento, California. Thousands of prospectors poured into California during the 1850s, panning for gold wherever rumors of a vein hit, pulling up stakes and generating boomtowns and ghost towns with dizzying speed. "Every few days news would come of the discovery of a brand-new mining region," Mark Twain wrote from California. "Immediately the papers would teem with accounts of its richness, and away the surplus population would scamper to take possession." Eventually word of new discoveries pulled prospec-

tors eastward from California. Tens of thousands of miners flooded into Colorado in 1859. Meanwhile prospectors in Nevada discovered the largest single vein in American history, the Comstock Lode, which would yield 350 million dollars worth of gold and silver during the 1860s and 1870s alone. Similar rushes transformed parts of Idaho in 1862 and Montana in 1864.

Western mining camps were extraordinary places. They were peopled by settlers from a variety of backgrounds. In the gold-country camps on the western slope of the Sierra Nevada, native-born Yankees lived among British subjects, Chinese immigrants, Mexicans, Spaniards, and African Americans. This was a male-dominated world of violence, vigilantism, and multicultural interaction. Alone or in small groups they would pan for gold in the beds of the rivers and streams that poured out of the Sierra Nevada mountains. This was known as placer mining. Once the surface gold had been captured, miners would shovel dirt into boxes or sluices to capture gold and silver by running water over it. Only a few miners struck it rich this way, although their stories captured the imaginations of thousands.

Marcus Daly, for example, came to America as a penniless Irish immigrant and struck it rich in the gold fields of California. But his biography says less about the prospects for success among individual miners than it does about the larger transformation in the mining frontier. With the wealth he accumulated on his own, Daly persuaded a group of San Francisco investors to back his plans to dig a silver mine deep into the ground at Butte, Montana. They did not find silver, but they did strike one of the largest veins of copper in the world. The Anaconda mine made Daly and his partners rich, but it also symbolized the changes that had taken place in western mining. Daly became the supervisor of a large group of engineers and wage laborers. Anaconda extracted and smelted its own ore, then shipped its high-grade copper around the world to cities and industries anxious to harness the power of electricity that was transmitted across copper wires. By 1883 the United States was the largest producer of copper on earth.

The world of the placer miners disappeared almost as quickly as it arose. As the years passed, the miners moved from west to east, into and then across the Sierra Nevada, following the news of new strikes in Idaho, Montana, Nevada, and Colorado. But as the surface riches were quickly snapped up, the remaining veins of gold and silver proved too deep for any one prospector to reach. It took heavy machines to get at the ore buried deep underground, and machinery required capital investments beyond the means of ordinary miners. Most of the wealth taken from the Comstock mines, for example, was extracted by corporations using powerful tools to dig deep into the earth. So mining corporations steadily bought up the settlers' claims and created a more permanent industrial presence in the western states. Mark Twain's experience was typical: having gone out to prospect for gold on his own, he ended up selling his labor for wages. "I went to work as a common laborer in a quartz mill," he explained, "at ten dollars a week and board."

Yet the mining camps, however brief their existence, represented a temporary alternative to the permanent inequalities of the industrial economy. As rough and violent as they were, the camps were also experiments in spontaneous democracy in which men came together, governed themselves, and agreed on the rules by which they would live. ●

But these hardy individuals did not settle an empty prairie. Waiting for them in the West were native peoples, some helpful and many hostile. And far from escaping the hierarchy of industrial capitalism, the settlers brought it with them. By the time the director of the U.S. Census declared the frontier "closed" in 1890, the political economy of the American West was composed of railroad tycoons and immigrant workers, commercial farmers and impoverished Native Americans.

The Overland Trail

"Left home this morning," Jane Gould wrote in her diary on April 27, 1862. Along with her husband, Albert, and their two sons, Jane loaded a covered wagon in Mitchell, Iowa, and joined a group of migrants on the Overland Trail to California (see Map 17–3). It would be a long and difficult journey. Albert got sick shortly after they left, and Jane had to nurse him, drive the wagon, and care for the children. The farther they traveled, the more distressed Jane became. The Overland Trail was littered with the remnants of wagon trains that had gone before, including discarded furniture, dried bones, and lonely graves. In early October the Goulds reached their new home in the San Joaquin Valley. Five months later, Jane's husband died.

A popular image pictures the West as a haven for rugged men who struck out on their own, but most migrants went in family groups, and the families were mostly middle class. Few poor people could afford the expense of the journey and still hope to buy land and set up a farm in the West.

The journey across the Overland Trail became safer over the years. In the late 1840s the U.S. government began building forts along the overland routes. Besides protecting migrants from Indians, the forts became resting points for wagon trains. By the 1850s Mormon settlers in Utah had built Salt Lake City into a major stopping point. Migrants came to rely on the facilities there to ease the journey. Also during the 1850s, the government began to pursue a long-term solution to the growing problem of Native American–white relations in the West.

The Origins of Indian Reservations

In 1851 more than 10,000 Native Americans from across the Great Plains converged on Fort Laramie in Wyoming Territory. All the major Indian peoples were

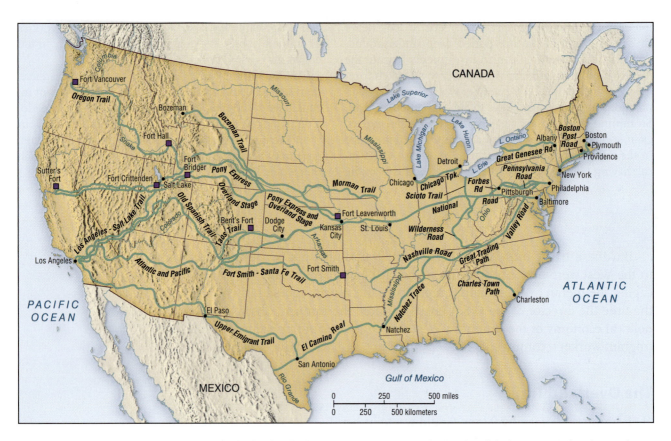

Map 17–4 The Overland Trail There was no transcontinental railroad until the late 1860s. Before then, and even thereafter, most settlers moved west on a series of well-developed overland trails.

represented: Sioux, Cheyenne, Arapaho, Crow, and many others. They came to meet with government officials who hoped to develop a lasting means of avoiding Indian–white conflict. Since the discovery of gold a few years earlier, white migrants had been crossing through Indian territory on their way to California, most of them already prejudiced against the Indians. U.S. officials wanted to prevent hostility between whites and Indians from breaking out into violence and to restrain the conflicts among Indians themselves. They proposed the creation of a separate territory for each Indian tribe, with government subsidies to entice the Indians to stay within their territories. This was the beginning of the reservation system, and for the rest of the century the U.S. government struggled to force the Indians to accept it.

From the start, the reservation system was corrupt and difficult to enforce. Agents for the Bureau of Indian Affairs cheated Indians and the government alike, sometimes reaping huge profits. But primarily, the reservations failed because not all Indians agreed to restrict themselves to their designated territories, leading to armed confrontations and reprisals.

By the late 1860s the tensions between Indians and whites were at a fever pitch, as Senator James R. Doolittle of Wisconsin discovered on a fact-finding mission through the West. In Denver he asked an audience of whites whether they preferred outright extermination of the Indians to a policy of restricting Indians to reservations. The crowd roared its approval for extermination. Army officers agreed. The government "must act with vindictive earnestness against the Sioux," General William Tecumseh Sherman declared.

Senator Doolittle and his colleagues resisted the calls for extermination, opting instead for a more comprehensive reservation policy. The government pursued this approach by means of two important treaties that divided the Great Plains into two huge Indian territories. The Medicine Lodge Treaty, signed in Kansas in October 1867, organized thousands of Indians across the Southern Plains. In return for government supplies, most of the Southern Plains peoples agreed to restrict themselves to the reservation. The Northern Plains Indians did not sign onto the reservation so readily. A treaty was drafted, but a band of holdouts demanded further government concessions. Inspired by their leader Red Cloud, the Indians insisted that U.S. forces abandon their forts along the Bozeman Trail. When the government agreed, Red Cloud signed the Fort Laramie Treaty in November 1868.

Red Cloud respected the treaties for the rest of his life, but they nevertheless failed. Most white settlers still preferred extermination to reservations, and not all the Plains Indians approved of the treaties. Nor did the U.S. Army abide by the reservation policy. Within weeks of Red Cloud's signature on the Fort Laramie Treaty, for example, the Seventh Cavalry led by Colonel George Armstrong Custer massacred Cheyennes at Washita, Oklahoma, on November 27, 1868. As long as the U.S. Army sustained the settlers' hunger for extermination, Indian "policy" was made on the battlefield rather than in government offices.

By 1870 it was clear that western Indians would not voluntarily retire to reservations and that the military could not force them into surrender. If any further

Indian Village Routed, Geronimo Fleeing from Camp Oil on canvas by Frederic Remington, 1896.

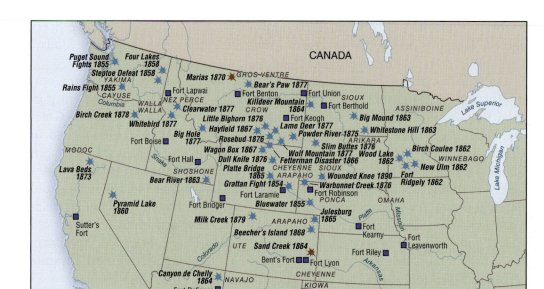

Map 17-5 Conflicts in the West In the late 19th century, battles between whites and Native Americans erupted all across the western half of the continent.

evidence of the Indian resistance was needed, it came in South Dakota, where, after discovery of gold in the Black Hills, thousands of whites poured onto Indian territory. When the Lakota Sioux rejected demands that they cede their lands to the miners, the government sent in the army, led by General Custer. Custer was an arrogant man, and he made two critical mistakes. First he divided his army in two, and then he failed to keep them in communication with each other. Custer and hundreds of his men were slaughtered at Little Bighorn, Montana, in 1876 by 2,000 Indian warriors led by Sitting Bull and Crazy Horse.

The Destruction of Indian Subsistence

Custer's Last Stand did not signal any change of fortunes for the Plains Indians. By the 1870s whites had learned that they could undermine Native American society most effectively by depriving Indians of their sources of subsistence, especially the bison. "Kill every buffalo you can," a U.S. Army colonel urged one hunter. "Every buffalo dead is an Indian gone." Federal authorities did not actually sponsor the mass killing of the bison; they merely turned a blind eye. Railroads joined the pro-

Ghost Dance, Wood Engraving, ca. 1890 The Ghost Dance swept across the Plains among Native Americans threatened with destruction by white settlement.

cess, sponsoring mass kills from slow-moving trains as they crossed the prairies. Some 13 million bison in 1850 were reduced, by 1880, to only a few hundred.

With their subsistence destroyed, Chief Sitting Bull and his starving men finally gave up in 1881. The Sioux war ended in 1890 with a shocking massacre of 200 Native American men, women, and children at Wounded Knee, South Dakota.

In the Northwest in 1877 the Nez Percés, fleeing from Union troops, set out on a dramatic trek across the mountains into Yellowstone in an attempt to reach Canada. The Nez Percés eluded government troops and nearly made it over the Canadian border. However, hunger and the elements did what the Union army had failed to do. Chief Joseph and his exhausted people agreed to go to their reservations.

Reformers who advocated reservations over extermination always believed that the Indians should be absorbed into the political economy of capitalism. By "confining the Indians to reservations," explained William P. Dole, Lincoln's Commissioner of Indian Affairs, "they are gradually taught and become accustomed to the idea of individual property." Most white settlers considered Native Americans an inferior race

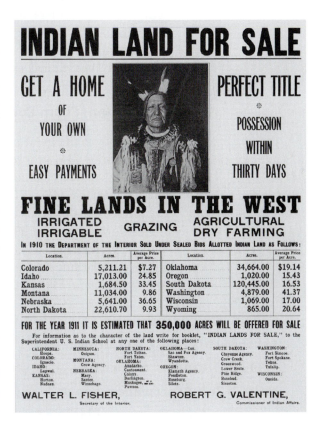

Indian Land For Sale Within a couple of decades of the passage of the Dawes Act, most Native American lands were sold to white settlers.

worthy of destruction. By contrast, Dole believed that "Indians are capable of attaining a high degree of civilization." But reformers like Dole equated civilization with the cultivation of "individual property." Accordingly, reformers set out to destroy Native American society. They introduced government schools on Indian reservations to teach children the virtues of private property, individual achievement, and social mobility.

The reformers' influence peaked in 1887 when Congress passed the Dawes Severalty Act, the most important piece of Indian legislation of the century. Under the terms of the Dawes Act, land within the reservations was broken up into separate plots and distributed among individual families. The goal was to force Indians to live like stereotypical white farmers. But the lands allotted were generally so poor, and the plots so small, that their owners sold them as soon as they were allowed. By the early twentieth century there were virtually no reservations left, except for a few parcels in the desert Southwest. With the Indians subdued, the path was cleared for the capitalist transformation of the West.

The Economic Transformation of the West

A few hundred civilians died in Indian attacks during the late nineteenth century. More than 5,000 died building the railroads. Lawless violence and wild speculation were very much a part of the western experience, as were struggling families, temperance reformers, and hardworking immigrants. By 1900 the West provided Americans with the meat and bread for their dinner tables, the wood that built their homes, and the gold and silver that backed up their currency. The West was being drawn into the political economy of global capitalism.

Cattlemen: From Drovers to Ranchers

The cowboy is the great mythic figure of the American West: a rugged individual, a silent loner who scorned society for the independence of the trail. Like many myths, this one has elements of truth. Cowboys were usually unattached men. They worked hard, but when their work was over they played just as hard, spending their earnings on a shave, a new suit of clothes, and a few good nights in town. Driving cattle was hard work, often dangerous, and even more often boring. Civil War veterans, emancipated slaves, displaced Indians, and Mexican vaqueros all became cowboys at various times. Cowboys were poorly paid, their work was unsteady, and their chances of reaching real independence were slim.

Longhorn cattle were as much a part of western legend as the cowboys who drove them. With the destruction of the bison and the westward spread of the railroads, it became possible to drive huge herds of Texas longhorns north onto the Great Plains. With relatively little capital, cattle herd-

> **The Great Pacific Railway is commenced. . . . Immigration will soon pour into these valleys. Ten millions of emigrants will settle in this golden land in twenty years. . . . This is the grandest enterprise under God!**
>
> GEORGE FRANCIS TRAIN

ers could make substantial profits. Cowboys drove gigantic herds, sometimes numbering half a million, to a town with a railroad connection from which the cattle could be shipped, such as Abilene, Wichita, or Dodge City, Kansas. Cattlemen sold half of their stock to eastern markets and the other half in the West, to Californians, or to the government, which purchased beef to feed soldiers and Indians on reservations.

But the Texas longhorn had several drawbacks that eventually led to its replacement. Most seriously, it carried a tick that devastated many of the grazing animals that came into contact with it. In addition, the longhorn took a long time to fatten up and never produced good beef. Wealthy investors began to experiment with hybrid cattle that did not carry the deadly tick, fattened up quickly, and produced higher quality meat. By the early 1880s investors were pouring capital into mammoth cattle-herding companies. At the same time it was becoming clear that the Great Plains were seriously overstocked. The grazing lands were depleted, leaving the cattle weak from malnutrition. In the late 1880s several severe winters devastated the sickly herds.

Open-range herding became so environmentally destructive that it was no longer economically feasible. In addition, long drives became increasingly difficult as farmers settled the plains and fenced in their lands. By the 1890s huge cattle companies were giving way to smaller ranches that raised hybrid cattle. The western railroad network was by then so extensive that it was no longer necessary to drive herds hundreds of miles to reach a railhead. Cowboys became ranch hands who worked for regular wages, like miners and factory workers.

In the mid-1880s, more than 7 million head of cattle roamed the Great Plains, but their numbers declined rapidly, and in their place came sheep. Sheep fed on the growths that cattle would not eat. In fact, the sheep ate so many grasses that they proved even more ecologically destructive than cattle. Nevertheless, by 1900 sheepherding had largely replaced the cattle industry in Wyoming and Montana and was spreading to Nevada. Sheepherding had one other crucial advantage: it did not interfere with small farmers as much as cattle driving did.

Commercial Farmers Subdue the Plains

Between 1860 and 1900, the number of farms in America nearly tripled, thanks largely to the economic development of the West. On the Great Plains and in the desert Southwest, farmers took up former Indian lands. From San Francisco to Los Angeles, white settlers poached on the estates of Spanish-speaking landlords, stripping them of their natural resources and undermining their profitability. Over time Hispanic ranchers gave way to Euro-American farmers. The Hispanic population of Los Angeles fell from 82 percent in 1850 to 19 percent in 1880. A similar pattern displaced the Mexican American landowners in New Mexico and Texas.

This ethnic shift signaled profound changes in the ecology and political economy of the West, driven by the exploding global demand for western products. Cattle ranchers were feeding eastern cities. Lumber from the Pacific Northwest found its way to Asia and South America. By 1890 western farmers produced half of the wheat grown in the United States, and they shipped it across the globe.

But farming in the arid West was different from farming in the East. To begin with, the 160-acre homesteads envisioned by eastern lawmakers were unrealistic:

farms of that size were too small for the economic and ecological conditions of western agriculture. From the beginning, western farmers were businessmen. To produce wheat and corn for the international market they needed steel plows, costly mechanical equipment, and extensive irrigation. To make these capital investments, western farmers mortgaged their lands. For mechanized, commercial agriculture to succeed on mortgaged land, western farms had to be much bigger than 160 acres.

Most western agricultural settlement took place not on government-sponsored homesteads but through the private land market. By some estimates land speculators bought up nearly 350 million acres of western lands from state or federal governments or from Indian reservations. Railroads were granted another 200 million acres by the federal government. The more farmers who settled in the West, the more agricultural produce they could regularly ship back East. Therefore, railroads set up immigration bureaus and advertised for settlers, offering cheap transportation, credit, and agricultural assistance, filling up the Great Plains with settlers from the East Coast and from Ireland, Germany, and Scandinavia. In 1890 the director of the Bureau of the Census reported that the frontier had at last been filled.

Changes in the Land

The trans-Mississippi West was no Garden of Eden waiting for lucky farmers to move in and reap the land's abundant riches. The climate, particularly in the Great Plains and the desert Southwest, was too dry for most kinds of farming. The sod on the plains was so thick and hard that traditional plows ripped like paper; only steel would do the job. With little wood or stone to build houses, farmers lived first in dugouts or sod houses. Fierce winter blizzards gave way to blistering summers, each rocked by harsh winds. Yet settlers seemed determined to overcome, and to overwhelm, nature itself. To build fences where wood was scarce, manufacturers invented barbed wire. Windmills dotted the prairie to pump water from hundreds of feet below ground. Powerful agricultural machinery tore through the earth, and new strains of wheat from Europe and China were cultivated to withstand the brutal climate.

The western environment was transformed. Wolves, elk, and bear were exterminated as farmers brought in pigs, cattle, and sheep. Tulare Lake, covering hundreds of square miles of California's Central Valley, was sucked dry by 1900. Hydraulic mining sent tons of earth and rock cascading down the rivers flowing out of the Sierra Nevada, raising water levels to the point where entire cities became vulnerable to flooding. The skies above Butte, Montana, turned grey from the pollutants released by the copper-smelting plants. Sheepherding destroyed the vegetation on the eastern slopes of the Rocky Mountains and the Sierra Nevada.

By the turn of the century, the bison had all but disappeared, and the Indians had been confined to reservations. Industrial mining corporations, profitable cattle ranches, and mechanized farms now dominated the West. The frontier was gone, and in its place were commercial farmers whose lives were shaped by European weather, eastern mortgage companies, commodity brokers, and railroad conglomerates. Cowboys sold their labor to cattle companies owned by investors in Boston and Glasgow. Mining and lumber corporations employed tens of thousands of wage laborers. Big cities sprang up almost overnight. San Francisco had 5,000 inhabitants in 1850, but by the time the Gold Rush was over, in 1870, there were 150,000 people living there. Denver was incorporated in 1861 but its population hovered at just below 5,000 until the railroad came in 1870. Twenty years later Denver had more than 100,000 inhabitants. Whatever it was in American mythology, the West was well on its way to becoming a part of an urban, industrial nation.

Conclusion

Rosa Cassettari and Andrew Carnegie never met, but together their lives suggest the spectrum of possibilities in industrializing America. Both were immigrants who, caught up in the political economy of industrial capitalism, made their way to the United States. Yet the same grand forces touched the two immigrants in different ways. Cassettari moved to a mining camp west of the Mississippi River before making her way to Chicago—the city that opened the West to the dynamism of industrial capitalism. Carnegie migrated, almost overnight, from the preindustrial world of Scotland to the heart of the Industrial Revolution in America—Pittsburgh, with its railroads, oil refineries, and steel mills. Cassettari struggled all her life and achieved a modest level of comfort for herself and her children. She did as well as most immigrants could hope for, and in that sense her biography reflects the realities of working-class life in industrial America. Cassettari's experience with failure—the harsh life of the mining camp and a bad marriage—impelled her to move on in search of something better. It was success, however, that made Carnegie itch for something different. By 1890, having made his millions, he remade himself by becoming a patron of culture. He moved to New York and traveled the world, befriending the leading intellectuals of his day. He built libraries and endowed universities. He had helped create an industrial nation. Now he set out to re-create American culture.

Further Readings

Alfred D. Chandler, *The Visible Hand: The Managerial Revolution in American Business* (1977). The standard account of the rise of corporate bureaucracy.

William Cronon, *Nature's Metropolis: Chicago and the Great West* (1991). Meticulously charts the way Chicago's influence stretched across much of the West.

Eric Hobsbawm, *The Age of Empire: 1875–1914* (1987). Establishes the global context for the industrial transformation of the United States.

Maldwyn Jones, *American Immigration*, 2nd ed. (1992). Unusually sensitive to the political and economic background to global migration.

David Montgomery, *The Fall of the House of Labor: The Workplace, the State and American Labor Activism, 1865–1925* (1987). Shows how the rise of big business changed the daily labor of the American working class.

David Nasaw, *Andrew Carnegie* (2006). Does an especially good job of putting Carnegie's life into the larger historical context.

Gregory Nobles, *American Frontiers: Cultural Encounters and Continental Conquest* (1997). A brief survey reflecting the latest scholarship in western history.

Heather Cox Richardson, *West From Appomattox: The Reconstruction of America After the Civil War* (2007). An intelligent and highly readable survey of American history in the late nineteenth century.

Richard White, *'It's Your Misfortune and None of My Own': A History of the American West* (1991) is a comprehensive survey by a leading historian of the West.

C. Vann Woodward, *Origins of the New South, 1877–1913* (1951) is one of the great works of American historical literature.

>> Timeline >>

▼ 1848

Taiping Rebellion spurs Chinese emigration to United States

Revolution in Austria-Hungary

Andrew Carnegie emigrates to United States

▼ 1851

Fort Laramie Treaty establishes Indian reservations

▼ 1856

St. Paul's boarding school opens

▼ 1857

Henry Bessemer develops process for making steel

▼ 1862

Pacific Railroad Act

Homestead Act

▼ 1865

First transatlantic telegraph cable begins operation

▼ 1867

Medicine Lodge Treaty

▼ 1868

Second Fort Laramie Treaty

Washita Massacre

▼ 1871

October: Great Chicago fire

Who, What

Review Questions

1. What were the major features of "global" capitalism in the late nineteenth century?

2. Describe the new social order of industrial America.

3. How did western Indians respond to westward expansion?

4. How was the West absorbed into the national and international market?

Websites

A Coal Miner's Work. http://people.cohums.ohio-state.edu/kerr6/courses/History563/A%20Coal%20Miner's%20Work.htm

The Chinese in California. http://memory.loc.gov/ammem/award99/cubhtml/cichome.html

The Northern Great Plains, 1880–1920. http://memory.loc.gov/ammem/award97/ndfahtml/ngphome.html

For further review materials and resource information, please visit www.oup.com/us/ofthepeople

▼ **1872**
Edgar Thomson Steel Works open near Pittsburgh

▼ **1873**
Financial panic, followed by depression

▼ **1876**
Custer's Last Stand at Little Bighorn

▼ **1878**
American Bar Association founded

▼ **1881**
Czar Alexander II of Russia assassinated

▼ **1882**
Chinese Exclusion Act

John D. Rockefeller forms Standard Oil trust

Edison Electric Company lights up New York buildings

▼ **1887**
Dawes Severalty Act

▼ **1890**
Jacob Riis publishes *How the Other Half Lives*

Massacre at Wounded Knee, South Dakota

Director of U.S. Census declares frontier "closed"

▼ **1893**
Financial panic, followed by depression

Common Threads

>> How did American culture in the late nineteenth century reflect the rise of big cities and big business?

>> What, if anything, is the difference between popular culture and high culture?

>> What was new about artistic realism?

>> Was culture a political issue in the late nineteenth century?

Cultural Struggles of Industrial America 1850–1895

>> Anthony Comstock's Crusade Against Vice

Anthony Comstock devoted most of his adult life to putting the owners of brothels, gambling dens, abortion clinics, and dance halls out of business. "You must hunt these men as you hunt rats," Comstock declared, "without mercy." There was little in his background to foreshadow such zeal. While still a young man Comstock moved from rural Connecticut to New York City, where he worked as a clerk in a dry goods store. White-collar careers of this sort were a familiar path for native-born Protestant men in the middle of the nineteenth century. Fame came to him in 1873 when the United States Congress enacted a statute that bore his name. The Comstock Law banned the production, distribution, and public display of obscenity. Thereafter, Comstock spent much of his life chasing down and prosecuting pornographers, prostitutes, and strippers.

Comstock and many like-minded citizens were genuinely disturbed by the municipal corruption that kept police departments from enforcing obscenity laws. To overcome this obstacle, reformers established private organizations with quasi-official authority. Among the most influential was Anthony Comstock's New York Society for the Suppression of Vice, commonly known as the SSV. Founded in 1873, the SSV was dedicated to "the enforcement of laws for the suppression of the trade in, and circulation of, obscene literature and illustrations, advertisements, and articles of indecent or immoral use." As head of the society, Comstock was appointed a special agent of the U.S. Post Office. Along with other SSV leaders, Comstock disregarded the rights of due process by entrapping his victims. But Comstock and others defended their actions by pointing out that the established legal procedures of the police and the judiciary were ineffective in preventing the sale of smut.

Comstock's chief concern was the protection of children. In his most famous book, *Traps for the Young* (1883), he warned that obscenity was enticing American youngsters into deviant ways by artificially nourishing youthful appetites and passions until they exerted "a well-nigh irresistible mastery over their victim." The evils that trapped America's children were concentrated in the cities that, in the late nineteenth century, attracted millions of young people. Urban life was relatively anonymous and it was also driven by vast amounts of cash. In the last third of the nineteenth century the income of nonfarm employees in America rose steadily, while prices declined. Except for the very poorest workers, urban Americans had more money to spend and more time to spend it than ever before. And if industrial workers enjoyed more leisure time, white-collar employees enjoyed even more. The big city offered Americans bawdy new entertainments that violated long-established standards of respectability. Pornography was not a new thing in the late nineteenth century, but it was more widespread than ever before.

For Comstock, cities were cesspools of vice and corruption, the breeding ground for immigrant slums thought to be devoid of "culture." At the time, many educated Americans thought that "culture" referred only to the great works of Western art, literature, and music. High culture, in this sense, was a healthy alternative to the sordid realities of urban and industrial America. Ironically, the best artists and writers of the late nineteenth century were "realists" who wanted art to reflect the gritty realities of everyday life. While Anthony Comstock tried to suppress the vices of the city, realists embraced them, translating them into compelling fiction and dramatic canvases.

In the second half of the nineteenth century, cultural clashes were as much a part of industrial capitalism as

continued

were class conflict and political upheaval. Rural Americans were often ambivalent about urban culture, attracted by its freedom but repelled by its licentiousness. Native-born Protestants, often genuinely concerned to help immigrants, were at the same time condescending and suspicious of immigrant folkways. Defenders of high culture resisted the lure of popular culture. Amateur sportsmen sniffed at the emergence of spectator sports. Victorian moralists assailed the collapse of traditional gender distinctions. Yet these struggles reflected the efforts of Americans to absorb the dramatic social transformations that accompanied the rise of industrial capitalism. ●

OUTLINE

The Varieties of Urban Culture

Americans both loved and hated the cities they lived in, and their mixed feelings were reflected in the variety of entertainments they embraced during the second half of the nineteenth century. They swooned over romanticized re-creations of the Plains wars on the western frontier, and they paid good money to watch nostalgic minstrel shows about plantation life in the Old South. But as the economy developed, the nation's love affair with the countryside gave way to popular entertainments that idealized the city as never before. These new entertainments rested more than ever on the technological marvels of American industry. Beginning in the 1880s, electricity lit up the big city after dark, making it possible to create new forms of urban "night life." By 1900 electricity was powering the trolleys and subways that brought tens of thousands of Americans into new "downtown" districts (see Figure 18-1). Stores, businesses, and factories were the hallmarks of the older downtowns. But leisure activities attracted tens of thousands to the new city centers. In growing numbers Americans went to theaters, music halls, concert saloons, baseball stadiums, and sports arenas. City life, long associated with poverty and crime, now came to mean fun and excitement as well.

Minstrel Shows as Cultural Nostalgia

In the late nineteenth century the western frontier became one of the most popular themes in American show business. As rugged pioneers gave way to wage earners, commercial farmers, and industrialists, the mythology of the West grew. The most spectacular example of this was Buffalo Bill Cody's hugely successful Wild West Show, which toured the country parading live Indians before delighted urban spectators. Audiences watched displays of horsemanship and highly stylized reenactments of the Plains wars. America's fascination with a romanticized frontier was one example of a popular nostalgia for ways of life that were thought to have been simpler than the life of the city. Nowhere was this nostalgia more obvious than in the minstrel shows.

Minstrel shows were the most significant form of public entertainment for most of the nineteenth century. During the 1830s and 1840s minstrel shows were dominated by white performers in blackface. Although the minstrels stereotyped plantation slaves as happy and carefree, the earliest performances were not as viciously racist as they became later. In the mid-1850s, however, the tone of blackface minstrel shows changed. As the slavery controversy forced white northerners to take sides on a divisive issue, popular troupes like New York's Christy Minstrels took the side of the slaveholders. During the Civil War and Reconstruction, minstrel shows attacked white reformers in the North who supported emancipation and black rights. They portrayed blacks with gross racial stereotypes and subjected

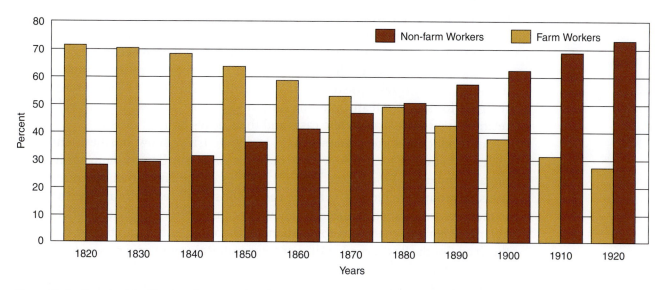

Figure 18–1 Growth of the Nonfarm Sector Underpinning the rise of urban culture was the emergence of a wage-earning labor force. Concentrated in cities, wage earners had cash at their disposal to spend on the amusements cities had to offer.

> Amusement is not only a great fact and a great business interest, it is also a great factor in the development of the national character. If a wise philanthropist could choose between making the laws of any people and furnishing their amusements, it would not take him long to decide. The robust virtues are nurtured under the discipline of work; if the diversions can be kept healthful, a sound national life will be developed. The ideals of the people are shaped, and their sentiments formed, to a large extent, by popular amusements.
>
> REVEREND WASHINGTON GLADDEN,
> *Applied Christianity,* 1886

abolitionists to ridicule. Minstrel troupes staged corrupted versions of *Uncle Tom's Cabin,* stripped the novel of its abolitionist theme, and reduced the plot to a simplistic story of beleaguered southern whites. Yet throughout the period, minstrel shows continued to poke fun at the aristocratic pretensions of cultural elites. Indeed, minstrel shows commonly combined racism with populism, lampooning elites by playing them in blackface wearing fancy clothes and putting on airs.

In the 1870s minstrel shows grew larger and more elaborate. J. H. Haverly led the way. He hired the most players, dressed them in the gaudiest costumes, placed them in the most spectacular sets, and had them perform the widest variety of numbers. He toned down the emphasis on blackface singers and plantation themes and added scantily clad women and off-color routines. Haverly expanded his audiences with extensive advertising. By 1881 he had theaters in New York, Brooklyn, Chicago, and San Francisco; three national minstrel troupes; and four touring comedy theaters. Of Haverly's three companies, two were white and one was black. There were other black companies as well. As national minstrel shows abandoned their commitment to authentic representations of southern life, blacks often took to the stage and kept the plantation theme alive, operating within the racial stereotypes established by prewar whites in blackface. The most famous black minstrel of the nineteenth century, Billy Kersands, drew huge audiences with his portrayals of ignorant and comical characters. Yet as the plantation theme became the preserve of black players, some of the early criticism of slavery crept back into the productions. When black minstrels romanticized the Old South, their nostalgia was reserved for slaves. Meanwhile, the largest and most successful minstrel shows retained their exclusively white casts and their heavy-handed racism.

As productions grew more ornate and expensive, show business entrepreneurs put smaller local troupes out of business or swallowed them up into national companies. From more than 60 troupes in the late 1860s, the number of minstrel troupes fell to just 13 by the early 1880s. Differences from one company to the next diminished as minstrel shows became uniform and somewhat bland. Yet, more popular than ever, they expanded their audiences into the far West and the deep South. By 1890 a handful of huge entertainment moguls controlled the minstrel shows.

Minstrel shows never lost their nostalgic appeal to rural America. However, by the late nineteenth century they looked more and more like vaudeville, an art form that was born and bred in the big city.

The Origins of Vaudeville

Unlike the minstrels, vaudeville shows did not rely on nostalgia. Rather, vaudeville and its cheaper cousins (concert saloons and dollar theaters) flourished in American cities after elites succeeded in distinguishing serious theater from variety shows. As the cost of a ticket to a Shakespeare production rose beyond the means of most working people, urban audiences turned to inexpensive houses that offered music, singing, sketches, and variety acts. At first the audiences in such theaters were rowdy and exclusively male. Yet these concert saloons and variety theaters attracted patrons from up and down the social scale. In 1883 a Chicago guidebook claimed that the city's variety theaters were patronized not only by "the lower class of society, but [by] journalists, professional men, bankers, railroad officials, politicians, and men of rank in society." Even so, there were no blacks.

Increasingly, however, there were women. Beginning in the 1880s, a handful of show business entrepreneurs tried to develop variety theaters that appealed to audiences with both men and women. The respectability of a mixed audience was one of the distinguishing signs of vaudeville. Vaudeville producers booked a variety of acts to appeal to a broad audience. They also developed continuous performances, which allowed patrons to come to a vaudeville show any time of the day or evening. Continuous performances kept the prices down, thereby increasing the size of the potential audience. Locating downtown in the heart of the city had the same effect. Theater owners also regulated smoking and, over time, banned alcohol consumption, thus promoting the image of family entertainment. Finally, they booked great opera singers or distinguished musicians for brief appearances, in a conscious effort to enhance vaudeville's reputation for respectability.

Billy Kersands African American minstrels such as Billy Kersands moderated the racism characteristic of the extremely popular white minstrels.

Growing audiences made it possible for vaudeville producers to construct huge and ornate theatrical "palaces" that housed ever more elaborate productions. The high cost of such theaters kept the number of competitors down. As a result, a handful of companies came to dominate the vaudeville theater industry, much as minstrel companies had become concentrated in the hands of a few owners. By the turn of the century, vaudeville was one of the most popular forms of public entertainment in American cities. But minstrel shows and vaudeville theaters were not the only places Americans went during their leisure time.

Sports Become Professional

As growing numbers of Americans went to the theater to be entertained, still more went to the baseball park or sports arena. For a significant segment of the urban population, sports became something to watch rather than something to do.

AMERICA AND THE WORLD

>> World's Fairs

To celebrate the accomplishments of urban and industrial society, the city of London hosted a spectacular world's fair at the Crystal Palace in 1851. Over the next 50 years the cities of the Western world became showcases for the technological and cultural achievements of industrial capitalism. By 1900 there had been expositions in Paris, Vienna, Brussels, Antwerp, Florence, Amsterdam, Dublin, and even Sydney, Australia. Most celebrated the achievements of the host countries and the civic pride of their sponsoring cities, as well as the triumph of technology and the progress of humanity. American fairs were no exception. Several major American cities—including St. Louis, San Francisco, and Chicago—sponsored world expositions in the late nineteenth and early twentieth centuries.

The first major world's fair in the United States took place in Philadelphia in 1876, timed to commemorate the centennial of American independence. In keeping with the theme of global interaction, the fair's sponsors asked the nations of the world to build pavilions of their own. The pavilions were arranged to reflect not the harmony of nations, but the differences among the world's "races." Americans were only beginning to develop such ideas in 1876, but the broad outlines of the racial categories were already evident. France and its colonies, "representing the Latin races," were grouped together, as were England and its colonies, "representing the Anglo-Saxon races," and "the Teutonic races," represented by Germany, Austria, and Hungary. Within 20 years, these racial categories would harden into an elaborate hierarchy that embraced all the peoples of the world.

Nowhere was this hierarchy more visible than at the greatest fair of the century, the World's Columbian Exposition in Chicago in 1893. Built on Lake Michigan several miles south of downtown, the Chicago fair had twice as many foreign buildings as its Philadelphia predecessor, covered 686 acres, and attracted 25 million visitors. The exposition was divided between the White City and the Midway Plaisance. The White City showcased American industrial might with immense steam engines and the latest consumer goods. But the Midway Plaisance boasted carnivals, the first Ferris wheel, games, and sideshows. It also featured an ethnographic exhibit providing a popular rendition of principles of scientific racism. The exhibit portrayed the "races" of the world in a hierarchy from the most civilized (Europeans) to the least civilized (Asians and Africans).

Where earlier forms of popular entertainment had romanticized preindustrial society and the rural life, the world's fairs celebrated the global economy, industrial enterprise, and urban life. The White City, the heart of the World's Columbian Exposition in Chicago, was an idealized vision of urban life. Rural simplicity had given way to the majestic city as the model for civilization. ●

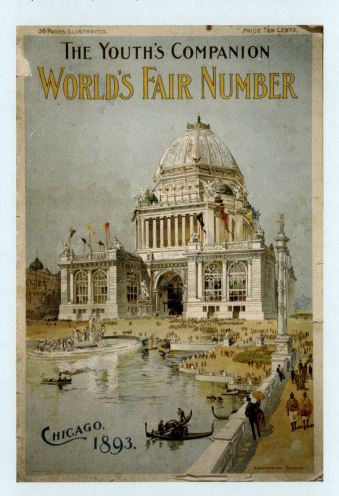

The Cover of *The Youth's Companion,* **World's Columbian Exposition at Chicago Issue, 1893** The World Columbian Exposition in Chicago was the largest of the world's fairs that became popular in the late 19th century. Among other things, they were celebrations of the technology and city life that were becoming the characteristics of modern, industrial civilization.

As the number of spectators increased, baseball and prizefighting became professionalized. Prizefighting had long been a disreputable amusement of shady bars and lower-class streets, but during the 1880s it became an organized sport attracting a huge national audience. Richard Kyle Fox, owner of the *National Police Gazette*, used his popular magazine and his considerable financial resources to transform boxing. Because Fox put up the prize money, he had the power to reform the sport. He made it both more profitable and more respectable, and he introduced standardized rules.

As prizefighting grew in popularity, entrepreneurs sponsored matches at indoor rings where they could control unruly audiences with police and security guards. Thereafter, as prizefighter John L. Sullivan explained in 1892, "the price of admission is put purposely high so as to exclude the rowdy element, and a gentleman can see the contest, feeling sure that he will not be robbed . . . or in any way be interfered with." Although prizefighting never completely lost its aura of disrepute, by the 1890s it was one of the most popular spectator sports in America, second only to baseball.

Like prizefighters, baseball players became professionals in the last half of the nineteenth century. By the 1860s baseball had become tremendously popular among city dwellers, particularly immigrants and their children. They formed leagues in urban neighborhoods all across the country. But not until 1869, when the Cincinnati Red Stockings went on tour and charged admission, did baseball become a professional spectator sport. Soon thereafter standardized rules appeared for the first time.

Within a decade the owners of eight baseball clubs had formed a National League that had all the earmarks of a corporate cartel. It restrained the power of players, restricted the number of teams to one per city, prohibited Sunday games, banned the sale of alcohol at ballparks, hired umpires, and set schedules and admission prices. Chafing under these restrictions, many players jumped to a new American Association that formed in 1882. The owners regrouped, however, and within a year the two leagues merged and quickly reinstated the restrictions on players. In reaction the players formed a league of their own but were unable to match the wealth and power of the owners. By the mid-1890s the National League controlled professional baseball.

Baseball idealized the principle of success based purely on merit. Objective statistics identified the best players without respect to their personal background. A model of ordered competition, the baseball meritocracy provided a useful lesson in the way capitalist society was supposed to work. Professional players became working-class heroes, many of them having risen from factories and slums. But professional baseball reflected the realities as well as the ideals of American capitalism. The owners' cartel prevented professional athletes from taking advantage of the market. In addition, baseball's meritocracy had no place for the merits of black players. Even the seating arrangements in ballparks reflected America's social divisions. Working-class fans sat in the bleachers, the middle class occupied the stands, and elites took the box seats.

The popularity of sports was reflected in the growing numbers of participants as well as spectators. As daily work became more sedentary, especially for white-collar workers, Americans spent more time in physical recreation. During the late nineteenth century, "the sporting life" became an American pastime. The

Women and Men on Bicycles in New York City, on Riverside Drive Prosperity and shorter working hours gave many middle-class Americans more leisure time than ever before. Bicycling was only one of the many physical activities that became wildly popular in the late 19th century.

popularity of bicycling exploded, for example, particularly after the invention of the modern "safety bike" in 1888. Within a decade there were 10 million bicycles in the United States. Men joined the YMCA or organized local baseball teams. At Harvard, Yale, and Princeton young men took up football, basketball, and rowing. At Smith, Vassar, and Berkeley young women played baseball, basketball, and tennis. In urban neighborhoods ethnic groups organized Irish, Italian, and German baseball teams. Women began riding bicycles, swimming, and playing golf and croquet.

But appearances were deceptive. The sports craze mirrored the inequalities and anxieties of industrial America. Men who believed that independence was a sign of masculinity became concerned that wage labor would make them soft and "feminine." A vocal segment of the American elite turned to athletic activities as an antidote to the supposedly feminizing tendencies of industrial capitalism. Theodore Roosevelt, the product of an old and wealthy New York family, and who became president of the United States, believed that "commercial civilization" placed too little stress on "the more virile virtues." There was, Roosevelt argued, "no better way of counteracting this tendency than by encouraging bodily exercise and especially the sports which develop such qualities as courage, resolution and endurance."

As baseball and prizefighting became popular and professional, elites reacted by glorifying the amateur ideal, embracing vigorous athletic activity for its own sake rather than for monetary reward. In the late nineteenth century wealthy Americans pursued the sporting life at elite colleges, exclusive racetracks, and private athletic clubs, country clubs, and yacht clubs. By the turn of the century, the most exclusive colleges in the Northeast had formed football's Ivy League, a designation that became synonymous with elite private universities.

The rigors of sport taught elite men how to face the rigors of business competition, weeded out the weak, and prepared society's leaders for the contest of daily life. Thus the elite's attraction to rugged sports reinforced a self-serving view of American society: in an increasingly global and competitive capitalism the best nations, like the best men, would rise to the top.

The most significant attempt to spread such values was the founding of the Young Men's Christian Association (YMCA) in 1851. By 1894 there were 261 YMCAs across the nation. A strong reform impulse sustained the YMCA movement. Its founders hoped that organized recreational activity would distract workers from labor radicalism. Classroom instruction and organized games would assimilate immigrants to the laws, customs, and language of the United States. Take away Anthony Comstock's fanatic tinge, and the YMCA can be seen as an extension of the movement to suppress vice: it hoped to provide wholesome amusements to young men who might otherwise succumb to the temptations of city life.

The Elusive Boundaries of Male and Female

Anthony Comstock saw the city as a place where traditional morality broke down, particularly standards of sexual propriety. In fact, the political economy of industrial capitalism and the triumph of wage labor compelled men and women to rethink traditional conceptions of masculinity and femininity. As they did so, spectacular new cities and newfound leisure time offered Americans unprecedented opportunities to test the conventional boundaries of sexual identity.

The Victorian Construction of Male and Female

Until the mid-1700s most European doctors believed that there was only one sex: females were simply inferior, insufficiently developed males. Sometime after 1750, however, scientists and intellectuals began to argue that males and females were fundamentally different, that they were "opposite" sexes. For the first time it was possible to argue that women were naturally less interested in sex than men or that men were "active" while women were "passive." Nature itself seemed to justify the infamous double standard that condoned sexual activity by men but punished women for the same thing.

In the nineteenth century, Victorians drew even more extreme differences between men and women. Taking its name from the long reign of Britain's Queen Victoria, the "Victorian" era is often stereotyped as an age of sexual repression and cultural conservatism. Like many stereotypes, the image of the puritanical Victorian is simplistic but not without a grain of truth. Victorian boys were reared on moralistic stories of heroes who overcame their fears. In this way boys were prepared for the competitive worlds of business and politics, worlds from which women were largely excluded. To be a "man" in industrial America was to work in the rough-and-tumble world of the capitalist market. Men proved themselves by their success at making a living and therefore at taking care of a wife and children.

Victorian men defined themselves as rational creatures whose reason was threatened by their overwhelming sexual drives. Physical exertion was an important device for controlling a man's powerful sexual urges. A growing number of physicians warned that masturbation was an unacceptable outlet for these drives. Medical experts urged men to channel their sexual energies into strenuous activities such as sports and, conveniently enough, wage labor. Masculinity was defined as the ability to leave the confines of the home and compete successfully in the capitalist labor market.

Where masculinity became a more rigid concept, femininity became less certain. Women's schools established their own sports programs. Thousands of women took up bicycling, tennis, and other physical activities. Yet at the same time the stereotype persisted that women were too frail to engage in the hurly-burly of business and enterprise. Lacking the competitive instinct of the male, the female was destined to become a wife and mother within the protective confines of the home. Just as men congregated in social clubs and sports teams, a "female world of love and ritual" developed. Middle-class women often displayed among themselves a passionate affection that was often expressed in nearly erotic terms. But genuinely passionate female sexuality was deeply disturbing to the Victorians. Evidence of sexual passion among women was increasingly diagnosed, mostly by male doctors, as a symptom of a new disorder called "neurasthenia."

Over time the differences between men and women were defined in increasingly medical terms. Victorian doctors redefined homosexuality as a medical abnormality, a perversion, and urged the passage of laws outlawing homosexual relations. The new science of gynecology powerfully reinforced popular assumptions about the differences between men and women. Distinguished male physicians argued that the energy women expended in reproduction left them unable to withstand the rigors of higher education. In extreme cases physicians would excise a woman's clitoris to thwart masturbation or remove her ovaries to cure neurasthenia.

On the assumption that motherhood was a female's natural destiny, doctors pressed to restrict women's access to contraception and to prohibit abortion. Before the Civil War many Americans tolerated abortion in the first three months of pregnancy, though they did not necessarily approve of it. This began to change as the medical profession seized control over the regulation of female reproduction. The American Medical Association (AMA, founded in 1847) campaigned to restrict the activities not only of quacks and incompetents but also of female midwives and abortionists. Doctors, most of whom were males, accepted prevailing assumptions about the maternal destiny of women. Hence doctors opposed attempts by women to interfere with pregnancy. The AMA supported passage of the Comstock Law, which outlawed the sale of contraception. Doctors also pushed successfully to criminalize abortion.

Victorians Who Questioned Traditional Sexual Boundaries

In a new economy based on wage labor large numbers of Americans, especially young men, now found themselves with cash and leisure time. The anonymity of huge cities gave them the opportunity to defy established standards of sexual behavior. Freed from the constraints of parents and the scrutiny of small-town life, wage earners frequented prostitutes in unprecedented numbers, attended shows that featured sexually provocative entertainers, read erotic novels, and purchased pornographic prints. Many Americans began to explore unconventional sexual practices.

The major venues of popular amusement flouted Victorian standards of propriety by using sexual titillation to attract and entertain audiences. Can-can girls, off-color jokes, and comedy skits focusing on the war of the sexes were increasingly popular. Even the styles of clothing that consumers purchased in mass quantities were a rejection of the stifling conventions of the Victorian middle class. Trousers got looser, starched collars disappeared, and women's dresses were simplified and became considerably more comfortable. The sensuous human body became an

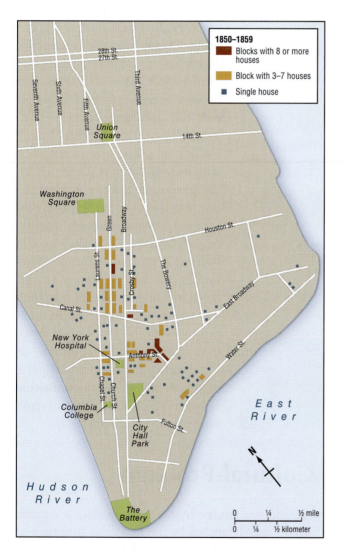
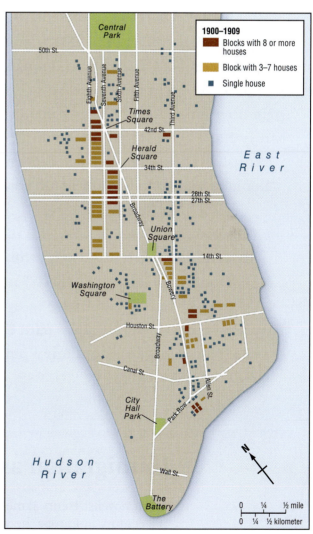

Map 18-1   Houses of Prostitution, 1850–1859 and 1900–1909 One measure of the sexual freedom characteristic of city life was the explosive increase in prostitution. As the demand for prostitution rose, so did attempts to suppress it. *Timothy J. Gilfoyle,* City of Eros *(New York: W. W. Norton, 1992), p. 33.*

object of fascination in much of the popular culture. Minstrels, musical variety shows, and the vaudeville theater all glorified female sexuality. For the first time male sports heroes were openly admired for their physiques.

There were homoerotic themes running through Horatio Alger's popular novels. Once rescued from rags and gainfully employed, Alger's hero typically set up house with a roommate. These households were fastidiously neat, and their inhabitants were thrifty and sober. The only difference from an ideal middle-class household was that both inhabitants were male. In one case, two male roommates, having both been saved and made respectable, actually "adopted" a little boy, a street urchin named "Mark the Matchboy." But the novels often moved beyond homoeroticism to the very different realm of pedophilia. Alger himself began his career as a Unitarian minister in Brewster, Massachusetts, but he was expelled from his pulpit for "the revolting crime of unnatural familiarity with boys." He left New England in disgrace and moved to New York, where he developed a keen interest in the problems of young boys who roamed loose on the city streets. Alger's charity work became the basis of his fiction. In most of his novels, the young heroes shared the same physical attributes. They were dirty but handsome. In most cases it was the boy's good looks that attracted the attention of the wealthy male patron. Alger's novels depicted the relationships between men and boys in terms reminiscent of a seduction.

> [I]n spite of his dirt and rags there was something about Dick that was attractive. It was easy to see that if he had been clean and well dressed he would have been decidedly good-looking. . . .
>
> When Dick was dressed in his new attire, with his face and hands clean, and his hair brushed, it was difficult to imagine that he was the same boy.
>
> He now looked quite handsome, and might readily have been taken for a young gentleman, except that his hands were red and grimy.
>
> "Look at yourself," said Frank, leading him before the mirror.
>
> "By gracious!" said Dick, staring back in astonishment, "that isn't me, is it?"
>
> "Don't you know yourself?" asked Frank, smiling.
>
> "It reminds me of Cinderella," said Dick, "when she was changed into a fairy princess."
>
> HORATIO ALGER,
> *Ragged Dick*

Immigration as a Cultural Problem

When novelist Henry James returned to the United States in 1907 after a quarter of a century in Europe, he was stunned and disgusted by the pervasive presence of immigrants in New York City. On the streetcars, he confronted "a row of faces, up and down, testifying, without exception, to alienism unmistakable, alienism undisguised and unashamed." James was one of the many native-born Americans who assumed that their culture was Protestant, democratic, and English speaking. They were deeply disturbed, therefore, by the arrival of vast numbers of immigrants who were none of those things, and by the way ethnic subcultures seemed to flourish in United States cities. Yet among immigrants and their children, an ethnic identity was often a sign of assimilation into a broader American culture.

Josiah Strong Attacks Immigration

"Every race which has deeply impressed itself on the human family has been the representative of some great idea," Josiah Strong wrote in *Our Country*. Greek civilization was famed for its beauty, he explained, the Romans for their law, and the Hebrews for their purity. The Anglo-Saxon race had two great ideas to its credit, Strong argued. The first was the love of liberty, and the second was "pure spiritual Christianity." Published in 1885, Strong's best-selling book was revised and reprinted in 1891 and serialized in newspapers across America. Strong spoke to the concerns of vast numbers of native-born Americans who saw themselves as the defenders of Anglo-Saxon culture. Strong was optimistic that as representatives of "the largest liberty, the purest Christianity, the highest civilization," the powerful Anglo-Saxon race would "spread itself over the earth."

> Go and see in our public schools the children of German, Irish, Bohemian, and Italian parents, waving the Stars and Stripes on the glorious Fourth, and you will fully appreciate the meaning of my statement, that education is solving the problem.
>
> RICHARD BARTHOLDT, 1896

But there was a problem. Strong and his followers believed that the Anglo-Saxon in America was threatened by the arrival of millions of immigrants. By 1900 more than 10 million Americans were foreign born. The typical immigrant, he warned, was not a freedom-loving Anglo-Saxon Protestant but a "European peasant." Narrow-minded men and women "whose moral and religious training has been meager or false," immigrants brought crime to America's cities and undermined the nation's politics. Immigrants voted in blocks, and their influence was enhanced by the fact that they were concentrated in big cities. "[T]here is no more serious menace to our civilization," Strong warned, "than our rabble-ruled cities."

At the core of the problem was the fact that immigrants could not be assimilated into the American way of life. "Our safety demands the assimilation of these strange populations," Strong wrote. But they were coming in such huge numbers that assimilation was becoming impossible (see Map 18–2). Worst of all—in Strong's view—the Catholic Church held millions of immigrants in its grip, filling their heads with superstition rather than "pure Christianity." It did not help that immigrants had large numbers of children. Through its elaborate network of parochial schools, the Catholic Church was training new generations to love tyranny rather than liberty.

Strong and his readers need not have worried. The millions of immigrants who came to the United States adapted quickly to American society. Indeed, Strong misread much of his own evidence. By cultivating the German vote or the Irish vote, for example, political machines went far toward assimilating immigrants into American political culture. Nor were immigrants as slavishly subservient to the Catholic

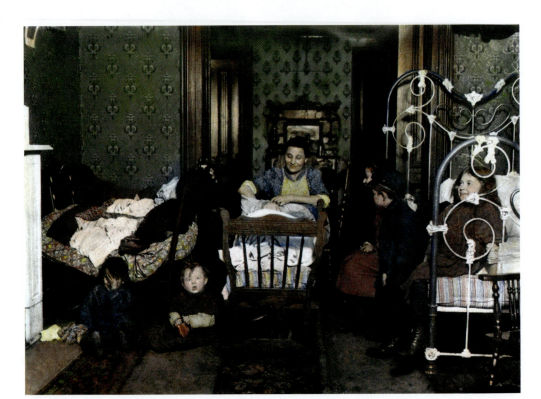

Immigrants Immigrants often crowded into "tenements," a new form of apartment building that actually improved living conditions for many of America's poor city dwellers.

Church as Strong thought. In the end, the church played an ambiguous role in the cultural history of American immigrants.

From Immigrants to Ethnic Americans

Critics like Strong scarcely noticed the regional and class differences that immigrants brought with them. In the middle of the nineteenth century, most immigrants came with loyalties to their regions and villages, but not to their nationality. In New York City German-speaking immigrants thought of themselves primarily as Bavarian or Prussian rather than as German. Irish immigrants identified with their home counties more than their native country. Immigrant churches across America were torn by such regional conflicts.

After immigrants arrived in the United States, however, regional differences began to decline. One reason was the growth of secular fraternal organizations. Fraternal organizations often began as mutual aid societies designed to help newcomers find jobs and housing. In 1893 mineworkers formed the Pennsylvania Slovak Catholic Union to help cover burial expenses for those killed in the mines. Most often, however, middle-class immigrants took the lead in forming fraternal organizations; in other cases local priests played prominent roles. Regardless of their leadership, about half of all immigrants eventually joined ethnic fraternal societies.

As they grew, fraternal organizations became national in their scope, as immigrants constructed a new "ethnic" identity that united all members under a single

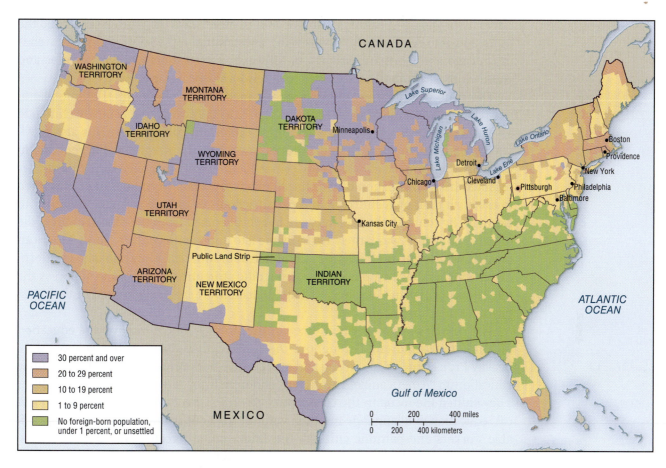

Map 18–2   Population of Foreign Birth by Region, 1880 *Clifford L. Lord and Elizabeth H. Lord,* Lord & Lord Historical Atlas of the United States *(New York: Holt, 1953).*

national rubric. In some cases immigrant businessmen led the drive toward the development of a unified ethnic identity. Marco Fontana, who ran the Del Monte company in California, encouraged the growth of an "Italian" identity among his workers. He found that regional loyalties hindered the efficient operation of his enterprises. Eventually, immigrants began to think of themselves as members of ethnic groups that shared the same national ancestry.

It was not merely coincidental that immigrants developed "national" identities in the United States. Nationalism was spreading throughout the Western world during the nineteenth century. While immigrants in America were coming to see themselves as Irish or Italian, the same thing was happening back home in Ireland and Italy. In the United States the Civil War had unleashed a wave of nationalistic fervor, and a series of liberal revolutions did the same thing in Europe. As the decades passed, immigrants brought to America an increasingly powerful sense of their ethnic identities.

The Catholic Church and Its Limits in Immigrant Culture

The Roman Catholic Church played a complicated role in the development of ethnic cultures among immigrants. In some cases churches were established to preserve Old World traditions. Local priests sometimes collected donations to build

German- or Italian-speaking churches. But in other ways the church smoothed the transition into American life by serving as a mutual aid society. Polish churches in Chicago and German parishes in Milwaukee used their women's groups and youth clubs as mutual aid societies for their local immigrants.

The church sometimes unintentionally sped the development of ethnic identities. The Irish became more devout in America as they came to rely on the church to assist them in resisting an overwhelmingly Protestant culture. Germans also gravitated toward the church and in the process overcame their regional differences. But the more they came to equate their German identity with Catholicism, the more they resented Irish domination of the church hierarchy. Thus German Catholics worked to establish their own churches and parish schools or to have sermons preached in German. By contrast, the Italians were largely alienated from the official church, the hierarchy of which was largely Irish. By the late nineteenth century North American bishops were trying to standardize Catholicism in America. They published uniform catechisms, established powerful bureaucratic structures, and tried to suppress the folk rituals of Italian Catholicism. Thus Italians were ironically united in their suspicion of the church.

The church's power was reinforced by the struggle for control over the education of immigrant children. Throughout the nineteenth century, public schools were heavily Protestant. Josiah Strong and other native-born reformers tried to use public education to "Americanize" immigrant children. They taught the Protestant Bible. They shifted the focus in the classroom away from the classics and toward "practical" education and language training, with the goal of turning immigrants into reliable workers and patriotic citizens. But immigrants fiercely resisted such efforts, and the bulwark of their resistance was the church.

During the second half of the nineteenth century both the Catholic and Lutheran churches established parochial school systems to protect immigrant children from the biases of public education. So comprehensive was the Catholic Church's effort that by 1883 all but two parishes in the city of Chicago had their own parochial schools. Ironically, parochial education contributed to assimilation among immigrants. Catholic or Lutheran schools in Irish or German parishes reinforced the growth of distinctively American ethnic identities and bound ethnicity to an increasingly standardized and Americanized Catholicism or Lutheranism.

Immigrant Cultures

Despite assimilation, the ethnic identities that immigrants developed in America remained distinctive. Irish Americans, for example, fused together songs from various parts of Ireland and added piano accompaniment. Similarly, Polish immigrant bands expanded beyond the traditional violin of their homelands by adding accordions, clarinets, and trumpets. But the results were still distinctively Polish American or Irish American music. Hundreds of immigrant theaters sprang up offering productions that adjusted traditional plot lines to the New World. Jewish plays told of humble peddlers who outwitted their prosperous patrons. Italian folktales emphasized the importance of the family. In these ways distinctive ethnic identities, adapted to urban and industrial America, developed.

One of the most distinctive features of immigrant culture was family size. At a time when middle-class families had only two or three children, immigrant families remained large. There were sound economic reasons for this. There were no child-labor laws restricting the employment of minors and few compulsory-education laws requiring children to attend school. Working-class families relied heavily on the incomes of their children, particularly teenagers. Children in the immigrant working class were expected to contribute to the economic well-being of their families.

At the turn of the century, Italian mothers in Buffalo, New York, had an average of 11 children. Among Polish wives the average was closer to eight. In Pennsylvania's coal-mining district, working-class immigrant women had 45 percent more children than native-born women. But the death rate among immigrant children was also high. In 1900, one out of three Polish and Italian mothers had seen one of their children die before his or her first birthday.

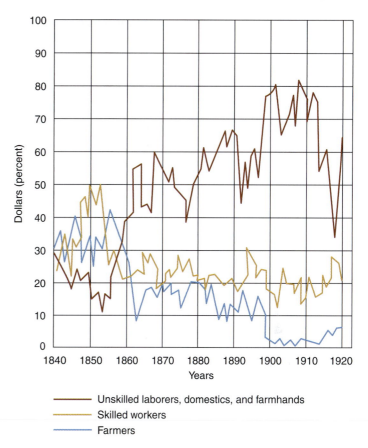

Figure 18-2 Working-Class Immigration, 1840–1920 *U.S. Bureau of the Census.*

As ethnicity developed in the late nineteenth century, class divisions were increasingly difficult to isolate from cultural distinctions. The middle class, for example, was overwhelmingly native born, white, Anglo-Saxon, and Protestant. The working class was, by contrast, African American, foreign born, Catholic, or Jewish. By 1900, 75 percent of the manufacturing workers in the United States were immigrants or the children of immigrants. In large cities, five out of six new manufacturing jobs were filled by immigrants and their children. In the South, wage laborers were overwhelmingly black sharecroppers. It was in this context that educated elites constructed a definition of high culture that would distinguish the middle classes from the allegedly uncultivated and uncultured working classes.

The Creation of High Culture

During the second half of the nineteenth century many leading intellectuals sought to isolate and define a tradition, *high culture,* that stretched through Western history from ancient Greece and Rome to the present. By the 1890s high culture embodied principles of social, cultural, and political hierarchy that were firmly installed in museums, libraries, and universities across the United States. A "Western tradition" had been created as an antidote to the new forms of popular culture that had emerged in the same decades.

High Culture Becomes Sacred

The leading advocate of high culture was an Englishman, Matthew Arnold. In *Culture and Anarchy*, published in 1869, Arnold promoted the study of "the best which has been thought and said in the world" as a source of stability amidst the "anarchy" of capitalist society. There could be no question as to which were "the best" works of art and literature. "Certain things are not disputable," *Harper's Magazine* declared in 1867. Authors such as Homer, Shakespeare, and Dante "are towering facts like the Alps or the Himalayas. . . . It is not conceivable that the judgment of mankind upon those names will ever be reversed." American elites looking for firm moral guidelines were establishing a canon of great cultural achievements and turning to it the way earlier generations had looked to holy scripture. Secular culture took on the qualities of the sacred.

> Culture [is] the great help out of our present difficulties; culture being a pursuit of our total perfection by means of getting to know, on all the matters which most concern us, the best which has been thought and said in the world; and through this knowledge, turning a stream of fresh and free thought upon our stock notions and habits.
>
> MATTHEW ARNOLD,
> *Culture and Anarchy*, 1869

Lurking beneath the sacred view of culture was the fear that the modern world had undermined traditional values, especially religious values. "Organizations are splitting asunder, institutions are falling into decay, customs are becoming uncustomary," one observer complained in 1865. Particularly troubling was the apparent decline in religious fervor. Middle-class men and women often confessed to a loss of their own faith.

The middle class never lost its faith entirely. On the contrary, Victorians retained their overwhelmingly Protestant orientation and their deep suspicion of Roman Catholicism. What they lost was a strong theology and missionary zeal. Victorians moved restlessly from one denomination to another, but few found the spiritual satisfaction or moral guidance they sought. As religious fervor waned, the Victorian middle class looked for comfort in more secular pursuits.

Thomas Wentworth Higginson typified this shift. Nurtured in the reform movements of antebellum New England, Higginson had been an abolitionist and supporter of women's rights. During the Civil War he commanded a famed regiment of African American troops. Fully engaged in the politics of his day, Higginson was equally at home in the literary culture of his native New England, turning to culture for relief from the sordid realities of urban life and industrial capitalism.

In 1871, two years after Matthew Arnold published *Culture and Anarchy*, Higginson made a strikingly similar case. Culture, he explained, "pursues" art and science for their intrinsic worth. It "places the fine arts above the useful arts." It sacrifices "material comforts" for the sake of a "nobler" life. At its best, Higginson believed, culture "supplies that counterpoise to mere wealth which Europe vainly seeks to secure by aristocracies of birth." Like Matthew Arnold, Higginson saw culture as a defense against materialism.

Higginson shared the Victorian conviction that culture was an attribute of the middle classes. At the top of the social order stood an increasingly dissolute and unrestrained capitalist class. At the bottom, poor working men and women lived lives utterly devoid of gentility and cultural refinement. Yet these very classes, the greedy capitalists at the top and the ignorant masses below, seemed to grow in influence as capitalism developed. To counteract this threat, American elites worked to transform American cities into centers of high art and cultural distinction.

The Emergence of a Cultural Establishment

In the early nineteenth century Shakespeare was the most popular playwright in America. Traveling through the country in the 1830s, Alexis de Tocqueville encountered Shakespeare even in "the recesses of the forests of the New World. There is hardly a pioneer's cabin but that does not contain a few odd volumes of Shakespeare." In established theaters, Shakespearean plays were performed more than any others, and the repertoire was not limited to a few classics. American audiences were familiar with a substantial body of Shakespeare's work.

A Shakespearean play was usually performed as the centerpiece of an entire evening's entertainment that included music, dancing, acrobats, magicians, and comedians. The show generally ended with a short humorous skit, or farce. Audiences attending these shows came from all walks of life, and they often made a noisy crowd. They generally preferred highly melodramatic renditions of Shakespeare in which the moral ambiguities were smoothed out and the lessons made sharp and clear. Ideally the ending was always satisfying. Good always triumphed over evil. Instead of committing suicide, Romeo and Juliet lived happily ever after. By 1850 Americans were so familiar with Shakespeare that politicians could safely make allusions to his plays without fear of losing an audience.

All of this changed in the second half of the nineteenth century. Shakespeare was redefined as high culture, and performances of his plays were separated from popular entertainment. This shift was evident as early as the 1850s, when a San Francisco theater announced that its production of *A Midsummer Night's Dream* would be performed by itself, with "NO FARCE." The entertainments that had once accompanied Shakespearean performances became the basis of the vaudeville theater, and theater audiences became segregated by class. The respectable classes retreated from the boisterous houses into quieter theaters, where the prices rose beyond the means of ordinary working people.

The same thing happened to opera and to orchestral music. Opera changed from an eclectic and highly popular art form to an elite entertainment. Italian immigrants who began arriving in the United States in the late nineteenth century noticed the difference. Back home opera was widely popular, and certain composers, Verdi in particular, were heroic figures whose work addressed the national aspirations of millions of Italians. But in America opera had become associated with high fashion and elite culture, and the opening of the opera season became synonymous with the opening of the "social season" among the very rich.

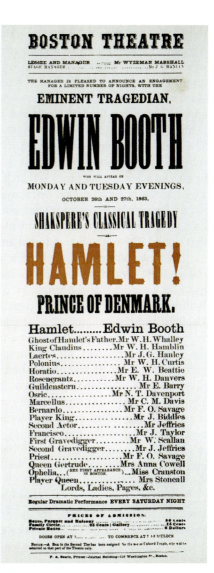

Advertisement for *Hamlet* Shakespeare was the most popular playwright in mid-19th-century America. This 1863 playbill advertised the appearance of one of the most popular Shakespearean actors of the time.

>> The Modern University

At the same time that American elites were endowing museums and libraries, they stepped up their commitment to the establishment of distinguished private universities. Cornell, Johns Hopkins, Vanderbilt, Stanford, and the University of Chicago all appeared between the late 1860s and the 1890s. Wealthy businessmen had good reason to endow great universities. The political economy of industrial capitalism rested on technological developments, which in turn depended on up-to-date scientific learning. Research universities played a central role in such developments and provided the training for the new business and engineering elite. And finally, corporate philanthropists agreed with many Americans that a great Western nation required great universities.

The new colleges reflected a new conception of how universities should be organized. Daniel Coit Gilman, the first president of the Johns Hopkins University in Baltimore, created specialized departments of history, English, and the various sciences that were responsible for recommending appointments and promotions and for developing courses. He encouraged the publication of academic journals and established the first university press in 1878. Gilman had created the modern university with a faculty of specialists dedicated to research and the training of other scholars. His innovations spread quickly and led to the undergraduate major; the system of numbered courses, unit requirements, and electives; and PhD programs with research seminars and dissertations based on original research.

In this new setting, the study of modern literature entered the college curriculum for the first time. Some professors, influenced by German scholarship, emphasized sentence structures, word roots, and forms of publication. This approach appealed to those who sought to make the study of literature into a science. But beneath the surface was a set of assumptions about the intrinsic superiority of western European languages. A leading Oxford scholar, Friedrich Max Müller, saw "an unbroken chain between us and Cicero and Aristotle." Müller and his American followers created a canon of great works that they believed defined culture of the "West." They also defined the study of literature as the preserve of specialists.

Leading scholars in the new "social sciences" of sociology, anthropology, and political science also divided the world into great and inferior nations. At the top stood the so-called Teutonic nations of western Europe and North America. This hierarchy, far from reflecting the biases of its creators, was grounded in the objective methods of pure science—or so anthropologists, sociologists, and professional economists claimed. Science was becoming the model for the production of all human knowledge.

As the modern university emerged it reflected the inequalities of the age. Only a tiny fraction of Americans attended college, most of them were men, most of the men were native born, and very few of those rose out of the working class. State universities and land-grant colleges were more open to a wider range of students, but in the late nineteenth century colleges and universities hardened rather than softened the barriers of caste and class. In the late twentieth century Americans would come to view widespread access to a college education as one of the great promises of democracy. But a century earlier the greatest seats of learning produced some of the most sustained attacks on democracy itself. ●

The Vanderbilt University Campus, ca. 1900 Founded in 1873, Vanderbilt was one of a large number of private and public universities established in the late 19th century.

Something similar was happening to orchestral music. In the first half of the nineteenth century local bands sprang up in thousands of communities across America (3,000 of them by 1860) with a repertoire that included popular and classical pieces. Beginning in the 1840s, classical music became the preserve of elite symphony orchestras in large cities.

Symphonies and opera companies cost a lot of money. Orchestras like the New York Philharmonic and the Chicago Symphony needed expensive new halls. Opera companies needed endowments. Serious theater needed generous patrons. Thus great infusions of private wealth were necessary to support lavish arts programs. In

Orchestra Hall in Chicago This is one of many stately auditoriums built to house America's major symphony orchestras in the second half of the 19th century. Pictured here are the Chicago Symphony Orchestra and Theodore Thomas, Auditorium Theater, 1897.

the late nineteenth century, the rich formed an alliance with leading performers and intellectuals to create a cultural establishment that endures to this day. Opera houses and symphony halls were built with and sustained by the patronage of the wealthy. They were the architectural embodiment of high culture.

Great cities required great museums as well. Americans built a stunning array of secular temples devoted to the world's great art. Major museums were founded in New York, Boston, Philadelphia, and Chicago in the 1870s. Spectacular new public libraries appeared at the same time. By 1900 many Americans had come to associate "culture" with impressive institutions lodged in major cities. By this reasoning, for example, the cultural life of Chicago was embodied not in the immigrant neighborhoods or the popular theaters, but in the Art Institute, Symphony Hall, and the Chicago Public Library.

Social Darwinism and the Growth of Scientific Racism

In 1859 Charles Darwin published his masterpiece of evolutionary theory, *On the Origin of Species*. Several scientists had already suggested that life had evolved over a long period of time, but Darwin offered the first persuasive explanation of how this might have taken place. He argued that a process of "natural selection" favored those biological changes that were most suited to the surrounding environment. In Darwinian theory, natural selection was the single most important explanation for the vast array of life forms on earth. American scientists were remarkably receptive to Darwinism. Asa Gray at Harvard and Joseph Le Conte at the University of California spread the evolutionary word in their influential textbooks on botany and geology. By 1900 virtually all the science textbooks used in American high schools embraced evolution.

Darwin's remarkable influence did not stop with the natural sciences. Social scientists applied the theory of natural selection to social evolution. This combination of social theory with evolutionary science was known as social Darwinism. Social Darwinists argued that human inequality was the outcome of a struggle for survival in which the fittest rose to the top of the social ladder. This theory made the rich seem more fit than the poor; it made blacks seem less fit than whites. To social Darwinists, inequality was the natural order of things. In this way Darwin's theory—one of the greatest scientific discoveries of all time—was twisted into a pseudoscientific defense of the new social order of industrial capitalism.

From the moment Darwin published his findings, the theory of natural selection was invoked to sustain a theory of African racial inferiority. Racists had argued that emancipation would force blacks to compete with their white superiors and that this competition would end in the disappearance of the African race. When the 1890 census seemed to show that the African American population was declining, racial theorists rushed into print with a series of influential studies claiming to show that blacks were withering under the strain of competition with whites. In 1892 biologist Joseph Le Conte weighed in with an article on "The Race Problem in the South." In conditions of free competition with whites, Le Conte argued, blacks faced either "extinction" or permanent subordination. Only the protection of whites could shield blacks from their natural fate.

Far more influential than the Le Conte article was Frederick L. Hoffman's full-length treatise, *Race Traits and Tendencies of the American Negro,* published in 1896. Hoffman's book quickly established itself as one of the most important studies of race relations written in the nineteenth century. Hoffman himself was a statistician, and the tables and figures scattered throughout his book gave it the authoritative air of the new social sciences. All of those numbers, Hoffman claimed, led to one inescapable conclusion: ever since they had left the protective cover of slavery, blacks had shown clear signs of moral degeneration and were doomed to poverty and social inferiority.

Social scientists like Hoffman prided themselves on their commitment to the truth as it was revealed in facts and statistics. Like advocates of high culture, sociologists and anthropologists claimed to have isolated the definitive truths of human society. But not all "realists" sought solace in the past or justified the inequalities of the present. The best American artists of the late nineteenth century openly embraced the realities of urban and industrial America.

Artistic Realism Embraces Urban and Industrial America

In the second half of the nineteenth century, artists and writers embraced the world that Anthony Comstock wanted to suppress, that Matthew Arnold wanted to escape, and that Thomas Wentworth Higginson wanted to fix. "This is the age of cities," writer Hamlin Garland declared. "We are now predominantly urban and the problem of our artistic life is practically one of city life." Artists like Garland called themselves "realists" and saw themselves as part of the first major artistic movement that was grounded in urban and industrial America. As writer Fanny Bates put it, the people of the cities "live more in realities than imagination."

The Triumph of Literary Realism

In April 1861 the *Atlantic Monthly* published a powerful story called "Life in the Iron Mills" by a writer named Rebecca Harding. Her story created a sensation. Rarely had the dreary lives of ordinary workers been presented in such relentless detail. In the decades to come, the best writers in America joined in the crusade to make fiction realistic. The leading spokesperson for realistic fiction was William Dean Howells, the author of one of the best-known realist novels, *The Rise of Silas Lapham,* and editor of the *Atlantic Monthly,* one of a handful of influential magazines that championed literary realism.

Realists tried to bridge the gap between "high" and "popular" culture by making great literature out of the details of everyday life. To "enjoy the every-day life," Sarah Orne Jewett explained in *Deephaven,* one must "find pleasure in thought and observation of simple things, and have an instinctive, delicious interest in what to other eyes is unflavored dullness." By writing about failed businessmen or runaway slaves, writers like Howells and Mark Twain hoped to reveal both courage and cowardice in the lives of ordinary men and women. This was the great achievement of Twain's *Huckleberry Finn.*

The characters in realistic novels were flawed men and women who struggled with the moral dilemmas they encountered in their daily lives. In Howells's best novel, Silas Lapham had to decide whether to mislead the men who wanted to buy his failing paint company. Huck Finn had to decide whether to turn in a runaway slave. Yet neither Lapham nor Finn was "heroic" in the way that earlier heroes were. Lapham was an ill-educated social climber who drank and talked too much. Huck Finn was a barely literate seeker of adventure who played hooky, spoke improper English, and spun absurd fantasies. In the end both Silas Lapham and Huck Finn made the right moral decisions, but neither found his decision easy to make, and Lapham suffered for having done so. Thus realism meant not merely the evocation of the themes of ordinary life, but the creation of characters who were psychologically complex and therefore more "realistic." For Henry James, psychological realism was the whole point and his characters—Isabel Archer in *Portrait of a Lady* is a good example—are among the most vivid and compelling in all American literature.

The realist movement was greeted with shock by the defenders of the genteel tradition of American letters. In March 1885 the public library committee of Concord, Massachusetts, banned *Huckleberry Finn* from its shelves, denouncing it as "the veriest trash." Members of the committee characterized Twain's masterpiece as "rough, coarse and inelegant, dealing with a series of experiences not elevating, the whole book being more suited to the slums than to intelligent, respectable people."

Realists dismissed such criticism as evidence of the "feminine" taste that prevailed in American letters, and they saw realism as a "masculine" alternative to sentimental writing that appealed to women novel readers. In their commitment to the unvarnished truth, realists thought of themselves as "virile and strong." But female realists also rejected the assumption, common to sentimental fiction, that women's lives should be bounded exclusively by the needs of their husbands and children. "The public demands realism and they will have it," the novelist Willa Cather declared. Louisa May Alcott wanted her female characters to be "strong-minded, strong-hearted, strong-souled, and strong-bodied." Realistic writers thus challenged the sentimental depiction of women as nervous, frail, and destined only for the domestic life.

Other authors, most notably Walt Whitman, pushed the radical possibilities of realism even further. Like most realists, Whitman aspired to "manly" writing. Through his poems he hoped "to exalt the present and the real, to teach the average man the glory of his daily walk and trade." He was the poet of the city who filled his verse with vivid details of urban life. For Whitman that meant he would embrace the "goodness" as well as the "wickedness" of modern America. Just as vaudeville flirted more and more openly with sexual titillation, Whitman wrote more and more openly about eroticism, as in this passage from *Leaves of Grass:*

> Have you ever loved the body of a woman?
> Have you ever loved the body of a man?
> Do you not see that they are exactly the same to all in all nations and
>   times all over the earth?
>
> If anything is sacred the human body is sacred,
> And the glory and sweet of a man is the token of manhood untainted,
> And in man or woman a clean, strong, firm-fibred body, is more beau-
>   tiful than the most beautiful face.

Thus Whitman, like so many realists, fused the themes of popular culture with the forms of "high" art.

Walt Whitman One of America's greatest poets, Whitman was a champion of the diversity and excitement of city life.

Painting Reality

In 1878 New York artist John Ferguson Weir declared that "art, in common with literature, is now seeking to get nearer the reality, to 'see the thing as it really is.'" Like the best writers of the post–Civil War era, the finest painters rejected romanticism. Winslow Homer and Thomas Eakins shifted the emphasis of American painting from sentiment to realism, from unspoiled nature to the facts of social life in urban and industrial America. Realists did not always paint the city, but even when they depicted rural life, or in Winslow Homer's case the life of the seafarer, realists generally avoided the romanticized scenes of nature that had been so popular in the early nineteenth century.

Winslow Homer was, in the words of one critic, a "flaming realist—a burning devotee of the actual." He left several important bodies of work, all realistic in different ways. A series of Civil War studies, notably *Prisoners From the Front* (1866), presented ordinary soldiers with ragged uniforms and worn, tired expressions. This was a sharp departure from a tradition of painting military men in heroic poses. As an illustrator for *Harper's Weekly,* the first successful mass-circulation magazine in America, Homer also drew realistic scenes of factories, railroad workers, and other aspects of industrial life.

Two of Homer's most enduring contributions were his sensitive depictions of African Americans and his remarkable portrayals of seafaring men struggling against nature. At a time when intellectuals were perfecting theories of black racial inferiority and minstrel shows presented blacks in the grossest stereotypes, Winslow Homer represented blacks as varied men and women who worked hard and struggled with dignity against the difficulties of everyday life. In the process, Homer produced some of his finest paintings.

Thomas Eakins was an even more thoroughgoing realist, determined to drain his paintings of all romantic sentiment. He wielded his paintbrush with the precision of a scientist in a laboratory. Indeed, in his effort to represent the human body with perfect accuracy, Eakins attended medical school. After studying for several years in Europe, Eakins returned to his native Philadelphia in 1870 and was soon shocking viewers with warts-and-all portraits of his own sisters. Eakins, one critic sniffed, "cares little for what the world of taste considers beautiful."

Eakins established his reputation with a series of lifelike paintings of rowers. Even at the beginning of his career, Eakins could render scenes with startlingly three-dimensional effects. In 1875, he shocked the art world once again with *The Gross Clinic,* a large canvas depicting the gruesome details of a surgical procedure. The selection committee for the 1876 Philadelphia Centennial Exposition rejected *The Gross Clinic* on the grounds that "the sense of actuality about it was . . . oppressive."

Eakins was fascinated by the human form. He photographed dozens of naked men and women and used some of them as the basis for full-scale paintings. *The Swimming Hole* (ca. 1884) was based on a photograph Eakins had taken. By 1886 the

The Swimming Hole Thomas Eakins was a pioneer in the artistic use of photography. By using photography as the basis for painting, and by using scenes from ordinary life as the basis of high art, Eakins demonstrated his commitment to artistic realism.

directors of the Academy had had enough. Eakins was fired after he pulled the loin-cloth from a male model posing before a group of female students.

Critics complained that Eakins was obsessed with nudity, but for Eakins himself the exact details of the human body were merely the entryway into a deeper exploration of the characters and personalities of his subjects. In the late 1880s and 1890s Eakins produced a number of portraits that were stunning both for their physiological accuracy and their psychological penetration. Like Winslow Homer's portrayals of blacks, Eakins's women were thoughtful and dignified. *Miss Amelia C. Van Buren* (1891) conveys its subject's intelligence and complexity with no sacrifice of accuracy. Eakins thereby did for painting what Henry James did for literature. Both demonstrated that distinguished works of art could be impressively realistic and at the same time deeply insightful.

Is Photography Art?

As city life became the subject matter of painters and writers, a major technological development—photography—created a new medium of artistic expression. The camera had been invented scarcely a generation earlier, in 1839, by a Frenchman named Louis Daguerre. By the early 1860s photographic technology had improved dramatically. For one thing, cameras had become more portable. Mathew Brady knew how to take advantage of it. In the fall of 1862 Brady mounted an exhibit of Civil War photographs in his New York gallery. This was the first time a large viewing public was able to see realistic pictures of the most gruesome facts of war. His exhibition had electrifying effects. By the 1880s journalists used photographs to heighten the reality, the sense of "truth," conveyed by their stories. The effect of Jacob Riis's *How the Other Half Lives,* published in 1890, was enhanced by the fact that he included a series of dramatic photographs documenting the misery of the urban poor. Photography had become part of the body of factual evidence.

The camera's eye inevitably fascinated realistic writers and artists. In the second half of the nineteenth century photography set the standard for accurate representation to which many artists aspired. Thomas Eakins, for example, used the camera to freeze images that he intended to paint on canvas. He photographed horses in motion to guide him as he painted. Eakins soon became a skilled photographer, producing hundreds of portraits of his subjects. He took numerous photos of the naked human form, and not always as a basis for later paintings. Eakins was one of the first artists to recognize the artistic element of photography itself. His work thereby raised questions that remain unanswered: Is a painting based on a photograph a work of art? Is photography art?

Some writers applauded the camera's capacity to capture the "truth." Writers as varied as Walt Whitman and Harriet Beecher Stowe used photographic metaphors to describe the effects they hoped to achieve with their words. But others were not persuaded that the photograph could ever be a genuine work of art. The camera captures only "the external facts," *The Galaxy* magazine declared, it "does not tell the whole truth."

Anthony Comstock worried a great deal about the difference between art and photography. Millions of copies of great and not-very-great works of art flooded the market in the late nineteenth century. Photographs of naked men and women suddenly became a new form of readily accessible pornography. "Is a photograph of an obscene figure or picture a work of art?" Comstock asked. "My answer is emphatically, No."

Civil War Photography Pioneered by Mathew Brady's New York studio, Civil War photography was part of a larger artistic movement toward realism. The photos were not simply graphic; the best of them were works of art.

Artists who paint nude portraits use lines, shadings, and colors in ways that "seem to clothe the figures"; their artistry diverts the viewers' attention from the nudity. Photographers have no such artistic devices at their disposal, Comstock explained. "A photograph of a nude woman in a lewd posture, with a lascivious look on her face," was to Comstock no work of art, for it lacked "the skill and talent of the artist."

Conclusion

When Comstock questioned whether photography could be art, he was participating in a larger debate about what counted as culture in the new world created by industrial capitalism. Did it include the popular culture of the city, or was American culture restricted to the nation's great libraries, universities, museums, and opera houses? And what was culture supposed to do for people? Americans argued over whether culture should maintain traditional values or boldly face up to the realities of the new political economy.

These cultural struggles easily spilled over into politics. Urban reformers proposed public policies to elevate the cultural level of slum dwellers. Elites convinced politicians to subsidize the construction of huge public libraries. Nevertheless, American politics in the late nineteenth century had not yet become cultural politics. The issues that brought Americans into the streets and into the voting booths remained, for the most part, economic issues. Just as American culture was transformed by the rise of cities and industry, the problems of industrial capitalism became the focus of American politics in the late nineteenth century.

Further Readings

John D'Emilio and Estelle Freedman, *Intimate Matters: A History of Sexuality in America* (1988). An innovative overview with important chapters on the late nineteenth century.

Elliot J. Gorn and Warren Goldstein, *A Brief History of American Sports* (1993). An intelligent introduction to the subject.

John Higham, *Strangers in the Land: Patterns of American Nativism, 1860–1925* (1955). The classic study of the response of native-born Americans to immigrants.

Lawrence Levine, *Highbrow/Lowbrow: The Emergence of Cultural Hierarchy in America* (1988). Traces the origins of the distinction between "high" and "low" culture in the nineteenth century.

John Matteson, *Louisa May Alcott and Her Father* (2007). A beautiful study of an important realist author.

Roy Rosenzweig, *Eight Hours for What We Will: Workers and Leisure in an Industrial City, 1870–1920* (1983). A pioneering work demonstrating the importance of leisure time to industrial workers.

David Shi, *Facing Facts: Realism in American Thought and Culture, 1850–1920* (1995). A broad, insightful overview.

Robert Toll, *Blacking Up: The Minstrel Show in Nineteenth-Century America* (1974). The first and still the best survey of the subject, especially good at tracing changes over time.

Alan Trachtenberg, *The Incorporation of America: Culture and Society in the Gilded Age* (1982). Shows the connections between culture and industrial society.

Who, What

>> Timeline >>

▼ 1851
YMCA is founded
First world's fair is held at Crystal Palace in London

▼ 1859
Charles Darwin publishes *On the Origin of Species*

▼ 1861
Rebecca Harding publishes "Life in the Iron Mills"

▼ 1862
Mathew Brady exhibits Civil War photos at his New York studio

▼ 1866
New York Athletic Club opens
Horatio Alger expelled from his pulpit in Brewster, Massachusetts

▼ 1869
Cincinnati Red Stockings charge admission to watch baseball games
Matthew Arnold publishes *Culture and Anarchy*

▼ 1870
Metropolitan Museum of Art and Boston Museum of Fine Arts are founded

▼ 1870s
National League is formed; baseball becomes professional

▼ 1871
Walt Whitman publishes *Democratic Vistas*

▼ 1873
New York Society for the Suppression of Vice (SSV) founded
Congress enacts the Comstock Law

▼ 1875
First Harvard-Yale football game is played
Thomas Eakins paints *The Gross Clinic*

▼ 1876
World's fair held in Philadelphia
Philadelphia Museum of Art founded
Daniel Coit Gilman becomes first president of Johns Hopkins University

Review Questions

1. In what ways was American culture "urbanized" in the late nineteenth century?

2. How did immigration affect American culture?

3. What were the major features of the high cultural establishment that developed in this period?

4. What was "artistic realism?"

5. Did American culture become more repressed or more eroticized in the second half of the nineteenth century?

6. In what ways did American culture reflect the patterns of race relations in the late nineteenth century?

Websites

On the Lower East Side. http://tenant.net/Community/LES/contents.html

The World's Columbian Exposition. http://xroads.virginia.edu/~MA96/WCE/title.html

For further review materials and resource information, please visit www.oup.com/us/ofthepeople

▼ **1878**
Johns Hopkins establishes the first university press

▼ **1879**
Art Institute of Chicago founded

▼ **1880s**
Richard Kyle Fox professionalizes prizefighting

▼ **1881**
Henry James publishes *Portrait of a Lady*

▼ **1883**
Anthony Comstock publishes *Traps for the Young*

▼ **1884**
Mark Twain publishes *The Adventures of Huckleberry Finn*
Thomas Eakins paints *The Swimming Hole*

▼ **1885**
William Dean Howells publishes *The Rise of Silas Lapham*
Josiah Strong publishes *Our Country*

▼ **1888**
Modern "safety" bike invented

▼ **1890**
Jacob Riis publishes *How the Other Half Lives*

▼ **1891**
Thomas Eakins paints *Miss Amelia C. Van Buren*

▼ **1893**
World's Columbian Exposition held in Chicago

▼ **1894**
Vaudeville producer B. F. Keith opens the New Theatre in Boston

▼ **1896**
Frederick L. Hoffman publishes *Race Traits and Tendencies of the American Negro*

Common Threads

>> How did both culture and politics reflect sharp distinctions between men and women? How did culture and politics break those distinctions down?

>> What was the overriding issue of American politics in the late nineteenth century?

>> Was American politics headed for a crisis in the 1890s?

The Politics of Industrial America 1870–1892

>> Luna Kellie and the Farmers' Alliance

Luna Kellie was the daughter of a railroad worker, but as a young girl she dreamed of one day raising a family on a farm of her own. Born in 1857, Luna grew up in towns along the Northern Pacific Railroad line. At one point her father did try to make a go of farming in Minnesota, but when the farm failed he moved the family to St. Louis, Missouri. There Luna met and married James T. Kellie. But she still hoped for a large family and a big house, so at the age of 18 Luna moved with her husband and their infant to a homestead in Hastings, Kansas.

Life on the prairie was a far cry from the dreams of Luna Kellie's youth. She gave birth to twelve children, two of whom died. They lived in an eight-by-twelve-foot sod house dug into the side of a hill. Overworked and exhausted, physically weakened by the strain of childbirth and constant work, Luna kept dreaming of a better future. She read an article in *Harper's* about the great geysers of Yellowstone and imagined a family trip. "Our trip never materialized," she recalled years later, "but we put in some happiest hours of life planning it."

What Luna Kellie imagined as a life of sturdy independence turned out to be an impoverished and isolated existence. It was an experience common to many American farmers, men and women alike. She tried to find connections with friends and neighbors wherever she could, but there was not much choice. Her family joined a Methodist church, but when an arrangement to care for a neighbor's cows in return for milk failed, Luna's husband became estranged from the church's pastor. Schools were even scarcer than churches, but Luna went out of her way to become active in the school district, where she took part in discussions over whether women should have the right to vote.

Luna and her husband were not able to make a go of their farm. Like many rural women, Luna shared the responsibility for managing the farm with her husband. She kept a garden, which helped feed the family and brought in extra income from the sale of chickens and eggs. As Luna taught herself how to maintain the livestock and grow fruit trees, her husband learned how to grow spring wheat

on the forbidding Kansas plains. But no matter how hard they worked, a lethal combination of declining prices and high interest rates clamped the farm down in perpetual debt. After seven years Luna and her husband lost the farm. They struggled to keep themselves afloat by raising chickens, sheep, and livestock.

The more Luna Kellie came to understand the burdens on farmers in the late nineteenth century, the more attracted she was to organized efforts to relieve their plight. She became active in the Farmers' Alliance, the largest and most powerful of all such efforts. Nor was Luna Kellie alone. On the contrary, she was but one of the 250,000 women who joined the Farmers' Alliance, making it the largest women's organization in the United States at the time.

Luna Kellie was one of a large number of rural women who became active in the Populist movement.

For Kellie, the Alliance held out the hope of realizing the dreams of her youth. It advocated education for the young, scientific farming, business methods, and organized cooperation among producers. The reforms the Alliance advocated would bring progress and prosperity to rural America. They would break down the stifling isolation of rural life, bringing farmers together in cooperative enterprises and at the same time linking rural Americans to the progressive world of cities and industry. For Kellie, and for thousands of other farmers, the mere existence of the Alliance already established many of those connections. In 1892, when the Nebraska

continued

633

>> **AMERICAN PORTRAIT** *continued*

Farmers' Alliance affiliated with the National Farmers' Alliance and Industrial Union, she was elected state secretary. Kellie worked as tirelessly on Alliance business as she had on her own farm. She wrote countless letters. She edited and set the type for articles for the Alliance newspaper.

Without ever setting foot outside her home, Luna Kellie found herself at the center of a vast network of farmers who learned from each other by discussing the issues of greatest concern to men and women like themselves. Those issues started from a basic concern for improving the lives of rural Americans, but the discussions quickly expanded into broader questions of political reform. For by 1892 the Farmers' Alliance had become the backbone for the most important political insurgency of the late nineteenth century, the Populist Party. ●

OUTLINE

Two Political Styles

There were two distinct political styles in late nineteenth-century America: one was partisan, the other was voluntary. Partisan politics included all the eligible voters who counted themselves as Democrats or Republicans, attended party parades and electioneering spectacles, and cast their ballots in record numbers. This was largely a world of men. The second political style, voluntarism, embraced a vast network of organizations, including women's assemblies, reform clubs, labor unions, and farmers' groups.

The Triumph of Party Politics

In the late nineteenth century American men voted along very strict party lines. Political parties printed and distributed their own ballots, and loyal Republicans and

Democrats simply dropped a party ballot in the appropriate box. Party allegiances and discipline were strict, and campaigns were carefully organized. At no other time in American history did voters ally themselves so tightly to the two major parties.

And never again would so large a proportion of American men participate in presidential elections. From the 1840s through the 1860s an average of 69 percent of those eligible voted in presidential elections. During the final quarter of the century, the average rose to 77 percent. The figures were less impressive in the South, although they followed the same general pattern. Between 1876 and 1892, nearly two out of three southern men cast ballots in presidential elections. In the North, 82 percent of men went to the polls every four years between 1876 and 1892. In the presidential elections of 1896 and 1900, northern voter turnout peaked at 84 percent.

Newspapers played a critical role in maintaining this level of political participation. Most editors were strong party advocates. Papers survived with the help of official advertisements and contracts to print ballots and campaign documents. Strong-willed editors such as Horace Greeley of the *New York Tribune* and William Cullen Bryant of the *New York Evening Post* became influential party leaders. Papers editorialized relentlessly in favor of their candidates and their party and slanted stories to show their party in the most favorable light. Some papers printed logos boasting of their partisan affiliation. "Republican in everything, independent in nothing," the *Chicago Inter Ocean* declared. Newspapers thus presented to their readers a starkly partisan world in which the difference between parties was the same as the difference between good and evil.

> A New England Village of olden time—that is to say, of some forty years ago—would have been safely and well governed by the votes of every man in it; but, now that the village has grown into a populous city, with its factories and workshops, its acres of tenements-houses, and thousands and ten thousands of restless workmen, foreigners for the most part, to whom liberty means license and politics means plunder . . ., the case is completely changed, and universal suffrage becomes a questionable blessing. Still we are told it is an inalienable right. Suppose for an instant that it were so, wild as the supposition is. The community has rights as well as the individual, and it has also duties. It is both its right and its duty to provide good government for itself, and, the moment the vote of any person or class of persons becomes an obstacle in doing so, this person or class forfeits the right to vote. . . .
>
> FRANCIS PARKMAN,
> "The Failure of Universal Suffrage," 1878

Spectacular political campaigns reinforced the partisan attachments promoted by newspapers. The parties organized political clubs to drum up enthusiasm for elections. Military marching companies organized the party foot soldiers as well. The clubs and marching groups in turn organized an endless series of competing party parades. Marchers rang bells, set off cannons, raised banners, and unfurled flags. Millions of American men, perhaps a fifth of all registered voters, participated in these huge spectacles.

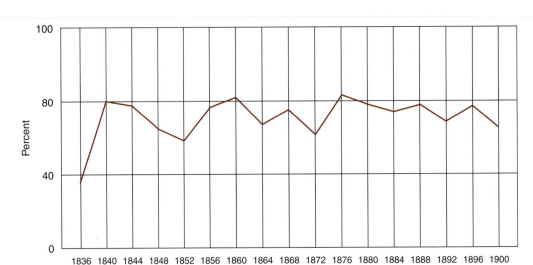

Figure 19-1 Percent of Eligible Voters Casting Ballots Between 1840 and 1896 a huge proportion—often 80 percent—of those eligible to vote did so in presidential elections. In the 20th century turnout dropped substantially.

Conspicuously absent from these events were the candidates themselves, particularly in presidential contests. Throughout the nineteenth century it was considered unseemly for presidential candidates to stump for votes. Those who did campaign—for example, Stephen Douglas in 1860, Horace Greeley in 1872, or James G. Blaine in 1884—were notoriously prone to losing the election. As the *Philadelphia Inquirer* explained in 1884, "It is better that the country should make its choice between the two candidates from what they know of their public records rather than from what they may learn of their personal appearance."

Masculine Partisanship and Feminine Voluntarism

Party politics was a largely masculine activity in the late nineteenth century. Both major parties functioned like fraternal organizations, and voting was increasingly referred to as a "manly" or a "manhood" right. Denying a man his right to vote was like denying his masculinity. If the electoral sphere of campaigns and voting was a man's world, the private sphere of home and family was widely understood as a woman's world. In practice, women always participated in the background of popular politics. They sewed the banners, decorated the meeting halls, prepared the food for rallies and picnics, and joined the parades dressed as symbolic representations of the Goddess of Liberty or some similarly feminine icon. Nevertheless, politically active women opted for a different style of politics.

The stereotypes of the public man and the private woman rested on the assumption that women were destined to remain at home as protectors of the family's virtue. By the middle of the century, increasing numbers of women used that female stereotype to develop their own form of political activism. Female virtue justified women's support for moral reform movements such as abolitionism and temperance. Thus many women entered the public sphere to protect the private sphere. By defining "the family" in broad terms, women expanded the horizons of political activity beyond the confines of the two-party system. In this way, a stereotype that initially restricted feminine political activity became a justification for women's increasing participation in public crusades.

Women pursued politics as representatives of voluntary associations that were dedicated to specific reforms, such as Sabbatarian laws that would prohibit working and drinking alcohol on the Sabbath, or the struggles against slavery, prostitution, and poverty. Because it grew out of voluntary associations rather than political parties, this style of political activity is known as voluntarism. Most of those who joined voluntary associations came from the educated middle class, and voluntary associations inevitably reflected the class biases of their members. By upholding the home as the special preserve of feminine authority, for example, reformers ignored the fact that working-class families depended heavily on the labor of children.

Sometimes women's associations copied the style of partisan politics, staging mass marches and rallies. But because many politically active women were critical of the emotional style of mass politics, voluntary associations concentrated less on rousing voters than on educating them and lobbying elected officials. Although men also joined voluntary associations, they were dismissed by mainstream politicians as "namby-pamby, goody-goody gentlemen." In the late nineteenth century, voluntarism was associated with feminine politics and party politics was associated with masculinity.

The Critics of Popular Politics

The combination of partisanship and voluntarism made American politics more "popular" than ever before. Women and men, blacks and whites, immigrants and the native born, working class and middle class all found places in the popular politics of

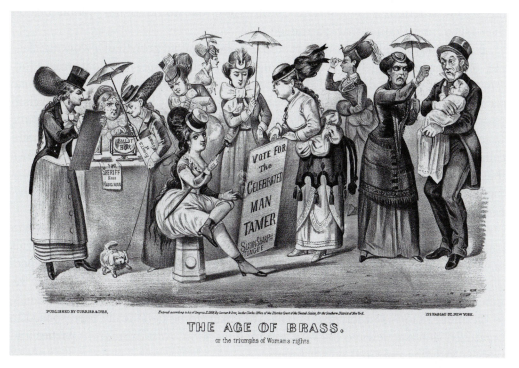

"Women on Top" A satirical cartoon from 1869 belittled the campaign for women's suffrage. Entitled "Women on Top," the image reflected the common assumption that electoral politics was strictly a masculine activity.

the late nineteenth century. But not all Americans appreciated popular politics. After the Civil War a small but influential group of conservatives reacted with disgust to the American rage for politics. Contemptuous of partisanship, they advocated a new style of nonpartisan politics and questioned the principle of universal suffrage. Because they laid the groundwork for a new style of politics that would prevail in the twentieth century, the critics were ahead of their time.

"Universal suffrage can only mean in plain English the government of ignorance and vice," Charles Francis Adams complained in 1869. Adams spoke for a traditional American elite that saw popular politics as a degradation of public life. To such men, economic independence was the precondition for political virtue, among voters and public officials alike. The fact that the American working class was made up largely of blacks, Asians, and Catholic immigrants only made matters worse.

But blatantly antidemocratic rhetoric was a losing proposition in the late nineteenth century. Elites who hoped to maintain political influence learned to avoid direct assaults on the principle of universal suffrage. Instead they became advocates of good government: government run by professionals rather than party bosses, and staffed by civil servants rather than party favorites. They became, in short, advocates of *nonpartisan* politics.

Nonpartisan politics was a reaction against the upheavals of urban and industrial development. Many elites were haunted by what they saw as the twin evils of radicalism and immigration. In the wake of the nationwide strikes of 1877, *The Nation* magazine, a reliable barometer of elite opinion, asked whether an "alien" proletariat had transformed universal suffrage from a democratic blessing into a nightmare for the "well-to-do and intelligent" classes. In 1881, supporters of good government organized the National Civil Service Reform League to prevent political parties from filling government positions with their supporters. Victory came two years later with the establishment of a Civil Service Commission that would assign federal jobs on the basis of merit rather than patronage.

But civil service reform would not stop the phenomenal growth of a working-class electorate made up largely of recent immigrants. Political opposition to immigration, known as nativism, had enjoyed some success in the 1850s, and in 1882 nativists had secured a congressional ban on the further immigration of Chinese. Anti-Catholicism spread across the country, especially in the Midwest in the late 1880s. Immigrants were Catholic and working class, so Yankee Protestants often saw working-class radicalism as a double threat. One nativist pointed to the "two lines" of foreign influence that were threatening the American republic. One line led to the radical politics of "agrarianism" and "anarchy." The second line tended toward Catholic "superstition." Both led "by different roads to one ultimate end, despotism!"

By the mid-1890s, as the number of immigrants from eastern and southern Europe increased, nativist rhetoric grew more racist. It was no longer merely radicals and Catholics who were swarming into the United States, but darker-skinned peoples from Italy, Russia, and eastern Europe. Social scientists wrote treatises on the inherent intellectual inferiority of such peoples, giving the imprimatur of science to the most vicious stereotypes. Italians were said to be genetically predisposed to organized violence, Jews to thievery and manipulation. Anti-immigrant parties and nativist societies appeared across America.

Throughout most of the nineteenth century, however, the critics of popular politics remained a vocal minority. Most Americans entered the political arena with

As the Number of Immigrants to America Swelled, So Did Opposition to Them This 1891 cartoon blames immigration for causing a host of social and political evils.

deep concerns over the problems of a society that was rapidly becoming more urban and industrial. Industrial capitalism generated the issues that dominated American public life in the late nineteenth century.

Economic Issues Dominate National Politics

By the late nineteenth century, Americans were accustomed to the idea that government should oversee the distribution of the nation's natural resources. After the Civil War, federal officials distributed public lands to homesteaders and railroads and granted rights to mining, ranching, and timber companies. During these same decades, the rise of big business led growing numbers of Americans to believe that the government should regulate the currency and also protect American commerce and workers from ruinous foreign competition. Given the even balance of the two major parties, it is not surprising that the outcome was a policy that split the difference. High protective tariffs protected workers, while the gold standard remained largely intact. Meanwhile the Supreme Court restricted the government's ability to regulate the domestic market. But this was never a stable compromise. On the contrary, struggles over economic policy were at the center of national politics throughout the late nineteenth century.

Weak Presidents Oversee a Stronger Federal Government

Starting in the mid-1870s, the Democrats and Republicans had nearly equal electoral strength, and from 1876 through 1896 not a single president enjoyed a full term during which his own party controlled both houses of Congress, nor did any

> In Grover Cleveland the greatness lies in typical rather than unusual qualities. He had no endowments that thousands of men do not have. He possessed honesty, courage, firmness, independence, and common sense. But he possessed them to a degree other men do not.
>
> ALLAN NEVINS

president during these years take office with an overwhelming electoral mandate. After Grant's re-election in 1872, no president was elected to two consecutive terms until 1900.

In some cases, a president took office already tainted by the process that put him there, as was certainly true of Rutherford B. Hayes's election in 1876. Hayes's fellow Republicans were annoyed by his efforts to conciliate the southern Democrats, who were conducting congressional investigations of his election, and frustrated by the president's contradictory position on civil service reform. Hayes forbade his party from raising money by assessing Republican officeholders, and he wrestled with the mighty Roscoe Conkling, Republican boss of New York City, for control of the New York Customs House—the most lucrative source of patronage in America. But although Hayes spoke for civil service reform, he acted the role of the party patron by lavishly rewarding his own supporters. Civil service reformers soon turned away from Hayes.

In 1877 Hayes took one important step toward strengthening the presidency. When railroad workers went on strike, Hayes dispatched federal troops to suppress them. This was an important precedent. Later presidents would often exercise their authority to intervene directly in disputes between workers and employers. But except for calling out the troops, Hayes's policy was to do nothing whatsoever to relieve the distress caused by the depression of the 1870s. Millions of Americans were suffering from the sharp fall in wages and prices, yet Hayes vetoed a bill that would have modestly inflated the currency. By 1880 the president was so unpopular that his fellow Republicans happily took him up on his offer not to run for reelection.

The results of the 1880 election were typical of the era. Republican James A. Garfield won the presidency by a tiny margin. He received 48.5 percent of the votes, and Democrat Winfield Hancock received 48.1 percent. As usual, the Republicans did best in New England, the upper Midwest, and the West. The Democrats swept the South but also took New Jersey, Nevada, and California. As a general rule, the Republicans appealed to southern blacks and to a northern middle class that was native born and overwhelmingly Protestant. The Democrats could count on strong support from working-class immigrants and southern whites.

As usual, economic issues dominated the 1880 campaign. But this did not mean that the Democrats and Republicans differed on economic policy. Both parties were addicted to the patronage system, so neither pressed for civil service reform. In theory the Democrats favored lower tariffs than the Republicans. In practice neither party advocated free trade and both parties had strong "protectionist" blocs (those who supported high tariffs to protect American business) as well as significant numbers who favored lower tariff rates. Neither party wanted to reverse the prevailing deflationary policies. Finally, while Republicans made periodic gestures in support of southern blacks, they had abandoned the freed people of the South. Thus Garfield's victory for the Republicans in 1880 did not foreshadow any major shifts in government policy.

On July 2, 1881, the president was shot by a lunatic who claimed to be a disappointed office seeker. Garfield died two months later, and Chester A. Arthur, the product of a powerful patronage machine, became president. The assassination that put him in office made it dangerous for the president to resist the swell of popular support for civil service reform. The Republicans in control of Congress did resist, however, and Democrats swept into office on a tide of resentment against Republican corruption and patronage. The following year Congress passed, and President Arthur signed, the landmark Pendleton Civil Service Act.

The Pendleton Act prohibited patronage officeholders from contributing to the party machine that gave them their jobs. More important, the law authorized the president to establish a Civil Service Commission to administer competitive examinations for federal jobs. Before the century ended, the majority of federal jobs were removed from the reach of the patronage machines. The Pendleton Act was a major turning point in the creation of a stable and professional civil service.

Although Arthur signed the Pendleton Act, he squandered his chance of gaining popular credit as a reformer by distributing lavish patronage to his supporters in a shameless bid for reelection in 1884. He likewise threw away an opportunity to lead the way on tariff reform. With the return of prosperity in the late 1870s and early 1880s, government coffers bulged with surplus revenues from import taxes. Cries for lower tariffs grew louder, but the president succumbed to the political manipulations of the high-tariff forces in Congress. The so-called Mongrel Tariff he signed in 1883 did nothing. Arthur was no more successful in his attempts to strengthen the navy or carry out an aggressive foreign policy. To make matters worse, the economy began to slow down again. Arthur approached the 1884 elections a tainted president. His fellow Republicans would not even renominate him.

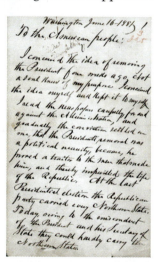

Letter from Charles Guiteau The original letter written by Charles J. Guiteau, in which he concludes "*I had no ill will to the president,*" after he shot President James Garfield to death in a Washington, DC, train station.

The Democrats nominated Grover Cleveland. In his brief career as mayor of Buffalo and governor of New York, Cleveland had developed a reputation as an honest man and a moderate. Cleveland, the first Democrat elected to the presidency in nearly 30 years, made reconciliation between the North and the South a theme of his administration.

Cleveland's conviction that the federal government should defer to southern whites derived in part from his commitment to local government. Accordingly, Cleveland was not an activist president. During his first two years in office he initiated no new programs, but neither did he thwart congressional moves to strengthen the authority of the central government. Cleveland approved legislation that raised the Agriculture Department to the status of a cabinet office and signed the Dawes Severalty Act of 1887, which placed the federal government in direct control over most Native Americans (see Chapter 17, "The Triumph of Industrial Capitalism"). In the same year, Cleveland signed the Interstate Commerce Act, the first federal legislation designed to regulate big business. It empowered a five-member Interstate Commerce Commission to curb monopolistic and discriminatory practices by railroads.

Another voice for Cleveland.

Republican Campaign Poster from the 1888 Presidential Election This poster assails the Democratic candidate, Grover Cleveland, on both personal and ideological grounds. Cleveland supported lower tariffs, and is therefore derided as an advocate of free trade. He had also fathered a child out of wedlock, hence the image of the infant.

Cleveland earned few points for merely signing laws passed by Congress, so when his fellow Democrats lost control of the House of Representatives in 1886, he decided to take the lead on some important issue. The issue he chose was the tariff. In December 1887, shortly before his reelection campaign was to begin, Cleveland devoted his annual message to Congress almost entirely to sharp reductions in the tariff. He insisted that he was not an advocate of free trade; he simply thought that the tariff was too high.

Having staked so much on tariff reduction, the president merely watched passively as Congress produced a doomed bill that was biased in favor of southern interests. When his own party included only a weak endorsement of tariff reform in the 1888 platform, Cleveland did nothing. Throughout his campaign for reelection, he spoke not one word on the subject. Cleveland went before the voters with no tariff reform, and little else, to show for his four years in office.

Running a skillful campaign on an overtly protectionist platform, the Republicans won back the White House in 1888. A Republican president, Benjamin Harrison, at last presided over a Republican majority in Congress. Making good on their campaign promises, Republicans enacted high tariff rates. The Harrison-McKinley Tariff of 1890 also gave the president the authority to raise or lower tariffs with nations that opened their markets to American businesses. Thus the legislation gave the president important new authority in the conduct of foreign affairs. Also in 1890 the Republicans passed the Sherman Anti-Trust Act, declaring it illegal for "combinations" to enter into arrangements that would restrain competition. By failing to define precisely what constituted a "restraint of trade," the Sherman Act left it to the probusiness courts to decide.

The Republicans received little credit for their efforts, and part of the problem was the president himself. Nicknamed "the human iceberg," Harrison was too stiff and pompous to rally the people. But the larger problem was the rising discontent among voters. In 1890 they put the Democrats back in control of the House of Representatives, and in 1892 they reelected Grover Cleveland president. Once again, however, a president took office without a popular majority. Cleveland was the last of a string of relatively weak presidents (see Table 19–1).

But the weakness of the executive did not indicate an inactive central government. In

 Table 19–1 Razor-thin Electoral Margins in the Gilded Age

Year	Popular Vote	% of Popular Vote	Electoral Vote
1876	4,036,572	48.0	185
	4,284,020	51.0	184
1880	4,453,295	48.5	214
	4,414,082	48.1	155
	308,578	3.4	—
1884	4,879,507	48.5	219
	4,850,293	48.2	182
1888	5,477,129	47.9	233
	5,537,857	48.6	168

addition to the Pendleton Act, the Interstate Commerce Act, and the Sherman Anti-Trust Act, the government tried to inflate the currency by modestly increasing the amount of silver in circulation. By maintaining high tariffs, politicians effectively protected the wage rates of workers and the economic security of businesses. Nevertheless, the weakness of the federal government left growing numbers of Americans with the impression that the political system could not solve the problems associated with the political economy of industrial capitalism.

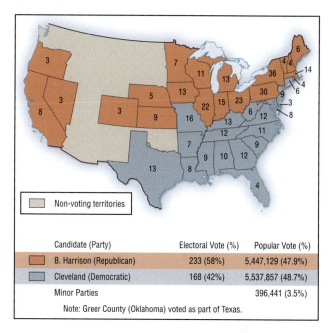

Candidate (Party)	Electoral Vote (%)	Popular Vote (%)
B. Harrison (Republican)	233 (58%)	5,447,129 (47.9%)
Cleveland (Democratic)	168 (42%)	5,537,857 (48.7%)
Minor Parties		396,441 (3.5%)

Note: Greer County (Oklahoma) voted as part of Texas.

Map 19–1 The Election of 1888

Government Activism and Its Limits

There are two standard themes in the political history of the late nineteenth century. The first theme stresses that government in this era was replete with corruption and bribery. The second theme emphasizes that the late nineteenth century was the great age of limited government and unregulated markets. After the retreat from Reconstruction, the government stepped back and allowed the new industrial economy to grow at its own rapid pace. There is a kernel of truth in each of these themes. Corruption was a real problem in late nineteenth-century politics, and the government's regulatory powers were trivial compared to what would come later. Nevertheless, government in the late nineteenth century did become somewhat more involved in the regulation of the economy. The conflicting impulses toward limited and active government can be seen most clearly in one of the most disruptive issues of late nineteenth-century American politics, the regulation of the currency.

Greenbacks and Greenbackers

People have always disagreed over how much money governments should produce and how they should produce it. During the eighteenth century, American colonists complained that there was not enough money in circulation to sustain their economic needs. In the first half of the nineteenth century, Americans fought over how much power the government should give to banks to regulate the amount of money in circulation. After the Civil War, capitalist development sparked another political debate over the role of government in the organization of the economy.

During the Civil War, the U.S. government printed $450 million worth of "greenbacks" to support the Union effort. Greenbacks were paper bills that were backed by the government's word, but not by the traditional reserves of gold or silver. When the war ended, most Americans agreed that the greenbacks should be withdrawn from circulation. But after the depression of the 1870s a growing number of Americans demanded that the government keep the greenbacks in circulation. Those who wanted to return to the gold standard by making greenbacks convertible for "specie"—gold or silver—were called *resumptionists,* that is, they

AMERICA AND THE WORLD

....

>> Foreign Policy and Commercial Expansion

Capitalist development reshaped American foreign policy just as it dominated domestic politics. In the 1860s William Henry Seward shifted the emphasis of American foreign policy from the acquisition of territory to the expansion of American commerce. As the secretary of state for Abraham Lincoln and Andrew Johnson, Seward argued for foreign and domestic policies that promoted industrial expansion. Prewar southern expansionism had dampened Seward's enthusiasm for the acquisition of more land: he came

to believe that "political supremacy follows commercial supremacy," and so he shifted his attention to the opening of American markets in Latin America, Canada, and the Pacific region, including Asia. Territorial expansion did not come to an end, but it took a back seat to commercial expansion.

In the late 1860s, as congressional Republicans struggled with President Johnson over Reconstruction, many of Seward's plans got caught in the crossfire. His biggest success came on April 9, 1867, when the Senate

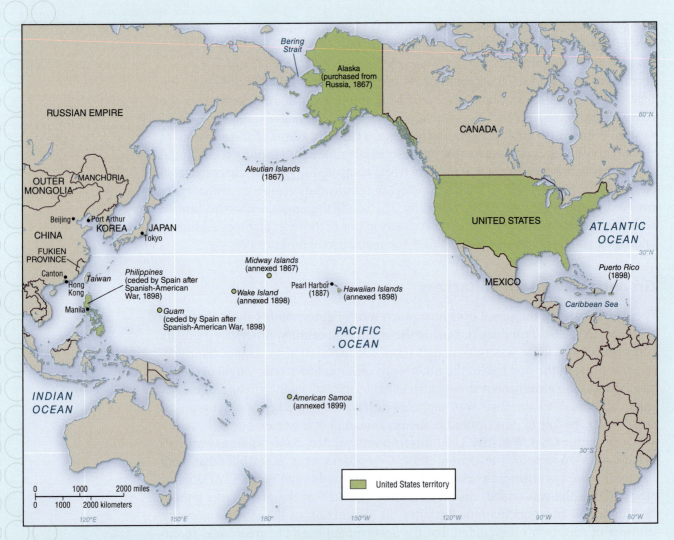

Map 19–2   American Expansion, 1857–1898 By the 1860s, Secretary of State William Henry Seward established the principle that American foreign policy would be driven by commercial interests.

ratified the treaty purchasing Alaska for $7.2 million. A few months later, however, the Senate blocked a treaty with Denmark for the purchase of the Virgin Islands. Seward likewise failed to win approval for a naval base in Santo Domingo and a treaty with Colombia giving the United States exclusive rights to build a canal across the isthmus of Panama. President Grant and Senator Charles Sumner revived long-standing American hopes of annexing Canada, but the Canadians seemed intent on cementing their ties to Great Britain.

European powers thwarted U.S. territorial ambitions in Latin America, but so did racist concerns about bringing large numbers of nonwhites into the United States. A rebellion in Cuba in 1868 heightened American interest in annexing the island. But Secretary of State Hamilton Fish had long resisted the idea of absorbing half a million Cubans of "every shade and mixture of color." Similar inhibitions led the Senate to reject President Grant's 1869 treaty with Santo Domingo.

Despite America's continued expansionist efforts, however, Seward believed that commercial rather than territorial expansion would drive American foreign policy in the future. Those commercial interests were increasingly global. Between 1860 and 1897 American exports tripled, surpassing $1 billion per year. After 300 years of trade deficits, in 1874 America's exports began to surpass its imports. Nearly 85 percent of those exports were agricultural commodities, but the growth of industrial exports was even more spectacular. Iron and steel exports jumped by 230 percent between 1888 and 1898. John D. Rockefeller's Standard Oil corporation shipped three-quarters of its kerosene overseas between the 1860s and the 1880s. In the 1880s, U.S. multinational corporations became a fixture of international commerce.

Aggressive secretaries of state reaffirmed Seward's commitment to commercial expansion. In 1886, for example, James G. Blaine worried openly that rapidly industrializing European nations were diverting Latin American commerce away from the United States. Concern for access to foreign markets pushed successive administrations to assert America's exclusive right to build a canal across Central America. The canal, President Harrison argued in 1891, "is the most important subject now connected with the commercial growth and progress of the United States." Hoping to thwart European commercial expansion by forging ties of friendship with Latin America, the United States convened the first Pan-American Conference in 1889.

Mexico provided the most vivid demonstration of U.S. commercial expansion. Although Americans had been buying up property in Mexico since before the Civil War, political instability limited Mexico's attractiveness as an investment. In 1876, however, Porfirio Díaz seized power in Mexico and began a reign of 35 years that proved a boon to American commercial interests. American investors quickly swarmed into Mexico, building railroads, selling life insurance, and digging oil wells. By 1910 Americans owned 43 percent of all the property in Mexico, more than Mexicans themselves owned.

United States attention also turned toward Asia and the South Pacific. In the 1880s the United States nearly went to war with England and Germany over disputed claims to Samoa. An 1876 reciprocity treaty gave Hawaiian sugar favored treatment on the American market, prompting a huge influx of Hawaiian sugar into the U.S. market (along with a backlash against the treaty by sugar producers on the mainland). By 1886, however, two-thirds of Hawaiian sugar was produced on American-owned plantations. Consequently, President Cleveland supported the treaty's renewal by referring to "our close and manifest interest in the commerce of the Pacific Ocean." By the 1890s American power in Hawaii had grown so great that it provoked among native Hawaiians a backlash that culminated in Queen Liliuokalani's ascension to the throne in January 1891. Two years later, Hawaiians favorable to the United States dethroned the queen. The Senate rejected the annexation treaty submitted by President Harrison, but eventually, under President William McKinley, Hawaii was annexed to the United States.

The United States treaded somewhat more cautiously in East Asia, where European powers had long-established ties. The United States negotiated treaties with Japan and Korea that substantially increased American access to Asian markets.

From 1865 to 1890 the Senate repeatedly rejected treaties negotiated by presidential emissaries, but a succession of powerful secretaries of state compensated for a succession of weak presidents. By the late 1880s America's extensive global interests began to shape the nation's military policy. In 1890 Congress approved the construction of the first modern warships, and the Supreme Court extended the president's control over "our international relations." The growing links between commercial and diplomatic interests were reviving the powers of the American presidency. ●

wanted the government to resume specie payments. Those who wanted the government to keep greenbacks in circulation to help inflate the currency were called greenbackers.

The supporters of the gold standard associated sound money with sound religion. In 1878, for example, the *Christian Advocate* compared greenbackers to atheists. And in fact, greenbackers were often radical critics of industrial society. They formed a Greenback-Labor Party, which garnered more than 1 million votes in the 1878 congressional elections and elected 14 members of Congress. But the sound-money forces won out, and in 1879 the $300 million in greenbacks that were still in circulation were made convertible into gold.

Supporters of inflation next took up the issue of "free silver." To counteract the deflationary trend, they argued, the government should add to the amount of money in circulation by allowing the unlimited coinage of silver. In 1878 the inflationists and sound-money forces in Congress passed the Bland-Allison Act authorizing the Treasury to purchase silver and mint it in amounts tied to the amount of gold being minted. With the return of prosperity in the 1880s the currency question died down, to be revived with the arrival of another severe depression in the 1890s.

> I do not believe that the power and duty of the General Government ought to be extended to the relief of individual suffering which is in no manner properly related to the public service or benefit. A prevalent tendency to disregard the limited mission of this [government] power and duty should, I think, be steadfastly resisted, to the end that the lesson should constantly be enforced that **though the people support the Government the Government should not support the people.**
>
> GROVER CLEVELAND

Growth of the Central Government

Despite the inevitable retrenchment that followed the Civil War, the size of the central government grew as new bureaucracies were created in the late nineteenth century. Congress consolidated the United States Geological Survey in 1879, established the Interstate Commerce Commission in 1887, and created the Department of Justice in 1870 and the Department of Agriculture in 1889.

The number of civilian federal employees rose from 53,000 in 1871 to 256,000 in 1901. These numbers reflected the emergence of a professional civil service. In 1883, when Congress passed the first civil service law, 13,780 federal jobs were "classified," meaning that applicants had to pass an exam to qualify. Fifteen years later, 89,306 federal positions were classified, amounting to nearly half of the jobs in the national government. This expansion of the number of civil service jobs substantially weakened the power of the Democratic and Republican parties. As the proportion of "classified" federal jobs swelled, the patronage well dried up.

By the turn of the century, however, only the rudiments of a modern federal government were in place. The Interstate Commerce Commission lacked the power to enforce its own rulings, so it was forced to rely on the courts, which were dominated by supporters of big business. The Sherman Anti-Trust Act was even weaker.

Few monopolies were threatened, much less broken up, by it. Finally, only about 15 percent of the wage-labor force was actually protected by the high tariffs. By 1900 the federal government had developed in important ways, yet it remained small and weak by later standards. Indeed, it was not the federal but rather the state and municipal governments that responded most aggressively to the problems of urban and industrial society.

States Regulate; Municipalities Reform

Even as Americans called on their government to do more and more, politicians proclaimed their opposition to the taxes and bureaucracies that active government required. The result was a jarring contradiction. At the state level, politicians enacted policies of retrenchment. In contrast to the steady expansion of the federal government, for example, late-nineteenth-century state legislatures passed fewer laws and lowered taxes.

But state politicians also established new regulatory bodies to govern the exploding municipalities of urban and industrial America. During the late nineteenth century, state officials often transferred municipal power from elected officials and party politicians to experts and specialists on unelected boards. Mayors, city council members, and aldermen lost much of their authority over budgets, schools, police, and parks. For example, reformers handed control of the police to commissions staffed by middle-class citizens rather than by working-class immigrants. Parks commissions, sanitation commissions, public health commissions, and transportation commissions were generally staffed by middle-class professionals who were appointed to their posts and who prided themselves on their "nonpartisan" approach to government. The quality and professionalism of police and fire services increased dramatically over the course of the nineteenth century.

As states retrenched, cities increased their property taxes to pay for streets, sewers, reservoirs, and public transportation. In the late nineteenth century city governments produced some of the great urban achievements of American history. Huge public parks, such as Central Park in New York and Golden Gate Park in San Francisco, sprang up across the country. At the same time, cities sponsored spectacular feats of engineering and architecture. New Yorkers built the Brooklyn Bridge; Chicagoans literally reversed the flow of the

Bird's-Eye View of Golden Gate Park San Francisco's Golden Gate Park, designed by Frederick Law Olmsted, was one of the most impressive of the great municipal parks built in cities across America in the late 19th century.

Chicago River. Municipal governments went a long way toward enhancing the civility and decency of urban life in America.

Yet Americans grew dissatisfied with their governments. Some were disgusted by corruption and inefficiency; others were offended by the hoopla of popular politics. To a significant number, government policies seemed inadequate to the demands of urban and industrial America. The powers of government grew slowly, but they were dwarfed by the private power of huge new corporations. Frustrated by piecemeal reforms, middle-class Americans turned to radical campaigns for social and economic transformation.

Middle-Class Radicalism

In the late nineteenth century a number of middle-class radicals argued that economic development had undermined individual liberty and equality. Yet while their attacks on capitalism were severe, their assumptions were surprisingly traditional. They were usually frightened, not motivated, by socialism. They often worried that if substantial reforms were not undertaken, a discontented working class would overthrow the reign of private property. Their radical critiques of industrial society exposed deep wells of discontent among Americans.

Henry George and the Limits of Producers' Ideology

Henry George was born in Philadelphia in 1839, the son of middle-class parents. Although his formal education was limited, George traveled extensively and read widely. Like many middle-class Americans of his generation, he was shocked by the fact that as the United States grew richer the number of poor people grew as well. He studied the problem for many years and in 1879 published his conclusions in a best-selling book called *Progress and Poverty*.

George's explanation rested on what historians have called producers' ideology. It started from the assumption that only human labor could create legitimate wealth. Anything of value, such as food, clothing, or steel rails, came from the world's producing classes. By contrast, stockbrokers, bankers, and speculators made money from money rather than from the goods they produced. Producers' ideology therefore deemed their wealth illegitimate. Starting from these premises, Henry George divided the world into two classes: producers and predators.

The harmony of capital and labor was a central theme of producers' ideology. Henry George dreamed of a world in which working people owned their own farms and shops, making them both capitalists and laborers. His critique of industrial capitalism thus harkened back to Thomas Jefferson's vision of a society of small farmers and independent shopkeepers. America used to be that way, George believed, but as society "progressed," the land was monopolized by a wealthy few. Producers were forced to go to work for wealthy landholders. Employers then invested in technology that increased the productivity of their workers, but they kept the added wealth for

> The tramp comes with the locomotive, and almshouses and prisons are as surely the marks of material progress as are costly dwellings, rich warehouses, and magnificent churches.
>
> HENRY GEORGE,
> *Progress and Poverty*, 1879

John F. Weir's 1877 Painting *Forging the Shaft: A Welding Heat* This painting graphically depicts the forms of industrial wage labor that Henry George feared. He advocated tax policies that would restore a Jeffersonian economy of small, independent producers.

themselves. Technology thus multiplied the wealth of the predators at the expense of the producers.

George's solution for the inequities of industrial society was a so-called Single Tax on rents. Because all wealth derived from labor applied to land, he reasoned, rents amounted to an unnatural transfer of wealth from the producers to the landlords. To thwart that transfer, George suggested taxing rents and improvements on land at prohibitive levels. This would discourage the accumulation of land by the landowning class. All other taxes would be abolished, including the tariffs that protected big business.

George presented his Single Tax as an alternative to the dangerous socialist doctrines that he thought were spreading among the working class. George attacked as "faulty" the socialist idea that there was an inherent conflict between labor and capital. He opposed government regulation of the economy, and he was a fiscal conservative, suspicious of proposals to counteract deflation by putting more money in circulation. Despite his apparent radicalism, George's popularity testified to the strength of middle-class concerns about the political power of the working class.

Edward Bellamy and the Nationalist Clubs

In 1888 Edward Bellamy, a 38-year-old Massachusetts editor, published a best seller with a critique of capitalism even more powerful than Henry George's. Bellamy's *Looking Backward* was a utopian novel set in the future. The plot revolves around Julian West, who goes to sleep in Boston in 1887 and wakes up in the year 2000.

AMERICAN LANDSCAPE

>> The "Crusade" Against Alcohol

A few days before Christmas in 1873, Dr. Diocletian Lewis arrived in Hillsboro, Ohio, to speak on the evils of alcohol. He had given the speech many times before, but on this occasion the women who came proved unusually responsive. Lewis told them how, when he was a boy, his mother saved his father from drink by persuading a local saloonkeeper to stop selling liquor. The next morning a group of Hillsboro women met for prayer and then marched through the town urging local merchants to stop selling liquor. Inspired by their success, the women kept up the pressure through the winter of 1873/1874.

The Crusade, as it came to be called, quickly spread to more than 900 towns and cities in 31 states and territories. The women closed down thousands of liquor stores and saloons and secured written pledges from hundreds of druggists and hotel keepers not to sell alcohol. With the dramatic success of the Crusade of 1873/1874, temperance was reborn as a movement dominated by women.

From these humble, almost accidental, beginnings, there grew one of the late nineteenth century's largest outlets for women's political activism. Under the auspices of the Woman's Christian Temperance Union, women took up causes that stretched well beyond the suppression of alcohol. Voting and office holding were restricted to men, but the WCTU expanded democratic participation to include tens of thousands of women. ●

His host, Doctor Leete, introduces West to the miraculous changes that have taken place. Technological marvels have raised everyone's standard of living. Boston has become a clean and orderly city. The great problems of industrial civilization have been solved. This was possible, Doctor Leete explains, because Americans had overcome the "excessive individualism" of the late nineteenth century, which "was inconsistent with much public spirit."

What about "the labor question?" Julian West asks. It had been "threatening to devour society" in 1887 when West fell asleep. Bellamy's critique of capitalism is contained in Doctor Leete's answer to West's question. In the early years of the American republic, the doctor explains, workers and employers lived in harmony. Upward mobility was common. This changed when "great aggregations of capital" arose. Like Henry George's, Bellamy's criticism of capitalism was grounded in traditional Jeffersonian ideals. For both authors the triumph of wage labor led to concentrations of wealth that undermined the harmony of capital and labor.

But where *Progress and Poverty* proposed the restoration of the simple virtues of Jeffersonian society, *Looking Backward* imagined a high-tech future in which consumer goods were provided in abundance. What got produced and what got consumed would no longer be left to the chaotic whims of the market. Instead, in Bellamy's ideal world production and consumption would be harmonized by an obscure process of centralized planning. The result would be a consumer's utopia of widespread abundance.

Where Henry George reasserted the values of hard work and self-restraint, Edward Bellamy embraced the modern cult of leisure. For Henry George, technology led to misery and inequality, but for Edward Bellamy, machines would free mankind from the burdens and inequities of the modern world.

In spite of these differences, Bellamy and George were both motivated by a profound fear of militant workers. *Looking Backward* catered to a middle-class craving for order amidst the chaos of industrial society. Decisions about what to produce were made collectively, and society as a whole owned the means of production. Yet Bellamy was contemptuous of socialism and called his vision "nationalism." Under nationalism, the restoration of social peace was so complete that there was little or no need for government. This vision inspired thousands of middle-class Americans to form "Bellamy Clubs" or "Nationalist Clubs," particularly in New England.

The Woman's Christian Temperance Union

"Edward Bellamy's wonderful book" likewise inspired Frances Willard, president of the Woman's Christian Temperance Union (WCTU). She called nationalism "the fulfillment of man's highest earthly dream." Fifteen years earlier such support would have been impossible. At first "conservatives" who wanted to restrict the WCTU's activity to the suppression of liquor dominated the organization. But Willard had grander visions, and so, apparently, did the WCTU's members. In 1879 they elected Willard their national president, a position she held until her death in 1898.

The temperance movement broadened its interests and grew steadily more radical and more popular. It embraced women's suffrage, workers' rights, and finally "Christian socialism." Nevertheless, the WCTU's appeal and its radicalism were restricted by its predominantly prosperous membership. The middle-class Protestant bias of the WCTU was consistent with its disdain for most forms of party politics.

To be sure, the WCTU convened huge rallies, but Willard contrasted them to party conventions. WCTU gatherings were depicted as clean, well-disciplined affairs with oratory that was substantive rather than bombastic. Unlike the major parties, the WCTU combined education with interest-group pressure. Willard and her associates gave speeches, wrote articles, published books and newspaper columns on the evils of drink, organized petition campaigns, and lobbied officeholders. The crusade against alcohol grew into a broad-ranging political campaign to alleviate the problems of a new industrial society. In this sense the WCTU was typical of American politics in the late nineteenth century.

Under Willard's direction the WCTU endorsed women's suffrage and formed an alliance with the country's largest labor union. Willard supported laws restricting the workday to eight hours and prohibiting child labor. Even the WCTU's attitude toward alcohol changed. By the 1890s Willard viewed drunkenness as a public health problem rather than a personal sin, a problem of political economy rather than individual failure. Accordingly, temperance advocates supported reforms designed to relieve poverty, improve public health, raise literacy, alleviate the conditions of workers, reform prisons, suppress public immorality, and preserve peace. In the end, Willard attributed the evils of liquor to the inequities of corporate capitalism.

Three factors explain the WCTU's success. The first was Frances Willard's paradoxically conservative approach to radical reform. Her justification for female political activism always came back to women's distinctive calling as protectors of the home. The second reason for the WCTU's success was its decentralized structure. Willard left the local chapters of the union free to adjust their activities to suit their particular needs. In the southern unions there was little talk of women's suffrage. Willard called this the "Do Everything" policy. Finally, the WCTU appealed to middle-class women who felt isolated by a culture that restricted them to the home. Women found in the WCTU a source of camaraderie as well as political activism. The WCTU dwarfed most other women's political organizations in the late nineteenth century. By the early 1890s, for example, the National American Woman Suffrage Association had 13,000 members; the less-radical General Federation of Women's Clubs had 20,000. The WCTU had 150,000 adult members and 50,000 in its young women's auxiliary. The only reform organization to attract more women was the Farmers' Alliance.

For all its success, however, temperance remained a middle-class reform movement. The organization rested on a constituency that was concentrated in cities, especially in the North. The WCTU did not attract many immigrants, for example. The official policy of religious toleration was undermined by the prejudices of middle-class members. For many temperance advocates immigrants were the Union's targets rather than its constituents, and the strong Protestant identity of the WCTU limited its appeal among working-class Catholics. One of its first major campaigns in the 1870s was aimed at replacing altar wine with grape juice in Christian services, a switch that Irish Catholics and German Lutherans were unwilling to make. As radical as it was, the WCTU would never reflect the interests of black sharecroppers, white tenant farmers, or immigrant workers. Nevertheless, like the Single-Taxers and the Bellamy Clubs, WCTU reformers reflected a growing sense that the American political system was unable to solve the problems of an industrial political economy.

Discontent Among Workers

Radicalized workers shared the conviction that mainstream politics could not confront the problems of industrial capitalism. Labor radicals began to question one of the premises of producers' ideology—that American democracy was secured by a unique harmony between capital and labor. Labor agitation often became violent, and employers demanded that government use its police powers to put down strikes. But if the harmony of capital and labor had been destroyed, advocates of the producers' ideology continued to search for a political solution to the labor problem.

The Knights of Labor and the Haymarket Disaster

Between 1860 and 1890 wages overall grew by 50 percent, but the bulk of the growth was confined to elite skilled and semiskilled workers in a handful of industries, such as printing and metalworking. The vast majority of workers suffered directly from the deflation and economic instability of the late nineteenth century. By 1880, 40 percent of industrial workers lived at or below the poverty line, and the average worker was unemployed for 15 to 20 percent of the year. To relieve their plight, American workers sought political solutions to economic problems.

The most important labor organization to emerge from the crisis of the 1870s was the Noble and Holy Order of the Knights of Labor. Founded in 1869, the Knights of Labor was inspired by the producers' ideology and admitted everyone from self-employed farmers to unskilled factory workers. It appealed to a nostalgic vision of a world dominated by ordinary working people. Nevertheless the Knights of Labor advocated a host of progressive reforms, including the eight-hour day, equal pay for men and women, the abolition of child and prison labor, inflation of the currency to counteract the deflationary spiral, and a national income tax.

By the late 1870s leaders realized that the union needed a strong national organization to hold various locals together. A new constitution, drawn up in 1878, required all members to pay dues and allowed the national organization to support local boycotts and thereby boost its credibility among workers. Thereafter the Knights grew rapidly, from 19,000 members in 1881 to 111,000 in 1885. True to the producers' tradition, leader Terence Powderly favored the consumer boycott over the strike. His approach proved most successful during the sharp recession of 1884, when trade union strikes were being broken. By 1886 membership in the Knights skyrocketed to more than 700,000.

Liberty *versus* Anarchy. In this image published in *Harper's Weekly* (September 4, 1886), cartoonist Thomas Nast depicted a massive female Liberty crushing the Haymarket defendants in her hands, presumably rescuing the republic in the process.

But the more the Knights of Labor grew, the more the strains among its members showed. The interests of shopkeepers and small-factory owners were very different from those of wage laborers. The critical issue dividing self-employed producers from wage-earning producers was the use of the strike as a weapon of organized labor. Self-employed producers preferred the consumer boycott, and so did the leadership of the Knights of Labor. By contrast, wage laborers saw the strike as their most powerful weapon.

With the return of prosperity, trade unions called for a nationwide strike for the eight-hour day. On May 1, 1886, workers across the country walked off their jobs in one of the largest and most successful labor walkouts in American history. In Chicago 80,000 workers went out on strike. The Chicago job action was largely peaceful until May 4, when, at an anarchist rally at Haymarket Square near downtown, someone from the crowd tossed a bomb into a line of police. One policeman was killed instantly, and seven more died within days. The number of civilian casualties was never determined. Although the bomb thrower was never identified, eight anarchists were tried for inciting violence, and four were put to death.

Anarchists—who questioned the legitimacy of all government power—had been active in Chicago for several years. Although they had little influence on the labor movement, their fiery rhetoric advocating the use of violence made them conspicuous.

At the Haymarket rally on the evening of May 4, anarchist speakers used the same violent rhetoric. Samuel Fielden, for example, urged his listeners to "throttle" and "kill" the legal system or else, he warned, "it will kill you." This remark provoked detective James Bonfield to rush 170 policemen to the dwindling rally, and into this crowd of policemen someone threw a bomb.

Haymarket was a turning point in American labor politics. With the support of its president, Terence Powderly, the Knights of Labor had tried to prevent its locals from supporting the May Day walkouts. Powderly had put himself into a bind. Members resented his failure to support the strikes, while outside the union a wave of revulsion against labor agitation swept the country. The Knights of Labor never recovered from the Haymarket disaster. Thereafter worker agitation split dramatically into two competing wings. Small farmers formed their own organizations, and wage laborers organized separately into industrial trade unions.

Agrarian Revolt

The late nineteenth century was a desperate time for American farmers, especially in the West and South. To compete they had to buy expensive agricultural equipment, often from manufacturers who benefited from tariff protections. Then they had to ship their goods to market on railroads that charged higher rates to small farmers than to big industrialists. When their goods reached a market, they faced steadily declining prices.

As the economy became global, southern cotton had to compete against cotton from India and the Near East. Western wheat competed with Russian and eastern European wheat. To keep up, farmers increasingly went into debt, and in a deflationary spiral the money they borrowed to plant their crops was worth more when it came time to pay it back, while their crops were worth less. Farmers mortgaged their homes and land. The proportion of owner-occupied farms declined while the number of tenants rose.

Farmers were traditionally opposed to active government, but they began to press for government action. But farmers were notoriously hard to organize. They were scattered over large sections of the country, they were committed to an ideology of economic independence, and they were traditionally hostile to government intervention. If American farmers were to pursue their political agenda effectively, they needed to overcome these and many other obstacles.

One of the first attempts to organize farmers was the Patrons of Husbandry, generally called the Grange. The Grange began to attract large numbers of farmers during the depression of the 1870s and claimed 1.5 million members by 1874. Consistent with producers' ideology, the Grange organized cooperatives designed to eliminate the role of merchants and creditors. By storing grain collectively, farmers held their products back from the market in the hope of gaining control over commodity prices. But inexperience made the Grange cooperatives difficult to organize and sustain. After 1875 their membership dwindled.

The National Farmers' Alliance and Industrial Union, known simply as the Farmers' Alliance, was much more effective than the Grange. Founded in Texas in 1877, the Farmers' Alliance spread rapidly across the South, the West, and the upper Plains states. The goal of the Alliance was not to restore rural America to Jeffersonian simplicity, but to bring American farmers into the modern world of industry and prosperity. The Alliance focused above all on education, broadly conceived. That meant public schools for their children and the spread of scientific agriculture and sound business practices among themselves. To spread the word, the Alliance built a remarkable network of newspapers and lecturers to help liberate individual farmers from their rural isolation. Yet the appeal of the Farmers' Alliance transcended politics and economic reform. For men and women alike the Farmers' Alliance offered a chance to escape the stifling isolation of rural life. It appealed to the desire among tens of thousands of farmers to claim a share in the progress and prosperity of American life.

Nevertheless, at its core the Alliance was a reform organization calling for a specific set of economic policies. Above all, the farmers wanted to inflate the currency, sometimes by the circulation of more silver currency, sometimes by the circulation of more paper currency, or "greenbacks," and sometimes by a combination of the two. Inspired by the successful example of highly organized corporations, especially railroads, the Farmers' Alliance also supported a system of cooperative "subtreasuries" that would allow farmers to pool their products and store them in warehouses until the best prices were available. In the meantime the Alliance cooperative would sustain its members through low-interest loans.

By the late 1880s the Farmers' Alliance had attracted millions of members, concentrated in the southern, western, and Plains states. Its potency was demonstrated at a huge meeting at Ocala, Florida, in 1890. The Ocala Platform supported a host of reforms that joined economic progress to democratic reform. In addition to planks calling

> [W]e meet in the midst of a nation brought to the verge of moral, political, and material ruin. Corruption dominates the ballot-box, the Legislatures, the Congress, and touches even the ermine of the bench. The people are demoralized; most of the States have been compelled to isolate the voters at the polling places to prevent universal intimidation and bribery. The newspapers are largely subsidized or muzzled, public opinion silenced, business prostrated, homes covered with mortgages, labor impoverished, and the land concentrating in the hands of the capitalists. The urban workmen are denied the right to organize for self-protection, imported pauperized labor beats down their wages, a hireling standing army, unrecognized by our laws, is established to shoot them down, and they are rapidly degenerating into European conditions. The fruits of the toil of millions are boldly stolen to build up the fortunes for a few, unprecedented in the history of mankind; and the possessors of these, in turn, despise the Republic and endanger liberty. From the same prolific womb of governmental injustice we breed the two great classes—tramps and millionaires.
>
> THE OMAHA PLATFORM,
> July 4, 1892

Kansas Farmers Organizing to Attend a Populist Party Gathering

for the free coinage of silver, lower tariffs, and a government system of subtreasuries, the platform also called for a constitutional amendment providing for direct election of senators. Finally, the Alliance called for strict government regulation, and if necessary direct government ownership, of the nation's railroad and telegraph industries.

The Farmers' Alliance steered clear of politics and instead judged political candidates by the degree to which they supported the reforms advocated in the Ocala Platform. But very little such support was forthcoming from either of the major parties. Farmers' Alliance members therefore formed their own third parties, with some success on the Great Plains in the election of 1890. Out of these initial forays into politics came the most significant third party of the late nineteenth century, the People's Party, otherwise known as the Populists.

The Rise of the Populists

On February 22, 1892, a huge coalition of reform organizations met in St. Louis, including Single Tax advocates inspired by Henry George, greenbackers who wanted an inflationary currency policy, representatives of the Knights of Labor, and members of the Farmers' Alliance. Together they founded the People's Party and called for a presidential nominating convention to meet in Omaha, Nebraska, on July 4. There they nominated General James B. Weaver of Iowa for president and drew up the famous Omaha Platform, a vigorous restatement of the proposals laid out two years earlier by the Farmers' Alliance. Like the Ocala Platform, the Omaha Platform demanded an inflationary currency policy and subtreasuries. The Populists also called for a graduated income tax, direct government ownership of the railroad and telegraph industries, and the redistribution of lands owned by the railroads.

In the 1892 elections the Populist presidential candidate won about 1 million votes, and the Populists elected several senators, representatives, governors, and state legislators. But there was no support among wage earners in the industrial centers of the North and East. The Populist platform, for all its talk of the unity of working people, was frankly incompatible with the interests of industrial workers, who favored the protective tariffs that shielded the industrial economy. Inflation would only undermine the value of their wages and raise the price of commodities, and income taxes would shift the tax burden from landowners and importers to wage laborers. Conversely, farmers who hired workers had every reason to oppose the eight-hour day and laws restricting child labor.

Southern Populists faced a particularly daunting challenge. They could not hope to win without the support of the largest class of impoverished farmers, black sharecroppers. But any attempt to build a multiracial alliance of white and black Populists was met with an avalanche of racial demagoguery from Democratic politicians. White Populists had a hard enough time overcoming their own racial prejudices. The Farmers' Alliance had always been strictly segregated, with the Colored Farmers' Alliance kept at arm's length from the central organization. And in truth the economic interests of the two groups were not always compatible. But for political purposes they did need one another, and this made some amount of cross-racial cooperation desirable. Leading black Populists were fully aware of the limits of any alliance they might enter into with white reformers. But the *need* for a coalition of whites and blacks had a tendency to contradict the entrenched racial prejudices of white farmers. It also made the extremist racial demagoguery of the Democratic Party all but inevitable. Third parties are hard to sustain in the best of circumstances, but in the face of such attacks Populism in the South could not survive.

Conclusion

After the Civil War the problems of industrial capitalism placed increasing strain on the political system. The two major parties were so closely matched in electoral strength that neither could risk bold new programs to meet the needs of a new political economy. So restless workers, desperate farmers, and an anxious middle class turned in increasing numbers to voluntary organizations, labor unions, and farmers' alliances.

The politics of industrial society reached a dramatic turning point in the 1890s. During that decade American voters went to the polls in record numbers. Organized farmers made their most radical demands; labor agitation reached a violent climax. And as night follows day, a conservative reaction set in. Movements to restrict the number of voters emerged, particularly in the South. Opponents of immigration made significant strides. The Supreme Court declared constitutional one of history's greatest social experiments, systematic racial segregation. In short, radicalism and reaction reached their peak in the 1890s. During the closing decade of the nineteenth century, a recognizably modern America was born.

Further Readings

Richard Franklin Bensel, *The Political Economy of American Industrialization, 1877–1900*. Argues that the Republican Party was the "agent" of industrialization.

Ruth Bordin, *Woman and Temperance: The Quest for Power and Liberty, 1873–1900* (1981). *Woman and Temperance* is the best single volume available on the subject.

Leon Fink, *Workingmen's Democracy: The Knights of Labor and American Politics* (1983). A case study, with broad implications, showing the connections between political mobilization and labor organization.

Walter LaFeber, *The New Empire: An Interpretation of American Expansion, 1860–1898* (1963). Links American foreign policy to commercial expansion.

Michael McGerr, *The Decline of Popular Politics: The American North, 1865–1928* (1986). Particularly strong on the culture of popular politics in the late nineteenth century.

Charles Postel, *The Populist Vision* (2007). Outstanding. The best book on populism.

John L. Thomas, *Alternative America: Henry George, Edward Bellamy, Henry Demarest Lloyd, and the Adversary Tradition* (1983). A sensitive examination of middle-class radicalism and its limits.

>> Timeline >>

▼ **1867**
United States purchases Alaska from Russia
Patrons of Husbandry (the Grange) founded

▼ **1869**
Noble and Holy Order of the Knights of Labor founded
Suez Canal opened

▼ **1870**
Department of Justice created

▼ **1872**
Grant reelected

▼ **1873**
"Crusade" against alcohol begins in Hillsboro, Ohio

▼ **1874**
WCTU is formed

▼ **1876**
Rutherford B. Hayes elected president
Porfirio Díaz seizes power in Mexico

▼ **1877**
Farmers' Alliance founded

▼ **1878**
Bland-Allison Act

▼ **1879**
Frances Willard becomes president of the WCTU
Henry George publishes *Progress and Poverty*

▼ **1880**
James Garfield elected president

▼ **1881**
Garfield assassinated; Chester Arthur becomes president
WCTU endorses women's suffrage

▼ **1883**
Pendleton Civil Service Act
"Mongrel Tariff"

Who, What?

Review Questions

1. Describe the two major "styles" of politics in the late nineteenth century.

2. What were the major issues in national politics in this period?

3. What did Henry George, Edward Bellamy, and Frances Willard have in common?

4. What did the Farmers' Alliance stand for?

For further review materials and resource information, please visit www.oup.com/us/ofthepeople

▼ **1884**
Grover Cleveland elected president

▼ **1886**
Nationwide strike for eight-hour day
Riot at Haymarket Square in Chicago

▼ **1887**
Interstate Commerce Act
Four Haymarket anarchists executed
Dawes Severalty Act

▼ **1888**
Benjamin Harrison elected president

Edward Bellamy publishes *Looking Backward*

▼ **1889**
United States convenes first Pan-American Conference
Department of Agriculture created

▼ **1890**
Harrison-McKinley Tariff
Sherman Anti-Trust Act
Ocala Platform

▼ **1891**
Queen Liliuokalani assumes the Hawaiian throne

▼ **1892**
Omaha Platform of the People's Party
Grover Cleveland reelected

▼ **1893**
Queen Liliuokalani overthrown

▼ **1898**
Frances Willard dies

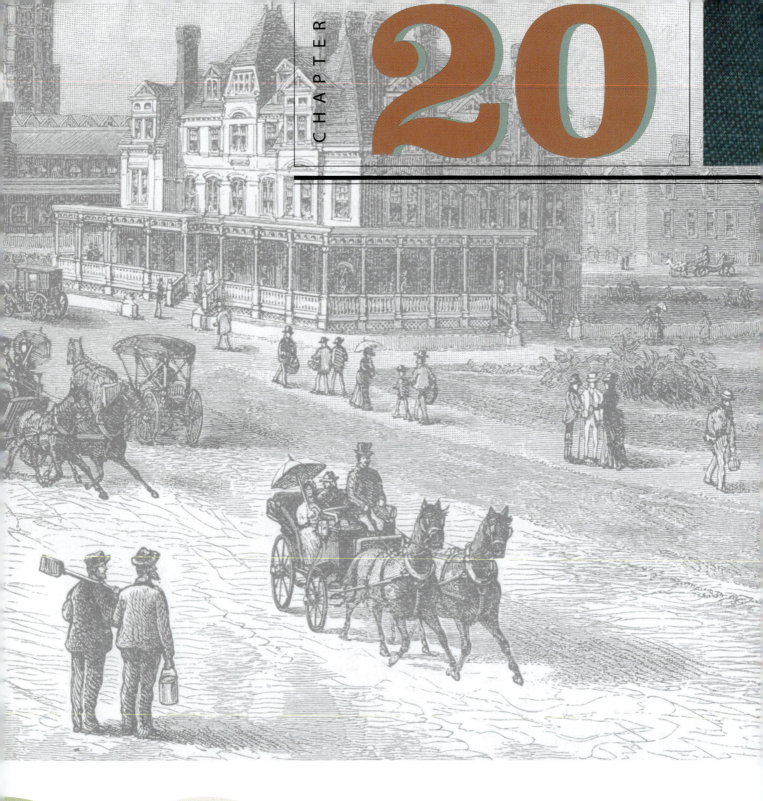

Common Threads

>> How did industrial ideals of efficiency and organization change democratic practice in America during the early 1900s?

>> Did the choices Americans made about how to run their economy set the United States on a course for overseas conflict?

>> What did it mean to be modern? How did the pace of technological change affect Americans' outlook?

Industry and Empire
1890–1900

I t was a short distance from the Arlington Hotel to the White House, and although it was icy and dark, J. Pierpont Morgan chose to walk. He pulled his scarf up around a scowling face known to millions of newspaper readers. He had not wanted to come to Washington. There were "large interests" that depended on keeping the currency of the United States sound, he told a Treasury official, and those interests were now in jeopardy. The commander in chief of the nation's bankers was going to meet the president to keep the United States from going bankrupt.

The events leading up to this urgent meeting stretched back five years to 1890, when business failures in Argentina toppled London's venerable Baring Brothers investment house and triggered a collapse in European stock prices. Depression spread through Britain, Germany, and France. Anxious European investors began selling off their substantial American holdings. For two years, good harvests staved off the inevitable, but in early 1893 the panic reached the United States. The Philadelphia and Reading Railroad folded in February. Fourteen thousand businesses soon followed, along with more than 600 banks.

Summer brought more bad news from abroad. The government of India stopped minting silver, causing U.S. silver dollars to lose one-sixth of their value. Wall Street went into another tailspin. In New York 55,000 men, women, and girls in the clothing industry were thrown out of work. Banks refused to cash checks, and coins of all kinds vanished from circulation. The governor of Nebraska instructed the police to deal leniently with the thousands of homeless poor people on the roads. Breadlines formed. "For thorough chaos I have seen nothing since the war to compare with it," the historian Henry Adams observed. "The world surely cannot remain as mad as it is."

For Grover Cleveland the madness was only starting. The anger of workers and farmers, simmering for decades, was boiling over. The president called Congress into special session and pledged to keep the dollar on the gold standard, but it was not enough. A wave of strikes swept the country. Unemployed workers battled police

on the Capitol grounds. By January 1895 so many panicky investors were cashing government bonds that the Treasury's gold reserve was half gone, and it looked as if the remainder might last only two weeks. Reluctantly, Cleveland asked his aides to open negotiations with Morgan.

Admired and reviled, Morgan was known as the preeminent financial manipulator of the late nineteenth century. Born to wealth in Hartford, Connecticut, he had been a Wall Street fixture since before the Civil War. Like his contemporaries, steelmaker Andrew Carnegie and oil magnate John D. Rockefeller, Morgan's skill lay in organization. He restructured railroads, rooting out corruption, waste, and competition and driving down wages. Instead of taking risks, he eliminated them. His style was to gather the leaders of warring firms for a meeting aboard his mammoth yacht, the *Corsair*, and strike a bargain that allowed everyone to profit. Cleveland was about to place the Treasury in this man's hands.

The president opened the meeting by suggesting that things might not be so bad; perhaps a new bond issue would stabilize the Treasury. No, Morgan replied flatly, the run on gold would continue until European investors regained confidence. As things stood, they had more faith in the House of Morgan than in the government. If the president agreed, Morgan would arrange a private loan and personally guarantee the solvency of the U.S. Treasury. After a stunned silence, the two men shook hands. News of the deal instantly calmed the bond markets. The crisis was over. The *New York Sun* reported that the deal struck between the country's political and economic

continued

chief executives "revived a confidence in the wealth and resources of this country," but Populist newspapers denounced it as a conspiracy and a "great bunco game."

Culminating two decades of economic turbulence, the Panic of 1893 permanently transformed the American political economy. Businessmen like Morgan created even larger corporate combinations and placed them under the control of professional managers. They used technology and "scientific management" to take control of the workplace and push laborers to work faster and harder. Workers resisted, and the 1890s witnessed brutal clashes between capital and labor. Looking for jobs and schools, country people moved to the city and found both promise and danger. Social mobility among African Americans aroused fears in whites, and southerners created a system of formal segregation, enforced by law and terror. Amid growing violence, industrial workers, Native Americans, and African Americans debated how best to deal with the overwhelming forces ranged against them.

The 1890s were also a turning point in American political history. After the 1896 election, many Americans voluntarily withdrew from the electoral process. Others were systematically removed from the voter rolls through a process known as "disfranchisement." African American leaders and union organizers urged their followers to turn away from politics in favor of "bread and butter" economic issues. Torchlight parades and flag raisings became scarce, and the masculine, public spectacle of nineteenth-century politics died out. Patriotism, once synonymous with partisanship, now became identified with the United States' global military and economic ambitions. Civic events featured army bands and cannon salutes. Newspapers conjured up foreign threats. As Americans became more conscious of their military power, they watched the horizon, fearing that well-being at home could hinge on events as far away as China.

Americans began to feel that their economy's links to the world—and the changes manufacturing and rapid communications brought to politics and daily life—separated the events of their times from everything that had happened before. Morgan's rescue required transactions on two continents, instantaneously coordinated by telegraph. The speed of industry, trade, and information, the ability of machines and technology to span distance and time created a sense that the environment and the future could be controlled. Many felt that the peoples who possessed this newfound control—the modern countries—stood apart from those living in other lands whose thought and action were not guided by science and the streams of information issuing from transoceanic cables.

Between 1890 and 1900 Americans made their country recognizably modern. Those with the means to do so enlarged, accelerated, and rationalized the settings of work and daily life. Financiers and giant corporations assumed control of the American economy. Huge cities grew. The significance of voting declined, and a decade that opened with a global economic catastrophe ended with a dramatic display of the global reach of U.S. power. ●

OUTLINE

The Crisis of the 1890s

Financial convulsions, strikes, and the powerlessness of government against wealth rudely reminded Americans of how much their country had changed since the Civil War. When Illinois sent Abraham Lincoln to Congress, Chicago's population was less than 5,000; in 1890 it exceeded 1 million. Gone was the America of myth and memory, where class tensions were slight, and upward (or at least westward) mobility seemed easy. Many Americans, a British diplomat noted, foresaw the imminent collapse of civilization: "They all begin with the Roman Empire and point out resemblances." Others, however, felt that the United States was passing into a new phase of history that would lead to still greater trials and achievements.

> Chicago is the product of modern capitalism, and, like other great commercial centers, is unfit for human habitation.
>
> EUGENE V. DEBS

Hard Times

Chicago in 1893 captured the hopes and fears of the new age. To celebrate the 400th anniversary of Columbus's discovery of America, the city staged the World's Columbian Exposition, transforming a lakefront bog into a gleaming vision of the past and the future, but just outside the exposition's gates lay the city of the present. In December 1893 Chicago had 75,000 unemployed, and the head of a local relief committee declared that "famine is in our midst." In the nation's second-largest metropolis, thousands lived in shacks or high-rise tenements in which each densely packed floor had only a single bathroom. Jobs were hard to find, and when groups of men gathered at the exposition's gates to beg for work, the police drove them away.

As the depression deepened, the Cleveland administration ordered troops to guard Treasury branches in New York and Chicago. Jobless people banded together into "industrial armies," many with decidedly revolutionary aims. Hundreds heeded the call of Jacob Coxey, a prosperous Ohio landowner and Populist. Coxey appealed in 1894 to the unemployed to march on Washington and demand free silver and a public road-building program that would hire a half-million workers. When Coxey set out with 100 followers, reporters predicted the ragged band would disintegrate as soon as the food ran out, but well-wishers turned out by the thousands to greet the Coxeyites and offer supplies for the trip.

Industrial armies set out from Boston, St. Louis, Chicago, Portland, Seattle, and Los Angeles. When Coxey arrived in Washington on May 1 with 500 marchers, Cleveland put the U.S. Army on alert. The march ended ignominiously. In front of the Capitol, police wrestled Coxey into a paddy wagon, and his disillusioned army dispersed. Still, after the march no one could deny that something was seriously wrong. Ray Stannard Baker, a reporter for the *Chicago Record,* acknowledged that "the public would not be cheering the army and feeding it voluntarily without a recognition, however vague, that the conditions in the country warranted some such explosion."

The Overseas Frontier

At noon on September 16, 1893, thousands of settlers massed along the borders of the Cherokee Strip, a 6-million-acre tract in northwestern Oklahoma. In the next six hours the population of Wharton, Oklahoma, grew from zero to 10,000 and the

AMERICA AND THE WORLD

>> ## Singer Sewing Machine Company

Before the Russian Revolution, St. Petersburg's grandest boulevard, the Nevskii Prospekt, was known according to one tourist for its "cathedrals, the grocery of Elisieff Brothers, and the Singer Sewing Machine Company's establishment." The headquarters of Kompaniya Singer was Russia's tallest building. Completed in 1904, the six-story tower was topped by an illuminated globe bearing the name Singer in gilded letters. It symbolized the global reach of one of America's preeminent manufacturers.

Isaac Merritt Singer did not invent the sewing machine; he invented a way to market it. Elias Howe, who applied for the first U.S. patent in 1845, invented a device with an oscillating eye-pointed needle that made a locking stitch fed continuously from spools mounted on an overhanging arm. It seemed a practical, labor-saving device, but Howe soon found that tailors and shoemakers who made a living by hand sewing had no use for it. His principal customers viewed the gadget with hostility.

Singer, a machinist from Rochester, New York, made Howe's device smaller, added a decorative cabinet, and sold it as an article for the home. He employed young women to demonstrate the machine in shop-front "sewing centers." Salesmen went door to door, and in the 1880s, Singer introduced buying on the "installment" plan, whereby customers could purchase a new machine by putting down a dollar a week. It was a "psychological fact, which has come to light in this sewing machine business," he asserted, that "a woman would rather pay $100" in installments "than $50 outright." By 1867, Singer was the largest manufacturer of sewing machines in the world, producing 43,000 a year.

The federal government aided this growth in two ways. The need for military uniforms during the Civil War outstripped the capacities of hand tailors, and Singer promoted machine sewing as a patriotic duty women could perform for the country. "We Clothe the Union Army," the company proclaimed. Secondly, the government imposed a 35 percent tariff on imported sewing machines, preventing European makers from challenging Singer in its home market.

With its domestic base secure, Singer expanded. By 1890, it had an international merchandising network that sold three-quarters of the world's sewing machines. A German consul general in Istanbul reported that Singer's "ingeniously organized selling apparatus, extending to the smallest places" gave it "an almost unassailable position."

The sales formula did not work everywhere. In India, agents complained that they were not allowed to speak to women. Chinese merchants were suspicious of the "iron tailor." The company had trouble collecting installments from Kyrgyz nomads, who never stayed put long enough to make payments. A Singer representative in Charkoff, Russia, was ordered to leave on the grounds that he was "a foreign Jew." In Japan, however, the adoption of Western-style military uniforms during the Sino-Japanese War (1894–1895) provided a ready market, and Japanese outfitters adopted the faster-moving treadle models. Europe, the Philippines, Mexico, and Russia all became significant markets.

Alarmed by Singer's success, European governments began protecting their colonial and home markets. In 1893, French courts ordered Singer to reveal information about its earnings and stock dividends. Other governments raised import taxes or set quotas to exclude American machines. Singer responded by forming separate national subsidiaries that could claim local, rather than American, origin. When the Spanish-American War broke out in 1898, the Singer offices in Madrid flew the Spanish flag and donated to the war fund. The locals were not fooled. The newspaper *El País* called Singer "an immense octopus whose tentacles encircle Spain and crushes it, snatching from it the savings of its workers in order to aggrandize the miserable, iniquitous, cowardly disgusting North American nation."

The company prided itself on bringing democracy and fair dealing to the world. In the Middle East, Singer machines carried the brand *Hurriya*, Arabic for "freedom." By the turn of the century, the company had over 4,000 branch offices, located on every inhabited continent. It opened a string of factories overseas, in Montreal (1882),

Floridsdorf, Austria (1882), Kilbowie, Scotland (1883), Podolsk, Russia (1902), and Wittenberg, Prussia (1904).

Growth slowed in the more tumultuous twentieth century. The agent in Teheran had to flee a revolution in 1907, and ten years later Red Guards stormed the St. Petersburg office with guns drawn. The mass armies deployed in World War I wore factory-made uniforms, and the postwar market for ready-to-wear clothing undercut demand. German bombers pounded the Scotland plant to rubble in 1941, and four years later the Soviet army smashed the Wittenberg factory.

Singer was a forerunner of a global commerce in consumer goods that the United States would dominate in the late twentieth century. Portable and practical, the machine itself had universal appeal, and its marketing was infinitely adaptable. In 1891, Singer's advertising department issued trading cards showing the peoples of the world in native costume. The images were strikingly different from racialized depictions common in that period. Although the fabrics and colors varied, the peoples of other cultures looked very much alike, each with their sewing machine, a global community of consumers. ●

last great land rush came to an end. The line of settlement that had been marked on census maps throughout the nineteenth century had ceased to exist.

Frederick Jackson Turner, a historian at the University of Wisconsin, explained the implications of this event. Steady westward movement had placed Americans in "touch with the simplicity of primitive life," he explained, and allowed the nation to renew the process of social development continuously. The frontier furnished "the forces dominating the American character," and without its rejuvenating influence, democracy itself might be in danger. Turner's thesis resonated with Americans' fears that modernity had robbed their country of its unique strengths. For the previous 10 years, Populists and financiers had worried that the end of free land would signal trials for free institutions. "There is no unexplored part of the world left suitable for men to inhabit," Populist writer William "Coin" Harvey claimed, "and now justice stands at bay."

That assertion turned out to be premature. More homesteaders claimed more western lands after 1890 than before, and well into the twentieth century new "resource frontiers"—oil fields, timber ranges, Alaskan ore strikes—were explored. Irrigation technology and markets for new crops created a bonanza for dry-land farmers. Nonetheless, the economic and social upheavals of the 1890s seemed to confirm Turner's contention that new frontiers would have to be found overseas.

While farmers had always needed to sell a large portion of their output abroad, until the 1890s manufactured goods had sold almost exclusively through domestic distribution networks. As the total volume of manufactured goods increased, the composition of exports changed. Oil, steel, textiles, typewriters, and sewing machines made up a larger portion of overseas trade. American consumers still bought nine-tenths of the output of domestic factories, but by 1898 the extra tenth was worth more than $1 billion (see Figure 20–1).

As American firms entered foreign markets, they discovered that other nations and empires guarded their markets with restrictive tariffs just as the United States did, to promote domestic manufacturing. Government and business leaders acknowledged that to gain a larger share of world trade, the United States might have to use political or military leverage to pry open foreign markets. Their social Darwinist view of the world—as a jungle in which only the fittest nations would survive—justified engaging in global competition for trade and economic survival.

Recognizing that a strong navy could extend America's economic reach, Congress authorized the construction of three large battleships in 1890. Four years later,

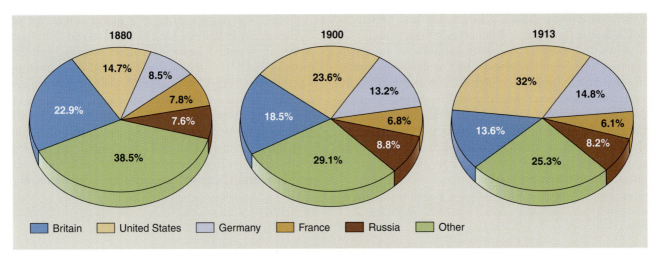

Figure 20–1 Relative Shares of World Manufacturing The United States was a significant industrial power by 1880, and by the turn of the century it moved into a position of dominance.

an official commission investigated the feasibility of a canal across Central America. A newly organized National Association of Manufacturers urged the government to open foreign markets. The administration created a Bureau of Foreign Commerce and urged U.S. consuls to seize opportunities to extend sales of American industrial products abroad.

Congress also knew that tariff rates could influence the expansion of trade. Before 1890, taxes on imports had been set high to raise revenue and to help domestic manufacturers by making foreign goods unaffordable. The Harrison-McKinley Tariff of 1890 did something different. It allowed the president to use the tariff to punish countries that closed their markets to U.S. goods or reward them for lifting customs barriers. This "bargaining tariff" put the full weight of the U.S. economy behind the drive to open markets around the world.

The United States began to reorganize itself to compete in a global marketplace. The struggle required the executive branch to enlarge the military and take on additional authority. It also meant that domestic industries had to produce higher-quality goods at less cost to match those being turned out in Germany or Japan. Employers and workers had to gear up for the global contest for profits.

The Drive for Efficiency

In mines, factories, and mills, production relied on the knowledge of skilled workers. Laborers used their knowledge to set work routines, assure their own safety, and bargain with managers who wanted to change the pace or conditions of work. As profits stagnated and competition intensified, managers tried to prevent labor from sharing control over production. In the struggle for control in the workplace, employers relied on three allies: technology, scientific management, and federal power. Workers resisted, organizing themselves and enlisting the support of their communities.

Advances in management techniques enabled employers to break routines favored by laborers and to dictate new methods. Frederick Winslow Taylor, the first "efficiency expert," reduced each occupation to a series of simple, precise move-

>> Pullman, Illinois

When economist Richard T. Ely first saw the industrial town of Pullman in 1885, he thought he was looking at the future. A planned suburb entirely owned by one company and inhabited by its employees, Pullman seemed "a forerunner of better things for the laboring classes." On broad streets named for famous inventors—Watt, Fulton, Morse, and, of course, Pullman—mechanics, shopkeepers, and company officials lived side by side in tidy homes with gas heat and indoor plumbing. Pullmanites shopped under the glass roof of the Arcade, the first indoor shopping mall, and benefited from a library, a theater, and a school provided by their employer. Surrounded by culture and natural beauty, Pullman workers were, by company estimate, 40 percent more refined, thrifty, and wholesome than other workers.

George Mortimer Pullman's name was synonymous with luxury. With the help of Andrew Carnegie, he had become the preeminent maker of passenger railroad cars. By the 1880s every railroad in the country used Pullman sleeping cars, dining cars, and observation cars.

In 1880 he decided to centralize his scattered factories into a single site on Lake Calumet, south of Chicago. He asked Solomon S. Beman, a young architect, and Nathan Barrett, a landscape designer, to build a model town around the plant. By the following year, there were 1400 dwellings, public parks, gardens, a hotel, a school, and a church, all designed in a gracious "secular gothic" style. By 1893 it was home to 12,000 residents.

Pullman was not designed as art or charity, but for business. Happy, healthy workers were expected to produce more, and in Pullman's estimate, they did. Modern sewers and plumbing made the air and water safe. The death rate in Pullman was less than half that in nearby neighborhoods. There were no saloons. Drinkers had to walk miles to one of the 30 taverns at the edge of the company property on Kensington Avenue.

The theater's management screened out "immoral" shows. An exhibit at the Columbian Exposition claimed Pullman was making a new kind of worker, "dis-tinct in appearance, in tidiness of dress, in fact in all the external indications of self-respect."

Other companies rushed to copy Pullman's success. Chocolate makers built Hershey, Pennsylvania, and near Cincinnati the producers of floating soap colonized the model town of Ivoryville. But the residents of Pullman were less enthusiastic. Despite low rents and spacious homes, most Pullmanites moved out within a year or two. Even those who stayed saw the arrangement as temporary. "We call it camping out," one woman told Ely. The town was nicer than any they had lived in before, but "the general complaint seems to be that they were too much under Mr. Pullman's thumb."

Pullman had no newspaper, no clubs, no elected officials. The school board was manned by company executives. When a group of women organized a charity, the company ordered it stopped. Political activity, especially on behalf of Democratic candidates, was discouraged. When shopkeeper John P. Hopkins put up a sign for Grover Cleveland, his lease was revoked. The town's one church was for "artistic effect" only. No congregation met there.

After staying several weeks, Ely concluded that "the idea of Pullman is un-American." It was impossible

continued

for the residents to escape the overshadowing power of the company, which owned the houses, the shops, even the streets. There was not a single piece of property that was privately owned, and leases could be terminated in 10 days. In the factories, workers assembled sumptuous railroad cars that only reminded them of the wealth they could not attain.

When the Panic of 1893 hit, Pullman laid off 2,000 of his 5,000 employees and cut wages to the others by 25 percent. Rents dropped in Chicago, but not in Pullman. Many residents could not afford rent or food, but there were no charities or municipal agencies to help. There was only the company.

Desperate workers organized in the spring of 1894 and joined Eugene V. Debs's American Railway Union (ARU). On May 11, they struck. George Pullman cut off credit for workers at the stores in the Arcade and then went on vacation. In June, Pullman workers asked the entire ARU to join the strike. "We struck because we were without hope," one worker told the convention. The ARU voted to make the strike national; ARU switchmen would refuse to switch Pullman cars onto trains.

The strike shut down 20 railroads in the West and Midwest. Almost no traffic moved through Chicago, the nation's hub. The U.S. attorney general vowed to meet the strike with force, and President Cleveland sent 2,000 troops to Chicago. Fighting between workers and soldiers broke out at the stockyards and in the Illinois Central switchyard. Troops fired into crowds of workers, killing 20 and wounding 60 others. Debs was jailed for "interfering with the mails." The union was broken. The town of Pullman remained peaceful, but residents saw, over the tops of their houses, a column of smoke rising from the Columbian Exposition. The White City was on fire.

Three years later, George Pullman died of a heart attack. His obituaries mixed praise for his achievements with criticism of his stubborn refusal to head off one of the bloodiest labor conflicts in U.S. history. The next year, the city of Chicago absorbed Pullman and the company town became a neighborhood where voters could choose their own aldermen. Efficient, paternal corporate rule gave way to the messy but democratic politics of a big city. A writer for *The Nation* noted that what working people wanted most was a chance to own a place of their own. "Mr. Pullman in his scheme for a model community for American workmen overlooked this peculiar American characteristic. Hence, in my humble opinion, these tears." ●

ments that could be easily taught and endlessly repeated. To manage time and motion scientifically, Taylor explained, employers should collect "all of the traditional knowledge which in the past has been possessed by workingmen" and reduce "this knowledge to rules, laws, and formulae."

Taylor's stopwatch studies determined the optimal load of a hand shovel (21.5 pounds), how much pig iron a man could load into a boxcar in a day (75 tons), how much the man should be paid (3.75 cents per ton), and how much he should eat (3500 calories). Even office work could be separated into simple, unvaried tasks. Taylorism created a new layer of college-educated "middle managers" who supervised production in offices and factories.

Although Taylorism accelerated production, it also increased absenteeism and worker dissatisfaction. Telephone operators had a 100 percent yearly turnover rate. Another new technique, "personnel management," promised to solve this problem with tests to select suitable employees, team sports to ward off boredom, and social workers to regulate the activities of workers at home.

As the nineteenth century ended, management was establishing a monopoly on expertise and using it to set the rhythms of work and play, but workers did not easily relinquish control. In the 1890s, the labor struggle entered a new phase. New unions confronted corporations in bloody struggles that forced the federal government to decide whether communities or property had more rights. Skilled workers asserted leadership over the labor movement, and they rallied to the cause of retaining control of the conditions of work.

A TAYLOR SYSTEM MACHINIST "UP-TO-DATE"

An argument without words

Taylorism Corporations used stopwatches and social workers to stretch each machine and worker to full capacity. The method was called "Taylorism."

Progress and Force

To accelerate production, employers aimed to seize full control over the workplace. They had private detective agencies at their disposal, the courts on their side, and federal troops ready to act. In Pennsylvania and Chicago this antagonism led to bloody confrontations.

In 1892 Andrew Carnegie's mill at Homestead, Pennsylvania, the most modern steelworks in the world, turned out armor plating for American warships and steel rails for shipment abroad. In June Carnegie's partner, Henry Clay Frick, broke off talks with the plant's American Federation of Labor–affiliated union and announced that the plant would close on July 2 and reopen a week later with a nonunion workforce. The union contended that Frick's actions constituted an assault on the community, and the town agreed. On the morning of July 6, as 300 armed guards tried to land from barges, they were raked by gunfire. Townspeople placed the company guards under arrest.

The victory was short-lived. A week later the governor of Pennsylvania sent in the state militia, and under martial law strikebreakers reignited the furnaces. Homestead became one of labor's most celebrated battles, but it broke the union and showed that corporations, backed by government, would defend their prerogatives at any cost.

The Pullman strike, centered in Chicago, paralyzed the nation's railroads for two weeks in the summer of 1894. It pitted the American Railway Union (ARU) against 24 railroads and the powerful Pullman Company over the company's decision to cut pay by 30 percent. The calm at the center of the strike was Eugene V. Debs, charismatic president of the ARU, who urged strikers to obey the law, avoid violence, and respect strikebreakers. When Cleveland sent in the army over the governor's protests, enraged crowds blocked tracks and burned railroad cars. Police arrested hundreds of strikers. Debs went to jail for six months and came out a Socialist. Pullman and Homestead showed that the law was now on the side of the proprietors.

Newspapers, magazines, and novels portrayed Pullman and Homestead as two more battles in an unending war against the savage opponents of progress. Frederic Remington, famous for his reporting on wars against the Navajo and Apache Indians, covered the Pullman strike for *Harper's Weekly*. In his account, rough-hewn cavalrymen, having defeated the Sioux, now came to rescue civilization from the unions.

The business elite's influence over cultural expression allowed it to define the terms of this contest, to label its enemies as enemies of progress. Workers did not object to efficiency or modernization, but they wanted a share of its benefits and some control over the process of change. With state and corporate power stacked against them, the workers' goals appeared beyond reach.

Just as the massacre at Wounded Knee in 1890 had ended the armed resistance of Native Americans, the violence at Homestead and Chicago signified that the struggle of industrial workers had entered a new phase.

Corporate Consolidation

In a wave of mergers between 1897 and 1904, investment bankers consolidated leading industries under the control of a few corporate giants. J. P. Morgan led the movement. His goal was to take industry away from the industrialists and give it to the bankers. Bankers, he felt, had better information about the true worth of an industry, and they could make better decisions about its future. Financiers could create the larger and leaner firms needed to take on foreign competitors.

Morgan's greatest triumph was the merger of eight huge steel companies, their ore ranges, rolling mills, railroads, and shipping lines into the colossal U.S. Steel. Announced in March 1901, the merger created the world's largest corporation. Its capital amounted to 7 percent of the total wealth of the United States (by comparison, Wal-Mart's total assets in 2008 amounted to one and one half percent of the gross national product). U.S. Steel's investors (Morgan especially) earned profits "greatly in excess of reasonable compensation," according to one government report.

Bankers outnumbered steelmakers on U.S. Steel's board, and they controlled the company. *McClure's* magazine reported that the new company was "planning the first really systematic effort ever made by Americans to capture the foreign steel trade." Morgan's son wrote to his stepmother that "Father is in the same category with Queen Victoria." He did not say what category his father's employees and customers fell into.

A Modern Economy

Grover Cleveland's bargain with Morgan revived the industrial economy, but farm prices, wages, and the president's popularity remained flat. Cash-strapped farmers in the West and South grumbled against the president's hard-money policies and cozy relationships with plutocrats like Morgan. Calling out troops to crush the Pullman strike cost Cleveland the support of northern workers. The escalating cycle of economic and political crises, farmer and labor insurgencies, middle-class radicalism, and upper-class conservatism fractured political parties. Democrats, Republicans, and Populists all called for stronger government action, but each party split over what action to take. In 1896 the "currency question" dominated a watershed election that transformed the two major parties and destroyed the third.

The year 1896 was the last time presidential candidates openly debated great economic questions in terms that had been familiar to voters since Thomas Jefferson ran for president in 1800; 1896 was also the first recognizably modern presidential election. It was the first time a successful candidate fully employed the advertising and fund-raising techniques of twentieth-century campaigns.

> **Whatever questions may at one time or another disturb the minds of the mass of men who hold the franchise in England, France, Germany, or other European countries, the plain people have never for a moment believed it possible that they were competent to settle currency and banking questions.**
>
> DR. ALBERT SHAW,
> political scientist, October 1896

Currency and the Tariff

The soundness of the dollar, which Morgan and Cleveland worked so hard to preserve, was a mixed blessing for Americans. Based on gold, the dollar helped sell American goods in foreign markets, especially in Europe, where currencies were also based on gold. The United States traded on a much smaller scale with countries—like Mexico or China—that used silver. "Without exception," Cleveland's secretary of commerce explained, "prices are fixed in the markets of countries having a gold standard." Gold, however, was valuable because it was scarce, and many Americans suffered from that scarcity. The low prices and high interest rates Populists complained of were a result of the gold standard.

Increasing the money supply would reduce interest rates and make credit more available. There were two ways to put more money in circulation: the government could print paper "greenbacks," or it could coin silver. "Free silver" advocates generally favored coining a ratio of 16 ounces of silver for each ounce of gold. Populists initially wanted greenbacks but later found silver an agreeable compromise. Western mining interests pushed silver as well. The Republican and Democratic parties officially endorsed the gold standard, but by 1896 each party had a renegade faction of silverites. To Americans in the 1890s, the crucial political issues—jobs, foreign trade, the survival of small farms, and the prosperity of big corporations—boiled down to one question: Would the dollar be backed by gold or silver? The election of 1896 was "the battle of the standards."

The Cross of Gold

A dark mood hung over Chicago as delegates arrived at the Democratic convention in July 1896. They had come to bury Cleveland and the party's commitment to the gold standard along with him. The draft platform denounced Cleveland for imposing "government by injunction" during the Pullman strike. When the platform

Victor Debreuil, *The Cross of Gold* (ca. 1896) Debreuil was known for his realistic still lifes of coins, greenbacks, and photographs. Artists and citizens in the 1890s used the "'money question" to ask what was valuable, true, and real in the modern age.

came before the full convention, delegates had to decide whether the party would stand for silver or gold and who would replace Cleveland as the candidate for president.

Both questions were decided when a former congressman from Nebraska, William Jennings Bryan, mounted the stage. Handsome and only 36 years old, he was an electrifying speaker. "You come and tell us that the great cities are in favor of the gold standard," he said. "Destroy our farms, and the grass will grow in the streets of every city in the country!" Bryan delivered his lines in the rhythmic cadence of a camp preacher. "We will answer their demand for a gold standard by saying to them"—he paused stretching out his arms in an attitude of crucifixion—"You shall not press down upon the brow of labor this crown of thorns. You shall not crucify mankind upon a cross of gold!" The hall exploded with cheers. Bryan won the nomination handily.

Two weeks later the Populists, meeting in St. Louis, also nominated Bryan. The Ocala and Omaha platforms, which imagined comprehensive changes in the money system and American institutions, had been reduced to a single panacea: silver. Republicans overwhelmingly adopted a pro-gold plank, drafted with the approval of J. P. Morgan, and nominated William McKinley, the governor of Ohio and a supporter of industry. The parties could hardly have offered two more different candidates or two more different visions of the future.

The Battle of the Standards

In one of the most exciting electoral contests since the Civil War, the candidates employed new techniques in radically different ways. McKinley ran like an incumbent: he never left his home. Instead, delegations came to him. Some 750,000 people from 30 states trampled McKinley's grass and listened to speeches affirming the candidate's commitment to high tariffs and sound money. The speeches were set in type and distributed as newspaper columns, fliers, and pamphlets throughout the country. The campaign used public relations techniques to educate the electorate on the virtues of the gold standard. Posters reduced the campaign's themes to pithy slogans like "Prosperity or Poverty," or "Vote for Free Silver and Be Prosperous Like Guatemala."

The genius behind the campaign was a Cleveland coal-and-oil millionaire named Marcus Hanna who bankrolled his publicity blitz with between $3 million and $7 million raised from industrialists. He assessed a share of the campaign's expenses from corporations and banks based on calculations of the profitability and net worth of each. The combination of big money and advertising revolutionized presidential politics.

With only $300,000 to spend, Bryan ran like a challenger even though his party occupied the White House. He logged 29,000 miles by rail and buggy and made more than 500 speeches in 29 states. Oratorical ability had won Bryan the nomination, but audiences were unaccustomed to hearing a candidate speak for himself, and many considered it undignified. "The Boy Orator has one speech," wrote an unsympathetic Republican, John Hay. "He simply reiterates the unquestioned truths that . . . gold is vile, that silver is lovely and holy."

Despite the scorn of eastern newspapers, industrialists genuinely feared the prospect of a Bryan presidency. "He has succeeded in scaring the gold bugs out of their five wits," Hay remarked. Factory owners threatened to close shop if Bryan won. Just before election day, the global markets that McKinley praised returned the favor. Crop failures abroad doubled the price of wheat in the Midwest, raising farm incomes and alleviating the anxieties that made farmers flock to Bryan. In the final tally, Bryan won the South and West decisively, but McKinley won the populous states of the industrial Northeast, as well as several farm states in the upper Midwest, capturing the Electoral College by a majority of 271 to 176.

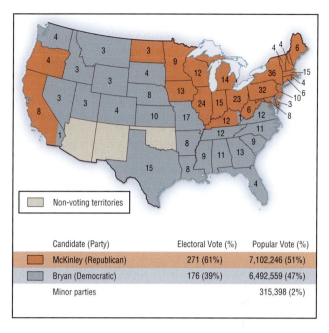

Candidate (Party)	Electoral Vote (%)	Popular Vote (%)
McKinley (Republican)	271 (61%)	7,102,246 (51%)
Bryan (Democratic)	176 (39%)	6,492,559 (47%)
Minor parties		315,398 (2%)

Map 20–1 The Election of 1896 William McKinley's "front-porch campaign" carried the northern industrial states, along with the key farm states of Iowa and Minnesota, securing a narrow victory over Bryan.

The election of 1896 changed the style of campaigns and shifted the political positions of both major parties. By pushing currency policies to improve the lives of workers and farmers, Bryan's Democrats abandoned their traditional commitment to minimal government that stretched back to Andrew Jackson. The Republicans recognized that the electorate would judge the president on his ability to bring prosperity to the country. Electoral democracy now had a distinctly economic cast. As president, McKinley asserted his leadership over economic policy, calling Congress into special session to pass the Dingley Tariff Act, which levied the highest taxes on imports in American history. He extended the reach of presidential power even more dramatically through an expansionist foreign and military policy.

In the election of 1896 fundamental economic questions—who is the economy supposed to serve? what is the nature of money?—were at stake in a closely matched campaign. No wonder voter turnout hit an all-time high. Administrative agencies took over those issues after the turn of the century, but Americans long remembered that raucous campaign when the nation's economic future was up for grabs. As late as the 1960s, schoolchildren still recited the Cross of Gold speech.

The Retreat from Politics

The economy improved steadily after 1895, but this latest business panic and its aftermath left lasting marks on corporate and political culture. Industrial workers made a tactical retreat in the face of a new political and legal climate. In the South, depression, urbanization, and the modernizing influence of railroads accelerated the spread of legalized racial segregation and disfranchisement. What was happening in the South was part of a nationwide decline of participatory politics. With the slackening of agrarian unrest and the exhaustion of resistance to corporate capitalism, politics lost some of its value. Voter participation declined, and Americans felt less of a personal stake in election campaigns. Disaffected groups—such as labor and African Americans—had to devise new ways to build community and express resistance.

> I want to give you niggers a few words of plain talk and advice. You might as well understand that this is a white man's country, as far as the South is concerned, and we are going to make you keep your place.
>
> WILLIAM C. OATES,
> Alabama governor, 1895

The Lure of the Cities

In the South as in the North, people left the countryside and moved to towns and cities. By 1900 one out of six southerners lived in town. With the lone exception of Birmingham, Alabama, southern cities were not devoted to manufacturing but to commerce and services. Doctors' offices, haberdasheries, dry goods stores, and groceries could be found near warehouses where cotton was stored, ginned, and pressed and near the railway station where it was shipped to textile mills.

The growth of villages and towns in the South was the product of rural decay. Crop liens, which gave bankers ownership of a crop before it was planted, and debt drove people from the countryside. The young and the ambitious left first, while older and poorer residents stayed behind.

While white newcomers settled on the outskirts of towns, African Americans moved into industrial districts along the railroad tracks. Cities became more segregated as they grew. By 1890 most blocks in the larger cities were either all black or all white. Still, towns offered things that were missing in the country, such as schools. A Little Rock, Arkansas, resident noted that newly arrived African American parents were "very anxious to send their children to school." Jobs were often available, too, although more frequently for women than for men. Men looked for seasonal labor at farms or lumber camps some distance from town. This meant families faced a tough choice between poverty and separation.

Despite setbacks, the newcomers gained a place for themselves in urban life. By 1890 every southern city had an African American business district with churches, insurance companies, lawyers, doctors, undertakers, and usually a weekly newspaper. Benevolent and reform organizations, sewing circles, and book clubs enriched community life. There were limits to how high educated African Americans could ascend. Professionals like lawyers, doctors, and nurses had to work within their community. Jobs on the bottom rung of the corporate ladder—clerk, salesman, telephone operator, stenographer, railroad conductor—were reserved for whites.

Inventing Jim Crow

In June 1892 Homer Plessy boarded the East Louisiana Railway in New Orleans for a trip to Covington, Louisiana. Having purchased a first-class ticket, he attempted to board the whites-only car and was arrested under a Louisiana law that required

African Americans and whites to ride in "equal but separate accommodations." Before Judge John H. Ferguson could try the case, Plessy's lawyer appealed on the grounds that the separate-car law violated the Constitution's Fourteenth Amendment.

When *Plessy v. Ferguson* came before the Supreme Court in April 1896, lawyers for the state of Louisiana argued that the law was necessary to avoid the "danger of friction from too intimate contact" between the races. In separate cars, all citizens enjoyed equal privileges. Plessy's lawyer, Albion Tourgée, replied that the question was not "the equality of the privileges enjoyed, but the right of the state to label one citizen as white and another as colored." In doing so, the government gave unearned advantages to some citizens and not to others. The issue for Tourgée was not racial conflict or even prejudice, but whether the government should be allowed to divide people arbitrarily. The court upheld the "separate but equal" doctrine. The Plessy decision provided legal justification for the system of official inequality that expanded in the twentieth century. Informal segregation had existed since the Civil War. People associated with members of their own race when they could, and when they could not—at work, in business, or when traveling—unwritten local customs usually governed their interaction. By the 1890s those informal customs were being codified in law. Railroads, as symbols of progress, were a chief point of contention.

Mary Church Terrell (1863–1954) Activist, suffragist, and educator, Terrell tried to unite the struggles for women's rights and civil rights. "A white woman has but one handicap to overcome," she wrote. "I have two—both sex and race."

The political and economic tensions created by the depression helped turn racist customs into a rigid caste division. Competition for jobs fed racial antagonisms, as did the migration into cities and towns of a new generation of African Americans, born since the war, who showed less deference to whites. New notions of "scientific" racism led intellectuals and churchmen to regard racial hostility as natural. Angry voters in many southern states deposed the coalitions of landowners and New South industrialists that had governed since Reconstruction and replaced them with Populist "demagogues."

Between 1887 and 1891 nine states in the South passed railroad segregation laws. Trains began pulling separate cars for African Americans, called "Jim Crow" cars after the name of a character in a minstrel show. Soon Jim Crow laws were extended to waiting rooms, drinking fountains, and other places where African Americans and whites might meet.

Segregation was also enforced by terror. The threat of lynching poisoned all relations between the races, and African Americans learned that they could be tortured and killed for committing a crime, talking back, or simply looking the wrong way at a white woman. Lynchings occurred most frequently in areas thinly populated by whites, but killings and mob violence also occurred in the largest cities. Between

Lynchings Were Public Spectacles When 17-year-old Jesse Washington was killed in Waco, Texas, in 1916, a crowd of several thousand, including the mayor, police chief, and students from Waco High, attended the event on the lawn of city hall. Afterwards, the murderers posed for a photograph and sold their victim's teeth for $5 apiece.

1882 and 1903, nearly 2,000 African American southerners were killed by mobs. Victims were routinely tortured, flayed, castrated, gouged, and burned alive, and members of the mob often took home grisly souvenirs like a piece of bone or a severed thumb.

Many African American southerners fought segregation with boycotts, lawsuits, and disobedience. Ida Wells-Barnett, a Nashville journalist, organized an international antilynching campaign (see Chapter 21, "A United Body of Action"). Segregation was constantly negotiated and challenged, but after 1896 it was backed by the U.S. Supreme Court.

The Atlanta Compromise

When Atlanta invited African American educator Booker T. Washington to address the Cotton States Exposition in 1895, northern newspapers concluded that a new era of racial progress had begun. The speech made Washington the most recognized African American in the United States. Starting with 40 students and an abandoned shack, Washington had built Tuskegee Institute into a nationally known institution, the preeminent technical school for African Americans. Washington was a guest in the stately homes of Newport and at Andrew Carnegie's castle in Scotland. When Atlanta staged an exposition to showcase the region's industrial and social progress, the organizers asked Washington to speak.

Washington's address stressed racial accommodation. It had been a mistake, he argued, to try to attain equality by asserting civil and political rights. "The wisest among my race understand that agitation of questions of social equality is the extremest folly," he said, "and that progress in the enjoyment of all the privileges that will come to us must be the result of severe and constant struggle rather than artificial forcing." He urged white businessmen to employ African American southerners "who have, without strikes and labor wars, tilled your fields, cleared your forests, built your railroads and cities." Raising his hand above his head, stretching out his fingers and then closing them into a fist, he summarized his approach to race relations: "In all things that are purely social, we can be as separate as the fingers, yet one as the hand in all things essential to mutual progress." The largely white audience erupted into applause.

Washington's "Atlanta Compromise" stressed the mutual obligations of African Americans and whites. African Americans would give up the vote and stop insisting on social equality if

Booker T. Washington With voting rights denied to African Americans, Booker T. Washington urged vocational education as the surest route to economic advancement.

white leaders would keep violence in check and allow African Americans to succeed in agriculture and business. White industrialists welcomed this arrangement, and African American leaders felt that for the moment it might be the best that could be achieved.

Disfranchisement and the Decline of Popular Politics

After the feverish campaign of 1896, elections began to lose some of their appeal. Attendance fell off at the polls. Some 79 percent of voters cast ballots in the battle of the standards; eight years later the figure was down to 65 percent. More visibly, the public events surrounding campaigns drew thinner crowds. Organizers fretted about apathy, which seemed to have become a national epidemic.

In the South, the disappearance of voters was easy to explain. As Jim Crow laws multiplied, southern states disfranchised African Americans (and one out of four whites) by requiring voters to demonstrate literacy, property ownership, or knowledge of the Constitution before they could register. Louisiana added the notorious grandfather clause, which denied the vote to men whose grandfathers were prohibited from voting.

Whites saw disfranchisement and segregation as modern, managed race relations. Demonizing African Americans enforced solidarity among white voters, who might otherwise have voted on local or class interests.

No new legal restrictions hampered voting in the North and West, but participation fell there, too. This withdrawal from politics reflected the decline of political pageantry as an element of cultural and social life, but it also reflected the disappearance of intense partisanship. For American men, the cliffhanger contests of the late nineteenth century provided a sense of identity that matched and strengthened ethnic, religious, and neighborhood identities.

A developing economy with new patterns of recreation, class relations, and community participation undermined the habits of partisanship, but so did the new style of campaigns. The emphasis on advertising, education, and fund-raising reduced the personal stakes for voters. Educated middle- and upper-class voters liked the new style, feeling that raucous campaigns were no way to decide important issues. They sought to influence policy more directly, through interest groups rather

 Table 20–1 The Spread of Disfranchisement

	State	Strategies
1889	Florida	Poll tax
	Tennessee	Poll tax
1890	Mississippi	Poll tax, literacy test, understanding clause
1891	Arkansas	Poll tax
1893, 1901	Alabama	Poll tax, literacy test, grandfather clause
1894, 1895	South Carolina	Poll tax, literacy test, understanding clause
1894, 1902	Virginia	Poll tax, literacy test, understanding clause
1897, 1898	Louisiana	Poll tax, literacy test, grandfather clause
1899, 1900	North Carolina	Poll tax, literacy test, grandfather clause
1902	Texas	Poll tax
1908	Georgia	Poll tax, literacy test, understanding clause, grandfather clause

than parties. Unintentionally, they discarded traditions that unified communities and made voters feel connected to their country and its leaders.

Organized Labor Retreats from Politics

Workers also withdrew from politics as organized labor turned away from political means and goals and redefined objectives in economic terms. As traditional crafts came under attack, skilled workers created new organizations that addressed immediate issues: wages, hours, and the conditions of work. The American Federation of Labor (AFL), founded in 1886, built a base around skilled trades, and grew from 150,000 members to more than 2 million by 1904. The AFL focused on immediate goals that would improve the working lives of its members. Its founder, Samuel Gompers, was born in London's East End and apprenticed as a cigar maker at the age of ten. Three years later his family moved to New York, where Gompers joined the Cigar Makers' International Union.

Although affiliated with the Knights of Labor, the cigar makers were more interested in getting higher wages than in remaking the economy. They concentrated on shortening work hours and increasing pay. High dues and centralized control allowed the union to offer insurance and death benefits to members while maintaining a strike fund. Gompers applied the same practices to the AFL. His "pure and simple unionism" made modest demands, but it still encountered fierce resistance from corporations, which were backed by the courts.

In the 1895 case of *In re Debs,* the Supreme Court allowed the use of injunctions to criminalize strikes. The court then disarmed one of the few weapons left in labor's arsenal, the boycott. In the 1908 case of *Loewe v. Lawlor,* popularly known as the Danbury Hatters case, the court ruled that advertising a consumer boycott was illegal under the Sherman Anti-Trust Act.

Gompers believed that *industrial unions,* associations that drew members from all occupations within an industry, lacked the discipline and shared values needed to face down corporations and government, and that unions organized around a single trade or craft would break less easily. However, because the AFL was organized by skill, it often ignored unskilled workers, who were often women or recent immigrants. Because employers used unskilled newcomers to break strikes or to run machinery that replaced expert hands, Gompers excluded a large part of the labor force. Organizers recruited Irish and German workers through their fraternal lodges and saloons while ignoring Italian, African American, Jewish, and Slavic workers. The union attacked female workers for stealing jobs that rightfully belonged to men.

Even leaders who rejected Gompers's philosophy and strategy built unions that represented the immediate interests of their members. Under the leadership of Eugene V. Debs, railroad workers merged the old railroad brotherhoods into the ARU in 1893. The United Mine Workers (UMW), founded in 1890, unionized coal mines in Pennsylvania, Ohio, Indiana, and Michigan. The ARU and the UMW were industrial unions that tried to organize all of the workers in an industry. These new unions faced determined opposition from business and its allies in government. "Our government cannot stand, nor its free institutions endure," the National Association of Manufacturers declared, "if the Gompers-Debs ideals of liberty and freedom of speech and press are allowed to dominate."

American Diplomacy Enters the Modern World

The Republican victory in 1896 gave heart to proponents of prosperity through foreign trade. Before the turn of the century, the new president announced, the United States would control the markets of the globe. "We will establish trading posts throughout the world as distributing points for American products," Senator Albert Beveridge forecast. "Great colonies, governing themselves, flying our flag and trading with us, will grow about our posts of trade." McKinley sought neither war nor colonies, but many in his party wanted both. Called "jingoes," they included Assistant Secretary of the Navy Theodore Roosevelt, John Hay, the ambassador to London, and Senators Beveridge and Henry Cabot Lodge. Britain, France, and Germany were seizing territory around the world, and jingoes believed the United States needed to do the same for strategic, religious, and economic reasons. Spain was the most likely target. Madrid clung feebly to the remnants of its once-vast empire, now reduced to Cuba, the Philippines, Guam, and Puerto Rico. Under Cleveland, the United States had moved away from confrontation with Spain, but McKinley, at first reluctantly but later enthusiastically, pushed for the creation of an American empire that stretched to the far shores of the Pacific.

> **Nobody wants to arouse America's anger. The United States is a rich country.**
>
> OSWALD FREIHERR VON RICHTHOFEN, German foreign minister, 1898

Sea Power and the Imperial Urge

Few men better exemplified the jingoes' combination of religiosity, martial spirit, and fascination with the laws of history than Alfred Thayer Mahan. A naval officer and strategist, he told students at the Naval War College that since the Roman Empire, world leadership had belonged to the nation that controlled the sea. Published in 1890, his book *The Influence of Sea Power upon History, 1660–1783* became an instant classic.

In his first paragraph, Mahan connected naval expansion and empire to the problem of overproduction that the United States faced. A great industrial country needed trade; trade required a merchant fleet; and merchant shipping needed naval protection and overseas bases. Colonies could provide markets for goods and congregations for Christian missionaries, but more importantly they offered a springboard for naval forces that could protect sea lanes and project power into the great land masses of Asia, Latin America, and Africa.

Mahan urged the United States to build a canal across Central America, allowing manufacturers on the Atlantic coast to "compete with Europe, on equal terms as to distance, for the markets of eastern Asia." He felt that naval bases should be established along routes connecting the United States with markets in Latin America and the Far East. Congress and the Navy Department began implementing these recommendations even before McKinley took office.

Mahan was not the only prophet who saw resemblances to the Roman Empire. Brooks Adams's *The Law of Civilization and Decay* (1895) spelled out the implications of the closing of the frontier: greater concentration of wealth, social inequality, and eventually collapse. To repeal this "law" the United States needed to seek a new frontier in Asia where it could regenerate itself through combat. Sharing the social

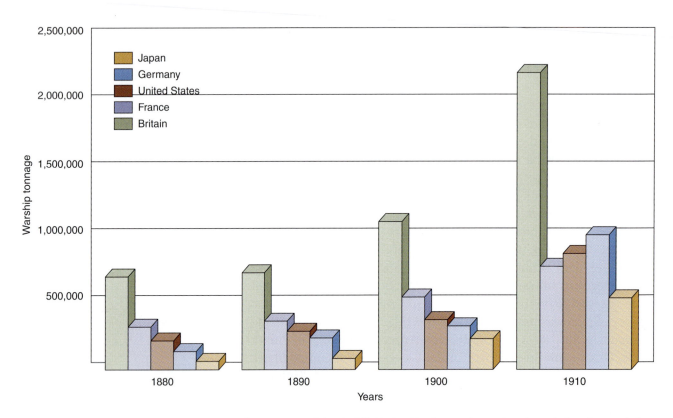

Figure 20-2 Warship Tonnage of the World's Navies Naval strength was the primary index of power before World War I. The United States held onto third place in the naval arms race, while Germany and Japan made significant gains. *Paul Kennedy,* Rise and Fall of the Great Powers *(New York: Random House, 1987), p. 203.*

Darwinist belief (see Chapter 18) that nations and races were locked in a savage struggle for survival, Mahan and Adams expected the United States to prevail and benefit from the approaching conflict.

If subduing continents with cross, Constitution, and Gatling gun appealed to anyone, it was Theodore Roosevelt. As a politician and strategist, Roosevelt paid keen attention to new ideas and forces that were magnifying the power of some nations and diminishing others. Imperialism seemed to him the essential characteristic of modernizing countries. He was the image of the modern frontiersman, a writer, soldier, and politician. Between stints in the state assembly and as New York City police commissioner, he raised cattle in the Dakota Territory, reading books by the campfire at night to the amusement of his fellow cowpunchers. Roosevelt was acutely conscious of how modern forces—globalized trade, instant communications, the reach of modern navies, and imperialism—had altered the rules of domestic and international politics. He sought to position the United States at the center of these modernizing currents, a place that would have to be earned, he felt, both on foreign battlefields and at home, where the material and technological gains of the nineteenth century had not yet been translated into the social and moral advancement that marked a true civilization.

The Scramble for Empire

For jingoes, China was the ultimate prize to be won in the global contest for trade and mastery. It had more people than any other country, hence more customers and more souls to be brought to Christ. The number of American missionaries in China doubled in the 1890s. Many of them came from the Student Volunteer Movement, which promised "the evangelization of the world in this generation" and had chapters on nearly every college campus. Even though no more than 1 or 2 percent of U.S. exports had ever gone to Chinese ports, manufacturers believed that if any country could absorb the output of America's overproductive factories, it was China. James B. Duke founded the British-American Tobacco Company based on "China's population of 450 million people, and assuming that in the future they might average a cigarette a day." In 1890 Standard Oil began selling kerosene in Shanghai. Fifteen years later, China was the largest overseas market for American oil. Mahan had predicted that China would be the arena for the coming struggle for industrial and military supremacy, and by 1897 he appeared to be right.

In 1894 Japan declared war on China, and within months it occupied Korea, Manchuria, and China's coastal cities. When the fighting

Missionaries in China Thanks to the work of missionaries in China, Mark Twain observed, "the people who sit in darkness . . . have become suspicious of the blessings of civilization."

was over, Western powers seized slices of Chinese territory. In November 1897, German troops captured the port of Qingdao on the Shandong Peninsula. An industrial area on the northeast coast, Shandong was the center of American missionary activity, investment, and trade. To Americans, the invasion of Shandong presaged the beginning of an imperial grab for territory and influence. In the 1880s European powers had carved up Africa. Now it appeared that the same thing was about to happen in China. "It is felt," the *Journal of Commerce* declared, "that we stand at the dividing of the ways, between gaining or losing the greatest market which awaits exploitation." The McKinley administration watched the events unfolding in China carefully, but in the winter of 1897/1898 the Departments of State and War had more pressing concerns closer to home.

War with Spain

While other European powers were expanding their empires, Spain was barely hanging on to the one it had. Since the 1860s its two largest colonies, Cuba and the Philippines, had been torn by revolution. Between 1868 and 1878 Cuban nationalists fought a prolonged war of independence. Spain ended the war by promising autonomy but not independence. U.S. officials wanted an end to Spanish rule, but their disappointment at this peaceful outcome did not last long. The McKinley Tariff and the Panic of 1893 ruined the island's chief export industry, sugar. Groaning under a crushing debt, Spain reneged on its promise, and in 1895 the rebellion resumed, quickly overrunning two-thirds of the island. The rebels practiced a "scorched earth" policy, dynamiting trains and burning plantations in an attempt to force Spain out.

Spain retaliated with a brutal campaign of pacification, killing nearly 100,000 civilians, but it was no use. The Spanish army was disintegrating. Cuban rebels, in full control of the countryside, prepared a final assault on the cities. U.S. officials, many of whom wanted to annex the island, now worried Cuba would gain full independence. McKinley explored the options of either purchasing it from Spain or intervening on the pretext of ending the "strife." William Randolph Hearst's *New York Journal* and other newspapers favored the latter, inciting readers with lurid stories of Spanish atrocities and Cuban rioting. Cuba sold newspapers. "Is there no nation," one editorialist asked, "wise enough, brave enough, and strong enough to restore peace?"

McKinley moved quickly toward confrontation. When riots erupted in the Cuban capital he asked the navy to send a warship to Havana. Theodore Roosevelt selected one of the newest battleships, the *Maine*. The arrival of the *Maine* reduced tensions for a while, but on February 15 an explosion ripped through the ship. Almost the entire crew of 266 perished. Navy investigators later concluded that the explosion had been internal, probably in the new oil-fired boilers, but the newspapers alternately blamed Spanish and Cuban treachery. Hearst printed a full-page diagram showing the ship being destroyed by a "sunken torpedo."

McKinley hesitated, mindful of the budget and the unfolding events in China, but Roosevelt ordered Commodore George Dewey's Asiatic Squadron to prepare for an attack on the Philippines. Congress appropriated $50 million for arms. Spanish emissaries tried to gain support from other European countries, but they were rebuffed.

In March the economic picture took a turn for the better, and McKinley sent Spain an ultimatum demanding independence for Cuba. On April 11 he asked Congress for authorization to use force, and Congress responded by passing a declaration of war. Expansionists such as Roosevelt, Mahan, and Adams would not have had their way if war had been less popular. Corporate interests favored it, immigrants and southerners saw it as a way to assert their patriotism, and newspapers found it made good copy. "We are all jingoes now," declared the *New York Sun*.

Neither side had many illusions about how the fighting would turn out. Going to war with Spain, novelist Sherwood Anderson wrote, was "like robbing an old gypsy woman in a vacant lot at night after the fair," but the war opened with a cliffhanger that even Hearst could not have invented. On May 1 news arrived that Dewey's Asiatic Squadron was in battle against the Spanish fleet in Manila Bay in the Philippines. The war had begun not in Cuba, but instead half a world away on the far edge of the Pacific Ocean. There the information stopped. The telegraph cable connecting Manila to the outside world had been cut. Official Spanish reports were vague, but they alleged that the Americans had suffered a "considerable loss of life." Dewey's squadron contained only two modern cruisers, but all of its ships were steel hulled in contrast with Spain's wooden vessels. For six anxious days the American public awaited word from the Far East.

It arrived in the early morning hours of May 7, interrupting a poker game in the newsroom at the *New York Herald*. The paper's Hong Kong correspondent had been at the battle. Dewey destroyed Spain's entire fleet of 12 warships without suffering a single serious casualty. The country went wild with relief and triumph. New York staged a parade on Fifth Avenue. A Dewey-for-president movement began. In Washington, McKinley consulted a map to see where the Philippines were. Roosevelt quit his job and ordered Brooks Brothers to make him a uniform.

The war in Cuba unfolded less spectacularly. The navy bottled up Spain's Atlantic fleet in the Bay of Santiago de Cuba. When the ships attempted to escape, American warships cut them to pieces. "Don't cheer, men," an officer ordered the gun crews. "Those poor devils are dying." A bit of drama was provided by the voyage of the USS *Oregon*, which left its West Coast base and traveled at top speed around the southern tip of South America in 68 days to join the Atlantic fleet too late for the fighting. Its journey, tracked by newspapers around the country, dramatized the need for a canal connecting the Atlantic and the Pacific.

In the years before the war, Congress had poured money into the navy but not the army, and it took some time before soldiers could be trained and equipped. Recruits were herded into camps in Florida without tents, proper clothing, or latrines. There were few medical supplies or doctors. In unsanitary camps, soldiers in woolen uniforms died of dysentery and malaria. Of the 5,462 U.S. soldiers who died in the war with Spain, 5,083 succumbed to disease, a scandal that forced the government to elevate the status of the surgeon general and to regard sanitation and disease prevention as important to national defense.

The army landed on the Cuban coast and marched inland to engage Spanish defenders. A cavalry general, Joseph Wheeler, an ex-Confederate from Alabama, urged his men on, yelling, "The Yankees are running! Damn it, I mean the Spaniards!" Roosevelt came ashore with the First Volunteer Cavalry, known as the "Rough Riders." He recruited, trained, and publicized the regiment, and afterwards he wrote its history, all with an eye to symbolism. An assortment of outlaws, cowboys, Ivy League athletes, New York City policemen, a novelist, and a Harvard Medical School graduate, its membership combined frontier heroism with eastern elite leadership. The regiment traveled with its own film crew and a correspondent from the *New York Herald*.

Spanish forces stubbornly resisted around the city of Santiago. Their Mauser rifles had a longer range and a faster rate of fire than American weapons. At San Juan Hill, 500 defenders forced a regiment of the New York National Guard to retreat. The all–African American 9th and 10th Cavalry took their place along with the Rough Riders, with Roosevelt cautiously waiting until Gatling guns could be brought up from the rear. "The negroes saved that fight," a white soldier reported. The capture of Santiago effectively ended Spanish resistance. When fighting ended in August, U.S. troops occupied Cuba, Guam, Puerto Rico, and the city of Manila. The war had lasted only four months.

As American and Spanish diplomats met in Paris to conclude a peace treaty, McKinley had to decide which occupied territories to keep as colonies. Congress, not wanting to inherit the island's $400 million in debt, had already resolved not to annex Cuba. McKinley decided that Guam and Puerto Rico would make ideal naval bases.

The president also seized the opportunity to annex the island nation of Hawaii. In 1893 American sugar planters, led by Sanford Dole, overthrew the islands' last queen, Liliuokalani, and petitioned for annexation (see Chapter 19). They were motivated by the Harrison-McKinley Tariff, which would ruin the planters financially unless they could somehow reconnect Hawaii's trade to the United States. Annexation was their best chance, and they had a powerful ally in the U.S. Navy. Mahan had identified the deep-water anchorage at Pearl Harbor, on Oahu, as a vital base. McKinley now decided to take up Dole's annexation offer.

The Philippines presented more of a problem. Its 7,000 islands were far from the United States and had a population of several million. What the United States needed was a naval base and a coaling station close to the China coast, but holding just one island would be impossible if another power controlled the others. Shortly after Dewey's victory, British and German warships anchored in Manila Bay, clearly intending to divide up whatever territory the United States did not claim. McKinley felt trapped.

"The United States, whatever it might prefer as to the Philippines, is in a situation where it cannot let go," he advised his negotiators.

One consideration McKinley did not take into account was that the Philippines had already declared independence. With Dewey's encouragement, rebels under the command of Emilio Aguinaldo had liberated the countryside surrounding Manila and laid siege to the city. At Malolos, 25 miles north of Manila, a national assembly, including lawyers, doctors, professors, and landowners from across the archipelago, issued a constitution. By the time the U.S. Army finally arrived in 1899, Filipinos throughout the country had overthrown the Spanish and rallied to their new government.

Spanish negotiators recognized Cuban independence and surrendered most of Spain's empire to the United States for free, but they gave up the Philippines only after the United States agreed to pay $20 million, or as an American satirist calculated, $1.25 for every Filipino. The treaty was signed December 10, 1898.

The Anti-Imperialists

Many prominent Americans opposed both the annexation of new colonies and the approaching war with the Philippines. During the treaty fight in Congress in January 1899, they tried to mobilize opinion against the treaty. The movement included ex-presidents Grover Cleveland and Benjamin Harrison, William Jennings Bryan, labor unionists including Samuel Gompers and Eugene Debs, writers such as Mark Twain and Ambrose Bierce, and industrialists including Andrew Carnegie. The anti-imperialists advanced an array of moral, economic, and strategic arguments. Filipinos and Hawaiians, they said, had sought American help in good faith and were capable of governing themselves. The islands could not be defended. Instead of using the Pacific Ocean as a barrier, U.S. forces would be exposed to attack at Pearl Harbor or Manila. Carnegie argued that imperialism distracted attention from domestic problems and took tax money that could be spent at home. White supremacists asked whether Filipinos would become citizens or be allowed to vote and emigrate to the mainland.

The most moving objections came from those who believed imperialism betrayed America's fundamental principles. "Could there be a more damning indictment of the whole bloated ideal termed 'modern civilization' than this amounts to?" William James asked. To Mark Twain imperialism was only the newest form of greed. "There is more money in it, more territory, more sovereignty, and other kinds of emolument, than there is in any other game that is played." Opponents of annexation organized an Anti-Imperialist League and lobbied for the rejection of the Paris Treaty.

Congress whittled away at anti-imperialist objections, banning Philippine immigration, placing the colonies outside the tariff walls, and promising eventual self-government. Jingoes had the momentum of military victory on their side. Anti-imperialists could not offer a vision comparable with naval supremacy, the evangelization of the world, or the fabled China market. On February 6, 1899, the U.S. Senate ratified the Paris Treaty and annexed the Philippines. A day earlier, on the other side of the world, the Philippine-American War began.

The Philippine-American War

McKinley believed he had annexed islands full of near savages "unfit for self-rule," but the Philippines by 1899 had an old civilization with a long tradition of resistance to colonialism. When Magellan discovered the islands in 1521, he found a literate

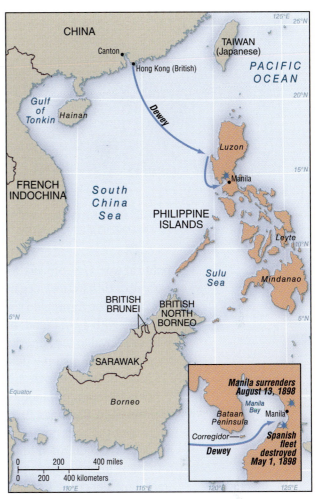

Map 20–2   Spanish-American War, Caribbean   Spanish-American War, Pacific

population linked by trade ties to India, Japan, and China. The Spanish converted most Filipinos to Catholicism and established schools and a centralized government. Manila's oldest university was older than Harvard. By 1898 much of the upper class, the *illustrados,* had been educated in Europe.

Dewey gave Aguinaldo his word that America desired no colonies. Aguinaldo continued to trust the Americans long after the arrival of fresh troops made it clear that the United States intended to stay. On February 4 an argument between American and Filipino sentries ended in gunfire. Aguinaldo was despondent: "No one can deplore more than I this rupture. I have a clear conscience that I endeavored to avoid it at all costs."

Kansas volunteers drove the Filipino armies into the mountains. Aguinaldo abandoned conventional warfare for a guerilla strategy, which proved effective. Some 4,000 Americans were killed during the war and another 3,000 wounded out of a total force of 70,000. Frustrated by guerilla conflict, American soldiers customarily executed prisoners, looted villages, and raped Filipino women. An American general on the island of Samar ordered his soldiers to kill everyone over the age of 10. One soldier wrote home, "No cruelty is too severe for these brainless monkeys, who can appreciate no sense of honor, kindness, or justice. I am in my glory when I can sight some dark skin and pull the trigger."

Kansas Volunteers Kansas volunteers on a firing line in Luzon, 1899. New technologies, such as stereoscope images and moving pictures, made the Philippine War vivid for Americans.

The army's preferred mode of torture was "the water cure," in which water was forced down a prisoner's throat until the abdomen swelled, and then forced out again by kicking. When Congress investigated these practices, military officials argued that in a savage war such measures were necessary. Filipinos were "half-civilized," they explained, and force was the best language for dealing with them.

Newspaper accounts of torture and massacres fueled opposition in the United States to the war, but just as the anti-imperialist movement gained steam, U.S. forces scored some victories. Recognizing that they were fighting a political war, U.S. officers took pains to win over dissidents and ethnic minorities. In early 1901 this strategy began to pay off. When American troops intercepted a messenger bound for Aguinaldo's secret headquarters, Brigadier General Frederick Funston came up with a bold (and, under the rules of war, illegal) plan. He dressed a group of Filipinos loyal to the American side in the uniforms of captured Filipinos, and, posing as a prisoner, Funston entered Aguinaldo's camp and kidnapped the president.

After three weeks in a Manila prison, Aguinaldo issued a proclamation of surrender. "Enough of blood, enough of tears and desolation," he pleaded. Resistance continued in Batangas Province, south of Manila, for another year. The U.S. Army increased the pressure by imposing the same reconcentration policies the United States had condemned in Cuba, and produced the same result. Perhaps as much as a third of the province's population died of disease and starvation. On July 4, 1902, President Theodore Roosevelt declared the war over.

The American flag flew over the Philippines until 1942, but the colony never lived up to its imperial promise. Instead of defending American trade interests, U.S. troops were pinned down in Philippine garrisons, guarding against sporadic uprisings and the threat of Japanese invasion. The costs of occupation far exceeded the profits generated by Philippine trade. The colony chiefly served as an outlet for American reformers and missionaries, who built schools, churches, and agricultural colleges. A small group of colonists sought statehood, but as the Philippines became more closely tied to the United States, Americans liked their colonial experiment less and less. Labor unions feared a flood of immigration from the islands, and farmers resented competition from Philippine producers; in 1933 Congress voted to phase out American rule.

The Open Door

As Americans celebrated their victories, European powers continued to divide China into quasi-colonial "concessions." An alarmed imperial court in Beijing began a crash program of modernization, but reactionaries within the government overthrew the emperor and installed the conservative "dowager empress" Ci Xi. In the countryside, Western missionaries and traders came under attack from local residents led by street-corner martial artists known as Boxers. In 1899, a British author, Charles Beresford, lectured across the United States promoting his book *The Breakup of China*. Large audiences turned out to hear what they already feared, that the approaching disintegration of China would mean the exclusion of U.S. trade. Just as the United States arrived at the gateway to the Orient, the gates were swinging closed.

Secretary of State John Hay watched events in China with growing apprehension. "The inherent weakness of our position is this," he wrote McKinley. "We do not want to rob China ourselves, and our public opinion will not allow us to interfere, with an army, to prevent others from robbing her. Besides, we have no army." Casting about for some means to keep China's markets open, McKinley turned to William Rockhill, a legendary career foreign service officer who had lived in China and had been the first westerner to visit Tibet. He, in turn, consulted his friend Alfred Hippisley, an Englishman returning from service with the British-run Chinese imperial customs.

Together, Rockhill, Hippisley, and Hay drafted an official letter known as the Open Door Note. Sent to each of the imperial powers, it acknowledged the partitioning of China into spheres, and it observed that so far none of the powers had closed its areas to the trade of other countries. The note urged each of the powers to continue this policy and to declare publicly their intention to keep their concessions open to the trade of the other powers.

The Open Door was mostly bluff. The United States had no authority to ask for such a pledge and no military power to enforce one. The foreign ministers of Germany, Japan, Russia, Britain, and France replied cautiously at first, agreeing to issue a declaration when the others had done so, but Hay adroitly played one power off another, starting with Britain and Japan, whose trade interests gave them a stake in the Open Door. Once the two strongest powers in China had agreed, France reluctantly acquiesced. Russia and Germany, rather than challenge the other powers, did likewise. Hay proclaimed the Open Door a diplomatic watershed on the order of the Monroe Doctrine. The United States had secured access to China without war or partition, but the limits of Hay's success soon became apparent.

In early 1900, the antiforeign Boxer movement swept through Shandong province. Armed Chinese attacked missions and foreign businesses, destroyed railroads, and massacred Chinese Christians. Empress Ci Xi recruited 30,000 Boxers into her army and declared war on all foreign countries. The Western powers rushed troops to China, but before they could arrive Chinese armies laid siege to Western embassies in Beijing. An international force of British, Russian, Japanese, and French troops gathered at Tianjin to march to the rescue. European powers appeared all too eager to capture the Chinese capital.

Without consulting Congress, McKinley ordered American troops into battle on the Asian mainland. Five thousand soldiers rushed from Manila to Tianjin. John Hay issued a second Open Door Note, asking the allied countries to pledge to protect China's independence. Again, the imperial powers reluctantly agreed rather than admit their secret plans to carve up China. On August 15, 1900, U.S. cavalry units under General Adna Chaffee reached Beijing along with Russian Cossacks, French Zouaves, British-Indian sepoys, German hussars, and Japanese dragoons. After freeing the captive diplomats, the armies of the civilized world looted the city. The United States was unable to maintain the Open Door in China for long. Russia and Japan established separate military zones in northeast China in defiance of the Beijing government and American protests, but the principle of the Open Door, of encouraging free trade and open markets, guided American foreign policy throughout the twentieth century. It rested on the assumption that, in an equal contest, American firms would prevail, spreading manufactured goods around the world, and American influence with them. Under the

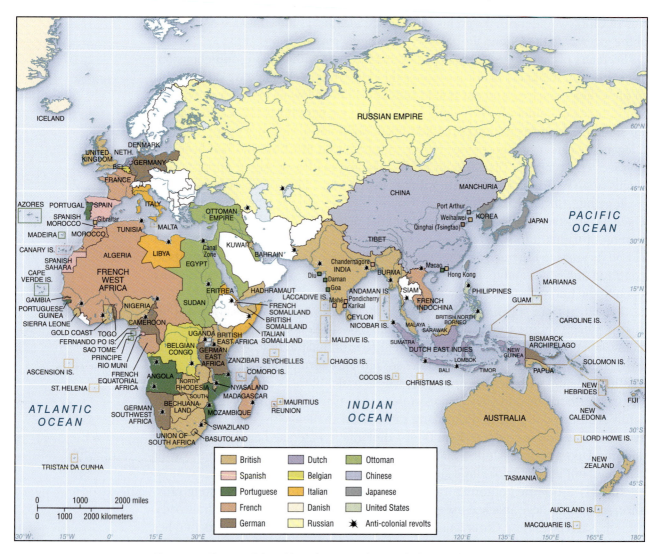

Map 20–3 The Imperial World Modern imperialism reached its apex between 1880 and 1945. Most of Africa, the Middle East, and Asia, a third of the world's population, was absorbed into global empires linked by telegraph and steamship to centers of government and commerce in London, Paris, Tokyo, and Washington, DC.

Open Door, the United States was better off in a world without empires, a world where consumers in independent nations could buy what they wanted. Just one year after the Spanish-American War, Hay's notes rejected imperial expansion in favor of trade expansion. This bold new strategy promised greater gains, but it placed the United States on a collision course with the great empires of the world.

Conclusion

In the turbulent 1890s the social and economic divisions among Americans widened. The hope that a solution to these divisions could be found outside the United States was short-lived. Imperialism promised new markets and an end to the wrenching cycle of depression and labor strife. The United States conquered an overseas empire and challenged other empires to open their ports to free trade, but the goal of prosperity and peace at home proved elusive.

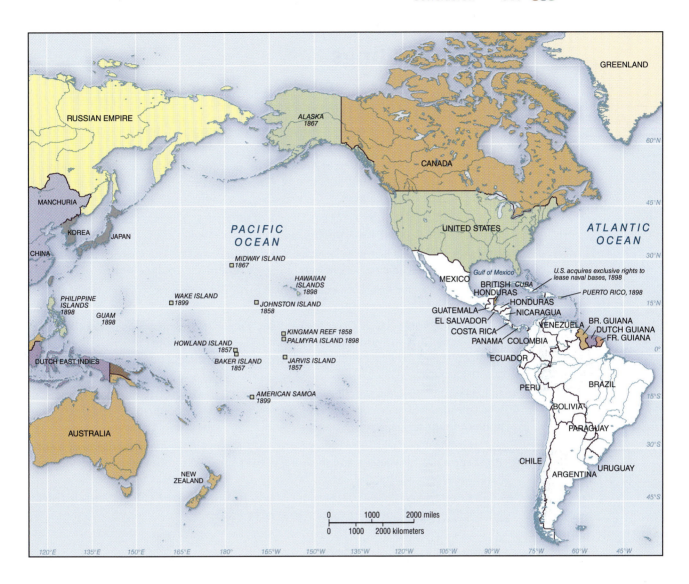

In many ways social Darwinism became a self-fulfilling prophecy, as competition rather than compromise prevailed. Workers and businessmen, farmers and bankers, middle-class radicals and conservatives, whites and African Americans saw each other as enemies. Racial segregation showed that middle ground, where whites and African Americans could meet on equal terms, had disappeared. Workers, farmers, African Americans, radicals, and reformers had to decide what was politically possible and devise new bargaining strategies.

Economic recovery and victory in global conflict closed the decade on an optimistic note. Prosperity, power, and technology seemed to have rewritten the rules of human affairs to America's advantage. Henry Adams, standing in the American exhibit at the Paris Exposition of 1900, contemplated a 40-foot dynamo—a "huge wheel, revolving within arm's length at some vertiginous speed, and barely murmuring"—and felt as if he had crossed a "historical chasm." The machine's silent force, scarcely understood or controlled and emanating from "a dirty engine house carefully kept out of sight," seemed a metaphor for the modern age.

Further Readings

Edward L. Ayers, *The Promise of the New South: Life After Reconstruction* (1992). A study of daily life, work, and politics in the turn-of-the-century South.

H. W. Brands, *The Reckless Decade: America in the 1890s* (1995). A lively look at some of the decade's noteworthy events and characters.

Ron Chernow, *The House of Morgan: An American Banking Dynasty and the Rise of Modern Finance* (1990). The life and business of J. P. Morgan and his heirs, the lions of Wall Street for more than a century.

James B. Gilbert, *Perfect Cities: Chicago's Utopias of 1893* (1991). The fears and dreams that led Chicago's elite to create the World's Columbian Exposition.

Robert Kanigel, *The One Best Way: Frederick Winslow Taylor and the Enigma of Efficiency* (1997). The most famous efficiency expert and how his system changed the world.

Stanley Karnow, *In Our Image: America's Empire in the Philippines* (1989). America's colonial venture in the Philippines from 1898 to 1986.

Paul A. Kramer, *The Blood of Government: Race, Empire, the United States, and the Philippines* (2006). To justify war and occupation, U.S. officials invented new theories of racial dominance and divided Filipinos into "civilized" Christians and "savage" Muslim and animist groups.

David L. Lewis, *W. E. B. Du Bois: Biography of a Race, 1868–1919* (1993). The story of the man who "pleaded with a headstrong, careless people to despise not Justice," and the era that produced him.

Louis Pérez, *The War of 1898: The United States and Cuba in History and Historiography* (1998). Pérez separates the motives and meaning of the Cuban War from the nationalist legends that have grown around it.

Nick Salvatore, *Eugene V. Debs: Citizen and Socialist* (1982). From the railroad yards to federal prison, the story of one of America's great labor leaders.

>> Timeline >>

▼ **1890**
Global depression begins
United Mine Workers founded
Battle of Wounded Knee ends Indian wars
Harrison-McKinley Tariff passed
Alfred T. Mahan publishes *The Influence of Sea Power Upon History, 1660–1783*

Standard Oil markets kerosene in China

▼ **1892**
Homestead strike

▼ **1893**
Financial crisis leads to business failures and mass unemployment
World's Columbian Exposition, Chicago
Cherokee Strip land rush
American sugar planters overthrow Queen Liliuokalani of Hawaii

▼ **1894**
Coxey's Army marches on Washington
Pullman strike
U.S. commission charts canal route across Nicaragua

▼ **1895**
Morgan agrees to Treasury bailout

National Association of Manufacturers founded
Brooks Adams publishes *The Law of Civilization and Decay*
Booker T. Washington gives "Atlanta Compromise" address
Revolution begins in Cuba
Japan annexes Korea and Taiwan

▼ **1896**
Plessy v. Ferguson declares "separate but equal" facilities constitutional
Mary Church Terrell founds National Association of Colored Women
William McKinley elected president

Who, What?

William Jennings Bryan 14
Booker T. Washington 18
Samuel Gompers 20
William Randolph Hearst 24

Taylorism 10
Gold standard 13
Separate but equal 17
Open Door 29

Review Questions

1. What new techniques and practices made U.S. industries more efficient?

2. What motivated Americans to seek an empire?

3. Why did some observers find the Pullman experiment "un-American"?

4. Which cities were the main centers of industry and culture in the 1890s?

5. How did the concept of individual rights evolve in reaction to new economic conditions? Name key figures who articulated a concept of democratic rights, and describe their ideas.

6. Contrast the arguments for empire with the rhetoric of the anti-imperialists. Which dangers to the nation and democracy did each side stress?

7. Why was the issue of currency so important to Americans in 1896? What was at stake?

For further review materials and resource information, please visit www.oup.com/us/ofthepeople

▼ **1897**
Germany captures Qingdao, on China's
  Shandong Peninsula
McKinley issues formal protest to Spain

▼ **1898**
Maine explodes in Havana's harbor
United States declares war on Spain
Dewey defeats Spanish fleet at Manila Bay
In the Treaty of Paris, Spain grants Cuba
  independence, cedes Guam, Puerto Rico,
  and the Philippines to the United States
Aguinaldo proclaims Philippine independence

▼ **1899**
Senate votes to annex
  Puerto Rico, Hawaii,
  and the Philippines
Philippine-American
  War begins
Hay issues first Open
  Door Note

▼ **1900**
Hay issues second Open Door Note
U.S. Army joins British, French, Russian,
  German, and Japanese forces in capture of
  Beijing

Great Exposition of Paris showcases
American technology
William McKinley reelected

▼ **1901**
Aguinaldo captured
McKinley assassinated; Theodore
Roosevelt becomes president

▼ **1902**
Roosevelt declares Philippine-American war
over

Common Threads

>> What political problems arose from the transition to an urban, industrial, and national society?

>> How did women's activism on social issues change the style and content of politics?

>> Why did party politics decline at the same time that national interest groups emerged?

>> How did the new interventionism transform the administration of cities and states?

>> In what ways did Progressivism enlarge the president's powers over foreign policy and the economy?

>> Alice Hamilton

O n an October morning in 1902, three distinguished friends, Maude Gernon of the Chicago Board of Charities, Gertrude Howe, kindergarten director at Hull-House, and Dr. Alice Hamilton, a professor of pathology at Northwestern University, stood over sewer drains catching flies. The prey was abundant, and the women methodically trapped dozens in test tubes. Hamilton organized the expedition in the midst of a typhoid epidemic. The disease ravaged Chicago's 19th Ward, a working-class neighborhood where Hull-House stood. To find out why, Hamilton investigated the surrounding tenement houses, which often had illegal outdoor privies rather than indoor plumbing. It was then that she noticed the flies. Army doctors in the Spanish-American War found a link between flies and poor sanitation and the spread of typhoid. Hamilton incubated her test tubes for several days, examined them under a microscope, and confirmed that Chicago's flies carried the typhoid bacillus.

When her findings appeared in the *Journal of the American Medical Association* a few months later, they touched off a furor. Hull-House attacked the Board of Health for failing to enforce the sanitary codes, and an inquiry discovered that landlords bribed sanitation inspectors to overlook the outhouses. Further investigations found that drinking water was pumped straight from Lake Michigan, without any purification, and that broken pumping equipment channeled raw sewage into the water mains. Through a chain of bribery and neglect, Chicago's city government was responsible for an epidemic that killed hundreds of people.

Hamilton, who grew up in affluent surroundings in Fort Wayne, Indiana, attended medical school at the University of Michigan, later going on to do advanced work in bacteriology and pathology at Leipzig and Munich. Despite her training, it was difficult for her to find work, but in Chicago she found support at Hull-House, a "settlement house" founded by women who wanted to live among the poor. Hamilton lived there for 22 years. Her work concerned occupational disease, which she began studying in Germany. In the United States she noticed a "strange silence on the subject" of job-related disease. Her early research linked the working conditions of Jewish garment workers to the tuberculosis that frequently claimed their lives.

After the typhoid scandal, Hamilton began looking into stories of poisoning among workers at the National Lead Company. Clouds of metallic dust filled the plant, and employees came home from work glistening with lead. The company refused to admit its high absenteeism had anything to do with the work. Hamilton interviewed workers' wives and priests in the neighborhood. One foreman told her that lead workers "don't last long at it. Four years at the most, I should say, then they quit and go home to the old country." "To die?" she asked. "Well," he replied, "I suppose that is about the size of it." Searching hospital records, she documented a pattern of chronic lead poisoning. Confronted with these findings, the company agreed to install ventilators and create a medical department. Hamilton pushed for state laws on occupational disease, and in 1911 Illinois became the first state to pass legislation giving workers compensation for job-related disability.

Hamilton's activism was noteworthy but not unique. She was one of millions of people in the early twentieth century who reshaped democracy by participating in a new type of politics. Responding to the challenges of immigration, industrialization, and urbanization, Americans agitated for change. They worked from outside the two-party system, forming their own organizations.

continued

>> **AMERICAN PORTRAIT** *continued*

Women, who did not have the vote, took the lead and created a new style of activism.

Some activists feared the uncontrolled power of corporations, while others feared the uncontrolled passions of the poor. Both called themselves progressives, and they shared certain understandings about democracy. They optimistically believed in people's ability to improve society, but they were pessimistic about the ability of people, particularly nonwhite people, to improve themselves. Science and religion, as Progressives understood them, supported these beliefs and justified the supervision of human affairs by qualified experts.

Although reformers accepted industry as a modern necessity, they were outraged by the worst consequences of industrialism: the trail of disease, waste, and corruption the factory system left behind. They sought a middle ground between revolutionary socialism and uncontrolled corporate capitalism. Finally, they belonged to a movement that had national reach. Progressivism, as it came to be called, was the first and perhaps the only reform movement experienced by all Americans. Wide-circulation magazines carried the agitation into every town and county. ●

 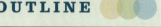
Toward a New Politics

Progressivism displaced the intensely partisan politics of the late nineteenth century. The political and economic crises of the 1890s left Americans disillusioned with traditional parties. A growing Socialist movement threatened to lead Americans in a more radical direction if moderate reform failed. Protestant churches became outspokenly critical of capitalism's abuses, and new interpretations of Christian ethics lent a moral urgency to reform. The mounting dangers of urban life, some of which

Alice Hamilton encountered, gave educated, affluent Americans a sense that civic problems needed to be dealt with immediately. Women took leading roles, using pressure groups to extend their influence while also seeking the vote.

Egged on by a national press, progressives organized at the local, state, and national levels to solve the problems of the new industrial world. Although they sometimes pined for the (probably imaginary) security of smaller towns and bygone eras, progressives recognized that large-scale industrial capitalism was here to stay. They worked as troubleshooters, laboring to make an erratic and brutal system more predictable, efficient, and humane. In pushing for reform, however, they were willing to enlarge the authority of the state and to use state power to tell people what was good for them. As reform gained momentum, mayors, governors, and presidential candidates identified themselves and their agendas as progressive.

> **A city is in many respects a great business corporation, but in other respects it is enlarged housekeeping. . . . May we not say that city housekeeping has failed partly because women, the traditional housekeepers, have not been consulted?**
>
> JANE ADDAMS,
> 1907

The Insecurity of Modern Life

Most people who lived in cities at the turn of the century had grown up in the country. They remembered living in communities where people knew each other, where many of the foods they ate and clothes they wore were made locally. These communities were less dependent on outsiders or big corporations. For many Americans, living in a modern metropolis meant depending on strangers. Meat and bread came not from a familiar butcher or baker, but from packinghouses hundreds or thousands of miles away. Tap water, fuel, and transportation to work were all supplied by

A Tale of Two Kitchens The house where Woodrow Wilson was born in 1856 (left) used food, fuel, water, and lighting supplied locally or even just outside the door. The kitchen in the house where he died in 1924 (right), used gas and electricity from hundreds of miles away, as well as food and appliances that came from national suppliers.

large, anonymous corporations. Unknown executives made decisions that affected the livelihoods, savings, and safety of thousands of people. City dwellers felt more sophisticated than their parents but also less secure.

City living carried risks. Inspecting a Chicago market, journalist Upton Sinclair found milk laced with formaldehyde, peas colored green with copper salts, and smoked sausage doctored with toxic chemicals. Druggists sold fraudulent cures for imaginary diseases. Dozens of patent medicines—including aspirin, cocaine, and heroin—advertised themselves as the remedies for everything from hay fever to cancer.

Even staying indoors involved hazards. Tenement blocks housing hundreds of people often had no fire escapes or plumbing. Tragedy reminded New Yorkers of these dangers on March 25, 1911, when fire engulfed the Triangle Shirtwaist Company on the top three floors of a ten-story building. Five hundred Jewish and Italian seamstresses were trapped; many jumped from ledges in groups, holding hands. In all, 146 died. Such episodes demonstrated that an unregulated economy could be both productive and deadly.

Government often added to the problem. Regulation supplied a pretext for kickbacks and bribery. In 1904 and 1905, journalist Lincoln Steffens uncovered corruption in state after state. In New York, insurance companies paid off state representatives and even a U.S. senator in return for favorable legislation. Trials in San Francisco disclosed that boss Abraham Ruef ruled the city with a slush fund donated by public utilities. The Minneapolis police, with the connivance of the mayor's office, protected brothels and gambling dens in return for bribes. Elections made the system less accountable, not more. By creating a demand for campaign funds and jobs, elections became invitations to graft.

The rising middle class found public and corporate irresponsibility particularly infuriating. In the stately Victorian "streetcar suburbs," business managers, accountants, engineers, lawyers, and doctors became conscious of themselves as a class, but they felt trapped between the two dominant social groups, the rich and the masses of wage laborers. "We do not like to acknowledge that Americans are divided into two nations," Jane Addams observed, but the tiny middle class could see itself as imperiled by both groups or, alternatively, as the only possible mediator between them. By virtue of their education and experience, members of the middle class had their own ideas on how organizations, such as utility companies, cities, and states, should run. Modern corporations had to have clear lines of authority, an emphasis on efficiency, and reliable sources of information. Yet these virtues were frustratingly absent from civic life.

The Decline of Partisan Politics

Participation in elections declined by choice and coercion. Nationally, 79 percent of the electorate voted in 1896, but four years later only 73 percent voted, and by 1904 the total fell to 65 percent. Literacy tests accounted for much of the decline in the South, but in all regions the old spectacular style of electioneering, with torchlit parades, mass rallies, and flagpole raisings, gave way to campaigns that were more educational and less participatory. "Listless" was how one observer described the 1904 turnout. "There is much apathy on the part of the public as regards the campaign—more than I have ever seen before." Worse from the parties' point of view, the voters who did turn out split their tickets. The ethnic and sectional loyalties that

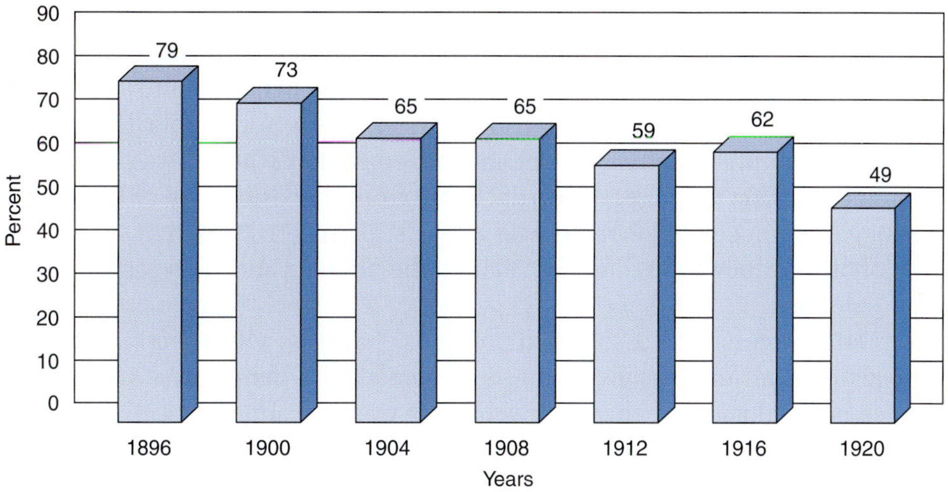

Figure 21-1   Voter Participation, 1896–1920 After the intense partisanship and high-stakes elections of the 1890s, campaigns became more "educational" and voters lost interest.

led people to vote a straight party ballot in the late nineteenth century seemed to be weakening.

Increasingly, Americans participated in politics through associations. Voluntary and professional societies took over functions that once belonged to the parties: educating and socializing voters and even making policy. These "interest groups" worked outside the system to gather support for a particular cause or proposal. Many were patterned after corporations, with a board of directors and state and local chapters. Built on the idea that reform was a continuous process, they strove for permanence. Some, like the National Association for the Advancement of Colored People (NAACP), the Salvation Army, and the Sierra Club, remain prominent after a century.

Social Housekeeping

The mounting clamor for social change aroused latent political strength in unexpected places. Women's social clubs had been nonpolitical before the turn of the century. Dedicated to developing public talents like art, speaking, reading, and conversation, they were typically highly organized, with local, state, and national chapters. A General Federation of Women's Clubs was formed in 1890. Within 10 years the urgency of social problems led many clubs to launch campaigns on behalf of free kindergartens, civil service reform, and public health. "Ladies," Sarah P. Decker announced at her inauguration as head of the federation in 1904, "Dante is dead. He has been dead for several centuries, and I think that it is time that we dropped the study of his inferno and turned attention to our own." Following her advice, clubwomen turned from developing public skills to exercising them.

A growing cohort of professional women also energized reform. The first generation of graduates from the new women's colleges had reached adulthood, and some, like Alice Hamilton, had attained advanced degrees at a time when few men went to college. These "new women," as historians have called them, had ambitions and values that set them apart from women of their mothers' generation. About half of the female graduates did not marry. Since career paths were closed to them, educated women found careers by finding problems that needed solving. Florence Kelley, trained as a lawyer, became Illinois' first state factory inspector and later directed the National Consumers League. Margaret Sanger, a New York public health nurse, distributed literature on birth control and sex education when it was illegal to do so. Sophonisba Breckinridge, with a doctorate from the University of Chicago, led the struggle against child labor. Female activists "discovered" problems, publicized them, lobbied for new laws, and then staffed the bureaus and agencies administering the solutions.

Women's professional associations, unions, business clubs, ethnic and patriotic societies, and foundations changed the practice of democracy. Activities that had once been considered charity or volunteer work became political. Some, such as the YWCA (1894) and the International Council of Nurses (1899), had a global reach. The experiences of women's clubs and associations taught activists the importance of cooperation, organization, and expertise. When women's clubs built a playground and donated it to the city or urged lawmakers to address an issue, they increased their own stake in the political system. They gave themselves new reasons to demand full citizenship.

The women's suffrage movement quietly built momentum in the early years of the century. Women had gained the vote in four states—Colorado, Wyoming, Utah, and Idaho—early on, but between 1896 and 1910 no other states adopted a women's suffrage amendment. The movement encountered stubborn opposition from the Catholic Church, machine politicians, and business interests.

Competing suffrage organizations joined forces under the National American Woman Suffrage Association (NAWSA). Led by Carrie Chapman Catt and Anna Howard Shaw, NAWSA developed a strategy based on professional lobbying and publicity. Suffragists appealed to clubwomen and middle-class reformers by cultivating an image of Victorian respectability and linking suffrage to moderate social causes, such as temperance and education. NAWSA eventually narrowed its constituency and became less democratic, but initially its strategy paid off. After 1910, five states adopted suffrage amendments in rapid succession, but the opposition rallied and defeated referendums in three eastern states.

Frustrated with the glacial pace of progress, Alice Paul's National Woman's Party adopted more radical tactics, picketing the White House and staging hunger strikes. Despite setbacks, women led the transformation of politics through voluntary organizations and interest groups and were on the threshold of even greater gains.

Evolution or Revolution?

The Socialist Party's swelling membership seemed to confirm its claims that the future would be revolutionary rather than progressive. At its founding meeting in Indianapolis in 1901, the party declared confidence in the inevitability of capitalism's downfall. By 1912, Eugene V. Debs, the party's candidate for president, garnered almost a million votes, some 6 percent of the total. "Gas and water" Socialists, who demanded public ownership of utilities, captured municipal offices in smaller cities across the country. In the Plains states, socialism drew strength from primitive Baptist and Holiness churches and held revival-style tent meetings. The party's stronghold was Oklahoma, where almost one-quarter of the electorate voted Socialist in 1914.

Although tinged with religion, Socialists' analysis of modern problems was economic. They maintained that the profit motive distorted human behavior, forcing people to compete for survival as individuals instead of joining to promote the common good. Driven by profits, corporations could not be trusted to look after the welfare of consumers or workers. Socialists demanded the collective ownership of industries, starting with ones that most directly affected the livelihoods and safety of people: the railroads and city utilities. Although their ambitions collided with corporate values, they had faith that America could make the transition without violence. Above all, they were sure socialism was coming, "coming like a prairie fire," a Socialist newspaperman told his readers. "You can see it in the papers. You can taste it in the price of beef."

"Social Gospel" clergymen preached this coming millennium. Washington Gladden, a congregational pastor from Columbus, Ohio; Walter Rauschenbusch, a Baptist minister from New York; William Dwight Porter Bliss, who founded the Society for Christian Socialists; and George Herron, an Iowa Congregationalist, were among the prominent ministers who interpreted the Bible as a call to social action. Their visions of the Christian commonwealth ranged from reform to revolution, but they all believed that corporate capitalism was organized sin, and that the church had an obligation to stand against it.

When the Industrial Workers of the World (IWW) talked about revolution they meant class war, not elections. Founded in 1905, the IWW unionized some of the most rugged individuals in the West: miners, loggers, and even rodeo cowboys (under the Bronco Busters and Range Riders Union). Gathering unskilled workers into "one big union," the Wobblies challenged both the AFL's elite unionism and the Socialists' gradualism. Membership remained small, fewer than 100,000, but the union and its leader, William "Big Bill" Haywood, had a reputation for radicalism. At IWW strikes in Lawrence, Massachusetts, and Paterson, New Jersey, strikers clashed with police and staged parades in which thousands of marchers carried red flags. To sensationalist newspapermen and anxious middle-class readers, these activities looked like signs of approaching class warfare.

Conservatives and reformers alike felt the hot breath of revolution on their necks, and socialism's greatest influence may have been the push it gave conservatives to support moderate reform. Theodore Roosevelt warned that unless something was done the United States would divide into two parties, one representing workers, the other capital.

The failure of the two parties to deal with urgent problems created a chance to redefine democracy. As the new century began, Americans were testing their political ideals, scrapping the old rules, and getting ready to fashion new institutions and laws to deal with the challenges of modern society.

The Progressives

Historians have found it difficult to define the progressives. They addressed a wide variety of social problems with many different tactics, but for people of the time the connectedness was apparent. A rally to end child labor, for instance, might draw out young lawyers, teachers, labor unionists, woman suffragists, professors, and politicians. "Scores of young leaders in American politics and public affairs were seeing what I saw, feeling what I felt," journalist William Allen White remembered. A series of overlapping movements, campaigns, and crusades defined the era from 1890 to 1920.

Progressivism was a political style, a way of approaching problems. Progressives had no illusions that wage labor or industrialism could be eliminated or that it was possible to re-create a rural commonwealth. Big cities and big corporations, they believed, were permanent features of modern life, but progressives shared an optimistic conviction that modern institutions could be made humane, responsive, and moral.

In choosing solutions, progressives relied on scientific expertise as a way to avoid the clash of interests. The generation raised during the Civil War knew democracy was no guarantee against mass violence. Rival points of view could be reconciled more easily by impartial authority. Like the salaried managers many of them were, progressives valued efficiency and organization. No problem could be solved in a single stroke. Instead, true remedies could be enforced only by persistent action.

Convinced that science and God were on their side, progressives did not balk at imposing their views on other people, even if democracy got in the way. Such measures as naming "born criminals" to be put on probation *before* committing a crime were called "progressive." To southern progressives "scientific" principles justified racial segregation. Popular opposition posed a strategic rather than a philosophical problem. Progressives demanded more democracy when it led to "good government," but if the majority was wrong, in their view, progressives handed power to unelected managers. The basic structure of American government and economy, they felt, should not be open to political debate.

More than anything else, progressives shared an urgency. "There are two kinds of people," Alice Hamilton learned from her mother, "the ones who say, 'Someone ought to do something about it but why should it be I?' and the ones who say, 'Somebody must do something about it, then why not I?' "Hamilton and other progressives never doubted that they were the second kind.

> I've come here to write the Uncle Tom's Cabin of the labor movement.
>
> UPTON SINCLAIR,
> Chicago, 1904

Social Workers and Muckrakers

Among the first to hear the call to service were the young women and men who volunteered to live among the urban poor in "settlement houses." Stanton Coit established the first on New York's Lower East Side in 1886, but the most famous was Hull-House, which opened in Chicago three years later. Its founders, Jane Addams and Ellen Starr, bought a run-down mansion at the center of an inner-city ward thick with sweatshops, factories, and overcrowded tenements. The women of Hull-House opened a kindergarten and a clinic, took sweatshop bosses to court, investigated corrupt landlords, criticized the ward's powerful alderman, and built the first public playground in Chicago.

Addams drew together at Hull-House a remarkable group of women with similar backgrounds. Florence Kelley organized a movement for occupational safety laws. Julia Lathrop headed the state's Children's Bureau. All three women were raised in affluent Quaker homes during or shortly after the Civil War, and their parents were all abolitionists. Like Alice Hamilton, all three attended college and afterward traveled or studied in Europe.

The Hull-House Choir in Recital, 1910 Chicago, according to Lincoln Steffens, was "loud, lawless, unlovely, ill-smelling, new; an overgrown gawk of a village." Addams and other settlement workers sought to tame this urban wilderness through culture and activism.

As the fame of Hull-House spread, women (and some men) organized settlement houses in cities across the country. By the turn of the century there were more than 100, and by 1910 more than 400. Reformers often began by using social science techniques to survey the surrounding neighborhoods, gathering information on the national origins, income, housing conditions, and occupations of the local people. Addams released *Hull-House Maps and Papers*, a survey of the 19th Ward, in 1895. One of the Progressive Era's most ambitious research projects was the Pittsburgh Survey, a massive investigation of living and working conditions in the steel city published in six volumes between 1909 and 1914. Survey data confirmed that the causes of poverty were social, not personal, contradicting a common belief that the poor had only themselves to blame. Settlements did "social work" rather than charity.

Surveys re-created a social world with statistics accompanied by maps, photographs, and in some cases three-dimensional models. In 1900, housing reformers in New York exhibited a scale cutaway model of a tenement block, allowing visitors to see from a bird's-eye perspective how overcrowding, the arrangement of rooms, and the size of air shafts contributed to disease and crime. Shelby Harrison, director of surveys for the Russell Sage Foundation, explained that the survey itself was reform. It relied "upon the correcting power of facts . . . plus such a telling of facts that will make them common knowledge. It is believed to be the American experience that people will act upon facts when they have them."

This statistical outlook motivated settlement workers to attack urban problems across a broad front. "If parks were wanted, if schools needed bettering," Jacob Riis wrote, "there were at the College Settlement, the University Settlement, the Nurses' Settlement, and at a score of other such places, young enthusiasts to collect the facts and urge them, with the prestige of their non-political organization to back them." Social workers labored to make food safe, repair housing, and sponsor festivals and pageants. Working conditions, especially for women and children, drew special attention, but employers, landlords, and city bosses were not the only targets. The "young enthusiasts" attacked working-class vices—gambling, saloons, and brothels. Supporters participated vicariously by reading *The House on Henry Street, The City Wilderness, Twenty Years at Hull-House,* and other popular books written by settlement workers.

The loudest voice of progressivism came from a new type of journalism introduced in 1902. In successive issues, *McClure's* magazine published Lincoln Steffens's investigation of graft in St. Louis, and Ida Tarbell's "History of the Standard Oil Company," sensational exposés that disclosed crimes of the nation's political and economic elite. As periodicals competed for a mass readership, the old partisan style of journalism gave way to crusades, celebrity correspondents, and "sob sister" features. The new ten-cent magazines, like *Everybody's, Cosmopolitan,* and *McClure's,* had national audiences and budgets big enough to pay for careful, in-depth investigations. The result was a type of reporting Theodore Roosevelt disdainfully called "muckraking." Readers loved it, and an article exposing some new corporate or public villainy could easily sell half a million copies.

Muckrakers named names. Upton Sinclair described the grisly business of canning beef. Ray Stannard Baker investigated railroads and segregation. Samuel Hopkins Adams catalogued the damage done by narcotics in popular medicines. Tarbell exposed Standard Oil's methods: camouflaged companies, espionage, sweetheart deals, and predatory pricing. The series ran in 24 straight issues and shattered the

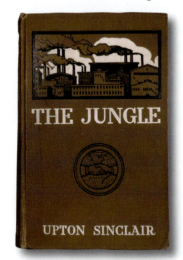

notion that industrial giants competed in a free market. Amid a national outcry, the Justice Department sued Standard Oil in 1906 for conspiracy to restrain trade.

The ten-cent magazines projected local problems onto a national canvas. Newspapers had covered municipal corruption before, but Steffens's series in *McClure's* revealed that bribery, influence peddling, and protection rackets operated in nearly every major city, and for the same reason: an insidious alliance between city officials and local monopolies. Magazines also carried news of progressive victories, allowing solutions adopted in Toledo or Milwaukee to spread quickly. Muckraking declined after 1912, the victim of corporate advertising boycotts and declining readership, but while it lasted, "public opinion" became a force that could shake politicians and powerful corporations.

Dictatorship of the Experts

For doctors, lawyers, and engineers, reform offered a chance to apply their skills to urgent problems. Not accidentally, the Progressive Era coincided with the rise in influence of the social sciences and the professions. Experts could mediate potentially violent conflicts between rival interests and eliminate the uncertainties of democracy. Scientific advances seemed to justify this faith. In just a generation, antiseptic

>> The Calorie

Just after breakfast on March 23, 1896, Professor Wilbur Atwater sealed a student in an airtight chamber in the basement of Wesleyan University's Judd Hall. The apparatus was described by the press as resembling a meat locker, a single room lined with copper and zinc. Atwater carefully recorded the change in temperature inside the cell while the student, A. W. Smith, rested, lifted weights, and ate measured portions of bread, baked beans, hamburger, milk, and potatoes. The device was a calorimeter, a tool previously used to measure the efficiency of engines and explosives.

The national press was riveted by the story of the "prisoner of science," but the results were even more startling. Atwater proved a theory European scientists had advanced 50 years earlier, that the human body had the thermodynamic properties of a machine. Both its intake— food—and its output—physical or mental exertion—could be measured in uniform units called calories. The discovery had immense military and industrial implications, allowing rations and wages to be calculated for maximum energy-producing efficiency. Congress voted funds to build a calorimeter in Washington, and government scientists compiled charts that proved another fact scientists had thought highly unlikely: all people, regardless of climate or race, need exactly the same number of calories to thrive. When it came to food, all men were created equal, after all.

Before the calorie, it was no more possible to measure appetite than to measure beauty or intelligence. Eating habits varied widely among cultures and individuals, and dietary knowledge was closer to a religion than a science. The calorie opened the way for the systematic study of nutrition. The discovery of vitamins in 1914 brought the machine theory of the body into question, but the calorie remained the only universal gauge of food consumption.

World War I provided the first practical applications. After Germany's invasion of Belgium in 1914 devastated the neutral country, a wealthy mining engineer, Herbert Hoover, organized American charities to prevent famine. The Belgium Relief used the calorie to ration food supplies, and soon Europeans learned to count what they ate by American numbers. When the United States entered the war, Hoover mobilized the country's food supply to feed the Allied armies. He particularly prized wheat, "the largest supply of calories available" for the war effort. American families were told how to count calories and save wheat by cleaning their plates and avoiding "overeating." Restaurants helpfully listed calorie counts on the menu.

In the wake of victory in 1918, Europe's ports opened to American relief shipments, and Hoover's organization commanded the food supply from central Europe as far east as Moscow. The calorie briefly even became a unit of currency. Immigrants could send a check from New York to their relatives in Poland or Lithuania to be cashed at food banks for a fixed number of calories. The newly formed League of Nations discussed using the calorie to rationalize the world's food supply, perhaps eliminating famines permanently.

Food *is* Ammunition—
Don't waste it.

UNITED STATES FOOD ADMINISTRATION

Calorie consciousness revolutionized global cuisine in the interwar years. The discovery that Japanese sailors could eat just as much as their British counterparts prompted the Imperial Navy to provision its ships with high-calorie pork and chicken dipped in batter (tempura). These new recipes, popularized as the national cuisine, became what we know today as Japanese food. Greek and Mexican cookbook writers added flour to increase calorie counts. But while nationalists used calories to assert entitlement to a full plate, newspapers around the world urged women to count calories to stay thin. The calorie measured the food needs of whole populations, rather than individuals, but despite doctors' warnings, "dieting" became a global fad.

To many people, quantification took all the pleasure out of eating. Dutch historian Johan Huizinga saw the calorie as a peculiarly American "Taylorism of the mind."

continued

Indian nationalist leader Mahatma Gandhi rejected the calorie as yet another imperial ploy to control the world's hungry masses, this time through science. Insisting that each body had its own needs and each food its own spiritual value, he made hunger and self-denial into weapons in the independence struggle.

Nutrition came to be seen as a solution to economic and political problems. A 1936 League of Nations report proposed that the global agricultural depression could be solved if surplus calories in the industrial countries could be exported to countries, such as China, with caloric deficits. The proposal led in 1942 to the creation of the Food and Agriculture Organization, the first component of the United Nations system. The United States fought World War II, President Franklin D. Roosevelt proclaimed, to guarantee "freedom from want."

Since ancient times, communities and nations have always kept a close eye on food supplies, but the calorie made food and nutrition an international concern. It implied that humanity had a single appetite, and that those who had food had obligations to those who did not, even if they were on opposite sides of the world. Back in the twentieth century, many a child who refused to eat his asparagus got a stern reminder of that duty. ●

techniques, X-rays, and new drugs generated a whole new understanding of disease. Electric light, recorded sound, motion pictures, radio, and flight confirmed science's ability to shape the future.

Social workers copied doctors, diagnosing each case with clinical impartiality and relying on tests and individual histories. Newly professionalized police forces applied the techniques of fingerprinting, handwriting analysis, and psychology to law enforcement. Dietitians descended on school cafeterias, banishing pierogies and souvlaki and replacing them with bland but nutritionally balanced meals. Reformers tried (but failed) to simplify spelling and bring "efficiency" to the English language.

Trust in science sometimes led to extreme measures. One was the practice of eugenics, an attempt to rid society of alcoholism, poverty, and crime through selective breeding. "We know enough about eugenics so that if the knowledge were applied, the defective classes would disappear within a generation," the president of the University of Wisconsin predicted. Persuaded that genetics could save the state money in the long run, the Indiana legislature passed a law in 1907 authorizing the forced sterilization of "criminals, idiots, rapists, and imbeciles." Patients with epilepsy, psychiatric disorders, or mental handicaps who sought help at state hospitals were surgically sterilized. Criminals received the same treatment. Seven other states also adopted the "Indiana Plan."

Behind the emphasis on expertise lay a thinly veiled distrust of democracy. Education was one example. Professional educators took control of the schools away from local boards and gave it to expert administrators and superintendents. They certified teachers and classified students based on "scientific" intelligence tests. To reformers, education was far too important to be left to amateurs, like teachers, parents, or voters.

Progressivism created new social sciences and made universities into centers of advocacy. Sociology was a product of the progressive impulse. The study of government became political science, and "scientific" historians searched the past for answers to modern problems. John R. Commons, Richard Ely, and Thorstein Veblen escaped from the old debates over classical theory and used economics to study how modern institutions developed and functioned. Legal scholars like Louis Brandeis and Roscoe Pound called for revising the law to reflect social realities.

This stress on expertise made Progressive-Era reforms different from those of the Gilded Age and earlier. Instead of trying to gain success at a single stroke—by passing a law or trouncing a corrupt politician—progressives believed in process. When they could, progressives set up permanent organizations and procedures that would keep the pressure on and make progress a habit.

Progressives on the Color Line

In her international crusade against lynching, Ida B. Wells-Barnett pioneered some of the progressive tactics of research, exposure, and organization. A schoolteacher in Memphis, Wells-Barnett documented mob violence against African Americans and mobilized opinion in the United States and Britain. Cities that condoned extralegal executions soon faced a barrage of condemnation from church groups and women's clubs. As her Afro-American Council took on national and then international scope, she joined forces with white suffragists, social workers, and journalists, but her cause fell outside of the progressive mainstream. Many reform groups sympathized with white southerners or wanted to avoid dividing their membership over race.

Reformers debated as to how much progress non-Anglo-Saxons were capable of, but they were inclined to be pessimistic. Eugenics gave white supremacy the endorsement of science. A new technology, the motion picture, showed its power to rewrite history from a racial viewpoint in D. W. Griffith's classic *Birth of a Nation* (1915), which romanticized the Klan's campaign of terror during Reconstruction. Policy was often based on assumptions about the capabilities of various races. Trade schools, not universities, were deemed appropriate for educating Filipinos and Hawaiians. Progressives took Native American children from their families and placed them in boarding schools. Electoral reform in Texas meant disfranchising Spanish-speaking voters.

Wells-Barnett was not alone in finding doors through this wall of racial ideology. William Edward Burghardt DuBois documented the costs of racism in *The Philadelphia Negro* (1898). The survey spoke the progressives' language, insisting that discrimination was not just morally wrong but inefficient, since it took away work and encouraged alcoholism and crime. DuBois transformed the politics of race as profoundly as Addams transformed the politics of cities.

Raised in Massachusetts, DuBois learned Latin and Greek in public schools. At 17, he went to Fisk University in Tennessee, where he "came in contact for the first time with a sort of violence that I had never realized in New England." He also had his first encounter with African American religion and gospel music. The songs he heard in church were "full of the voices of the past." DuBois later studied at Harvard and Berlin.

Ida B. Wells-Barnett with Her Children Ida Wells-Barnett, journalist and activist, made lynching an international issue through her writing and speaking tours.

DuBois and Booker T. Washington came to espouse opposing visions of African Americans' place in the United States. Both emphasized the importance of thrift and hard work. DuBois, however, rejected Washington's willingness to accept legal inequality. Gradually, DuBois came to believe that the Atlanta Compromise (see Chapter 20) led only to disfranchisement and segregation. He disliked the way Washington's influence with white philanthropists silenced other voices. Five years after the Atlanta speech he opened a sustained attack on Washington's "Tuskegee Machine."

In *The Souls of Black Folk* (1903), DuBois argued that the strategy of accommodation contained a "triple paradox": Washington had urged African Americans to seek industrial training, build self-respect, and become successful in business, while asking them to stop striving for higher education, civil rights, or political power. How could a people train themselves without higher education or gain self-respect without having any of the rights other Americans enjoyed? How could African Americans succeed in business without having the political power to protect themselves or their property? Economic, political, and educational progress had to move together. Like other progressives, DuBois insisted on the importance of process and organization. African Americans could not stop demanding the vote, equality, or education.

In July 1905, DuBois and 28 prominent African American leaders met on the Canadian side of Niagara Falls (no hotel on the U.S. side would admit them) to organize a campaign against racial violence, segregation, and disfranchisement. The Niagara Movement was one of several such organizations. In 1909, Wells-Barnett, Addams, and other reformers created the National Association for the Advancement of Colored People to carry on the fight in the courts. In 1915 the NAACP won a Supreme Court decision outlawing the grandfather clause, which denied the vote to descendants of slaves, but another 40 years passed before it succeeded in overturning *Plessy v. Ferguson*.

Progressives in State and Local Politics

Progressives were of two minds about the public. Walter Lippmann, a journalist and reformer, could write fondly of "the voiceless multitudes," and contemptuously of the "great dull mass of people who just don't care." Progressives' tactics betrayed this split

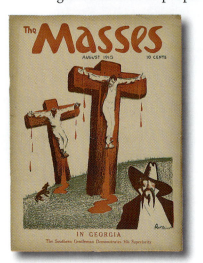

vision. To bring the cities under control, they made city government less democratic and more "businesslike." Reforms at the state level, however, expanded voters' power to initiate legislation and remove corrupt officeholders. In both cases, the changes enlarged the influence of the small-town and urban-middle-class reform constituency while reducing that of immigrants and the working class.

Redesigning the City

The machine politicians who ran American cities proved remarkably adaptable to changing conditions. To immigrants and factory workers, the local boss was one of the few people looking out for the average person. He rushed to fire scenes to aid homeless victims. He distributed turkeys in poor neighborhoods at Christmas. When a family member was jailed or thrown out of work, the machine politician stood ready to post bail or find a job. Jane Addams acknowledged that for popularity, she could not compete with Johnny Powers, the local ward boss, this "big manifestation of human friendliness, this stalking survival of village kindness."

Powers and other aldermen sheltered the brothels, saloons, and gambling dens that, in Addams's view, exploited honest workers. Hull-House organized to beat Powers in 1895, and in reacting to defeat the reformers revealed their frustrations with democracy. The reformers nominated an Irish bricklayer, William Gleeson, on the assumption that the 19th Ward's working-class voters would prefer a candidate of their own status. But voters said they wanted someone grander to represent them, and Powers, with his big house and diamond buttons, seemed just the type. Gleeson was thoroughly trounced. Addams was "puzzled, then astounded and indignant" at the outcome.

With officials like Powers in charge, corporations could do what they liked, so long as they padded the right wallets. "If you want to get anything out of the council," the

> Four years ago, the city of Galveston was almost wiped from the face of the earth. . . . Today, Galveston is practically a new city, with more advantages than were enjoyed in the days before the storm, a more economical administration, and a better financial showing than has ever been known in the history of the city.
>
> *WASHINGTON POST,*
> June 10, 1904

"Annual Parade of the Cable-Trolley Cripple Club," from *The Verdict,* **March 20, 1899** Injuries caused by privately run utilities led to demands for public supervision of essential services.

head of the Chicago Chamber of Commerce advised, "the quickest way is to pay for it—not to the city, but to the aldermen." City machines lost their appeal not by providing too few services, but too many. As tax burdens grew, wealthier voters clamored for reform. Progressives set out to replace paternalism with efficient, scientific administration.

After the depression of 1893, scores of associations sprang up to criticize municipal government. The structure of many cities resembled the federal system in miniature. A mayor, elected by the whole city, presided over a council of representatives from each neighborhood, or ward. This system diluted the influence of the "better classes" and allowed a few powerful wards to rule the city. In 1899 Louisville's Conference for Good City Government proposed a new model, later known as the "strong mayor" system. It gave more power to the mayor and required each council member to represent the whole city. Two years later, after a hurricane and tidal wave destroyed Galveston, Texas, the devastated city experimented with an even bolder plan. The recovery would be managed by a commission of five elected officials, each of whom managed a city department. Des Moines, Iowa, copied and improved on Galveston's design, and by 1911 some 160 cities had commission governments.

The commission resembled a corporate board of directors. Professionalism and accountability, the skills that made for business success, could make a city run, too. This philosophy led Detroit voters to elect Ford Motor Company's chief efficiency expert, James Couzens, as mayor. Other cities, led by Dayton, Ohio, tried to improve on the city-commission plan by placing local government in the hands of an unelected "city manager."

Middle- and upper-class professionals led this revolution in city government, and they gained the most from it. The new city officials could explain where tax money was spent, and they responded to criticisms from leading citizens and newspapers, but there were no turkeys at Christmas. Getting a job or help from the city meant filling out the proper forms. Reform administrations targeted urban "vice," which included the whole range of working-class recreations. Voters also learned that businesslike efficiency did not lower taxes. Budgets continued to grow along with the public's demand for services.

Reform Mayors and City Services

While commissioners rewrote the rules, a new breed of reform mayors cleaned up their cities. Samuel "Golden Rule" Jones, a Welsh immigrant who earned a fortune in the Pennsylvania oilfields, won election three times as independent mayor of Toledo. He enacted the eight-hour day for city employees, pushed for public ownership of city utilities, and staged free concerts in the parks. Like Tom Johnson in Cleveland and Hazen Pingree in Detroit, Jones worried less about inefficiency and saloons and more about utilities. Milwaukee, Schenectady, and other cities bought or regulated the private monopolies that supplied lighting, garbage removal, water, and streetcars.

Figure 21-2   Percentage of the Population Living in Cities, 1890–1920 Cities and towns underwent dramatic growth around the turn of the century. Offices, department stores, and new forms of mass entertainment—from vaudeville to professional sports—drew people to the city center. Railroads and trolleys allowed cities to spread outward, segregating residents by class. *Kennedy,* Rise and Fall of the Great Powers, *p. 200.*

The reform mayor's efforts to humanize the urban environment were supported by architects and engineers who endeavored to improve urban life through the arrangement of public space. A City Beautiful movement sought to soften the urban landscape with vistas, open spaces, and greenery. The District of Columbia, with its commission government, broad avenues, and parks adjacent to federal buildings, furnished a model of city planning, and Congress sought to make it a model of municipal reform as well by introducing a model child-labor law, slum-clearance plan, and school system, but representatives from the industrial North and the segregated South found it easier to agree on parks and monuments than on social legislation. Spatial arrangement performed social and educational functions indirectly. Well-ordered scenes were designed to Americanize and uplift immigrant city dwellers. New York enacted zoning laws in 1916, and "city planners" joined the ranks of specialists by organizing themselves as a profession.

Progressivism and the States

Reform at the state level varied by region. The East mimicked the tactics and agenda of urban reform. New York's progressive governor, Charles Evans Hughes, passed laws prohibiting gambling and creating a state commission to regulate utilities. In southern states, progressivism often meant refining the techniques of segregation and disfranchisement, freeing white voters to disagree among themselves about schools or crime. Lynching and mob assaults on African Americans were weekly occurrences in the Progressive Era. White leaders justified segregation and violence in terms used to justify urban reform in the North: the "better classes" had an obligation to rein in the excesses of democracy.

States in the West and Midwest produced the boldest experiments. Oregon introduced the secret ballot, voter registration, and three measures originally proposed by the Populists: the initiative, recall, and referendum. The initiative allowed voters to place legislation on the ballot by petition; the referendum let the legislature put proposals on the ballot; and the recall gave voters the chance to remove officials from office before the end of their terms. In his inaugural address as governor of New Jersey, Woodrow Wilson observed that Oregon had brought "government back to the people and protect[ed] it from the control of the representatives of selfish and special interests." Other states soon adopted all or part of the "Oregon system."

The best known of the progressive governors was Robert M. "Fighting Bob" La Follette, whose model of state government came to be known as the "Wisconsin Idea." Elected governor in 1900, La Follette pushed through a comprehensive program of social legislation. Railway and public-utility commissions placed the state's largest corporations under public control. A tax commission designed a "scientific" distribution of the tax burden, including an income tax. Other commissions regulated hours and working conditions and protected the environment. Wisconsin also implemented the direct primary, which allowed party nominees to be chosen directly by the voters rather than by party caucuses.

Few machine politicians had as much personal power as the reform governors did. Wisconsin papers reserved the term "demagogue" for La Follette, but the demagogic reform governors dispelled much of the public's cynicism and brought policy making out of the "smoke-filled rooms." By shaking up city halls and statehouses, progressives made government more responsive to demands for reform, but they

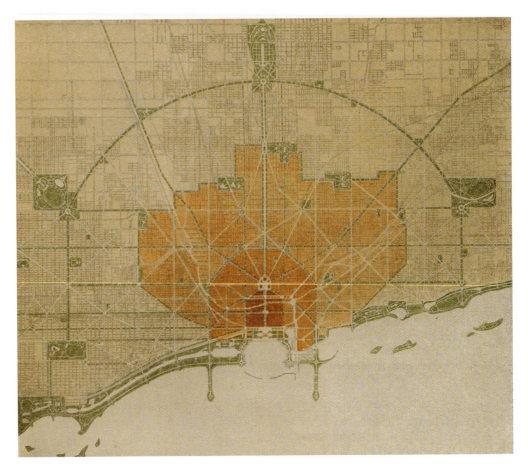

Daniel Burnham's City Plan for Chicago, 1909 Through comprehensive planning, Burnham sought to save cities from "the chaos incident to rapid growth." He drafted designs for Washington, Cleveland, San Francisco, and Manila.

knew that social problems did not respect city and state boundaries. National corporations and nationwide problems had to be attacked at the federal level, and that meant capturing the White House.

The President Becomes "The Administration"

If Theodore Roosevelt stood at the center of the two great movements of his age, imperialism and progressivism, it was because he prepared himself for the part. The Roosevelt family was one of the oldest in New York and wealthy enough to afford comfort, but Theodore embarked instead on a series of pursuits that were unusual for a man of his class. After graduating from Harvard in 1880, he married, started law school, wrote a history of the War of 1812 (he would write four other works, including the four-volume *Winning of the West*), bought a cattle ranch in the Dakota Territory, and, most surprisingly, ran for the state legislature.

Roosevelt's political bid stunned his family and friends, who believed government was no place for gentlemen. Roosevelt himself described his colleagues as "a stupid, sodden, vicious lot, most of them being equally deficient in brains and virtue." Avoiding the "rough and tumble," he argued, only conceded high offices to those less fit to lead. Albany's politicos hardly knew what to make of the young swell who appeared at the capitol wearing a monocle and carrying "a gold-headed cane in one hand and a silk hat in the other." Roosevelt's flair for publicity got him noticed, and in 1886 the Republican Party nominated him for mayor of New York. He finished a poor third, behind the Tammany nominee and the Socialist candidate.

A turn as head of New York's board of police commissioners from 1895 to 1897 deepened Roosevelt's commitment to reform. The commission supervised an army of 38,000 policemen. Muckraking journalists Lincoln Steffens and Jacob Riis showed Roosevelt the dismal tenement neighborhoods that housed Irish and Italian immigrants. Roosevelt's crackdown on saloons and corruption in the police department earned him a reputation as a man who would not be intimidated, even by his own party's bosses, and when McKinley captured the presidency he named Roosevelt assistant secretary of the navy. The Spanish-American War catapulted him to national fame, and in quick succession he became governor of New York, vice president, and then president of the United States.

Roosevelt believed that to restore democracy—"genuine democracy"—America needed a mission. "We must have a genuine and permanent moral awakening without which no wisdom of legislation or administration really means anything." He spoke more often about the responsibilities, duties, and character of citizens than about their choices. In the White House, he set out to find great tasks—principles to be upheld, isthmuses to be cut, and lands to be conserved—that inspired a spirit of common purpose and tested the national will. In the process, he rewrote the president's job description, seizing new powers for the executive branch and turning the presidency into "the administration."

> **Theodore Roosevelt began the work of turning the American mind in the direction which it had to go in the Twentieth Century.**
>
> WALTER LIPPMANN

The Executive Branch Against the Trusts

Roosevelt approached politics the way Addams approached poverty, studying it, living in its midst, and carefully choosing his battles. His fear of radicalism was borne out in September 1901. President William McKinley was shaking hands at the Pan American Exposition in Buffalo, New York, when a man thrust a pistol into his chest and fired twice. The assassin, Leon Czolgosz, came from the Cleveland slums and claimed to seek vengeance for the poor.

Roosevelt entered the White House at the age of 42, the youngest man to attain the presidency. He was the first president to call himself a progressive, and the first, according to Lippmann, "who realized clearly that national stability and social justice had to be sought deliberately and had consciously to be maintained," and that "the promise of American life could be realized only by a national effort."

Unsatisfied to be merely the standard-bearer of his party, he set out to remake the executive as the preeminent branch of government, the initiator of legislation, molder of public opinion, and guardian of the national interest at home and abroad. "I believe in a strong executive," he explained, "I believe in power." Instead of asking Congress for legislation, he drafted bills and lobbied for them personally. He believed federal administrators should intervene in the economy to protect citizens or to save business from its own short-sightedness. McKinley had already decided action against the trusts was necessary, but his plans were not as bold as his successor's.

Challenging the corporations would be no easy task. Roosevelt took office less than a decade after J. P. Morgan rescued the federal Treasury. In an 1895 decision, the Supreme Court gutted the Sherman Act, one of the few laws that allowed federal action against monopolies. The underfunded Interstate Commerce Commission possessed only theoretical powers. Roosevelt admitted to Congress that "publicity is the only sure remedy which we can now invoke." He used it to the limit. Wall Street took notice when in his first inaugural he asserted that trusts "are creatures of the State, and the State not only has the right to control them, but it is duty bound to control them." In 1903 Roosevelt established a Department of Commerce and Labor that required annual reports, making corporate activities transparent.

The Justice Department revitalized the Sherman Act with vigorous prosecutions of the worst offenders. To send a message to Wall Street, Roosevelt selected cases for maximum publicity value. Attorney General Philander Knox filed suit against J. P. Morgan's holding company, Northern Securities. Morgan expected that the matter could be settled in the usual way, and his attorney asked how they might "fix it up." "We don't want to fix it up," Knox replied. "We want to stop it." When the Court handed Roosevelt a victory in 1904, Americans cheered.

With this case, Roosevelt gained an undeserved reputation as a "trust buster." Although he opposed serious abuses, he distinguished between good and bad trusts, and believed government should encourage responsible corporations to grow. His thinking mirrored that of progressive writers like Herbert Croly, editor of *The New Republic*, who imagined a professionalized, central government staffed by nonpartisan experts who would monitor the activities of big corporations to assure efficiency and head off destructive actions.

Not all progressives agreed. Louis Brandeis and Woodrow Wilson envisioned a political economy of small, highly competitive firms kept in line by regular applications of the Sherman Act. To Roosevelt, there was no going back to an economy of small businesses. Only large combinations could compete on a world scale. It was government's obligation not to break them up but to regulate them. He secured passage of the Hepburn Act (1906), which allowed the commission to set freight rates and banned "sweetheart" deals (of the kind Standard Oil enjoyed) between carriers and favored clients. The Elkins Act (1910) regulated telephone, telegraph, and cable communications. The Pure Food and Drug Act (1906) responded to Upton Sinclair's stomach-turning exposé of the meatpacking industry by making it a crime to ship or sell contaminated or fraudulently labeled food and drugs. Under Roosevelt, the federal government gained the tools to counterbalance the power of business. It grew to match its responsibilities. The number of federal employees almost doubled between 1900 and 1916.

The Square Deal

Roosevelt's exasperation with big business reached a peak during the coal strike of 1902. The United Mine Workers represented 150,000 miners in the coalfields of eastern Pennsylvania. The miners, mostly Polish, Hungarian, and Italian immigrants, earned less than $6 a week, and over 400 died yearly to supply the coal to run railroads and heat homes. Seventy percent of the mines were owned by six railroads, which in turn fell under the control of the usual financiers—Morgan and Rockefeller, among others. The owners refused to deal with the union, declaring it a band of outlaws. When the miners struck in May 1902, they had the public's sympathy. Editorials, even in Republican newspapers, urged the president to take the mines away from the owners.

The "gross blindness of the operators" infuriated Roosevelt. Coal was the only fuel for heating, and a strike might cause hundreds to freeze. After failing to get the sides to negotiate, he invited union officials and the operators to Washington so that he could personally arbitrate. John Mitchell, head of the mine workers, eagerly accepted the president's offer, but the owners flatly refused.

For Roosevelt this was the final straw. He drew up plans for the army to move into the coalfields and place the mines under government control. The owners capitulated, agreeing to submit the dispute to a federal commission. The result was a compromise: miners received a 10 percent increase in pay and a nine-hour workday, but owners did not have to recognize the union.

Roosevelt's direct action made the federal government a third force in labor disputes. For the first time a strike was settled by federal arbitration, and for the first time a union had struck against a strategic industry without being denounced as a revolutionary conspiracy. The government would no longer automatically side with the corporations. Instead, Roosevelt offered an understanding: "We demand that big business give the people a square deal; in return, we must insist that when anyone engaged in big business honestly endeavors to do right, he shall be given a square deal."

Theodore Roosevelt Theodore Roosevelt ran in 1912 at the head of a new Progressive Party ticket. His candidacy split the Republicans, allowing Wilson to gain a plurality.

Conserving Water, Land, and Forests

When Roosevelt felt important issues were at stake, he seldom accepted the limits of his office. He enraged Congress by stretching the definitions of presidential power, nowhere more so than in the area of conservation. When Congress sent him a bill to halt the creation of new national forests in the West, Roosevelt first created or enlarged 32 national forests then signed the bill. To stop private companies from damming rivers, he reserved 2,500 of the best hydropower sites by declaring them "ranger stations." The energy behind his program came from Gifford Pinchot, the chief forester of the United States, who saw conservation as a new frontier. Unsettled, undeveloped lands were growing scarce, and Pinchot convinced the president that hope for the future lay in using the available resources more efficiently. Forests, deserts, and ore ranges were to be used, but wisely, scientifically, and in the national interest.

One of the first victories for the new policy of resource management was the Newlands Reclamation Act (1902), which gave the Agriculture Department authority to build reservoirs and irrigation systems in the West. In the next four years, 3 million acres were "reclaimed" from the desert and turned into farms. To prevent waste, Roosevelt put tighter controls on prospecting, grazing, and logging. Big lumber and mining companies had few complaints about rationalized resource administration, but small-scale prospectors and ranchers found themselves shut out of federal lands. Naturalists, like John Muir (see feature), also resisted, pointing out that nature was to be appreciated, not used.

By 1909, conservation had become a national issue. Hikers, sightseers, and tourism entrepreneurs drawn to the new parks and forest reserves were forming a powerful constituency. By quadrupling the acreage in federal reserves, professionalizing the forest service, and using his "bully pulpit" to build support for conservation, Roosevelt helped create the modern environmental movement.

TR and Big Stick Diplomacy

Imperial and commercial expansion put new strains on foreign and military policy after the turn of the century. U.S. investors wanted Washington to use its leverage to protect their overseas factories and railroads against civil wars and hostile governments. Diplomatic and military budgets grew to meet these demands. The diplomatic corps replaced political cronies with trained professionals. Commercial attachés issued reports on foreign business conditions. Conducting foreign relations was no longer a matter of weathering "incidents" but of making policy.

Roosevelt's view of world affairs flowed from his understanding of the past and the future. Global trade and communications, he believed, united "civilized" nations. His foreign policy aimed to keep the United States in the mainstream of historical processes such as commerce, imperialism, and military (particularly naval) modernization. He felt a duty to interfere with "barbarian" governments in Asia, Latin America, or Africa that blocked progress. The United States had an obligation, he felt, to overthrow governments and even seize territory when it was acting in the interests of the world as a whole.

Building an interoceanic canal topped Roosevelt's list of foreign-policy priorities. A canal would be a hub of world trade and naval power in the Atlantic and

AN AMERICAN LANDSCAPE

>> The Hetch Hetchy Valley

When landscape painter Albert Bierstadt visited in 1875, he saw a panorama of waterfalls. The canyon walls towered 2,500 feet above a wide, forested meadow populated by herds of elk. Twenty-five years later, San Francisco's mayor James Phelan beheld the perpendicular cliffs and the pure glacier water tumbling into the Tuolumne River and saw his city's answer to the problems of "monopoly and microbes."

The Hetch Hetchy Valley hypnotized naturalists and hydraulic engineers equally because of its magnificence and its location. It was only 152 miles from San Francisco, close enough to lure visitors or, alternatively, to channel its waters to the city. A village of less than a thousand in 1848, the City by the Bay was by 1900 the nation's ninth largest, with 340,000 people. Only water kept it from growing larger.

Hemmed in by ocean on three sides, San Francisco faced a chronic scarcity of water. As the Gold Rush swelled the population, farsighted entrepreneurs bought up all available water supplies and formed the Spring Valley Water Company, which held a monopoly on the city's water for 60 years. Water tycoons supported the city's political machine, led by "Boss" Abe Ruef. The company's water was neither cheap nor safe, a liability demonstrated by occasional outbreaks of cholera and typhus.

When voters elected Phelan at the head of a reform ticket in 1897, they expected him to do something about water. What the Republican mayor wanted to do was to dam the Hetch Hetchy and build an aqueduct across the Central Valley, thus breaking the monopoly and making water an abundant, safe public utility.

Local and national obstacles stood in the way. The city's board of superintendents, controlled by Ruef, sided with Spring Valley and thwarted efforts to build a city reservoir. But it was even harder to get permission from the federal government. Hetch Hetchy was located in Yosemite National Park, one of the first nature preserves, created in 1890 to save its peaks

and waterfalls from wanton destruction. The parks system itself was new, and the philosophy of conservation—how to preserve natural resources, and for what purposes—was evolving rapidly. Phelan found an ally in Gifford Pinchot, who filled the newly created office of chief forester.

continued

Albert Bierstadt, *Hetch Hetchy Canyon* (1875)

Pinchot's father had made millions in the lumber trade, and Gifford studied scientific forestry in France, where timber was seen as a crucial strategic and economic resource. The job of forestry was "to grow trees as a crop," he argued, and the two principal threats to any resource were inefficient use and monopoly control. On this point he and Phelan saw eye to eye. The few hikers who might enjoy Hetch Hetchy's magnificence were clearly less important than the need "to supply pure water to a great center of population."

Natural and political disasters worked to Phelan's advantage. After the great 1906 earthquake and fire destroyed San Francisco's downtown and vividly demonstrated the need for a water supply, Congress passed a waiver allowing the city to apply to use part of Yosemite's land. The following year, a lurid scandal led to a bribery conviction for Ruef and disgrace for his followers. But just as the way seemed clear, an outpouring of petitions and letters urged the secretary of the interior to save the Hetch Hetchy.

The campaign was orchestrated by the 1,000-member Sierra Club and its ascetic founder, John Muir. A wilderness explorer and naturalist, Muir gained a national following through his writings on the transcendent, spiritual aspects of the natural world. "Dam Hetch Hetchy!" he remonstrated. "As well dam for water tanks the people's cathedrals and churches." Historians have characterized the debate between Muir and Pinchot as a contest between rival concepts of environmentalism—conservation for use versus preservation for nature's sake—but the two men also represented opposing interpretations of democracy and the dangers it faced in the modern world.

"Conservation is the most democratic movement this country has known for generations," Pinchot believed. The Hetch Hetchy project would replace unbridled corporate power with management of natural resources for the public good.

Democratic values were scientific values: efficiency, expertise, and "the greatest good, for the greatest number, for the longest time." For Muir, nature was a refuge where democratic values could survive amid the "gobble gobble" culture of self-interest and scientific progress. The valley had to be preserved not just to save the trees, but to "save humans for the wilderness." Only there could people share the nonmaterial values in which democracy took root.

Because people were essential to their vision of the valley, the Sierra Club did not advocate leaving the area pristine. They imagined roads and hotels, managed by the park service, that would make Hetch Hetchy a weekend retreat for harried city dwellers. The public outcry threw dam advocates off balance, but eventually they were able to cast the "nature lovers" as unwitting tools of the water and power monopolies.

The Roosevelt administration wavered, but in 1913, Phelan got his dam. Muir died a year later. Today the Hetch Hetchy aqueduct delivers 300 million gallons of water a day to San Francisco. But the battle for the valley gave birth to a modern environmental movement. When municipal and mining interests encroached on the Yosemite and Yellowstone preserves in the following decades, they were opposed by a national constituency that saw both activism and wilderness as national legacies. ●

Pacific, and Roosevelt aimed to prevent French or British engineers from building it. He negotiated a deal to buy out a failed French venture in the Colombian province of Panama.

A civil war in Colombia complicated his plans. In 1902 American diplomats brokered a peace between modernizers led by José Marroquín and traditionalists who wanted to isolate the country from outside influences. The fundamentalists fiercely opposed the canal, which would thrust Colombia into the crossroads of world trade. Marroquín favored it, but he knew war would erupt again unless the Americans gave Bogotá full control over the canal. For Roosevelt, control was not negotiable.

In the spring of 1903 Panamanian senators, upset by the rejection of the U.S. offer, began conspiring to secede. Panama had had revolutions before, but the United States had always stepped in to preserve Colombia's sovereignty. Together with Philippe

Map 21–1   Growth of Public Lands Responding to a national conservation movement, Roosevelt set aside public lands for use as parks and managed-yield forests. The National Park Service was founded in 1916.

Bunau-Varilla, who represented shareholders in the French company, the Panamanians lobbied U.S. officials to support their plot. Bunau-Varilla predicted a revolution for November 3, thereby assuring that the rebels, the Colombian army (which had been bribed into surrendering), and U.S. warships would all be on hand.

The revolution went off without a hitch, and Roosevelt presented the new Panamanian government a treaty that gave less and took more than the one offered to Colombia. The president was defensive about his behavior, claiming that he had acted "with the highest, finest, and nicest standards of public and governmental ethics." Congress launched an investigation. "I took the canal and let Congress debate," Roosevelt said, "and while the debate goes on the canal does also." Engineers, led by George W. Goethals, removed a mountain to let water into the isthmus and built another to shore up an artificial lake. Colonel William C. Gorgas defeated malaria and yellow fever, reducing the death rate in Panama to below that of an average American city. The canal, a 50-mile cut built at a cost of $352 million and more than 5,600 lives, opened in 1914.

Once construction was under way, Roosevelt acted to protect the canal from other powers. Poverty in the Caribbean states created opportunities for imperial governments to establish bases on Panama's doorstep. In 1902 Germany came close to invading Venezuela over an unpaid loan, but Roosevelt stepped in to mediate. When the Dominican Republic reneged on its loans two years later, four European nations laid plans for a debt-collecting expedition.

Roosevelt went before Congress in December 1904 and announced a policy later known as the Roosevelt Corollary. It stipulated that when chronic "wrongdoing or impotence" in a Latin American country required "intervention by some civilized nation," the United States would do the intervening. Its language captured the president's worldview. White "civilized" nations acted; nonwhite "impotent" nations were acted upon. The following month the United States took over the Dominican Republic's customs offices and began repaying creditors. The economic intervention turned military in 1916, when the United States landed marines to protect the customs from Dominican rebels. U.S. troops stayed until the early 1920s.

By enforcing order and administrative efficiency in the Caribbean, Roosevelt extended progressivism beyond the borders of the United States; the movement gained footholds in the Far East, too. In 1906 the U.S. federal courts took the unusual step of creating a court outside the United States, in Shanghai, China, to control prostitution in the American community there.

Taft and Dollar Diplomacy

Enormously popular at the end of his second term, Roosevelt chose his friend, William H. Taft, to succeed him. Taft gained national attention as a circuit judge with decisions that enlarged federal power to regulate trusts. As governor general of the Philippines he brought municipal reform to Manila. Taft easily defeated William Jennings Bryan in the 1908 election, and as president he began consolidating Roosevelt's gains. He sent to the states constitutional amendments for the direct election of senators and the income tax. His administration increased antitrust enforcement and levied the first tax on corporations. Satisfied that his legacy would continue, Roosevelt left for a tour of Africa.

In the Caribbean, Taft put the Roosevelt Corollary into action. The United States bought up the debts of Honduras and Nicaragua. Taft persuaded four New York banks to refinance Haiti's debt to prevent German intervention there. Taft intended "dollar diplomacy" to replace force as an instrument of policy, "substituting dollars for bullets," but in most cases, dollars preceded bullets. For Caribbean nations, American protection meant high import taxes. A revolt usually followed. Marines went into Honduras and Nicaragua in 1912. They stayed in Central America until 1933.

Dollar diplomacy also aimed to harness economic power for diplomatic purposes. Shortly after his inauguration, Taft mobilized a consortium to finance China's Chinchow-Aigun railway. Railroads were instruments of power in North China, and Taft felt he could drive a wedge between the imperial powers—Britain, Russia, and Japan—and compel them to resume open-door trade. Instead, they joined forces against the United States and the Open Door. Despite the setback, Taft still believed military force was outmoded and economic power was what mattered.

Taft disappointed both conservatives and progressives in his party. He first urged Congress to reduce the tariff, but then signed the Payne-Aldrich Tariff in 1909,

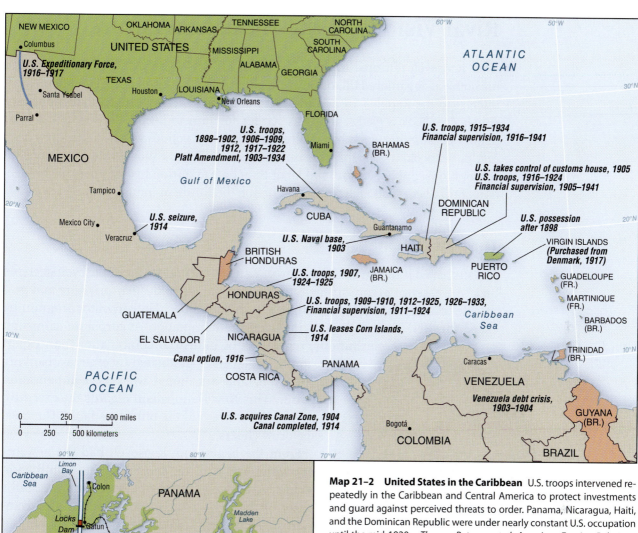

Map 21–2   United States in the Caribbean U.S. troops intervened repeatedly in the Caribbean and Central America to protect investments and guard against perceived threats to order. Panama, Nicaragua, Haiti, and the Dominican Republic were under nearly constant U.S. occupation until the mid-1920s. *Thomas Paterson et al.,* American Foreign Relations *(D.C. Heath, 1995), vol. 2, pp. 55, 40.*

which raised rates on steel, cotton, silk, and other important imports. Taft's secretary of the interior, Richard Ballinger, sided with ranchers and miners who opposed Roosevelt's resource-management policies. When Pinchot fought back, Taft fired him. When the Ballinger-Pinchot affair brought the party's divisions into the open, Roosevelt began to believe his country needed him back.

Rival Visions of the Industrial Future

After Roosevelt returned in 1910, Pinchot, La Follette, Croly, and others trooped to his home at Sagamore Hill to complain about Taft. The former president denied his interest in the Republican nomination, but a friend acknowledged that "no thirsty sinner ever took a pledge that was harder for him to keep." Roosevelt reentered politics because his views had evolved, and because politics was what he knew best. Just 54 years old, his energy was undiminished. He took more radical positions on corporations, public welfare, and labor than he had during his presidency. The election of 1912 became a race that would define the future of industrial America.

The New Nationalism

At a sunbaked junction in Osawatomie, Kansas, in August 1910, Roosevelt declared that "the essence of any struggle for liberty . . . is to destroy privilege and give the life of every individual the highest possible value." He laid out a program he called the New Nationalism. It included the elimination of corporate campaign contributions, regulation of industrial combinations, an expert commission to set tariffs, a graduated income tax, banking reorganization, and a national workers' compensation program. "This New Nationalism regards the executive power as the steward of the public welfare." The message drew cheers.

From the beginning, Roosevelt had the newspapers while Taft had the delegates. The nomination fight tested the new system of direct primaries. Taft's control of the party machinery gave him an advantage in states that chose delegates by convention, but in key states Roosevelt could take his campaign to the voters. When the convention met in Chicago in June 1912, Taft's slim but decisive majority allowed him to control the platform and win over undecided delegates. Grumbling that he had been robbed, Roosevelt walked out.

Roosevelt returned to Chicago in August to accept the nomination of the newly formed Progressive Party. The delegates were a mixed group. They included Hiram Johnson, the reforming governor of California; muckraking publisher Frank Munsey; imperialist senator Albert Beveridge; and J. P. Morgan's business partner George W. Perkins. The party platform endorsed the New Nationalism, along with popular election of senators, popular review of judicial decisions (which would allow the voters to second-guess the courts), and women's suffrage. Women served as delegates, and Jane Addams gave the speech seconding Roosevelt's nomination. The gathering had an evangelical spirit. Roosevelt spoke apocalyptically. "Our cause is based on the eternal principles of righteousness," he said. "We stand at Armageddon and we battle for the Lord."

The 1912 Election

Meanwhile in Baltimore the Democratic convention nominated a former college professor and governor of New Jersey. Like Roosevelt, the young Woodrow Wilson defied his family's expectations by pursuing a political career. He took an unusual route. Obtaining a doctorate in government from Johns Hopkins University in 1886, he published his first book, *Congressional Government,* at the age of 28. It advocated reforming the federal structure by enlarging the power of the executive branch. As a professor and later president of Princeton University, he became a well-known lecturer and commentator for the new national political magazines like *Harper's* and *The Atlantic.* In 1910 he won election as governor of New Jersey and enacted a sweeping program of progressive reforms. For Democrats, smarting from a string of defeats under Bryan's leadership, Wilson offered a new image and the ability to unite the South and the East under a progressive program.

With Roosevelt in the race, Wilson had to stake his own claim to the progressive constituency. With the help of Louis Brandeis, Wilson devised a program called the New Freedom. It challenged Roosevelt on his fundamental approaches to the economy and politics. Simply regulating the trusts, Wilson argued, would not make the economy friendly to consumers, workers, or small entrepreneurs. Instead, it would create a paternalistic bureaucracy. Wilson wanted antitrust laws that would allow a lean but powerful government to return competition and economic mobility to the marketplace. Both men agreed on the importance of a strong executive, but they had different economic formulas. Roosevelt appealed to a collective, national interest, while Wilson stressed the needs of individual consumers and investors. The political philosophy and style of New Nationalism was evangelical, aiming to inspire people to work for the common good. Wilson appealed to reason and self-interest.

On election day, Wilson won fewer votes than Bryan had in any of his races, but the split in the Republican Party gave him a plurality. He won 42 percent of the popular vote, compared to 27 for Roosevelt, 23 for Taft, and 6 for Debs. Although his margin was thin, Wilson could interpret Taft's repudiation and the large combined vote for the progressive candidates as a mandate for change. "What the Democratic Party proposes to do," he told his followers, "is to go into power and do the things the Republican Party has been talking about doing for sixteen years."

The New Freedom

Within a year and a half of his inauguration, Wilson produced one of the most coherent and far-reaching legislative programs ever devised by a president.

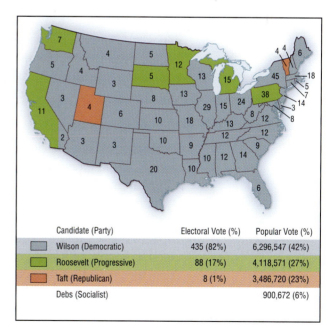

Candidate (Party)	Electoral Vote (%)	Popular Vote (%)
Wilson (Democratic)	435 (82%)	6,296,547 (42%)
Roosevelt (Progressive)	88 (17%)	4,118,571 (27%)
Taft (Republican)	8 (1%)	3,486,720 (23%)
Debs (Socialist)		900,672 (6%)

Map 21–3   The Election of 1912 The election pitted rival visions of progressivism against each other. The decentralized regulation of Wilson's "New Freedom" had more appeal than Roosevelt's far-reaching "New Nationalism."

Drawing on his long study of congressional politics, he seized the advantage of his party's majority and exercised an unprecedented degree of personal control through the majority leaders in both houses. The New Freedom advocated lower tariffs, increased competition, and vigorous antitrust enforcement. Three monumental bills passed through Congress in rapid succession.

The first bill was the Underwood-Simmons Tariff (1913), which made the first deep cuts in tariff rates since before the Civil War. The bill overturned one of the cornerstones of Republican economic policy, the protectionist tariff, and it helped farmers and consumers by lowering prices and increasing competition, but Wilson argued that its real beneficiaries would be manufacturers. Lower tariffs would help persuade other countries to reduce taxes on imports from the United States, he reasoned, opening new markets for American-made goods. Wilson created an expert Tariff Commission in 1916 to carry tariff bargaining to a new level. The most-favored-nation policies it implemented (and which remain standard practice) induced European powers to open their empires to American goods. The Singer, Ford, and Camel brand names began appearing in bazaars, souks, and godowns from Caracas to Mandalay. The Underwood-Simmons Tariff also permanently shifted the revenue base of the federal government from taxes on imports to taxes on income.

Wilson's next target was the banking system. When Steffens and Lippmann investigated banking for *Everybody's* magazine in 1908, they found its structure was "strikingly like that of Tammany Hall: the same pyramiding influence, the same tendency of power to center on individuals who did not necessarily sit in the official seats, the same effort of human organization to grow independently of legal arrangements." Money poured into investment houses but scarcely trickled to western farmers. The Federal Reserve Act of 1913 set up a national board to supervise the system and created 12 regional reserve banks in different parts of the country. Banks were now watched to assure that their reserves matched their deposits. The system's real advantage was the flexibility it gave the currency. The Federal Reserve Board could put more dollars into circulation when demand was high and retire them when it subsided. Regional banks could adjust the money supply to meet the needs of different parts of the country. The system broke Wall Street's stranglehold on credit and opened new opportunities for entrepreneurship and competition.

Finally, Wilson attacked the trusts. He established the Federal Trade Commission (FTC), an independent regulatory commission assigned to enforce free and fair competition. It absorbed the functions of Roosevelt's Bureau of Corporations, but it had more far-reaching powers, including the right to subpoena corporate records and issue cease-and-desist orders. The Clayton Antitrust Act (1914) prohibited price fixing, outlawed interlocking directorates, and made it illegal for a company to own stock in its competitor. To enforce these provisions citizens were entitled to sue for triple the amount of the actual damages they suffered. In 1916 Wilson produced another crop of reform legislation, including the first national workers' compensation and child-labor laws, the eight-hour day for railroad workers, and the Warehouse Act, which extended credit to cash-strapped farmers.

These programs furthered Wilson's goal of "releasing the energies" of consumers and entrepreneurs, but they also helped business. Businessmen headed many of the regulatory boards, and the FTC and Federal Reserve Board brought predictability and civility to unruly markets. The New Freedom implemented reform without resorting to the elaborate state machinery that the New Nationalism envisioned or that European industrial nations were assembling. The New Freedom linked liberal reform to individual initiative and the free play of markets.

Conclusion

By 1900 America's political economy had outgrown the social relationships and laws that served the rural republic for most of the nineteenth century. Squeezed between the indifference of corporate elites and the large, transient immigrant communities that controlled urban politics, middle-class reformers created a new style of political participation. They experimented with the structure of decision making at the municipal and state levels and vested the state with responsibility for the quality of life of its citizens. Progressives challenged but never upset the system. Above all, they wanted managed, orderly change. Science and the pressure of informed opinion, they believed, could overcome resistance without open conflict.

The progressive presidents continued this movement on the national stage. Roosevelt and Wilson touted their programs as attacks on privilege, but both presidents helped position the federal government as a broker among business, consumer, and labor interests. "Democracy is now setting out on its real mission," William Allen White observed, "to define the rights of the owner and the user of private property according to the dictates of an enlightened public conscience." In less than two decades, the federal government overcame its reputation for corruption and impotence and adapted to a new role at the center of economic and social life. The concept of a "national interest" that superceded individual and property rights and needed to be protected through continuous action was now firmly ingrained. The president's leadership now extended beyond the administration to Congress and public opinion. These achievements created a modern central government just at the time when military, diplomatic, and economic victories made the United States a global power. War and its aftermath would curtail the progressive movement, as the consensus favoring a strong central government would be tested by events unfolding in Europe.

Further Readings

Jane Addams, *Twenty Years at Hull-House* (1910). In her autobiography, Addams urges respect for the traditions of immigrants and action against the causes of crime and poverty.

Harry Bruinius, *Better for All the World: The Secret History of Forced Sterilization and America's Quest for Racial Purity* (2006). In 1927, the Supreme Court upheld state laws that sterilized women against their will. Eugenic policies, which had their origins in the Progressive Era, remained in force for much of the twentieth century.

John Milton Cooper Jr., *The Warrior and the Priest: Theodore Roosevelt and Woodrow Wilson in American Politics* (1983). A dual biography of the progressive presidents compares their backgrounds, philosophies, and political styles.

Maureen A. Flanaghan, *Seeing with Their Hearts: Chicago Women and the Vision of a Good City, 1871–1933* (2002). Beginning with the Great Fire in 1871, women organized to rebuild a safer, cleaner, and more orderly Chicago.

Louise W. Knight, *Citizen: Jane Addams and the Struggle for Democracy* (2005). Knight analyzes Addams's complex attitude toward democracy and her search for a politics of justice and equity.

J. Anthony Lukas, *Big Trouble: A Murder in a Small Western Town Sets Off a Struggle for the Soul of America* (1997). The anxiety and tension of the Progressive Era West comes to the surface in the trial of three labor leaders for the murder of a former governor of Idaho.

Michael E. McGerr, *A Fierce Discontent: The Rise and Fall of the Progressive Movement in America, 1870–1920* (2005). Traces the rise and fall of a middle-class movement that veered between desperation and utopianism.

Kevin Starr, *Inventing the Dream: California Through the Progressive Era* (1985). The century's first decade in a state that was defining a distinct local identity through planning, art, and reform.

Robert H. Wiebe, *The Search for Order, 1877–1920* (1967). This classic study of progressivism traces the movement's origins to the middle class's yearning for a lost Eden of small towns and personal relationships.

Who, What?

>> Timeline >>

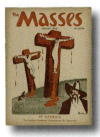

Review Questions

1. Were the progressives' goals conservative or radical? How about their strategies?

2. Why did reformers feel that privately owned utilities caused corruption?

3. What were the Oregon system and the Wisconsin Idea?

4. Theodore Roosevelt has been called the first modern president. In what ways did he change the presidency?

5. Did the progressives' emphasis on research and documentation indicate their respect for public opinion, or not?

6. Choose one level of government—local, state, or federal—and describe three key progressive reforms.

Websites

San Francisco Public Utilities Commission, "Hetch Hetchy Virtual Tour," http://www.creatf .com/hetchy/watershedtour.html

Sierra Club, "Hetch Hetchy: Time to Redeem a Historic Mistake," http://www.sierraclub .org/ca/hetchhetchy/

Ida B. Wells, "Lynch Law in Georgia," 1899, http://www.loc.gov/exhibits/odyssey/educate/ barnett.html. Read the exposé of racial violence that inspired a worldwide antilynching movement.

For further review materials and resource information, please visit www.oup.com/us/ofthepeople

---

▼ **1905**
U.S. takes over Dominican customs
Industrial Workers of the World founded
Roosevelt mediates end to Russo-Japanese War

▼ **1906**
Hepburn Act passed, allowing the Interstate Commerce Commission to set freight rates
Pure Food and Drug Act requires accurate labeling

▼ **1907**
Indiana passes forcible sterilization law

▼ **1908**
William H. Taft elected president

Supreme Court upholds maximum-hours laws for women in *Muller v. Oregon*

▼ **1909**
Payne-Aldrich Tariff goes into effect
NAACP founded

▼ **1910**
Taft fires chief forester Gifford Pinchot
Elkins Act authorizes Interstate Commerce Commission to regulate electronic communications
Roosevelt announces the New Nationalism

▼ **1911**
Triangle Shirtwaist Company fire

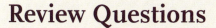

▼ **1912**
U.S. troops occupy Nicaragua
Woodrow Wilson elected president

▼ **1913**
Federal Reserve Act reorganizes banking system
Underwood-Simmons Tariff

▼ **1914**
Panama Canal completed
Clayton Act strengthens antitrust enforcement

▼ **1916**
New York City enacts zoning laws
Federal workers' compensation, child-labor, and eight-hour-day laws passed

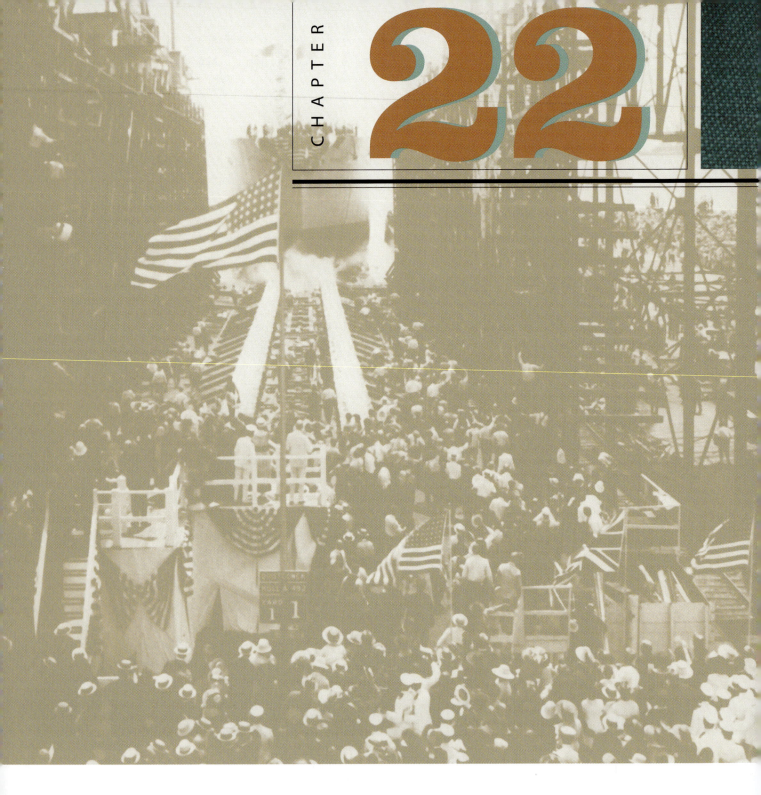

CHAPTER 22

Common Threads

>> As a progressive, Wilson was committed to order, efficiency, and gradual reform. How did his policies toward Mexico and Europe reflect this commitment?

>> Both the Philippine-American War of 1899 and U.S. involvement in World War I in 1917 pro-

voked dissent at home. Why did the government tolerate opposition in the first case but suppress it in the second?

>> How did the repression of the war years set the stage for the Red Scare and the Ku Klux Klan?

>> Walter Lippmann

Walter Lippmann had just arrived in Brussels in July 1914 when the trains suddenly stopped running. At the station, "crowds of angry, jostling people, carrying every conceivable kind of package" were trying to leave the city. This looked, he confided in his diary, like the beginning of a war. Four weeks earlier, Austria-Hungary's crown prince, Archduke Ferdinand, had been shot as he drove through the Serbian city of Sarajevo. Austria threatened to attack unless Serbia found and punished the terrorists. Russia mobilized to come to Serbia's defense. As stock markets tumbled and banks collapsed, Lippmann found himself caught up in a conflict between the world's most powerful states: Austria and Germany on one side, Russia, France, and Britain on the other. As land borders closed, he escaped across the channel to England.

In the twilight of August 4, he stood with an anxious crowd on the terrace outside the House of Commons, as Britain's foreign minister, Sir Edward Grey, asked Parliament for a war resolution. In Berlin, the Reichstag declared war on France. "We sit and stare at each other and make idiotically cheerful remarks," Lippmann wrote, "and in the meantime, so far as anyone can see, nothing can stop the awful disintegration now. Nor is there any way of looking beyond it: ideas, books, seem too utterly trivial, and all the public opinion, democratic hope, and what not, where is it today?"

Twenty-four years old, Lippmann had come of age in the Progressive Era. As a student at Harvard, he came to believe that reason and science would allow his generation to "treat life not as something given but as something to be shaped." After graduation, he set out to become a journalist, studying under Lincoln Steffens and helping to start a magazine called the *New Republic*. "It was a happy time, those last few years before the First World War," he later remembered; "the air was soft, and it was easy for a young man to believe in the inevitability of progress, in the perfectibility of man and of society, and in the sublimation of evil."

The European war crushed those hopes. Just days after Lippmann left Belgium, German armies sliced through the neutral nation in a great wheeling maneuver that aimed to encircle the French army, but before the ring could be closed, reserve troops from Paris, many of them rushed to the front in taxicabs, struck the German flank and stopped the advance at the Marne River in northeastern France. By November, the Western Front had stabilized into the bloody stalemate that would prevail for the next four years, absorbing between 5,000 and 50,000 lives a day. The machine gun defeated all attempts to break through the enemy's trench lines. Colossal artillery, poison gas, submarine warfare, aerial bombardment, and suicide charges would each be used in desperate bids to break the deadlock, and all would fail.

The carnage horrified Americans. German soldiers terrorized Belgian civilians in retaliation for guerilla attacks, killing over 5,000 hostages and burning the postcard medieval city of Louvain. The gruesome tragedy of war in the heart of the modern world made Americans feel simultaneously fortunate and guilty to be so uninvolved. "We Americans have been witnessing supreme drama, clenching our fists, talking, yet unable to fasten any reaction to realities," Lippmann told his readers. "We are choked by feelings unexpressed and movements arrested in mid-air." For three years, Americans watched as a civilization they had admired sank into barbarism. They recoiled from the war's violence and the motives behind it, and they debated what, if anything, they could do to stop it.

When the United States entered the fight in 1917, it mobilized its economy and society to send an army of a million to Europe. The war disrupted and culminated

continued

>> **AMERICAN PORTRAIT** *continued*

the progressive movement. In the name of efficiency, the state stepped in to manage the economy as never before, placing corporations under federal supervision but allowing them profits and a measure of autonomy. The war transformed many of the most controversial items on the progressive social agenda—women's suffrage, prohibition of alcohol, restrictions on prostitution—into matters of national urgency. The federal government used its control of the mails to punish political dissenters. On the battlefield, American forces brought swift triumph, but victory failed to impose a new stability. Defeated powers collapsed into revolution and anarchy. New ideologies threatened American ideals. The experience of war brought home the dangers of a modern, interdependent world, but it also revealed the United States' power to shape the global future. ●

 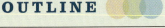
The Challenge of Revolution

Like other progressives, Wilson saw threats arising from rapid change in the industrial world. Revolution, militarism, and imperial rivalries threatened global stability just as surely as labor wars, reckless corporations, and corrupt officials threatened the republic internally. Wilson opposed radicalism at home and abroad, and he tried to fashion institutions and processes to foster orderly change. Stability, like reform, was not a goal but a process, but Wilson also believed it had to be forced on those who resisted. Opponents "who will not be convinced," he wrote, deserved to be "crushed."

Imposing order, the president believed, was both a duty and an opportunity for the United States. An expanding commercial power like the United States had talent, technology, and capital to share. "Prosperity in one part of the world ministers to prosperity everywhere," he declared, but it could only do so in safe markets. Imperialism and revolution endangered the trade necessary for peace in the world and growth at home. It was the government's duty to assure the safety of goods and investments in order to secure American prosperity and its benefits for the world.

This combination of idealism and self-interest, humanitarianism and force, produced a seemingly contradictory foreign policy. Wilson renounced "dollar diplomacy," only to use Taft's tactics himself in China. He atoned for the imperialism of prior administrations, but he intervened repeatedly in Central America. Secretary of State William Jennings Bryan negotiated a series of conciliation, or "cooling-off," treaties that required arbitration before resorting to war, but Wilson was seldom willing to submit his own policies to arbitration. He believed the United States had a mission to promote democracy, yet he considered many peoples—including Filipinos—unready to govern themselves.

These contradictions are explained by Wilson's view of history. As he saw it, modern commerce and communications were creating a global society with new rules of international conduct. Meanwhile, relics of the past—militarism and revolution—threatened to "throw the world back three or four centuries." Resolving the struggle between the past and the future would require "a new international psychology," new norms and institutions to regulate conflict. Wilson's sympathies lay with Britain and France, but with Europe aflame, the United States, the sole voice of reason, had to remain aloof. "Somebody must keep the great economic processes of the world of business alive," he protested. He was also preoccupied with matters closer at hand. In April 1914, American troops invaded Mexico in an attempt to overthrow its revolutionary government.

> **We intend to teach the Mexicans to elect good men.**
>
> WOODROW WILSON

The Mexican Revolution

In May 1911, rebels took control of Mexico City, ending over three decades of enforced order and rapid industrialization under the dictatorship of Porfirio Díaz. Díaz and a clique of intellectuals and planners known as the *científicos* had spanned the country with railroads and made Mexico one of the world's leading oil exporters. They confiscated communal lands, forcing Indians to farm as tenants on commercial *haciendas*. Foreign investment poured in, and by 1911 Americans owned 40 percent of the property in the country. Mexicans grew to resent foreign businessmen and the regime's taxes. When Francisco Madero's revolt broke out, the army folded, Díaz fled to Spain, and power changed hands in a nearly bloodless coup.

The fall of Díaz gave the United States little cause for concern: Madero held an election to confirm his presidency. But in February 1913, just two weeks before Wilson's inauguration, General Victoriano Huerta seized power and had Madero shot. Mexican states raised armies and revolted against Huerta's regime, beginning one of the twentieth century's longest and bloodiest civil wars. In the mountains south of Mexico City, Emiliano Zapata led a guerilla resistance. Meanwhile along Mexico's northern border, Venustiano Carranza organized a constitutionalist army.

Wilson denounced Huerta, gave arms to Carranza's soldiers, and sent 7,000 marines to occupy Mexico's largest port city, Veracruz, in April 1914. The invasion radicalized the revolution, unifying all sides against the United States. When Carranza deposed Huerta a few months later, he promised to nationalize U.S. oil fields. Still determined to "put Mexico on a moral basis," Wilson pressured Carranza to resign while providing arms to his enemy, Francisco "Pancho" Villa. Villa briefly seized the capital at the end of 1914, but Carranza counterattacked, driving Villa's army north toward the border. Reluctantly, Wilson recognized the Carranza government and cut ties to Villa. Stung by Wilson's betrayal, Villa crossed the border and attacked the 13th Cavalry outpost at Columbus, New Mexico, killing 17 Americans and stealing horses and guns.

Furious, Wilson sent 10,000 troops under General John J. Pershing into Mexico. Pershing never found Villa, but the invasion once again unified Mexicans against the United States. Wilson now faced a choice between declaring war or giving up the hunt. He ordered Pershing home. After three years of trying to bring democracy and stability to Mexico, Wilson had nothing to show for his efforts. Carranza was seeking German arms, the civil war still raged, and American property was more in danger than ever. Wilson's failure to tame revolution and nationalism in Mexico foreshadowed disappointments he would experience in trying to bring order to the rest of the world.

Bringing Order to the Caribbean

In principle, Wilson opposed imperialism, but his desire to bring order to neighboring countries led him to use force again and again. He sent the marines into more countries in Latin America than any other president. Marines quashed a revolution

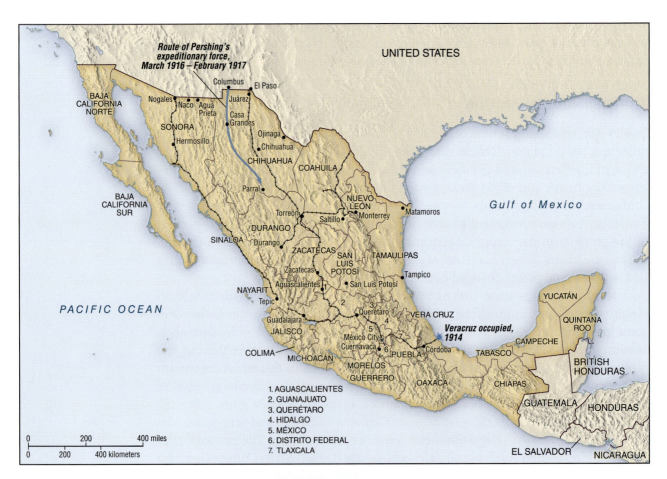

Map 22–1 Mexican Invasion Routes to Veracruz General John Pershing led 10,000 troops together with observation aircraft and a convoy of trucks 419 miles into Mexico on a fruitless hunt for Francisco Villa's band. Federal forces loyal to Carranza confronted Pershing near Parral, bringing the U.S. advance to a halt.

in Haiti in 1915, then occupied the country. They landed in the Dominican Republic the following year to supervise an election, and stayed to fight a guerilla war until 1924. Wilson kept marines in Honduras, Panama, and Nicaragua, and briefly sent troops into Cuba.

Progressive senators wondered why Wilson busted trusts and reorganized banks at home but put the marines at their service abroad. Senators Robert La Follette and George Norris argued that revolutions might be necessary in some countries to protect the rights of the many against the power of the few. On August 29, 1914, some 1,500 women, dressed in black, marched down Fifth Avenue in New York City to oppose wars in the Caribbean and Europe. Peace advocates, like Jane Addams, saw signs that the United States was being drawn toward war.

A One-Sided Neutrality

As German armies crossed Belgium in August 1914, Woodrow Wilson declared a policy of strict neutrality and called on Americans to "be impartial in thought as well as in action." The war took him by surprise, and like Addams he found it "incredible" that civilized nations could display such savagery. His first worry was that America's immigrant communities would take sides. Shortly after the crisis began, 450 steelworkers from Gary, Indiana, enlisted in the Serbian army. Irish Americans, who wanted independence for their homeland, sided with Germany against England. The Allies (Britain, France, Italy, and Russia) and the Central powers (Germany, Austria-Hungary, and Turkey) each used propaganda to manipulate U.S. opinion.

Wilson dispatched his closest aide, Colonel Edward House, to Europe with offers to broker a peace agreement. Privately the president believed that a German victory would be a catastrophe. Protected by Britain's control of the seas, the United States had expanded its influence during the previous century. If the Allies were defeated, he told his brother-in-law, "the United States, itself, will have to become a military nation, for Germany will push her conquests into South America." With Europe and possibly Asia controlled by a single power, the United States would be vulnerable and alone.

Modern warfare and commerce made true neutrality difficult, and in the implementation a bias became clear. The belligerent powers desperately needed everything the United States had to export. As purchasing agent for France and Britain, J. P. Morgan's firm soon became the world's largest customer, buying more than $3 billion worth of armaments, food, textiles, steel, chemicals, and fuel. Factories hired extra shifts, and farm prices rose to an all-time high. U.S. loans to the Allies grew to $2.5 billion by 1917, but the Central powers received only $127 million in credit. Trade with the Central powers meanwhile sank from $170 million to less than $1 million by 1916. An Allied victory would make the United States the world's leading creditor, while defeat might mean financial collapse. Although the United States had not formally taken sides, the American economy was already in the war on the side of the Allies.

Wilson's response to the British and German naval blockades reinforced the tilt toward the Allies. Both sides violated the "freedom of the seas" by imposing blockades, Britain with mines and warships, Germany with submarines. Wilson considered Britain's violation justifiable, but he reacted differently toward Germany. Britain's surface fleet was able to capture civilian ships as required by international law, but a German *Unterseeboot* or U-boat—a small, fragile submarine with a crew of only 32 men—could not do that without giving up the stealth and surprise that were its only weapons.

The *Lusitania*'s Last Voyage

Germany posted advertisements in American newspapers warning passengers not to travel on ships bound for the war zone; Americans were horrified by the targeting of ships carrying civilians. The State Department was divided. Robert Lansing, the department's counselor, condemned submarine attacks as an offense against law and morality, but Bryan wanted to bar Americans from traveling on belligerent ships. Wilson sided with Lansing and declared that Germany would be held to "strict accountability" for American lives or property.

On the afternoon of May 7, 1915, submarine U-20 sighted the luxury liner *Lusitania* off the coast of Ireland. A torpedo detonated against the starboard side behind the bridge. In 18 minutes the massive ship broke apart and sank. Of almost 2,000 pas-

sengers aboard, 1,198 drowned, including 94 children. Among the drowned were 124 Americans. The newspapers reacted with rage and horror, but Wilson's advisers again disagreed on how to respond. Bryan wanted to balance a protest with a denunciation of Britain's violation of neutral rights. Wilson ignored him and demanded that submarine warfare stop altogether. He hinted that unless his demands were met, the United States would break relations.

Public opinion was equally divided. Lippmann told a friend in England that "the feeling against war in this country is a great deal deeper than you would imagine by reading editorials." When Germany promised not to attack passenger liners without warning, Wilson accepted this pledge as a diplomatic triumph. It momentarily restored calm, but official and public opinion had turned against Germany. The *Lusitania* crisis, Lippmann predicted, "united Englishmen and Americans in a common grief and a common indignation" and might "unite them in a common war."

The Drift to War

The *Lusitania* disaster opened a gap between progressives on the issue of the war. Peace advocates such as Addams, Bryan, and La Follette urged a stricter neutrality. Others believed war, or preparations for war, were justified. Theodore Roosevelt clamored for it. He endorsed the preparedness campaign mounted by organizations like the National Security League and the American Defense Society. Thousands of preparedness supporters marched down New York's Fifth Avenue under an electric sign declaring "Absolute and Unqualified Loyalty to our Country."

Preparedness leagues, headed by businessmen and conservative political figures, called attention to the state of the armed forces, equipped only for tropical wars, and lacking trucks, planes, and modern arms. The preparedness campaign appropriated patriotic rituals once reserved for elections. Wilson himself led the parade in

AMERICAN LANDSCAPE

>> Plattsburg Training Camp

Dawn rose over Lake Champlain as a special train pulled onto a siding near the old army barracks at Plattsburg, on the lake's New York side. The passengers, young men in their 20s and early 30s, some in civilian clothes, others already in uniform, filed from the cars and stood at attention on the platform. These were no ordinary recruits. They included diplomat and Morgan partner Willard Straight, Thomas Miller, a 29-year old congressman, Raynal C. Bolling, a top executive at United States Steel, southern plantation owners, Ivy League professors, the editor of *Vanity Fair,* and the mayor of New York.

They were there for four weeks of push-ups, forced marches, and intensive military training, although none had actually enlisted in the army. Drill sergeants called them "tourists," but the recruits saw themselves as the bearers of a new martial spirit. "This was young America," one observed, "a very decent sort of thing, a thing even thrilling to touch shoulders with for a little time."

The camp was conceived in New York's Harvard Club by an alliance of generals, businessmen, and professors. Leonard Wood, commander of the army's eastern division, wanted to create an army reserve that could be used in a foreign war. University presidents suggested that he organize a summer military camp for college students. Students needed the discipline and exercise, and the army needed educated commanders. The president of Harvard explained that the camps would train "a class of men" that would supply "a large proportion of the commissioned officers" in the next war. Private businessmen provided funds, and the first college camps bivouacked at Gettysburg, Pennsylvania, and Monterey, California, in the summer of 1913.

When war erupted in Europe the following summer, young business leaders clamored for a camp of their own. Over a thousand people jammed the Harvard Club on June 14, 1915, five weeks after the *Lusitania* disaster, to hear Wood announce the Businessmen's Military Training Camp at Plattsburg. Word spread through alumni societies and professional associations, and 1,300 of "the best and most desirable men" signed up. Plattsburg emptied "the whole table at Delmonico's," one organizer beamed. Young men from the wealthiest and most prestigious families shelled out $30 for a khaki uniform and mess kit.

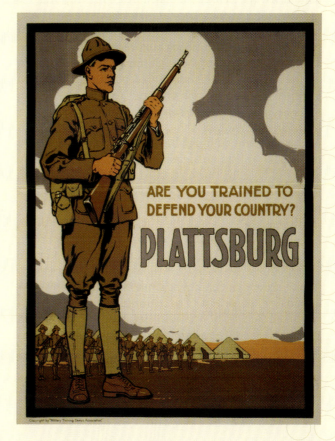

ARE YOU TRAINED TO DEFEND YOUR COUNTRY? PLATTSBURG

The press sniped at this new fashion for militarism, but Willard Straight replied that the camp's organizers "do not propose to militarize the American nation. They seek rather to civilize the American military." Harvard was out to show West Point how to run an army, but two weeks of close-formation drill was enough to give the "tourists" a new respect for professional soldiers. The recruits answered reveille at 5:55 A.M. After breakfast and inspection, calisthenics and drill began at 7:25 and went until supper. Top college athletes found it gruelling. Regular infantry marched 30 miles in a day, but at the end of four weeks the recruits could barely manage 10.

At evening campfires, recruits discussed politics, war, and what the Plattsburg experience meant. Theodore Roosevelt, who had three sons and a nephew at the camp, came one evening to denounce "the professional pacifist, the poltroon, and the college sissy" who were

continued

trying to keep the United States out of the war. Some recruits agreed with Roosevelt that the United States must be prepared for war, but others saw preparedness as a way to avoid war. They agreed that young Americans, and particularly the rich, could benefit from military drill.

Over the previous decades, the upper class had detached itself from American society, retreating into exclusive schools, neighborhoods, and recreational enclaves, a process known as "social closure." Aloofness undermined its claim to leadership in a democratic society, and nowhere more than in the military. The officers and men of the regular army came from the rural South and West, from farming and working-class families. Few in the corporate elite sent their children to West Point and almost none to the enlistment depots. The heroes of the coming war would become the elected leaders of the future, and Plattsburg was Wall Street's chance to claim a share of military glory.

Recruits talked about the wholesome, democratic influence of military training. It instilled "discipline, manliness, and that comradeship in a high common purpose which grows so slack . . . in a society governed by purely economic conditions," one observed. A millionaire looked like anyone else in uniform, and a journalist remarked that "each reservist left his worldly goods, his 'pull,' his record of past performances at home." Just as in sports, the only standard was how well one performed now. The camp included a large number of college ath-letes, including Yale fullback Frank Butterworth; Hamilton Fish Jr., the captain of Harvard's football team; and his coach, Percy Haughton. Not surprisingly, recruits saw what one described as the "obvious parallel between a football team and an army, and between the training of a fullback and a first-rate squad leader." War, he wrote, was the "real game."

In articles written afterwards, and memoirs many years later, the recruits remembered the emotions stirred by watching the flag lowered at sunset to the solemn strains of a bugle sounding retreat. "There is a fine restraint in military ceremony," Harvard philosophy professor Ralph Barton Perry noted, "that enables the purest product of New England self-repression to *feel*." "I do not believe that anyone in the camp," John J. McCloy, an Amherst college student who would become an adviser to five presidents, told a friend, "no matter how tired or blue he felt, ever 'stood retreat' without having a tiny thrill run up his spine." Like McCloy, many of the young men at Plattsburg fought in World War I, served the federal government in World War II, and ran law firms, industries, embassies, and government agencies during the cold war. For them, Plattsburg was the beginning of America's adventure in world leadership. "Plattsburg was not just a military training camp," historian Kai Bird later wrote, "it was, in a way, a secular retreat for a whole generation. There, amid simple, material surroundings, the upper class elite underwent a conversion experience of patriotism." ●

Washington in 1916, wearing a red tie, white trousers, and a blue blazer. "What a picture," Mrs. Wilson remembered, "as the breeze caught and carried out the Stars and Stripes!"

Hundreds of young Americans, positive that a German victory would mean the defeat of civilization, went to Paris to enlist. The French army soon had an American Volunteer Corps and a squadron of American fliers, the Lafayette Escadrille, whose exploits filled American newspapers. Magazines reprinted the romantic poems of Alan Seeger, a Harvard graduate who volunteered for the foreign legion. While Americans slept "pillowed in silk and scented down," Seeger wrote, "I've a rendezvous with death/At midnight in some flaming town." Wilson increasingly felt that to shape the world order to come after the war, Americans would have to meet that rendezvous.

The Election of 1916

Although Wilson increasingly felt the United States would need to enter the fight, he campaigned for reelection under the slogan "He kept us out of war." The preparedness issue reunited Theodore Roosevelt and the Republicans behind Supreme Court

Justice Charles Evans Hughes, who attacked Wilson for failing to defend American honor in Mexico and Europe. Woman suffragists campaigned against Wilson. They whistle-stopped across the country in a train called the *Golden Special* and picketed the White House with signs asking, "Mr. President? How long must women wait for liberty?" Although the Republicans remained dominant, Hughes proved an inept campaigner. He won pivotal states in the North and East—New York, Pennsylvania, and Illinois—but lost in the South and West. Wilson won narrowly; a shift of a few thousand votes in California would have cost him the election. Republicans controlled the House and the Senate. Still, reelection freed Wilson to pursue a more vigorous foreign policy. As Lippmann realized, "What we're electing is a war president—not the man who kept us out of war."

The Last Attempts at Peace

After the election, Wilson launched a new peace initiative. Looking for an opening for compromise after years of stalemate, he asked each of the belligerent powers to state its war aims. Each insisted on punishing the other and enlarging its own territories. Going before Congress in January 1917, the president called for a "peace without victory," based on self-determination of all nations and the creation of an international organization to enforce peace.

Germany toyed with accepting Wilson's proposals but decided to wait. With the defeat of Russia in 1917, it could begin shifting armies from the eastern front to France. U-boats once again torpedoed British passenger liners and American merchant ships. In late February, British naval intelligence officers showed the U.S. ambassador in London a telegram from the German foreign minister, Arthur Zimmermann, plotting an alliance with Mexico. The Zimmermann Telegram provoked alarm in the West, where antiwar feeling had been strongest. If Wilson did not declare war now, Roosevelt declared, he would "skin him alive."

Americans disagreed then, as historians do today, on why the United States went to war. Critics pointed to the corporate interests that stood to gain. Publicly and in private, Wilson stressed two considerations: the attacks on American ships and the peace settlement. The treaty conference afterward would settle scores of issues in which American interests would be involved. Unless it took part in the conflict, Wilson told Jane Addams, the United States would have to shout "through a crack in the door."

War Aims

Rain was falling on the evening of April 2, 1917, as Wilson went to ask Congress for war. Some onlookers on Pennsylvania Avenue cheered and waved paper flags while others stared silently at the president's limousine. The war, Wilson told the assembly, was in its last stages. American armies could bring it to a merciful end. The United States had tried to stand apart, but it had failed. Neutrality had provided no safety for travelers or trade. The only hope for avoiding future wars that might pose even graver dangers to the nation was to place the United States in a position to dictate the peace, to establish a "concert of free peoples." This would be a war to end all wars, to make the world safe for democracy.

In urging Congress to vote for war, the president explicitly rejected the aims of the Allies. "We have no quarrel with the German people," he said of the nation that would soon be at the receiving end of U.S. artillery. His argument was with the kaiser and all other emperors and autocrats who stood in the way of his plan for a new world order. Wilson realized, however, that imperial France and Britain did not stand for democracy or self-determination either. "We have no allies," he claimed, but the United States would fight with Britain and France as an "associated power."

Edward House assembled a secret committee, known as the Inquiry, to draft a peace proposal that would be both generous enough to show "sympathy and friendship" to the German people and harsh enough to punish their leaders. Made up of economists, historians, geographers, and legal experts, it met in the cramped offices of the American Geographical Society in New York. House named Lippmann as the group's secretary. Working day and night, the Inquiry produced a set of 14 recommendations that redrew the boundaries of Europe, created a league of nations, and based peace on the principles of freedom of the seas, open-door trade, and ethnic self-determination.

The Fight in Congress

During the ovation after Wilson's speech to Congress, one senator stood silently, his arms folded across his chest. La Follette told his colleagues that if this was a war for democracy, it should be declared democratically. The country had voted only five months earlier for the peace candidate for president, and there were strong reasons to suspect a declaration would fail a national vote. Representatives who polled their districts found that voters opposed American entry, in many places by two to one. Midwestern farmers, William Allen White reported from Iowa, "don't seem to get the war."

Prowar representatives blocked La Follette's move for a referendum and brought the declaration to a vote on April 6, when it passed by a margin of 82 to 6 in the Senate and 373 to 50 in the House. As debate turned to questions of how to pay for the war and who would fight in it, divisions resurfaced. Wilson wanted universal conscription, the first draft since the Civil War. The 1917 draft law deputized 4,000 local boards to induct men between 18 and 45. Both supporters and opponents believed the draft would mold citizens. It would "break down distinctions of race and class," said one representative, turning immigrants into "new Americans." La Follette countered that the new Americans would be like the new Germans, militarist "automatons" indoctrinated by the army.

Wilson and the Draft Lottery The AEF was the first U.S. army chosen primarily by conscription. The selective service registered 24 million men and chose 3 million of them—some through a draft lottery—to enlist.

Newspapers and politicians denounced the antiwar progressives as traitors who belonged either in jail or in Germany. They had too few votes to stop conscription, but they managed to make an exemption for conscientious objectors and to reduce some taxes on sugar, bread, and coffee used to pay for the war. The voices of opposition were soon silenced by patriotic calls for unity at all costs. There was little room in wartime America for dissent or divided loyalties. "I pray God," Wilson avowed, "that some day historians will remember these momentous years as the years which made a single people of the great body of those who call themselves Americans."

Mobilizing the Nation and the Economy

News of the war declaration, carried in banner headlines on Easter Sunday, 1917, set the nation abuzz with activity. William Percy, a college student from Mississippi, rushed home to Greenville and found women "knitting and beginning to take one lump of sugar instead of two, men within draft age were discussing which branch of the service they had best to enter, men above draft age were heading innumerable patriotic committees and making speeches." Wilson recognized that he was asking for an unprecedented effort. Raising an army of over 3 million, supplying it with modern equipment, and transporting it across submarine-infested waters to France were herculean feats. By midsummer, there were more men at work building barracks than had been in both armies at Gettysburg. Americans would spare from their dinner plates and send to Europe 1.8 million tons of meat, 8.8 million tons of grain, and 1.5 million tons of sugar. Factories that produced sewing machines, automobiles, and textiles would retool to make howitzers and tanks.

> We need more business not less. . . . Now is the time to open the throttle.
>
> HOWARD E. COFFIN,
> War Industries Board member
> and founder of Hudson Motors,
> April 1917

Accomplishing these tasks placed tremendous strains on the American people and economy. Wilson and others feared that it could widen political divisions and destroy the achievements progressives had made in the previous 15 years, but others felt that sharing the sacrifices of war would consolidate the gains. "We shall exchange our material thinking for something quite different," the General Federation of Women's Clubs predicted. "We shall all be enfranchised, prohibition will prevail, many wrongs will be righted." Lippmann hoped war would bring a new American revolution. "We are living and shall live all our lives now," he predicted, "in a revolutionary world."

Enforcing Patriotism

Authorities dealt severely with dissent. Suspicions about the loyalties of ethnic communities and rumors of German saboteurs fed the hysteria. There had already been mysterious explosions. On July 30, 1916, across the river from New York City, the largest arms storage facility in the country blew up, perforating the Statue of Liberty with shrapnel. Thousands of pounds

of shells and guns bound for Russia were lost. Four days after Wilson declared war, saboteurs struck again, blowing up a munitions factory outside of Philadelphia and killing 112 workers, mostly women and girls. Federal agents rounded up large numbers of aliens, but the fear of internal enemies persisted.

Congress gave the president sweeping powers to suppress dissent. The Espionage Act (1917) and the Sedition Act (1918) effectively outlawed opposition to the war and used the postal service to catch offenders. Although there was no link between the labor movement and sabotage, unions were the prime target. The Justice Department raided the Chicago offices of the Industrial Workers of the World and sent 96 leaders to prison on charges of sedition. William D. "Big Bill" Haywood was sentenced to 20 years. Eugene V. Debs, leader of the Socialist Party, received 10 years for telling Ohioans they were "fit for something better than slavery and cannon fodder."

States also passed laws criminalizing activity deemed unpatriotic. Indiana's Council for Defense licensed citizens to raid German homes, prevent church services in German, and make sure German Americans conserved meat and wheat and bought war bonds. Towns, schools, and clubs with German-sounding names changed them. East Germantown, Indiana, became Pershing. Hamburgers became "liberty sandwiches." School systems in the Midwest that for decades had taught math and science in German stopped teaching the language altogether. Americans who had once proudly displayed their ethnicity now took pains to disguise it.

Pacifist faiths encountered their own ordeals. Some sects had come to America to avoid conscription in Germany or Russia. Many could not comply even with the conscientious objector statute, which required submission to military control. Fifteen hundred Mennonites fled to Canada to avoid being placed in camps. Thirty-four Russian Pentecostals were arrested in Phoenix, Arizona, turned over to the army, court-martialed, and sent to Leavenworth.

The government's propaganda effort was managed by the Committee on Public Information (CPI) under former muckraker George Creel. It made films, staged pageants, and churned out display ads, billboards, posters, leaflets, and press releases. The CPI sold the war by telling Americans they were fighting to save their own homes. One poster showed a fleet of German bombers passing over a shattered, headless Statue of Liberty. Like Wilson, however, propaganda distinguished between Germany and the German people. The CPI distributed leaflets in German offering "Friendly Words to the Foreign Born." It cast immigrants as potential patriots, and women as symbols of progress and sacrifice. Creel drafted Charles Dana Gibson, whose "Gibson Girl" ads personified glamour, to depict women as mothers, nurses, and patriotic consumers. Advertising mobilized American thought on behalf of the war effort and, in the process, advanced progressive agendas.

Regimenting the Economy

The first prolonged conflict between industrial nations, World War I introduced the public to the term "total war." By 1917 all of the resources, manpower, and productive capacities of the combatants had been mobilized. It soon became clear that the economy of the United States would have to be planned and centralized in new ways.

The navy planned a vast shipyard on Hog Island, near Philadelphia, with 250 buildings, 80 miles of railroad track, and 34,000 workers. When finished it would be larger than Britain's seven largest shipyards combined, but in April 1917, Hog Island was 847 acres of swamp. Steelmaker Charles M. Schwab, in charge of the project, signed contracts for machinery, cement, steel, and timber. Manufacturers loaded materials on trains headed east. The result was the Great Pile Up, the biggest traffic jam in railroad history. Without enough workers to unload, stationmasters began to back cars up on sidings in Philadelphia. Within weeks cars could get no closer than Pittsburgh or Buffalo, and loads were being dumped on the outskirts of cities. Schwab begged the railroads to cooperate, to no avail. The voluntary system had failed, and on January 1, 1918, Wilson nationalized the railroads.

The Hog Island fiasco demonstrated the need for supervision of the economy. Wilson created a War Industries Board (WIB) to regulate prices, manufacturing, and transport. The job was enormous. After the first WIB administrator had a nervous breakdown, Wilson found the overseer he needed in Bernard Baruch, a Wall Street financier, who believed in regulation by "socially responsible" businessmen. He recruited corporate executives to fill top positions and paid them a dollar a year. The president of the Aluminum Company of America became chairman of the WIB's

Hog Island Shipyard Building the massive shipyard at Hog Island was a major feat. The railroad network broke down under the strain, leading Wilson to nationalize the railroads.

aluminum committee, and a former top executive of John Deere was named to head the agricultural implements section.

The dollar-a-year men regimented the economy and put business at the service of government, but they also guaranteed profits and looked after their own long-term interests. One of their innovations, the "cost-plus" contract, assured contractors the recovery of costs plus a percentage for profit. Under these arrangements, the Black and Decker Company used its factories to make gun sights, Akron Tire made army cots, and the Evinrude Company stopped making outboard motors and turned out grenades. Each company built up revenues to launch new product lines after the war. Standardization also helped industry. The WIB set standard designs and sizes for everything from shirts to lug nuts, ridding the economy of wasteful diversity. One steel executive observed, "We are all making more money out of this war than the average human being ought to."

Not all businesses submitted willingly to "war socialism." The Ford Motor Company had just set up a national dealer network, and it refused to stop making cars. When other automakers followed suit, the board threatened to cut off the industry's supply of coal and steel, amounting to "confiscation of the industry," one carmaker sputtered. After months of negotiations, the auto manufacturers agreed to cut production by three-fourths. The delay hurt. When American troops went into battle they had a grand total of two tanks.

The war economy was a culmination of two movements: Wall Street's drive for corporate consolidation and the progressives' push for federal regulation. Businessmen recognized that the WIB could rationalize the economy. These "New Capitalists" wanted to end cutthroat competition and make business predictable. They encouraged workers to identify with the company through stock sharing and bonus plans. The WIB's example of government-industry cooperation would serve as a model in crises that would face the nation in future decades.

The Great Migration

The war economy gave Americans new choices and opportunities. As factories geared up, corporate managers faced a shortage of labor. The draft took eligible employees from the cities, and the usual source of new workers—Europe—was sealed off by a screen of U-boats. Elbert Gary, head of U.S. Steel, wanted to import laborers from China, but other employers found a ready supply in the South. In small towns and rural junctions, labor recruiters arrived offering free rides to the North and well-paid employment on arrival. Large manufacturers came to rely on the labor of former sharecroppers. Westinghouse employed 25 African Americans in 1916; by 1918 it employed 1,500. The Pennsylvania Railroad recruited 10,000 workers from Florida and Georgia. In some northern cities, a thousand migrants were arriving each week. This massive movement from the rural South to the urban North and West came to be called the Great Migration.

Lynchings, intimidation, and a declining southern economy encouraged migration. Almost half a million people came north during the war years—so many that some counties emptied out, creating panic among whites left behind. Mississippi lost 75,000 workers, leaving farms without tenants and delivery wagons without drivers. "We must have the Negro in the South," the Macon, Georgia, *Telegraph* pined. "It is the only labor we have. . . . If we lose it, we go bankrupt." Southern states banned recruiters. In some places, migrants encountered violence, provoking still more migration. "Every time a lynching takes place in a community down south," one observer noted, "you can depend on it that colored people will arrive in Chicago within two weeks."

African American workers moved into jobs at the bottom of the pay scale: janitors, domestics, and factory hands. Rent, groceries, and other necessities were substantially more expensive in the cities. Still, African American workers could earn wages 70 percent higher than what they were used to at home. Almost no one went back. The new arrivals adapted to the rhythms of city life. "South State Street was in its glory then, a teeming Negro street with crowded theaters, restaurants, and cabarets," Langston Hughes wrote of Chicago in 1918. "Midnight was like day. The street was full of workers and gamblers, prostitutes and pimps, church folks and sinners." To Carl Sandburg this vibrant community was "spilling over, or rather being irresistibly squeezed out into other residence districts."

Archibald Motley, Jr., *Nightlife* (1943) In his paintings, Archibald Motley captured the vibrancy and freedom of Chicago at the height of the Great Migration. Motley grew up in the "Back of the Yards" neighborhood during World War I and began sketching in poolrooms, churches, and gambling halls before attending the Art Institute.

Housing was scarce, and African American renters found their options limited to overcrowded districts wedged between industrial zones and unfriendly white neighborhoods. W. E. B. DuBois noted that residential patterns in Philadelphia changed dramatically. At the turn of the century African Americans had lived in many neighborhoods, but by the end of the war they were concentrated in one area, the Seventh Ward. Ghetto neighborhoods were both expensive and decrepit. On Chicago's South Side, rents were 15 to 20 percent higher than in white neighborhoods, and the death rate was comparable to that of Bombay, India. White property owners and real estate agents worked to create the ghettos and enforce their boundaries. On Chicago's South Side, the Hyde Park Property Association organized to "Make Hyde Park White." A real estate agent explained that African American homeowners "hurt our values." When discrimination failed to deter "undesirables," they used dynamite. From 1917 to 1919 there were 26 bombings of African American residences in Chicago. On July 2, 1917, in East St. Louis, an arms manufacturing center in southern Illinois, competition for housing and political offices led a mob of white workers to attack "Black Valley," an African American neighborhood along the Southern Railroad track. Forty-seven people were killed and six thousand left homeless.

After East St. Louis, white mobs found African American neighborhoods less easy to attack. When a mob invaded a Washington, DC, ghetto three years later, residents fought back with guns. "New Negroes are determined to make their dying a costly investment for all concerned," an African American newspaper explained drily. "This new spirit is but a reflex of the Great War." The New Negro, urban, defiant, demanding rather than asking for rights, became the subject of admiring and apprehensive reports. Police kept files on suspected militants, but northern cities offered a mobility and anonymity that translated into freedom.

Reforms Become "War Measures"

On August 3, 1917, thousands of protestors marched in New York under signs demanding "Why not make America safe for democracy?" In the wake of the East St. Louis outrage, the NAACP urged Congress to outlaw lynching as a "war mea-

sure." African Americans were not alone in using the president's language to justify reform. Carrie Chapman Catt told Wilson that he could enact women's suffrage "as a 'war measure' and enable our women to throw, more fully and wholeheartedly, their entire energy into work for their country." Advocates of progessive change demanded that the United States practice at home the ideals it fought for abroad.

Suffragists hitched their cause to the national struggle. Catt's National American Woman Suffrage Association (NAWSA) abandoned its strategy of lobbying state by state and worked to identify women with the national cause. Members sold liberty bonds and knitted socks for the Red Cross, making clear that they expected to be rewarded with a constitutional amendment. Alice Paul's National Woman's Party (NWP) picketed the White House gate with signs quoting Wilson's demand for all peoples to "have a voice in their own governments." When Wilson announced his support in 1918, he cited women's war service as the reason. The Nineteenth Amendment was finally ratified in 1920, "so soon after the war," according to Jane Addams, "that it must be accounted as the direct result of war psychology."

As it had for African Americans, the shortage of labor increased opportunities for women. Although fewer than 1 in 20 women workers were new to the labor force, many took jobs previously considered "inappropriate" for their sex. Women replaced men as bank tellers, streetcar operators, mail carriers, and in heavy-manufacturing firms. Many of these opportunities vanished as soon as the war was over, but in rapidly expanding sectors like finance, communications, and office work women made permanent gains. By 1920, more than 25 percent labored in offices or as telephone operators, and 13 percent were in the professions. The new opportunities made work a source of prestige and enjoyment for women. Alice Hamilton remarked on the "strange spirit of exaltation among the men and women who thronged to Washington, engaged in all sorts of 'war work' and loving it." Army General Order 13 set standards for women's work, including an eight-hour day, prohibitions on working at night or in dangerous conditions, and provisions for rest periods, lunchrooms, and bathrooms. The government also empowered women consumers, encouraging them to report on shopkeepers who charged above the official price.

Wilson authorized a National War Labor Board to intervene in industries "necessary for the effective conduct of the war." The board set an unofficial minimum wage. For the first time the federal government recognized workers' rights to organize, bargain collectively, and join unions. Unskilled workers earned higher real wages than ever before. When the Smith and Wesson Company refused to acknowledge its workers' right to bargain collectively, the army seized the factory and recognized the union. There were limits, however, to how far the administration would go to keep workers happy. When skilled machinists at the Remington Arms plant in Bridgeport, Connecticut, made demands the board considered excessive, Baruch threatened to have them drafted and sent to France.

Prohibition did not please workers either, but beer, wine, and spirits were early casualties of war. The Anti-Saloon League and the Woman's Christian Temperance Union had assembled a powerful antiliquor coalition by 1916. Congress would have passed Prohibition without war, but in the rush to mobilize, temperance became a patriotic crusade. Military regulations prohibited liquor first in the vicinity of army camps. Finally, in 1919 the states ratified the Eighteenth Amendment, banning the "manufacture, sale, or transportation of intoxicating liquors." At midnight on January 28, 1920, the Anti-Saloon League celebrated the dawn of "an era of clear thinking and clean living." America was "so dry it couldn't spit," according to Billy Sunday. He overstated the case. By some estimates, after the ban illegal speakeasies in New York outnumbered the saloons they replaced. Bootleggers and smugglers slaked American thirsts, but liquor prices rose and consumption declined. Americans never again drank anything like the average two and a half gallons of pure alcohol per person annually imbibed before Prohibition.

The war also lent patriotic zeal to antivice crusaders. During the Progressive Era, muckrakers exposed the police-protection rackets that allowed gambling dens and brothels to thrive. Within days of the declaration of war, reformers identified prostitutes as enemies of the health of American troops. Gonorrhea afflicted a quarter of the Allied forces in France, and middle-class Americans were appalled. When French premier Georges Clemenceau offered brothels for the American army, the secretary of war told his aide, "Don't show this to the president or he'll stop the war." Before 1917, reformers targeted commercial vice as a source of political and social corruption, but afterward they directed their efforts at women as carriers of disease.

The army acted against liquor and prostitution to protect the welfare of soldiers, but it shrank from challenging racial injustice even when lives were at stake. At training camps in the South, it was often unclear who had more authority, uniformed African American soldiers or white local officials. Clashes could easily turn violent. A riot in Houston in August 1917 began when soldiers from nearby Camp Logan rushed to the aid of an African American woman being beaten by police. Before it was over, 20 policemen and soldiers were dead and 54 soldiers received life sentences in the largest court-martial in U.S. history.

After the Houston riot, African American units were dispersed across the country. They were not allowed to assemble in full companies or join their officers until they were in France. Training was continually interrupted by menial assignments like road building or freight handling. The army remained segregated. Worse, many southern communities used military discipline to strengthen their own Jim Crow laws. Encouraged by the army's "work or fight" order, which required draft-age men to either enlist or get a job, states and localities passed compulsory work laws that applied to women and older men. The laws were intended to keep laborers in the fields and servants in the kitchens at prewar wages.

In the "war welfare state" created by full mobilization, the government served as a mediator among labor, industry, and other organized interests. Social activism became a matter of lobbying federal agencies who could either dictate sweeping

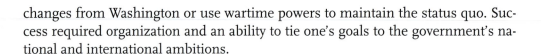

changes from Washington or use wartime powers to maintain the status quo. Success required organization and an ability to tie one's goals to the government's national and international ambitions.

Over There

When the U.S. Senate took up the enormous war budget the president submitted in April 1917, the finance committee questioned Major Palmer E. Pierce about what would be done with all of that money. "Clothing, cots, camps, food, pay," he replied, "and we may have to have an army in France." "Good Lord!" exclaimed Senator Thomas Martin of Virginia. "You're not going to send soldiers over there, are you?" After the horrors of the Somme and Verdun, where men were fed to the Spandau guns by the tens of thousands, it hardly seemed reasonable to send Americans to such a place. "One would think that, after almost four years of war, after the most detailed and realistic accounts of murderous fighting, . . . it would have been all but impossible to get anyone to serve," one veteran later recalled. "But it was not so, we and many thousands of others volunteered."

Americans went to France optimistically believing they could change the war and the peace. Trench warfare was not for them. They planned to fight a war of movement, sweeping in formations across open fields, as Americans had at Antietam and Gettysburg. The Europe they expected to see would confirm their opinion that their immigrant ancestors had made the right choice. To a remarkable degree, they got the war they wanted. Europeans watched their civilization destroy itself in the Great War, but Americans saw theirs rising. Soldiers, "doughboys," said so in their letters, echoing the words of their leaders, their newspapers, and the volumes of poetry they carried with them into battle.

> This western-front business couldn't be done again, not for a long time. . . . This took religion and years of plenty and tremendous sureties and the exact relation that existed between the classes.
>
> F. SCOTT FITZGERALD,
> *Tender Is the Night*

Citizens into Soldiers

Enlisting, training, and transporting soldiers began in a rush. Camps housing 400,000 recruits went up in the first 30 days. A Wisconsin man saw Fort Sheridan "alive with enthusiastic recruits, with an atmosphere somewhat like that of a college campus on the eve of a big game." To Secretary of War Newton D. Baker's surprise, conscription went smoothly, and soon 32 camps were in operation, housing 1.3 million men. Commander John J. Pershing arrived in France in June along with 40,000 men and the first of some 16,000 women who would serve in the American Expeditionary Force (AEF).

Neither the Wilson administration nor the Allies initially anticipated that soldiers would be the United States' main contribution to the war effort. Britain urgently needed financial support, and Wilson advanced $200 million immediately, the first of an eventual $10 billion in loans to the Allies. Funds, food, and ammunition were needed more urgently than men, but that changed in October 1917, when German and Austrian forces smashed through the Italian lines at Caporetto, capturing 275,000 men and finishing the war on that front. When the Bolshevik Revolution curtailed Russian resistance in the east in November, Britain and France saw that by the next spring Germany would be able to mass its armies on the line between Ostend and Switzerland and break through to Paris. The war became a race between the United States and Germany to see who could place the most men on the Western Front in 1918.

To get troops to the war the United States needed ships, but the American merchant fleet was smaller in 1917 than it was during the Civil War. For a time the United States had to cut back draft calls because it lacked ships to transport soldiers. Men shared berths, sleeping in shifts. The navy, meanwhile, cured the U-boat problem. The addition of the American destroyer fleet allowed the Allies to convoy effectively for the first time, cutting losses dramatically and banishing submarines from the sea lanes. When a torpedo was sighted, destroyers would sprint to the far end of the wake and deploy depth charges in a circle around the U-boat. By July 18, some 10,000 troops a day boarded the "Atlantic Ferry" for the ride to France.

The Fourteen Points

In December 1917, the Inquiry sent the president a memorandum titled "The War Aims and the Peace Terms It Suggests." Wilson redrafted it and presented it to Congress on January 8, 1918. The Fourteen Points outlined U.S. objectives, but more fundamentally they offered a different basis for peace than any that had been proposed up to that point. Unlike nineteenth-century wars waged for limited territorial or political objectives, the Great War was a total war, fought for unlimited aims. The principal belligerents—Britain, France, Russia, Germany, and Austria-Hungary—were global empires whose trade and law spanned continents and oceans. Germany hoped not only to defeat Britain but also to take its empire. France wanted to destroy Germany's future as a great power, economically and militarily. Wilson replaced these imperial visions of total victory with a peace based on limited gains for nations, instead of empires.

The Fourteen Points were grouped around four themes: national self-determination; freedom of the seas; enforcement of peace by a league of nations; and open diplomacy. The Inquiry's memorandum included a thick sheaf of maps marked with new European boundaries based on national, ethnic identities. The new state of Poland, for instance, should govern only territories with "indisputably Polish populations." Point three restated the Open Door, urging international free trade. Wilson thus hoped to eliminate what he saw as the two leading causes of war, imperial and commercial rivalry. By calling for an end to secret diplomacy, he aimed to appeal directly to the people of Europe, over the heads of their governments. The expectation was that the hope of a just peace would weaken the enemy nations' will and inspire the Allies to fight harder. Creel printed 60 million copies and had them distributed around the world. Planes dropped copies over Germany and Austria.

Wilson hoped the Fourteen Points would dispel not only the old dream of empire but also the new one of socialist revolution. On November 7, two months before Wilson presented the points to Congress, Russian workers overthrew the Provisional Government of Alexander Kerensky. The one-party regime of the Bolsheviks, led by Vladimir Lenin, summoned workers everywhere to rise against their governments and to make peace without indemnities or annexations. "The crimes of the ruling, exploiting classes in this war have been

countless. These crimes cry out for revolutionary revenge." In December, Lenin revealed the contents of the secret treaties, unmasking the imperial ambitions of the Allies. He sued for peace based on the principle of self-determination. The Council of People's Commissars allocated 2 million rubles to encourage revolutions around the world and called "upon the working classes of all countries to revolt."

Two world leaders—Lenin and Wilson—now offered radically different visions of the new world order, and Lenin was putting his into effect. The Bolsheviks' contempt for democracy angered Wilson, but he continued to hope that the revolution would move in a more liberal direction and that Russia would stay in the war. Those hopes ended with the Treaty of Brest-Litovsk, signed by Russia and Germany in March 1918. The treaty showed the fearful price of defeat in modern war. Russia lost the Ukraine, Poland, and Finland, three-quarters of its iron and steel, one-quarter of its population, and most of its best farmland. Those assets went to the Germans, who began integrating them into their war machine. With its eastern front secure, Germany began transferring 10 divisions a month to the west.

Wilson was the first, but not the last, American president to be haunted by the specter of a German-Russian alliance, uniting the immense war-making resources of Europe and Asia. Wilson's strategic vision replaced Alfred Thayer Mahan's. Sea power threatened U.S. security less, in Wilson's view, than the great land powers of Eurasia. He refused to recognize the Bolshevik government, and he sent 7,000 American troops to Russia to support anti-Bolshevik forces on the eastern front. U.S. and Japanese forces invaded Siberia from the east. The Bolshevik government now counted the United States among its enemies. Meanwhile, the battle for the control of Europe was about to begin.

The Final Offensive

The German high command knew the spring offensive would be the last. Their exhausted economy no longer could supply food or ammunition for a sustained effort. Breadlines, strikes, and industrial breakdowns foreshadowed the chaos that would follow defeat. Risking everything, the German commander Erich Ludendorff launched his offensive on March 21, 1918. Specially trained shock troops hurled the British Fifth Army back to Amiens. In May they penetrated French lines as far as Soissons, 37 miles from Paris. As gaps opened in the lines, French general Ferdinand Foch and General

Douglas Haig of Britain appealed urgently to Pershing to put American troops under British and French command. Pershing opposed the idea. Born in Missouri six months before the Civil War began, the AEF's commander had attended West Point at a time when cadets learned tactics by studying Shiloh and Chickamauga. He wanted the American army to play its own part in the war.

Pershing criticized European commanders for remaining on the defensive when the war could be won only by "driving the enemy out into the open and engaging him in a war of movement." Imagining himself a General Grant replacing European McClellans, he saw trenches not as protection against modern weaponry but as symbols of inertia. Pershing favored massed assaults on the main German force in which the sheer numbers of American troops would overwhelm the enemy. Infantry commanders, he decided, "must oppose machine guns by fire from rifles." In envisioning Europe's war as a replay of the U.S. Civil War, Pershing revealed a habit of mind that would typify American geopolitical thinking for the next century: the belief that Americans could understand the world through the prism of their own experience. He was not alone in wanting a clean, decisive alternative to trench warfare. Billy Mitchell, head of the army's aviation section, noted that while the Allies had been "locked in the struggle, immovable, powerless to advance for three years . . . we could cross the lines of these contending armies in a few minutes in our aeroplanes."

The German onslaught interfered with Pershing's plans. On May 27, German divisions pierced French lines at Château-Thierry and began advancing on Paris at a rate of 10 miles a day. The French government considered whether to abandon the capital or surrender. Bowing to urgent requests, Pershing threw the AEF into the breach. It was springtime in France as column upon column of fresh American troops filled the roads from Paris to the front. Photographs show doughboys marching to meet the enemy across fields of wildflowers. "We are real soldiers now and not afread [sic] of Germans," John F. Dixon, an African American infantryman from New York, wrote home. "Give my love to Claypool, Mary, June, and Grace. Tell them I say war is more than a notion. Our boys went on the battlefield last night singing." Ahead of them lay five German divisions, poison gas, minefields, rolling artillery barrages, and machine guns emplaced in interlocking fields of fire. The Americans stopped the Germans, but at a fearful cost. The marine brigade that took Belleau Wood suffered 4,600 casualties, half the force. Without artillery or tanks, they assaulted machine gun nests head-on, with rifles. The Americans stopped the German drive.

By mid-July, the initiative passed to the Allies. On September 12, Foch allowed Pershing to try his tactics against the St. Mihiel salient, a bulge in the French lines which, unknown to the Allies, the Germans had already begun to evacuate. The doughboys raced behind the retreating enemy past their planned objectives, even outdistancing their own supply wagons. Pershing was delighted. St. Mihiel had vindicated his strategy, and he yearned for another chance. It came two weeks later, at the battle of the Meuse-Argonne.

Ten miles northwest of Verdun, the Argonne Forest contained some of the most formidable natural and man-made defenses on the Western Front. Atop parallel ridges lay three fortified trench lines, *Stellungen*—barriers of concrete pillboxes, barbed wire, artillery, and observation posts—named for Wagnerian witches, Giselher, Kriemhilde, and Freya. Half a million German troops had defended these fortifications for four

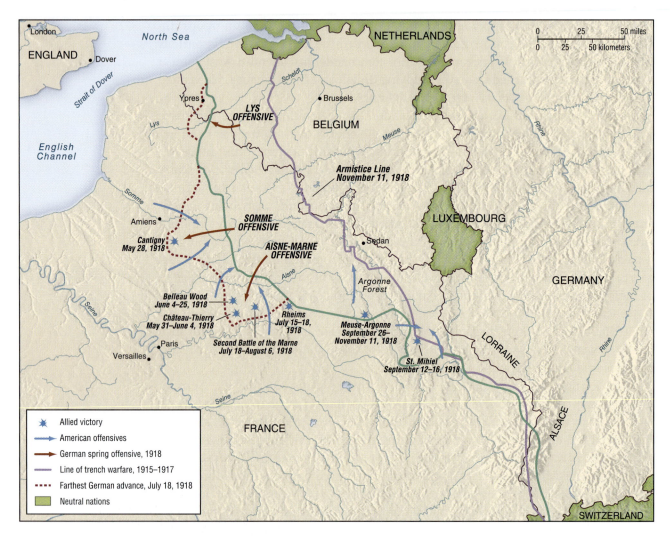

Map 22–2 Western Front, 1918 On the western front, the opposing armies fought from trenches fortified with earthworks and barbed wire. The parallel trench lines stretched thousands of miles from the North Sea to Switzerland.

years. Against this force, Pershing arrayed the American First Army, 1,031,000 men. The average doughboy at the Meuse-Argonne had a total of four months of training, and some had as little as 10 days. Pershing's battle plan called for overwhelming the German defenses with speed and numbers, breaching the Giselher Stellung, and reaching the second trench line, 10 miles inside the German front, the first day.

"Moving slowly forward, never heeding the bursting shells, nor gas, we followed a road forking to the left . . . into no man's land. It was soon noticed that we were in the bracket of a German barrage," a soldier wrote from the battlefield. Breaking through the first line of German trenches after a day and a half, the battle turned into a deadly crawl up the Romagne Heights into the teeth of the Kriemhilde Stellung. "We came to the spot where the fellow was hit during the night—he had one boot and leg blown off," Lt. Robert Sawyer of Texas wrote in his diary. "The dead seemed to be in hundreds, though I am quite sure it was my imagination." In two weeks of fighting, 26,277 Americans died. French soldiers reported seeing the American dead lying in rows, cut down by machine guns as they marched in formation. American divisions "suffer wastage out of all proportion to results achieved," a British observer noted. Finally, on November 10, American troops reached their objective and dynamited the rail line connecting the cities of Metz and Sedan. Meanwhile, Germany announced that it would accept the Fourteen Points as the basis for an armistice and negotiations. At 11:00 A.M. on November 11, 1918, the guns fell silent.

American intervention had been decisive. The American economy, two and a half times the size of Germany's, lent its immense industrial and agricultural productivity to the Allies at a crucial moment. American naval strength and manpower also tipped the balance. Pershing failed to transform strategy—it remained a mechanized war of attrition until the end—but by striking the final blow, Americans had the illusion that their way of war had been triumphant. American losses, 116,516 dead, were smaller than the British (908,371), the French (1.4 million), or the Germans (1.8 million), but they still show the colossal destructiveness of the kind of industrial war fought on the Western Front. In just six months, the United States suffered twice as many combat deaths as in the Vietnam War and almost a third as many as in World War II.

The Western Front From 1914 to 1918, the western front was the largest metropolis on earth, in Robert Cowley's phrase, an "unreal city" whose inhabitants—8,000 of whom died each day—worked in an industry of destruction.

While they fought on the same battlefields, Americans and Europeans fought two vastly different wars. The Americans' war, swift and victorious, bore almost no resemblance to the European experience, a prolonged catastrophe that consumed an entire generation. For Europeans, the mental world of the prewar era, with its optimistic faith in modernity, in the ability of science and democracy to create a better future, vanished forever. Confidence in the inevitability of progress became a distinctive feature of U.S. culture in the postwar era. In much of the world "American" became almost synonymous with "modern," but not everywhere. In the East another political and economic system shouted its claim to the future.

Revolutionary Anxieties

Americans celebrated the armistice with bonfires, automobile horns, church bells, and uplifted voices. New York's Metropolitan Opera interrupted a performance to sing the anthems of the Allied nations. Wilson told Congress that "everything for which America fought has been accomplished," but he observed that the situation in Russia cast doubt on the durability of peace. Even before the armistice, German revolutionaries took power in Bavaria. Over the next months, revolutions broke out throughout eastern Europe. From the trenches of Flanders to the Sea of Japan, not a single government remained intact, and in Moscow the new Soviet state towered above the ruins of the old regimes.

> **The Department of Justice has undertaken to tear out the radical seeds that have entangled American ideas in their poisonous theories.**
>
> ATTORNEY GENERAL
> A. MITCHELL PALMER,
> 1920

Wilson in Paris

For Wilson, the moment he had planned for in 1917 had arrived—the United States could help set the terms of peace—but war had exhausted the president. Confident that the public would view the nation's victory as his victory, he committed mistakes. Had he remained in Washington, some historians have argued, he could have taken credit for the achievements of his negotiators while keeping a close eye on his critics. Instead, he went to Paris, staking the treaty's success on his own popularity. He passed up a chance to include in the delegation a prominent Republican, like Lodge, who could guide the treaty through Congress afterwards. A member of the British cabinet, Winston Churchill, observed that "if Mr. Wilson had been either simply an idealist or a caucus politician, he might have succeeded. His attempt to run the two in double harness was the cause of his undoing."

In December 1918, Walter Lippmann, now an army captain, watched Wilson's triumphal entry into Paris. Crowds lined the streets, and as the procession crossed the Pont du Concorde into the center of the city, a great cheer went up, echoing off the walls of the Chamber of Deputies. "Never has a king, never has an emperor received such a welcome," *L'Europe Nouvelle* declared. For the next month, Wilson toured France, Italy, and Britain with cries of "Viva Veelson" ringing in his ears. An Italian mayor compared his visit to the second coming of Christ. "They say he thinks of us, the poor people," a workingman remarked, "that he wants us all to have a fair chance; that he is going to do something when he gets here that will make it impossible for our government to send us to war again. If he had only come sooner!"

By the time he arrived for the treaty talks at the Palace of Versailles, two of the Fourteen Points had already been compromised. Britain refused to accept the point on freedom of the seas, which would thwart the use of the Royal Navy in a future conflict. Wilson's own actions also undercut his position on point six, respect for Russia's sovereignty, since American troops were occupying Russian Siberia. Wilson was unable to prevent Britain, France, and Japan from dividing Germany's colonies among themselves and imposing harsh peace terms. Germany had to sign a humiliating "war guilt" clause and pay

Council of Four Peace Conference Ending WWI The Big Four. From left to right, David Lloyd George of Great Britain, Vittorio Orlando of Italy, Georges Clemenceau of France, and Woodrow Wilson of the United States gather outside Hotel Crillon before the Paris Peace Conference in 1919.

$33 billion in reparations, enough to cripple its economy for decades. "God gave us the Ten Commandments and we broke them," Clemenceau quipped. "Wilson gave us the Fourteen Points—we shall see."

Wilson concentrated on the League of Nations, which might make up for the treaty's other weaknesses and provide some safety against the rising tide of revolution. He took the lead in drafting the League Covenant, which committed each member to submit disputes to arbitration and pledged them to take action against "any war or threat of war."

The Senate Rejects the League

To many observers in the United States the Treaty of Versailles betrayed the goals Americans had fought to attain. "This is Not Peace," declared the *New Republic*. Congress saw the League of Nations less as a way to prevent wars than as a guarantee that the United States would be involved. Americans were "far more afraid of Lenin than they ever were of the Kaiser," Lippmann wrote. "We seem to be the most frightened lot of victors the world ever saw." To Republican leaders, like Henry Cabot Lodge, the United States' best bet was to look to its own security, keep its options open, and work out its international relations independently rather than as part of an alliance or league.

In early March 1919, before the treaty was concluded, Lodge and 38 other senators—more than enough to defeat the treaty—signed a petition opposing the League of Nations. James A. Reed of Missouri said the covenant would turn American foreign policy over to foreigners. Editorials described scenarios in which American troops would be automatically summoned to settle blood feuds in the Balkans. Wilson knew he would have to fight, but he believed that in the end the Senate would not reject the treaty.

>> The Influenza Pandemic of 1918

The 57th Vermont Pioneer Infantry marched for hours through the rain on the night of September 29, 1918, from Camp Merritt, New Jersey, to open ferries that carried them down the Hudson to Hoboken, where they boarded the U.S.S. *Leviathan* for the trip to France. The 9,000 tired and wet soldiers and 200 nurses aboard the country's largest and fastest troop transport were nervous about U-boats they might encounter in the Atlantic, but they had a deadlier enemy, one that came on board with the men of the 57th.

Within hours of embarkation, every bed in the ship's infirmary was full, and every patient had symptoms that were all too familiar to military doctors: aches in the legs and back, nosebleed, and, in extreme cases, the blue lips and ears, the thin, gasping breaths that indicated advanced pneumonia. But though doctors recognized the signs, they knew nothing about how to treat or prevent Spanish influenza. They could only comfort patients and try, futilely, to separate the sick from the well on the overloaded ship. By the time it arrived in France, 1,700 passengers were down with "the flu." Ninety had died during the passage and 200 more would perish within days of landing.

The 1918 pandemic affected nearly every spot on the globe, killing over 30 million people, far more than died in the world war. Called Spanish because the king of Spain was the first well-known figure to die, the flu was first observed at Fort Riley, Kansas, where the virus may have jumped from pigs to humans. War and commerce accelerated its spread. Men from all of Europe and colonial nations in Asia and Africa came together in the trenches and then carried the disease by steamship and locomotive to every continent. In August the flu mutated into an exceptionally lethal strain. Patients showed signs of massive pneumonia and usually died within three days.

It spread westward across North America, following the path of the railroads, and within weeks encircled the world in a fatal embrace, killing 6 million in India, 200,000 in Japan, and 675,000 in the United States. In Cincinnati, Ohio, and Harbin, China, farmers noticed that the disease killed hogs in the same proportion that it killed humans, roughly one in ten. A steamer from San Francisco put in at Tahiti on November 16, and within the next three weeks 10 percent of the population died. Isolated habitations newly tied to global conduits of trade and communications were hit hardest. The virus arrived in Eskimo villages on postal dogsleds and by camel caravan to Arabian towns. Australia closed its ports in a vain effort to shut out the disease.

At the Paris Peace Conference, delegate and Plattsburg veteran Willard Straight died, and President Wilson, Walter Lippmann, Edward House, and the entire American delegation were sick. When Wilson spoke of war and revolution as contagions spreading across the world, it was a terror his audience knew well. At the height of the pandemic in Philadelphia, churches, schools, saloons, and theaters were shut; San Francisco required everyone to wear surgical masks in public. Trolley cars were used as hearses, and the dead were interred in mass graves. Katherine Anne Porter, who nearly died, described the "noiseless houses with the shades drawn, empty streets, the dead cold light of tomorrow."

World war aroused a fervid nationalism, but the pandemic revealed that parliaments and autocrats were equally powerless in the face of catastrophe on this scale. Citizens accused their governments of apathy. The British Raj was in "a state of coma," the Bombay *Chronicle* complained. At Cartwright, on Canada's Labrador Coast, a minister wrote bit-

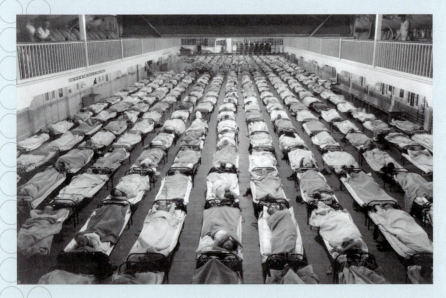

terly of his "resentment at the callousness of the authorities, who sent us the disease by mail-boat, and then left us to sink or swim." American soldiers in Brest took up red flags and mutinied, demanding to be released from flu-infested Camp Pontanezen.

One of the first acts of the new League of Nations in 1920 was to establish an international health organization to track the movement of epidemics. Agents at port cities collected reports of influenza, typhus, smallpox, cholera, and other plagues and sent them by telegraph to centers at Geneva and Singapore, allowing quarantines to be established or lifted when danger had passed. Quarantines disrupted trade, and League members wanted to control panic as much as disease. In 1948, the service became the World Health Organization (WHO), an affiliate of the United Nations.

Nearly a century later, air transport and global food-supply chains have made every epidemic into a potential pandemic. Outbreaks of communicable disease—or live-stock infections, such as mad cow disease—touch off a global response. In March 2003, a strange pneumonia appeared in China, Canada, Viet Nam, and Singapore, reviving memories of the 1918 flu. A WHO doctor, an Italian tending an American patient in a Hanoi hospital, identified it as a new virus: Severe Acute Respiratory Syndrome (SARS). The WHO issued travel alerts, established quarantine procedures at airports, and dispatched epidemiological teams to trace the outbreak to its source. National governments resisted, attempting to conceal the extent and danger of the disease from the media, but the WHO prevailed and the outbreak was contained. Still, experts counted us lucky. No cure has yet been found for viral diseases, and had SARS spread at the rate of the Spanish flu, the toll would have numbered in the millions. In April 2009, a lethal flu virus—transferred, like the 1918 strain, from pigs—emerged in Mexico and spread through New York and Toronto to the rest of the world. Once again, the WHO mobilized a global response. For disease trackers, 1918 remains the benchmark, the standard for how destructive a modern plague can be—and might be again. ●

In September, Wilson went "over the heads" of Congress and stumped for the treaty on a nationwide tour. He assured listeners in Sioux Falls that "the peace of the world cannot be established without America." He promised the citizens of Salt Lake City that China's independence would be respected. Traveling more than 8,000 miles and speaking before large audiences without loudspeakers took a toll on the president's health. After a speech in Pueblo, Colorado, he became so ill that he was rushed back to Washington, where he suffered a stroke that left him paralyzed on his left side and unable to concentrate for more than a few minutes a day. Mrs. Wilson and the president's physician kept his condition a secret and refused to allow anyone to see him.

It was at this moment, with Wilson secluded in the White House, that the Senate voted against ratification. Down to the end, Wilson refused to allow Senate Democrats to accept any modifications. Even Lippmann's *New Republic,* which had been a mouthpiece for the Wilson administration throughout the war, called the treaty's demise "desirable and wholesome." Lodge and the Republicans were not ready to retreat into isolation, but they preferred diplomatic strategies that employed the United States' economic strength rather than its relatively weak military. They also saw Latin America as more critical than Europe to U.S. security. Lodge even toyed briefly with the idea of two leagues, one for each hemisphere.

Meanwhile, European governments organized the League of Nations without delegations from the United States or the Soviet Union. Over the next decade, U.S. influence abroad grew enormously. American automobiles, radios, and movies could be seen in far corners of the globe. However, the United States was cautious in its diplomatic dealings in Europe and Asia, in order to avoid being drawn into what the *New York Tribune* called the "vast seething mass of anarchy extending from the Rhine to the Siberian wastes."

Red Scare

On May 1, 1919, a dozen or more mail bombs were sent to prominent Americans: J. P. Morgan, John D. Rockefeller, senators, cabinet officials, and Supreme Court Justice Oliver Wendell Holmes. None of the explosive packages reached its intended target, but one injured a maid in the home of Senator Thomas Hardwick and another exploded at the residence of Attorney General A. Mitchell Palmer in Washington, nearly injuring Franklin and Eleanor Roosevelt, who lived next door. Investigations later showed that the bombings were the work of lone lunatics, but many people quickly concluded that the United States was under attack. Since the Russian Revolution, newspapers, evangelists, and government officials had fed fears of Bolshevism. "The blaze of revolution was sweeping over every American institution," Palmer alleged, "licking at the altars of the churches, leaping into the belfry of the school bell, crawling into the sacred corners of American homes."

Revolutions in Europe terrified conservatives in the United States and led them to look for Soviet terrorists, particularly among immigrants and unionized workers. They drew no distinctions among Socialists, anarchists, Communists, and labor unionists; they were all "red." Seattle's mayor called in the army to break a dockworkers strike. When steelworkers in Gary, Indiana, struck for higher wages and shorter hours in September 1919, Judge Elbert Gary, president of U.S. Steel, denounced them as followers of "anarchy and Bolshevism" and other doctrines "brought directly from Russia." During the war they had worked 12 hours a day, 7 days a week, for an average wage of $28 a week. Enlisting the help of local loyalty leagues, Judge Gary broke the strike.

Using the patriotic rhetoric of the war, industry leaders labeled strikers as dangerous aliens. They persuaded allies in the courts to take action, and a series of Supreme Court decisions made union activity virtually illegal. In 1919 the Court allowed antitrust suits to be filed against unions, and it later outlawed boycotts and picketing. Then, in January 1920, a series of crackdowns known as the Palmer raids rounded up and deported 250 members of the Union of Russian Workers. In one night, 4,000 suspected Communists were arrested in raids across the country; some said this was not enough. "If I had my way with these ornery, wild-eyed Socialists and IWWs," evangelist Billy Sunday allowed, "I would stand them up before a firing squad and save space on our ships."

The most notorious case associated with the "Red Scare" began in May 1920 when Nicola Sacco and Bartolomeo Vanzetti, a shoemaker and a fish peddler, were arrested for robbing a shoe company in South Braintree, Massachusetts. Two men died of gunshot wounds during the robbery, and ballistics experts claimed that the bullets came from Sacco's gun. The trial, however, focused less on the evidence than on

The Sacco and Vanzetti Trial The trial of Sacco and Vanzetti, depicted here by Ben Shahn, came to symbolize the arbitrary injustices of the Red Scare. Their trial became an international cause celebre.

the fact that the defendants were Italian and anarchists. The state doctored evidence and witnesses changed testimony, but the judge favored the prosecution. The appeals lasted six years, during which protests for their release mounted. As the day of the execution approached, labor parties organized worldwide boycotts of American products. Riots in Paris took 20 lives. Uruguayan workers called a general strike. Governments called on the president to intervene, but on August 23, 1927, Sacco and Vanzetti died in the electric chair.

Americans who had talked in 1917 about making the world safe for democracy now seemed ready to restrict their own freedoms out of fear. Lippmann found it "incredible that an administration announcing the most spacious ideals in our history should have done more to endanger fundamental American liberties than any group of men for a hundred years." By the end of 1920, the original terror subsided, but labor unions and social radicals would have to fend off the charge of communism for decades to come.

Conclusion

Wilson tried to lead America toward what he called a new world order, a world where nations and international law would count more than empires and where the United States could light the way toward progress, stability, and peace. What he failed to recognize was that for many Americans this future was filled with terrors as well as promise. The strains of war had introduced new divisions in American society. Progressivism, which had given coherence and direction to social change, was a spent force. The growth of federal administration, the new powers of big business, internal migrations, and new social movements and values added up to what Lippmann called a "revolutionary world." Many of the changes that began during the war had not fully played out, nor were their consequences apparent, but Americans entered the 1920s with a sense of uneasiness. They were aware that their nation was now the world's strongest, but they were unsure about what that might mean for their lives.

Further Readings

Nancy K. Bristow, *Making Men Moral: Social Engineering During the Great War* (1996). Reformers and women's groups used military training to mold men into model citizens.

John Eisenhower, *Intervention! The United States and the Mexican Revolution, 1913–1917* (1993). The story of the U.S. occupation of Veracruz and Pershing's search for Pancho Villa.

Meirion Harries, *The Last Days of Innocence: America at War, 1917–1918* (1997). Lively anecdotal history of the war years.

David M. Kennedy, *Over Here: The First World War and American Society* (1980). An examination of the home front during World War I.

Edward G. Lengel, *To Conquer Hell: The Meuse-Argonne, 1918* (2008). The experience of combat in the American sector of the Western Front.

N. Gordon Levin Jr., *Woodrow Wilson and World Politics* (1968). Levin analyzes progressive president's response to the disorder of world politics.

Erez Manela, *The Wilsonian Moment: Self-Determination and the International Origins of Anticolonial Nationalism* (2007). The global reaction to Wilson's revolutionary doctrine of self-determination.

H. C. Peterson and Gilbert C. Fite, *Opponents of War, 1917–1918* (1957). On wartime peace movements and the Wilson administration's attempts to suppress dissent.

Linda R. Robertson, *The Dream of Civilized Warfare: World War I Flying Aces and the American Imagination* (2003). While infantrymen died by the thousands for a few yards of mud, Americans dreamed of soaring above the Western Front and winning the war in the skies.

Ronald Steel, *Walter Lippmann and the American Century* (1980). More than any other journalist, Lippmann shaped American foreign policy in the twentieth century.

Who, What?

>> Timeline >>

▼ **1911**
Mexican Revolution begins

▼ **1912**
Woodrow Wilson elected president

▼ **1914**
U.S. troops occupy Veracruz, Mexico
World War I begins

▼ **1915**
U.S. troops occupy Haiti (until 1934)
Lusitania sunk

▼ **1916**
U.S. forces invade Mexico in search of Pancho Villa
U.S. forces enter the Dominican Republic
Woodrow Wilson reelected.

▼ **1917**
Russian czar abdicates; parliamentary regime takes power

U.S. declares war on Germany
East St. Louis riot
Houston riot
October Revolution overthrows Russian government; Lenin takes power

▼ **1918**
Wilson announces U.S. war aims: the Fourteen Points
Wilson nationalizes railroads

Review Questions

1. Did the war help or hurt the progressive movement?

2. Allied commanders wanted to use American troops as a reserve, but Pershing wanted his soldiers to enter the battle as an army. Why was that so important to him?

3. Did Senate Republicans reject the League of Nations because they wanted the United States to withdraw from the world, or because they wanted to deal with the world in a different way?

4. Managing the pace of change posed a tricky problem for leaders in the early twentieth century. How did Wilson try to control the dynamic of social and political change? What methods of change was he unwilling to accept?

5. Why were American leaders so much more concerned about sedition and dissent during World War I than they were during the Civil War or World War II?

6. How did mobilization for war advance the progressive agenda? In what ways did it set progressives back?

Websites

Carrie Chapman Catt. From American National Biography Online. A powerful advocate for peace and women's suffrage, she and Alice Paul orchestrated the state-by-state campaign for the nineteenth amendment.

From the Home Front and the Front Lines. Library of Congress online exhibit. The Veterans History Project draws together diaries, oral histories, photographs and other artifacts from America's twentieth century wars. http://www.loc.gov/exhibits/treasures/homefront -home.html

For further review materials and resource information, please visit www.oup.com/us/ofthepeople

Sedition Act outlaws criticism of the U.S. government
U.S. troops stop German advance
Wilson sends troops to Siberia
Armistice ends fighting on the Western Front

Influenza pandemic peaks in September

▼ **1919**
Eighteenth Amendment outlaws manufacture, sale, and transport of alcoholic beverages
Versailles Treaty signed in Paris
Mail bombs target prominent government and business figures
Gary, Indiana, steel strike
U.S. Senate rejects Versailles Treaty

▼ **1920**
Nineteenth Amendment secures the vote for women
Palmer raids arrest thousands of suspected Communists
Sacco and Vanzetti arrested on charges of robbery and murder

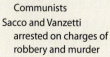

Common Threads

>> How did the Industrial Revolution continue to affect culture and politics, as well as the economy?

>> What differentiated the modern culture of the 1920s from the popular culture of the Gilded Age and the Progressive Era?

>> Why did individualism continue to be such an important force in American life?

>> How did the Republican New Era of the 1920s mark a break from the progressive politics of the 1900s–1910s?

>> What were the long-term implications of a political and cultural order so dependent on material prosperity?

The Modern Nation

1920–1928

>> "The Queen of the Waves"

On August 6, 1926, Gertrude Ederle walked across the beach at Cape Gris-Nez on the French coastline. Her body and her bright red swimsuit were heavily greased. At 7:00 A.M., the 19-year-old from New York City plunged into the water and began to swim toward the coast of England.

"Trudy," the daughter of a German immigrant butcher, was a champion distance swimmer who had won medals at the 1924 Olympics, but no woman had ever completed the long, hazardous swim across the English Channel. In fact, only five men had accomplished the feat. Ederle herself had tried and failed the year before. Exhausted, she had been pulled from the water by her coach, who rebuked her for playing the ukulele instead of practicing hard in the preceding weeks.

This time was different. Despite the tides, the chill water, and the threat of sharks, Ederle persevered, spurred on by her competitive instincts, her eagerness to please her mother, and her father's promise to buy her a new car, a roadster, if she succeeded.

Inspired by thoughts of that roadster, Ederle fought the choppy waves and hunted for a favorable tide. Finally, after 14 hours and 31 minutes in the water, she came ashore at Kingsdown, England, at 9:40 P.M. Ederle had become the first woman to swim the channel and had made the crossing faster than any of the men before her. "I am a proud woman," Trudy announced as she walked up the English beach.

Back in the United States, newspapers trumpeted Ederle's stunning achievement in page-one headlines and analyzed it in editorials. Ederle came home to a tumultuous ticker tape parade in New York. "No President or king, soldier or statesman," reported the *New York Times*, "has ever enjoyed such an enthusiastic and affectionate outburst of acclaim by the metropolis as was offered to the butcher's daughter . . . hailed as the 'Queen of the Waves.'" President Calvin Coolidge sent his congratulations. Trudy was overwhelmed with offers to endorse products and to appear on stage and in the movies.

Gertrude Ederle's enormous reception said a great deal about the United States in the 1920s. Once again at peace, America could afford to indulge an interest in the exploits of a long-distance swimmer. The nation's dynamic industrial economy seemed effortlessly to produce plenty of roadsters, movies, and prosperity.

Ederle herself exemplified a new national culture, rooted in the needs of the booming consumer economy, that broke sharply with the forms and conventions of the past. Emphasizing the importance of pleasure, this modern culture celebrated leisure activities such as dancing, channel swimming, ukulele playing, and other diversions. The ukulele-playing Ederle loved "all normal pleasures, including a jazzy dance now and then." The new culture glorified the purchase and consumption of material goods such as the roadster Ederle wanted and the merchandise she advertised. The teenage swimmer embodied still other aspects of the new culture—its fascination with youth, its endorsement of a more indulgent, child-centered family life, and its infatuation with pleasure-seeking, independent, nontraditional women.

Ederle—the solitary swimmer and enthusiastic consumer—also exemplified the resurgent individualism that shaped the politics of the 1920s. It was no wonder that President Coolidge, a staunch Republican, congratulated Ederle. She seemed to prove that individuals could still achieve great things and find happiness in an increasingly organized, centralized, bureaucratized society.

In the euphoria of the ticker tape parade, it was easy to conclude that Americans welcomed the emerging cultural and political order as much as they welcomed Trudy Ederle. In fact, many people were troubled by the changes of the 1920s. The modern order did not reflect the values of millions of Americans. Neither did it speak to the social and economic inequalities that plagued national life. As a result the new cultural and political order faced a powerful backlash, just as Ederle faced a hostile tide in the English Channel. Nevertheless, like the swimmer, the new culture and politics seemed to overcome all opposition as the decade moved to a close. ●

759

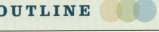
A Dynamic Economy

By and large, the 1920s were a prosperous time for America. After a recession during 1920 and 1921, the economy continued to grow. Consumer prices remained steady throughout the decade, and jobs were plentiful; the unemployment rate went as low as 1.8 percent in 1926. Wages jumped: the nation's net income—the value of its earnings from labor and property—leapt from $64.0 billion in 1921 to $86.8 billion in 1929. This prosperity was driven by the dynamism of the evolving industrial economy. New technologies, increased efficiency, a maturing automobile industry, and new businesses all contributed to the economic gains.

Despite the general prosperity, the transformation of the economy involved defeats for organized labor and decline for many farmers. The relative weakness of agriculture and the strength of industry helped to turn the United States into a predominantly urban nation. In the prosperous 1920s, as always, industrial capitalism was a transforming force.

The Development of Industry

Several long-term factors shaped the development of American industry in the 1920s. In their continuing quest for more efficient

> The man who builds a factory, builds a temple. The man who works there, worships there.
>
> PRESIDENT CALVIN COOLIDGE, January 1925

production, businessmen made use of a flood of new technologies and other innovations. The federal government issued more patents for new inventions—421,000 of them—than in any preceding decade. The industrial economy also made greater use of technical expertise. During the 1920s, the number of engineers in the country nearly doubled.

The switch from coal to electricity, under way since the 1910s, was an important innovation in factories. By the end of the 1920s, electricity powered more than two-thirds of American manufacturing plants. Henry Ford's car company pioneered another critical innovation, the system that became known as Fordism or mass production. By the 1910s, Ford, like other American manufacturers, used interchangeable parts, simple and accurate machine tools, and electric power to speed output at its Highland Park factory complex in Detroit, Michigan. However, auto production was slowed by traditional manufacturing practice. Frames, transmissions, and other key subassemblies remained in place on stands while teams of workers moved from one stand to another to work. Eager to meet the rising demand for the popular Model T car, Ford's managers reversed the process by "moving the work to the men." Beginning in 1913, the Ford plant added conveyor belts and chains to send subassemblies past groups of stationary workers. Instead of making an entire engine or subassembly, a worker might tighten a few bolts or install a single part. The results were astonishing: in 1914, Ford produced 300,000 Model Ts; in 1923, the company produced more than 2 million. Other manufacturers raced to copy Fordism, the company's techniques.

Ford Assembly Line Mass production at work: the assembly line at the Ford Motor Company plant in Dearborn, Michigan, 1928.

Mass production, electrification, and other innovations spurred an extraordinary increase in productivity for American industry. Output per worker skyrocketed 72 percent from 1919 to 1929.

Along with increased productivity, the rise of several industries drove the economy. Auto production now dominated as textiles, railroads, iron, and steel had earlier. In 1921, there were 9.3 million cars on American roads. By 1929, the figure had reached 23 million. By producing all those cars, auto manufacturers stimulated demand for plate glass, oil, gasoline, and rubber.

Other sectors of the industrial economy also grew rapidly. The demand for processed foods, household appliances, office machinery, and chemicals increased dramatically. Emerging industries such as aircraft demonstrated their potential economic importance.

Arguably the first powered, fixed-wing flight had occurred in December 1903, when Wilbur and Orville Wright brought their "Flyer" to the beach at Kitty Hawk, North Carolina. With Orville lying at the controls, the fragile plane flew 120 feet in 12 seconds. But the civilian airplane industry did not take off until the 1920s. Aircraft production rose from less than 300 in 1922 to more than 6,000 in 1929. By then, fledgling airlines were flying passengers on scheduled flights.

The Trend Toward Large-Scale Organization

The development of industry reinforced the trend toward large-scale organization that was basic to U.S. capitalism (see Chapter 17). Only giant corporations, with thousands of employees and hundreds of millions of dollars in capitalization, had the financial resources to pay for mass production. A wave of mergers meant that these big businesses controlled more factories and assets than ever. By 1929, corporations produced 92 percent of the nation's manufactured goods.

The largest firms also benefited from more efficient organizational structures. When the recession of 1920 and 1921 left big corporations with too many unsold goods, companies reorganized. Now top managers, aided by financial, legal, and other experts, oversaw the work of semiautonomous divisions that supplied different markets. At General Motors, for example, the Chevrolet division produced huge numbers of relatively inexpensive cars, while the Cadillac division turned out a smaller number of expensive cars. The new organizational system made corporations more flexible, efficient, and responsive to changes in consumer demand.

Corporate growth was not confined to industry. Chains such as A. & P. grocers and F. W. Woolworth's variety stores increased their share of the nation's retail sales from 4 percent to 20 percent. Just 1 percent of the nation's banks managed nearly half of the country's financial assets. By 1929, just 200 corporations held about one-fifth of national wealth.

Giant firms and their leaders had often been the targets of suspicion, hostility, and reform during the Progressive Era, but the decade's prosperity led many Americans to soften their attitude toward business. There were fewer calls to break up or regulate giant corporations. Big businessmen had seemed to be selfless, patriotic supporters of the U.S. effort in World War I. Now their companies were apparently leading the nation into a new period of economic well-being. To ensure a better image, businessmen paid for extensive public relations campaigns that stressed their commitment to ethical behavior and social service. Basking in the glow of public approval, big business confidently forecast a central role for itself in the nation's destiny. "The modern business system, despised and derided by innumerable reformers, will," a businessman predicted, "be both the inspiration and the instrument of the social progress of the future."

The Transformation of Work and the Workforce

Businessmen's quest for productivity had sweeping consequences for American workers. Industrial efficiency was not just a matter of electricity and machines. To speed up production, the managers at Ford and other factories had to change the nature of work.

Accordingly, the spirit of scientific management continued to sweep through American industry. Laboring under ever-tighter supervision, workers were pushed to work faster and harder. In textile mills, for instance, workers faced the "stretch-out," the requirement that they tend more looms than before. Ford's system of mass production shared Frederick Winslow Taylor's determination to simplify and regiment labor. The result of that determination was less-satisfying work. Instead of making a whole engine, a Ford assembly line worker might spend his day turning a few nuts on one engine after another. In 1913, the company's labor turnover rate soared to 380 percent as unhappy workers quit their jobs.

As production became more efficient, the nation experienced a net loss of about a million jobs in manufacturing, coal mining, and railroading. The growth of other kinds of employment more than compensated for this decrease, however. The ranks of white-collar workers increased 80 percent from 1910 to 1930, when nearly one worker in three did white-collar work rather than manual labor. The nation had already begun a long evolution from an industrial economy based on manual labor to a postindustrial economy based on white-collar work in sales and service.

Economic development also encouraged the continuing, gradual movement of women into the paid workforce. By the end of the 1920s, women made up a majority of clerical workers. In 1900, 22.1 percent of women had worked for pay; by the 1940s, the percentage would reach 27.1 As in the past, most women workers were unmarried.

Despite these changes, women still faced discrimination in the workplace. Overwhelmingly concentrated in low-wage occupations such as domestic service, factory work, and agriculture, they were paid less than men who did comparable work. Female sales workers, for example, earned between 42 and 63 percent of the wages paid to their male counterparts. Hardly any women held high-level managerial jobs. Moreover, there was still resistance to the idea that women should work outside the home. Most people continued to believe that a woman's place was in the home, especially if she had children. Many men feared that paid labor would make women too independent. Only economic necessities—families' need for income and employers' need for workers—reconciled American society to women's employment in the 1920s.

The Defeat of Organized Labor

The American labor movement did not respond effectively to the transformation of work and the workforce. In an age of increasing economic organization, workers became less organized. In 1920 nearly one nonagricultural worker in five belonged to a union. By 1929, little more than one in ten was a union member. The labor movement was especially weak in the developing mass-production industries such as automobiles and steel and barely addressed the growing ranks of clerks and other white-collar workers.

The weak state of organized labor partly resulted from prosperity. Earning relatively good wages, many workers were less interested in joining unions. To show that unions were unnecessary, corporations promoted welfare capitalism, a set of highly publicized programs ranging from lunch-hour movies to sports teams to profit-sharing plans supposedly beneficial to workers. Many firms created company unions purported to represent the interests of workers. But as it became clear that these groups did not give employees a real voice in management, their membership dwindled.

While some firms tried to win over their workers with baseball teams and company unions, many employers used tougher tactics to battle the labor movement. Management crusaded for the "open shop"—a workplace free of labor organization—and found an ally in the judicial system. Rulings by the U.S. Supreme Court such as *Duplex Printing Press Co. v. Deering* (1921) and *Bedford Cut Stone Co. v. Journeymen Stone Cutters' Assn.* (1927) made it easier for lower courts to grant injunctions against union activities. State and federal courts issued injunctions to stop unions from striking and exercising their rights and allowed businesses to sue unions for damages. Businesses used old antiunion tactics such as the demand that workers sign "yellow-dog contracts" promising not to join a union.

The labor movement also hurt its own cause. The leadership of the major national organization, the AFL, was increasingly conservative and timid. The heads of the AFL, mostly white males of western European extraction who represented skilled crafts, had little interest in organizing women workers and wanted nothing to do with socialists, radical unionists, or African American workers. The AFL was slow to admit or even pay attention to the Brotherhood of Sleeping Car Porters, the assertive union of African American workers organized in 1925 under socialist A. Philip Randolph. Despite pleas from Randolph and others, the AFL failed to organize unskilled workers, many of whom were African Americans or white immigrants from eastern and southern Europe.

Weakened by internal divisions, welfare capitalism, the open-shop crusade, and the courts, the labor movement did not challenge the ongoing transformation of industrial labor. Nationwide, the number of strikes and lockouts dropped from 3,411 in 1920 to 604 in 1928. All too often, these labor actions ended in defeat for workers.

The Decline of Agriculture

Against the backdrop of national prosperity, American agriculture continued its long decline. Prices for basic crops such as cotton and wheat fell, and the number of farms dropped.

The larger story of decline obscured important signs of growth and health. Some agricultural sectors were as dynamic as industry, and for the same reasons—increased efficiency promoted by new technologies and large-scale organization. Mechanization, including the introduction of such tractors as the huge Fordson built by the Ford Motor Company, made farm labor more efficient. So did the increasing development of irrigation systems since the turn of the century. By the 1920s, the irrigated farms of the Southwest were producing bumper crops of cotton, fruits, and vegetables. The Southwest also witnessed the rise of huge farms with hundreds and even thousands of acres, whose owners could afford mechanization and irrigation. These innovative "factories in the fields" depended on the old-fashioned exploitation of farm labor, as well as on size and technology. In California's Imperial Valley and elsewhere, migrant workers labored in harsh conditions for low pay in order to create modern, large-scale agriculture.

Ironically, the dynamism of the agricultural economy created a problem for many American farmers. Midsize farms, too big to be run by their owners alone and too small to make mechanization practical, could not compete with the vast "factories in the fields." Increased efficiency, meanwhile, led to bumper crops that did not always find a market at a good price. Farmers were hurt by changes in Americans' diet, such as declining consumption of bread and potatoes, and by the rise of competitors overseas. Producing too much, American farmers could not export enough of their surplus crops to foreign countries. The resulting glut reduced the price of farm products. As their incomes lagged behind those of urban workers, farmers yearned for the return of high pre–World War I agricultural prices that would restore parity between city and country.

Farmers' purchasing power did improve toward the end of the decade, but the basic reality did not change. As a Georgia farmer observed, "The hand that is feeding the world is being spit upon."

The Urban Nation

The woes of agriculture contributed to a long-term shift in the geographical distribution of the American population. For the first time, according to the federal census of 1920, a majority of Americans—54 million out of 105 million—lived in urban territory. This did not mean the United States had become a nation of big cities. The census defined "urban territory" as places with as few as 2,500 people. Many "urban" areas were really small towns little removed from rural life. Nevertheless, the population of the United States was no longer predominantly rural.

The decline of farming spurred this transformation. As agricultural prices fell, millions of Americans fled the nation's farms. While the total U.S. population increased by 17 million during the 1920s, the farm population actually declined by more than 1.5 million.

At the same time, the dynamic growth of the industrial economy

***Arrangement—New York*, ca. 1925** The city—modernistic and smoky—loomed over the new culture of the 1920s: Czech-American artist Jan Matulka's vision of New York City.

swelled the population of towns and cities. In the 1920s, factory production was still centered in urban areas. Manufacturing gave many cities their identity. Detroit was becoming the "motor city." Akron, Ohio, was the home of the nation's rubber production. Pittsburgh, Pennsylvania, and Birmingham, Alabama, symbolized the steel industry. Most of the new white-collar jobs were located in cities. Corporations also put their headquarters in cities, especially the two largest, Chicago and New York.

The rise of the automobile contributed to the emergence of the urban nation as well. The car made it practical for Americans to live in suburbs and drive into the city to work and to shop. In the 1920s, the suburban lifestyle was still reserved mostly for the well-to-do. Elite suburbs, such as Grosse Pointe and Ferndale outside Detroit, and Beverly Hills, Glendale, and Inglewood outside Los Angeles, grew explosively. The transformation of the countryside into suburbs was a powerful symbol of the new urban nation.

A Modern Culture

The 1920s saw the full emergence of a modern culture that had been gradually taking shape for decades. But Americans now felt themselves surrounded by something fundamentally new—a term they used over and over to describe their world. So perfectly symbolized by Gertrude Ederle, the new culture extolled the virtues of modernity and pleasure. Rooted in the nation's economic development, the new culture reflected both the needs of businessmen who had to sell the goods rolling off assembly lines and the desires of Americans with more money and free time than ever. Supported by advertising and installment buying, the culture of leisure and consumption offered spectator sports, movies, popular music, radio, and sex. The new culture entailed new views of gender, family life, and youth and placed renewed emphasis on the old values of individualism in an increasingly organized society.

The Spread of Consumerism

Encouraged by big business, many Americans increasingly defined life as the pursuit of pleasure. They were invited to find happiness in leisure and consumption rather than in work. This philosophy of consumerism saturated American society by the end of the decade.

The increased efficiency and profitability of the economy enabled American employers to allow their workers higher wages and more leisure hours. Some employers, most notably Ford, also raised wages in order to hold on to workers alienated by the drudgery of mass production. And Ford himself intentionally increased workers' pay to enable them to buy the products of modern factories. As a result, the incomes of workers and other employees reached a new high in the 1920s. Factory workers' real wages rose 19 percent from 1914 to 1923.

> Every morning, Every evening,
>   Ain't we got fun/
>
> Not much money, Oh but honey,
>   Ain't we got fun
>
> RICHARD A. WHITING, RAYMOND B. EGAN, AND GUS KAHN, 1921

Many workers had more time to enjoy their wages. For salaried, middle-class workers, the annual vacation had become a tradition by the 1910s. Although blue-collar workers seldom enjoyed a vacation, they spent less time on the job. Some employers, including Henry Ford, instituted a five-day workweek during the 1920s. More commonly, businesses shortened their workday. As a result, the average workweek fell from 47.4 hours in 1920 to 44.2 in 1929. "The shorter work day brought me my first idea of there being such a thing as pleasure," said one young female worker. "Before this time it was just sleep and eat and hurry off to work."

A change in attitude accompanied these changes in wages and workdays. The work ethic seemed less necessary in a prospering economy. Thanks to Fordism and Taylorism, work was less satisfying, too. In these circumstances, people justified pleasure as an essential antidote to labor. As early as 1908, a magazine announced that "Fun Is a Necessity." Many Americans now agreed.

The advertising industry encouraged the new attitude toward pleasure. Although advertising agencies had first appeared in the 1850s and 1860s, the business did not reach maturity until the 1920s. During the 1920s, ads appeared everywhere—in newspapers and magazines, on billboards and big electric signs. Major advertising agencies such as J. Walter Thompson and Batten, Barton, Durstine, and Osborn became concentrated in New York City, home to so many corporations. Impressed by successful ad campaigns for Listerine antiseptic and mouthwash and Fleischmann's yeast, big business increasingly turned to advertising agencies to sell goods and services. Expenditures for advertising leaped from $682 million in 1914 to nearly $3 billion by 1929.

Advertising, like the new culture, optimistically embraced change and trumpeted the new. Ad men believed they were bringing the benefits of modernity to Americans. According to advertisements, purchasing the right products would solve people's problems, make up for the drudgery of work, and bring fulfillment. To enthusiastic ad men, advertising became as important as the products it sold. In his best-selling book, *The Man Nobody Knows* (1925), ad executive Bruce Barton portrayed Jesus Christ as a great advertiser, who had turned his disciples into a sales force "that conquered the world" with the new product, Christianity.

Along with advertising, business used installment loans to encourage Americans to buy goods and services "on time." Credit buying spread so rapidly that the nation's total consumer debt more than doubled from 1922 to 1929. As a result, the sales of such consumer goods as pianos, washing machines, and automobiles boomed. Americans had bought just 181,000 automobiles in 1910; they bought 4,455,000 in 1929. Thanks to the availability of another kind of loan, the mortgage, more Americans were able to invest in a home of their own. Spending on new private housing jumped from $1.2 billion in 1915 to $2.0 billion in 1920 and then to

"Would your husband marry you again?" Like this advertisement for Palmolive Soap, advertising in the 1920s often sold products by making consumers feel insecure and inadequate.

a staggering $5.0 billion by 1924. All this loan-driven spending helped power the economic prosperity of the 1920s.

New Pleasures

The culture of the 1920s offered many pleasures, especially sports, movies, popular music, and radio. Gertrude Ederle was part of a golden age for spectator sports. Although people still avidly played games themselves, they also passively observed other people's games more than ever before. Tennis, boxing, and auto racing flourished during the decade. The American Professional Football Association, which became the National Football League, played its first season in 1920. Although crowds packed stadiums for college football games, baseball remained the most popular American sport. A huge network of minor-league baseball teams covered the nation. Meanwhile, the popularity of major-league baseball surged, thanks in part to the exploits of the New York Yankees' home run–hitting outfielder, Babe Ruth.

While spectator sports enthralled millions, another passive pleasure, the movies, was undeniably the most popular consumer attraction of the 1920s (see Table 23–1). Little more than a novelty when first shown in the mid-1890s, silent films had rapidly matured into a big business commanding the loyalty of millions of Americans. In city neighborhoods in the 1900s, crowds packed into stuffy "nickelodeons"—converted storefront theaters that showed short, silent one-reel films for the low price of a nickel. The movies quickly became longer and more sophisticated. Spreading through the cities and into the suburbs, theaters became larger and more elegant. By the 1920s, lavish movie "palaces," such as the Roxy in New York and the Tivoli in Chicago, evoked the Orient and other exotic faraway places. Nationwide, attendance doubled from 40 million a week in 1922 to 80 million a week in 1929.

Booming attendance fueled the growth of a handful of corporations, including Warner Brothers and RKO, that dominated the film industry. By the 1920s, the center of movie production had shifted from New York to Hollywood, California. As the film industry began to be called "Hollywood," the business grew still bigger toward the end of the decade, when film studios learned how to synchronize sound and moving images in such films as *The Jazz Singer* of 1927.

 Table 23–1 Spending for Recreational Services, 1909–1929

Year	Total (millions of dollars)	Motion Picture Theaters (millions of dollars)	Spectator Sports (millions of dollars)
1909	377	###	###
1914	434	###	###
1919	806	###	###
1921	911	301	30
1923	1082	336	46
1927	1405	526	48
1929	1670	720	66

Historical Statistics of the United States, Millennial Online Edition (Cambridge: Cambridge University Press, 2008), Table Dh309–318.

= No Data

It was fitting that one of the first "talking pictures" was about the impact of jazz. Popular music in general and jazz in particular played an important role in the new consumer culture. Created by African Americans in the 1910s, jazz was a rhythmically and harmonically innovative music that featured improvised solos and a hot beat. The new music emerged in various places around the country, but its first great center was the streets, brothels, and dives of New Orleans. The Louisiana city was home to the first major jazz composer, Jelly Roll Morton, and to the first jazz superstar, trumpeter and singer Louis Armstrong. As jazz became nationally popular, Morton, Armstrong, and the focus of jazz moved on, as did so many African Americans, to Chicago and New York City (see Chapter 22).

***The Jazz Singer* Premiere** The dazzling allure of a new pleasure—the "talking picture"—draws a big opening-night crowd to Warners' Theatre, New York City, October 6, 1927.

The new music quickly attracted white Americans, especially the young, who yearned for something more daring than the relatively sedate popular music of the day. Even the name—a reference perhaps to speed or sexual intercourse—conjured up pleasure and liberation. Soon white musicians were contributing to the evolution of the music. For many whites, jazz summed up a period seemingly dominated by the pursuit of liberating pleasures. The 1920s became known as the "Jazz Age," after the title of a 1922 book of short stories by F. Scott Fitzgerald.

The great popularity of jazz and other musical genres was made possible by the phonograph, originated by Thomas Edison in the 1870s and modified by other inventors. In the 1920s, the electrical recording microphone dramatically improved the sound quality of records and made the new music accessible to millions of Americans.

A newer technological innovation, the radio, also allowed Americans to hear popular music. After Italian inventor Guglielmo Marconi transmitted the first radio waves through the air in 1895, a series of innovations made possible the inauguration of commercial radio broadcasting in the United States by 1920. The federal government began licensing radio stations the next year.

Like the movies, radio quickly became corporatized big business. By 1923, there were more than 500 stations. In 1926, the first permanent network of stations, the National Broadcasting Company (NBC), took to the airwaves. Americans tuned in to hear broadcasts of live music, news, sports, and soap operas. To meet the demand for radios, manufacturers turned out more than 2 million sets a year by 1925. Radio, like the movies, played a key role in disseminating the values of consumerism, as corporations rushed to advertise their products by sponsoring radio programs.

A Sexual Revolution

Along with such new pleasures as radio and movies, the modern culture offered a new attitude toward an old pleasure, sex. By the 1920s, Americans' sexual attitudes and behavior were clearly changing. People openly discussed sex and placed a new emphasis on the importance of sexual satisfaction, primarily in marriage. And there were signs of greater sexual exploration among unmarried young people.

In the nineteenth century, Americans, especially middle-class Victorians, had tended to maintain a discreet silence about sex. But that silence gave way in the twentieth century. During the Progressive Era, reformers forced the public discussion of such sexual issues as prostitution and venereal disease. The reformers, anxious to limit and control extramarital sexual behavior, hardly wanted to glorify sexual pleasure. But they helped pave the way for a more open and approving depiction of sexuality.

The popular amusements of the 1910s and 1920s inundated Americans with sexual images. From the beginning, the movies explored sexual topics in such films as *The Anatomy of a Kiss* and *A Bedroom Blunder*. Some popular music featured suggestive songs about sex such as "It's Tight Like That" and "I Need a Little Sugar in My Bowl." Popular dances such as the grizzly bear, the shimmy, and the turkey trot promoted close physical contact or sexually suggestive steps. The contrast with the culture of the late nineteenth century was startling. As early as 1913, a magazine concluded that "Sex O'Clock" had struck in the United States.

The increased openness about sex reflected the growing belief that sexual pleasure was necessary and desirable, particularly within marriage. Married couples increasingly considered intercourse as an opportunity for pleasure as well as procreation. Experts insisted that healthy marriages required sexual satisfaction for both partners.

The new view of marital sexuality helped to change attitudes toward contraception. By the 1910s, an emerging grassroots movement, led by socialists and other radicals, promoted sex education and contraceptives, which were largely illegal. The crusade's best-known figure was the fiery former nurse and socialist organizer, Margaret Sanger, who coined the term "birth control." Although Sanger once had to flee the country to avoid prosecution, birth control gradually became respectable—and widely practiced—in the 1920s.

Despite the growing belief in the importance of sexual satisfaction, most adult Americans still condemned premarital sex. Nevertheless, premarital intercourse apparently became more common. Many couples believed that intercourse was acceptable if they were "in love" and intended to marry. There was also an apparent increase in "petting"—sexual contact short of intercourse.

While changing some of their attitudes about sexual behavior, most heterosexual Americans still condemned homosexuality. Nevertheless, a sexual revolution was under way.

Changing Gender Ideals

Shifting sexual attitudes were closely tied to new gender ideals. By the 1920s, Americans' sense of what it meant to be female was changing. Since the late nineteenth century, Americans had been talking about the independent, assertive "New

Woman" who claimed the right to attend school, vote, and have a career. The "New Woman" of the 1920s was now a sexual being, too. An object of male desire, she was also a fun-loving individual with desires of her own.

The sexual nature of women was central to a new movement, known as feminism, that had emerged in the 1910s. The feminists, like earlier female reformers, were generally white, well-educated, Protestant, urban women. Concentrated in New York's Greenwich Village, the feminists broke with the older reformers by insisting on sharing the sexual opportunities and satisfactions that men had presumably long enjoyed. Unlike the older generation of activist women, the feminists were unwilling to give up marriage and children in order to have careers outside the home. Feminism insisted on women's right to pleasure and satisfaction in all phases of life, from the most public to the most intimate.

Small in number, the feminists commanded a great deal of attention. Several of their ideas and practices were too radical for many American men and women. Much of the nation rejected altogether some feminists' decision to retain their maiden names in married life or to explore sexual relationships outside of marriage. Most fundamentally, many Americans were unwilling to accept the feminist insistence on full equality with men.

Nevertheless American culture proved rather open to the more liberated view of female sexuality that emerged from feminism, experts, and the movies. The most popular image of the American woman of the 1920s was the vivacious young "flapper," with her short skirt, bound breasts, and bobbed hair. The flapper was likely to wear cosmetics and to smoke cigarettes—practices once associated only with prostitutes.

Notions of masculinity were also changing. With the growing emphasis on female needs and desires, men were urged to be attentive and responsive and to focus on the home. As the world of work became less satisfying, experts told men to look for fulfillment in family life. The family man of the 1920s, unlike the stereotypical Victorian man, was not supposed to be a distant, stern patriarch. Instead, he was a companion to his wife and a doting friend to his children.

In practice, many men still defined themselves in terms of their work rather than their domestic life. Moreover, American society still regarded women as the primary caretakers of children. Despite the clear change in domestic values, many men were still relative outsiders in the home.

The Family and Youth

Changing gender ideals were directly related to a reconsideration of family life and youth. Although whole families still labored together in California fields and North Carolina textile mills, most Americans no longer regarded the family as a group of productive workers. Child-labor laws increasingly made sure that boys and girls spent their time in school rather than in the workplace. The family became primarily a unit of leisure and consumption. The home was the place where men, women, and children found pleasure and fulfillment, where they used their Fleischmann's yeast and Listerine mouthwash and congregated around the radio.

Reflecting the values of the modern culture, parents became more likely to indulge their children, who enjoyed more toys, possessions, spending money, and pleasures than had earlier generations. The automobile gave young people more

AMERICAN LANDSCAPE

>> "Flaming Youth" on Campus

College and university campuses were the laboratories for "flaming youth." During the 1920s, male and female college students created a distinctive youth culture within the larger modern culture. Campus life reflected central features of twentieth century society: the desire for individual freedom and the need to cope with organization. The culture of the "advance guard of the younger generation" also reflected the uneven development of American democracy in the Jazz Age.

On one level, higher education was anything but democratic. Traditionally, colleges and universities were for the elite. In 1899, only 238,000 students—little more than 2 percent of Americans aged 18 to 24—enrolled in institutions of higher learning. Only 85,000 of those students were women. But as the dynamic economy demanded educated white-collar workers, more middle-class families found the means to send their sons and daughters to college. By 1929, 1.1 million students—7.2 percent of 18- to 24-year-olds—were enrolled. Thanks to changing attitudes toward women, 480,000 female students were on campus.

The development of public-supported colleges and universities made this growth possible. In just three years from 1919 to 1922, enrollments doubled from 3,000 to 6,000 at the University of Illinois and from 4,000 to 8,000 at Ohio State University. Less elitist than leading private institutions, the public schools were at the forefront of a more democratic student culture.

That culture celebrated independence. "To me the Jazz Age signifies an age of freedom in thought and action," explained a coed at the University of Denver. "The average young person of today is not bound by the strict conventions which governed the actions of previous generations." Liberated from the constraints of home and workplace, college students had the space to pursue their desires. "We were big-eyed with wanting," said Hoagy Carmichael, a student at Indiana University, "with making fun."

On campuses across the country, students held "petting parties." They forced college officials to tolerate racy new dances such as the toddle, the shimmy, the Charleston, and the black bottom. By the end of the decade, about two out of three students defied Prohibition (see Chapter 22) by drinking on and off campus. Public drunkenness was no longer a scandal. Women students engaged in the "unladylike," sexually suggestive practice of smoking. "College," sniffed a dean at Princeton, "has unfortunately become a kind of glorified playground . . . a paradise of the young."

Students' quest for pleasure shaped their politics. While Carmichael and his friends paid little attention to most public issues, they believed strongly in individual rights. Students regarded sex and other satisfactions as a private matter. College newspapers criticized Prohibitionists and other moral reformers who wanted to regulate individual behavior.

Even as they reflected the individualist values of the modern culture, college students adapted to the growing power of organization. Collegiate life became more bureaucratic as administrators coped with rising enrollments. Students themselves turned to organizations in the 1920s. Nationwide, the number of fraternities and sororities shot up during the decade. By 1930 about one student in three belonged to a fraternity or sorority; Hoagy Carmichael joined Kappa Sigma. On many campuses, Greek houses included most student leaders and set the tone of campus fashion for the

"barbs," the barbarians who made up the rest of the student body.

Fraternities and sororities were places where college students could try out smoking and other freedoms. But the Greek system also forced its members to come to terms with organization. As the campus newspaper at Cornell University explained, the fraternity "crushes individuality." Initiation rites and hazing taught new members that they were expected to conform to the norms of the group. The distinctive culture of "flaming youth," like the new national culture, embraced organization as well as freedom, conformity as well as individualism. ●

mobility, too. With their new freedom, they could begin to create their own separate culture. One sign was the dramatic spread of petting among high-school youth, newly free from parental control.

Most adults accepted this situation partly because they admired and envied youthfulness. The modern culture, unhappy with work and anxious for fun, glorified youth. In 1923 the writer Samuel Hopkins Adams, writing under a pseudonym, published the novel *Flaming Youth*, about sexually adventurous, fast-living young people; the title became a catchphrase for the youth culture of the 1920s.

The Celebration of the Individual

The emphasis on the individual, so evident in changing views of sex, gender, family, and youth, was a fundamental aspect of the modern culture. In addition to Gertrude Ederle and Babe Ruth, Americans admired a host of sports heroes and heroines, including tennis player Helen Wills Moody, boxer Jack Dempsey, golfer Bobby Jones, and football running back Red Grange. In the 1920s, the movie industry increasingly focused public attention on the distinctive personalities of stars. Individualism was basic to the "New Woman," too.

The resurgence of individualism was not surprising. The belief in the importance of the individual was deeply engrained in the American culture. Paradoxically, the development of industrial capitalism intensified the importance of both individuals and organizations. As corporations grew larger and produced more, these giant firms needed to stimulate consumerism, the gratification of individual needs and desires.

There were serious obstacles to true individualism in the 1920s. Powerful organizations, including corporations, controlled individual life. Even the most famous individual exploit of the decade depended on organization. On May 20–21, 1927, Charles A. Lindbergh flew his monoplane, the *Spirit of St. Louis,* from New York City to Paris. This first nonstop solo crossing of the Atlantic made Lindbergh an international symbol of what an individual

First Nonstop Solo Transatlantic Flight Charles A. Lindbergh pictured in front of the *Spirit of St. Louis* just before taking off from Roosevelt Field, New York, for Paris, on May 20, 1927.

could accomplish, but Lindbergh's feat relied on a group of businessmen who put up the money and a corporation that built the plane. Organization and individualism, the new and the old, were interdependent in the 1920s.

The Limits of the Modern Culture

The modern culture had clear limits in the 1920s. For millions of Americans, much of the consumer lifestyle was out of reach. The spread of the new values was as limited as the spread of prosperity. Many Americans, among them artists and intellectuals, were unwilling to define their lives by the pursuit of pleasure, leisure, and consumption. For them modern society, with its emphasis on all things new, including the "New Negro," the "New Woman," and the "New Era," represented an unwelcome abandonment of old values. In different ways, fundamentalist Christians, immigration restrictionists, and the Ku Klux Klan demanded a return to an earlier United States. Mexican Americans, African Americans, and others found that the new culture, like the old, treated them like second-class citizens.

> I feel most colored when I am thrown against a sharp white background. . . . Among the thousand white persons, I am a dark rock surged upon, and overswept, but through it all, I remain myself. When covered by the waters, I am; and the ebb but reveals me again.
>
> ZORA NEALE HURSTON,
> 1928

The Limits of Prosperity

Despite the general aura of prosperity, low incomes and poverty persisted in the 1920s. As late as 1928, six out of ten American families made less than the $2,000 a year required for the "basic needs of life." Despite the housing boom, most American household heads—52 percent in 1930—still did not own their own home.

These statistics were not simply a reflection of the difficult lives of rural Americans. In the towns and cities of the increasingly urban nation, there was still a stark divide between middle- and upper-class existence on one hand, and working-class reality on the other. In their pioneering anthropological study of a small midwestern city in the 1920s, Helen and Staughton Lynd discovered that the "division into the working class and business class . . . constitutes the outstanding cleavage in Middletown." The working class of "Middletown"—it was in fact Muncie, Indiana—had less money and leisure to enjoy the new culture. As the Lynds reported in *Middletown* (1929), about a third of the city still did not own automobiles.

The "Lost Generation" of Intellectuals

Many artists and intellectuals felt alienated from the United States of the 1920s. For white, mostly male writers and artists who came of age during World War I, the conflict represented a failure of Western civilization, a brutal and pointless exercise in destruction. Its aftermath left these Americans angry at what the poet Ezra Pound called "an old bitch gone in the teeth . . . a botched civilization." It also left them alienated and rootless. In a nation supposedly devoted to individualism, they did not feel free. They were, as the writer Gertrude Stein described them, a "Lost Generation." Some of them, such as Stein and her fellow writer Ernest Hemingway, left the United States for Paris and other places in Europe.

However prosperous and peaceful, the postwar years did not reassure the Lost Generation about the course of American life. Artists and intellectuals argued that the nation had not changed much at all. In such works as *Winesburg, Ohio* (1919), novelist Sherwood Anderson portrayed a still-repressive society that denied people real freedom and individuality. The acid-tongued critic H. L. Mencken, editor of the magazine the *American Mercury,* condemned a provincial and parochial culture still dominated by the "booboisie" and its rural values.

At the same time, other American artists and intellectuals feared that their country had changed too much. Although excited by the potential of the machine, they criticized the routinized work and superficial pleasures of modern life. In his 1922 novel *Babbitt,* Sinclair Lewis satirized a midwestern Republican businessman whose consumerism made him a conformist, not an individualist. F. Scott Fitzgerald, in such fiction as *This Side of Paradise* (1920) and *The Great Gatsby* (1925), conveyed the sense of loss and emptiness in the lives of fashionable "flaming youth" in the "Jazz Age."

From a different angle, 12 southern intellectuals, including Allen Tate, Robert Penn Warren, Donald Davidson, and John Crowe Ransom, attacked the modern culture in *I'll Take My Stand: The South and the Agrarian Tradition* (1930). Their essays offered a spirited defense of the rural, traditional culture and lamented an industrial consumer society that demeaned work and exalted individualism.

The artists and intellectuals did not set off a mass rebellion against modern culture, but they did express the ambivalence and uneasiness many people felt. In different and contradictory ways, artists and intellectuals laid out an agenda for Americans as they came to terms with modern, consumer society in the decades to come.

Fundamentalist Christians and "Old-Time Religion"

For many Americans of faith, the rapid growth of the modern culture promoted a sense of profound and unsettling change. "The world has been convulsed," declared *Presbyterian Magazine.* "The most settled principles and laws of society have been attacked." The new culture was troubling because it was so secular. American society seemed to define life in terms of material satisfaction rather than spiritual commitment. Many Protestants, feeling that their own churches had betrayed them, resented the influence of liberal Protestants who had tried to accommodate their faith to the methods and discoveries of science and scholarship.

Fundamentalists, or opponents of liberalism, took their name from *The Fundamentals,* a series of essays by conservative Protestant theologians that appeared beginning in 1909. Fundamentalists emerged all around the country, but they were strongest in rural areas and in the South and West. By the end of World War I, fundamentalists dominated the Southern Baptist Convention and were fighting liberals for control of the northern churches.

Fundamentalists rejected liberalism above all for its willingness to question the historical truth of the Bible. The fundamentalist movement urged people to return to biblical, patriarchal, and denominational authority, to what came to be called "old-time religion."

The high point in the fundamentalist-liberal battle came in a courtroom in Tennessee in 1925. That year, a high-school biology teacher, John Scopes, defied a new state law banning the teaching of "any theory that denies the story of the divine creation of man as taught in the Bible, and that teaches instead that man has descended from a lower order of animals." Scopes's trial became a national media event. The chief lawyer for the prosecution was William Jennings Bryan, the former Democratic presidential candidate and secretary of state who had become a leading crusader for fundamentalism. While Bryan was a longtime champion of rural America, Scopes's attorneys—Clarence Darrow and Dudley Field Malone—represented the city and modern culture. (Malone had helped to finance Gertrude Ederle's swim across the English Channel.) In a dramatic confrontation, Darrow called Bryan to the stand and forced him to concede that the Bible might not be literally accurate. Although Scopes was convicted and fined, the fundamentalists lost some credibility and Bryan died soon after. In the next several years, other southern and western states passed antievolution laws, but similar measures failed in the more urbanized Northeast.

The Scopes trial did not end the war between fundamentalism and liberalism. Fundamentalists were numerous. Their hostility to liberal Protestantism and modern culture would affect American life for decades to come.

Nativists and Immigration Restriction

While fundamentalist Christianity sought a return to old-time religion, a resurgent nativist movement wanted to go back to an earlier, supposedly more homogenous America. As mass migration from Europe to the United States resumed after World War I, nativist feeling revived among Americans from western European backgrounds. Thanks to the Russian Revolution and the domestic Red Scare, they associated immigrants with anarchism and radicalism and derided southern and eastern Europeans as inferior races that would weaken the nation.

Responding in 1921, Congress overwhelmingly passed a law temporarily limiting the annual immigration from any European country to 3 percent of the number of its immigrants who had been living in the United States in 1910. This quota sharply reduced the number of new immigrants from southern and eastern Europe, but nativists wanted even tougher action. Congress responded with the National Origins Act of 1924. This limited the annual intake from a European country to 2 percent of the number of its immigrants living in the United States in 1890—a time when there were few southern and eastern Europeans in America. The act also excluded Japanese immigrants altogether. The legislation had the desired effect: immigration fell from 805,000 arrivals in 1921 to 280,000 in 1929 (see Table 23–2).

Scopes Trial The battle between liberalism and fundamentalism: Clarence Darrow, lawyer for John Scopes in his 1925 trial for teaching evolution, confronts chief prosecutor William Jennings Bryan on the witness stand.

The Rebirth of the Ku Klux Klan

Nativism and fundamentalism helped spur another challenge to the new cultural order of the 1920s. In 1915, the Ku Klux Klan, the vigilante group that had terrorized African Americans in the South during Reconstruction, was reborn in a ceremony on Stone Mountain, Georgia, and it enjoyed explosive growth after World War I. The "Invisible Empire" borrowed the rituals of the nineteenth-century Klan, including its costume of white robes and hoods and its symbol of a burning cross. Like the old Klan, the twentieth-century version was driven by a racist hatred of African Americans, but the new Klan took on new targets, including Jews, Roman Catholics, immigrants, religious liberalism, and change in general.

The Invisible Empire condemned modern culture, charging that the nation now valued "money above manhood." Klan rallies rang with denunciations of big business. Above all, the Klan condemned pleasure, "the god of the young people of America." The Klan was hostile to the new gender ideals, to birth control and freer sexuality, and to the independence of youth. Klansmen and Klanswomen yearned for an earlier America in which white Protestant males had power over women, youth, and other groups and had nothing to fear from big business.

The Klan's tactics were a blend of old and new. Seeing themselves as an army of secret vigilantes, some Klan members supported the age-old tactics of moral regulation—intimidation, flogging, and sometimes lynching—in order to scare people into good behavior. At the same time, much of the Invisible Empire repudiated violence and used the latest advertising techniques to boost its membership.

For several years, the Klan proved extraordinarily successful. Despite its extremist views, the Invisible Empire had a mainstream membership, flourishing in every region, in cities as well as the countryside. At its peak, the organization enrolled perhaps 3 to 5 million secret members. Because so many politicians sympathized with the Klan or feared its power, the organization had considerable political influence. Working with both major parties, the order helped to elect governors, senators, and other officials.

Table 23–2 The Impact of Nativism: Immigration, 1921–1929

	Arrivals (in thousands)		
Origin	**1921**	**1925**	**1929**
Eastern Europe and Poland	138	10	14
Southern Europe	299	8	22
Asia	25	4	4
Mexico	31	33	40
Total	805	294	280

Historical Statistics of the United States, (Cambridge: Cambridge University Press), I, 401. Itemized groups do not add up to totals.

KKK Parade, August 19, 1925 Members of the Ku Klux Klan marching down Pennsylvania Avenue in Washington, DC, to celebrate the organization and its defense of "traditional" values.

At the height of its power, however, the Invisible Empire collapsed under the weight of scandal. The Klan seemed lawless and hypocritical when its leaders were revealed to be caught up in financial scandal, alcohol, pornography, adultery, kidnapping, and murder. Most people realized they had nothing to fear from such Klan targets as Communists, unions, and Jews. Millions of Americans, however uneasy about the new culture, had no desire to support prejudice, lawbreaking, and violence in a futile attempt to go back to the past. The Klan's membership dropped precipitously in the late 1920s.

Mexican Americans

Despite the activities of immigration restrictionists and the Klan, the United States became in some ways more diverse than ever. Perhaps a million to a million and a half Mexicans entered the United States legally or surreptitiously between 1890 and 1929. Many left to avoid the upheaval of the Mexican Revolution of 1910 (see Chapter 22) and to escape the agricultural transformation that made it difficult for the rural poor to earn a living off the land. Meanwhile, the dynamic U.S. economy created opportunities for impoverished Mexican immigrants. Ironically, the restrictionist immigration legislation of the 1920s helped ensure that Mexicans would find work in the United States. Unable to get enough European or Asian workers, employers turned eagerly to Mexico as a source of cheap seasonal labor. In particular the Southwest's rapidly developing economy needed Mexican workers for mines, railroads, construction gangs, and, above all, farms.

Mexican American Workmen Laborers pause for the camera while making adobe bricks at the Casa Verdugo, Glendale, California, ca. 1920.

Like a large number of immigrants from Europe, many Mexican migrants did not plan to stay in the United States. They traveled back and forth to their homeland, or returned permanently. Gradually, however, many chose to stay as they developed economic and family ties in the United States. The National Origins Act, which made it costly, time consuming, and often humiliating for Mexicans to cross the border, also encouraged migrants to remain in the United States. As a result, the official Mexican population of the United States rose from 103,000 in 1900 to 478,000 by 1920. At the turn of the century, the majority of immigrants lived in Texas and Arizona, but California, with its booming agricultural economy, rapidly became the center of the Mexican population. The city of Los Angeles, growing phenomenally in the early twentieth century, attracted perhaps 190,000 Mexicans by 1930.

Mexican immigrants, like so many other ethnic groups in the United States, wrestled with complex questions about their national identity. Were they still Mexicans or had they become Americans or some unique combination of the two nationalities? In varying degrees, the migrants clung to their old national identities and adapted to their new home.

Mexican Americans, eager to hold onto the advantages they had won by birth and longtime residence in the United States, feared that the newcomers would compete for jobs and cause native-born whites to denigrate all Mexicans alike. The immigrants, in turn, often derided Mexican Americans as *pochos*—bleached or faded people—who had lost their true Mexican identity.

Nevertheless, ethnic Mexicans created a distinctive culture in the United States. For all their differences, they shared a sense of common cultural origins and common challenges. In a white-dominated society, they saw themselves as *La Raza*—The Race—set apart by heritage and skin color.

Poverty and discrimination also contributed to a sense of common Mexican American identity. In many towns and cities, ethnic Mexicans were effectively segregated in certain neighborhoods—*barrios*—in poor conditions. Largely ignored by corporations marketing goods nationwide, Mexican Americans supported their own businesses, listened to their own Spanish-language radio programs, and bought records made by their own musicians. Anglo-American prejudice also tended to drive Mexicans together. Many whites stereotyped them as a lazy and shiftless race who would take jobs from native-born workers and who could not be assimilated into American life and culture. Still other white Americans, drawing on the reform techniques of the Progressive Era, wanted to "Americanize" ethnic Mexicans by teaching them English and middle-class values and homemaking practices.

Their sense of common identity encouraged Mexican Americans to struggle for economic progress and equal rights. In 1928, farm workers in California created La Unión de Trabajadores del Valle Imperial (Imperial Valley Workers Union) in a successful fight for higher wages. A year later, Mexican American businessmen and professionals in Texas formed the League of United Latin American Citizens (LULAC) in Texas.

African Americans and the "New Negro"

Like Mexican Americans, African Americans found the new cultural terrain of the United States appealing but unsatisfying. They enjoyed and helped to create the new culture, but it did little to alter discrimination against blacks. In both South and North, African Americans still lived with economic and political inequality.

While discrimination had not changed, many African Americans insisted that they had. The decade that talked about the "New Woman" also talked about the "New Negro." The term went back to the late nineteenth century; in 1900, Booker T. Washington titled one of his books *A New Negro for a New Century*. By the 1920s, the increased use of "New Negro" reflected a fresh sense of freedom as African Americans left the southern countryside for cities. It was also the product of frustration as African Americans encountered inequality along with opportunity in urban areas. The "New Negro" was militant and assertive in the face of mistreatment by whites. "The time for cringing is over," said an African American newspaper.

The "New Negro" was also defined by a profound sense of racial difference. Applauding the distinctiveness of their life and culture, African Americans spurred the Harlem Renaissance. Harlem, the section of upper Manhattan in New York where many African Americans had moved since the turn of the century, became a center of artistic and intellectual creativity. Novelists such as Zora Neale Hurston, Jessie Fauset,

Claude McKay, Jean Toomer, and Dorothy West; poets such as Langston Hughes, Sterling Brown, and Countee Cullen; and artists such as Aaron Douglas and Augusta Savage produced a new birth of African American creativity. In different ways, these women and men explored and celebrated the nature of American blackness in 1920s America and its origins in Africa.

The militance of the "New Negro" was reflected in the development of the NAACP, which turned increasingly to African American leadership. The organization's key figure, W. E. B. DuBois, became more critical of whites and more determined that white-dominated nations should return Africa to African control. The NAACP also pushed the cause of African American civil rights more aggressively and attacked the white primary system that denied African Americans any say in the dominant Democratic Party organizations of the South. The NAACP continued a longtime antilynching campaign, which bore fruit in the 1920s, as southern whites were increasingly embarrassed by vigilante justice.

For a time, the NAACP's efforts were overshadowed by the crusades of Marcus Garvey. A Jamaican immigrant to New York City, Garvey founded the Universal Negro Improvement Association (UNIA), which became the largest African American activist organization of the 1920s. Less interested in political rights and integration, Garvey focused on African American pride and self-help and on Africa. He exalted "a new Negro who stands erect, conscious of his manhood rights and fully determined to preserve them at all times." So Garvey urged African Americans to develop their own businesses and thus become economically self-sufficient. Like DuBois, he insisted that the imperial powers give up their colonial control of the African continent. Sure that blacks could never find equality in a white-dominated nation, Garvey believed African Americans should return to Africa.

While the NAACP attracted mostly middle-class members, UNIA developed a vast following among the African American working class. In 1919, Garvey launched an economic self-help project, the Black Star Line, which, he promised, would buy ships and transport passengers and cargo from the United States to the West Indies, Central America, and Africa. Many of his followers invested in the Black Star Line, but it collapsed due to mismanagement. Garvey himself was indicted for mail fraud in connection with the project. By the end of the decade, federal authorities had deported him to Jamaica, and the UNIA had lost its mass following.

As the fate of the UNIA suggested, militance could be costly for African Americans. The NAACP also saw its membership drop dramatically during the decade. Nevertheless, African Americans' struggles laid the groundwork for more successful struggles in the future.

African American Activism Marcus Garvey presides at the 1922 UNIA convention, Liberty Hall, New York City.

A "New Era" in Politics and Government

The economic and cultural transformations of the 1920s shaped American democracy in profound but contradictory ways. Modern culture helped empower ordinary people and transform the style of politics. But organized groups—big business above all—affected public life more decisively. Reflecting this balance of power, a succession of conservative Republican presidents monopolized the White House during the decade. In a decade so fascinated by all things "new," the Republicans inevitably claimed to represent a "New Era" in American politics and government. But in fact, the Republican ascendancy of the 1920s mostly meant the return of an older vision centered on minimalist government, individualism, and a less internationalist foreign policy. The mix of old ideology and new political styles failed to galvanize the democratic system in a prosperous time: the 1920s became an age of apathy and low voter turnout.

> **Men do not live by bread alone. Nor is individualism merely a stimulus to production and the road to liberty; it alone admits the universal divine inspiration of every human soul.**
>
> HERBERT HOOVER, *American Individualism*, 1922

The Modern Political System

In some ways, the cultural changes of the 1920s stimulated equality. The celebration of feats such as Ederle's Channel crossing reinforced the idea that the individual could make a difference in politics, too. The emphasis on female freedom and empowerment encouraged women to exercise their newly won right to vote.

The modern culture also hastened the emergence of a political style taking shape since the late nineteenth century. Copying big business, politicians used advertising to appeal to the electorate. In the Gilded Age, voters had been active participants, joining clubs and marching in parades during campaigns. Now, citizens were political consumers choosing candidates just as they chose mouthwash or automobiles.

The shift to advertising was necessary, too, because the major parties' control over the media had dramatically decreased. Traditionally partisan, many newspapers now took a more independent stand. The new radio stations and movie theaters had no political affiliations at all. With the decline of intense partisanship, political ad campaigns focused more on the personality and activities of individual candidates than on the parties themselves.

Economic and cultural change also benefited big business and other organized groups. In Washington, Congress was besieged by lobbyists from corporations, business groups, professional organizations, and single-issue pressure groups such as the Anti-Saloon League. Organizations employed a political style that emphasized the use of supposedly objective, nonpartisan facts to educate legislators and voters. Unorganized Americans had less chance of influencing the political process.

The new, less partisan politics did a poor job of mobilizing voters on election day. Nationwide, voter turnout fell from 79 percent for the presidential election of 1896 to just 49 percent in 1920 and 1924. A number of factors accounted for this drop-off: African Americans in the South had been effectively disfranchised, and newly enfranchised women were less likely to vote than men, but white male turnout dropped dramatically, too.

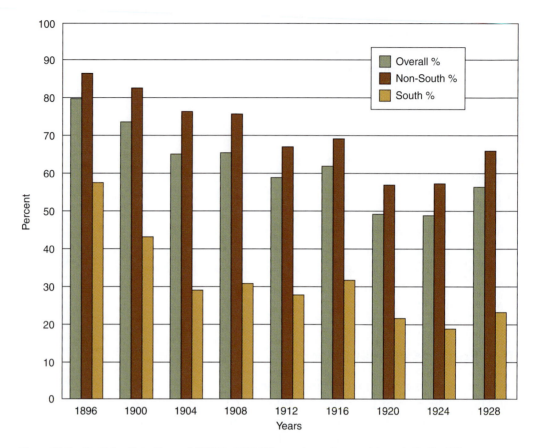

Figure 23–1   Declining Voter Turnout, 1896 to 1928 Why was turnout so much lower in the South?

The Republican Ascendancy

The chief beneficiaries of the new politics were the Republicans. Determined to win back the White House in 1920, the Republican Party chose an uncontroversial, conservative ticket. Handsome and charismatic, presidential nominee Warren G. Harding of Ohio had accomplished little during a term in the Senate. His running mate, Governor Calvin Coolidge of Massachusetts, was best known for his firm stance against a strike by the Boston police the year before.

The Republican ticket was not imposing, but neither was the opposition. The Democratic presidential nominee, Governor James M. Cox of Ohio, was saddled with the unpopularity of the Woodrow Wilson administration. His running mate, Franklin Roosevelt of New York, was a little-known cousin of former president Theodore Roosevelt who had served as assistant secretary of the navy.

While the Democrats ran an ineffective campaign, the Republicans made excellent use of advertising. And Harding neatly appealed to the reaction against Wilson's activist government, offering a return to "normalcy" after the progressive innovations that had disrupted American society during and after the war.

Harding won a huge victory with 60.3 percent of the popular vote, a new record; he won 37 states for a total of 404 electoral votes. The Republican Party substantially increased its majorities in the House and the Senate.

The Harding administration was plagued by revelations of fraud and corruption, some involving the so-called Ohio Gang, political cronies from Harding's home state. The director of the Veterans' Bureau, caught making fraudulent deals with federal property, went to prison. One of the Ohio Gang, fearing exposure of the group's influence-peddling schemes, committed suicide in 1923. The revelations shook the president, who complained about "my damn friends, my God-damn friends."

Harding died suddenly of a misdiagnosed heart attack in August 1923, but the scandals continued. Congressional hearings revealed that former secretary of the interior Albert B. Fall had apparently accepted bribes in return for leasing U.S. Navy oil reserves at Teapot Dome, Wyoming, and Elk Hills, California. Teapot Dome, as the scandal came to be called, eventually earned Fall a fine and a jail term. In 1924, another member of Harding's cabinet, Attorney General Harry Daugherty, resigned because of his role in the Ohio Gang.

The Teapot Dome Scandal The revelations of governmental corruption threatened to roll over politicians of both parties in 1923 and 1924.

The parade of scandals damaged the reputation of the dead president, but they did not seriously harm his party or his successor, Calvin Coolidge. The former vice president—so reserved in public that he was called "Silent Cal"—proved well suited to the political moment. The picture of rectitude, Coolidge restored public confidence in the presidency after the Harding scandals.

In 1924, Coolidge easily won the presidency in his own right against the Democrat John W. Davis, a colorless, conservative corporate lawyer from West Virginia, and the standard-bearer of the new Progressive Party, Senator Robert M. La Follette of Wisconsin. The choice, insisted Republicans, was either "Coolidge or Chaos." Holding onto the White House and to their majorities in Congress, the Republicans continued their ascendancy.

The Politics of Individualism

In office, the Republicans practiced the politics of individualism. Eager to serve big business, they denounced the activist, progressive state and called instead for less government and more individual freedom. Coolidge declared that "the chief business of the American people is business." Harding bluntly summed up the Republican prescription for America: "Less Government in Business and More Business in Government."

Despite such slogans, Republicans sometimes used government power to spur economic development. The Federal Highway Act of 1921 provided federal matching grants to improve the nation's roads, and the Fordney-McCumber Tariff of 1922 restored high taxes on imports to shelter American producers from foreign competition.

These measures were exceptions, however. Above all, the Harding and Coolidge administrations called for "economy"—reduced government spending and lower taxes. The Republicans also condemned budget deficits and pledged to reduce the national debt; they succeeded on all counts. Federal expenditures dropped from $6.4 billion in 1920 to $3.1 billion in 1929. Congress repeatedly cut income and other taxes, but the federal government still produced annual budget surpluses and reduced its debt.

Republicans' commitment to minimal government was obvious in their lax enforcement of Progressive Era legislation. During the Harding and Coolidge administrations, the federal government made only weak attempts to carry out Prohibition. Harding himself kept a private stock of liquor in the White House. The Republicans also allowed the regulatory commissions of the Gilded Age and the Progressive Era to atrophy. The Interstate Commerce Commission (ICC) and the Federal Trade Commission (FTC) were effectively controlled by the businesses they were supposed to regulate.

Herbert Hoover, the secretary of commerce in both the Harding and Coolidge administrations, had a more activist view of the government's role in the economy than either of his bosses. Trained as an engineer, Hoover had become a national hero by supervising the government's effort to relieve famine in Europe during and after World War I. Sensitive to business interests, Hoover used the Commerce Department to promote "associationalism"—organized cooperation among business trade groups. However, businessmen did not trust one another enough to make voluntary cooperation effective, and Hoover did not advocate federal action to force them to cooperate. Afraid of too much government, Hoover believed above all in what he called "American individualism."

Republican Foreign Policy

After America's intense involvement in international affairs during World War I, the 1920s were a period of relative withdrawal. No crisis thrust foreign policy to the center of American life. Nevertheless, the United States, the world's greatest economic power, played an active role around the globe.

The aftermath of World War I, like other postwar periods, found Americans eager to reduce the size of the military and to avoid new conflict. Horrified by the "Great War," women's groups and religious organizations joined a surging international peace movement. Activists' calls for disarmament helped push the Harding administration to organize the Washington Naval Conference of 1921–1922. In the first international arms-reduction accord, the United States, Great Britain, and Japan agreed to scrap some of their largest ships and, along with France and Italy, promised to limit the tonnage of their existing large ships, abandon gas warfare, and restrict submarine warfare.

The peace movement was less successful in its second goal, outlawing war. In 1928, the United States and 14 other countries signed the Kellogg-Briand Pact foreswearing war as an instrument of national policy. Enthusiastically received in the United States and elsewhere, the measure nevertheless contained no effective mechanism to stop a nation from going to war. U.S. membership in a world court, the third major goal of the peace movement, was not achieved in the 1920s. Too many Americans believed that the court, like the League of Nations, would undermine U.S. sovereignty.

While Americans debated membership in the court, the U.S. economy became increasingly bound up in the world economy. American investment grew substantially overseas during the 1920s, American bankers made major loans around the world, and Ford and other American companies exported their products around the world. More U.S. corporations became multinational firms by building plants overseas.

The growth of American economic activity abroad complicated the foreign policy priorities of the Harding and Coolidge administrations. In the 1920s, the United States had more interests than ever to protect overseas, but the American people were wary of government action that might lead to war. Many Americans were also

AMERICA AND THE WORLD

>> "Jazz-band partout!"

Even as political leaders pulled back from an activist foreign policy, American culture spread across the world in new ways. The rapid diffusion of jazz music epitomized the powerful global impact of the new, modern culture emerging in the United States. As early as 1920, a popular French song proclaimed *"Jazz-band partout!"*—"Jazz band everywhere!": "They're jazz bands by day, by night/ They're jazz bands everywhere/ It's all the rage in Paris, it makes men crazy."

Jazz itself was the product of globalization: the new music resulted from the long-term encounter between the musical cultures that Europeans and Africans had brought to the Americas. As World War I ended, jazz became, in turn, an agent of U.S. musical globalization. African American musicians had been part of the American army sent to France in 1917. The pioneering "Hell Fighters" band of the 369th Infantry Regiment, led by the orchestra leader Lt. James Reese Europe, helped introduce the French to the new music. After the war, some of his musicians returned to Europe. Meanwhile, American jazz groups began to tour overseas. Both the white musicians of the Original Dixieland Jazz Band and the African American musicians of Will Marion Cook's Southern Syncopated Orchestra visited England in 1919. Sam Wooding's band for the Chocolate Kiddies revue began an extended tour in 1925 that took African American jazz to Germany, Scandinavia, Spain, the USSR, and South America. Meanwhile, phonograph records conveyed the excitement of this swinging, hot music throughout the world.

The new sounds from America had a profound but complicated impact on listeners overseas. Noble Sissle, one of James Reese Europe's musicians, reported the dramatic effect of a jazz "spasm" at a Hell Fighters concert in France: "The audience could stand it no longer; the 'jazz germ' hit them and it seemed to find the vital spot, loosening all muscles and causing what is known in America as an 'eagle rocking fit. . . .'" Jazz seemed at once primitive and modern to the French. On one hand, it conjured up fantasies about African American sensuality and the mysteriousness of the African jungle. On the other, jazz conveyed the excitement of modern life in the industrial age. "The jazz band is the panting of the machine, the trepidation of the automobile. . . ." said a French critic. Above all, jazz seemed quintessentially American to its French audience. The music, a French writer observed, "has helped us finally to discover and to understand the United States." And so French audiences responded enthusiastically. "All through France, the same thing happened," Noble Sissle happily observed. "Then I was . . . satisfied that American music would one day be the world's music."

That was a worrisome prospect for some French musicians and writers. "[D]oes the whole world," one complained, "have to be American?" A number of French creative artists feared that jazz would simply sweep French music away: the French song, the *chanson,* would no longer be heard in the cafes and concert halls of France. "The violins have left and jazz is king!" lamented a French poet. "The French *chanson* is truly very sick . . . could it die?" But the *chanson* did not die: jazz did not simply Americanize France. Just as white and black Americans had heard and absorbed each other's music for generations, so French musicians accommodated, modified, and reinterpreted American jazz. By the mid-1930s, the greatest jazz-guitar player in the world was a French Gypsy, Django Reinhardt, whose many records incorporated French popular music as well as the distinctive, traditional sounds of the Gypsies.

Jazz was indeed *partout.* The music was one sign of the internationalization of the new American culture in the 1920s. It was a reminder, too, that the United States could not simply remake the world in its own image, musical and otherwise. ●

American Pianist Eubie Blake (1883–1983) and singer Noble Sissle (1889–1975), who helped bring jazz, the new American music, to Europe.

"NO MORE WAR" A meeting of the Washington State branch of the Women's International League for Peace and Freedom, 1922.

The "New Era" in Politics Meets the New Culture of Pleasure President Warren G. Harding and New York Yankees slugger Babe Ruth at a ball game in Yankee Stadium, 1923

uneasy about imperialism, the nation's continuing military role in its own possessions and in supposedly sovereign nations.

In these circumstances, the Harding and Coolidge administrations tried to pull back from some of the imperial commitments made by presidents Taft and Wilson in the 1910s. The U.S. Marines withdrew from the Dominican Republic in 1924. They also withdrew from Nicaragua in 1925 but returned the next year when the country became politically unstable.

The Harding and Coolidge administrations also attempted to promote a stable world in which American business would thrive. During the 1920s, the United States was involved in negotiations to increase Chinese sovereignty and thereby reduce the chances of conflict in Asia. The United States also tried to stabilize Europe in the years after World War I. With the quiet approval of Republican presidents, American businessmen intervened twice to help resolve the controversial issue of how much Germany should be expected to pay in reparation to the Allies.

Extending the "New Era"

The Republicans' cautious foreign and domestic policies proved popular. There was no serious challenge to the Republican ascendancy as the decade came to a close. In fact, the backlash against modern culture hurt the Democrats more than the Republicans. The Democratic Party depended on support not only from nativists, fundamentalists, and Klansmen, but also from their frequent targets—urban Catholics and Jews. The antagonism among these constituencies helped doom the Democrats' chances in the 1924 and 1928 elections.

In 1928, the Democrats nominated Al Smith, the governor of New York, for president. The first Irish Catholic presidential nominee of a major party, Smith displeased fundamentalists and nativists. Moreover, his brassy, urban style—his campaign theme song was "The Sidewalks of New York"—alienated many rural Americans. Smith represented a new generation of urban, ethnic Democrats who were ready to use activist government to deal with social and economic problems. Their brand of urban liberalism would be influential in later years, but Smith's politics and background could not galvanize a majority of voters in 1928.

Meanwhile, Herbert Hoover, the Republican nominee, polled 58.2 percent of the popular vote and carried 40 states for a total of 444 electoral votes—the Republicans' largest electoral triumph of the decade. Moreover, the Republicans increased their majorities in both the House and the Senate. "The New Era" would continue.

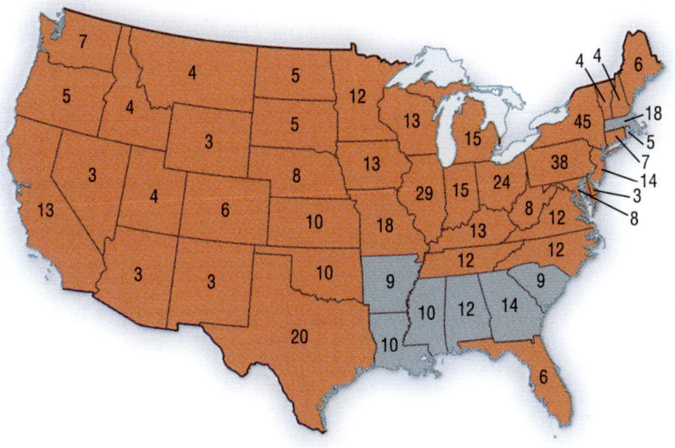

Conclusion

The Republicans' victory in 1928 underscored the triumph of modern culture. Just as Gertrude Ederle overcame the tides in the English Channel, the "New Era" swept past the challenges of nativists, fundamentalists, and Klansmen . As Hoover prepared to take over the White House, the appeal of the modern culture, rooted in the needs of the industrial economy, appeared undeniable. It offered a renewed sense of individual worth and possibility. It promised new freedom to women and youth. It held out an alluring vision of material pleasures—a life devoted to leisure and consumption—to all Americans.

Nevertheless, the modern culture and its Republican defenders were vulnerable. The political "New Era" of the 1920s was especially dependent on the state of the economy. Perhaps more than ever before in American history, the nation's dominant value system equated human happiness with the capacity to pay for pleasures. What would happen if Americans lost their jobs and their purchasing power? The new culture and the "New Era" had survived the dissent of alienated and excluded Americans in the 1920s. It would not survive the sudden end of prosperity.

Candidate (Party)	Electoral Vote (%)	Popular Vote (%)
Hoover (Republican)	444 (82%)	21,391,993 (58%)
Smith (Democratic)	87 (17%)	15,016,169 (41%)
Thomas (Socialist)		267,835 (1%)
Minor parties		62,890 (-)

Map 23–1   The Election of 1928 Herbert Hoover's landslide victory extends the Republican "New Era."

Further Readings

Susan Currell, *American Culture in the 1920s* (2009). A concise introduction to the emerging modern culture of the 1920s.

David Greenberg, *Calvin Coolidge* (2006). A brief, positive assessment of this Republican president.

Thomas Hine, *The Rise and Fall of the American Teenager* (2000). A useful, wide-ranging account.

Edward J. Larson, *Summer for the Gods: The Scopes Trial and America's Continuing Debate over Science and Religion* (1997). A vivid narrative account of the battle over evolution in Tennessee.

Jackson Lears, *Fables of Abundance: A Cultural History of Advertising in America* (1994). Puts the developments of the 1920s in broader context.

Robert S. Lynd and Helen Merrell Lynd, *Middletown: A Study in Contemporary American Culture* (1929). This pioneering sociological study of Muncie, Indiana, charts the spread of modern culture in an American community.

Nancy MacLean, *Ku Klux Klan: The Making of the Second Ku Klux Klan* (1994). Portrays the Klansmen's hostility to the modern culture.

David Nasaw, *Going Out: The Rise and Fall of Public Amusements* (1993). The evolution of movies, sports, and other amusements that helped to constitute the consumer culture of the 1920s.

George Sánchez, *Becoming Mexican American: Ethnicity, Culture, and Identity in Chicano Los Angeles, 1900–1945* (1993). A sensitive exploration of the Mexican encounter with life in the United States.

Who, What?

Review Questions

1. What caused the transformation of the industrial economy in the 1910s and 1920s? How did that transformation benefit or harm different economic groups such as big business, workers, and farmers?

2. Why did the modern culture emerge in the 1920s and not before?

3. How did views of sexuality, gender, family, and youth change in the 1920s? Why was individualism so important to the modern culture?

>> Timeline >>

▼ **1913**
Introduction of assembly line at Ford Motor Company

▼ **1918**
End of World War I

▼ **1919**
Black Star Line founded by Marcus Garvey
Original Dixieland Jazz Band and Will Marion Cook's Southern Syncopated Orchestra bring jazz to England

▼ **1920**
Commercial radio broadcasting
Warren G. Harding elected president

▼ **1922**
Fordney-McCumber Tariff
Sinclair Lewis, *Babbitt*

▼ **1923**
Teapot Dome scandal
Calvin Coolidge succeeds Harding as president

▼ **1924**
National Origins Act

4. Why was there such a widespread backlash against the modern culture of the 1920s? Why did the backlash fail?

5. Why did the Republican Party dominate the emerging political system of the 1920s? How did Republican policies reflect the economic and cultural changes of the decade?

6. Did the United States become more or less democratic a nation in the 1920s?

7. How would the emergence of consumer culture shape the United States beyond the 1920s?

Websites

Emergence of Advertising in America, 1850–1920 (http://library.duke.edu/digitalcollections/eaa/) is a huge searchable database of advertisements and pamphlets.

A Guide to Harlem Renaissance Materials, from the Library of Congress (http://www.loc.gov/rr/program/bib/harlem/harlem.html), provides a jumping-off point to a variety of collections about African American life and culture.

The Margaret Sanger Papers Project of New York University (http://www.nyu.edu/projects/sanger/) offers a selection of the birth control advocate's writings and speeches.

Prosperity and Thrift: The Coolidge Era and the Consumer Economy, an American Memory project of the Library of Congress (http://memory.loc.gov/ammem/coolhtml/coolhome.html), is an outstanding multimedia collection on politics and society in the 1920s.

The Red Hot Jazz Archive (http://www.redhotjazz.com/) offers a history and plenty of examples of the new music of the 1920s.

Women Working, 1800–1930, a project of the Harvard University Library Open Collections program (http://ocp.hul.harvard.edu/ww/), includes many items from the 1920s among its digitized books, pamphlets, photographs, and other materials.

For further review materials and resource information, please visit www.oup.com/us/ofthepeople

▼ **1925**
Founding of the Brotherhood of Sleeping Car Porters
Bruce Barton, *The Man Nobody Knows*
Scopes trial

▼ **1926**
Gertrude Ederle's swim across the English Channel

▼ **1927**
Charles Lindbergh's solo transatlantic flight

▼ **1928**
Kellogg-Briand Pact
Herbert Hoover elected president

▼ **1929**
Stock market crash

▼ **1932**
Franklin Roosevelt elected president

Common Threads

>> Contrast government's response to the Depression against its actions in earlier "panics" in 1893 and 1877.

>> How did Franklin D. Roosevelt's Democratic Party differ from the one that nominated William Jennings Bryan or Woodrow Wilson?

>> How did the New Deal redefine what it meant to be "liberal" or "conservative"?

>> Margaret Mitchell

Margaret Mitchell wrote her first and only book, *Gone with the Wind*, to earn extra money, and she was more than a little surprised when it became a runaway best seller as soon as it was published in June 1936. Stores sold out before the first shipments arrived. At a bookstore appearance fans tore buttons from Mitchell's coat to keep as souvenirs, and crowds gathered outside her Atlanta apartment. In four days, almost 1,200 letters from admiring readers arrived.

Most wrote to tell Mitchell how her story had renewed their faith in themselves. For an urban, industrial society in the depths of the century's worst economic crisis, *Gone with the Wind* conjured up a rural past in which Americans struggled and triumphed. Mitchell's fiercely determined heroine, Scarlett O'Hara, survived the collapse of her world in the Civil War through sheer force of will. "I'm going to live through this," Scarlett resolved at her lowest point, "and when it's over, I'm never going to be hungry again." Her eventual triumph reaffirmed the values of self-reliance and individualism at a time when many Americans wondered if those values still mattered.

In 1936 the Great Depression—the worst economic collapse in United States history—was nearly seven years old. The stock market crash in October 1929 preceded an uninterrupted four-year decline in nearly every sector of the economy. On farms across America hard work was rewarded with failure and poverty. In cities and towns there was little work to be found. Since the time of Andrew Jackson, Americans had grown to feel that democracy rested on shared values of individualism, private property, and a capitalist market economy. Now, with millions unemployed, these principles, and the relationship between them, were openly questioned. Politicians had few answers, and Americans felt alone and vulnerable.

The popularity of *Gone with the Wind* suggests that even in the depths of the Depression Americans still clung to the promise of individual opportunity. "We Americans have all been taught, from childhood, that it is a sort of moral obligation for each of us to rise, to get up in the world," the writer Sherwood Anderson explained. Steeped in the precepts of individualism, impoverished Americans blamed themselves for the economy's failure. "It's my own fault," explained a wheat farmer who worked hard his whole life only to lose his farm and move in with relatives. "I wasn't smart enough." Everywhere the theme of individual responsibility was reinforced. *Gone with the Wind* echoed advice books, newspapers and magazines, radio shows and movies that encouraged Americans to confront the Great Depression by working harder than ever. "In the final analysis," one advertisement from 1932 declared, "we are responsible for our own defeats and our own victories."

While millions of Americans were heartened by Scarlett's old-fashioned individualism, other readers turned to updated versions of American values. Atop the nonfiction bestseller list of 1937 sat Dale Carnegie's *How to Win Friends and Influence People*, a book that told readers how to become rich and famous. Carnegie, born poor on a Missouri farm, reinvented himself by moving to New York and adopting the last name of a steel tycoon. He sprinkled his writings with the names of celebrities ("Martin Johnson, the African explorer" and "Arnold Reubens . . . originator of the four-decker sandwich") who overcame their own setbacks by following a few simple steps. Where Scarlett O'Hara represented the lone heroine overcoming adversity as an individual, Carnegie's hero was a team player, an "organization man" who knew how to manipulate others for his personal advantage.

One figure, especially, captured the tension between old and new versions of American individualism in his viselike

continued

grip. In 1938 Action Comics introduced Superman, who in his first year thwarted two European wars, foiled evil businessmen and insane scientists, and rescued helpless politicians by the planeload. He was the creation of two Cleveland teenagers, Jerry Siegel and Joe Shuster, who sold the rights to the comic for a quick $130. Superman's dual identity reflected the split personality of Dale Carnegie's mild-mannered manipulator. Clark Kent, reared in rural Kansas, was a big-city organization man, a reporter for a large daily paper. But beneath his grey flannel suit he was Superman, who could right society's wrongs in a single bound. In an early issue, he turned his super strength against the Depression, tearing Metropolis's slums apart with his bare hands and forcing city officials to rebuild. The "man of the future" revived the fantasy of the rugged individual able to remake society on his own terms.

Society's emphasis on individual responsibility had important implications for the way voters and politi-cians responded to the economic disaster. For the first four years of the Depression, the federal government offered solutions that relied on individuals' willingness to help each other and themselves. But the persistence of the Depression strained the public's faith, and in 1933 the administration undertook a dramatic series of experiments to relieve the plight of individuals. These experiments, known collectively as the "New Deal," per-manently changed the relationship between Americans and their government. Voters relied on elected officials not just to represent their interests, but to protect their livelihoods. Yet by the late 1930s the ingrained suspi-cion of big government began to revive, and the New Deal ground to a halt. Margaret Mitchell and her char-acter Scarlett ended the decade in triumph. In 1939 she was immortalized on screen in the Technicolor film version of *Gone with the Wind*, which swept the 1940 Academy Awards. ●

OUTLINE

The Great Depression

In the fall of 1929 declining confidence in the stock market sent tremors throughout the economy. By Thursday, October 24, panic had set in as brokers rushed to unload their stocks. Prices rallied briefly, but on October 29, "Black Tuesday," stock values lost over $14 billion, and within the month the market stood at only half its precrash worth. Hundreds of corporations and thousands of individuals were wiped out. On Wall Street, the symbol of prosperity in the 1920s, mounted police had to hold angry mobs back from the doors of the stock exchange. Although the crash did not cause the ensuing depression, it did expose underlying weaknesses and shatter the confidence President Herbert Hoover relied on for recovery. His optimistic speeches would echo hollowly over the ensuing years of widespread unemployment, hunger, and homelessness.

Causes

No single factor explains the onset or persistence of the Great Depression. No one among the politicians, bureaucrats, business leaders, and others responsible for addressing the problem had a clear idea of why things had gone so wrong. Economists and historians still debate the issue today. Yet, even if no definitive account can be given, it is clear that structural flaws in the national and international economies along with ill-conceived government policies were at fault.

In the 1920s the base of the economy had begun to shift. No longer was it driven by steel, coal, textiles, railroads, and other heavy industries. Now, new industries that sold complex consumer goods like automobiles became the driving force. In addition to cars, sales of radios, clothing, processed foods, and a whole range of consumer products grew dramatically. This shift toward a vibrant new consumer-oriented economy was fueled by favorable business conditions, job growth, and plentiful credit that allowed consumers, mainly those in the relatively small middle class, to purchase more and more goods and services. The limits of this market had, however, been reached even before the Great Crash. When the stock market fell, the collapse of purchasing power caused by mass unemployment and the loss of savings slowed the transition to the new economy.

> Now everyone will get back to work instead of cherishing the idea that it is possible to get rich overnight.
>
> ALFRED P. SLOAN,
> Chairman, General Motors,
> October 27, 1929

A rickety credit and financial system added to the problems of the late 1920s. Even in good times banks failed by the hundreds. For banks in rural areas these failures could be traced to persistently low farm prices, but all over America financial institutions suffered from inept and even criminal management. Banks were virtually unregulated, and in the boom atmosphere of the 1920s many bet depositors' money on stocks or large, risky loans. Bank failures magnified the impact of the crash; many thousands lost money they thought was safely saved.

Like banks, corporate finance was free from regulation and given to misrepresentation, manipulation of stock prices, and corrupt insider deals. Few could be sure whether investments were going into sound companies or worthless paper.

Government missteps and poor policies also had a role. The Republican administrations of the 1920s were committed to reducing government interference in the economy, lowering taxes on the wealthy, and reducing spending. As a result, little was done to address the banking mess, the problems of farmers, or the growing reliance on credit. The Federal Reserve could have dampened speculation in stocks or, after the Depression began, expanded the currency to promote growth. Concerned more about keeping the dollar strong than maintaining employment, the Harding and Coolidge administrations throttled back spending and the money supply, worsening the eventual collapse.

The Depression was magnified by an international economy still reeling from the effects of World War I. Under the peace terms, Germany owed $33 billion in reparations to Britain and France, who in turn owed billions in war debts to the United States. Only U.S. bank loans to Germany made these huge payments possible, so throughout the 1920s funds that could have created jobs and industries went instead into this financial merry-go-round. The cycle was broken at the onset of depression in the United States. European nations attempted to protect themselves by devaluing their currencies and raising trade barriers. The result was a steady decline in their economies that made payments on reparations or loans impossible. The whole cycle reached a breaking point in 1931, and the international financial system came crashing down, bringing with it many more American banks and helping to further deepen the economic crisis.

Descending into Depression

The Great Depression was a year old when an unemployed worker in Pottstown, Pennsylvania, sat down and wrote a harsh letter to President Hoover. "I am one of the men out of work," he explained, "but the rich don't care so long as they have full and plenty." With winter coming on he pleaded with Hoover to speed up aid to "the struggling starving working class [of] under nourished men, women, and children." Such misery, he added, "really is alarming [in] this so called prosperous nation."

The statistics alone were alarming. Between 1929 and 1933 every index of economic activity showed a steadily worsening slide. The gross national product shrank from $104.4 billion in 1929 to $74.2 billion in 1933. The combined incomes of American workers fell by more than 40 percent. Bank failures increased, from 640 in 1928 to 2,294 in 1931. A *New York Times* index of business activity dropped from 114.8 in June of 1929 to 63.7 in March of 1933. Both exports and imports fell by more than two-thirds.

As business activity collapsed, joblessness skyrocketed. Periodic bouts of unemployment had always been a feature of capitalist economies, even in good times. What distinguished the Great Depression was the extent and duration of unemployment. At the lowest point of the slump in the early 1930s, between 20 and 30 percent of wage earners were out of work. In some cities the jobless percentage was much higher, with Chicago and Detroit approaching 50 percent, Akron 60 percent, and Toledo a crushing 80 percent. In 1933, the Bureau of Labor Statistics estimated that as many as one in three workers, more than 12,600,000 Americans, were unemployed.

Behind the grim statistics lay terrible human costs. In the spring of 1930, as the first Depression winter came to an end, breadlines

Table 24–1 Labor Force and Unemployment, 1929–1941 (Numbers in Millions)

Year	Labor Force	Unemployment	
		Number	% of Labor Force
1929	49.2	1.6	3.2
1930	49.8	4.3	8.7
1931	50.4	8.0	15.9
1932	51.0	12.1	23.6
1933	51.6	12.8	24.9
1934	52.2	11.3	21.7
1935	52.9	10.6	20.1
1936	53.4	9.0	16.9
1937	54.0	7.7	14.3
1938	54.6	10.4	19.0
1939	55.2	9.5	17.2
1940	55.6	8.1	14.6
1941	55.9	5.6	9.9

Source: *United States Department of Commerce*, Historical Statistics of the United States (1960), p. 70.

appeared in major cities. Apple peddlers crowded street corners hoping to earn a few nickels to replace some of their lost wages. The unemployed could be seen in the thousands, Sherwood Anderson wrote, "men who are heads of families creeping through the streets of American cities, eating from garbage cans; men turned out of houses and sleeping week after week on park benches, on the ground in parks, in the mud under bridges." Unemployed men and women stood in lines at factory gates desperately seeking work, at soup kitchens hoping for a meal, and at homeless shelters that were already overflowing.

The basic necessities—food, clothing, and shelter—were suddenly hard to get. "I have always been able to give my family a decent living," a struggling father in Seattle explained, "until economic conditions got so bad I was unable to make it go any longer." Schoolteachers reported growing numbers of students were listless from hunger. Big-city hospitals began receiving patients suffering from nutritional disorders, including children with rickets, a disease caused by a deficiency of vitamin D. Deficient diets caused another disease, pellagra, to reappear in many parts of the South. *Fortune* magazine ran an article on Americans who had actually starved to death. Embarrassed mothers sent children to school in rags. Men wrapped newspapers beneath their shirts as protection from the cold or put cardboard in their shoes to cover the holes. Desperate families, their savings gone, unable to pay the rent, "doubled up" by moving in with relatives. More and more tenants were evicted; more and more banks foreclosed on mortgages. Apartments stood vacant and homes went unsold, yet by 1932 more than a million homeless men, women, and children occupied shantytowns on the outskirts of towns and cities or slept in doorways and alleys. Hoboes appeared everywhere, traveling railroads and highways in a constant search for something to eat, somewhere to live, someplace to work.

Farmers faced a double catastrophe of economic and environmental disaster. Farmers in the Plains states and the West aggressively increased production in the 1920s and then watched helplessly as the markets for corn, wheat, beef, and pork collapsed in the wake of the crash. Between 1929 and 1932, the income of American farmers dropped by two-thirds. Then the drought struck. Between 1930 and 1936, the rains all but stopped in large parts of the South, the Southwest, and the Great Plains. Exposed by decades of wasteful farming practices, the earth dried up and blew away. Spectacular dust storms carried topsoil hundreds of miles through the air, giving a new name— the Dust Bowl—to a large swath of the Southern Plains. Dust and depression ripped thousands of farm families from the land in Texas, Kansas, Oklahoma, and Arkansas, sending these "Okies," "Arkies," and "Texies" off to California in search of work.

The Great Depression affected nearly everyone in America, but it was most severe for those already disadvantaged. While the environmental shock of the Dust

Effects of the Dust Bowl Drought and modern agriculture churned the Great Plains into silica powder that was carried by windstorms. Over half the patients in Kansas hospitals in 1935 suffered from dust pneumonia.

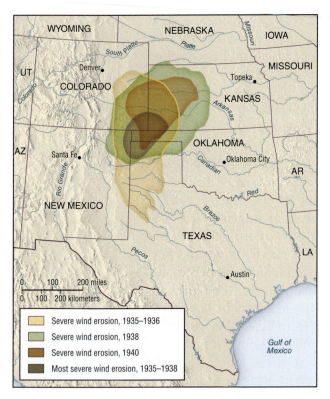

Map 24–1 Extent of the Dust Bowl The Dust Bowl of the 1930s eventually spread across thousands of square miles of the Southern Plains.

Bowl affected many poor white farmers, the larger agricultural depression was even more devastating for sharecroppers on the southern cotton lands, workers in the wheatfields of the Midwest, and the vast migrant labor pools that traveled up and down the East and West coasts picking fruits and vegetables. In cities, African Americans, who held the least secure jobs, found themselves pushed from menial service tasks and unskilled work by desperate white workers.

By 1932 private charities, the major social safety net before the Depression, failed to meet the needs of desperate citizens. Ethnic organizations such as the Bohemian Charitable Association or Jewish Charities in Chicago had been a bulwark against adversity for members of their own groups. Now they found themselves overwhelmed. Summing up the state of charities, Arthur T. Burns, the president of the Association of Community Chests and Councils, flatly declared that "the funds we have are altogether inadequate to meet the situation."

Public monies were just as scarce. Only eight states provided any form of unemployment insurance; most of it was meager. Such state welfare agencies as existed tended to be poorly funded in the best of times and were now stretched beyond their limits. Entire cities slid toward insolvency as their tax bases dwindled. Many states were expressly forbidden by their constitutions to borrow for social welfare expenditures. Frustrated politicians and citizens looked to the federal government for a solution, but beyond pensions for veterans, little existed in the way of a social welfare state. There was no social security for the elderly and disabled, no federal unemployment insurance for those who lost their jobs, and no food stamps to relieve hunger.

The federal government thus found itself under unprecedented pressure to do something, anything, to relieve the Depression. Even bankers and businessmen abandoned their resistance to a strong central government. The president of Columbia University suggested a dictatorship might provide more effective leadership. Others warned of social revolution if the government did not act. Most of the pleas for federal action were aimed at the administration, and Herbert Hoover himself came to symbolize the failures of the federal government. The newspapers that jobless men wrapped themselves in were called "Hoover shirts"; shantytowns were "Hoovervilles." In the popular imagination, Hoover and the Great Depression became inseparable.

Hoover Responds

In many ways, Hoover was ideally qualified to handle this emergency. He had experience with natural and human catastrophes. Orphaned at a young age, Hoover grew up in small-town America and worked hard to educate himself. He was trained

A Hooverville in Seattle, Washington As the Depression deepened, the homeless settled in "Hoovervilles" on the edge of city centers.

as an engineer at Stanford University, then roamed the world building and managing mining operations. He became a millionaire by his mid-20s. Like many other young progressives, Hoover sought to apply skills from the business world to solve social problems. He won fame as an administrator of emergency relief, saving Belgium from starvation during World War I and overseeing rescue efforts during the Great Mississippi Flood of 1927.

He came into the presidency with a well-developed theory on the role of government in a modern economy. His vision centered on the belief that complex societies required accurate economic information, careful planning, and large-scale coordination. At the same time, Hoover rejected the idea that a large and overbearing government could provide these services without crushing the creativity and flexibility essential to a capitalist economy. His political philosophy, associationalism, envisioned a federal government empowered to gather information and encourage voluntary cooperation among businesses but forbidden to intervene further. This voluntarist dream fit well with the dominant ideology of America, and it was no surprise that Hoover easily won the presidency in 1928.

Once in office Hoover lost no time in implementing his ideas. One of his first achievements was the Agricultural Marketing Act of 1929, designed to raise farm incomes and rationalize production. Since the turn of the century, farmers had been plagued by a "paradox of plenty." Modern techniques produced more food and fiber than Americans could consume, so the more farmers grew, the less they earned. The bill established a Federal Farm Board to establish cooperatives for purchasing and distributing surplus crops. It issued $500 million in loans to stabilize prices, but it did not limit production or dictate prices.

When the market crashed, Hoover's initial response was consistent with his overall vision. His goal was to get business to promise to cooperate to maintain wages and investment. In 1931, as banks were failing at a rate of 25 a week, he encouraged the formation of the National Credit Corporation, in which banks were urged to pool resources to stave off collapse. Rather than distribute unemployment insurance or poor relief, he tried to persuade companies not to lay off workers and to contribute to charities for the homeless and unemployed. But the breadth and depth of the Depression overwhelmed all of Hoover's schemes. Crop prices fell so low that farmers began to blockade cities and demand adequate compensation for their crops.

Hoover had never failed before in his life, and he worked tirelessly to fight the Depression. By 1932, he reluctantly conceded the need for more aggressive government programs, even at the risk of deficit spending. He proposed a Reconstruction Finance Corporation (RFC) authorized to loan $2 billion to revive large corporations. Plans to increase government revenues and allow the Federal Farm Board to distribute surpluses to the needy were also enacted. But it was too little too late. The Depression was three years old and showed no signs of lifting.

The Republican administration's policies did not simply fail to relieve the Depression but, rather, increased its severity. Unable to control members of his own party, Hoover watched helplessly as Congress passed the Hawley-Smoot Tariff in 1930. The tariff raised import duties to their highest level in history, stifling hopes that international trade might help the economy and wreaking untold damage on the weak nations of Europe. Despite the president's misgivings about the tariff, he signed the bill into law. At the same time, Hoover opposed other measures that might have relieved poverty or stimulated recovery. He vetoed massive public works bills sponsored by congressional Democrats. Finally, Hoover's stubborn commitment to the gold standard and a balanced budget choked off hopes of a turnaround.

Hoover, whose popularity had plummeted as the Depression deepened, reinforced his reputation as a cold and aloof protector of the privileged classes by his response to the Bonus Marchers in 1932. In 1924 Congress had issued the veterans of World War I a "bonus" to be paid in 1945. But as the Depression threw millions out of work, veterans asked to have their bonuses paid early. In the summer of 1932, veterans formed a "Bonus Expeditionary Force" to march on Washington. Arriving on freight cars and buses, over 20,000 Bonus Marchers encamped on the Capitol grounds. "Families were there galore, just couples and families with strings of kids," one marcher remembered. Hoover ordered the army to remove the march-

The Bonus Army Expeditionary Force, or Bonus Marchers The Bonus Marchers arrived in Washington, DC, in the summer of 1932 to ask Congress to pay World War I veterans' payments early.

ers. General Douglas MacArthur exceeded his orders and attacked the marchers with tanks and mounted cavalry. Major George S. Patton, sabre drawn, galloped through the encampment, setting fire to the miserable tents and shacks of the veterans. Among those he attacked was Joseph T. Angelino, who won the Distinguished Service Cross in 1918 for saving Patton's life. Americans were shocked by photographs of MacArthur calmly sipping coffee and standing in a pool of blood. Hoover's silent support solidified his reputation for callousness.

As Congress struggled to devise policies to relieve unemployment and suffering, Hoover flatly dismissed the "futile attempt to cure poverty by the enactment of law." Arrogant and aloof, the president questioned the integrity and suspected the motives of everyone who disagreed with his policies. By the end of his presidency the "Great Humanitarian" had become sullen and withdrawn. It was a dispirited Republican Convention that met in Chicago to nominate Hoover for reelection in 1932.

The First New Deal

When the Democratic Convention chose a presidential candidate in 1932, Franklin Delano Roosevelt flew from Albany, New York, to Chicago to accept the nomination in person, a dramatic gesture in an age new to air travel and personal politics. "I pledge myself," he told the enthusiastic crowd, "to a new deal for the American people." The phrase stuck, and, ever since, the assortment of reforms enacted between 1933 and 1938 has come to be known as the New Deal. The programs came in two great waves commonly referred to as the "first" and "second" New Deals. The first commenced with the Hundred Days, a three-month burst of executive and legislative activity following FDR's inauguration. The first New Deal continued through 1934.

> **TVA is more an example of democracy in retreat than democracy on the march.**
>
> REXFORD TUGWELL,
> New Deal economist

The Election of 1932

The Depression reached its lowest depths as the 1932 election approached, and the Republicans seemed headed for disaster. Their inability to develop a legislative program to attack the Depression had already cost them control of the House. But the Democrats had to overcome serious internal divisions if they were to take advantage of the situation.

Throughout the 1920s the Democratic Party had been split along cultural lines between the ethnically diverse, wet (i.e., anti-Prohibition), urban wing concentrated in the North and the East, and the Anglo-Saxon Protestant, rural southern and western wings. Ideological divisions on a whole range of issues separated northeastern business Democrats from western populists, and urban progressives from southern conservatives.

The leading candidate for the Democratic nomination, New York's Governor Franklin D. Roosevelt, had the background to overcome many of these divisions. He came from an upstate rural district and his interest in conservation endeared him to many westerners. He had built ties to the southern Democrats while serving as Woodrow Wilson's assistant secretary of the navy and, during the 1920s, as a sometime resident of Warm Springs, Georgia. As governor of New York he built a strong record of support for progressive social reforms that appealed to urban liberals.

Roosevelt turned out to be the ideal candidate. As a distant cousin of Theodore Roosevelt, he had a recognizable name. FDR also had immense personal charm. Despite having been crippled by polio since 1921, he proved a tireless campaigner and would go on to become one of the most visible of modern presidents. He was a born patrician, a blue-blooded member of the American aristocracy, raised in wealth and educated at Groton and Harvard. Yet he spoke in clear, direct language that ordinary Americans found persuasive and reassuring.

During the campaign, Roosevelt simultaneously embraced old orthodoxies and enticed reformers with hints of more radical changes. He promised to cut government spending and provide government relief for the poor. How he would do both, FDR declined to say, but it hardly mattered. In November 1932, the Republicans were swept out of office in a tide of popular repudiation. FDR and the Democrats took control of the national government with the promise of "a new deal" for the American people.

Behind the scenes during the campaign, Roosevelt worked hard to develop a program to fight the Depression. While governor of New York, FDR had recruited intellectuals who provided him with an influential diagnosis of the Great Depression. Known as the "Brains Trust," they attempted to convince Roosevelt that the Depression was caused by the economy's fundamental defects. The core of the problem, they told FDR, was the maldistribution of wealth within the United States. Because the rich held onto too large a share of the profits of American industry, the economy was producing much more than Americans could consume.

Despite the influence of the Brains Trust, Roosevelt never fully bought their ideas or allowed any one group to dominate his thinking. It was FDR's comfort with experimentation and chaos that would hold his administration together and make it capable of confronting the confusing persistence of the Depression. Where Hoover had retreated into dogmatism, FDR endorsed "bold, persistent experimentation." Above all, he ordered his officials, "try something." And rather than trying to unite his followers behind a single idea or policy, Roosevelt seemed to enjoy watching his advisers feud. He acted as a dealmaker, arranging the final bargains and compromises for the exhausted combatants. The president, one adviser said, was "the boss, the dynamo, the works."

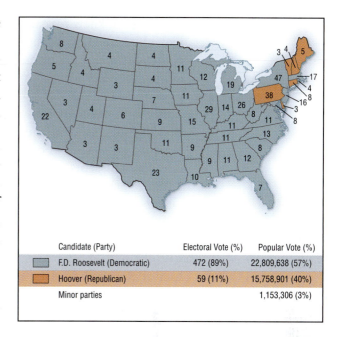

Candidate (Party)	Electoral Vote (%)	Popular Vote (%)
F.D. Roosevelt (Democratic)	472 (89%)	22,809,638 (57%)
Hoover (Republican)	59 (11%)	15,758,901 (40%)
Minor parties		1,153,306 (3%)

Map 24–2 The Presidential Election of 1932 By November 1932 most American voters blamed the Depression on Hoover and the Republicans. The Democrats, led by FDR, swept into office by huge electoral margins.

FDR Takes Command

As the president-elect and his advisers discussed their approach to the Depression in the weeks before the inauguration, the ailing American banking system took a sharp turn for the worse. In mid-February the governor of Michigan declared an eight-day bank holiday. In one of the nation's most important manufacturing states, nearly a million depositors could not get their money. Stock prices dropped on the news, and the anxious rich began shipping their gold to safer countries. Panic struck and banks saw their funds fly out of the tellers' windows at an alarming rate. On the morning of the inauguration New York and Illinois, the two great centers of American finance, joined most of the other states in calling a bank holiday. The New York Stock Exchange and Illinois Board of Trade also closed. To many, it seemed like the end of the American economy that had so recently been the envy of the world.

With commerce at a standstill the nation turned expectantly to the new president: Roosevelt did not disappoint. "First of all," he declared, "let me assert my firm belief that the only thing we have to fear is—fear itself, nameless, unreasoning, unjustified terror." In another time and place such words might have sounded empty, but in the midst of a frightening financial collapse FDR's speech revitalized the nation almost overnight.

Roosevelt knew reassuring words alone would not end the crisis. On the day he took office, the new president declared a national bank holiday to last through the end of the week. He immediately instructed his new secretary of the Treasury to draft emergency legislation and called Congress into special session. When Congress convened on March 9, the drafting team had finished a bill, barely, and presented one pencil-marked copy for its consideration. Congress was ready to act. Breaking all precedent, the House unanimously shouted its approval of the bill after less than one half hour of debate; that evening the Senate voted to do the same with only seven dissents, and the president signed it into law that night. The Emergency Banking Act was a modest reform. It gave the Treasury secretary the power to determine which banks could safely reopen and which had to be reorganized. It also enabled the RFC to strengthen sound banks by buying their stocks.

On Sunday night, a week after taking office, FDR went on national radio to deliver the first of his many "fireside chats." Sixty million people tuned their radios to hear Roosevelt explain, in his resonant, fatherly voice, his measures to address the banking crisis. He assured Americans that their money would be "safer in a reopened bank than under the mattress." This was a tremendous gamble because the government was not completely sure how solid most banks truly were, but it worked. The next day, 12,756 banks reopened, some in style. Five thousand customers of the Consolidated National Bank of Tucson, Arizona, were welcomed into a lobby decked with flowers and a band playing "Happy Days Are Here Again." The run stopped and deposits began flowing back into the system. The immediate crisis was over.

Once the banking crisis had been resolved in March 1933, Roosevelt wanted to ensure that the financial system would remain sound for the long run. He moved to restrict banks' speculations while guaranteeing their profitability. The Glass-Steagall Banking Act of 1933 imposed conservative banking practices nationwide. Chancy loans, stock investments, and shady business practices by banks were outlawed, and close federal oversight guaranteed the stability of the U.S. banking system until Glass-Steagall was repealed in 1999. In addition, the newly created Federal Deposit Insurance Corporation protected deposits. Two years later, the Banking Act of 1935 reorganized the Federal Reserve, bringing the entire system under more centralized and democratic control. Together, these laws established the credibility of the U. S. banking sys-

FDR Photographed During One of His Fireside Chats Hoover broadcast his speeches on radio, but Roosevelt's "fireside chats" took advantage of the intimacy of the new medium.

tem. One reason the banking system had become so vulnerable was its ties to the unregulated securities markets. So in 1933 the administration sponsored a Truth in Securities Act that required all companies issuing stock to disclose accurate information to all prospective buyers. The following year Congress passed the Securities and Exchange Act. Where the 1933 law regulated companies, the 1934 legislation regulated the markets that sold stocks. It prohibited inside trading and other forms of manipulation. It gave the Federal Reserve Board the power to control how much credit was available and it established the Securities and Exchange Commission, which quickly became one of the largest and most effective regulatory agencies in the country.

Federal Relief

Roosevelt's unemployment programs departed sharply from Hoover's relief strategies. In May, Congress passed a bill providing a half billion dollars for relief and creating the Federal Emergency Relief Administration (FERA) to oversee it. Lacking the organization to dispense money across the nation, the federal government passed on funds to existing local and state agencies. Headed by Harry Hopkins, a shrewd social worker and Roosevelt confidant from New York, FERA distributed money at a terrific rate. As winter came on, however, Hopkins convinced Roosevelt that only a massive new federal program could avert disaster. At FDR's request, Congress created the Civil Works Administration (CWA), which employed 4 million men and women. During the winter, the CWA built or renovated over half a million miles of road and tens of thousands of schools and other public buildings. When spring came the CWA was eliminated—Roosevelt did not want the nation to get used to a federal welfare program—but FERA continued to run programs on a smaller scale.

Roosevelt generally came to relief only out of necessity, but he was enthusiastic about one program, the Civilian Conservation Corps (CCC). FDR believed that life in the countryside and service to the nation would have a positive moral impact on the young men of the cities and those "wild boys" whom the Depression had compelled to roam the nation. The CCC employed these young men building roads and trails in the national parks. By the time the program was discontinued in 1942, it had dramatically transformed America's public lands and employed over 3 million teenagers and young adults.

The Farm Crisis

"I don't want on the relief if I can help it," a Louisiana farm woman wrote to the first lady, Eleanor Roosevelt, in the fall of 1935. "I want to work for my livin.'" But she was desperate. She asked Mrs. Roosevelt to send money to save the family cow "for my little children to have milk." One child was sick and the doctor was no longer

Eleanor Roosevelt Eleanor Roosevelt wrote a syndicated newspaper column, personally inspected government projects, and acted as a presidential adviser, all new roles for a first lady.

able to give her the medicine "unless we pay him some for he is in debt for it." The landlord was threatening to evict them unless they got a mill plow, which they could not afford. She had turned to the first lady because of Mrs. Roosevelt's reputation for caring about the poor, but political realities would limit what the first lady, or her husband, could do to help this woman and thousands like her.

By the spring of 1933, farmers in many parts of the country were desperate. Prices of basic commodities like corn, cotton, wheat, and tobacco had fallen so low that it was not even worth the cost of harvesting. The banking crisis left farmers without access to the necessary credit to continue, and millions faced the stark prospect of foreclosure, homelessness, or dust storms.

FDR saw a stark "imbalance" between city and country as a root cause of the Depression. While the land remained the only real source of wealth, modern cities absorbed all of the countryside's water, produce, talent, and population. The Dust Bowl was a consequence of this ecological distortion. His aim was to restore a more even pattern of development across the landscape, with small manufacturing towns, suburbs, and farms linked to centers of culture and commerce. The New Deal program that came closest to fulfilling each of these goals was the Tennessee Valley Authority, or TVA. While campaigning for the presidency, Roosevelt had endorsed the proposal by Senator George Norris of Nebraska to develop the Muscle Shoals property along the Tennessee River. Norris's dream was realized when Congress created the TVA within the first Hundred Days. The TVA was a "corporation clothed with the power of government but possessed of the flexibility and initiative of a private enterprise." According to its administrator, it aimed to change the environment, the economy, the way of life, and the "habits, social, economic, and personal" of a region that spanned nine states.

One of the most ambitious projects of the entire New Deal, the TVA was also astonishingly successful. The dams eventually built by the TVA served many purposes. They controlled flooding in the Tennessee Valley, created reservoirs for irrigation, and provided cheap hydroelectric power. Electricity not only made life more comfortable for millions of farm families, it also made it possible for industry to move into new areas, thus bringing jobs to some of the poorest parts of the country. Jesus "is the greatest thing that can happen to any man," a Tennessee preacher testified, "but the next greatest thing is electricity."

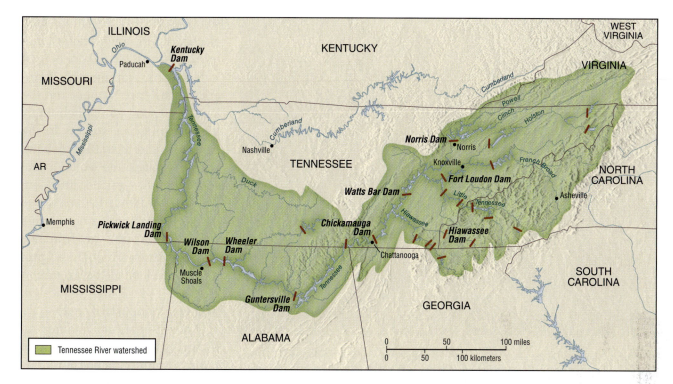

Map 24–3   TVA Projects The Tennessee Valley Authority (TVA) was one of the most ambitious of all New Deal projects. A network of dams provided electricity, irrigation, and flood control to many of the poorest regions of the South.

The TVA took responsibility for soil conservation, reforestation, improved navigation, and the manufacture of fertilizer and aluminum. During the course of the Roosevelt administration, the poor, mountainous region along the Tennessee–North Carolina border went from growing cotton to manufacturing aircraft and components for nuclear weapons. The average income of the area's residents increased tenfold. As a comprehensive, centrally planned development scheme, the TVA came closest to the Brains Trusters' vision of how a modern "democracy on the march" should work. But it was an exception among New Deal programs, which tended to be more fragmented and improvisational.

Headed by Henry Wallace, founder of the Pioneer Hi-Bred Corn Company, the Agriculture Department was an idea factory in the first Hundred Days. An emergency farm bill gave Wallace broad powers to control production, buy up surpluses, regulate marketing, and levy taxes. Conservation and reclamation projects drained swamps, irrigated deserts, and altered the weather, planting a "shelterbelt" of forest across the Great Plains to break the force of windstorms. The Agricultural Adjustment Act established a system of subsidies, price controls, and production limits that turned agriculture into a regulated industry. After 1933, farmers, once fiercely independent, essentially worked for the federal government. The New Deal farm system permanently altered the American diet by making processed grains, grain-fed meat, sugar, and dairy products cheap and plentiful relative to unsubsidized fresh vegetables, fruits, and fish.

In many respects, however, the New Deal did little for the rural poor. Price supports and production controls helped farmers who owned their own land. Similarly,

The Norris Dam New Dealers idolized civil engineering projects such as the Norris Dam, which they saw as symbols of a new national consensus. "A river has no politics," David Lilienthal explained. "Development anywhere helps everyone everywhere."

soil conservation, irrigation, rural electrification, and various long-term reforms tended to benefit independent commercial farmers. Subsistence farmers and the landless poor—overwhelmingly Mexican migrant workers in the Far West, and tenants and share-croppers, black and white, in the cotton South—gained little. Indeed, an unintended consequence of New Deal production limits was to take work away from the poorest Americans. These programs accelerated the migration of poor, often barely educated, people into industrial cities.

Native Americans suffered an especially severe form of rural poverty. Shunted onto reservations in the late nineteenth century, by 1930 the majority of American Indians were landless, miserably poor, and subjected to the corrupt paternalism of the Bureau of Indian Affairs. Alcoholism, crime, and infant mortality were all more common on reservations than they were even among the poorest whites. John Collier, FDR's commissioner of Indian affairs, was determined to correct the situation, and the Indian Reorganization Act of 1934 gave him the power to try. Collier reversed decades of federal attempts to assimilate Native Americans into the cultural mainstream. Under the New Deal, forced land sales ended, and reservations were actually enlarged. Tribal democracy replaced bureaucratic authority. But Congressional opponents, even western liberals, resented Collier's attempts to preserve traditional culture. Even on its own terms Collier's plan could be only partially successful. What worked for Pueblo communities might not work for the Navajo, for example. And Indians themselves were divided over policies and goals. As a result, while the New Deal relieved some poverty among Native Americans, it did not develop a satisfactory long-term solution.

The Blue Eagle

FDR had no fixed plan for industrial recovery and preferred to wait until business interests could agree on one before acting. Congress, however, moved independently to pass a bill aimed at spreading employment by limiting the workweek to 30 hours. Heading off what he thought an ill-conceived plan, Roosevelt put forward his last proposal to become law in the first Hundred Days: the National Industrial Recovery Act. It mandated that business, labor, and government officials negotiate a "code" restructuring each industry into a national cartel. The code would set trade practices, wages, hours, and production quotas. The hope was to raise prices by limiting production while simultaneously protecting the purchasing power of workers. The NIRA reversed decades of antitrust law. Organized labor received protections from Section 7(a) of the act, which guaranteed unions the right of collective bargaining. Finally, $3.3 billion was earmarked for jobs creation through a Public Works Administration.

The NIRA was a bold idea, but it suffered from many of the same problems as Hoover's earlier schemes. It quickly brought together representatives from hundreds of industries to draw up their respective codes, but the process tended to be dominated by business. Few strong unions existed, and the government lacked expertise in industrial management. Smaller businesses were shut out, leaving America's largest corporations to write the codes in their interest. For a time in 1933 and 1934 the NRA's Blue Eagle, the symbol of compliance with the codes, flew proudly in the windows of shops and factories. Soon, however, dissatisfaction with the program dampened enthusiasm, and by 1935 the eagle had come to roost atop a shaky and unpopular agency.

The Second New Deal

The first Hundred Days had been extraordinary by any standard. Congress had given the president unprecedented power to regulate the economy. The financial system had been saved from collapse. Federal relief had been extended to the unemployed. The agricultural economy was given direct federal support. A "yardstick" for the nation's public utilities had been created by the TVA. And a bold experiment in industrial planning had been attempted. Almost everyone was dazzled by what had happened, but not everyone was pleased. Critics pointed out that much of this legislation was poorly drafted, overly conservative, or downright self-contradictory. If Hoover had been too rigid, FDR struck even his admirers as hopelessly flexible. By 1935 the New Deal was besieged by critics from all directions. But rather than becoming demoralized, Roosevelt responded to political criticism and judicial setbacks by keeping Congress in session throughout the hot summer of 1935. The result was another dramatic wave of reforms known as the second New Deal.

Critics Attack from All Sides

In May 1935 one of William Randolph Hearst's emissaries traveled to Washington to warn Roosevelt that the New Deal was becoming too radical. Hearst had long been one of the most powerful newspaper publishers in America, and like many businessmen he had "no confidence" in Roosevelt's advisers. But by 1935 Roosevelt was losing patience with the business community. Saving capitalism had

> Those taxes were never a problem of economics. They are politics all the way through. . . . With those taxes in there, no damn politician can ever scrap my social security program.
>
> FRANKLIN DELANO ROOSEVELT

AMERICAN LANDSCAPE

>> Angola, Louisiana

"Angola was a pleasant place to live back then," Patsy Spillman remembers of her childhood in the 1930s. "You could get inmates as cooks, yard boys, house boys; you could have two or three of them if you wanted." "It was wonderful," her sister JoAn agrees. "I was the princess, and my daddy and mother were the king and queen, and we had servants, and we didn't want for anything." There were occasional problems. Once, a convict put rat poison in the girls' milk. Another time, the Himel family down the road had their throats slit by a prisoner attempting to escape. JoAn and Patsy were the daughters of John Spillman, a guard "captain" at the Louisiana State Penitentiary at Angola. Their home was a plantation house inside the prison.

Apart from the striped uniforms, Angola in the 1930s resembled a pre–Civil War plantation, 18,000 treeless acres of cotton and sugarcane bounded on one side by the Tunica Hills and on the other three by the earthen levees holding back the Mississippi River. Inmates, organized into work gangs, slept in military-style "camps" and rose before dawn to chop cotton and cane and refine sugar in the prison's own mill, the Pelican State Factory. Guards, all of whom were white, flogged prisoners, most of whom were black, with a leather strap, an average of three beatings a day between 1928 and 1940. "Angola was probably the closest thing to a feudal system in America at the time," one warden observed, "the guard captains being the lordly aristocrats and the inmates as the downtrodden serfs."

To the warden and the state, the prison's main purpose was to turn a profit, not to reform prisoners or even to keep them alive. With the economy in crisis, the voters and legislators wanted to lower property taxes while increasing state spending on roads, education, and jobs. To save money, Governor Huey Long demanded that that prison system be self-supporting, or even return revenue to the state. Democratic pressures created the system of convict slavery at Angola.

Before 1928, many southern states had a "convict lease" system that allowed planters and private businesses to rent chain gangs of prisoners. In the 1930s that system disappeared, as Long and other governors realized that the state could as easily reap the proceeds for itself. While two-thirds of American workers were unemployed, convict laborers nationwide produced $75 million a year in shirts, shoes, cement, license plates, and other goods and services. Inmates at Angola were treated as state property and taken from the prison to repair roads, tend gardens at the governor's mansion, and even to perform minstrel shows. To maximize gains, prisoners at Angola worked 60 hours a week and were paid two cents a day. They grew their own food, slept in unheated barracks, used the same bucket for a toilet and to hold drinking water, and had no medical care. Epidemics regularly swept through the camps. In the 1930s, an average of 41 prisoners died each year.

No walls stood between the prisoners and the outside. The prisoners guarded themselves. Fewer than 20 free captains, along with 600 "trusty" convicts with rifles, guarded over 4,000 prisoners. Trusties were rewarded for shooting prisoners who stepped over the "deadlines" that surrounded work areas. Chase teams of mounted men hunted down escapees with dogs. Survivors were "hotboxed" in tiny airless cells at the notorious Red Hat camp, where they received only bread and water. Desperation drove prisoners to keep trying. On September 10, 1933, 12 prisoners took advantage of a Sunday baseball game to shoot a captain and two trusties and steal a car. They were rounded up in hours. The following year, 15 Red Hats working an okra field brandished wooden pistols and disarmed two trusties, but other guards shot them down.

The system established in the 1930s has proven surprisingly resilient. Voters continue to demand that prisons turn a profit. When the population topped 4,000 inmates in the 1950s, the prison was deemed overcrowded. Today it has 5,100; over half are lifers and 87 are awaiting execution. Prisoners still work

Blues legend Huddie Ledbetter, known as Leadbelly, served time in Angola, where he was discovered by music producers.

five days a week, raising soybeans and cattle instead of sugar. Pay has risen to two cents an hour. The prison's revenue streams are now adapted to the region's tourist economy. Vacationers can explore a museum on the site of the old Red Hat camp and attend an annual rodeo, where convicts ride bulls to the delight of a paying audience. In 1976, inmates began publishing a newspaper, *The Angolite,* which won a Pulitzer Prize for reporting on prison life. Its editor likes to quote the essayist William Hazlitt, who wrote that "We are all, more or less, slaves of opinion." ●

always been one of Roosevelt's goals, but shortsighted businessmen and financiers never appreciated his efforts. They had their own reasons for detesting the New Deal, and in the long run they proved more potent critics than all of Roosevelt's radical opponents combined.

The fate of the Communist Party illustrates the difficulties radicals faced during the New Deal. On the one hand, the 1930s were "the heyday of American Communism," as perhaps a quarter of a million Americans, disillusioned with capitalism, joined the Communist Party (CPUSA). The Communists organized labor unions and took the lead in defending the Scottsboro Boys, a group of nine young African American men falsely accused of raping two white women in Alabama. Yet the party's appeal was greatest after 1935, when, on orders from the Soviet Union, it adopted a "popular front" strategy in support of the New Deal. Thus, the Communists were most popular when they surrendered their revolutionary aims. Most of those who joined had left the party by the end of the decade.

Populist radicals gave Roosevelt more trouble. Father Charles Coughlin was a Catholic priest in Detroit who attracted listeners to his weekly radio show by blaming the Depression on international bankers and Wall Street. His solution was to nationalize the banking system and inflate the currency. FDR was careful not to anger Coughlin, and at first the radio priest defended Roosevelt and blamed the New Deal on Communist and Jewish influence in Washington. But by 1935 Coughlin turned on the president. He formed his own organization, the National Union for Social Justice, which pressured Congress to enact further reforms.

A California physician, Dr. Francis Townsend, offered an agenda especially popular among older Americans devastated by the Depression. Through a transaction tax of 2 percent, the government would fund retirement pensions of $200 per month. By requiring the elderly retirees to spend all of their pensions each month, the program was supposed to pump money into the economy and thereby stimulate a recovery. "Townsend clubs" advocating this scheme sprang up across the country and a *Townsend National Weekly* spread the word. Huey Long's "Share Our Wealth" program was more comprehensive than Townsend's and more popular than Father Coughlin's. As governor of Louisiana, Long slapped steep taxes on the oil industry which he used to build or renovate roads, schools, hospitals, and Louisiana State University. In the process, he amassed nearly dictatorial powers, controlling the legislature and the state police. Long was a loyal but critical supporter of FDR during the first Hundred Days. But by 1934 he was proposing his own alternative to the New Deal.

Long believed that the Depression was caused by the maldistribution of income. Consequently, his program for recovery called for the radical redistribution of wealth through confiscatory taxes on the rich and a guaranteed minimum income of $2,500 per year. Townsend's, Coughlin's, and Long's plans all rested on a crucial kernel of truth about the condition of the American economy. The currency did need to be inflated. Elderly Americans were indeed desperate, and wealth was unequally distributed. Roosevelt eventually defused these movements by adopting parts of their programs.

The business community's rising hostility concerned FDR as he prepared for his 1936 campaign. It would be several years before bankers would even admit the New Deal had saved the financial system. Wall Street never admitted it. And after some initial gestures of cooperation, most industrialists became vocal critics of the NIRA. As criticism of the New Deal grew, a conservative U.S. Supreme Court moved to strike down many of the key laws of the first Hundred Days. On May 27, 1935, in *Schechter Poultry Corporation v. United States,* the Court invalidated the NIRA. The case had been brought by a small New York poultry company, but it was financed by larger companies interested in killing the Blue Eagle. The justices ruled the NIRA unconstitutional and did so in a way that made it difficult for Congress to regulate the national economy to any significant degree. Roosevelt feared the setback portended the elimination of most of his achievements, and his fears were borne out in January 1936, when the Court overturned the Agricultural Adjustment Act.

The Second Hundred Days

FDR loved a good fight. No longer concerned about attracting the support from business, the president welcomed criticism and shot right back. After 1935 the rhetoric became noticeably more radical. When the Supreme Court invalidated the NIRA, Roosevelt kept Congress in session through the sweltering Washington summer and forced through a raft of legislation in a "second Hundred Days," which marked the beginning of the second New Deal.

A few of the new proposals were designed to salvage pieces of the NIRA and AAA or to silence radical critics. Hoping to undermine the "crackpot ideas" of Huey Long, Roosevelt proposed a Revenue Act that would encourage a "wider distribution of the wealth." The Revenue Act raised estate and corporate taxes and pushed personal income taxes in the top bracket all the way up to 79 percent. Despite the political motives behind the bill, it made certain economic sense. Before the 1935 Revenue Act, most New Deal programs had been financed by regressive sales and excise taxes. Thereafter, programs were funded with progressive income taxes that fell most heavily on those best able to pay.

The first New Deal had been preoccupied with the dire emergency of 1933. The second New Deal left a more enduring legacy. The administration put the finishing touches on its program to ensure the long-term security of the nation's financial system and extend the relief programs that had helped so many to survive. It put in place a social security system that became the centerpiece of the American welfare state for the remainder of the century, and it allied itself with organized labor, thereby creating a new and powerful Democratic Party coalition. By the time Congress adjourned in late August 1935, the most important achievements of the New Deal were in place.

Social Security for Some

Bolstered by big Democratic gains in the 1934 elections, FDR pursued a massive effort to fund work relief by sponsoring the Emergency Relief Appropriations

Bill. Providing nearly $5 billion, more than the entire 1932 federal budget, it was called by some members of his administration the "Big Bill." This appropriation breathed new life into the relief programs of the first New Deal and created a new Works Progress Administration (WPA), headed by Harry Hopkins. The WPA lasted for eight years, employing as many as 3.3 million Americans. WPA workers built infrastructure: bridges, schools, libraries, and sewer systems, the Blue Ridge Parkway across Virginia and the Carolinas, and over 800 airports. The WPA commissioned artists to decorate post offices, and historians to collect the stories of mill workers and former slaves. At Indiana University, the WPA paid undergraduates to build a student union. WPA lexicographers wrote a Hebrew-English dictionary. "There are rabbis who are broke," Hopkins explained. The program was hugely popular.

Critics complained with some justice that the WPA put people to work on meaningless "make-work" jobs or that many of the workers were incompetent to perform the jobs they were given. Political corruption was a more serious problem. WPA officials, especially at the local level, often used the agency as a patronage machine. Party regulars were sometimes favored with public works projects, and individual jobs were awarded on the basis of party loyalty. Corruption was not rampant, but there was enough of it to provide ammunition to the WPA's opponents. In many states, particularly in the South, local officials openly discriminated against African Americans. The WPA was never able to employ all those who needed work, but for millions of Americans it provided a critical source of immediate relief from the very real prospect of hunger and misery.

In addition to short-term relief, the New Deal created a permanent system of long-term economic security. In 1932 there were no national programs of unemployment insurance, workers' compensation, old-age pensions, or aid to needy children. The states were only slightly more able to care for citizens. As a result, most Americans had little or no protection from economic calamity.

The Social Security Act of 1935 took a critical first step toward providing such protection. It established matching grants to states that set up their own systems of workers' compensation, unemployment insurance, and aid to families with dependent children. Even more importantly, the federal government itself created a huge new Social Security system that guaranteed pensions to millions of elderly Americans. FDR insisted that it be funded as an insurance plan with payroll taxes paid by employees and employers. He hoped that this would protect the system from the political attacks that welfare programs commonly encountered.

Most New Dealers hoped to go much further. Secretary of Labor Frances Perkins wanted to include agricultural laborers and domestic servants, mostly women and African Americans, in the new Social Security system. But that would have provoked enough opposition from southern conservatives to kill the entire program. The administration also preferred federal rather than state programs of workers' compensation and unemployment insurance. There was, however, no federal bureaucracy in place that could have run such programs, and in any case there was fierce opposition to the idea of taking such programs away from the states.

Local and factional opposition thus limited the New Deal's plans for nationalized social welfare and economic security. Welfare and insurance programs were weaker in the South than in the North and weaker for women and African Americans than for white men. Despite such strong opposition, the New Deal actually accomplished a great deal. By 1939 every state had established a program of unemployment insurance and assistance to the elderly. Welfare bureaucracies across the country were professionalized to meet the demands of the federal system. Almost overnight the Social Security system became the federal government's first huge social welfare bureaucracy. More Americans than ever before were thereby protected from the ravages of unemployment, disability, poverty, and old age.

Labor and the New Deal

The 1930s saw unions take a new role in America's political economy. During that decade the number of Americans organized in unions leaped by the millions, and by 1940 nearly one in four nonfarm workers was unionized. Labor organizations overcame resistance from employers to enroll workers in the economy's core industries, including steel, rubber, electronics, and automobiles. Unions also became key players in the Democratic Party. None of the leading New Dealers, Roosevelt included, had anticipated this in 1932. Nevertheless, in critical ways the New Deal fostered the growth of organized labor and its inclusion in the Democratic electoral coalition.

The Roosevelt administration had never adopted the past government attitude of outright hostility toward unions. Rather, over the course of the 1930s FDR moved from grudging acceptance to open support for organized labor. Across the country, workers responded to the change. Section 7(a) allowed unions to launch huge organizing drives, and labor began to flex its muscle with a spontaneous wave of strikes. Mill workers in the South launched brave, but doomed, strikes against textile manufacturers. Dockworkers in San Francisco organized a tremendously successful general strike throughout the city. At the same time, the NIRA inspired a talented group of national leaders, in particular John L. Lewis of the United Mine Workers, Sidney Hillman of the Amalgamated Clothing Workers, and David Dubinsky of the International Ladies' Garment Workers.

Employers fought back against this new worker militancy. They used all the methods to intimidate workers—espionage, blacklisting, and armed assault—that had worked so well in earlier decades. But when it became clear that the federal government would now protect workers seeking to organize and bargain collectively, employers formed company unions to thwart independent action by workers themselves. By 1935 the employers seemed to be winning, particularly in May when the Supreme Court declared the NIRA, including Section 7(a), unconstitutional. In 1935 militancy among workers declined and the unionization drive seemed to be stalled. But the hopes of organized labor were kept alive by an influential and imaginative liberal senator from New York named Robert Wagner.

Wagner took the lead in expanding the limited protections of Section 7(a) into the National Labor Relations Act, also known as the Wagner Act. Although he had few ties to organized labor, Wagner believed workers had a basic right to join unions. He also hoped that effective unions would stimulate the economy by raising wages, thereby building consumer purchasing power. Like Section 7(a), the Wagner Act guaranteed workers the right to bargain collectively with their employers, but it also outlawed company unions, prohibited employers from firing workers after a strike, and restricted many of the other tactics traditionally used by companies to inhibit the formation of unions. Most importantly, the Wagner Act created the National Labor Relations Board (NLRB) to enforce these provisions. In the summer of 1935 FDR, perhaps convinced that businessmen could not be counted on to support industrial planning, declared the Wagner Act "must" legislation, and the bill became law.

While Wagner and his colleagues moved in Congress, John L. Lewis and Sidney Hillman took another course. In 1935 they pressed the conservative leadership of the American Federation of Labor to accept the principle of industrial unions, which would organize workers in an entire sector of the economy such as steel. The traditionalists of the AFL rejected the idea and held fast to the notion that workers should be organized by their crafts rather than by whole industries. Thwarted by the AFL leadership, Lewis, Hillman, and their allies formed a rival organization that eventually became the Congress of Industrial Organizations (CIO).

The CIO proceeded to organize some of the most powerful and prosperous industries in the country. Although none of these efforts depended on the Wagner Act for their initial success, the government's new attitude toward organized labor played an important role. For example, when the United Automobile Workers initiated a series of "sit-down strikes" against General Motors, neither FDR nor the Democratic governor of Michigan sent in troops to remove workers from the factories that they were occupying. This sent a powerful message to the leaders of industry and helped to win the strike against the most powerful corporation in America. In addition, the NLRB protected the new unions from an employer counterattack during the recession that hit the economy in 1937.

Thus by the late 1930s a crucial political alliance had been formed. A newly vigorous labor movement had become closely associated with a reinvigorated national Democratic Party. Thanks to this alliance, American industrial workers entered a new era. Having won the ability to organize with the help of the government, industrial workers used their power to increase wages, enhance job security, improve working conditions, and secure their retirements. Organized labor now had a stake in preserving the system from economic collapse. As much as the banking and financial reforms of the first New Deal, the successful unionization of industrial workers helped stabilize American capitalism.

The New Deal Coalition

Franklin Roosevelt believed that to overcome his varied opposition and win his bid for reelection he needed to create a coalition far broader than that of 1932. By 1936, the Democratic Party was transformed in fundamental ways. For the first time since the Civil War, a majority of voters identified themselves as Democrats, and the Democrats remained the majority party for decades to come. FDR achieved this feat by forging a powerful coalition between the competing wings of the party. In the end, however, the same coalition that made the New Deal possible also limited its progressivism.

The rural South had been overwhelmingly Democratic for a century, but urban voters in the North became the party's new base. This shift was well under way during the 1920s, when Al Smith's two presidential bids attracted ethnic blue-collar voters. Symbolism and substance attracted the urban working class to the New Deal. FDR offered prominent ethnic Americans an unprecedented number of federal appointments. Jews and Catholics (Italian as well as Irish) served Roosevelt as advisers, judges, and cabinet officers. More importantly, thousands of working-class city dwellers found relief from the Depression through jobs with the CWA, the WPA, or the CCC. Those same New Deal programs generated a flood of patronage appointments that endeared Roosevelt to local Democratic machines. Finally, FDR's support for labor was reciprocated by the unions. The CIO alone poured $600,000 into Roosevelt's campaign, replacing the money no longer forthcoming from wealthy donors, and its members formed an army of volunteers to help get out the vote. Thus the Democratic Party became, by 1940, the party of the urban working class.

The New Deal's programs also help to explain a dramatic shift of allegiance among African American voters. Since Reconstruction, southern blacks had supported the party of Lincoln, but as they migrated to the urban North they gained voting strength and abandoned the Republican Party. By 1936 northern blacks voted overwhelmingly for FDR, even though the Democrats were weak on the issue of civil rights. The New Deal included no legislation against discrimination, and FDR silently allowed Congress to reject antilynching laws. New Deal agencies did, however, offer more assistance to poor, unemployed African Americans than previous federal programs. And some New Dealers such as Harold Ickes, Harry Hopkins, and Will Alexander committed themselves to equal rights. Mary McLeod Bethune, a prominent African American educator and close friend of Eleanor Roosevelt, served the New Deal as director of the National Youth Administration's Office of Negro Affairs, which gave jobs and training to some 300,000 young African Americans. Besides controlling her own Special Negro Fund, Bethune successfully pressured other New Deal administrators to open their programs to blacks. With perhaps a million African American families depending on the WPA by 1939, black voters had solid economic reasons for joining the New Deal coalition.

A similar logic explains why women reformers threw their support to the Democrats in the 1930s. Once again, FDR had no feminist agenda, and New Deal programs discriminated against women by offering lower pay and restricting jobs by sex. But as with African Americans, women benefited in unprecedented numbers from New Deal welfare and jobs programs. For the first time in American history, a woman, Frances Perkins, was appointed to the cabinet. "At last," said Molly Dewson, director of the Women's Division of the Democratic National Committee, "women had their foot inside the door."

The most prominent female reformer associated with the New Deal was Eleanor Roosevelt. She was in many ways the last great representative of a woman's reform tradition that flourished in the Progressive Era. She had worked in a settlement house and campaigned for suffrage and progressive causes. Eleanor and Franklin made a remarkable political couple. Millions of Americans read Eleanor's opinions in her weekly newspaper column, "My Day." She became for many Americans the conscience of the New Deal, the person closest to the president who spoke most forcefully for the downtrodden. Her well-deserved reputation for compassion protected her husband in at least two ways. Liberals who might have been more critical of the New Deal instead relied on Eleanor Roosevelt to push the president in the direction of more progressive reform. At the same time, conservatives who were charmed by FDR's personality blamed all the faults of the New Deal on his wife. "It was very simple," one southern journalist explained. "Credit Franklin, better known as He, for all the things you like, and blame Eleanor, better known as She, or 'that woman,' for all the things you don't like." This way, southern conservatives reasoned, "He was cleared, She was castigated, and We were happy."

Although four years of the New Deal had not lifted the Depression, the economy was making headway. Jobs programs had put millions of Americans to work; the banking crisis was over; the rural economy had been stabilized. Based on this record and the backing of his powerful coalition of southern whites, northern urban voters, the labor movement, and many other Americans, FDR won reelection by a landslide in 1936. He captured over 60 percent of the popular vote and, in the Electoral College, defeated his Republican opponent Alf Landon in every state but Maine and Vermont. Landon, the governor of Kansas, even lost his home state. The new Democratic coalition also won sweeping command of the Congress. Seventy-six Democratic senators faced a mere 16 Republicans. In the House, the Democratic majority was even stronger, 333 to 89. Roosevelt now stood at the peak of his power.

Crisis of the New Deal

When the members of the new Congress took their seats in 1937 it seemed as if Roosevelt was unbeatable, but within a year the New Deal was all but paralyzed. A politically costly fight to "pack" the Supreme Court at last gave Roosevelt's conservative opponents a winning issue. A sharp recession further encouraged the New Deal's enemies and provoked an intellectual crisis within the administration itself. In 1938, when the Republicans regained much of their congressional strength, the reform energies of the New Deal were largely spent. Within a year the nation turned its attention to rising threats from overseas.

> **Last Spring I thought you really intended to do something. Now I have given it all up. Henceforward I am swearing eternal vengeance on the financial barons and I will do every single thing I can to bring about communism.**
>
> INDIANA FARMER TO FDR,
> October 16, 1933

Conservatives Counterattack

With conservative opponents vanquished, it seemed as if New Dealers could finish the job begun in 1933. Administration progressives like Frances Perkins hoped that legislation already passed could now be strengthened.

FDR himself appeared to be poised to launch the next great wave of New Deal reforms, but one apparently immovable barrier stood in the way: the U.S. Supreme Court. The Court had already struck down the NIRA and the AAA, and recent rulings made it seem that neither Social Security nor the Wagner Act were safe from the Court's nine "old men." Before he went on, Roosevelt wanted to change the Court. He had not yet had the opportunity to appoint any new justices, and pundits joked that the elderly judges refused to die. Sure that a constitutional amendment supporting his program would take too long or fail, FDR launched a reckless and unpopular effort to "reform" the Court. He proposed legislation that would allow the president to appoint a new justice for every sitting member of the Court over 70 years of age. This "court packing" plan, as Roosevelt's opponents labeled it, would have given the president as many as six new appointments.

Conservatives had long complained of FDR's "dictatorial" powers, and the court plan seemed to confirm their warnings. They formed the National Committee to Uphold Constitutional Government and skillfully cultivated congressional allies, allowing Democrats to take the lead in opposing the court reform. Even the New Deal's allies refused to campaign for the president's bill, and it took all of his political power and prestige to keep it before a hostile Congress. By the end of the summer of 1937, it was over and the bill defeated.

Ironically, Roosevelt eventually won his point. Several of the justices soon retired, giving FDR the critical appointments he needed to swing the Court in the administration's favor. The Supreme Court backed away from its narrow conception of the role of the federal government; nevertheless, FDR's court plan proved a costly mistake. The defeat of court reform emboldened the president's opponents. In November 1937 the administration's critics issued a Conservative Manifesto calling for balanced budgets, states' rights, lower taxes, and the defense of private property and the capitalist system. It heralded the themes around which conservatives would rally for the remainder of the century. In some cases, opposition was purely a matter of interest group pressure, but behind the manifesto lay some hard political realities that drove the conservatives into opposition.

Southern congressmen, for example, were motivated by a desire to preserve white privilege. Federal programs that offered alternatives to subsistence wages disturbed entrenched systems of political and economic dominance. Southern conservatives blamed the New Deal. "You ask any nigger in the street who's the greatest president in the world. Nine out of ten will tell you Franklin Roosevelt," one white southerner declared. "That's why I think he's so dangerous."

In the rural South and West there were growing fears that the New Deal was becoming too closely tied to the urban working class in the Northeast. To counteract this trend, conservatives appealed to the deeply rooted American suspicions of central government. Still, conservatives were not strong enough to block all New Deal legislation. Farm-state representatives needed Roosevelt's support. In late 1937 the administration succeeded in passing housing and farm tenancy reforms. In 1938 Congress passed the Fair Labor Standards Act, requiring the payment of overtime after 40 hours of work in a week, establishing a minimum wage, and eliminating child labor. Even with flagging support, FDR could enact proposals blocked during the Progressive Era.

However, the 1938 congressional elections gave the conservatives the strength they needed to bring New Deal reform to an end. The president tried to purge leading conservatives by campaigning against them, but the attempt failed. Republicans gained 75 seats in the House and were now strong enough in the Senate to organize an effective anti–New Deal coalition with southern Democrats. By then, a jolting recession had created a crisis of confidence within the New Deal itself.

AMERICA AND THE WORLD

>> The Global Depression

In 1930, mulberry trees covered the hills of the Japanese islands of Hokkaido and Honshu. In parts of Japan, two-thirds of the cultivated land was fodder for the silkworms that produced Japan's leading export. Over 2 million families depended on silk, which went chiefly to the United States, where it was made into the fashionable stockings worn by American women.

The silk market was the one bright spot in Japan's economy after World War I. Chinese consumers had boycotted Japan to protest land grabs during the war. In 1923, an earthquake followed by fires and a tidal wave leveled Tokyo and Yokohama. Japan was not alone: in much of the world, economies stagnated in the 1920s under the burden of war reparations and war loans. One of the worst-hit was Italy, where lingering unemployment contributed to the rise of Benito Mussolini's fascist government in 1922. But the New York Stock Exchange crash triggered a global depression. As the world's leading creditor, producer, and consumer, the United States exported its financial disaster to the world.

Countries tied to a single commodity or to the American market suffered most. After the crash, American women stopped buying stockings, and the price of silk dropped by three-quarters. By the end of 1931, Japanese silk farmers were broke; by the next year, they were starving. Similar catastrophes unfolded in the rubber-growing regions of Malaya and the coffee farms of Guatemala. International prices for Australian wool, Cuban sugar, Canadian wheat, and Egyptian cotton plummeted. Brazil, unable to export coffee, used it to fuel locomotives. Everywhere, it seemed, the environment and the economy joined forces to destroy farmers. In Rwanda a famine aggravated by the loss of tin exports killed 40,000. In China, 25 million people fled when the Yangtze River broke its banks in 1935.

The disruption of trade intensified conflict in India, Africa, and other areas under imperial rule. Unable to collect taxes at the ports, colonial governments imposed head taxes or government monopolies that shifted burdens onto the rural poor. The distress of the peasantry intensified demands for independence in India, and Mohandas Gandhi's satyagraha, civil resistance, reached a peak in 1932, when 32,500 nonviolent protestors filled the jails. The French government of Indochina (Vietnam) forced rice farmers to pay taxes in gold. Uprisings against French rule grew in frequency and violence as the Depression wore on, as did insurgencies against the U.S. colony in the Philippines. In the industrial countries, jobless people stood in breadlines and built shanties near the centers of civilization and culture. More than 2 million workers were unemployed in Britain. American loans to Germany dried up in 1930, and by the end of the year two out of every five Germans were out of work. This catastrophe, together with a hyperinflation that wiped out the savings of most of central Europe's middle class, silenced the voices of political moderates. This was the worst economic crisis in memory, and voters demanded extreme action. Each country now looked out for itself, marshaling scarce resources and forming self-contained economies known as autarkies. Under nationalist leaders Getulio Vargas and José Félix Uriburu, Brazil and Argentina restricted trade and steered investment into industry. The Soviet Union, already cut off from the capitalist world, built "socialism in one country." Japan merged its colonies in Taiwan, Korea, and Manchuria into a "Greater East Asia Co-Prosperity Sphere." The 1932 Ottawa Accords merged Britain, its empire, Canada, and Australia into

continued

No Fireside Chat José Uriburu broadcasting shortly after taking power in a military coup in 1930. Uriburu's dictatorship began a period of Argentina's history known as "the infamous decade."

a self-contained economic bloc. In Germany, this policy was called *Grossraumwirtschaft,* the economics of large areas. It was the policy of the National Socialist (Nazi) Party led by Adolf Hitler.

Autarky exacted heavy demands on citizens, requiring them to sacrifice prosperity, liberty, and lives for the nation. Efficiency was more important than democracy, and regimes around the world became more ruthless and less free. Even to Americans, dictatorships had a high-tech, modern sheen. "If this country ever needed a Mussolini," Senator David A. Reed remarked, "it needs one now." In 1927, an Indiana automaker unveiled a new streamlined model, the Studebaker Dictator. FDR and other American leaders drew the connections between global trade, autarky, repression, and war. "If goods don't cross borders," Secretary of State Cordell Hull observed, "armies will." As another global war loomed, they recognized it as a contest between dictatorship and democracy, but also as a conflict between economic systems. The outcome would mean either autarky or a New Deal for the world. ●

The Liberal Crisis of Confidence

During the 1936 campaign Roosevelt was stung by the conservative criticism of his failure to balance the budget. He had leveled the same charge against Hoover four years earlier, but the demands of the Depression made it difficult and dangerous to reduce government spending. Furthermore, deficit spending seemed to be helping resuscitate the economy.

Hoping to silence his conservative critics after his reelection, Roosevelt ordered a sharp cutback in relief expenditures in 1937. On top of an ill-timed contraction of the money supply ordered by the Federal Reserve and the removal of $2 billion from the economy by the new Social Security taxes, Roosevelt's economy measure had a disastrous effect. Once again, the stock market crashed and industrial production plummeted. Even the relatively healthy automobile, rubber, and electrical industries were seriously hurt. Instead of being silenced, opponents carped about the "Roosevelt Recession" and accused the administration of destroying business confidence.

Among the president's advisers, the competition between the budget balancers and the deficit spenders intensified. This was an important turning point in the intellectual history of the New Deal, as well as of twentieth-century American politics. Until 1938, the orthodoxy that associated economic health with balanced budgets was firmly entrenched in government and the business community. Experience with the recession of 1937–1938 converted young New Dealers to the newer economic theories associated with John Maynard Keynes, the great English economist. During periods of economic stagnation, Keynes argued, the government needs to stimulate recovery through deficit spending. The goal of fiscal policy was no longer to encourage production, but rather to increase purchasing power among ordinary consumers. Roosevelt himself never fully embraced these theories, but more and more members of his administration found them attractive. Moreover, the massive inflow of government funds during World War II brought breathtaking economic revival and seemed to confirm the wisdom of Keynesian economics. Until the 1980s, presidents of both parties subscribed to

Keynesian theory, although they differed on what kind of government programs federal spending should buy.

Conclusion

The New Deal did not bring an end to the Depression, and this was undoubtedly its greatest failure. Nevertheless, FDR achieved other important goals. "I want to save our system," he told a White House visitor in 1935, "the capitalistic system." By this standard, the New Deal was a smashing success. By allowing Americans to survive the worst collapse in the history of capitalism while preserving core freedoms, the New Deal reaffirmed democracy at a time when most of the industrialized world chose dictatorship. The New Deal also created a system of security for the vast majority of American people. National systems of unemployment compensation, old-age pensions, and welfare programs grew from the stout sapling planted during the 1930s. Farm owners received new protec-tions, as did the very soil of the nation. Workers were granted the right to organize, hours of labor were limited, child labor ended, and wages held above the bare mini-mum. Moreover, the financial system was stabilized and made more secure, to the benefit of investors, deposi-tors, and the economy as a whole.

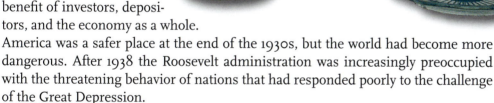

America was a safer place at the end of the 1930s, but the world had become more dangerous. After 1938 the Roosevelt administration was increasingly preoccupied with the threatening behavior of nations that had responded poorly to the challenge of the Great Depression.

Further Readings

Ben S. Bernanke, *Essays on the Great Depression* (2000). A distinguished economist com-pares the strategies different nations used to attack the economic crisis and finds that those who abandoned the gold standard first recovered faster.

Alan Brinkley, *The End of Reform* (1995). An intellectual history of the "internal crisis" of the New Deal.

Lizabeth Cohen, *Making a New Deal: Industrial Workers in Chicago, 1919–1939* (1990). This work successfully combines labor history with the history of popular culture.

James Goodman, *Stories of Scottsboro* (1994). A highly readable retelling of one of the most notorious trials of the 1930s through the eyes of various participants.

David E. Hamilton, *From New Day to New Deal: American Farm Policy from Hoover to Roosevelt, 1928–1933* (1991). How economists in Washington dealt with a farm crisis that had no explanation in economic theory.

Ellis W. Hawley, *The New Deal and the Problem of Monopoly: A Study in Economic Ambivalence* (1966). One of the first and most authoritative economic histories of the New Deal.

Richard Hofstadter, *The American Political Tradition* (1948). The critical chapter on FDR is a classic that anticipated later treatments of the broker state.

David M. Kennedy, *Freedom from Fear: The American People in Depression and War* (1999). A strong recent synthesis of the period from 1933 to 1945.

William E. Leuchtenberg, *Franklin D. Roosevelt and the New Deal* (1963). Still the best short survey of the New Deal and the president who made it.

Arthur Schlesinger Jr., *The Age of Roosevelt*, 3 vols. (1957–1960). A literary and scholarly masterpiece of heroic history.

Amity Shlaes, *The Forgotten Man: A New History of the Great Depression* (2008). This revisionist account criticizes FDR for the New Deal's excesses and defends Hoover's noninterventionist approach.

Who, What?

Herbert Hoover 797

FDR 801

Huey Long 809

Eleanor Roosevelt 814

The New Deal 800

CCC 803

TVA 804

Social Security 811

Wagner Act 812

Autarkies 817

>> Timeline >>

▼ **1928**
Herbert Hoover elected president

▼ **1929**
Stock market crash

▼ **1930**
Hawley-Smoot Tariff enacted

▼ **1931**
National Credit Corporation authorized

▼ **1932**
Franklin Roosevelt elected president

▼ **1933**
FDR declares a bank holiday
First Hundred Days
Emergency Banking Act passed
Economy Act passed

Civilian Conservation Corps (CCC)
United States goes off the gold standard
Agricultural Adjustment Act (AAA)
Emergency Farm Mortgage Act
Tennessee Valley Authority (TVA)
Truth in Securities Act

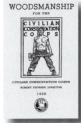

Review Questions

1. Did the stock market crash cause the Great Depression?

2. How did Roosevelt's philosophy of government differ from Hoover's?

3. What setbacks caused FDR to launch a second New Deal?

4. Compare the American response to the Depression to that of Britain, Germany, and Japan. Why did other industrial countries choose different paths?

5. What were Franklin Roosevelt's attributes as a leader? What aspects of his style inspired confidence or animosity?

6. Histories of the Depression focus on national statistics and large-scale programs. How could you retell the story of the 1930s from a local, personal perspective?

Websites

PBS, "Jim Crow Stories." The 1930s were years of struggle for African Americans in the segregated South. Hear of these experiences firsthand, from those who lived through them. http://www.pbs.org/wnet/jimcrow/stories.html

WBUR Radio, "Haunting the Quabbin." What happens when a federal dam project comes to an area? The Quabbin Reservoir brought water and power to Boston and created jobs for some, but whole towns lay at the bottom of the valley flooded by the new dam. http://www.insideout.org/documentaries/hauntingquabbin/

For further review materials and resource information, please visit www.oup.com/us/ofthepeople

National Industrial
   Recovery Act (NIRA)
Glass-Steagall Banking
   Act
Farm Credit Act

▼ **1935**
Second Hundred Days
NIRA declared
   unconstitutional
National Labor
   Relations Act
Social Security Act

▼ **1936**
AAA overturned
Gone with the Wind published
FDR reelected

▼ **1937**
FDR announces "court packing" plan
Economy goes into recession

▼ **1938**
Second Agricultural Adjustment Act
Fair Labor Standards Act

New Deal opponents win big in Congress

▼ **1939**
Administrative Reorganization Act
British actress Vivien Leigh stars in *Gone with the Wind*
Britain and France declare war on Germany

Common Threads

>> What strategic and domestic issues were at stake in the debate over American entry into the war?

>> Did the war consolidate, or overturn, New Deal reforms?

>> In what ways did the war generate economic opportunities and highlight issues of civil rights?

>> A. Philip Randolph

"Who is this guy Randolph," Joseph Rauh wondered, and "what the hell has he got on the President of the U.S.?" It was June 1941 and Rauh, a government attorney, had just been instructed to draft a presidential order prohibiting discrimination on grounds of "race, color, creed, or national origin" in defense industries. It was a radical departure from decades of official support for legalized racism. It would use the economic muscle of the federal government to overturn job segregation nationwide, and in the process make enemies for President Franklin Roosevelt. Rauh was enthusiastic, but he couldn't understand why FDR, with his reliance on southern votes, would even consider it. The president was bending to pressure, Rauh learned, from African Americans led by a charismatic organizer named A. Philip Randolph.

Raised in Florida and educated at New York's City College, Randolph had founded the largest African American labor union, the Brotherhood of Sleeping Car Porters, in 1925. Porters traveled the railroads as baggage handlers and valets, and during the Depression years Randolph's influence extended into every downtown station and rural depot reached by the Brotherhood's magazine, the *Messenger*.

In 1941, it looked to Randolph like only a matter of months before the United States entered the war raging in Europe and Asia. He believed, according to FBI informants, "that Negroes make most fundamental gains in periods of great social upheaval." War would create an opportunity to achieve equality, but only if African Americans demanded it. "The Negro sat by idly during the first world war thinking conditions would get better," he told an audience in Oklahoma City. "That won't be the procedure during the duration of this conflict."

In January 1941, Randolph called for African Americans to march to Washington to demand an end to job discrimination. Only 3 percent of workers in war industries were people of color. "The administration leaders in Washington will never give the Negro justice," he declared, "until they see masses, ten, twenty, fifty thousand Negroes on the White House lawn." The March on Washington Movement (MOWM) was largely bluff. No buses were chartered, and there were no plans for where the thousands would sleep and eat, but Roosevelt and the FBI believed it enough to try to head it off.

A protest march would embarrass the government, and Roosevelt had the power to accede to Randolph's demands. Using the leverage of federal defense contracts, the president could desegregate a large portion of the economy without even asking Congress. He opened negotiations with Randolph through Eleanor Roosevelt. The organizers agreed to cancel the march in return for a presidential directive—Executive Order 8802—establishing a Fair Employment Practices Committee to assure fairness in hiring.

It was a victory for civil rights and for Randolph personally. If the Emancipation Proclamation had ended physical slavery, the New York *Amsterdam News* declared, E.O. 8802 ended "economic slavery." Within a year, thousands of African Americans would be working at high-tech jobs in aircraft factories and arms plants. Randolph had recognized that war created an opening for changing the economic and political rules of the game. The social upheaval of war touched all Americans. The armed forces sent millions, to serve and fight, everywhere from the Arctic to the tropics. Millions of others left home to work in plants producing war materiel. Government stepped in to run the economy, and corporations, labor, the states, and universities fashioned new relationships to the federal government. The war stimulated revolutionary advances

continued

in science, industry, and agriculture. The United States itself became the foremost military and economic power in a world destroyed by war.

These changes enlarged the discretionary powers of the federal government and particularly the presidency. Americans willingly, even eagerly, accepted personal sacrifices and greater federal authority as part of the price of victory. As the March on Washington Movement proved, the president's enhanced powers could enlarge the freedoms and opportunities enjoyed by Americans, but they could also restrict individual liberties. Many Japanese Americans spent the war imprisoned in "relocation centers," and just six months after Roosevelt signed Executive Order 8802, the FBI placed Randolph's name on a list of persons to be placed in "custodial detention" in the event of a national emergency. The war unsettled the economy and society, enlisting all Americans in a global crusade and arousing both idealism and fear. ●

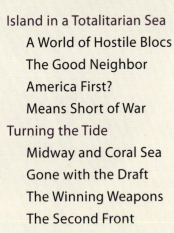

OUTLINE

Island in a Totalitarian Sea

Randolph's movement capitalized on a world crisis that reached back to the treaty that ended World War I. The Depression heightened international tensions, turning regional conflicts in Africa, Europe, and Asia into tests of ideology and power. In 1937 Japan attacked China. Two years later when Germany invaded Poland, France and Britain declared war, beginning World War II in Europe. As with the last war, Americans had time to reflect on the origins of the world crisis before it affected them directly. Most blamed the conflict on the failures of the Versailles Treaty and the desperation caused by the global Depression. Nations and empires were solving economic problems with military force.

Americans were divided, however, on how their country ought to respond. Isolationists believed the United States should stay out of war and secure the Western Hemisphere against attack. But Roosevelt and other internationalists believed the United States had to support the nations fighting Germany and Japan. The alternatives reflected different visions of America's role in the world and responsibilities at home. Internationalists saw a free-trading open-door world economy as a solution to international conflict. Isolationists worried about growing federal power and the ambitions of Britain and the Soviet Union. The threat of fascism forced Americans to ask whether their own economy and government could measure up in the competition between nations.

Internationalists and isolationists both knew war would change American society. The future of world politics and the world economy would be shaped by America's choice of allies and war aims. In 1940, most Americans opposed aid to the enemies of fascism, fearing that giving such aid would lead the United States to become involved. When France's defeat left Britain to fight alone, the polls shifted as more Americans saw aid to Britain as an alternative to U.S. involvement. Japan's attack on Pearl Harbor in December 1941 ended a debate that divided the nation.

> **If Hitler destroys freedom everywhere else, it will perish here. Ringed around by a world hostile to our way of life, we should be forced to become a great military power.**
>
> *FORTUNE* MAGAZINE,
> June 1941

A World of Hostile Blocs

The Depression destroyed the liberal international order based on free trade. For a century, governments around the world had favored policies that increased the movement of goods, people, and investment across borders. The steamship and telegraph accelerated that trend. In many respects, the world economy was more "globalized" before World War I than it is today. Movement toward an open-door world slowed during World War I and the 1920s, and then stopped completely with the Depression. World trade shrank from almost $3 billion a year in 1929 to less than $1 billion in 1933. Empires and nations began to restrict the movement of goods, capital, and people, and to regiment their societies in the pursuit of national self-sufficiency. Everywhere, it seemed, governments became more ruthless and less free.

Dictators enticed their followers with visions of imperial conquests and racial supremacy. Mussolini promised to build a new Roman Empire in Africa and the Mediterranean. Japanese schoolchildren learned that they belonged to a "Yamato race," purer and more virtuous than the inferior peoples they would one day rule. In Germany, Hitler built a state based on racism and brutality. Urging Germans to defend themselves against the *Untermenschen,* subhumans, in their midst—Jews, Gypsies, homosexuals—he suspended civil rights, purged non-Aryans from government and the professions, and compelled art, literature, and science to reflect the Nazi Party's racial conception of the world. A secret police, the Gestapo, hunted down enemies of the regime, and a Nazi army, the SS, enforced party rule.

Jews were the main target of Nazi terror. In 1935, the Nuremberg Laws stripped Jews of citizenship and outlawed intermarriage with members of the "Aryan race." On the night of November 9, 1938, Nazi stormtroopers and ordinary citizens rampaged throughout Germany, burning synagogues and destroying Jewish shops, homes, and hospitals, killing 100 Jews and arresting 30,000 more. *Kristallnacht,* the "night of the broken glass," alerted Americans to the scale of the terror. Until then FDR thought international opinion would restrain Hitler. Now he was no longer sure.

The American president grew apprehensive as Germany, Italy, and Japan, together known as the Axis powers, sought to solve their economic problems through military conquest. Italy invaded Ethiopia in 1935. In July 1937, Japan attacked China. The following year, Hitler's troops marched into Austria. Roosevelt worried the Axis would soon control most of Europe and Asia, but American leaders had an even darker fear, one they scarcely breathed: that in a world of rival economic blocs, totalitarianism would outcompete democracy. Free markets and free labor might be no match for the ruthless, modern efficiency of the fascist states. The United States would be, Assistant Secretary of State Adolf Berle worried, "an old-fashioned general store in a town full of chain stores." It would have to regiment its own citizens just to keep up. The United States would be forced to enlist industry, labor, and agriculture into a "state system," *Fortune* magazine predicted, "which, in its own defense, would have to take on the character of Hitler's system."

The Good Neighbor

Some believed the United States ought to retreat into its own self-contained sphere, and in the early 1930s policy briefly took that direction. The Hawley-Smoot Tariff of 1930 blocked most imports, but within a year, FDR reversed course and began pushing trade as the answer to America's economic problems. He reacted mainly to the vision of his single-minded secretary of state, Cordell Hull. A conservative former senator from Tennessee, Hull believed the Open Door was the cure for dictatorship and depression. The best way to ensure peace, he argued, was to give all countries equal access to the world's markets. In a world of empires and blocs, Hull's formulation turned an old foreign policy tradition, the Open Door, into a bold plan for building international peace and prosperity.

Using loans and the lure of the vast American market, Roosevelt and Hull slowly began to reopen markets in Latin America. The "Good Neighbor" policy—encouraging trade and renouncing the use of force—actually began with Herbert Hoover. FDR expanded the policy and made it his own. A new Export-Import Bank financed transactions, and a Reciprocal Trade Act lowered tariffs. Hull surprised the Pan American Conference at Montevideo, Uruguay, in 1933 by approving a declaration that no nation had the right to intervene in the affairs of another. Good Neighbor policies undermined German and Japanese economic ventures, and Latin American governments invited the FBI to track down Axis agents on their soil.

In 1938, after absorbing Austria, Hitler demanded part of Czechoslovakia's territory. Czechoslovakia's allies, Britain and France, agreed to negotiations, and in a meeting at Munich in September they yielded to Hitler's demands. FDR cabled Hitler a last-minute appeal for restraint, but he accepted the final decision. The victors of World War I feared that a small war over Czechoslovakia would escalate into a larger one. After World War II, the term "Munich" came to symbolize the failure of attempts to appease aggressors, but in 1938 Americans were unsure how best to guard their freedoms in a hostile world.

America First?

As the Axis threat grew, Roosevelt pushed for a buildup of U.S. forces, but Congress and the public disagreed. Disillusioned by the results of the last war, the public earnestly wanted to stay out of the conflicts in Europe and Asia. Polls indicated that more than 70 percent believed the United States had been tricked into World War I. Half a million students pledged that if another war came, they would refuse to serve. Senator Gerald P. Nye charged that the munitions industry was lobbying for war. Pacifists, economic nationalists, and veterans groups, backed by the *Chicago Tribune* and the Hearst newspapers, comprised a powerful isolationist constituency that aimed to prevent the United States from being drawn into hostilities.

From 1935 to 1937, Congress passed annual Neutrality Acts prohibiting loans and credits to nations engaged in war. The action took place against the backdrop of the Spanish Civil War in which Fascist forces, aided by Germany and Italy, fought against democratic, Loyalist forces aided by the Soviet Union. The war aroused passions in the United States, and some 3,000 Americans volunteered to fight with the Loyalists. Precisely for that reason, Congress decided to stay out of the conflict. The Neutrality Acts restricted the president's ability to aid the enemies of fascism just as Munich made the danger clear.

After the fall of 1939, Roosevelt watched his worst nightmare come true, as the United States became an island in a world dominated by force. The Soviet Union signed a nonaggression treaty

Charles Lindbergh and the America First Committee campaigned against involvement in Europe's war. With Britain's defeat likely, they urged neutrality and defense of the Western Hemisphere as the only chance to keep America safe.

with Germany. The full terms of the Nazi-Soviet pact were secret, leading diplomats to fear the worst, a totalitarian alliance stretching from the Rhine to the Pacific. In September, German armies struck Poland, using tanks and dive-bombers to slice deep into the interior. Reporters used the new term *Blitzkrieg,* "lightning war," to describe the German tactics. Hitler and Soviet leader Josef Stalin split Poland between them. Britain and France declared war on Germany.

The following April, Nazi armies invaded Denmark and Norway. On May 10, 1940, Hitler launched an all-out offensive in the West. Tank columns pierced French lines in the Ardennes Forest and turned right toward the English Channel. France folded along with Belgium and the Netherlands. Britain stood alone against the German onslaught. Roosevelt now had to reckon with the possibility that Britain might surrender, placing the British fleet, control of the Atlantic, and possibly even Canada in Hitler's hands. Already the German air force, the *Luftwaffe,* was dueling for control of the skies over southern England.

Determined to shore up this last line of defense, Roosevelt used his powers as commander in chief to bypass the Neutrality Acts. In June 1940, he submitted a bill to create the first peacetime draft in American history. He declared army weapons and supplies "surplus" so they could be donated to Britain. In September 1940, he traded Britain fifty old destroyers for leases to eight naval bases in Newfoundland, Bermuda, and the Caribbean.

The isolationists now found themselves isolated. Sympathy for Britain grew as radio audiences heard the sounds of air attacks on London. Two-thirds of the public favored the draft, but isolationists were not ready to give up. In September 1940, the America First Committee launched a new campaign that urged Americans to distance themselves from Europe and prepare for their own defense. Charles A. Lindbergh and Senator Burton Wheeler headlined America First rallies. The only reason for the United States to become involved, Lindbergh argued, "is because there are powerful elements in America who desire us to take part. They represent a small minority . . . but they control much of the machinery of influence and propaganda."

Roosevelt worried the 1940 election would become a referendum on intervention. Isolationist senator Robert Taft was a leading contender for the nomination, but the Republicans chose Wendell L. Willkie, an anti–New Deal internationalist. In his acceptance speech, Willkie endorsed the draft and expressed sympathy for Britain. With defense and foreign policy issues off the table, the only thing Willkie had to offer was a younger, fresher face. FDR won an unprecedented third term by a 5-million-vote margin.

Means Short of War

British prime minister Winston Churchill waited until after election day to broach the delicate but urgent issue of war finances. Britain had been buying arms on a "cash and carry" basis, but it was now out of funds. The Neutrality Act prohibited new loans, but without arms Britain would have to surrender. FDR gave his cabinet a weekend to come up with a plan, and the following Monday he produced the answer himself. Instead of loaning money, the United States would lend arms and equipment. Roosevelt compared the idea to lending a garden hose to a neighbor whose house is on fire. "There would be a gentleman's obligation to repay," but since there would be no loans, it would not violate the Neutrality Act. Lend-Lease, as the program came to be called, put the U.S. "arsenal of democracy" on Britain's side and granted FDR unprecedented powers to arm allies. The Lend-Lease bill, H.R. 1776, passed the Senate by a two-to-one margin in 1941.

Repayment took the form of economic concessions. Hull saw Lend-Lease as a chance to crack one of the largest autarkic blocs, the British Empire. He insisted that in return for aid, Britain had to discard the Ottawa Accords and open its empire to American trade. Churchill's economic adviser, John Maynard Keynes, reluctantly agreed. Britain was now, at least formally, committed to the Open Door. Later that year Churchill and Roosevelt met aboard the cruisers *Augusta* and *Prince of Wales* off the Newfoundland coast to issue a declaration of war aims, the Atlantic Charter. It assured all nations "victor and vanquished" equal access to the trade and raw materials of the world.

In June 1941, Hitler stunned the world again by launching a lightning invasion of the Soviet Union. Three million men backed by 3,000 tanks slashed through the Soviet defenses and rolled toward Moscow and Leningrad. Secretary of War Henry Stimson predicted that in three months the Axis would control Europe and Asia, but George C. Marshall, the army's chief of staff, reckoned that this might be a turning point. If the Soviet army could hold the area between Moscow and the Black Sea, the Germans would have a long winter. Roosevelt shared his optimism. The eastern front took pressure off Britain and gave the Allies a real chance to defeat Hitler. Roosevelt extended Lend-Lease aid to Moscow. The German columns advanced without interruption, but to the dismay of Hitler's officers, Russian soldiers did not respond to *Blitzkrieg* as French and Polish soldiers had. "Even when encircled, the Russians stood their ground and fought," a Nazi general reported.

German U-boats concentrated on severing Britain's lifelines, sinking half a million tons of shipping a month. To ease the burden on the British navy, Roosevelt fought an undeclared naval war against Germany in the western Atlantic. The U.S. Navy convoyed merchant ships as far as Iceland, where British destroyers took over. FDR said he was offering "all aid short of war," but it was not far short. In September a U-boat fired torpedoes at the USS *Greer,* and the destroyer threw back depth charges. Roosevelt ordered aggressive patrols to expel German and Italian vessels from the western Atlantic. In the Battle of the Atlantic he had crossed the line from neutrality to belligerency, and he appeared to be seeking an incident that would make it official.

Japan, meanwhile, probed into Southeast Asia. In 1939, Japanese militarists had adopted a "go south" strategy, planning to capture oil fields in the Dutch East Indies and encircle China. Because the Philippines, a U.S. territory, lay across the invasion route, the question for the Japanese was not whether to declare war on the United States, but when. In July 1941, Japanese troops established bases in French Indochina. Roosevelt saw this as a threat, but, preoccupied with war in Europe, he wanted to forestall war in the Pacific. U.S. diplomats opened talks with Japan while Marshall dispatched a fleet of B-17s in an attempt to deter an attack. When Japanese troop convoys moved into the South China Sea, Hull broke off negotiations and cut off U.S. oil exports, Japan's only source of fuel. On November 27, Marshall warned army and navy commands in Hawaii and the Philippines to expect "an aggressive move by Japan" in the next few days. The Philippines, Thailand, and Malaya were the likely targets.

On Sunday afternoon, December 7, Americans listening to the radio heard that aircraft "believed to be from Japan" had attacked U.S. bases at Pearl Harbor in Hawaii. At 7:40 A.M. Hawaii time, 181 planes had bombed and strafed the airfields on Oahu, destroying or damaging more than 200 planes on the ground. Bombers then made a run at the 96 ships of the U.S. Pacific Fleet anchored next to each other. Three torpedoes struck the battleship *Oklahoma,* capsizing it with 400 crew members aboard. Alongside her the *Maryland* went down, spreading flaming oil over the shallow waters. A bomb exploded in the *Arizona*'s forward magazine, breaking the ship in half and killing over a thousand men. Hours later, more bad news came from the Philippines, where Japanese bombers also caught American planes on the ground. The following day, President Roosevelt appeared before Congress to ask for a declaration of war against Japan. Only one representative, Montana's Jeannette Rankin, voted no. On December 11, Germany honored its alliance with Japan and declared war on the United States.

Some historians have argued that Roosevelt knew of the approaching attack but withheld warnings, in order to draw the United States into war. In fact, naval authorities at Pearl Harbor anticipated an attack but expected it to come in a different form. They doubted that Japan had the ability or audacity to

Pearl Harbor Japan's attack on the U.S. Navy's principal Pacific base at Pearl Harbor brought the United States into World War II. For Japan, it was the opening phase of a campaign to capture European and American colonies in Asia.

project air and sea power across the Pacific in secrecy. When Japanese planes destroyed American aircraft on the ground in the Philippines nine hours after the Pearl Harbor attack, Douglas MacArthur observed that the bombers must have been flown by Germans. Such preconceptions blinded commanders to the warning signs.

Turning the Tide

For the Allies there was only bad news in the first half of 1942. Japanese invaders walked over the numerically superior British and Dutch armies in Southeast Asia and captured the American islands of Guam and Wake. In February, the "impregnable" fortress of Singapore surrendered, with most of the Australian and Indian armies still inside. Japan's Combined Fleet commanded the waters between Hawaii and India, striking at will. MacArthur declared Manila an open city and staged an Alamo-style defense of the Bataan Peninsula and the fortress island of Corregidor.

Few could see it, but the tide was beginning to turn. The Soviets stopped the German advance in front of Moscow. On April 18, U.S. Colonel James Doolittle's B-25 bombers raided Tokyo. Roosevelt wanted to hold the line in the Pacific while coming to the aid of Britain and the Soviet Union as soon as possible. This meant stopping Japan, creating an American army, and putting it into action on the other side of the Atlantic. None of those jobs would be easy.

Midway and Coral Sea

"We can run wild for six months or a year," Admiral Isoroku Yamamoto prophesied before designing the victorious attack on Pearl Harbor, "but after that I have utterly no confidence." Panic-stricken Americans imagined enemy landings in California,

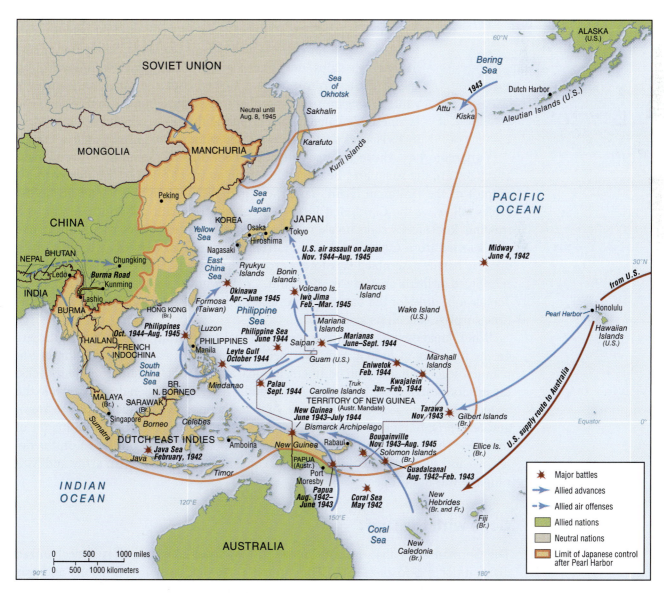

Map 25–1   World War II in the Pacific, 1942–1945 Japan established a barrier of fortified islands across the western Pacific. U.S. forces penetrated it westward from Hawaii and from Australia northward through the Solomon Islands to the Philippines.

> Through the haze I saw Marines stumble and pitch forward as they got hit. I then looked neither right nor left but just straight to my front. The farther we went, the worse it got.
>
> EUGENE B. SLEDGE,
> Battle of Peleliu, September 1944

but Japan's strategy was never so ambitious. It called for fortifying a defensive screen of islands in the western Pacific and holding the Allies at bay until they sued for peace. "The fact that the Japanese did not return to Pearl Harbor and complete the job was the greatest help for us," Chester W. Nimitz, the U.S. Pacific commander, later remembered, "for they left their principal enemy with time to catch his breath, restore his morale, and rebuild his forces."

After the Doolittle raid, the Japanese realized their error and laid plans to lure the U.S. Pacific Fleet into battle. The increase in radio traffic helped Commander Joseph Rochefort, who had already partly succeeded in breaking the Japanese codes. In late April, he was confident enough to tell Nimitz that Japan was planning an attack on Port Moresby on the island of New Guinea. Nimitz dispatched two carriers, *Lexington* and *Yorktown,* to intercept the invasion convoy and its carrier escorts. The Battle of Coral Sea was the first between carrier task forces, an entirely new type of sea battle. Sailors never saw the enemy's ships, only their aircraft, which struck with devastating speed. Planes from *Yorktown* turned back the Japanese transports while *Lexington*'s dive bombers dispatched the carrier *Shoho*. The Japanese retaliated, fatally crippling the *Lexington* and ripping a hole in *Yorktown*'s deck. The two sides withdrew after fighting to a draw.

Yamamoto next chose to attack the U.S. fleet directly. Sending a diversionary attack toward the Aleutians, he aimed his main attack at Midway, the westernmost outpost of the Hawaiian chain. Yamamoto gambled that Nimitz would divide his forces, allowing the Combined Fleet to crush the remnant guarding Hawaii. But trusting Rochefort's code breakers, Nimitz knew the real target was Midway. He also learned from Coral Sea that aircraft, not battleships, were the winning weapons. He hastily assembled task forces around the carriers *Hornet* and *Enterprise* and reinforced airfields on Midway and Oahu. Crews worked night and day to repair the *Yorktown* in time for the battle. The American fleet was still outnumbered, but this time surprise was on its side.

When Japanese aircraft encountered stiff resistance from Midway's flak gunners on the morning of June 4, they returned to their carriers and prepared for an unplanned second attack. With bombers, bombs, and aviation fuel littering their decks, Japan's four carriers were vulnerable. Defending Zeros had been drawn down to the water by a U.S. torpedo bomber attack. At that moment dive bombers from *Yorktown* and *Enterprise* burst out of the clouds. They destroyed three carriers in a matter of minutes. The mighty Combined Fleet ceased to exist. Midway put Japan on the defensive and allowed the United States to concentrate on building an army and winning the war in Europe.

Gone with the Draft

The German army that overran France in May 1940 consisted of 136 mechanized divisions of 17,000 men each. The United States had only five divisions and was still using horse cavalry. "Against Europe's total war," *Time* observed, "the U.S. Army looked like a few nice boys with BB guns." Realizing the danger, military officials drew up plans for a 10-million-man force. As in World War I, the United States had to find ways to house, equip, and transport the army, but this time it would be five times larger. By December 1941, 2 million men and 80,000 women had enlisted. A year later the total exceeded 5 million.

Buses rolled into the new camps and unloaded recruits in front of drill instructors. Boot camp aimed to erase the civilian personality and replace it with an instinct for obedience and action. Selectees, as they were called, learned that there were three ways of doing things: the right way, the wrong way, and the army way. Eugene Sledge left college to join the marines and found himself standing in line at a camp in San Diego. "Your soul may belong to Jesus," his drill instructor bellowed, "but your ass belongs to the Marines." After 13 weeks of calisthenics, close-order drill, road marches, and rifle practice, he was assigned to the infantry.

The 99th Pursuit Squadron, Known as the Black Eagles The Black Eagles trained at the Tuskegee Institute and engaged the Luftwaffe in the skies over North Africa.

Recruits hungered for a weekend pass, but in base towns in the South and West, where many bases were located, there was little for them to do except loiter on street corners and look for trouble. The War Department joined several charities in creating the United Services Organization (USO), to provide a "home away from home" with meals, dances, movies, and wholesome entertainment. Still, wherever there were large numbers of men on leave, soldiers fought with each other and with the locals. Distinctions of apparel and race could stimulate violence. Southerners lynched African American soldiers for wearing their uniforms. In 1943, riots erupted in Harlem after police arrested an African American soldier in uniform. The same year, sailors in Los Angeles attacked Mexican American shipyard workers who wore distinctive "zoot suits." In both cases the clothes signified a disruption of the established social order, a process accelerated by the war.

The army leadership struggled to preserve its racial traditions amid wartime changes. Like the multiethnic imperial armies of Britain and France, the U.S. Army consisted of segregated units, some with special functions. The Japanese American 442nd Regimental Combat Team and the marines' Navajo "code talkers" became well known. African Americans served in the army in segregated units, and until 1942 they were excluded from the navy altogether. Roosevelt ordered the services to admit African Americans and appointed an African American brigadier general, Benjamin O. Davis, but injustices remained. Even blood plasma was segregated in military hospitals.

Two issues aroused the most anger among African Americans: exclusion from combat and the treatment of soldiers at southern bases. Many GIs in uniform experienced the indignity of being refused service at restaurants where German prisoners of war were allowed to eat. Mutinies and race riots erupted at bases in Florida, Alabama, and Louisiana where African American soldiers were housed separately and denied furlough privileges. The army responded by sending African American GIs to the war theaters.

Though desperately short of infantrymen, the army kept African Americans out of frontline units and assigned them to menial chores. Combat symbolized full citizenship, and the NAACP pressed Roosevelt to create African American fighting units. An African American infantry division, the 92nd, went into battle in Italy; three air units—among them the 99th Pursuit Squadron, known as the Tuskegee Airmen—flew against the *Luftwaffe;* and one mechanized battalion, the 761st Tanks, received a commendation for action in the Ardennes. However, most African Americans went into the line individually as replacements, as during the Battle of the Bulge in late 1944. Racially mixed units aroused few complaints in the field, the NAACP noted; resistance to desegregation came mainly from Washington.

With manpower in short supply, the armed forces reluctantly enlisted women. Congress passed legislation creating the Women's Army Corps (the WACs) in 1942. The navy signaled its reluctance in the title of its auxiliary, the Women Accepted for Volunteer Emergency Service (WAVES). Eventually more than 100,000 women served as mechanics, typists, pilots, cooks, and nurses, but the unusual feature of the U.S. forces was not how many women served, but how few. Nearly every other warring country mobilized women for industry and combat, leaving the state to perform traditionally female jobs: caring for children, the sick, and the elderly, functions that continued after the war. Publics in Europe, Canada, and Australia came to accept this government role, but in the United States "welfare" continued to be associated with poor relief.

The Winning Weapons

During World War II weapons technology advanced with blinding speed. The quality of a nation's weapons often depended on how recently they had moved from the drafting table to mass production. Entering the war late, the United States gained a technological edge. American factories tooled up to produce models using the latest innovations, but many of these would not reach the fighting fronts until 1943 or later.

Until then, troops had to make do with weapons that were outclassed by their Axis counterparts. Marines went into action on Guadalcanal wearing World War I–era helmets and carrying the 1903 Springfield rifle. Japan's Zero was substantially faster and lighter than any American fighter. After 1943, the advantage began to pass to the Americans. The M1 rifle was the finest infantry weapon in the war. Artillery was precise and lethal, and American crews were skilled practitioners of the devastating "time-on-target" technique, which delivered shells from several directions simultaneously, leaving no place to hide. In the air, the elegant P-51 Mustang, a high-speed ultra-long-range fighter, could escort bomber groups from Britain as far as Berlin.

It dominated the French skies after D-Day. American four-engine bombers—the B-17 Flying Fortress and the B-24 Liberator—were superior in range and capacity to German or Japanese air weapons. In 1944, the B-29 Superfortress, with its 141-foot wingspan, 10-ton bomb load, and awesome 4,200-mile range, took to the skies over the Pacific. Uniquely adapted to city-busting raids, the Superforts incinerated one Japanese city after another. American tanks, however, remained inferior to their German counterparts throughout the war, owing to the army's failure to recognize the importance of this weapon.

Lawrence Beall-Smith, *Task Force Hornets* (1943) Carrier warfare was unique to the Pacific theater, where opposing fleets used aircraft to strike each other across vast expanses of ocean.

Quantity was often a substitute for quality, however, and American designers sometimes cut corners to make a product that could be mass produced. The results were impressive. When Allied troops landed in France in 1944, they enjoyed a superiority of 20 to 1 in tanks and 25 to 1 in aircraft. When Roosevelt set a production target of 50,000 aircraft in 1940, the Germans considered it a bluff, but American factories turned out almost 300,000 planes during the war. Often, abundance resulted in attrition tactics that pitted American numbers against Axis skill. An American soldier in Salerno asked a captured German lieutenant why he had surrendered. "The Americans kept sending tanks down the road," the German replied. "Every time they sent a tank, we knocked it out. Finally, we ran out of ammunition, and the Americans didn't run out of tanks."

Americans also developed a number of secret weapons. The War Department funded defense laboratories at Johns Hopkins, MIT, Harvard, and other universities, forging a permanent link between government, science, and the military. American and British scientists invented one of the first "smart" bombs, the proximity fuse, which set its own range by bouncing a radio signal off its target. To keep it from falling into Axis hands, Allies used it only for the air defense of London, on ships in the Pacific, and in the worst moments of the battles of Iwo Jima and the Bulge. Collaboration between American and British scientists produced improvements in sonar and radar, penicillin, and the atomic bomb.

The Manhattan Project that produced the atomic bomb was the war's largest military-scientific-industrial enterprise. In 1939, Albert Einstein warned Roosevelt that the Germans might invent a nuclear weapon. The National Academy of Sciences concluded that a weapon of "superlatively destructive power" could be built, and General Leslie R. Groves was put in charge of the project, which eventually employed 600,000 people and cost $2 billion. World War II's marriage of technology and war changed warfare, and it also changed science. Researchers and inventors had once worked alone on problems of their own choosing. Now they worked in teams at government-funded laboratories on problems assigned by Washington.

The Second Front

To reassure Britain and the Soviet Union, FDR adopted a "Europe First" strategy, holding the line against Japan while directing the main effort at Nazi Germany. The Allies had little in common except that Hitler had chosen them as enemies. Britain was struggling to preserve its empire. The Soviet Union had once been allied with Germany and had a nonaggression pact with Japan. Roosevelt needed to keep this shaky coalition together long enough to defeat Hitler. His greatest fear was that one or both of the Allies would make a separate peace or be knocked out of the war before the American economy could be mobilized. Stalin and Churchill each had their own opinions about how to use American power, and their conflicting aims produced bitter disputes over strategy.

As the Nazis closed in on the Soviet oil fields during 1942, Stalin pleaded with Britain and the United States to launch an invasion of France. Roosevelt and Marshall also wanted a second front. Since the Civil War, U.S. military doctrine had favored attacking the main body of the enemy's army, which could be done only in northern Europe. But to the British, the idea of a western front evoked the horrors of the trench warfare of World War I. Britain could not sustain those losses a second time in a century. Instead, Churchill wanted to encircle the Nazi empire and attack the "soft underbelly" of the Axis from the Mediterranean.

Concerned about U-boats and the inexperience of American troops, FDR reluctantly accepted Churchill's plan. A month after Pearl Harbor he had promised Stalin a second front "this year." In late 1942, he postponed it to the spring of 1943. Finally, in June 1943, he told Stalin it would not take place until 1944. The delays reinforced Stalin's suspicions that the capitalist powers were waiting for the USSR's defeat.

Instead of invading Europe, the Americans chose a softer target, North Africa, and troops commanded by Lt. Gen. Dwight Eisenhower landed in Algeria and Morocco on the morning of November 8, 1942. As they advanced east to link up with British forces attacking into Tunisia, German tank divisions under General Erwin Rommel burst through the Kasserine Pass and trapped American columns in high, rocky terrain. Panicky troops fled, blowing up their ammunition stores. One GI described the Panzers as "huge monsters, with a yellow tiger painted on their sides." Once through the pass, Rommel briefly had a chance to encircle and defeat the Allied forces, but his Italian commanders ordered him to advance in another direction. The Americans and British regrouped for a counterattack.

Ernie Pyle, the popular war correspondent, reassured American readers that "though they didn't do too well in the beginning, there was never at any time any question about American bravery." Eisenhower was not so sure. He sacked the commander responsible for defending the Kasserine and replaced him with Maj. Gen. George S. Patton. The army increased basic training from 13 to 17 weeks and reviewed its doctrine and weapons. For Patton, the Kasserine debacle showed that firepower delivered by air, tanks, and artillery was more reliable than infantry. His preference for technology over bravery became ingrained in American strategy.

Map 25-2　World War II in Europe, 1942–1945 While the Soviets reduced the main German force along the eastern front, the British and American Allies advanced through Italy and France.

Allied forces captured Tunis and Bizerte on May 7, bagging 238,000 German and Italian prisoners. Rommel escaped to fight the Americans again in France a year later. At that time he would encounter a different American army, larger, more experienced, and equipped with the newest weapons. As it mobilized to fight the Axis, the United States was changing too. Industry and people were shifting around. Government took on new functions, and industry shifted into high gear.

Organizing for Production

To defeat regimented, totalitarian enemies, Americans had to gear their economy for war. Big government and corporations made possible the "miracle of production" that was winning the war and raising living standards. During the height of the Depression, FDR had never been bold enough to use deficit spending to stoke up the economy (a technique economists call a "Keynesian stimulus"), but during the war, half the money the federal government spent was borrowed, and nobody complained. The economy boomed. War contracts created 17 million new jobs. Industrial production doubled. The employment dial reached "full" in 1942 and stayed there until Japan surrendered.

> When Hitler put his war on wheels, he rolled it right down our alley.
>
> GEN. BREHON B. SOMERVELL

War industries worked by a new set of rules. Contractors depended on the government for financing, materials, and labor. New war plants, built at taxpayer expense, went up in towns that had seen little industry before. As industry moved, workers moved with it, changing jobs, migrating to the new boomtowns, and organizing themselves into a powerful political and economic force.

A Mixed Economy

The Roosevelt administration added new war agencies to control prices, assign labor, and gear up industry. It dusted off the tried-and-true methods from World War I—dollar-a-year men and "cost plus" contracts—and added new incentives, such as tax breaks for retooling and federal loans and subsidies. "You have to let business make money out of the process," Secretary of War Henry Stimson explained, "or business won't work." Sometimes it still wouldn't, and the government seized at various times the steel industry, the railroads, the coal mines, and even a department store chain.

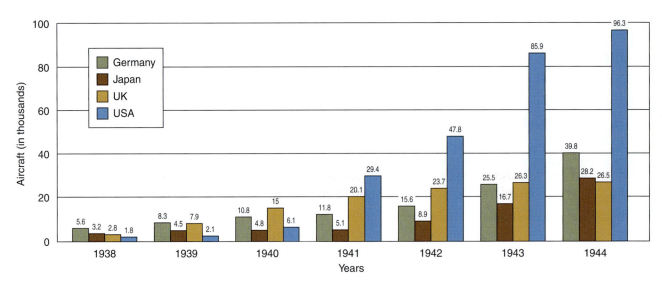

Figure 25–1 Number of Military Aircraft Produced U.S. production of military equipment lagged at first, but once in high gear it dwarfed that of the rest of the world. *I. C. B. Dear,* The Oxford Companion to World War II *(Oxford University Press, 1995), p. 22.*

A View of a Military Aircraft Facility in Long Island, New York, October 1942 Mass produced weapons allowed U.S. forces to win by attrition, wearing down the enemy with sheer weight and numbers.

Output soared. A Ford plant at Willow Run, Michigan, turned out a fleet of B-24s larger than the whole *Luftwaffe*. Cargo ships, which took longer than a year to build in 1941, were coming out of the Kaiser Shipyards in an average of 56 days. Entirely new industries such as synthetic rubber and Lucite (a clear, hard plastic used for aircraft windshields) appeared overnight. Industrial techniques applied to agriculture—mechanization and chemical herbicides and pesticides—raised output by one-third with 17 percent fewer farmers. Enterprising corporations patriotically increased their market share. Coca-Cola's mobile bottling plants followed the front lines, creating a global thirst for their product. Wrigley added a stick of gum to each K ration and made chewing gum a national habit.

Business leaders regained the prestige they had lost during the Depression. Major corporations like General Electric, Allis-Chalmers, and Westinghouse ran parts of the super-secret Manhattan Project. Edwin Witte, a member of the National War Labor Board, called this partnership "a mixed economy, which is not accurately described as either capitalism or socialism." Witte was sure that "individual initiative, work, and thrift count as much as ever" in the new economy, but he could not say how.

Most business was still small; 97 percent of manufacturing, for example, came from firms with just a few hundred employees. During the war, however, Congress and the administration drew a line between large high-tech firms, its partners in the business of national defense, and "small business" that had to be mollified with tax breaks and loans. "Small business" acquired its own federal agency and lobbying groups, while major corporations such as Boeing and General Electric negotiated long-term contractual relationships with the federal government. World War II permanently divided the economy into separate "government" and "market" sectors, each with its own rules and ways of dealing with Washington.

Industry Moves South and West

Although Detroit got its share, the bulk of war contracts went to states in the South and Southwest and on the Pacific Coast, shifting industry's center of gravity. Airplanes flown in World War I came from Dayton, Ohio, and Buffalo, New York, but the B-29 Superfortress, the most advanced plane at the end of World War II, was made in Seattle, Washington, Omaha, Nebraska, Wichita, Kansas, and Marietta, Georgia. The Manhattan Project's largest facilities at Oak Ridge, Tennessee, Hanford, Washington, and Los Alamos, New Mexico, likewise broke the historic pattern that had concentrated industry in the Northeast and Midwest.

There were several reasons for this shift. Industries that needed power gravitated to the huge hydroelectric grids created by the New Deal. Aluminum plants went up along the Tennessee and Columbia rivers to take advantage of abundant power from federal dams. The federal government also encouraged construction in the middle of the country to lessen the danger from enemy bombers. Corporations

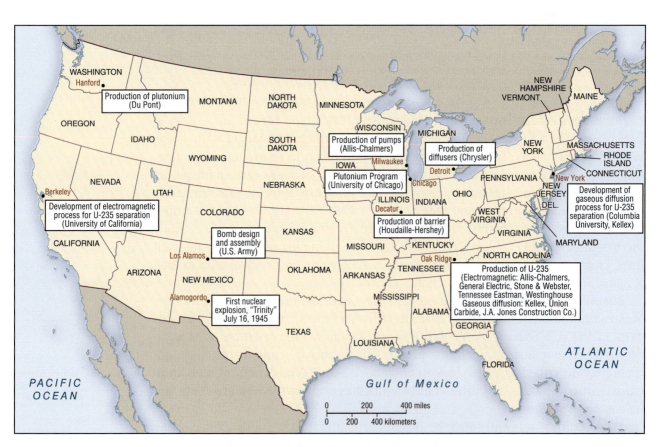

Map 25–3   The Manhattan Project   The Manhattan Project created a new kind of collaboration between industry, government, and science. In a pattern of federal spending that would continue after the war, much of the new infrastructure was located in the South and West.

moved south and west to find low-wage nonunion workers. Powerful southern and western senators, who controlled military appropriations, also steered new factory development into their states.

The results were visible. The population of the West increased by 40 percent. Towns became cities overnight. The population of San Diego doubled in 1942. Los Angeles, Houston, Denver, Portland, Seattle, and Washington, DC, became wartime boomtowns. While "old" industries such as automobiles and steel remained the mainstay of the economy above the Mason-Dixon Line, the Sunbelt states of the South and West became the home of the gleaming industries of the future: plastics, aluminum, aircraft, and nuclear power.

Few people objected to government direction of the economy when it meant new jobs and industry in regions that had been poor. A 1942 Gallup poll showed that two-thirds of Americans wanted the federal government to register all adults and assign them to war work as needed. The Office of Price Administration enlisted women consumers to enforce price ceilings, and thousands wrote in to inform on their local grocers. Citizens volunteered for scrap drives, bond drives, and blood drives, and they dug victory gardens. The war effort was so popular that the administration did not worry much about propaganda. Roosevelt and other war managers—many of them former progressives—had learned a lesson from World War I: in gaining public support, inducements worked better than coercion.

New Jobs in New Places

As it had during World War I, the need for workers pushed up wages, brought new employees into the workforce, and set people on the move in search of better opportunities. It also swelled the ranks of organized labor from 10 million to almost 15 million between 1941 and 1945. The federal government enlisted labor as a partner in the war effort. Unions grew because of a federally mandated "maintenance of membership" policy, by which new employees automatically joined the union. Through the National Defense Mediation Board, the Roosevelt administration encouraged cooperation, furthering a process begun by the New Deal. When wildcat locals of the United Auto Workers struck North American Aviation plants in Los Angeles in 1941, Stimson sent the army to break the strike, but the NDMB then forced management to accept the union's wage demands. Through a combination of carrots and sticks, federal administrators encouraged a more collaborative, managerial style of union leadership. Unions did not have to struggle for membership or recognition; in return, they curbed militant locals and accepted federal oversight. Decision making moved from the one-story brick "locals" that dotted factory districts around the country to the marble headquarters of national unions in Washington, DC.

People moved to jobs, rather than the other way around, and some 4 million workers, taking with them another 5 million family members, migrated to the new sites of war production. "Scarcely a section of the country or a community of any size escaped the impact of this great migration," according to an official report. Some 200,000 Mexican *braceros* crossed the border to harvest crops. San Francisco's African American population doubled in a single year. At the peak of the migration, African Americans were arriving in Los Angeles at a rate of 300 to 400 a day. By leaving Mississippi to take a factory job in Los Angeles, a sharecropper could increase his salary six- or sevenfold. Migrants moved into cities crowded

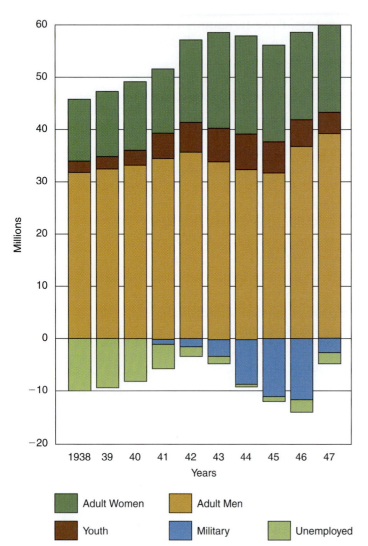

Figure 25–2 Makeup of U.S. Labor Force, 1938–1947 *Dear,* Oxford Companion to World War II, *p. 1182.*

with newcomers, families of overseas military personnel, ex-farmers seeking industrial jobs, and refugees from Europe.

Workers were generally happy with higher wages, but many would have been glad to have a decent place to live. New York, which had plenty of housing, suffered from unemployment while new factories were located in places with no housing. There were no rooms to rent within miles of Willow Run. In southern and western towns, workers "hot bedded"—slept in shifts in boardinghouses—or lived in cars. Frustrations over the housing shortage sometimes boiled over into racial conflict. In 1943, when the federal government constructed 1,000 units in Detroit, mob violence erupted over who would take possession of the dwellings. After two days of rioting, federal troops occupied the city. Housing remained a chronic problem throughout the war and for several years afterward.

Women in Industry

"Rosie the Riveter," the image of the glamorous machinist laboring to bring her man home sooner, was largely a creation of the Office of War Information. Industry needed workers, and the OWI promised women that running heavy machinery was no more difficult than using kitchen appliances. Some 36 percent of the wartime labor force was female, but that was only marginally higher than the peacetime figure. Few women left housework to take a job in an aircraft factory solely for patriotic reasons. Instead, the war economy shifted women workers into new roles, allowing some to move from service jobs into industry and those with factory jobs to take better-paid positions.

The number of manufacturing jobs for women grew from 12 million to 16.5 million, with many women moving into heavy industry as metalworkers, shipwrights, and assemblers of tanks and aircraft, jobs that had been off-limits before. Employers had once refused to hire women for such heavy labor, but under the pressures of wartime they found that machinery could take away some of the physical strain and actually improve efficiency. Women worked coke ovens in the hottest parts of steel plants; they operated blast furnaces and rolling mills. For many women, the war offered the first real chance for mobility.

Even so, employers did not offer equal pay. Unions either refused women membership or expelled them when the war ended. Employers gave little help to women trying to juggle job and family. The Lanham Act provided the first federal support for day care, but the 2,800 government centers were not nearly enough. "Latchkey children," left home alone while their mothers worked, were said to be a major problem. Experts saw female labor as necessary for the war effort but dangerous in the long run. "Many of them are rejecting their feminine roles," a social worker complained. "They wish to control their own fertility in marriage, and say they never wanted the children which had been thrust upon them." After the war, women were expected to yield their jobs to returning servicemen. They were blamed for neglecting their duties and encouraging juvenile delinquency, a backlash that had begun to build even before the war ended.

Between Idealism and Fear

In the movies Americans marched to war (and war plants) singing patriotic tunes by George M. Cohan, but in real life this war was noticeably free of high-minded idealism. Americans had already fought once to end all wars and keep the world safe for democracy. They were not ready to buy that bill of goods again. Journalist John Hersey asked marines

Flush riveting of aluminum wing panels required a steady hand. War industries employed thousands of women.

on Guadalcanal what they were fighting for. "Scotch whiskey. Dames. A piece of blueberry pie. Music," they replied. Things were no clearer on the home front, where to writer Dwight Macdonald the war seemed to represent "the maximum of physical devastation accompanied by the minimum of human meaning." In one wartime advertisement, Goodyear Rubber Company asked, "What can you say to those whose hearts bear the aching burden of this conflict? That their sons have died in a noble cause? That the nation mourns with them?" Obviously not.

If Americans weren't sure what they were fighting for, they knew what they were fighting against: totalitarianism, gestapos, and master races. Throughout the war and after, totalitarianism provided a powerful symbol of what America and Americans ought to oppose. The president of the U.S. Chamber of Commerce denounced the New Deal as "fascist" and "totalitarian." Labor unions and civil rights groups used the same words to brand their enemies, but wartime rhetoric also held Americans to a higher standard of tolerance. "Religion makes no difference, except to a Nazi or somebody as stupid," Frank Sinatra explained in *The House I Live In* (1945), before bursting into song: "All races and religions; that's America to me."

Wartime leaders struggled to fill the inspirational vacuum, crafting some of the twentieth century's most stirring restatements of

> If Hitler wins, down with the blacks! If the democracies win, the blacks are already down.
>
> W. E. B. DUBOIS, 1941

the democratic creed. Winston Churchill spoke of the destiny of the "English-speaking peoples," a global community with an inheritance of liberty and culture to protect. In his State of the Union address in January 1941, Franklin Roosevelt aspired to a world based on the "Four Freedoms": freedom of speech, freedom of worship, freedom from want, and freedom from fear. A month later, *Life* magazine published an essay by its founder, Henry Luce, entitled "The American Century." Coming before the United States had entered the war, at a moment when the Allies were falling back, it confronted defeatism with a powerfully optimistic vision. It foresaw a globalization of democracy, "a sharing with all people of our Bill of Rights, our Dec-

laration of Independence, our Constitution, our magnificent industrial products, our technical skills." Luce put science and material abundance on a par with democracy among the gifts America had to offer the world. The administration responded with a bold plan for applying the Four Freedoms in practice. Vice President Henry Wallace proclaimed that in the "Century of the Common Man," nations would "measure freedom by standards of nutrition, education and self-government." He equated democracy—as American leaders would do in the postwar period—with schools, jobs, food, and a New Deal for the world.

African Americans sought to attain the four freedoms in an atmosphere of increasing racial hostility. Detroit was just one of many cities in which rapid economic growth touched off racial conflict. In Maryland, Michigan, New York, and Ohio white workers engaged in "hate strikes" to prevent the hiring of African American workers. Over 3,000 white employees of a naval shipyard burned African American neighborhoods in Beaumont, Texas, in June 1943. Curfews, rumors of riots, and white citizens' committees kept many other cities on edge.

African Americans responded by linking their struggle for rights in the United States to the global war against fascism. Thurgood Marshall, chief counsel for the NAACP, compared the Detroit rioters to "the Nazi Gestapo." In 1942, the *Pittsburgh Courier* launched the "Double V" campaign explicitly to join the struggles against racism and fascism in a fight for "victory at home as well as abroad." "Defeat Hitler, Mussolini, and Hirohito," it urged, "by Enforcing the Constitution and Abolishing Jim Crow." Membership in the NAACP grew tenfold during the war. In Chicago, students and activists inspired by the nonviolent tactics of Indian nationalist Mohandas Gandhi organized the Congress of Racial Equality (CORE), which desegregated restaurants and public facilities in the North. The NAACP won a legal victory in the Supreme Court case of *Smith v. Allwright* (1944), which invalidated all-white primary elections.

The experience of war may have been the greatest catalyst to change. Many African American veterans returned from the war determined not to accept discrimination any longer. Amzie Moore came back to Cleveland, Mississippi, after serving in the army and was elected head of the local NAACP chapter. "Here I am being shipped overseas," he said of his service in the Pacific, "and I been segregated from this man who I might have to save or he save my life. I didn't fail to tell it." The war prepared Moore and a generation of African Americans for the struggle ahead.

Japanese Internment

Idealism was no match for fear, and in the days after Pearl Harbor, panicky journalists, politicians, and military authorities perpetrated an injustice on American citizens of Japanese descent. Ominous signs reading "Civilian Exclusion Order" went up in California and the Pacific Northwest in February 1942. They instructed "Japanese aliens and non-aliens" to report to relocation centers for removal from the Pacific Coast "war zone." The Western Defense Command of Lt. Gen. John L. DeWitt and the *Los Angeles Times,* believing the Japanese planned to invade the West Coast, aroused the public against the Japanese "menace." FBI investigators found no suspicious plots and told the president so, but the press continued to print rumors. "The Pacific Coast is officially a combat zone," columnist Walter Lippmann observed. "There is plenty of room elsewhere for [the Japanese] to exercise his rights." Responding to the press, DeWitt, and the California congressional delegation, FDR ordered the relocation.

Internees and civil-liberties lawyers challenged the legality of confining American citizens without charge or trial. Fred Korematsu, a welder from San Leandro, California, took a new name and had his face surgically altered in a futile attempt to stay out of the camps. When he was arrested, the American Civil Liberties Union used his case to challenge the exclusion order. Supreme Court Justice Hugo Black upheld the evacuation policy as justified by "military necessity." In January 1947, the army's Western Defense Command applauded the record of the evacuation program and suggested that it could be used as a model for the treatment of suspect populations during the next national emergency.

No Shelter from the Holocaust

The United States might have saved more of the victims of Hitler's "final solution" had it chosen to do so. A combination of fear and anti-Semitism and a desire to avoid unwanted burdens led American leaders to dismiss the Holocaust as someone else's problem. The State Department, worried that spies and saboteurs would sneak in among the refugees, erected a paper wall of bureaucratic restrictions that kept the flow of immigrants to a trickle. Refugees found it easier to get a visa from China than from the United States. In 1939, the *St. Louis* steamed from Hamburg with 930 Jewish refugees aboard. American immigration officials refused to let the refugees ashore because they lacked proper papers—papers that would have had to be furnished by their Nazi persecutors. The ship and its passengers returned to Germany.

Once it began, Nazi Germany's systematic extermination of the Jews made news in the United States. Stories in the *New York Times* as early as 1942 described the deportations and concluded that "the greatest mass slaughter in history" was under way. At Auschwitz, Poland, in the most efficient, high-tech death camp, 2,000 people an hour could be killed with Zyklon-B gas. Jewish leaders begged War Department officials to bomb the camp or the rail lines leading to it. The city of Auschwitz was bombed twice in 1944, but John J. McCloy, the assistant secretary of war, refused to target the camp, dismissing it as a humanitarian matter of no concern to the army. Roosevelt, who also knew of the Holocaust, might have rallied public support for Hitler's victims. His inaction, according to historian David Wyman, was "the worst failure of his presidency."

>> Manzanar

Jeanne Wakatsuki's exile into internment began with a Greyhound bus ride from Los Angeles across the Mojave Desert. When the shades came up a mile from her destination, she saw "a yellow swirl across a blurred, reddish setting sun. The bus was being pelted by what sounded like splattering rain. It wasn't rain. This was my first look at something I would soon know very well, a billowing flurry of dust and sand churned up by the wind through Owens Valley." Its lakes and rivers emptied by the Los Angeles aqueduct, Owens Valley was a man-made desert.

Temperatures ranged from 115 degrees in summer to well below freezing in winter. On an alkali flat beneath the towering Inyo Range, workmen were building the Manzanar Relocation Camp, 600 wood and tar paper barracks that would soon house more than 10,000 people. Each family received 20 square feet of floor space and an iron cot and army blanket for each member. Prisoners made the other furnishings themselves, filling burlap bags with straw for mattresses, making privacy screens from newspaper, crafting chairs and tables from spare lumber.

The prisoners fed themselves. They tilled the dry soil and planted tomatoes, turnips, radishes, watermelons, and corn. They also raised cattle, pigs, and poultry, making the camp self-sufficient in both meat and vegetables. "People who lived in Owens Valley during the war still remember the flowers and lush greenery they could see from the highway as they drove past the main gate," Wakatsuki later wrote. Prisoners opened repair shops, laundries, a newspaper, a clinic, and a cemetery. They practiced medicine and law. The Manzanar Co-Op, which sold retail and mail-order goods, did $1 million in business in 1944.

Manzanar was like a small city, except that it was surrounded by wire and armed guards. The camp administrators created a network of informants to spy on inmates. In December 1942, four prisoners beat up a man suspected of being an informant. When one was arrested, a group of prisoners demonstrated in front of the administration building to demand his release. Nervous guards fired into the crowd, killing two young men and wounding eight others. "You can't imagine how close we came to machine-gunning the whole bunch of them," a camp official explained. "The only thing that stopped us, I guess, were the effects such a shooting would have had on the Japs holding our boys in Manila and China."

It was the last "uprising" at the camp. Administrators censored the newspaper, prohibited expressions of Japanese culture, and required all meetings to be conducted in English. The community within the camp remained forever divided. Young men denounced their elders for respecting the law even when it was unjust. Administrators, with their persistent questionnaires, separated the angry from the docile and drew up blacklists.

Defiance was severely punished. Over 8,000 internees who would not renounce the emperor were separated from their families and sent to a camp at Tule Lake, California, and 263 young men who refused military service went to federal prison. Still, the majority of draft-eligible men in the camps served in the armed forces, many in intelligence and combat roles. The separation of the loyal from the disloyal, and the placement of so many in positions of trust, removed all justification for continuing to hold

loyal Japanese Americans, apart from the political embarrassment their sudden release would cause.

Those who could—college students who gained admission to eastern universities, workers with contracts elsewhere, those who joined the armed forces—left, leaving only the very old and the very young. "What had to be endured was the climate, the confinement, the steady crumbling of family life," Wakatsuki wrote in her memoir, *Farewell to Manzanar*. "In such a narrowed world, in order to survive, you learn to contain your rage and your despair, and you try to re-create, as well as you can, your normality, some sense of things continuing." ●

When American soldiers penetrated Germany in 1945, they gained a new understanding of what they were fighting for and against. On April 15, Patton's Third Army liberated the Buchenwald death camp. Radio commentator Edward R. Murrow described the scene for listeners in the United States: the emaciated, skeleton-like survivors, the fetid piles of the dead, the ovens. "I pray you to believe what I have said about Buchenwald," he said. "I have reported what I saw." Eisenhower ordered photographs and films to be taken, and he brought German civilians from the surrounding communities to witness the mass burial, by bulldozer, of the corpses. Many GIs doubted that the things they had witnessed would be believed. "We got to talk about it, see?" one told reporter Martha Gellhorn. "We got to talk about it if anyone believes us or not."

Americans went into the First World War flushed with idealism and became disillusioned in victory's aftermath. The Second World War followed the reverse trajectory. Americans slowly came to see that their shopworn ideals offered what little protection there was against the hatred and bigotry that afflicted all nations, including their own. Rose Mclain of Washington State wrote her husband in the Pacific to promise "that our children will learn kindness, patience, and the depth of love . . . that they shall never know hate, selfishness and death from such [a war] as this has been."

Closing with the Enemy

"The Americans are so helpless," Joseph Goebbels, Hitler's propaganda minister, exclaimed in 1942, "that they must fall back again and again upon boasting about their matériel." After the North Africa campaign, the United States made good on its boasts. The American army was small—only 5 million compared to Germany's 9 million—but it was amply supplied and agile. Tactics emphasized speed and firepower, a combination suited to a nation so fond of the automobile. In 1944 and 1945 the United States carried the war to Japan and into the heart of Europe with a destructiveness never before witnessed. As the war drew to a close, Americans began to anticipate the difficulties of reconstructing the postwar world and to create institutions to structure a global economy at peace.

Taking the War to Europe

Using North Africa as a base, the Anglo-American Allies next attacked northward into Italy, knocking one of the Axis powers out of the war. In Sicily, where the Allies landed in July 1943, Patton applied the mobile, aggressive tactics he had advocated since 1940. Slicing the island in half with a thrust from Licata to Palermo and trapping a large part of the Italian army, he swung east to Messina but arrived too late to block the Germans' escape. The defeat shook Italy. Parliament deposed Mussolini and ordered his arrest. German troops took control and fiercely resisted the Allied landings at Salerno in September. Winter rains stopped the Anglo-American offensive south of Rome. "Vehicles were bogged above the axles," General Mark Clark grumbled, "the lowlands became seas of mud, and the German rearguard was cleverly entrenched in the hills." American troops finally broke through to Rome on June 5, 1944.

> At the suggestion of Dr. Conant, the Secretary agreed that the most desirable target would be a vital war plant employing a large number of workers and closely surrounded by workers' houses.
>
> MINUTES,
> Interim Committee of Scientific Advisers to the Secretary of War, May 31, 1945

The assault on France's Normandy coast the next day, D-Day, finally created the second front the Soviets had asked for in 1942. Early on the morning of June 6, 1944, the Allied invasion armada, thousands of supply and troopships and hundreds of warships, assembled off England's Channel coast and began the run into beaches designated Juno, Gold, Sword, Utah, and Omaha. Hitler had fortified the beaches with an "Atlantic Wall" of mines, underwater obstacles, heavy guns, and cement forts. Americans waded ashore on the lightly held Utah Beach without much difficulty, but on Omaha the small boats headed straight into concentrated fire from shore batteries. The boats unloaded too soon, and men with full packs plunged into deep water. Floating tanks equipped with rubber skirts overturned and sank with crews inside. Commanders briefly considered calling off the attack, but soldiers in small groups began moving inland to outflank German firing positions. By the end of the day, they held the beach.

Eisenhower's greatest fear was another Italy. The hedgerow country behind the beaches contained the most defensible terrain between the Channel and Germany. Each field and pasture was protected by earthen mounds topped with shrubs, natural walls that isolated troops. When a column of GIs crossed a hedgerow, "the Germans could knock off the first one or two, cause the others to duck down behind the bank and then call for his own mortar support," according to one infantryman. "The German mortars were very, very efficient." However, just as had happened on Omaha Beach, the defects of the generals' strategy were compensated by the initiative of men at the lowest ranks of the army. On their own, tankers experimented with devices to gouge holes through the hedgerows. Sergeant Curtis G. Culin crafted a set of tusks out of steel girders from a German roadblock. Thus equipped, "rhino" tanks could burst into an enemy-held enclosure and cover infantry following through the gap. By the end of the month the U.S. advance broke through the German defenses and captured the critical port city of Cherbourg.

Once in the open country, highly mobile American infantry chased the retreating enemy across France to the fortifications along the German border. There, in the Ardennes Forest, where panzers had pierced French lines in 1940, Hitler's armies rallied for a final desperate counterattack. Thirty divisions, supported by 1,000 aircraft, hit a lightly held sector of the American lines, broke through, and opened a "bulge" 40 miles wide and 60 miles deep in the Allied front. Two whole regiments were surrounded and forced to surrender, but the 101st Airborne, encircled and besieged at Bastogne, held on to a critical road junction, slowing the German advance and allowing the Allies to bring in reinforcements. The Battle of the Bulge lasted a month and resulted in more than 10,000 American dead and 47,000 wounded, but the German army had lost the ability to resist.

Island Hopping in the Pacific

To get close enough to aim a knockout blow at Japan, the United States had to pierce the barrier of fortified islands stretching across the western Pacific. The army and the navy each had a strategy, and the two services bickered over supplies and the shortest route to Tokyo. Gen. Douglas MacArthur favored a thrust northward from Australia through the Solomon Islands and New Guinea to retake the Philippines. Nimitz preferred a thrust across the central Pacific to seize islands that could be staging areas for an air and land assault on Japan.

Mitchell Jamieson's *Burial Grounds* (1944) Wartime censors carefully spared the American audience images of the anonymous, mass death of modern war, but scenes such as this one in Normandy always followed major battles.

By November 1943, MacArthur's American and Australian forces had advanced to Bougainville, the largest of the Solomon Islands and the nearest to the Japanese air and naval complex at Rabaul. Jungle fighting on these islands was especially vicious. Atrocity stories became self-fulfilling, as each side treated the other without mercy, killing prisoners and mutilating the dead. Both sides fought with "a brutish, primitive hatred," according to Eugene Sledge, whose marine comrades kept gold teeth and skulls as trophies. Air attacks pulverized Rabaul's airfields and harbor in early 1944, opening the way for an advance into the southern Philippines.

Meanwhile, Nimitz launched a naval attack on Japan's island bases. With 11 new aircraft carriers, each holding 50 to 100 planes, the Fifth Fleet attacked Tarawa, a tiny atoll that contained 4,500 Japanese troops protected by log bunkers and hidden naval guns. Coral reefs snagged landing craft, forcing troops to wade ashore under heavy fire. Americans were shocked by the scale of the losses, more than 3,000 dead and wounded, for such a small piece of territory, but it was only one of many island battles. "Island hopping" from Tarawa to the Marshall Islands and then to the Marianas, American forces bypassed strongly held enemy islands and moved the battle lines closer to Japan.

The Allied capture of Saipan, Tinian, and Guam in July 1944 brought Japan within range of B-29 bombers. General Curtis LeMay brought his 21st Bomber Command to Saipan in January 1945 and began launching a new kind of air offensive against Japanese cities. LeMay experimented with low-level attacks using a mix of high explosives (to shatter houses) and incendiaries (to set fire to the debris). The proper mix could create a "firestorm," an inferno in which small fires coalesced into a flaming tornado hundreds of feet high. On the night of March 9, 1945, LeMay sent

334 bombers to Tokyo to light a fire that destroyed 267,000 buildings. The heat was so intense that the canals boiled, oxygen was burned from the air, and 83,000 people died from flames and suffocation. In the following months LeMay burned more than 60 percent of Japan's urban areas. Americans felt city busting was justified, but, as historian Ronald Spector has written, bomber crews "realized that this was something new, something more terrible than even the normal awfulness of war."

Building a New World

As the war progressed across Europe and the Pacific, Allied leaders met to discuss their visions of the world after victory. Meeting in Casablanca in 1943, Roosevelt and Churchill agreed to demand the unconditional surrender of the Axis powers, to give the Allies a free hand to set the terms of peace. No country planned for peace as carefully or extensively as the United States. The State, War, and Navy departments undertook a comprehensive survey of the world, examining each country and territory to determine its importance to the United States. The planners had only sketchy ideas about where future threats would come from, but based on experience they believed that American security would depend on having a functioning international organization, a global system of free trade, and a worldwide network of American military bases.

The loosely organized League of Nations stood little chance of maintaining the peace in the 1930s. Roosevelt envisioned a stronger organization led by regional powers who would act as "policemen" within designated spheres of influence. The new organization would disband empires, placing "trusteeships" over colonial territories preparing for self-government. The world after victory would be a world of nations, not empires or blocs. In September 1944, delegates from 39 nations met at the Dumbarton Oaks estate in Washington, DC, and sketched out a plan for a United Nations (UN) organization comprising a general assembly, in which all nations would be represented, and an executive council made up of the United States, China, the Soviet Union, Britain, and France.

To American leaders, the lesson of the 1930s had been that without prosperity there could be no peace. They wanted to remove the economic conditions that caused desperate people to follow dictators into war. A true victory, they imagined, would create an open-door world, in which goods and money could move freely, eliminating the need or justification for conquest. In 1943, before the UN existed as an organization, the United States created the United Nations Relief and Rehabilitation Administration (UNRRA) to provide food and medicine to areas retaken by the Allies. The Bretton Woods Conference (see feature) set conditions for a postwar expansion of trade. The army established schools at major universities where officers studied languages and discussed strategies for instilling a democratic culture in enemy nations. The invasion of Italy provided a first test of these techniques, and the United States drew on its resources as an immigrant nation to staff civil-affairs units with Italian-speaking officers.

Military planners were not ready to stake America's future security entirely on trade or international organizations. Pearl Harbor had shown that the Atlantic and Pacific oceans offered no protection against aggression. Military leaders could imagine aircraft and rockets striking deep into the American heartland without warning. Beginning in 1943, they laid plans for a global system of military bases from

AMERICA AND THE WORLD

>> Bretton Woods

As Allied armies struggled for control of Normandy in late June 1944, 300 economists, diplomats, and translators from 44 nations converged on the Mount Washington Hotel in Bretton Woods, New Hampshire. Army MPs were still tacking carpet and painting the lobby as they arrived. The hotel had gone out of business during the Depression, but a new owner, David Stoneman, reopened it in early 1944 in the hope that skiing would become popular once the war was over. With most big hotels already converted into barracks, this remote, run-down hotel was one of the few places where the United States could host a global conference.

Roosevelt and Churchill convened the conference to deal with the staggering economic problems that would follow the war. International trade had collapsed; several major world currencies—the franc, the mark, and the yen—were or soon would be valueless; Britain and the Soviet Union were approaching bankruptcy; and two-thirds of the world's gold reserves were held by one country, the United States. Allied leaders also recognized that peace in the postwar world would require a global system in which every nation could control its economic future.

Preventing a renewed Depression required each nation to combat unemployment, applying all its monetary

and trade resources for self-recovery. Reporter I. F. Stone noted that the new international economy would have to accommodate this "positive governmental interference" in ways that the gold standard had never allowed. Every nation would need a welfare state, and no nation could be allowed to fail. "Prosperity is indivisible," Treasury Secretary Henry Morgenthau warned at the conference's opening session.

The use of gold as an international currency had expanded trade in the nineteenth century, but in the twentieth century it amplified economic crises and political instability by radically reducing consumption and employment in debtor countries. By the 1930s, the world economy had broken into rival blocs, each settling accounts using a different metal or currency (sterling, gold, the yen, etc.). To knit together an indivisible prosperity, the conferees at Bretton Woods needed to find substitutes for gold and empire: a new way to settle international debts, encourage trade expansion, and still allow national governments to pursue full employment.

Two strong personalities vied to be the architect of the postwar order. John Maynard Keynes, the brilliant British economist, wanted to create a global currency unit, the "bancor," that would allow a centralized

world bank to expand or shrink the money supply as needed. The chief of the American delegation, Harry D. White, held that a world currency would be unnecessary if every lira, zloty, and balboa could be converted into U.S. dollars. Convertibility was the economic equivalent of a military alliance, and the United States should "attract other currencies into its orbit of influence."

The conference debated these proposals for a month. The United States' massive gold reserves gave its delegation a strong hand. White's assistant, Dean Acheson, settled a controversy over the location of the new world financial institutions—in Washington—by explaining simply "you fellows will have to give way in this matter, you know, if the fund is

continued

to go through." The conference's final resolutions were nearer to White's vision than to Keynes's.

The International Monetary Fund would manage international accounts. It fixed the relationship between gold and the dollar at $35 an ounce and pegged all other currencies to the dollar at fixed rates of exchange. The system brought an unprecedented predictability to international trade: the profits of Mexican wheat farmers no longer depended on the value of the peso but only on the value of wheat. The International Bank for Reconstruction and Development (later known as the World Bank) would promote growth and trade, Keynes explained, and "raise the standard of life and condition of labor everywhere."

Between them, the "Bretton Woods institutions" possessed broad powers to manage the global movement of capital. The IMF held to the system of fixed exchange rates until 1973, after which it managed the float of currencies against one another. IMF and World Bank loans have financed an expanding repertoire of development projects and reforms. By the 1990s, an international antiglobalization movement criticized the Bretton Woods institutions for enforcing international trade rules at the expense of local business, cultural diversity, and the environment. In 1944, however, critics of the new system objected that the plan gave national governments far too much leeway. The plan, columnist Walter Lippmann complained, provided "almost unlimited domestic freedom and diversity at the expense of international conformity and stability." After the straitjacket of the gold standard, the new rules seemed slack.

Contention between global and local interests began right there in the lobby at the Mount Washington. When deliberations went into overtime, delegates told the reservations clerk they needed three more days to straighten out the planet's finances. Stoneman went to Morganthau and explained that he had a hotel to run, other guests had booked rooms, and the conferees would have to leave. Morgenthau replied that the army could seize the hotel, if necessary. The hotel keeper caved. Score one for the forces of globalization. ●

---

the Azores to Algiers, Dhahran, Calcutta, Saigon, and Manila, encircling the vast Eurasian land mass. Planners could not say who the next enemy would be. Germany, Japan, the Soviet Union, and even Britain might present future threats. With such an extensive base network, the United States could act against any challenger before it could strike. If the United States attacked *before and not after a series of Munich conferences,*" one admiral explained, "the personal following of any future Hitler would be limited to a few would-be suicides." Britain and the Soviet Union looked upon this base system warily, suspecting they might be its targets, but American leaders were willing to take diplomatic risks to attain the security they felt they required.

The Fruits of Victory

Despite rumors of the president's failing health, Americans elected Franklin Roosevelt to a fourth term in 1944 by a margin of 53.5 percent to 46 percent for the challenger Thomas E. Dewey. On April 12, 1945, less than three months after his inauguration, Roosevelt died suddenly of a cerebral hemorrhage at Warm Springs, Georgia. "Mr. Roosevelt's body was brought back to Washington today for the last time," reporter I. F. Stone wrote on April 21, 1945. "Motorcycle police heralded the procession's approach. The marching men, the solemn bands, the armored cars, the regiment of Negro soldiers, the uniformed women's detachments . . . the coffin covered with a flag. . . . In that one quick look thousands of us said goodbye to a great and good man, and to an era." In Paris, French men and women offered condolences to American GIs. Flags flew at half staff on Guadalcanal, Kwajalein, and

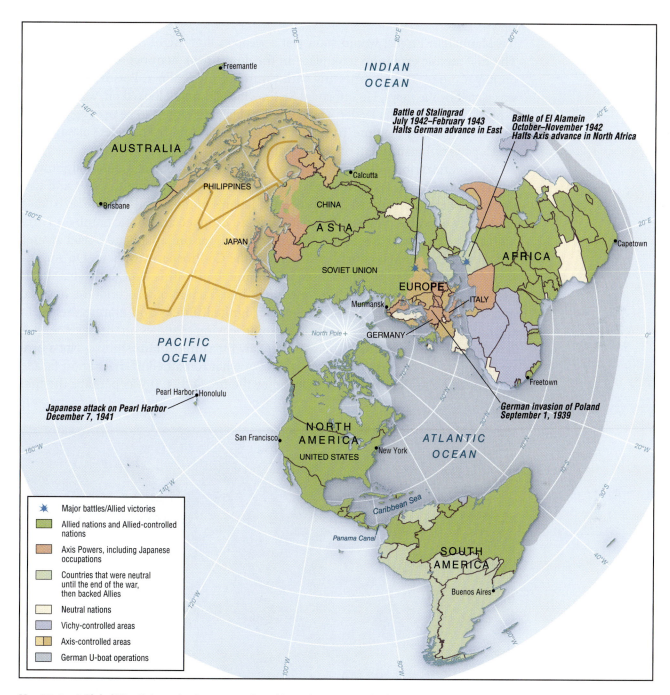

Map 25–4   A Global War Polar-projection maps such as this one became popular during the war and afterwards became the symbol of the United Nations. This perspective shows the war's geopolitical logic, the struggle on two fronts for control of the large central land mass of Eurasia.

Tarawa. The president died just days before Allied troops in Europe achieved the great victory for which Roosevelt had struggled and planned. On April 25, American and Soviet troops shook hands at Torgau in eastern Germany. On April 30, with Soviet soldiers just a few hundred yards away, Hitler committed suicide in his Berlin bunker. On May 8, all German forces surrendered unconditionally.

Harry S. Truman, the new vice president and former senator from Missouri, was now commander in chief. Shortly after he took office, aides informed him that the Manhattan Project would soon test a weapon that might end the war in Asia. The first atomic explosion took place in the desert near Alamogordo, New Mexico, on July 16, 1945. Truman, meeting with Churchill and Stalin at Potsdam, Germany, was elated by the news. He informed Stalin while Churchill looked on, watching the expression of the Soviet leader. The bomb had been developed to be used against the Axis enemy, but by the time Truman learned about it, American leaders already saw it as a powerful instrument of postwar diplomacy.

As American forces neared the Japanese home islands, defenders fought with suicidal ferocity. On Okinawa, soldiers and civilians retreated into caves and battled to the death. GIs feared the invasion of Japan's home islands, where resistance could only be worse. Then on August 6, a B-29 dropped an atomic bomb on Hiroshima. Two days later the Soviet Union declared war on Japan, and Soviet armies attacked deep into Manchuria, heartland of the Co-Prosperity Sphere. On August 9, the United States dropped a second atomic bomb, this time on Nagasaki. It detonated 1,900 feet above Shima Hospital. In a fraction of a second, the hospital and nearly a square mile of the city center ignited. Bricks and granite melted in the nuclear fire. People were vaporized, some leaving shadows on the pavement. A few days later a French Red Cross worker saw the ruins of Hiroshima. "Not a bird or an animal to be seen anywhere. . . . On what remained of the station facade the hands of the clock had been stopped by the fire at 8:15. It was perhaps the first

V-J Day Jubilant crowds greeted V-J Day in New York. Many soldiers newly returned from Europe were on their way to the Pacific.

time in the history of humanity that the birth of a new era was recorded on the face of a clock."

Conclusion

Emperor Hirohito announced Japan's unconditional surrender on August 14. In New York, crowds celebrated, but in most of the world there was silence and reflection. Thirty million people had been killed; great cities lay in ruins. At the end of the war, the United States' economic, scientific, and military mastery reached a pinnacle never attained by any of the great empires of history. Two-thirds of the world's gold was in American treasuries; half of the world's manufactured goods were made in the United States. At its height, imperial Britain controlled 25 percent of the world's wealth. In 1945, the United States controlled 40 percent. America's air armada, almost 80,000 planes, 10 times the size of the *Luftwaffe,* dominated the skies; its naval fleet had more ships than the navies of all its enemies and allies combined. Senator Claude Pepper asked Navy Secretary James Forrestal where he intended to put all of the 1,200 warships at his disposal. "Wherever there's a sea," Forrestal replied. Then there was the atomic bomb. The rest of the world looked for signs of how the United States would use its formidable wealth and power.

The war's sudden end meant Americans had to reconvert to a "peacetime" economy, preferably one more stable and prosperous than the depression economy of the 1930s. A. Philip Randolph predicted government would have to take a larger role in raising wages and stimulating key industries, such as housing, if soldiers returning home were to find jobs and goods to buy. The future looked tenuous. America could either succumb to "a native variety of fascism" in the postwar period, or open an era of expanding rights, democracy, and material abundance.

Further Readings

Thomas Childers, *Wings of Morning* (1995). A historian reconstructs the lives and war experiences of the last B-24 crew shot down over Germany.

I. C. B. Dear, *The Oxford Companion to World War II* (1995). Easily the best single-volume reference work on the war. Contains full descriptions of battles and campaigns, biographies of leading figures, chronologies, maps, and as many statistics as you could want.

Michael D. Doubler, *Closing with the Enemy: How GIs Fought the War in Europe, 1944–1945* (1994). World War II has been seen as a "general's war," but Doubler explains how the tactics that beat the Nazis came from the bottom up. The U.S. Army's ability to listen to the lowliest GIs was its best asset.

Doris Kearns Goodwin, *No Ordinary Time: Franklin and Eleanor Roosevelt: The Home Front in World War II* (1994). The story of the nation at war through the eyes of the family that led it.

E. B. Sledge, *With the Old Breed at Peleliu and Okinawa* (1990). A classic memoir, the story of a marine infantryman's war in the Pacific told with candor and feeling.

Ronald H. Spector, *Eagle Against the Sun: The American War with Japan* (1985). A comprehensive history of the Pacific War from a leading military historian.

Who, What?

Charles Lindbergh 828

Chester W. Nimitz 832

Benjamin O. Davis 833

George S. Patton 836

Braceros 841

Rosie the Riveter 842

Atomic bomb 835

Internment 845

City busting 849

>> Timeline >>

▼ 1930
Hawley-Smoot Tariff constricts trade
Depression becomes global

▼ 1933
Hitler becomes chancellor of Germany
President Roosevelt devalues the dollar
The United States recognizes the Soviet Union

▼ 1934
Reciprocal Trade Act passed
Export-Import Bank created

▼ 1935
Congress passes first Neutrality Act

▼ 1937
War begins in Asia

▼ 1938
Mexico nationalizes oil fields
Munich agreement gives Hitler Sudetenland

▼ 1939
War begins in Europe

▼ 1940
Germany defeats France, Netherlands, Belgium
Destroyers-for-bases deal between the United
   States and Britain

▼ 1941
Lend-Lease passed
Executive Order 8802 ends discrimination in
   defense industries
Roosevelt and Churchill sign Atlantic Charter
Germany invades the
   Soviet Union
Japan attacks the
   United States at
   Pearl Harbor
United States declares
   war on Axis powers

Review Questions

1. Which was more important to victory at Midway, planning or luck?

2. Why did the population of the West grow so rapidly during the war?

3. Contrast isolationist and internationalist viewpoints. Did they imagine different futures for the United States?

4. Thurgood Marshall worried about the emergence of "gestapos" in America. What did he mean?

5. According to American leaders, what caused World War II? How did their answers to that question affect their plans for the postwar world?

6. The government used propaganda and repressive laws to control domestic opinion during World War I. Why was there no repeat of those policies in World War II?

7. Some historians blame Roosevelt for luring the United States into war. How might that historical view be rooted in the isolationist/internationalist debate?

Websites

American Radioworks, Public Radio International, "Radio Fights Jim Crow," http://americanradioworks.publicradio.org/features/jim_crow/. During the war years, civil rights activists and the federal government producd a radio series that tried to mend racial divisions and unite the nation to win the war.

Franklin Roosevelt, "State of the Union Address: The Four Freedoms," January 6, 1941, http://millercenter.org/scripps/archive/speeches/detail/3320. Hear and read Franklin Roosevelt's statement of war aims.

Smithsonian Air and Space Museum, "Black Wings: African American Pioneer Aviators," http://www.nasm.si.edu/interact/blackwings/.

For further review materials and resource information, please visit www.oup.com/us/ofthepeople

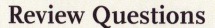
WAR GARDENS FOR VICTORY
GROW VITAMINS AT YOUR KITCHEN DOOR
Enter VICTORY GARDEN CONTEST

▼ **1942**
Philippines fall to Japan
Internment of Japanese Americans begins
Battles of Coral Sea and Midway turn the tide in the Pacific
Allies land in North Africa

▼ **1943**
Allies land in Sicily
Churchill and Roosevelt meet at Casablanca

U.S. troops advance to Bougainville
Marines capture Tarawa

▼ **1944**
U.S. troops capture Rome
Allied landings in Normandy
U.S. troops capture Saipan
Bretton Woods Conference
Roosevelt reelected for fourth term

▼ **1945**
Roosevelt dies

Harry S. Truman becomes president
Germany surrenders
Truman meets Churchill and Stalin at Potsdam
Atomic bombs dropped on Hiroshima and Nagasaki
Japan surrenders

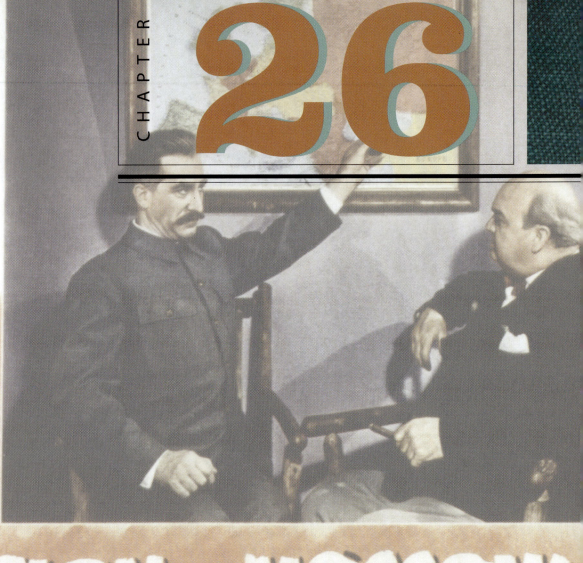

A
WARNER
BROS.
Picture

MISSION to MOSCOW

Common Threads

>> Why did friction over Germany, Poland, and the Mediterranean turn into a cold war affecting the entire world?

>> How did the need for constant vigilance interfere with democratic values?

>> The specter of the Depression hung over postwar economic planners. How did they try to avoid another decline as they reconverted the war economy?

The Cold War

1945–1952

>> Esther and Stephen Brunauer

Esther Caukin and Stephen Brunauer were an American success story. Born in California in 1901, Esther benefited from the increasing opportunities for women in the twentieth century. She graduated from Mills College, earned a doctoral degree from Stanford, and became an administrator for the American Association of University Women. In 1931, she married Stephen Brunauer, a successful chemist who had come to the United States from Hungary in Eastern Europe.

The Brunauers were patriots who hated fascism. In the 1930s, Esther tried to educate Americans about the threat from Adolf Hitler's Germany. When World War II came, she went to work in the U.S. State Department. Stephen also worked for the government as an explosives expert in the navy. After the war, he traveled to Hungary to gather scientific intelligence for the government and to help Hungarian scientists emigrate to the United States. With fascism defeated and their careers well launched, the Brunauers had succeeded. Like most Americans, they could have looked forward to a happy, prosperous future. But then it all went wrong.

In 1947 a congressman accused Esther of being one of the "pro-Communist fellow travelers and muddle heads" in the State Department. One of her speeches, he said, was "echoing Soviet propaganda." That year, a federal agency refused to let Stephen attend a meeting about atomic energy because he had once, as a student in the 1920s, belonged to the Young Workers' League, a group with Communist ties. Somehow, even though they hated Communism as much as they hated fascism, the Brunauers found their patriotism questioned.

Then things got worse. On March 13, 1950, Senator Joseph McCarthy of Wisconsin charged Esther and Stephen with espionage and links to known Communists. Esther, McCarthy testified, had engaged in "Communist-front activities"; Stephen had access "to some of the topmost secrets" of the U.S. military and constituted "a grave security risk of the highest order." McCarthy demanded that the subcommittee subpoena federal records in order to find out whether the Brunauers were Communists

who had betrayed their country. Stephen immediately denied he had ever been a Communist. "I am a loyal American," Esther insisted.

Two weeks later Esther took the witness stand to defend herself and her husband before the subcommittee. Rejecting McCarthy's charges, she accused the senator himself of betraying American values. His sudden and unfounded attack was, she said, "in violation of the traditions of fairness which are among our oldest heritages." Esther revealed how much McCarthy's accusations had already hurt her family. Since the 13th, they had received "anonymous telephone calls at all hours of the day and night, accompanied by threats and profanity." "Get out of this neighborhood, you Communists," one caller warned, "or you will be carried out in a box." "We are all upset and bewildered," Esther reported. "All of you who have families . . . how would you feel if it were happening in your home." Esther finished her testimony by offering letters of support from a senator, a former senator, and a college president. Dismissing McCarthy's charges, the college president, who was a brother of General Dwight D. Eisenhower, maintained that it was "un-American" to call Esther a "Communist sympathizer."

A majority of the subcommittee agreed. In July, the subcommittee's report concluded that McCarthy's charges against the Brunauers were "contemptible," "a fraud and a hoax." But the damage had been done. Despite the subcommittee report, there was enough doubt about the Brunauers that the State Department and the navy were no longer willing to risk keeping such controversial people on the job. In 1951 the navy suspended Stephen from his position, and the State Department suspended Esther from hers. Esther fought her suspension but found herself charged with "close and habitual association" with

continued

>> AMERICAN PORTRAIT *continued*

her husband. In 1952, the State Department fired her as a "security risk." The real reason for her dismissal, Esther told the press, was "political expediency." Their careers destroyed, the Brunauers left Washington to try to rebuild their lives out of the spotlight in Illinois.

How had it happened? How had the optimism of 1945 degenerated into suspicion? Those were questions that most Americans could have asked in one way or another. Like the Brunauers, Americans lived in a country and a world that had been saved from ruin. At home, the economic boom of World War II had swept away the Great Depression. Abroad, the United States had helped to destroy the threat of fascism. Understandably, Americans could have expected the postwar world to be stable and safe.

Before two years had passed, however, a tense peacetime confrontation with the Soviet Union disrupted American life. Convinced that the Soviets intended to expand their power and spread Communism across Europe, U.S. leaders challenged their former allies. While this "cold war" developed, Americans also faced the task of maintaining prosperity in peacetime. Organized labor, women, and African Americans struggled to preserve and extend their rights and opportunities. President Harry Truman and the Democratic Party struggled as well to preserve their power and implement a liberal agenda.

However unsettling, the cold war was not an aberration. The confrontation with Communism was deeply rooted in the core values of American democracy at the close of World War II. Truman and other leaders saw the Soviet system as inimical to free institutions, civil rights, and the capitalist system revived by the New Deal. Moreover, they worried that if a Communist coalition became too strong, the United States would have to defend itself by regimenting the economy and restricting individual rights—effectively turning America into a "garrison state." To contain Soviet expansion, the U.S. government took unprecedented peacetime actions—massive foreign aid, new alliances, a military buildup—that helped to transform the political economy in the 1940s and beyond.

Dramatic though they were, the new American policies did not prevent the cold war from widening and intensifying. By 1950, the nation was fighting a hot war on the other side of the world in Korea. By then, too, Americans knew that the Soviet Union had nuclear weapons that could conceivably devastate the United States. In turn, the Truman administration stepped up military spending and developed more powerful nuclear weapons. As the cold war seemed to spiral out of control, fear gripped American society. A frenzied search for Communist subversives at home threatened civil liberties and destroyed the careers of Esther and Stephen Brunauer. They suffered more than most people, but in one way or another, the cold war unsettled the lives of all Americans for years to come. ●

OUTLINE

Origins of the Cold War

In a span of two years, the United States and the Soviet Union went from a wartime alliance to the protracted rivalry known as the cold war. The sweeping, long-term consequences of the cold war made it particularly important for Americans to understand the origins of the conflict. From the outset, the United States and the Soviet Union tried to pin the blame for the cold war on each other. For a long time, Americans wanted to believe that the Soviet Union, authoritarian and expansionist, was solely responsible. However, historians have gradually offered a more critical perspective, and they generally agree that actions by both countries caused the cold war.

> One way of life is based upon the will of the majority, and is distinguished by free institutions, representative government, free elections, guarantees of individual liberty, . . . The second way of life is based upon the will of a minority forcibly imposed upon the majority. It relies upon terror and oppression.
>
> HARRY S. TRUMAN,
> March 1947

Ideological Competition

There is less agreement about the precise sources of the conflict. Ideological, political, military, and economic factors all clearly played a role. Ever since the founding of the Soviet Union toward the end of World War I, Soviets and Americans were ideological adversaries. They had essentially different political systems. The Soviet Union (the USSR) was committed to Communism and socialism, the United States to democracy and capitalism. Despite their differences, the two countries fought as allies in World War II. Wartime decisions, especially about the arrangement of the postwar world, laid the groundwork for animosity after 1945. In peacetime, the Soviet Union and the United States were the only countries strong enough to threaten each other, and the recent experience of both countries showed that with modern arms enemies could strike with devastating suddenness. Moreover, they had quite different political, military, and economic ambitions. By 1947 those different goals produced open antagonism. With the United States' vow to combat the spread of Communism, the cold war was under way. The Union of Soviet Socialist Republics (USSR) emerged from the Russian Revolution of 1917 and the civil war that followed. Vladimir Lenin's Bolshevik Party introduced a socialist economy in which the state—the government—owned factories and farms. At home, the Soviet Union practiced forms of economic and social regimentation Americans recognized from Nazi Germany and imperial Japan, limiting individual rights, including freedom of speech and religion, and achieving a self-contained autarkic economy. Abroad, the new nation endorsed the revolutionary overthrow of capitalism.

The Soviets' Marxist ideology obviously set them at odds with American ideals. The vast majority of Americans favored a capitalist economy, in which private citizens owned property. They celebrated individualism, freedom of speech, freedom of religion, and democratic government based on free elections. Communists believed all modern societies would eventually eliminate religion and private property and value the collective good over the rights of the individual.

Nevertheless, open conflict between the two countries was not inevitable. While American leaders hated Communism, the USSR was weak and hemmed in by powerful neighbors, Germany in the west and Japan in the east. It posed no military threat to the United States in the 1920s and 1930s. The Soviets could even be helpful to American interests. President Franklin Roosevelt, eager to promote trade and restrain Japanese expansion, officially recognized the Soviet Union in 1933.

Uneasy Allies

World War II demonstrated that, despite their differences, the United States and the Soviet Union could become allies. After the German invasion of the USSR and the Japanese attack on Pearl Harbor, the United States and the Soviets were thrown together in the war against fascism in 1941. Still, they were uneasy allies at best. For many Americans, the lesson of the war was that the United States could not tolerate aggression. No new dictator should ever be able to take over other European countries unopposed, as Hitler did, nor should any single power be allowed to dominate Eurasia. By 1945 some Americans already equated the Soviets with the Nazis by denouncing totalitarianism or "Red Fascism."

Each country had experiences that underlay its determination to protect itself from future disasters. American leaders believed autarkic trade blocs had caused both the Great Depression and the war that followed, and they resolved to rebuild the world

A WARNER BROS. Picture

MISSION to MOSCOW

economy as a single system, with reduced trade barriers and uniform rules. Soviet leaders feared a repeat of the last two wars, in which Poland and Eastern Europe had been staging areas for invasions that claimed millions of Russian lives. But the lessons they drew from war led them to opposite solutions: American leaders favored an interdependent system, with open borders allowing goods, information, and people to move freely; Soviet leaders felt only a closed system and tight controls on its periphery would give it real protection.

Wartime decisions also aggravated tensions between the United States and the Soviet Union. In 1943 the American government created ill feeling by excluding the Soviets from the surrender of Italy to the Allies. The delay of the Allied invasion of France until 1944 embittered the Soviets, who were desperately resisting the Germans at the cost of millions of lives. The American government further strained relations by sharing news of its secret atomic bomb project with the British but not with the Soviets.

Decisions about the postwar world led to trouble as well. At a conference in Yalta in the Soviet Union in February 1945, Franklin Roosevelt, Josef Stalin, and British prime minister Winston Churchill proposed a self-contradictory vision of the postwar world. The "Big Three" supported national self-determination, the idea that countries should decide their own future. They also agreed that countries should act collectively to deal with world problems. They laid plans for the United Nations, an organization that would encourage states to cooperate in keeping the world secure. But they also believed powerful nations should dominate other nations within a "sphere of influence." In these areas—Latin America and the Pacific for the United States; Africa and the Middle East for Britain; and Eastern Europe for the Soviet

Union—each power could act independently and limit the self-determination of smaller states. Clearly, spheres of influence and unilateral action conflicted with democracy, self-determination, and collective action.

The conflict was made apparent when the three leaders dealt with the critical issue of the future of Poland, the Soviets' neighbor to the west. Despite talk of self-determination and democracy, Stalin wanted to install a loyal Polish government. He could not risk an independent Poland that might become a gateway for another

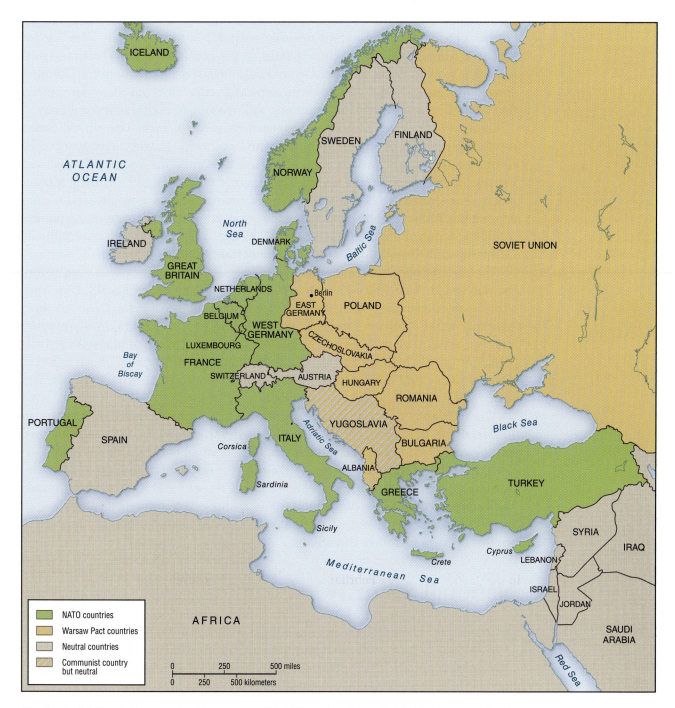

Map 26–1 Cold War in Europe, 1950 Five years after World War II, the cold war had divided Europe into hostile camps, with NATO members allied with the United States and Warsaw Pact signers tied to the Soviet Union.

invasion. Churchill and Roosevelt, however, favored a self-governing Poland under its prewar leaders. Stalin agreed to elections but came away feeling that Roosevelt had given him a free hand in Poland. This lack of clarity set the stage for future misunderstandings.

From Allies to Enemies

The United States' ambitions for global military and economic security appeared threatening to the Soviet Union. To prevent a future Pearl Harbor, the Pentagon erected a chain of air and naval bases that encircled Europe and Asia. The Bretton Woods agreement placed the United States at the center of a global economy with rules that worked to the disadvantage of controlled, socialist economies. The Roosevelt administration did not see these steps as antagonistic, but Stalin recognized that their effect was to cage his ambitions within a ring of bombers and dollars.

Disagreements over Germany sharpened these suspicions. The United States wanted defeated Germany to rejoin the world economy. Having been attacked by Germany twice in the last 50 years, the Soviets wanted the country divided and weakened forever. In the end, the Big Three agreed to split it into four zones of occupation. The United States, the USSR, Great Britain, and France would each administer a zone. Although Berlin lay within the Soviet zone, the four conquering powers would each control a section of the capital. The Big Three also agreed that eventually Germany would be reunified, but they did not indicate when or how.

The uncertainties and contradictions of Yalta led to disagreements even before the war ended. When Vice President Harry Truman succeeded Roosevelt in April 1945, he objected to the Soviets' attempt to take tight control of Poland. Promising to "stand up to the Russians," the new president held a tense meeting in Washington with the Soviet Foreign Minister, V. M. Molotov. With "words of one syllable," the president "gave it to him straight 'one-two to the jaw.'" "I have never been talked to like that in my life," Molotov answered. "Carry out your agreements," snapped Truman, "and you won't get talked to like that."

When Truman met with Stalin and the British prime minister in Potsdam in July, relations were more cordial. Because Soviet troops occupied most of Eastern Europe and much of Germany, there was little Truman could do about Stalin's actions there. There was no progress on planning the future reunification of Germany. But Truman learned during the meeting that the test of the atomic bomb in Nevada had been a success. The new weapon would increase U.S. influence everywhere in the world. Sailing home to the United States, he called Stalin "an S.O.B.," but admitted that "I guess he thinks I'm one too."

National Security

After the war, relations between the United States and the Soviet Union deteriorated. Although Stalin was still committed to overthrowing capitalism, his immediate concerns were in Eastern Europe and along the southern border with Turkey and Iran. The Soviet leader also wanted to keep Germany and Japan from menacing his country again. As an added measure of security the USSR built a completely self-reliant economy. The United States, by contrast, did not have to worry about securing its borders or supplies. Equipped with nuclear weapons, the United States was stronger than any rival. But American leaders feared that impoverished and vulnerable states around the world would voluntarily align themselves with Soviet power. Every election in Europe, coup in the Middle East, or uprising in Asia had the potential to add a piece to a future Communist war machine. Recalling the collapse of empires and alliances in the late 1930s, they could imagine chains of events that could leave the United States suddenly alone and vulnerable.

The Truman Doctrine

To avoid this dismaying scenario, American leaders favored the quick reconstruction of nations, including Germany and Japan, within a world economy based on free trade. They also needed military bases to keep future aggressors far from American shores. The opposing needs and interests of the Soviet and U.S. systems soon translated into combative rhetoric. In February 1946 Stalin declared capitalism and Communism incompatible. A month later, Winston Churchill, the former British prime minister, spoke at Fulton, Missouri. Introduced by Truman, Churchill ominously declared that "an Iron Curtain has descended across the Continent" of Europe. Central and Eastern Europe, the former prime minister warned, "lie in the Soviet sphere." Churchill called for an alliance against this menace.

In February 1946, George Kennan, an American consul in Moscow, sent the State Department a long telegram reflecting a new attitude. The Soviet leadership, he explained, believed "there can be no permanent peaceful coexistence" between capitalism and socialism. Stalin and his regime were sure that capitalist nations, beset by internal problems, would attack socialist nations. Acting on this fear, the USSR would, Kennan insisted, try to penetrate and destabilize other nations and align them with the Communist bloc. The Communist system needed to expand to survive.

More concerned than ever, Truman took aggressive steps to counter apparent Soviet expansion in the Mediterranean. The USSR had been pressing Turkey for control of the Dardanelles, a key waterway. Meanwhile in Greece, a civil war pitted Communist guerillas against a monarchist government backed by Britain. By 1947 the British could no longer afford the war and wanted to pass the burden to the Americans. Truman told Congress on March 12, 1947, that the world faced a choice between freedom and totalitarianism. "The free peoples of the world look to us," he insisted. "If we falter in our leadership, we may endanger the peace of

> We may be likened to two scorpions in a bottle, each capable of killing the other, but only at the risk of his own life.
>
> J. ROBERT OPPENHEIMER, 1953

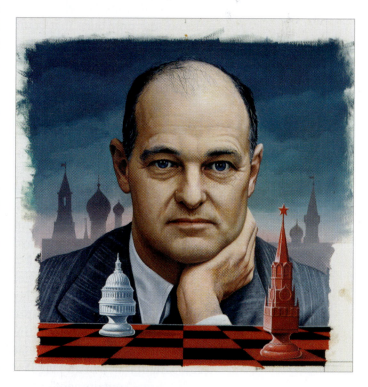

***George Kennan* by Ned Seidler** George Frost Kennan emerged as the principal strategist, author of the containment doctrine.

Iron Curtain In Winston Churchill's image, an "iron curtain" divided Europe, but soon similar barriers would mark the frontiers of containment in Asia and the Middle East.

the world—and we shall surely endanger the welfare of this Nation." The president announced what became known as the "Truman Doctrine." The United States must "support free peoples who are resisting attempted subjugation by armed minorities or by outside pressures." The speech, observed *Life* magazine, was "a bolt of lightning." Congress voted overwhelmingly to send aid to Greece and Turkey.

The crisis marked a turning point. In 1947, Walter Lippmann coined the term "cold war" to describe the American-Soviet confrontation. There was no formal declaration of war, but with the announcement of the Truman Doctrine, confrontation had certainly begun. Dividing the world into good and evil, the United States was ready to support "free peoples" and oppose Communism. Former allies were now bitter antagonists.

Was the confrontation inevitable? There is no way for historians to prove other outcomes were not possible, but it is difficult to see how the United States and the Soviet Union could have avoided friction. They had a history of hostility, and they both possessed great military power. It is harder to be sure that the form confrontation took—the cold war—was inevitable. It was the product of choices, such as Truman's decision to give aid to Greece, and perceptions, such as Kennan's conclusion that the Soviets were bent on expansion. Those choices and perceptions were not the only ones that could have been made. With good reason, Americans would wonder for decades whether the cold war could have been different.

Containment

As the United States implemented strategies for containing Soviet expansion through a combination of diplomatic, economic, and military moves, the scope of the confrontation widened to include the entire world. In 1949 China's civil war ended in a Communist victory. In 1950, just five years after the end of World War II, the United States went to war again, this time to save a non-Communist regime in South Korea. As the cold war spread, it became more dangerous. When the Soviets exploded their own atomic bomb, the United States also dramatically stepped up military spending and built a hydrogen bomb. As the arms race spiraled, the cold war seemed frighteningly out of control.

Committed to opposing Soviet and Communist expansion, the Truman administration had to figure out just how to fight the cold war. Once again, the diplomat George Kennan helped give expression to American thinking about the confrontation with the Soviets. Writing under the pen name "X," he argued that "the main element of any United States policy toward the Soviet Union must be that of a long-term, patient but firm and vigilant containment of Russian expansive tendencies."

The term "containment" aptly described American policy for the cold war. The United States worked to hold back the Soviets for the next 40 years, but "containment,"

AMERICAN LANDSCAPE

>> Dhahran

In the years after World War II an American city grew in the Arabian Desert. Starting with just 92 pioneers in 1942, Dhahran grew into a city of over 5,000 Americans, working and living in air-conditioned offices, clubhouses, movie theaters, and homes that looked, according to the *New York Times,* as if they had been lifted from Florida by magic carpet.

The clean, modern facilities inside the American zone contrasted sharply with the ragged tents and desert heat outside. Although larger than most, Dhahran was like thousands of compounds built all over the world during the cold war to house the expatriates who staffed the corporate headquarters, military bases, and embassies that looked after the United States' global interests.

America's interest in Arabia was oil. In the 1930s, U.S. companies struck a bargain with Ibn Saud, patriarch of a nomadic clan, securing rights until 2005 to any petroleum found in an area twice the size of Texas. When a huge reserve was found near Dhahran in 1938, pipelines, refineries, and machine shops sprang up overnight, making the oil consortium, known as ARAMCO, into the largest U.S. private overseas investment. And as the company grew, so did the power of its partner, Ibn Saud. By the late 1940s, Americans began to refer to the company's territory as "Saudi Arabia."

Before World War II, the Saud family was one of several Bedouin clans vying for control over the Arabian Peninsula. With oil wealth, Saud transformed his chieftaincy into a monarchical state, centralizing authority, raising taxes, and using radio to spread Wahabism, a puritanical faith that rejected liberal, pluralist Islamic practices in favor of Koranic literalism and a strict code of Sharia justice. Punishments for minor offenses included stoning and amputation. Saud's decrees allowed no labor unions, prohibited music and the education of women, and forced nomadic Arabs into settlements.

Oil money financed these policies, but ARAMCO officials refrained from criticizing Saudi rule. The king's relationship with the company was, the crown prince explained, "founded on mutual profit, with both parties respecting the rights of the other."

In the atmosphere of the cold war, security for the company and the Saudi regime became vital U.S. interests. The U.S. Pacific Fleet consumed nearly three-quarters of ARAMCO's oil, and the remainder fuelled European construction under the Marshall Plan. If rebels or the Soviets cut off Saudi oil, Defense Secretary James Forrestal warned, Americans would be reduced to driving four-cylinder cars. The residents of Dhahran were supplying an essential ingredient of the American way of life, and making a million dollars a day for the company in the process.

With its tennis courts and ranch homes, Dhahran looked like a suburb of Houston or Miami. It had its own

continued

Dhahran, 1952 The "American Camp" at Dhahran was a complete American suburb, with a golf course, Little League, tract homes, and segregated schools.

PTA and scout troop, a country club, libraries, and television station. It resembled American cities in another way, too. It was racially segregated. Outside the gates of the American colony, ARAMCO built an "intermediate camp" to house 2,000 Italian and Palestinian skilled workers. Further out lay the "coolie camp," a squalid settlement of wood and grass huts housing the 14,000 Arabs who drilled the oil, laid the pipe, and paved the roads.

Each settlement had its own separate electrical and water systems, schools, and clinics, except for the Arab camp, which had none of those things. The American colony had the country's only swimming pools and hospitals. No Arabs allowed. The clearest distinction between the nationalities was in climate. Americans could live, work, and shop entirely in air-cooled surroundings, but Arabs dug ditches and hauled loads in temperatures averaging 120 degrees in the shade for a starting wage of 90¢ a day. "For most Americans," one observer noted, differences of language and religion "and fear of local diseases made friendship with the Arabs hard to establish."

Arabs resented being third-class citizens in their own country, but complaints were not tolerated in Saud's kingdom. Americans drank liquor and appeared in public unveiled, flouting Sharia laws that Saud's religious police sternly enforced in the Arab community. Bedouin shepherds complained that pipelines fenced them in. Literate Arabs resented United States support for Israel. By the early 1950s, occasional flashes of violence in the workplace unsettled the community. In the autumn of 1953, Dhahran erupted in a general strike as 13,000 Arabs walked off the job to protest the arrest of workers attempting to organize a union. The U.S. community met the challenge, manning the pumps to keep the oil flowing. Together with Saud's U.S.-trained police they broke the strike.

ARAMCO and the king recognized the strike as a wake-up call and responded with a combination of paternalism and force. The company raised wages to over a dollar a day and built a hospital and concrete dormitories for Arab workers. Saud built a modern military equipped with U.S. jets and tanks. More Saudis took white-collar positions in the company, but the number of Americans living in the country continued to grow. Executives continued to hope that the American example would make Saudi society more tolerant, progressive, and democratic, but the company adapted readily to the kingdom's autocratic customs. ARAMCO refused to hire Jews, for fear of offending their hosts. The company helped the king seize lands from rival tribes, and from neighboring Yemen.

An opportunistic partnership between an American industry and an antidemocratic monarchy had become a permanent alliance. The cold war created many such relationships, and U.S. officials worried that so many of America's allies were dictators and kings rather than elected leaders. But the Soviet threat, they believed, did not allow the United States to choose its friends. That time would come when the danger had passed. ●

as Kennan described it in 1947, was still a vague concept. Truman and his successors had to decide just where and when to contain the Soviet Union, and they also had to decide what combination of diplomatic, economic, and military programs to use.

One thing became clear quickly. Containment would not rely primarily on the United Nations. Like the United States, the Soviet Union had a veto over actions by the United Nations Security Council. From the beginning, they used the veto to frustrate American efforts. The United Nations would become another arena for rivalry, not an instrument of American policy.

Truman and his advisors revolutionized American policies on foreign aid, overseas alliances, and national defense. Soon after the decision to help Greece and Turkey, the United States confronted a ruined Europe which Winston Churchill described as "a rubble-heap, a charnel house, a breeding ground of pestilence and hate." Fearing an impoverished Europe would embrace Communism, Truman and his advisors were determined to help rebuild. In a speech at Harvard University in June 1947, Truman's new secretary of state, General George C. Marshall, proposed a "European Recovery Plan" to combat "hunger, poverty, desperation and chaos" and to promote "political and social conditions in which free institutions can exist." The

Soviets declined to join and refused to allow Eastern European countries to participate, but 16 nations eagerly supported what became known as the "Marshall Plan."

"The Marshall Plan saved Europe," Truman boasted. From 1948 to 1952, $13 bil-
lion from the United States went to boost agricultural and industrial output,
increase exports, and promote economic cooperation. Whole cities were re-
built. By 1950, participating countries had already exceeded prewar production by 25 percent. Politically, prosperity helped stabilize Western European
governments and weaken the region's Communist parties. In the process,
Western European nations were bound more tightly to the United States.

Whatever the weather
We only reach welfare
together

Containment required more than aid. It also demanded the kind of
military alliances that the United States historically avoided. Such entangle-
ments, Americans had long believed, might drag the nation into unnecessary wars. But facing the challenge of the cold war, leaders now saw alliances
as a way of preventing, rather than provoking, armed conflict. In 1949, the
United States joined 10 Western European nations and Canada to form the
North Atlantic Treaty Organization (NATO). Under the NATO agreement,
an attack on any member nation would be treated as an attack on all. To
strengthen the American commitment to Western Europe, Congress appropriated $1.3 billion in military aid for NATO countries, and Truman ordered Ameri-
can troops to the Continent. General Dwight D. Eisenhower, the commander of
the Allied invasion of France in World War II, agreed to become the supreme commander of NATO forces.

Containment also required a government organized for vigilance. In 1947 Congress passed the National Security Act, creating a Central Intelligence Agency (CIA)
to gather and assess information for the president and a National Security Council
(NSC) to advise him on military and political threats. The act placed the army, navy,
and air force under a single command, the Joint Chiefs of Staff, and a single cabinet
secretary, the secretary of defense. The term "national security" was itself a novelty;
it provided a blanket justification for responses to all kinds of threats, actions including election rigging, proxy wars, and other "covert operations" by the CIA. Congress
briefly considered requiring all young men to undergo military training. Instead it
passed a new Selective Service Act the draft for men between 19 and 25.

Taking Risks

Containment entailed risks. There was always the chance that the simmering conflict could boil over into a world war. One particularly dangerous hot spot was Berlin. In 1948, the Americans, British, and French began to unify their zones of occupation in Germany into a single unit under a new currency, the deutschmark. Faced
with a revived anti-Communist western Germany, Stalin sealed off his own German
zone of occupation. On June 24, the Soviets cut road and rail transport into Berlin,
the jointly occupied German capital. Truman figured Stalin was bluffing, and as
the sole nuclear power, the United States could call the bluff. "We stay in Berlin,
period," Truman snapped. But the 2.5 million citizens of the American, British, and
French sectors were at risk of running out of food and coal. Sending an armed supply convoy through the Soviet blockade could provoke a shooting war.

Instead, the Truman administration supplied Berlin by air. American transport
planes carried 2,500 tons of food and fuel a day. Along with this massive airlift, the

Truman administration sent to Britain two squadrons of B-29 bombers: significantly, the kind of planes that dropped the atomic bombs on Japan. In May 1949 the Soviets ended the blockade. Put to the test, the strategy of containment had worked. U.S. countermeasures had seemingly deterred Soviet expansion. But the risks were plain.

The dangers became even greater for the United States later that year. In early September, American planes found radioactivity in the air over the Pacific, evidence that the Soviet Union had exploded an atomic bomb. The U.S. monopoly of nuclear weapons, which had boosted Truman's confidence, was over. Suddenly, the confrontation with the Soviets had potentially lethal consequences for the American people. It was now, a Republican senator somberly observed, "a different world."

Global Revolutions

The cold war soon spread from Europe to shape the politics of the whole world. Civil and postcolonial strife in Asia, Africa, the Middle East, and Latin America came to be seen as part of the conflict between the nuclear superpowers.

In China, the nationalist government of Jiang Jieshi had waged a civil war against Mao Zedong's Communist rebels since the 1920s. Both sides joined forces to fight the Japanese during World War II, but while combat experience strengthened the Communists, it weakened Jiang's corrupt and unpopular regime. When Japan surrendered, U.S. forces helped Jiang regain control of Chinese cities and Truman urged the two sides to reach a permanent settlement, but the civil war resumed. Congressional Republicans saw China as a key cold war battleground, but Truman doubted the United States could influence the outcome in this vast, populous, rural country. He sent the nationalists $2 billion in aid but refused to send troops. In December 1949 the defeated nationalists fled the Chinese mainland for the island of Taiwan, and Republicans angrily blamed the administration for the "loss" of China.

With most of Asia now in Communist hands, American strategists began to rethink containment. Before 1949, the danger zones were in the world's industrial heartlands, Europe and Japan. Now it seemed that brushfire wars could spread nearly anywhere. Resentful peasants manned Mao's armies, and the rural "third world" seemed especially vulnerable. To implement containment in Latin America, Truman organized a coordinated defense, known as the Rio Pact, through which the United States would provide training, weapons, and advisers for Latin American militaries. The Organization of American States (OAS), created in 1948, promoted stability and economic development from its headquarters in Washington.

Territories formerly of little interest to American strategists, such as Southeast Asia and Africa, became vital to national security. Although the Truman administration favored self-determination, it tolerated Latin American dictatorships, European colonial dominion, and South Africa's white supremacist state because these undemocratic regimes opposed Communism.

Korea

With the United States working to hold off Communism at so many points, it was probably not surprising that the nation was eventually drawn into war. Nevertheless, the news that U.S. troops were in battle in Korea startled Americans in 1950,

AMERICA AND THE WORLD

>> Underdevelopment

As the opening acts of the cold war unfolded, a second global drama, in some ways more consequential, played out in Asia, the Middle East, and Africa. Subjugated peoples struggled for and claimed independence, and European colonial systems crumbled. By the end of the 1940s, for the first time in history, a majority of the world's people lived in nations, instead of empires.

Decolonization ripped apart systems of authority and trade. After years of conflict, new nations often gained little but freedom. They inherited economies without industry or markets, governments with no schools, roads, or tax collectors, and restless populations living in deep poverty. The Truman administration recognized that, although the movement toward nationalism could not be stopped, with luck, it might be managed.

In the fourth point of his 1949 inaugural address, Truman announced a "bold new program for making the benefits of our scientific advances and industrial progress available for the improvement and growth of underdeveloped areas." The "Point Four" program was the United States' first global foreign aid program, but Truman's real innovation was in redefining terms. By calling the new nations underdeveloped, Truman asserted that nations were entitled to growth, that all nations would one day be fully developed.

National leaders eagerly accepted the new terms. Truman "hit the jackpot of the world's political emotions," *Fortune* magazine reported. Delegations from Ecuador, Pakistan, and Egypt lined up to ask for technical assistance. "America's attitude is our salvation," an Afghan prince declared. "We are free of the threat of great powers using our mountain passes as pathways to empire. Now we can concentrate our talents and resources on bettering the living conditions of our people."

While nationalists struggled for freedom from outside interference, development made it the obligation of every responsible government to open the door to foreign experts. Countries that had expelled foreign advisers a few years earlier welcomed teams of economists from the World Bank and the Ford Foundation. UN commissions on food, health, and education measured each nation's progress toward universal goals that would mark its arrival as a fully modern state. Development directed the nationalist energies into economic channels and away from political actions that might endanger U.S. interests. It was Point Four's purpose, Secretary of State Dean Acheson noted, to "use material means to a non-material end."

Nationalist leaders also remarked on how material changes altered the spiritual and cultural outlook of people. Hydroelectric dams were the temples of modern India, declared Prime Minister Jawaharlal Nehru at the dedication of an enormous water project modeled on the TVA. "When we undertake a big work, our minds open out a little." Some contended that development might replace the cold war with a peaceful competition to modernize the world under rival economic theories.

Others argued that poverty went beyond aid, technical knowledge, or even states of mind. A Brazilian delegate at the first Point Four conference explained that poverty was caused by the terms of trade: Latin American agricultural exports steadily declined in value, while manufactured imports from the United States steadily increased in price. Economies became wealthy and technically advanced, in other words, by pushing others into backwardness. Development created underdevelopment.

But the success of the Marshall Plan and Japan's reconstruction gave Americans tremendous confidence in

Ways of Sharing "know-how"

RESEARCH AND LABORATORIES

TECHNICAL LIBRARIES AND FILM SERVICES

ON-THE-JOB TRAINING

INTERNATIONAL CONFERENCES

DEMONSTRATION OF METHODS

EXCHANGE OF TEACHERS AND STUDENTS

continued

their ability to make over whole societies. In the 1950s, social scientists devised theories of "nation building." For their own convenience, academic specialists divided the world into three parts, each with a distinct set of problems: a democratic, developed "first world," a Communist "second world," and the underdeveloped "third world," which contained most of the nations and two-thirds of the people on earth.

If the United States could ease the third world's ascent, MIT economist Walt W. Rostow predicted, it could create "an environment in which societies which directly or indirectly menace ours will not evolve." Military strategies against guerilla insurgencies increasingly employed development techniques to stabilize governments and win (in Mao Zedong's phrase) the "hearts and minds" of the people.

Aid officials often said that development and democracy went together. As peasants became consumers and workers, they would demand more choice in how they lived their lives and who their leaders were. By giving freely of its resources and know-how, America could "export democracy." But in practice, development programs seldom asked ordinary people what kind of progress they wanted. Aid reinforced a centralized state, channeling funds to unelected planning commissions and economic experts who made decisions that affected millions of people.

By the 1960s, "nation building" by planners and social scientists had become central to U.S. containment strategy. The long U.S. struggle in Vietnam, which began with military aid in 1950 and ended with defeat in 1975, would test the theory that stimulating development would increase democracy and security. That idea, Henry Kissinger later concluded, was "clearly wrong."

But by then, a system of national and international institutions to guide the development of nations was already in place. Leaders and electorates around the world judged national success by the statistical yardstick of economic growth. While few people fully accepted Truman's hunch that prosperity would guarantee peace, even fewer were ready to reject it entirely. Underdevelopment had taken a permanent place on the agenda of global problems. ●

because the conflict was so far from areas considered strategically important. But the Korean War was firmly rooted in the logic of the cold war.

Korea, a peninsula bordering China and the Soviet Union, had been liberated from the Japanese in 1945. American and Soviet troops jointly occupied the territory, splitting it into two zones at the 38th parallel. American policy makers opposed the popular nationalist Kim Il Sung, who was a Communist, and acted unilaterally to install a regime in the southern zone under Syngman Rhee, an anti-Communist. By 1948, Korea effectively had two governments, each claiming jurisdiction over the whole. In June 1950, after incidents along the 38th parallel, Kim's army, led by Soviet-made tanks, invaded the South.

Truman responded boldly. By itself, South Korea was not strategically important, but the president and his advisors believed the Soviet Union was behind the North Korean attack. After the "loss" of China, the Truman administration could not afford another Communist victory in Asia. "By God," the president swore, "I am going to let them have it!" His administration secured approval from the United Nations for international action in Korea. Troops from 15 countries eventually fought under the UN flag, but nine-tenths of the UN force in Korea came from the United States. America was at war then—or was it? Claiming that the conflict was only a "police action," Truman never asked Congress for a declaration of war. For the first time, but not the last, a president committed troops to battle in the cold war without regard for the Constitution.

At first, the fighting did not go well. U.S. troops, unprepared and understrength, fell back toward the coast. But in the summer, General Douglas MacArthur used the U.S. Navy's control of the seas to put troops ashore at Inchon on the west coast of South Korea, deep behind enemy lines. North Korea's main armies were cut off and destroyed. Within weeks, the South had been reclaimed.

Then Truman and his advisers made a fateful decision. Rather than just contain Communism, they wanted to roll it back. Truman gave the order to invade North Korea and reunify the peninsula. Mac-Arthur, who privately thirsted for war with the Chinese Communists, pushed northward, ever closer to China. Fearing an American invasion, the Chinese issued warnings, sent their forces into North Korea, and then, on November 25, unleashed a massive attack on UN troops. MacArthur's shattered army fled to South Korea and regrouped to defend it.

The Korean "police action" settled into a troubling stalemate. A frustrated MacArthur wanted to expand the war effort and fight back aggressively, but the chastened Truman administration, giving up on reunification, was prepared to accept the old division at the 38th parallel. That was too much for MacArthur, who broke the U.S. military's unwritten rule against public criticism of civilian leaders. "There is no substitute for victory," MacArthur lectured in 1951. Truman, fed up, fired his popular general in April. Meanwhile, the war dragged on.

The Korean stalemate underscored difficult realities of the cold war. Containment had the potential to sacrifice American lives in minor, nondecisive wars. Since each conflict had to be stopped short of nuclear disaster, U.S. troops also had to be prepared, as the saying went, to "die for a tie"—to fight for something less than victory. In this kind of conflict, leaders had to sustain the confidence of allies, undecided nations, and citizens at home that, despite setbacks, the West would eventually win. Psychology was more important than territory.

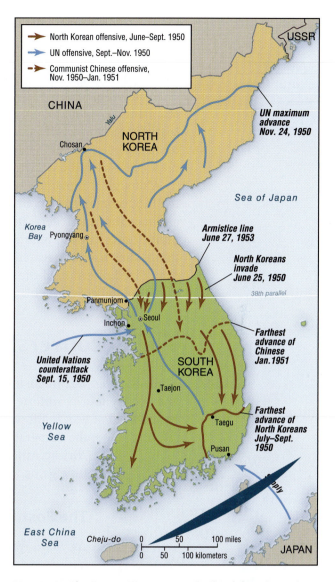

Map 26–2 The Korean War, 1950–1953 The shifting lines of advance mark the back-and-forth struggle that would end with stalemate and the division of Korea.

NSC-68

Before Korea, the Truman administration tried to balance its international and domestic agendas—limiting spending on the military, for instance, to boost economic recovery. By the 1950s, containment became the first priority. Escalating the U.S. effort, the administration challenged revolutionary movements even in peripheral areas, such as Southeast Asia. Colonial struggles, such as the Vietnamese rebellion against their French overlords, came to be seen as critical challenges to the non-Communist West.

In April 1950, the National Security Council approved a secret guideline known as NSC-68. Citing a growing list of threats and the "possibility of annihilation," it stipulated that the United States should triple defense spending, impose order in the postcolonial areas, and seek more powerful weapons. Truman worried about the cost, but the Korean War soon convinced him. By 1952, defense expenditures had nearly quadrupled, to $44 billion. Meanwhile, the armed forces grew—reaching 3.6 million by 1952—along with the list of combat theaters, now including Vietnam. Over the objections of J. Robert Oppenheimer, the director of the Manhattan Project, Truman ordered the building of "the so-called hydrogen or superbomb." Successfully tested in November 1952, the atom-fusing, thermonuclear bomb had far more explosive power than the atomic bomb, but it did not stop the arms race. Less than a year later, the USSR had its own "H-bomb."

Although it remained top secret until the 1970s, NSC-68 profoundly changed the U.S. economy and political system. The military buildup was paid for with deficit financing, and federal borrowing generated jobs and growth, particularly in the Sunbelt areas of the South and West. To fight the cold war, Americans accepted things they had long feared: secrecy, debt, alliances, a massive standing army, and centralized direction of the economy. Each of these innovations magnified the role of the federal government.

The Reconversion of American Society

While the cold war intensified, domestic policy focused on restoring the economy and society to a peacetime footing. "Reconversion" was a welcome process for a nation tired of war, but it was also a cause for worry. Americans feared a return to the desperate economic conditions of the 1930s. Labor, women, and African Americans, especially, wanted to hold on to and extend wartime gains.

> **We are living in a period in which there are going to be witch-hunts, hysteria, and red-baiting by the most vicious group of congressmen that have gathered under the dome of the Capitol.**
>
> WALTER REUTHER,
> labor union president, 1947

The Postwar Economy

As World War II ended, it seemed likely that the economy would slide back into depression. Millions of unemployed servicemen returned home at a time when government was cutting spending. The disaster never came. Unemployment rose to almost 4 percent the year after the war but never approached the double-digit rates of the 1930s. Despite brief downturns, the economy remained vibrant. This resilience reflected several factors, including veterans' choices, the federal role, the gradual transformation of industry, and U.S. economic dominance. Returning veterans did not strain the economy, partly because half of them went to school rather than work. Under the GI Bill of 1944 the federal government paid for up to three years of education for veterans. Spending by the federal government also helped to prevent a return to the economic conditions of the 1930s. With the end of World War II, federal expenditures decreased dramatically, but the government was still spending far more than it did during the 1930s. The GI Bill illustrated how that spending stimulated the economy. Pumping nearly $14.5 billion into the educational system, the bill encouraged colleges and universities to expand. As veterans swelled enrollments, institutions hired new faculty. Entire new educational systems, such as the State University of New York, were created.

Reconversion accelerated economic transformations that World War II started. In the late 1940s, industrial production was still concentrated in the Northeast and Midwest but there were already signs of change. Military spending helped shift factories and population toward the South and West. In the 1940s, the population of the western states grew by 50 percent while the population of the East grew by only 10 percent. The nature of the economy was changing, too. Oil and natural gas replaced coal as the principal source of power. New industries, such as plastics, electronics, and aviation, were growing rapidly.

Finally, the dominance of the United States in the world economy facilitated reconversion. At the end of World War II, the U.S. economy was roughly the size of the European and Soviet economies combined. As late as 1950, America, with only 6 percent of the world's population, accounted for a staggering 40 percent of the value of all the goods and services produced around the globe. Demand for American exports provided jobs but also stoked inflation. Ultimately production caught up, and by the late 1940s, the economy was beginning a prolonged peacetime boom.

The Challenge of Organized Labor

Organized labor had never been more powerful than at the end of World War II. One-third of nonagricultural civilian workers belonged to unions. The Democratic Party paid attention to the interests of influential unions such as the Congress of Industrial Organizations (CIO), and after pledging not to strike during World War II, organized labor was eager to test its clout. Workers wanted wage increases to cope with inflation and reward workers for their contribution to wartime profits. In Europe and Japan, unions were gaining control over the way corporations did business, and some American unionists wanted a similar role in management. Not surprisingly, corporations were reluctant to give up any of their power or profits. Along with conservatives in Congress, they branded the unions as agents of Communism.

The result was a huge wave of strikes as soon as the war ended in August 1945. At the start of 1946, 2 million workers were on strike. Machinists in San Francisco, longshoremen in New York City, and other workers across the country called a record 4,985 strikes that year. "[L]abor has gone crazy," an anxious Truman told his mother.

Significant work stoppages took place in automobile factories, coal mines, and railroad yards. Late in 1945, the United Auto Workers (UAW) struck General Motors (GM) for a 30 percent raise in hourly wages, access to the company's account books, and more say in company decisions. UAW vice president Walter Reuther insisted that higher wages would stimulate consumption without forcing the company to raise prices. GM rejected union interference in management decisions. When the strike finally ended after 113 days, the UAW won only some of its wage demands. It marked a turning point for labor. Unions never again made such bold demands to participate in management, and instead focused on pay and benefits.

The coal and railroad strikes were even more contentious than the GM work stoppage. Members of the United Mine Workers (UMW) and the railway unions refused to accept arbitration by the federal government. As the coal supply dwindled, power systems suffered "brownouts," and railroad passengers were stranded. The situation tested the strong relationship, forged in the New Deal, between the Democratic Party and organized labor. Truman ordered federal takeovers of both the mines and the railroads. "Let Truman dig coal with his bayonets," snarled John L. Lewis, leader of the

Containment on the Home Front. Although Congress passed the Taft-Hartley Act in 1947 to forestall an impending coal strike, United Mineworkers leader John L. Lewis ignored the act and struck anyway.

UMW. But the strikes came to an end in May. Much of the public applauded the president's action. Many Americans believed that Lewis, Reuther, and the other union leaders had become too powerful, arrogant, and demanding for the good of the country.

Counting on the public's unhappiness with unions, probusiness Republicans in Congress soon moved to limit the power of organized labor, which had been boosted by the Democratic New Deal. In 1947, a coalition of Republicans and conservative, mostly southern, Democrats passed the Taft-Hartley Act, a sweeping modification of federal labor law. The measure made it easier for employers to hire nonunion workers and to oppose the formation of unions. The bill also limited unions' right to organize and engage in political activity. Most humiliating of all, it compelled union leaders to swear that they did not belong to the Communist Party.

Despite these setbacks, workers and unions still prospered. Landmark contract negotiations between the UAW and GM offered a peaceful and lucrative model of labor relations. In 1948 the UAW won guaranteed cost-of-living adjustments, known as COLAs, and an annual wage increase tied to rises in worker productivity. In the so-called Treaty of Detroit, signed in 1950, the UAW obtained other increases and a pension plan in an unusually long-term contract lasting five years. The UAW contracts replaced confrontation with cooperation and strikes with security. In return for pensions and protection against inflation, the autoworkers gave management stable, predictable labor relations over the long term.

The Treaty of Detroit ended a difficult period for organized labor. Thanks to such lucrative contracts as the Treaty of Detroit, many workers were more secure than ever before, but reconversion also limited the power of organized labor. Aggressive strikes produced mixed results, public hostility, and government interference. Reconversion revealed the limits of the Democratic Party's support for labor as well. With the end of the strike wave, unions effectively abandoned their demand to participate in management in postwar America.

Opportunities for Women

Reconversion also posed special challenges to the status of American women. During World War II, the shortage of male labor had expanded women's opportunities for employment. Working women prized the income and the sense of satisfaction they gained from performing jobs traditionally monopolized by men. But there was a widespread belief, encouraged by employers and government officials, that women should surrender jobs to returning veterans. The number of women in the labor force dropped 13 percent from 1945 to 1946, but reconversion did not send displaced female workers home for good. Three-quarters of the women who wanted to stay at work after the war managed to find jobs.

Women's role in the postwar workplace was the product both of their desire and of financial necessity. Most, of course, needed to earn a living for themselves or their families. By 1953 the number of women in the workforce matched the level of 1945. A higher percentage of women were employed than before World War II. The number in nontraditional jobs increased, too. More women than ever before were skilled craftspersons, forepersons, physicians, and surgeons.

The number of married women in the postwar labor force was especially notable. The cultural prejudice against women's employment had always applied most strongly to married women and mothers, but economic realities overcame cultural prejudices. Increasingly, employers needed women workers. By 1947 there were already more married women than single women in the wage labor force.

The armed forces, like civilian employers, initially cut back the number of women in the ranks when the war ended, but reconversion did not cause a return to the prewar days when women had almost no place in the military. Congress granted women permanent status in the armed forces and merged the separate women's military organizations, such as the Women's Army Corps, into the regular armed services.

Despite these gains, women continued to face discrimination. The majority had to settle for traditionally female, traditionally low-paying jobs in offices, stores, and factories. Women's hourly pay rose only half as much as men's pay in the first years after the war. In the military, women were largely confined to noncombatant roles such as nursing. There were no women generals.

Secretarial Pool Despite official discouragement, large numbers of women worked in offices and other settings after World War II.

Women faced discrimination in the larger society as well. There was little interest in women's rights. After a meeting with female activists, Truman dismissed a constitutional amendment guaranteeing equal rights for women as a "lot of hooey." Despite the lack of support for women's rights, women's opportunities were gradually expanding in the years after World War II; the combination of women's desires and the economy's needs was slowly promoting the feminization of the labor force.

Civil Rights for African Americans

Like women, African Americans had made significant gains during World War II. They had filled new roles in the military and higher-paying jobs in the civilian economy, and aggressively pushed their demand for civil rights. Like women, African Americans sought to preserve and extend these rights and opportunities in the face of substantial resistance.

Several factors, including economic change, legal rulings, and wartime experiences, stimulated the drive for equal rights and opportunities after World War II. By the end of the war, the transformation of the southern economy was undermining the system that segregated African Americans and denied them the right to vote. As the mechanization reduced the need for field hands, African Americans continued to leave farms for the region's growing cities and for the North and West. One of the fundamental rationales for segregation—the need for an inexpensive and submissive labor force to work the fields—was disappearing. The developing southern economy also attracted white migrants from other regions, people less committed to segregation and disfranchisement. Meanwhile, the African American migrants to northern and western cities increased African American votes and political influence in the nation.

In fighting the Nazis during the war and the Communists afterwards, the United States dedicated itself to universal freedoms. The United Nations Declaration on Human Rights committed member states to guarantee rights to education, free movement, assembly, and personal safety. Truman often stated that disregard for human rights was "the beginning of tyranny, and too often, the beginning of war." But Kennan noted that, since the United States did not respect the rights of its own citizens, such statements only "invite charges of hypocrisy against us." African Americans appealed to the UN, the courts, and the press to recognize these commitments.

During the 1940s, a series of decisions by the U.S. Supreme Court struck at racial discrimination and encouraged African Americans to challenge inequality. In *Smith v. Allwright* in 1944, the court had banned whites-only primary elections. In *Morgan v. Virginia* in 1946, the court ruled that interstate bus companies could not segregate passengers. In *Shelley v. Kraemer* in 1948, the court banned restrictive covenants, the private agreements between property owners not to sell houses to African Americans and other minorities. These and other court decisions made discriminatory practices vulnerable and raised the possibility that African Americans might have a judicial ally in their struggle for justice.

African Americans' war experiences also encouraged them to demand more from the United States. Veterans, having fought for their country, now expected it to give them justice. Reconversion could not mean a return to the old days of discrimination. "Our people are not coming back with the idea of just taking up where they left off," an African American private wrote. "We are going to have the things that are rightfully due us or else."

That kind of determination spurred civil rights activism after World War II. In the South, African Americans increasingly demanded the right to vote after *Smith v. Allwright*. The National Association for the Advancement of Colored People (NAACP), the oldest civil rights organization, set up citizenship schools in southern communities to show African American voters how to register. The campaign was driven, too, by individual and spontaneous actions. In July 1946 Medgar Evers, a combat veteran who had just reached his 21st birthday, decided to try to vote in the Democratic Party's primary election in Decatur, Mississippi.

Such activism met resistance from whites deeply committed to disfranchisement and segregation. A white mob kept Evers from voting in 1946. In Georgia, whites killed an African American voter. More often, they manipulated registration laws to disqualify voters. A voter who wanted to register might have to answer such questions as "How many bubbles are there in a bar of soap?" Nevertheless, African American voter registration in the South, only 2 percent in 1940, rose to 12 percent by 1947. With that widening margin came the election of a few African American officials and improved service from local government.

While the campaign for voting rights went forward, civil rights activists fought segregation in all parts of the country. The interracial Congress of Racial Equality (CORE) took the lead in protesting public discrimination. To test the Supreme Court's decision in *Morgan,* CORE sent an integrated team of 16 activists on a two-week bus trip through the upper South, where they met with violence and arrests. Activists hardly dented segregation in the South in the 1940s, but they had more success promoting antidiscrimination laws in the North. By 1953, fair-employment laws had been adopted in 30 cities and 12 states.

Slain American Civil Rights Activist Medgar Evers (1925–1963) Medgar Evers fought for democracy in France and Germany, and then returned to fight for it again in Mississippi.

Activists also pressured Truman to support civil rights. In the spring and summer of 1946, picketers marched outside the White House with signs that read, "SPEAK, SPEAK, MR. PRESIDENT." Racial discrimination was an embarrassment for a nation claiming to represent freedom and democracy around the world, but support for civil rights was a political risk for a politician dependent on white support. Nevertheless, Truman took significant steps.

In the fall of 1946, a presidential committee report, *To Secure These Rights,* called for strong federal action against lynching, vote suppression, job discrimination, and civil rights violations, including segregation in the armed forces. Admitting that "there is a serious gap between our ideals and some of our practices," Truman insisted "this gap must be closed." Furious white southern politicians and newspapers said Truman was "stabbing the South in the back."

African Americans, meanwhile, kept the heat on Truman. To protest discrimination in the military, A. Philip Randolph, the head of the Brotherhood of Sleeping Car Porters, proposed a boycott of the draft. Warned that he would be accused of treason, he replied that "if that is the only way we can get democracy, we will have to face it." In July 1948 Truman responded with Executive Order 9981, creating a committee to phase out discrimination in the military. At the same time, Truman established the Fair Employment Board, which moved more slowly against discrimination in federal hiring.

During the Truman years, the most publicized blow to racial inequality came not from the White House but the baseball diamond. When the Brooklyn Dodgers called up infielder Jackie Robinson from the minor leagues in 1947, he became the first African American man in decades to play in the majors. A strong, self-disciplined former soldier, Robinson took taunts and beanballs on the field and death threats in the mail. Fast, powerful, and exciting, he finished the season as the National League's Rookie of the Year. Robinson's success paved the way for increasing numbers of African American players in the majors over the next several years.

Robinson's success also spelled the end of the Negro Leagues, the organizations created when African Americans were banned from the major leagues. As would sometimes be the case, integration undermined distinctly African American institutions. Nonetheless, the achievements of Robinson, Larry Doby, and other pioneering African American major leaguers sent a powerful message for civil rights and underscored the limits of reconversion. On the whole, African Americans preserved and sometimes managed to expand their wartime gains while still encountering injustice and inequality in almost every aspect of daily life. In one respect, at least, African Americans, women, and organized labor shared a common experience in the first years after World War II. For each of these groups, reconversion turned out to be better than feared and worse than hoped. African Americans, women, and workers all struggled to preserve and expand their rights and opportunities in the political economy of the late 1940s. They all confronted the limits of their power to change the society around them.

The Frustrations of Liberalism

During the Great Depression, liberalism, in the form of Franklin Roosevelt's New Deal, had reshaped American democracy, thrusting the federal government more deeply than ever into economic and social life. But the liberal Democratic agenda, with its calls for further federal activism, had stalled during World War II. In the first years after the war, it met with more frustration. Liberals and the Democratic Party strained to show that they had answers for a nation no longer facing an economic or military emergency. Harry Truman struggled to prove that he was a worthy successor to Roosevelt.

The Democrats' Troubles

An accidental president, Harry Truman faced skepticism from many Americans. Liberals wondered whether he shared their ideals. They were incensed when he fired FDR's trusted aide Henry Wallace after Wallace criticized Truman's policy toward the USSR. Conservatives and moderates also had doubts about his agenda. During the Depression, Americans had been willing to endorse government interventions in the economy, but in a fairly prosperous peacetime, people felt less need for government and more need for individual freedom.

The president embraced more of liberalism than the liberals expected. Shortly after he took office in 1945, he presented a legislative program that included proposals on education, employment, insurance, social security, and civil rights. Yet a full-employment bill, reflecting the liberal belief that the federal government should take responsibility for securing jobs and prosperity, met overwhelming conservative and moderate opposition. Watered down by Congress, the resulting Employment Act of 1946 created a Council of Economic Advisors for the president but did nothing to increase the economic role of the federal government.

> I'm "not familiar with the term 'cold war.'"
>
> 46 PERCENT OF AMERICANS, Gallup poll, December 1948

Truman and the liberals suffered an even sharper defeat over the president's sweeping proposal for a national health insurance system that would guarantee medical care to all Americans. The plan gave the federal government powers to manage the insurance system and set doctors' and hospitals' fees. Conservatives and the medical profession promptly condemned Truman's proposal as "the kind of regimentation that led to totalitarianism in Germany." The bill failed, and so did most of Truman's domestic proposals.

Nevertheless, the federal role in national life continued to grow in cold war America. Medical care offered a notable example. The Veterans Administration established a vast network of federal hospitals to care for returning soldiers. In 1946, the Hill-Burton Act appropriated federal money for the construction of hospitals. That same year, Congress created a research lab, later called the Centers for Disease Control, in Atlanta, Georgia, to monitor infectious diseases. Congress also reorganized the National Institutes of Health in 1948 and established the National Institute of Mental Health in 1949. Even though national health insurance was defeated, the federal role grew.

While Truman struggled with domestic and foreign policy, he became increasingly unpopular. "To err is Truman," went the joke. The president looked weak and ineffective to some Americans, tyrannical and overbearing to others. "Had Enough?" asked Republicans. Many had. In the 1946 congressional elections, the voters gave the Republicans a majority in both the House of Representatives and the Senate for the first time in 16 years.

Truman's Comeback

The 1946 elections seemed to point toward Truman's defeat two years later, but the president managed a stunning comeback. It began with the Republican majority that took control in Congress in 1947. Led by Senator Robert Taft of Ohio, they hoped to beat back New Deal liberalism and substitute a different understanding of American democracy. Refuting "the corrupting idea that we can legislate prosperity, legislate equality, legislate opportunity," Taft wanted "free Americans freely working out their destiny." The Taft-Hartley Act was a blow to liberals and the administration, but Republicans found themselves hamstrung by Americans' ambivalence about liberalism. Few were enthusiastic about bold new programs such as national health insurance, but there was little sentiment to roll back the New Deal. Americans clearly wanted to hold on to the benefits they had. Besides Taft-Hartley, the Eightieth Congress did not accomplish much, and soon Truman was campaigning against a "do-nothing Congress."

Nevertheless, things looked bad for Truman. By March 1948 only 35 percent of the people approved of his performance. Moreover, his party was splitting apart. On the left, his former secretary of commerce Henry Wallace was running for president as a "Progressive." On the right, Democratic governor Strom Thurmond of South Carolina was running as a "Dixiecrat," appealing to white supporters of segregation. Losing Democratic votes to both Wallace and Thurmond, Truman seemed certain to lose in November. Or so his Republican opponent, Governor Thomas E. Dewey of New York, thought. Dewey believed a moderate, uncontroversial campaign would do the trick, but Truman worked to pull the New Deal majority back together. Climbing aboard his railway car, Truman visited more than half the states on a "whistle-stop" campaign. The president reached out to African Americans, labor, farmers, senior citizens, and other beneficiaries of New Deal liberalism. "Give 'em hell, Harry," the crowds shouted, and he did. He hammered home the difference between the Democrats' and Republicans' visions of the political economy. "The Democratic Party puts human rights and human welfare first," he declared. "These Republican gluttons of privilege . . . want a return of the Wall Street economic dictatorship."

On election day, Wallace and Thurmond received only a million votes each. Dewey attracted fewer votes than he had four years before. Holding together Roosevelt's coalition, Truman won the presidency in his own right with only 49.5 percent of the vote (see Map 26–3). Moreover, the Democrats recaptured the House and the Senate. The triumph did not last long. Like Taft two years before, Truman soon discovered that an election victory did not mean a mandate. In his State of the Union address in January 1949, Truman declared that "every individual has a right to expect from our Government a fair deal." But the president's "Fair Deal" legislation made little headway in Congress. Despite Truman's comeback, the liberal vision, so influential in the 1930s, could not dominate the politics of cold war America.

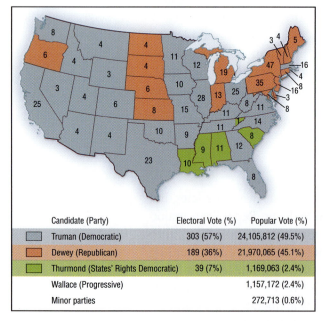

Candidate (Party)	Electoral Vote (%)	Popular Vote (%)
Truman (Democratic)	303 (57%)	24,105,812 (49.5%)
Dewey (Republican)	189 (36%)	21,970,065 (45.1%)
Thurmond (States' Rights Democratic)	39 (7%)	1,169,063 (2.4%)
Wallace (Progressive)		1,157,172 (2.4%)
Minor parties		272,713 (0.6%)

Map 26–3 The 1948 Presidential Election Segregationist and progressive candidacies were expected to undermine the Democratic majority, but the Roosevelt coalition returned Truman to the White House for a second term.

Fighting the Cold War at Home

While conservatives and liberals battled over domestic policy, the cold war increasingly intruded into every aspect of life. As the drafters of NSC-68 had hoped, the billions of dollars in defense expenditures stimulated economic growth, but in the short run, the main by-product was fear. Doubt and insecurity pervaded American culture in the late 1940s. Americans added a new fear of nuclear weapons to their old fear of immigrants. Above all, society succumbed to a largely irrational dread of hidden traitors in Hollywood, Washington, the universities, and the public library. To fight the cold war at home, anti-Communist crusaders such as Joe McCarthy hunted for disloyal Americans. By the 1950s, McCarthyism was a powerful force capable of destroying the lives of thousands of Americans, including Esther and Stephen Brunauer.

Doubts and Fears in the Atomic Age

Despite the U.S. triumph in World War II, American culture was surprisingly dark and pessimistic in the late 1940s. The rise of fascism, the Holocaust, and the bombings of Hiroshima and Nagasaki raised troubling questions about the direction of progress and the innate goodness of humankind. The cold war did nothing to calm those concerns. Even the welcome prosperity of the reconversion period did not soothe Americans' sense of doubt. People felt insignificant and powerless in an age of giant corporations, big unions, big government, and superbombs.

Americans revealed their unease in a variety of ways. Not long after the announcement of the Truman Doctrine in 1947, people suddenly began seeing lights in the sky. There were reports of "flying saucers" over 35 states and Canada. Some Americans even believed the federal government was covering up the truth about these unidentified flying objects. In a nuclear-armed world, columnist Joseph Alsop observed, the saucer scare was a reminder that "man-made horrors are quite real, quite imminent possibilities."

Meanwhile, Hollywood films explored popular fears. In 1946, *The Best Years of Our Lives* traced the difficult, sometimes humiliating readjustment of three returning veterans. The same year, *It's a Wonderful Life* told the story of a small-town banker forced to accept the disappointment of his unfulfilled dreams. Both films expressed reservations about the morality of capitalism and the chances of achieving happiness in the modern world. A new cinematic genre, film noir, offered an even darker view of individuals trapped in a confusing, immoral world. "I feel all dead inside," confessed the detective in *The Dark Corner* (1946). "I'm backed up in a dark corner and I don't know who's hitting me."

Nuclear weapons were perhaps the greatest source of fear. The unprecedented power of the atomic bomb dominated the popular imagination. For many Americans, this was the Atomic Age. They dealt with their anxiety about the new age in a variety of ways. Some people tried dark attempts at humor. Americans drank "atomic cocktails" and danced to the "Atomic Polka." American women wore the new "bikini," the explosively scanty two-piece bathing suit named for the Pacific atoll where the United States tested the H-bomb. The Soviets' development of the atomic bomb and then the hydrogen bomb was impossible to laugh away.

Americans' fear was also reflected in the hardening of attitudes toward foreigners. In 1945, a welcoming nation eased the immigration process for the foreign wives of American servicemen by passing the War Brides Act, but as the cold war intensified, other potential migrants met a hostile reception. The Immigration and

Nationality Act of 1952 tightly restricted immigration, particularly from Asia. It also kept out Communists and homosexuals and allowed the deportation of American citizens suspected of disloyalty.

The Anti-Communist Crusade

Americans may have feared disloyalty most of all. Many believed the real Communist threat came from within their own country. Historians debate the origins of this second "Red Scare." Some trace the anti-Communist crusade to a conservative reaction against the rising power of labor, African Americans, women, and other disempowered groups. Others blame the Truman administration for stoking fear to justify unprecedented military activity and spending. Although the new Red Scare was not solely a political creation—anti-Communism had deep roots in American culture—politicians in both parties gave domestic anti-Communism its particularly dangerous form.

The crusaders had to search hard for Communists at home. The Communist Party of the United States of America (CPUSA), a legal political party, was tiny and losing followers. Infiltrated by FBI and police informants, it never received more than a microscopic 0.3 percent of the popular vote. Just to be sure, the Truman administration charged 12 party leaders with violations of the Smith Act, which had criminalized membership in "a group advocating . . . the overthrow of the government by force." In 1949, 11 were convicted and sent to jail.

Open Communists posed less of a threat than secret ones, and in fact, self-professed former Communists and spies were seen as the most reliable informants on the hidden network of traitors presumed to be operating throughout the country. The hunt for these "subversives" was led by the House of Representatives' Un-American Activities Committee (HUAC). In 1947 HUAC held hearings on supposed Communist plots in Hollywood. The film industry cooperated, but eight screenwriters, a producer, and a director cited their First Amendment rights and declined to

The Subway **(1950)** Modernist painter George Tooker captured the claustrophobic anxiety of the McCarthy era in paintings like *The Subway* and *Government Bureau (*1956). In popular fiction and noir films, social conformity only thinly concealed a mounting hysteria.

testify. The "Hollywood Ten" were convicted of contempt of Congress and sent to jail for up to a year. Hollywood got the message. Film studios "blacklisted"—refused to hire—writers, directors, and actors even remotely suspected of Communist ties. Avoiding controversial subjects, the studios put out overwrought anti-Communist movies such as *The Red Menace* and *I Was a Communist for the FBI.*

Afraid of looking "soft" on Communism, the Truman administration encouraged the idea that there was a real problem with domestic Communism. "Communists," declared Truman's attorney general, Tom Clark, "are everywhere—in factories, offices, butcher shops, on street corners, in private businesses—and each carries with him the germs of death for society."

Late in 1946 the president set up a committee to investigate "employee loyalty." The next year he created a permanent loyalty program. Any civil servant could lose his or her job by belonging to any of the "totalitarian, Fascist, Communist or subversive" groups listed by the attorney general. The loyalty program proceeded with little regard for due process. People accused of disloyalty could not challenge evidence or confront their accusers, and they were presumed guilty until they proved their own innocence. Although only about 300 employees were actually discharged, Truman's loyalty program helped create the impression that there must be a serious problem in Washington.

The Hunt for Spies

There was, in fact, spying going on inside the federal government. The Soviet Union, just like the United States, carried out espionage abroad. The Canadian government found evidence of a spy ring that had passed American atomic secrets to the Soviets during World War II. Through its intercepts of Soviet communications, the CIA had a good idea of the scale of the spying and who was involved, but for its own reasons, the agency chose not to share this information with Congress, prosecutors, or even the president.

Thanks to information from the Canadian case, the FBI began to suspect Alger Hiss, an aide to the secretary of state, was a Soviet agent. Hiss was quietly eased out of his job. Then, in 1948, HUAC took testimony from Whittaker Chambers, an editor of *Time* magazine who claimed to have been a Soviet agent in the 1930s. Chambers accused Hiss of passing secret documents. Educated at elite schools before joining the Roosevelt administration, Hiss epitomized New Deal liberalism. He denied the charges and said he had never even met Chambers. He initially appeared more credible than the rumpled Chambers, an admitted perjurer, but Congressman Richard Nixon of California, a Republican member of HUAC, forced him to admit that he had in fact known Chambers under an alias. With help from the FBI, Chambers charged that Hiss had given him secret information in the 1930s. In front of reporters, Chambers pulled rolls of microfilm out of a hollowed-out pumpkin on his Maryland farm. The film contained photographs of secret documents. Hiss could not explain these "Pumpkin Papers." Under the statute of limitations, it was too late to try Hiss for spying, but it was not too late to indict him for lying to Congress. Hiss's perjury trial ended in a hung jury in 1949, but a second jury convicted him in January 1950. While Hiss sat in prison for almost four years, Chambers wrote a best seller and Nixon became a senator. The case was a great triumph for Republicans and conservatives and a blow to Democrats and liberals.

As the Hiss case ended, another scandal stimulated Americans' fears. In early 1950, British authorities arrested Klaus Fuchs, a physicist who had worked at the U.S. nuclear research facility in Los Alamos, New Mexico. The investigation led eventually to David Greenglass, who worked on the atomic bomb project, and his brother-in-law, Julius Rosenberg. Julius, a former member of the CPUSA, and his wife Ethel were convicted of conspiring to steal atomic information, in a trial that was controversial owing to its anti-Semitic overtones and because the act protecting atomic secrets became law after the spying allegedly took place. Though they had two young sons, both Rosenbergs were sentenced to death. Ignoring appeals for clemency from around the world, the federal government finally electrocuted the Rosenbergs in June 1953.

There now seems little disagreement that the USSR obtained American nuclear secrets, but the impact was probably not as great as conservatives feared or as small as liberals insisted. Most likely, espionage sped up the Soviets' work on an atomic bomb that they would have eventually produced anyway.

The Rise of McCarthyism

Two weeks after Hiss's conviction, one week after Truman's announcement of the decision to build the hydrogen bomb, and just days after the arrest of Klaus Fuchs, Senator Joseph McCarthy of Wisconsin suddenly and spectacularly took command of the anti-Communist crusade. Speaking to the Republican Women's Club of Wheeling, West Virginia, the previously obscure senator claimed to have names of 205 Communists working in the State Department. In fact, McCarthy had no new information. Instead, he dredged up a handful of old accusations, including the ones against the Brunauers.

Nevertheless, McCarthy was instantly popular and powerful. Frightened by new geopolitical and technological dangers, many people wanted to believe in a senator bold enough to fight back. Some shared McCarthy's resentment of privileged elites—New Dealers, diplomats, scientists—the powerful figures he derided as "egg-sucking phony liberals" and "bright young men . . . born with silver spoons in their mouths." For some Americans—immigrants, midwesterners, Catholics, and fundamentalists—support for McCarthy was a way to prove that they were more patriotic than educated or wealthy elites. "McCarthyism" was a way to assert local, civic control over national cultural life. Even Democratic legislators voted for the Internal Security Act of 1950, which forced the registration of Communist and Communist-front groups, provided for the deportation of allegedly subversive aliens, and barred Communists from defense jobs. Refusing to "put the Government of the United States in the thought control business," Truman vetoed the bill, but Congress overrode his veto.

Eventually, McCarthy went too far. Angry that one of his aides, David Schine, had not received a draft deferment, the senator launched an investigation of the army. The secretary of the army, Robert T. Stevens, refused to cooperate and claimed that McCarthy had tried to get preferential treatment for Schine. In April 1954, before a television audience of 20 million people, McCarthy failed to come up with evidence of treason in the army. When he tried unjustifiably to smear one of the army's young lawyers as a Communist, the senator was suddenly exposed. "Have you no sense of decency, sir, at long last?" asked the army's chief counsel, Joseph Welch. It was an electric moment. The Senate hearings came to no judgment, but Americans did. McCarthy's popularity ratings dropped sharply. By the end of the year, the Senate finally had the courage to condemn him for "unbecoming conduct."

The fall of McCarthy did not end McCarthyism. Schools forced teachers to sign loyalty oaths. Faculty members at several universities lost their jobs, and deans passed the names of suspect students to the FBI. Communism had become a useful charge to hurl at anything that anybody might oppose—labor unions, civil rights, even modern art. Politicians and communities attacked nonrepresentational, abstract expressionist artists as "tools of the Kremlin" and "our enemies." To protect themselves, groups policed their own membership. Labor unions, led by Reuther and other liberals, drove out Communist leaders and unions. The Cincinnati Reds renamed their team the "Redlegs" to make sure no one associated the world's oldest professional baseball team with Communism.

Across the country, Americans became more careful about what they said out loud. Many Americans had come to believe, along with McCarthy, that the civility and routines of democracy, the attention to rights and fairness, left America exposed to a ruthless adversary not bound by similar codes of conduct. Even as the Senate was censuring McCarthy, James Doolittle, the heroic World War II aviator, handed the Central Intelligence Agency a report on counterespionage and countersubversion. It explained that America faced "an implacable enemy whose avowed objective is world domination by whatever means and at whatever cost." "There are no rules in such a game," it concluded. "If the United States is to survive, long-standing American concepts of 'fair play' must be reconsidered."

Conclusion

By the time Esther Brunauer lost her job in 1952, the cold war had disrupted American life. To contain Communism, the United States had made unprecedented commitments that transformed the nation's economy. American society sorted through the unfinished business of reconversion, including the role of government and the rights and opportunities of labor, women, and African Americans. Despite these changes, the cold war had widened and intensified. Just seven years after dropping the first atomic bomb on Japan, Americans were again at war in the Far East and were forced to live with the threat of their own nuclear annihilation. They lived, too, with the frenzied search for subversives. American society seemed to be out of control.

As Esther and Stephen Brunauer moved back to Illinois to find peace and rebuild their lives, other Americans needed peace as well. They wanted the fighting in Korea to end. Anxious to avoid a nuclear holocaust, they wanted the confrontation with the Soviets to stabilize. Meanwhile, American society adjusted to a postwar economy, sorting out the role that government, labor, race, and gender would have in the new cold war order.

Further Readings

Kai Bird and Martin J. Sherwin, *American Prometheus: The Triumph and Tragedy of J. Robert Oppenheimer* (2005). Oppenheimer, the genius behind the Manhattan Project and a victim of McCarthyism, personified the contradictions of the early cold war.

Richard M. Fried, *Nightmare in Red: The McCarthy Era in Perspective* (1990). Provides a concise overview of the anti-Communist crusade.

William Graebner, *The Age of Doubt: American Thought and Culture in the 1940s* (1991). Probes the fears and insecurities that shaped American society during the cold war.

Alonzo L. Hamby, *Man of the People: A Life of Harry S. Truman* (1995). A full biography of the first cold war president.

Melvyn P. Leffler, *A Preponderance of Power: National Security, the Truman Administration, and the Cold War* (1992). One of several important conflicting accounts of the origins of the cold war.

Nelson Lichtenstein, *The Most Dangerous Man in Detroit: Walter Reuther and the Fate of American Labor* (1995). Examines the hopes and frustrations of the labor movement after World War II.

David M. Oshinsky, *A Conspiracy So Immense: The World of Joe McCarthy* (1983). An engaging, evenhanded biography of the most famous anti-Communist crusader.

Arnold Rampersad, *Jackie Robinson: A Biography* (1997). Explores the complicated man who integrated major league baseball.

Allen Weinstein, *Perjury: The Hiss-Chambers Case* (1978). Provides a thorough, controversial study of one of the most controversial episodes of the cold war.

Who, What?

>> Timeline >>

▼ 1945
Yalta conference
Harry S. Truman inaugurated
Potsdam Conference
Industrial strikes break out

▼ 1946
Winston Churchill's "Iron Curtain" speech
George Kennan's "long telegram" on Soviet expansionism

Employment Act of 1946
Morgan v. Virginia
Election of Republican majorities in House and Senate

▼ 1947
Announcement of Truman Doctrine
Beginning of Federal Employee Loyalty Program
CORE's "Journey of Reconciliation"
Integration of major league baseball by Jackie Robinson
HUAC Hollywood hearings

Rio Pact
Taft-Hartley Act
National Security Act
Presidential commission reports on civil rights

▼ 1948
Shelley v. Kraemer
Congressional approval of Marshall Plan
Truman's Executive Order 9981
Beginning of Berlin crisis

Review Questions

1. How did the National Security Act change the executive branch?

2. Why did Truman see Korea as important enough to defend?

3. Why were struggles in the workplace more intense in the late 1940s than during the Depression or World War II?

4. McCarthyism attacked government, science, education, theater, and Hollywood. Does this pattern reveal anything about the nature of American anxiety in the 1950s?

5. Two-thirds of the world's peoples gained their independence between 1945 and 1961. How did the cold war affect this movement toward nationhood?

6. In the 1950s and 1960s, historians debated the question of who started the cold war. In the 1990s, it became more interesting to ask *when* it started. Why the change, and what questions might historians today ask?

Website

America Abroad Media, "Banking on the Future: Global Development and the World Bank," http://www.americaabroadmedia.org/programs/view/id/52. Since World War II, the World Bank has worked to rebuild countries ravaged by war and colonialism and to create a unified world economy. It carries on the mission Truman launched with his Point Four address.

For further review materials and resource information, please visit www.oup.com/us/ofthepeople

Selective Service Act
Truman elected
   president

▼ **1949**
Formation of North
   Atlantic Treaty
   Organization
Communist takeover of mainland China

▼ **1950**
NSC-68
Alger Hiss's conviction for perjury

Joe McCarthy's speech in Wheeling, West
   Virginia
Treaty of Detroit
Beginning of Korean War
Internal Security Act of 1950

▼ **1951**
Truman fires General
   Douglas MacArthur

▼ **1952**
Immigration and
   Nationality Act

Test of hydrogen bomb

▼ **1953**
Execution of Ethel and
   Julius Rosenberg

▼ **1954**
Army-McCarthy
   hearings

Common Threads

>> Did the character of the cold war change from the 1940s to the 1950s?

>> Why did consumerism change the way Americans lived?

>> Why did diversity and individuality survive in the 1950s?

>> What was the impact of the Eisenhower administration on democracy?

>> How would the emerging discontents of the 1950s affect society and politics in the next decades?

The Consumer Society
1945–1961

>> Gene Ferkauf

At the end of World War II, Harry Ferkauf owned two luggage stores in midtown Manhattan in New York City. An immigrant Jewish man from Eastern Europe, he haggled with customers over prices in the old way and made a decent living. He did not want or expect much more. After all, he had barely kept his business alive during the Great Depression.

Harry's son, Eugene, who managed one of the stores, was unwilling to accept the old limits. After the war, Gene began offering discounts on luggage, watches, and other goods. Local storeowners resented this low-priced competition. Father and son argued frequently over Gene's strategy. In 1948, Gene quit the business and put all his savings into his own discount store on East 46th Street that would compete with the full-priced stores of the other merchants.

Gene envisioned a new kind of store, where customers could buy appliances and other goods without haggling, at low, fixed prices. Discounting his merchandise by a quarter and even a third, Gene could not make much money from a single sale. But if he sold enough televisions and refrigerators, he would earn more than his father ever had. On opening day, crowds filled the small shop and spent $3,000. Harry, who usually took in about $50 a day, was impressed.

In a few years, Gene had five successful discount stores in and around New York City. The business was called "E. J. Korvettes"—E for Eugene, J for his partner Joe Zwillenberg, and Korvettes after the small, quick Canadian warships of World War II. Korvettes appealed to a new generation, more optimistic than the older generation that had survived the Depression. Eager to buy televisions and other appliances, these younger people were unafraid to go into debt. Prosperous, they were leaving their parents' neighborhoods in the city for new suburbs. Gene Ferkauf understood these people; he was one of them. He, too, moved from his small $75-a-month urban apartment in Brooklyn to a $75,000 suburban "mansion" in Jamaica, Queens.

Gene had made it big. Closing the stores in New York, Korvettes built suburban stores in several states. In 1955,

the partnership became a corporation. Gene had left his father's world behind.

Gene Ferkauf's success reflected one of the central developments that shaped American society after World War II. Along with the cold war, economic prosperity transformed the nation in a host of ways. Just as Gene left his father's world behind, American society left behind the sense of economic limits and constraints that characterized the Great Depression and the war. The 1950s marked the culmination of the nation's long transformation into a full-fledged consumer society. Gene Ferkauf profited because mainstream culture celebrated consumption and pleasure instead of work and self-restraint and because televisions and suburbs defined the consumer lifestyle.

The emergence of the consumer society strongly affected American culture and politics. The prosperous 1950s helped to produce a more homogeneous, seemingly more harmonious society, characterized by decreasing class differences, changing gender relations, and a baby boom. Enjoying the benefits of consumerism, American voters demanded less from government. In later years, American culture would look back nostalgically at the 1950s as a prosperous golden age, but the consumer society had its conflicts, failures, and limits. In different ways, many Americans chafed against the conformity and constraints of the 1950s. The benefits of the consumer society did not reach every group; consumerism did not solve the problem of racial inequality or end the cold war. By the close of the decade, many Americans worried about the inadequacies of the consumer society, even as they enjoyed its benefits. ●

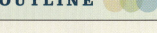
Living the Good Life

Consumerism was not a new development: much of the consumer lifestyle existed by the 1920s (see Chapter 23). But it was only in the 1950s that consumer values and habits finally dominated the American economy and culture. Never before had so many Americans had the chance to live the good life.

They tended to define that "good life" in economic terms. A dynamic, evolving economy provided more leisure and income. Sure of prosperity, Americans had the confidence to spend more of their time and money in the pursuit of pleasure. Millions of people lived the dream of home ownership in new suburbs, bought flashy automobiles, purchased their first televisions, and enjoyed a new openness about sex.

Economic Prosperity

Consumerism could not have flourished without prosperity. Despite three short recessions, the 1950s were a period of economic boom. The economy grew solidly, and the gross national product—the value of all the country's output of goods and services—grew at an average of 3.2 percent a year.

Several major factors spurred this economic growth. The shortage of consumer goods during and just after World War II had left Americans with money to spend. Because of the cold war, the federal government was also ready to spend money. Washington's expenditures for the defense buildup and foreign aid helped to stimulate the demand for American goods and services. Robust capital spending by the nation's businesses also helped ensure economic growth. At the same time, the industrial economy was evolving. Traditional heavy manufacturing—the production of steel and automobiles—was still crucial to national prosperity, but newer industries such as electronics, chemicals, plastics, aviation, and computers became increasingly important.

> See the USA in your Chevrolet
> America is asking you to call
> Drive your Chevrolet through the USA
> America's the greatest land of all.
>
> CHEVROLET COMMERCIAL JINGLE,
> 1950

The emergence of the computer business was especially significant for the long-term transformation of the economy. In 1946, two engineers at the University of Pennsylvania, J. Presper Eckert Jr. and John William Mauchly, completed the first fully electronic digital computer, loaded with hot bulky vacuum tubes. The Electronic Numerical Integrator and Computer (ENIAC) weighed more than 30 tons and filled a large room. Then Eckert and Mauchly produced the UNIVAC 1 (Universal Automatic Computer), a more advanced machine that was used to count census data in 1951 and presidential election returns in 1952.

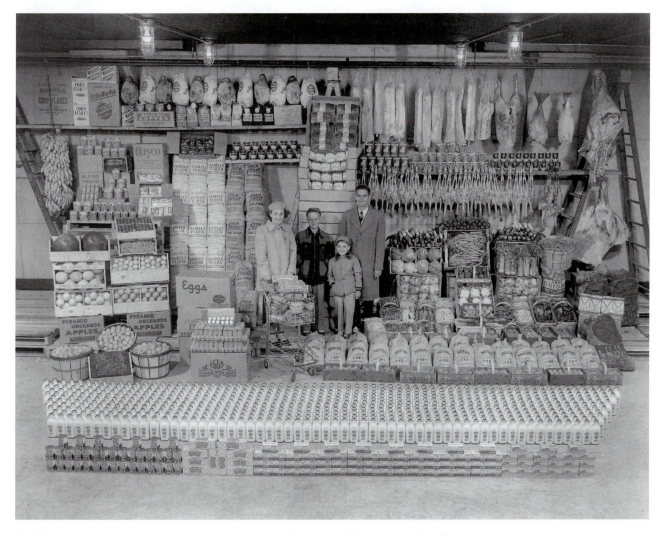

The New Affluence All the groceries consumed by a white-collar DuPont Chemical worker, his wife, and their two children in 1951.

ENIAC The first fully electronic digital computer fills a room in 1946.

As tiny solid-state transistors replaced vacuum tubes, computers became smaller, more powerful, and more common. By 1958, American companies were producing $1 billion worth of computers a year. Because computers were still so large and expensive, they were used mostly by universities, corporations, the Department of Defense, and other federal agencies. By 1961, there were about 10,000 computers in use, and the nation was on the brink of the computer age.

As American industry continued to evolve, the nation's distribution and service sectors played a larger economic role than ever before. While the number of manufacturing jobs barely changed, employment in retail stores like E. J. Korvettes increased 19 percent. Jobs in the service sector, such as restaurants, hotels, repair shops, hospitals, and universities, jumped 32 percent. The United States had begun to develop a postindustrial economy, less dependent on production and more dependent on service and consumption.

Economic prosperity greatly benefited big business. New corporations such as E. J. Korvettes emerged and grew. Thanks to a wave of mergers, established corporations became still larger. By 1960, corporations earned 18 times as much income as the rest of the nation's businesses combined.

Prosperity also boosted corporations' popularity. Even liberals, once critical of corporate power, now celebrated the benefits of large-scale business enterprise. Businessmen exuded confidence. "What is good for the country is good for General Motors, and vice versa," Charles Wilson, the head of GM, supposedly announced.

Benefiting from prosperity, American workers enjoyed high employment, low inflation, and rising incomes. Typically, less than 5 percent of the workforce was out of a job at one time. Wages rose dramatically. Factory workers' average hourly pay more than doubled between 1945 and 1960. Moreover, consumer prices rose less than 2 percent per year. As a result, the percentage of Americans living in poverty fell from as much as 30 in the late 1940s to 18 in 1959.

The economy also gave Americans more leisure time. By the 1950s, the 40-hour workweek was commonplace in American factories. Many workers now looked forward to two- or three-week paid annual vacations. As life expectancy increased and the economy boomed, more and more Americans could expect to retire at age 65 and then live comfortably off their pensions and Social Security.

Workers' well-being produced labor peace, which in turn stimulated prosperity. After the contentious relations of the 1940s, workers and employers were more likely to resolve their differences without strikes and lockouts. When the relatively aggressive Congress of Industrial Organizations (CIO) merged with the American Federation of Labor (AFL) to become the gigantic AFL-CIO in 1955, the union movement seemed to become more bureaucratic and complacent. "American labor never had it so good," crowed a trade union leader. Workers and corporations alike had the means to live the good life.

The Suburban Dream

For growing numbers of people, the good life meant a house in the suburbs. Most Americans had never owned their own homes. Suburbs had been mainly for the well-to-do. But entrepreneurship, efficient construction methods, inexpensive land, and generous federal aid made possible a host of affordable-housing developments outside the nation's cities. Along with Gene Ferkauf and his family, much of America moved to the suburbs in the 1950s.

William J. Levitt's pioneering development, Levittown, illustrated how entrepreneurship, low-priced land, and new construction techniques fueled a suburban housing boom. Levitt came back from military service in World War II with an optimistic vision of the future. He wanted to make houses affordable for middle-class and working-class people. Drawing on his military experience and on the assembly-line techniques of automaker Henry Ford, he intended to build houses so efficiently that they could be sold at remarkably low prices. Levitt bought 1,000 acres of cheap farmland not far from a Korvettes on New York's Long Island. He put up simple houses, with prefabricated parts, no basements, and low price tags. The original Cape Cod–style house cost $7,990, an appealing price for young couples trying to finance their first home.

Like Korvettes, Levittown quickly became a huge success. Buyers signed 1,400 contracts for houses on a single day in 1949. The development grew to 17,500 dwellings housing 82,000 people. Levitt soon built more Levittowns, as did imitators all around the country.

The federal government helped develop the suburbs. To make home ownership more affordable, the government allowed buyers to deduct mortgage interest payments from their federal income taxes. Federal legislation also guaranteed loans to the millions of military veterans. To help make commuting practical, the National System of Defense Highways Act of 1956 encouraged the construction of freeways connecting cities and suburbs.

Under such favorable conditions, the United States quickly became a nation of suburban home owners. As the rate of home ownership increased 20 percent between 1945 and 1960, nearly one-third of Americans lived in places like Levittown. The suburban dream had become an everyday reality.

AMERICAN LANDSCAPE

>> Levittown, New York

For many Americans, the first Levittown epitomized the virtues and defects of suburbia, consumerism, and democracy in post–World War II America. The new community seemed to be a democratic triumph, a visual reminder of upward mobility and equality of condition. The male heads of Levittown households tended to be prosperous blue-collar workers, veterans of World War II reaching for middle-class status for their growing, baby boom families. As an observer noted, Levittown was a "one-class community." Most households had an annual income of about $3,500 to $4,000, just enough to afford a place in the suburb.

From another angle, Levittown seemed less democratic. The suburb was notable for who didn't live there. Amid all the young families, there were few teenagers or senior citizens. There were hardly any African Americans, either.

The homogeneity of Levittown was no accident. The developer, William Levitt, had planned it that way. Levittown's first four-room Cape Cod houses came in only five models that differed very little from each other. To

The Suburban Dream. A young family stands proudly in front of a typical house in 1950s Levittown.

observers, the houses and streets of the new development all appeared to be the same. In fact, William Levitt even admitted that he had once gotten lost in all the look-alike streets of his suburb. The uniform style and cost of the houses ensured that the new development would attract only one class of residents. So-called restrictive covenants—special clauses in housing deeds—ensured that only whites bought property in Levittown.

Levitt also tried to impose uniform behavior on his residents. Community rules forbade putting up fences or hanging out the wash on weekends. Some of the residents themselves promoted conformity in Levittown. They wrote the local newspaper to attack neighbors who broke the rules. A nonconformist could expect to be labeled a "commie" or a "Russkie."

In Levittown, as in the rest of America, there was a heavy emphasis on domesticity. The design of the community and its houses reflected the domestic values of the period. The small Cape Cod homes encouraged family "togetherness." With so little private space, family members congregated around the kitchen table or in front of the TV in the living room. The wives of Levittown were expected to spend weekdays doing domestic tasks at home, rather than working at a paying job. That was how Levitt could assume these women would not need to hang out laundry on the weekends. Because the kitchen was supposed to be the center of women's lives, that room was placed at the front of the Cape Cod houses in Levittown.

The design of Levittown also supported men's domestic role. Former apartment dwellers found they had to spend time at home mowing their new lawns. Moreover, Levittown had few traditionally masculine public places—bars, firehouses, ball fields, and the like. Instead, the community promoted family togetherness away from home with plenty of playgrounds and swimming pools for children and their parents. As the local property owners association concluded, "Levittown is a child-centered community."

Despite the power of conformity, Levittown also revealed the survival of individuality in America. In time, the suburb became less homogeneous. With each succeeding year, the Levitts offered houses with a bit more variety. In 1949, they replaced the Cape Cod model with new ranch-style houses. The following years saw new features, including carports. As the 1950s wore on, residents turned houses into expressions of their individual tastes. They built garages and patios. They added rooms, gardens, signposts, and distinctive paint jobs. Despite the rules, they put up fences. "The houses take on the personalities of their owners," wrote a suburban resident.

In this way, as in others, Levittown was a product of 1950s America. This pioneering suburb revealed the power of domesticity and conformity. Levittown also demonstrated both the limits of democracy and the persistence of individuality in the consumer society. ●

The Pursuit of Pleasure

The consumer society depended on Americans' eagerness to pursue pleasure. Businesses made sure that nothing would prevent Americans from buying goods and services. If their wages and salaries were not enough, consumers could borrow. Along with federally guaranteed mortgage loans, people could now get credit cards. In 1950, the Diners Club introduced the credit card for well-to-do New Yorkers. By the end of the decade, Sears Roebuck credit cards allowed more than 10 million Americans to spend borrowed money. In 1945, Americans owed only $5.7 billion for consumer goods other than houses. By 1960, they owed $56.1 billion.

In the 1950s, discount stores such as Korvettes made shopping seem simpler and more attractive, and so did another new creation, the shopping mall. In 1956, Southdale, the nation's first enclosed suburban shopping mall, opened outside Minneapolis, Minnesota. Consumers bought meals more easily, too. The first McDonald's fast-food restaurant opened in San Bernardino, California, in 1948. Taken over by businessman Ray Kroc, McDonald's began to grow into a national chain in the mid-1950s.

To get to McDonald's, the Southdale Mall, Korvettes, and Levittown, Americans needed cars. In the 1950s, automobiles reflected Americans' new sense of affluence and self-indulgence. Big, high-compression engines burning high-octane gasoline powered ever-bigger cars stuffed with new accessories—power steering, power brakes, power windows, and air-conditioning. Unlike the drab autos of the Great Depression, the new models featured "Passion Pink" and "Horizon Blue" interiors and two-tone and even three-tone exteriors studded with shiny chrome.

Automakers used that chrome to solve one of the main problems of a consumer society—getting people who already had plenty to want to buy even more. How could

Icons of the Consumer Society The first enclosed mall in the United States—Southdale, outside Minneapolis, Minnesota.

Detroit persuade Americans to trade in old cars that were running just fine and purchase new ones? The answer was what General Motors' chief designer called "dynamic obsolescence," the feeling that last year's model was somehow inadequate. So the automakers changed chrome, colors, and tail fins from year to year (see Table 27–1).

More than ever, automakers offered cars as a reflection of a driver's identity. The car of the 1950s clearly announced its owner's affluence. General Motors' line of cars rose up the socioeconomic ladder, from the ordinary Chevrolet, to the more prosperous Pontiac, Oldsmobile, and Buick, all the way up to the sumptuous success symbol, the Cadillac.

Automobiles also spoke to gender identities. Detroit designed the interior of cars to appeal to women. Inside, the autos of the 1950s seemed like living rooms. The exterior offered men power and sexuality. Automakers tried to make them feel like they were flying supersonic jets. While the back of a 1950s car looked like the winking afterburners of a jet, the front spoke to something else. The chrome protrusions on 1950s Cadillacs were known as "Dagmars," after the name of a large-breasted female television star. A car, as a Buick ad promised, "makes you feel like the man you are."

It was not remarkable that the chrome on a Cadillac would make Americans think of a television star. In the 1950s, television became a central part of American life. Technological advances made TV sets less expensive. As sales boomed, there were new opportunities for broadcasters. By 1950, the Federal Communications Commission (FCC) had licensed 104 TV stations, mostly in cities. By 1960, 90 percent of the nation's households had a television (see Table 27–2). In 15 years, TV had become a part of everyday life.

 Table 27–1 Automobiles and Highways, 1945–1960

Year	Factory Sales (in 1,000s)	Registrations (in 1,000s)	Miles of Highway Completed (in 1,000s)
1945	69.5	25,796.9	3,035
1946	2,148.6	28,217.0	5,057
1947	3,558.1	30,849.3	15,473
1948	3,909.2	33,355.2	21,725
1949	5,119.4	36,457.9	19,876
1950	6,665.8	40,339.0	19,876
1951	5,338.4	42,688.3	17,060
1952	4,320.7	43,823.0	22,147
1953	6,116.9	46,429.2	21,136
1954	5,558.8	48,468.4	20,548
1955	7,920.1	52,144.7	22,571
1956	5,816.1	54,210.9	23,609
1957	6,113.3	55,917.8	22,424
1958	4,257.8	56,890.5	28,137
1959*	5,591.2	59,453.9	32,633
1960	6,674.7	61,682.3	20,969

*Denotes first year for which figures include Alaska and Hawaii.

Source: *Historical Statistics of the United States, Millennial Online Edition* (Cambridge University Press, 2008), Table Df347–352 and Table Df213–217

From its early days, television reinforced the values of consumer society. Advertisements for consumer products paid for programming that focused mainly on pleasure and diversion. Nightly national news broadcasts lasted only 15 minutes. There were operas, documentaries, and live, original dramas in what some critics consider television's golden age, but most of the broadcast schedule was filled with variety shows, sports, westerns, and situation comedies. As television undermined the popularity of radio and movie theaters, the three major broadcasting companies quickly created TV networks and dominated the new industry.

American culture also became more open about sexuality. Dr. Alfred C. Kinsey of Indiana University commanded enormous public attention with two pioneering academic studies—*Sexual Behavior in the Human Male* (1948) and *Sexual Behavior in the Human Female* (1953). To his readers' surprise, Kinsey reported that Americans were more sexually active outside of marriage than had been thought. The Supreme Court contributed to sexual openness by overturning a ban on a film version of D. H. Lawrence's often erotic novel, *Lady Chatterley's Lover,* in 1959. The new candor about sexuality was epitomized by *Playboy* magazine, first published by Hugh Hefner in December 1953. Featuring pictures of bare-breasted women, *Playboy* presented sex as one part of a hedonistic consumer lifestyle complete with flashy cars, expensive stereos, and fine liquor.

Table 27–2 Television, 1941–1960

Year	Television Stations	Households with Television Sets (in 1,000s)
1941	2	—
1945	9	—
1950	104	3,875
1955	458	30,700
1960	579	45,750

Source: George Thomas Kurian, *Datapedia* (Lonham, MD: Bernan Press, 1994), pp. 299–300.

A Homogeneous Society?

The spread of consumerism reinforced a sense of sameness in America during the 1950s. It seemed as if the United States was becoming a homogeneous society whose members bought the same products, watched the same TV shows, worked for the same corporations, and dreamed the same dreams. Some observers worried that Americans had become conformists willing to sacrifice their individuality in order to be like one another. Declining class differences strengthened the feeling that people were becoming more alike, as did a rush to attend church and have children. Along with the renewed emphasis on religion and family, Americans faced pressure to conform to gender roles.

Nevertheless, the United States remained a heterogeneous society. While class and ethnic differences among whites decreased, race remained a powerful divider. Despite fears of conformity, the nation still encouraged difference and individuality.

The Discovery of Conformity

In the years after World War II, sociologists and other writers noticed a disturbing uniformity across American society. A variety of factors promoted homogeneity. During the frenzied search for domestic Communists, people did not want to risk accusations by appearing different or unusual. Moreover, as corporations merged and small businesses disappeared, Americans worked for the same giant companies. Levittown and the other new suburbs intensified the sense of homogeneity. In 1957, one writer described suburbanites as "people whose age, income, number of children, problems, habits, conversations, dress, possessions, perhaps even blood types are almost precisely like yours."

Americans, some observers believed, actually wanted to be like one another. In *The Lonely Crowd* (1950), sociologist David Riesman argued that instead of following their own internalized set of values, Americans adjusted their behavior to meet the expectations of the people around them. In *The Organization Man* (1956), William H. Whyte Jr. suggested that the conformist white-collar workers of big corporations were making the United States more like the totalitarian Soviet Union.

> Little boxes on the hillside
>
> Little boxes made of ticky tacky
>
> Little boxes on the hillside, little boxes all the same
>
> There's a green one and a pink one and a blue one and a yellow one
>
> And they're all made out of ticky tacky and they all look just the same.
>
> MALVINA REYNOLDS'S SONG ABOUT SUBURBIA, "LITTLE BOXES" (1962)

The Decline of Class and Ethnicity

The apparent decline of social class differences reinforced the sense of homogeneity. By the 1950s, the old upper class—the families of the Gilded Age industrialists and financiers—no longer single-handedly controlled and managed America's big businesses. Thanks to the Great Depression and income and inheritance taxes, the largest American fortunes were smaller than at the beginning of the twentieth century. As sociologist C. Wright Mills argued in *The Power Elite* (1956), an interlocking group of military, political, and economic managers ran the nation's institutions. But this rather drab group didn't have the bold swagger or the dynastic ambitions of the Gilded Age robber barons.

Meanwhile, the ranks of American farmers continued to decrease. As agriculture became more efficient and corporatized, the number of farms fell from more than 6 million in 1944 to just 3.7 million in 1959. Although manual and service workers remained the nation's largest occupational group, they seemed to be a less distinctive social class. In this era of labor peace, well-paid blue-collar workers appeared content with American society. Labor leaders endorsed consumerism and anti-Communism. Some observers argued that American workers had become essentially middle class in their buying habits and social values. The middle class itself was burgeoning. By 1960, the white-collar sector made up 40 percent of the workforce.

Even ethnic differences no longer seemed significant. Whites from different national and religious backgrounds mixed together in the new suburbs. The rate of intermarriage between ethnic groups increased. Anxious to prove their loyalty during the cold war, newer Americans were reluctant to emphasize their origins. Ethnicity had apparently disappeared in the national melting pot of the consumer society.

Many Americans, especially powerful ones, had long wanted to believe that the United States was a unified society devoted to middle-class values. In the 1950s, there was probably more basis for this belief than ever before.

The Resurgence of Religion and Family

A renewed emphasis on religion and family contributed to the homogeneity of American society. The nation's political leaders, fighting the cold war, encouraged religiosity. Freedom of religion, they insisted, differentiated the United States from allegedly godless Communist nations. To underscore the national commitment to religion, the federal government put the words "In God We Trust" on all its currency. Meanwhile, denominations adapted religion to the consumer society. Charismatic preachers such as Roman Catholic bishop Fulton J. Sheen and Protestant evangelist Billy Graham used television to bring religion to Americans in a new way.

Partly as a result, Americans became more involved with organized religion. In 1945, 45 percent of the nation belonged to one religious denomination or another; by 1960, that figure had reached 61 percent. Weekly church attendance increased, too, reaching a peak of 49 percent in 1958. By 1960, there were 64 million Protestants, 42 million Roman Catholics, and fewer than 6 million Jews (see Table 27–3).

American culture also celebrated what *McCall's* magazine christened family "togetherness." Manufacturers promoted TV viewing as a way of holding families together. Detroit presented its big automobiles as "family" cars.

"Togetherness" meant the nuclear family, with a mother, a father, and plenty of children. After decades of decline, the birthrate rose unexpectedly in the 1940s. Beginning in 1954, Americans had more than 4 million babies a year. Thanks to new drugs, nearly all these infants survived. Antibiotics reduced the risk of diphtheria, typhoid fever, influenza, and other infections. The Salk and Sabin vaccines virtually wiped out polio. As a result, the average number of children per family went from 2.4 in 1945 up to 3.2 in 1957, and the population grew by a record 29 million people to reach 179 million.

Like the religious revival, the "baby boom" of the 1940s and 1950s is somewhat difficult to explain. For more than 100 years, Americans had reduced the size of their families in order to ease burdens on mothers and family budgets and to provide more attention, education, and material resources to children. The economic prosperity of the cold war era may have persuaded couples that they could afford to have more children. Prosperity alone did not explain why American culture became so much more

 Table 27–3 Religious Revival and Baby Boom, 1945–1960

Year	Membership of Religious Bodies (in 1,000s)	Live Births (in 1,000s)
1945	71,700	2,858
1946	73,673	3,411
1947	77,386	3,817
1948	79,436	3,637
1949	81,862	3,649
1950	86,830	3,632
1951	88,673	3,823
1952	92,277	3,913
1953	94,843	3,965
1954	97,483	4,078
1955	100,163	4,104
1956	103,225	4,218
1957	104,190	4,308
1958[1]	109,558	4,255
1959[2]	112,227	4,245
1960	114,449	4,258

[1]Includes Alaska.
[2]Denotes first year for which figures include Alaska and Hawaii.
Source: George Thomas Kurian, *Datapedia* (Lanharn, MD: Bernan Press, 1994), pp. 37, 146.

child centered during these years. In his *Common Sense Book of Baby and Child Care* (1946), pediatrician Benjamin Spock urged parents to raise their children with less severity and more attention, warmth, tenderness, and fun. *Baby and Child Care* outsold every other book in the 1950s except, not surprisingly, the Bible.

Maintaining Gender Roles

As many social differences seemed to disappear, American culture nevertheless reemphasized the distinctions between the sexes. During the baby boom, women were expected to be helpful wives and devoted mothers. Men were encouraged to define themselves primarily as family providers.

The 1950s underscored the differences between genders in a variety of ways. Blue became the color for boys and pink the color for girls. Standards of beauty highlighted the physiological differences between women and men. The image of the slim girlish flapper of the 1920s had long since faded away; now more voluptuous actresses such as Dagmar, Jayne Mansfield, and Marilyn Monroe defined femininity.

Nevertheless, gender roles grew more similar during the 1950s. Society stressed a man's domestic role more than before. Experts urged husbands to do some of the housework and to spend more time nurturing their children, although few men lived up to the new ideal.

Female roles evolved more dramatically. To help pay for the consumer lifestyle, many wives had to leave the domestic sphere and find a job. In 1940, 15.6 percent of married women were in the paid workforce. By 1960, that percentage had nearly doubled to 31.0, and women made up more than one-third of the labor force. Gene Ferkauf's wife, while taking care of their child, helped publicize the first Korvettes store. Most women held clerical and sales positions. Thanks to the spread of labor-saving devices, fewer women took the traditional female job of domestic servant.

To a degree, American culture supported the expanding role of women outside the home. In the cold war competition with the Soviets, Americans celebrated the supposedly greater freedom and opportunity for women in the United States. Television featured situation comedies with feisty women, such as Lucy Ricardo in *I Love Lucy* and Alice Kramden in *The Honeymooners,* who got out of line and stood up to their husbands.

Nevertheless, women had little help coping with jobs and bigger families. Congress voted an income tax deduction for child-care costs in 1954, but little first-class child care was available. At work, women were expected to watch men get ahead of them. Women's income was only 60 percent of men's in 1960.

American culture strongly condemned women and men who strayed outside conventional gender norms. *Modern Woman: The Lost Sex,* a 1947 best seller by Marynia Farnham and Ferdinand Lundberg, censured feminism as the "deep illness" of "neurotically disturbed women" with "penis envy." Psychologists and other experts demonized lesbians and gay men. As police cracked down on gay bars, unmarried men risked accusations of homosexuality. The dominant culture expected males to be heterosexual husbands and fathers. Those roles, in turn, made men more likely to conform to social expectations. "Once a man has a wife and two young children," the writer Gore Vidal observed, "he will do what you tell him to."

Persisting Racial Differences

In spite of the many pressures toward conformity, American society remained heterogeneous. Although suburbanization broke down ethnic differences among whites, it intensified the racial divide between those whites and African Americans. The nation's suburbs were 95 percent white in 1950. As whites moved into Levittown and other suburbs, African Americans took their place in cities. By 1960, more than half of the black population lived in cities, where they were typically kept out of white neighborhoods.

Native Americans, living on their reservations, were also set apart. In 1953, Congress did try to "Americanize" the Indians by approving the termination of Indians' special legal status as sovereign groups. Termination meant the end of the traditional rights and reservations of more than 11,000 Native Americans. The new policy was intended to turn them into members of the consumer society.

It did not turn out that way. As reservations became counties in the 1950s and early 1960s, Indians had to sell valuable mineral rights and lands to pay taxes. Despite short-term profits, tribes faced poverty, unemployment, and social problems. Encouraged by the federal government's new Voluntary Relocation Program, about one in five Native Americans moved to the city. Some tribes, including the Catawba, the Coquille, the Klamath, and the Menominee, began long legal fights to reclaim tribal status. But whether they lived on reservations or on crowded city blocks, the nation's quarter of a million Indians remained largely separate and ignored.

The increasing migration of Puerto Ricans also reinforced the multiracial character of American society. Beginning in the 1940s, a large number of Puerto Ricans, who were U.S. citizens, left their island hoping for more economic opportunity on the mainland. By 1960, the Puerto Rican population in the mainland United States had reached 887,000, two-thirds of it concentrated in the East Harlem section of New York City. These new migrants found opportunities in the United States, but they also found separation and discrimination.

Mexican immigration further contributed to racial diversity. After 1945, increasing numbers of Mexicans left their impoverished homeland for the United States, particularly the booming Southwest. Congress, bowing to the needs of southwestern employers, continued the Bracero Program, the supposedly temporary wartime agreement that had brought hundreds of thousands of laborers, or *braceros,* to the United States. Meanwhile, illegal Mexican migration increased dramatically.

Like other Mexican migrants before them, the newly arrived met a mixed reception. As in the years before World War II, Mexicans already living in the United States worried that the new migrants would compete for jobs, drive down wages, and feed American prejudice. Many white Americans did indeed deride them as *mojados,* or "wetbacks," because so many had supposedly swum the Rio Grande River to get into the United States illegally. Mexican Americans feared that the federal government would use the provisions of the Internal Security Act of 1950 and the Immigration and Nationality Act of 1952 to deport Mexicans and thereby break up families. The government's intention became clear in 1954 with the launching of Operation Wetback, which sent more than 1 million immigrants back to Mexico in that year alone.

About 3.5 million Mexican Americans were living in the United States by 1960. The great majority worked for low wages in the cities and on the farms of the Southwest. Many continued to live in *barrios* apart from whites. Because of Operation Wetback and other instances of prejudice, some Mexican Americans became more vocal about

The Plight of Mexican "Wetbacks" Illegal immigrants taken off freight trains in Los Angeles, after two days without food or water, in 1953. They were probably sent back to Mexico.

their circumstances and their rights. The League of United Latin American Citizens denounced the impact of the Immigration and Nationality Act. More outspoken was the American GI Forum, an organization of Mexican American veterans formed when a funeral parlor would not bury a deceased comrade in Three Rivers, Texas, in 1949. Such assertiveness made it all the harder for white Americans to ignore the presence of Mexican Americans in the consumer society.

The experiences of Hispanics, Mexican Americans, Native Americans, and African Americans underscored the continuing importance of race in the United States. Mostly living apart, whites and nonwhites faced different conditions and different futures. Prosperity and consumerism did not change that reality. As long as race was such a potent factor in national life, the United States would never be a homogeneous society. In the 1960s, white Americans would have to face that fact.

The Survival of Diversity

Along with race, a variety of forces ensured the survival of diversity. Despite the appearance of suburbs and discount stores all over the country, the states continued to differ from each other. As in the past, internal migration and the expansion of national boundaries promoted diversity. During the 1950s, more than 1.6 million people, many of them retired, moved to Florida. As a result, the state increasingly played a distinctive national role as a center for retirement and entertainment.

Meanwhile, other Americans moved westward. During the 1950s, California gained more than 3 million new residents. California earned a reputation as the pioneer state of the consumer society, the home of the first Disneyland amusement park and the first McDonald's.

The admission of two new states highlighted the continuing diversity of the United States. In 1959, Alaska and Hawaii became, respectively, the 49th and 50th states in the Union. Racially and culturally diverse, climatically and topographically distinctive, they helped make certain that America was not simply a land of corporations and Levittowns.

Popular music also exemplified the continuing diversity of the United States. Big swing bands gave way to such popular singers as Frank Sinatra and Patti Page. Jazz split into different camps—traditional, mainstream, and modern. Country music, rooted in white rural culture, included cowboy songs, western swing, honky-tonk, bluegrass, and the smooth "Nashville sound." A range of African American musical forms, including blues, jazz, and vocal groups, became known as "rhythm and blues" (R & B). Gospel music thrilled white and African American audiences. Mexican Americans made Tejano music in Texas, and Cajuns played Cajun music in Louisiana, and German and Polish Americans danced to polka bands in Illinois and Wisconsin.

R & B collided with country music to create rock and roll. By 1952, white disc jockey Alan Freed was playing R & B on his radio show, "Moondog's Rock 'n' Roll Party," out of Cleveland. In 1954, a white country group, Bill Haley and the Comets, recorded the first rock-and-roll hit, "Rock Around the Clock." Rock and roll produced both African American and white heroes in its first years—Chuck Berry, Fats Domino, Jerry Lee Lewis, and Buddy Holly, among others.

The biggest rock-and-roll sensation of all was a young white singer and guitar player, Elvis Presley. Born in Mississippi and raised in near poverty in Memphis, Tennessee, Presley drew on a variety of musical genres to create a distinctive personal style in an age of supposed conformity. "Who do you sound like?" he was asked. "I don't sound like nobody," he said.

Because of Presley and other musicians, the sound of American popular music was anything but homogeneous. Because of the distinctiveness of Florida, California, Alaska, Hawaii, and other states, the United States was hardly monolithic. In these ways, at least, American society remained diverse after World War II.

The Eisenhower Era at Home and Abroad

Prosperity encouraged Americans to demand less from government in the 1950s. In a period of rapid social change and continuing international tensions, most people wanted reassurance rather than boldness from Washington. The politics of the decade were dominated by President Dwight D. Eisenhower, a moderate leader well suited to the times. His middle-of-the-road domestic program, "Modern Republicanism," appealed to a prosperous electorate wary of government innovation. But Eisenhower's anti-Communist foreign policy did little to diminish popular anxieties about the cold war in the short run and laid the groundwork for trouble in the Middle East and Southeast Asia in the long run.

"Ike" and 1950s America

Eisenhower, a charismatic military hero with a bright, infectious grin, would have been an ideal public figure in almost any era of American history, but the man known affectionately as "Ike" was especially suited to the 1950s. The last president born in the nineteenth century, he had successfully accommodated the major changes of the twentieth. Raised on the individualistic values of the rural Midwest, Eisenhower adopted the bureaucratic style of modern organizations. He succeeded in the military after World War I, not because he was a great fighter or strategist, but because he was a great manager. A believer in teamwork, Eisenhower was the quintessential "organization man." As a commander in

> **Would it not be better to compete in the relative merits of washing machines than in the strength of rockets? Is this the kind of competition you want?**
>
> VICE PRESIDENT RICHARD NIXON TO SOVIET PREMIER NIKITA KHRUSHCHEV, "Kitchen Debate," Moscow, July 24, 1959

Mamie and Dwight Eisenhower The first lady and the president were reassuring figures in the turbulent transition to the Cold War and consumerism in the 1950s.

World War II, Eisenhower worked to keep sometimes fractious allies together. After the war, he deepened his organizational experience as president of Columbia University and then as the first commander of the armed forces of NATO.

Just as he accommodated the rise of big organizations, Eisenhower accommodated the extension of the nation's commitment abroad. Ike had grown up among people who often feared American involvement in the world's problems. But his military career rested on his acceptance of an activist role for the United States around the world.

Eisenhower easily fit the dominant culture of the 1950s. He was an involved, loving husband and father. In a society zealously pursuing pleasures, he was famous for his many hours on the golf course. His wife, Mamie, eagerly wore the "New Look" fashions inspired by designer Christian Dior and avidly watched television soap operas.

Nominated for president by the Republicans in 1952, Eisenhower ran against Adlai Stevenson, the liberal Democratic governor of Illinois. Stevenson, witty and eloquent, was no match for Eisenhower. Running a moderate, conciliatory campaign, the former general avoided attacks on the New Deal and promised to work for an end to the Korean War. Meanwhile, his tough-talking running mate, Senator Richard Nixon of California, accused Stevenson of being soft on Communism. The Republican ticket won big with 55 percent of the popular vote and 442 electoral votes. The Republican Party took control of the White House and both houses of Congress for the first time in 20 years.

Modern Republicanism

Eisenhower advocated Modern Republicanism for the American political economy. This philosophy attempted to steer a middle course between traditional Republican conservatism and Democratic liberalism. With a conservative's faith in individual freedom, the president favored limited government and balanced budgets, but Eisenhower the organization man believed that Washington had an important role to play in protecting individuals. Eisenhower also recognized that most Americans did not want to give up such liberal programs as Social Security and farm subsidies.

Accordingly, the Eisenhower administration limited the reach of the government by decreasing regulation of business and cutting taxes for the wealthy. With the Submerged Lands Act of 1953, the federal government turned over offshore oil resources to the states for private exploitation. With the Atomic Energy Act of 1954, Washington allowed private firms to sell power produced by nuclear reactors.

Nevertheless, the Eisenhower administration did little to undermine the legacy of the New Deal and the Fair Deal. Eisenhower went along with increases in Social Security benefits and farm subsidies. Despite his belief in balanced budgets, his administration produced several budget deficits. Federal spending, including the highway program, helped fuel the consumer economy.

Modern Republicanism frustrated liberals as well as conservative "Old Guard" Republicans, but many Americans appreciated the president's moderation. "The public loves Ike," a journalist observed. "The less he does the more they love him."

Eisenhower's popularity was confirmed at the polls in 1956. In a repeat of 1952, Eisenhower and Nixon defeated Adlai Stevenson again. This time Eisenhower won an even bigger victory, with 58 percent of the popular vote and 457 electoral votes.

An Aggressive Cold War Strategy

Like President Harry Truman before him, Eisenhower was committed to opposing Communism at home and around the world. The president helped the crusade against alleged Communist subversives and tolerated its excesses. He refused to criticize the tactics of Senator Joseph R. McCarthy in public and declined to stop the execution of the convicted atomic spies, Julius and Ethel Rosenberg, in 1953. Eisenhower denied the security clearance that J. Robert Oppenheimer, the former director of the Manhattan Project, needed to continue work on the government's nuclear projects. Thousands of other alleged security risks also lost their federal jobs during the Eisenhower era.

While Truman had pledged only to contain further Communist expansion, Eisenhower and his advisers talked aggressively of rolling back Soviet power in Europe and freeing already "captive peoples" from Communism. Secretary of State John Foster Dulles threatened "instant, massive retaliation" with nuclear weapons in response to nuclear and even nonnuclear Soviet aggression. To support this threat, the U.S. military adopted the "New Look" strategy, named after Mamie Eisenhower's favorite fashions, that de-emphasized costly conventional armies and increased the nuclear arsenal with long-range bombers, missiles, and the first nuclear-powered submarines. Not surprisingly, the New Look stirred fears of nuclear war.

The president also used the CIA to counter Communism by stealthier means. At the president's direction, the CIA carried out secret activities once considered unacceptable: as a presidential commission observed, the cold war was "a game" with "no rules." At home, the agency explored the possible uses of lysergic acid diethylamide—the dangerous hallucinogenic drug known as LSD—by using it on hundreds of unwitting Americans. Some of them went mad and at least one killed himself. Abroad, the agency gave secret aid to pro-American regimes and ran secret programs against uncooperative governments.

In August 1953 a covert CIA operation, code-named Ajax, orchestrated a coup that removed Mohammad Mossadeq, the nationalist prime minister of oil-rich Iran. Eisenhower and Dulles feared that this "madman," who had nationalized Iran's oil fields, would shut out U.S. business and open the way for Communism and the Soviet Union. The young Iranian monarch, Shah Mohammad Reza Pahlavi, who had effectively ceded power to Mossadeq, now reclaimed it. The shah gratefully accepted $45 million in U.S. aid, turned his back on the Soviets, and made low-priced oil available to American companies.

The next year, PBSUCCESS, a secret CIA operation modeled on Ajax, overthrew another foreign leader. Eisenhower and Dulles worried that a "Communist infection" in the Central American nation of Guatemala could spread to the United States–controlled Panama Canal and farther north to Mexico. In fact, the Soviet Union had made no effort to help Guatemala's new president, Jacobo Arbenz Guzmán, who supported the redistribution of land and threatened the interests of a powerful

The "New Look" of Defense in the Eisenhower Era A ceremony honors the production of the 1,000th B–47 Stratojet, the long-range bomber capable of delivering nuclear weapons in an attack on the Soviet Union.

American corporation, United Fruit. In June, PBSUCCESS used misleading "disinformation," a small force of Guatemalan exiles, and CIA-piloted bombing raids to persuade Arbenz Guzmán to resign.

More openly, Eisenhower intensified efforts to shape perceptions of American culture and values abroad. In 1953, the administration gathered various information and propaganda efforts together in a new United States Information Agency (USIA), overseen by the State Department. Active in 76 countries by 1960, the agency published pamphlets, promoted the exchange of visitors with other nations, beamed the radio broadcasts of Voice of America around the world, and collaborated with the CIA on propaganda and psychological warfare. The growth of the USIA underscored that the cold war was a global struggle about culture and ideas as well as military power.

Avoiding War with the Communist Powers

Despite its tough talk, the Eisenhower administration tried to avoid direct confrontation with the two major Communist powers, the People's Republic of China and the Soviet Union. Eisenhower knew he had to end the Korean conflict. As he promised in his 1952 campaign, Eisenhower traveled to Korea to observe conditions firsthand and then pushed to end the military stalemate that ultimately killed 33,629 Americans. A cease-fire agreement in July 1953 left the United States without a victory. Although North and South Korea remained divided, the agreement ended a costly, difficult war. It was, Eisenhower declared, "an acceptable solution."

Ending an old war with one Communist power, the Eisenhower administration avoided a new conflict with the other. In October 1956, Hungarians, spurred on by American propaganda broadcasts, rose up against their pro-Soviet government. The Soviet Union sent troops to break the rebellion. Despite talk of "captive peoples" and "massive retaliation," the Eisenhower administration did not intervene to help the Hungarian rebels.

Fundamentally, Eisenhower would not break with Truman's policy of containment. Cautious about military confrontation with the Soviets and the Chinese, Eisenhower declined to unleash nuclear weapons that would "destroy civilization." Although he dispatched CIA agents to conduct covert operations, the president was more reluctant than Truman to send American soldiers into open battle.

At the same time, Eisenhower, like Truman, knew the cold war was an economic and political fight. The Eisenhower administration maintained foreign aid programs and fought a propaganda war with the Soviets. In front of a model American kitchen in Moscow in 1959, Vice President Richard Nixon and Soviet leader Nikita Khrushchev argued the merits of their two systems. Not surprisingly, Nixon turned this "Kitchen Debate" into a celebration of the prosperity and freedom of the consumer society.

AMERICA AND THE WORLD

>> Popular Music as a Cold War Weapon

By the 1950s, music, like other forms of popular entertainment, had long served as a vehicle for spreading American culture around the world. It was only natural, then, for the United States government to make popular music a weapon in the cold war struggle against Communism.

The State Department particularly used jazz, a uniquely American improvised music, to sell a democratic image of the United States. In 1955, Washington's worldwide radio service, the Voice of America, began broadcasting *Music U.S.A.*, hosted by Willis Conover. "Jazz is a cross between total discipline and anarchy," Conover explained. "The musicians agree on tempo, key and chord structure but beyond this everyone is free. . . . It's a musical reflection of America." Conover also believed that jazz, largely created by African Americans such as the trumpeter and singer Louis Armstrong and the composer and bandleader Duke Ellington, sent the true message of racial equality in the United States. "Jazz corrects the fiction that America is racist," Conover insisted.

Music U.S.A. became a remarkable hit. The show soon reached an audience of about 30 million people in 80 countries. "Conover's daily two-hour musical program has won the United States more friends than any other activity," declared an Egyptian weekly in 1959. Conover himself saw the show's popularity as a sign of the spread of American values. "[P]eople in other countries love jazz because they love freedom," he observed. "Jazz also helps them to believe that America is the kind of country that they want to believe it is."

Washington sent well-known jazz musicians on overseas concert tours sponsored by the president's Special International Program for Cultural Relations and overseen by the State Department. The most popular touring jazzman was Louis "Satchel Mouth" Armstrong, who became known as "Ambassador Satch." Beginning in 1956, the African American trumpeter and singer won over white audiences in Europe and black audiences in Africa. "I feel at home in Africa . . .," Armstrong proclaimed. "I'm African-descended down to the bone, and I dig the friendly ways these people go about things." "Through his superb jazz musicianship," a Kenyan newspaper wrote, "Satchmo has given expression to the often inarticulate feelings of his people, once oppressed, but now, although there are blots on the record, moving rapidly towards full and equal citizenship of the great country he represents."

Armstrong's message and music disturbed the Soviet Union. Concerned about the impact of jazz around the world, the Soviet leadership also worried that the music made its own young people rebellious back home. Soviet composers, visiting the United States in 1959, denounced Armstrong's music as "vulgar," "unnatural," and "a long way from good taste." When cheering throngs welcomed "this son of our African race" to the Congo in 1960, the Soviets charged that Ambassador Satch was only there to "distract" the African nation from the reality of white

continued

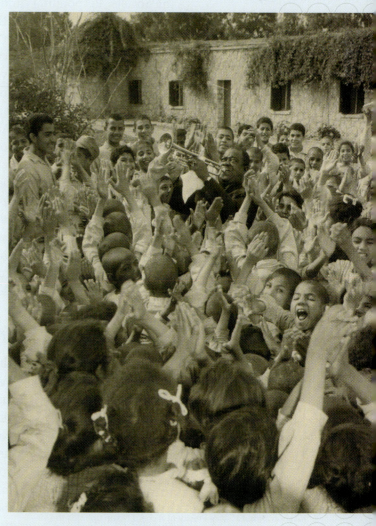

"Ambassador Satch" Jazz trumpeter Louis "Satchel Mouth" Armstrong represents the United States in Cairo, Egypt, 1961.

European power. The State Department happily declared Armstrong "the most effective unofficial goodwill ambassador this country had."

Armstrong usually played his propaganda role to perfection. He dodged difficult questions about the identity and the loyalty of black Americans. "Do you feel like an American in Africa or an African in America?" he was asked. "I just feel in place, man." But during the Little Rock crisis in 1957, this African American rebelled against his role. The trumpeter was outraged by white treatment of black students and by President Eisenhower's reluctance to intervene. "The way they are treating my people in the South, the government can go to hell," Armstrong fumed. "It's getting so bad, a colored man hasn't got any country." Armstrong refused to represent the United States on a scheduled trip to Moscow. "The people over there ask me what's wrong with my country," he demanded, "what am I supposed to say?"

As the State Department discovered, jazz, in the person of Louis Armstrong, really was the sound of democratic freedom, and therefore impossible to control completely. "[M]usic," Armstrong concluded, "is stronger than nations." ●

The Eisenhower administration took some modest steps to improve relations with the Soviets. Responding cautiously to the Soviets' interest in "peaceful coexistence," Eisenhower told the United Nations that he wanted to pursue disarmament and the peaceful use of atomic power. The president proposed an "Atoms for Peace" plan in which an international agency would experiment with nonmilitary uses for nuclear materials. The Soviets, however, dragged their feet.

The president made another attempt at improving relations with the Soviets. In July 1955, Eisenhower joined Khrushchev in Geneva, Switzerland, for the first meeting between an American president and a Soviet leader since World War II. Eisenhower's proposal for "Open Skies"—a plan to allow each side to fly over the other's territory—sparked some optimism about American-Soviet relations. That optimism ended by May 1960, when the Soviets shot down an American U-2 spy plane flying high over the USSR. After the Eisenhower administration denied the entire affair, Khrushchev triumphantly produced the captured pilot, Francis Gary Powers, along with pieces of the plane. The U.S.-Soviet rivalry would continue.

"Kitchen Debate" Vice President Richard Nixon upholds the virtues of the consumer society in an argument with Soviet leader Nikita Khrushchev at an exhibition in Moscow in 1959.

Crises in the Third World

Although Eisenhower worried most about the fate of Western Europe, his administration increasingly focused on the threat of Communist expansion in Africa, Asia, Latin America, and the Middle East. These relatively rural, unindustrialized regions, which made up the so-called third world, were enmeshed in the confrontation between the "first world" of industrialized, non-Communist nations and the "second world" of industrialized, Communist countries. Plagued by poverty, violence, and civil war, many third world societies struggled to break free from imperial domination.

Under Khrushchev, the Soviet Union tried to exploit third world discontent and conflict. Anxious to preserve America's influence and access to natural resources, the Eisenhower administration stood ready to counter Soviet moves with the techniques of containment—aid, trade, and alliances. Eisenhower offered increased foreign aid to third world countries and tried to stimulate trade with them. He also pursued closer military ties, including individual defense pacts with the Philippines, South Korea, and Taiwan.

Eisenhower's approach to the third world was sorely tested in Southeast Asia. When he took office in 1953, the United States continued to support France's war to hold on to Vietnam and its other Southeast Asian colonies. Despite vast American aid, the French could not defeat the nationalist forces of the Viet Minh, led by the Communist Ho Chi Minh and helped by the mainland Chinese. By 1954, the Viet Minh had surrounded French troops at Dien Bien Phu in northern Vietnam. Unwilling to fight another land war in Asia, Eisenhower refused to send American troops and rejected the use of atomic bombs. Without further help from the United States, France surrendered Dien Bien Phu in May.

In 1954, peace talks at Geneva produced an agreement to cut Vietnam, like Korea, in half. Ho Chi Minh's forces would stay north of the 17th parallel; his pro-French Vietnamese enemies would stay to the south of that line. The peace agreement stipulated that a popular election would unite the two halves of Vietnam in 1956. Certain that Ho Chi Minh and the Communists would win the election, the United States refused to sign the agreement. The president feared that a Communist takeover of Vietnam would deprive the West of raw materials and encourage the triumph of Communism elsewhere. Comparing the nations of Asia and the Pacific to "a row of dominoes," Eisenhower explained that the fall of the first domino—Vietnam—would lead to the fall of the rest, including Japan and Australia.

Instead, the Eisenhower administration worked to create an anti-Communist nation south of the 17th parallel. To protect South Vietnam, the United States joined with seven nations to create the Southeast Asia Treaty Organization (SEATO) in 1954 (see Map 27–1). To ensure South Vietnam's loyalty, the Eisenhower administration backed Ngo Dinh Diem, an anti-Communist who established a corrupt, repressive government. The United States sent military advisers and hundreds of millions of dollars to Diem.

By thwarting the Geneva Accords and establishing an unpopular regime in the South, Eisenhower ensured that Vietnam would be torn by civil war in the years to come. In the short run, however, Eisenhower had avoided war and seemingly stopped the Asian dominoes from falling.

Eisenhower soon confronted another crisis in the Middle East. Gamal Abdel Nasser, who had seized power in Egypt in 1954, emerged as a forceful spokesman for Arab nationalism and Middle Eastern unity. Fearing that Nasser would open the way for Soviet power in the Middle East, John Foster Dulles withdrew an offer to aid the Egyptians. Nasser struck back by taking over the British- and French-owned Suez Canal in 1956. In retaliation, Britain and France, with Israel's cooperation, moved against Nasser. As Israeli troops fought their way into Egypt in October, Britain and France stood ready to take back the Suez Canal. Eisenhower, fearing the invasion would give the Soviets an excuse to move into the Middle East, threatened the British, French, and Israelis—U.S. allies—with economic sanctions. They soon withdrew.

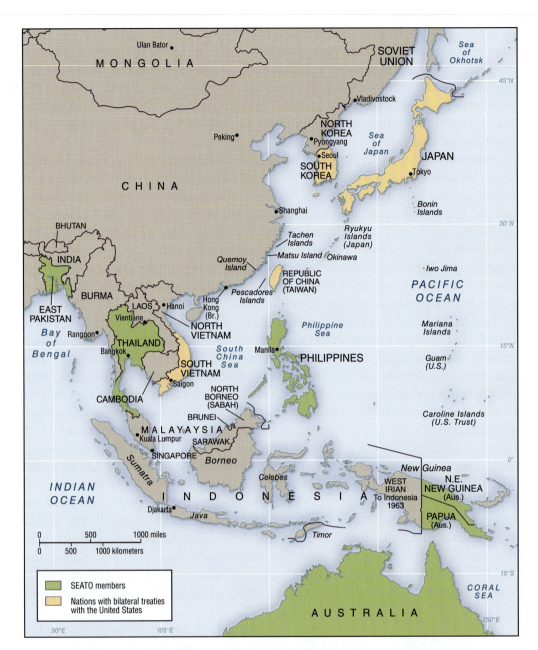

Map 27–1 America's Cold War Alliances in Asia Members of SEATO (the Southeast Asia Treaty Organization) and signers of other treaties with the United States. Through these pacts, the Eisenhower administration hoped to hold back the threat posed by Communist mainland China.

The Suez crisis was a pivotal moment. Before a joint session of Congress in January 1957, Eisenhower promised that the U.S. would intervene to protect any Middle Eastern nation threatened by "power-hungry Communists." The president implemented this "Eisenhower Doctrine" by sending troops to Lebanon the next year. In 1959, the United States joined with Turkey and Iran to create a Middle Eastern defense alliance known as the Central Treaty Organization (CENTO) for its geographical position between NATO and SEATO.

Eisenhower had helped to stabilize the Middle East and Southeast Asia temporarily, but he had also drawn the United States more deeply into these crisis-ridden regions and increased the odds of future trouble. In the 1960s and 1970s, the United States would have to deal with Eisenhower's legacy in the third world.

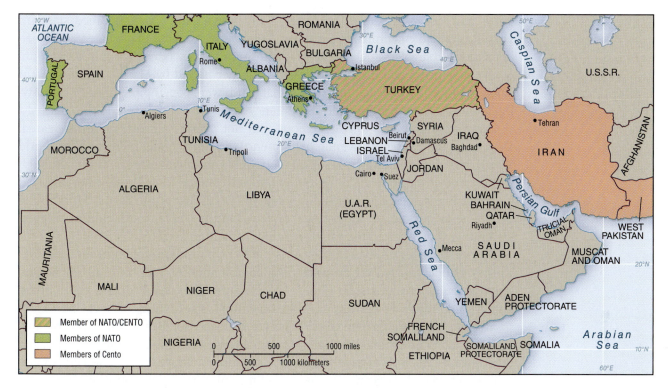

Map 27–2 America's Cold War Alliances in the Middle East Located between the members of NATO and SEATO, the members of CENTO (the Central Treaty Organization) joined with the United States to deter the threat of international Communism sponsored by the Soviet Union to the north.

Challenges to the Consumer Society

While the Eisenhower administration managed crises abroad, American society confronted challenges at home. In different ways, a rebellious youth culture, the alienated beat movement, a nascent environmental movement, and the divisive civil rights struggle upset the stability of the Eisenhower era. They demonstrated that consumerism had not solved all the nation's problems or won over all of its citizens.

Rebellious Youth

"Never in our 180-year history," declared *Collier's* magazine in 1957, "has the United States been so aware of—or confused about—its teenagers." In the 1950s, the emergence of a distinct youth culture, built around rock and roll, customized cars, comic books, and premarital sexual exploration, troubled many adults. The youth culture was the culmination of a trend apparent since the 1920s and 1930s. As more and more teenagers attended high school, they were segregated in their own world. Within that world, they developed their own values and practices. In the 1950s, young people claimed rock and roll as their own music. They wore blue jeans; they read comic

> America when will you be angelic?
> When will you take off your clothes?
> When will you look at yourself through the grave?
>
> ALLEN GINSBERG,
> "America" (1956)

books and teen magazines. Expressing their individuality, boys modified standard Detroit cars into customized "hot rods." Teens were attracted to alienated and rebellious movie characters such as the troubled son played by James Dean in *Rebel Without a Cause* (1955) and the motorcycle-gang leader played by Marlon Brando in *The Wild One* (1953). Worried adults feared that youth were copying the movies and defying authority. A wave of juvenile delinquency appeared to be sweeping the country.

Many young people were rebellious, but not nearly as much as adults feared. Despite all the publicity, juvenile delinquency did not actually increase after World War II and neither did rates of sexual intercourse among teenagers. Girls, although restless and attracted to such figures as James Dean and Elvis Presley, never played a very visible role in the male-dominated youth culture of the 1950s. Most young people never questioned the political system. On the whole, youth culture exaggerated rather than rejected the values of adult, consumer society.

The early career of Elvis Presley illustrated the boundaries of youthful rebellion. Presley's appeal rested on an unsettling combination of rock-and-roll music and open sexuality. Presley's style—his sensual mouth, disheveled "duck's ass" haircut, and gyrating hips—powerfully amplified the music's sexuality.

Despite his appeal to teenagers, Presley remained relentlessly polite and soft spoken, devoted to his parents and deferential to interviewers. Buying a pink Cadillac and other luxury cars, he was caught up in the consumer culture. Like Gene Ferkauf and millions of other Americans, Presley joined the suburban migration when he bought his house, Graceland, on the outskirts of Memphis, Tennessee. Presley was a new version of the old American dream of upward mobility.

Still, many adults blamed Presley, rock and roll, and mass media for the spread of dishonesty, violence, lust, and degeneration among young Americans. One popular television program showed Presley only from the waist up. To get rid of blue jeans and other teenage fashions, high schools imposed dress codes on their students. There was a crusade against comic books, teen magazines, and movies that were supposedly "brainwashing" teenagers. In well-publicized hearings from 1954 to 1956, the Senate's Subcommittee to Investigate Juvenile Delinquency focused attention on the corrupting power of the mass media.

A Less-than-rebellious Youth Culture As his father Vernon looks on, rock and roll star Elvis Presley kisses his mother, Gladys, on the eve of his induction into the army in 1958..

However, the campaign against youth culture had little impact in a society devoted to free speech and consumerism. Television networks, movie studios, record labels, and comic book companies did not stop catering to teenagers with spending money. Many adults found youth culture appealing.

The Beat Movement

A second group of rebels was smaller in numbers but a bit older and much more critical of American society. The beat movement, which emerged in New York City in the 1940s, expressed a sense of both alienation and hope. The term "beat" itself referred to a feeling of physical and emotional exhaustion and also to a state of transcendence, the "beatific."

Worn down by contemporary culture, the beats searched hopefully for a way to get beyond it.

Uptown at Columbia University and downtown in Greenwich Village, Allen Ginsberg, Jack Kerouac, John Clellon Holmes, William Burroughs, and others wanted, as one of them put it, "to emote, to soak up the world." Beats explored their sexuality, sampled mind-altering drugs, and investigated the spirituality of Eastern religions. In a society captivated by bright colors, "beatniks" declared their alienation from consumerism by wearing black. Kerouac captured the spirit of their odyssey in his novel about a trip across America, *On the Road* (1957). During the decade, San Francisco emerged as a center of beat culture. There, Allen Ginsberg published his long poem, "Howl" (1956), which evoked the beats' sense of alienation: "I saw the best minds of my generation destroyed by madness, starving hysterical naked, . . ."

Few in number, the beats sometimes seemed absurd, but their dark vision of America attracted a great deal of attention. The beat movement was a clear sign of budding dissatisfaction with consumer society, conventional sexual mores, and politics as usual.

The Rebirth of Environmentalism

A rebirth of environmental consciousness was one more indication of worry about consumerism. By the late 1950s, Americans were more concerned about the environment than at any time since the Progressive Era at the beginning of the twentieth century. The environmental threat was obvious in the cities. A well-publicized pall of smog seemed to hang perpetually over Los Angeles, so dependent on cars instead of subways and trains. Americans could no longer ignore the fact that their large, flashy automobiles, the symbol of the consumer society, were polluting the air.

The environmental threat was obvious in the countryside, too. Even as they moved into new suburban developments built on old farms, some Americans lamented the disappearance of undeveloped land. They began to criticize society's cavalier attitude toward the natural world. In the mid-1950s, environmentalists, led by the Sierra Club and the Wilderness Society, successfully blocked the construction of the Echo Park Dam in the upper basin of the Colorado River because the project would have inundated a national park, the Dinosaur National Monument. A new environmental movement, determined to protect wilderness lands from development, emerged from the battle.

The Struggle for Civil Rights

The African American struggle for civil rights also challenged the Eisenhower era. By the 1950s, segregation was under increasingly effective attack in the courts and on the streets. Focusing on public schools, the NAACP assaulted the discriminatory legacy of the Supreme Court's *Plessy v. Ferguson* ruling of 1896 (see Chapter 20). In 1951 the organization's special counsel, Thurgood Marshall, combined five school lawsuits, including African American welder Oliver Brown's challenge to the constitutionality of a Kansas state law that allowed cities to segregate their schools. Because of the law, Brown's eight-year-old daughter, Linda, had to ride a bus 21 blocks to a "colored only" school even though there was a "white only" school just three blocks from home. When the Brown case reached the Supreme Court in December 1952, Marshall attacked the *Plessy* argument that justified "separate but equal" facilities for whites and African Americans. As a result of segregation, Marshall maintained, Linda Brown and other African Americans received both an inferior education and a feeling of inferiority. He concluded that segregation violated the citizenship rights guaranteed by the Fourteenth Amendment.

In May 1954, the Court, led by new Chief Justice Earl Warren, handed down its ruling in *Brown v. Board of Education, Topeka, Kansas.* Overturning the *Plessy* decision, the justices ruled unanimously that public school segregation was unconstitutional under the Fourteenth Amendment. "Separate but equal has no place," Warren announced. African Americans and white liberals were jubilant. The ruling was, an African American newspaper exulted, "a second emancipation proclamation." Marshall himself foresaw the dismantling of school segregation before the end of the decade.

It did not work out that way. When the Supreme Court ruled on the enforcement of its decision in 1955, the justices turned to local school boards, dominated by whites, to carry out the integration of the schools. Federal district courts were to oversee the process of desegregation, which should occur with "all deliberate speed." In other words, school segregation had to end, but not right away.

Taking heart from this ruling, many whites refused to give up Jim Crow. For some white southerners, as one put it, a "reasonable time" for the end of segregation would be "one or two hundred years." In 1956, 101 congressmen signed a "Southern Manifesto" calling on their home states to reject the *Brown* ruling. Amid calls for massive resistance to desegregation, White Citizens' Councils formed in southern states to prevent schools from integrating. Some states passed laws intended to stop school integration. There was violence, too. In October 1955, white Mississippians killed Emmett Till, a 14-year-old black boy from Chicago, who had supposedly whistled at a white woman. Till was shot in the head, bludgeoned, and wired to a factory fan.

Map 27–3 African Americans Attending Schools with White Students in Southern and Border States, 1954
The small percentages indicate just how successfully segregation had separated the races before the Supreme Court ruled in *Brown v. Board of Education, Topeka, Kansas* in 1954.

African Americans, encouraged by the court's action, were ready to fight even harder against segregation. In Montgomery, Alabama, the NAACP wanted to test the state law dictating segregation on the city's buses. On December 1, 1955, Rosa Parks, a 42-year-old African American tailor's assistant and NAACP official "tired of giving in," boarded a bus to go home from work. Local custom required an African American to give up her seat to a white passenger and move to the back of the bus, but when the bus driver told her to move, Parks would not get up. As she said, "my feet hurt." More than that, she wanted to find out "once and for all what rights I had as a human being and a citizen." The angry driver thought she had none; he had Parks arrested.

Seizing on Parks's arrest, African American men and women began to boycott the city's bus system. Twenty-six-year-old Martin Luther King Jr., pastor of the Dexter Avenue Baptist Church, agreed to lead the boycott. The son of a noted Atlanta preacher, King was already developing a brilliant oratorical style and a philosophy of nonviolent protest against segregation.

The boycott met immediate resistance. The city outlawed carpools and indicted the leaders; African American homes and churches were bombed. In November 1956, however, the U.S. Supreme Court ruled Alabama's bus-segregation law unconstitutional. By then, the boycott had cost the bus company and downtown store owners dearly, and the white community had lost the will to resist. The city settled with the boycotters and agreed to integrate the buses. "We just rejoiced together," one of the boycotters remembered. "We had won self-respect."

Montgomery showed that a combination of local activism and federal intervention could overcome Jim Crow in southern communities. It established a charismatic new leader with a powerful message, and it soon brought forward a new civil rights organization, when King helped found the Southern Christian Leadership Conference. For one journalist, Montgomery "was the beginning of a flame that would go across America."

The flame did not travel easily. In 1957, the school board of Little Rock, Arkansas, accepted a federal court order to integrate the city's Central High School, but in September the state's segregationist governor, Orval Faubus, called out National Guard troops to stop black students from enrolling. Even after meeting with President Eisenhower, Faubus would not order the troops away from the school. When he finally did remove the soldiers, an angry mob of whites made it impossible for the African American students to stay. "Two, four, six, eight," cried the mob, "we ain't going to integrate."

Little Rock created a dilemma for the president. Not a believer in racial equality, Eisenhower wanted to avoid the divisive issue of civil rights. He privately opposed the *Brown* ruling and gave only mild support to the weak Civil Rights Act of 1957, which offered no real protection for African Americans' right to vote.

An Unlikely Criminal Arrested for refusing to give up her bus seat to a white passenger, Rosa Parks poses for her official "mug shot" in December 1955.

The president knew, however, that his government was being defied in Little Rock and humiliated around the world. The Soviets, he complained, were "gloating over this incident and using it everywhere to misrepresent our whole nation." So Eisenhower sent in troops of the crack 101st Airborne of the U.S. Army. With that protection, nine African American students went to Central High.

Like the Montgomery bus boycott, Little Rock demonstrated that a combination of federal action, however reluctant, and African American courage could triumph over "massive resistance." The Central High crisis showed, too, how the cold war helped tip the balance against segregation. Competing with the Soviets for support from the multiracial third world, no president could afford the embarrassment of racial inequality at home. Segregation and discrimination would continue to upset the stability of Eisenhower's America. It was, the president concluded, "troublesome beyond imagination."

An Uneasy Mood

Little Rock, Arkansas, September 1957 African American student Elizabeth Eckford braves a hostile crowd of white students to integrate Central High School, September 6, 1957.

Youth culture, the beat movement, the environmental movement, and the civil rights struggle contributed to an uneasy mood in America by the end of the 1950s. Even people who did not share the beats' values worried that the consumer society was flawed. Some intellectuals believed that "softheaded high living" had left the nation "cultureless." For the critic Lewis Mumford, modern automobiles were "fantastic and insolent chariots" and suburbs were "a low-grade uniform environment from which escape is impossible." Consumerism itself could seem like a trap. In his best seller *The Hidden Persuaders* (1957), Vance Packard played on the fears that advertisers were manipulating American consumers.

Americans were troubled, too, by signs of corruption in the consumer society. In 1958, they learned that record companies had paid Alan Freed and other disc jockeys to play particular records on the radio. The same year, Americans were shocked by revelations that contestants on popular TV quiz shows had secretly been given the answers to questions in advance.

While Americans worried about whether the consumer society was corrupt, they wondered whether it could meet the challenge of the cold war. In October 1957, the Soviet Union sent *Sputnik,* the world's first satellite, into orbit, setting off a wave of fear in the United States. If the Soviets could send up a satellite, they could be ahead in nuclear weapons and economic growth too. Americans felt suddenly more vulnerable.

Sputnik intensified concerns about the quality of American education. A diverse and growing student population, along with rising parental demands, had strained the nation's schools. Now Americans worried that the schools were not preparing children to compete with the Soviets in science and technology. In 1958, Congress, previously reluctant to provide aid to schools, passed the National Defense Education Act. To win what Senator Lyndon Johnson called the "battle of brainpower," this wide-ranging measure promoted instruction in science, math, and foreign languages, supported construction of new schools, and offered loans and fellowships to students.

Sputnik forced Washington to accelerate the space program. The first U.S. satellite launch collapsed in flames—*Flopnik,* the world's press called it. At the end of January 1958 the government successfully launched its first satellite, *Explorer I.* Later that year, Congress created the National Aeronautics and Space Administration (NASA) to coordinate space exploration. These initiatives did not wipe away fears about the fate of a society caught up in consumerism and the cold war, however. "What we are really worried about," one magazine emphasized, "is that the whole kit and caboodle of our American way of life—missiles and toasters, our freedoms, fun, and foolishness—is about to go down the drain."

Eisenhower did little to change the national mood. Slowed by poor health, the president now seemed old and out of ideas. In 1960, he even had to create a Commission on National Goals to help figure out what the country should do. A few days before the end of his presidency in January 1961, Eisenhower fed the uncertain mood with a somber warning in his farewell address. Noting that cold war spending had built up the military and the defense industry, he cautioned against allowing this "military-industrial complex" to gain too much power. "We must never

"The Helicopter Era" Cartoonist Herblock lampoons President Dwight Eisenhower's apparent lack of involvement in the nation's problems.

let the weight of this combination endanger our liberties or democratic processes," Eisenhower cautioned. It was a stunning admission that the cold war might destroy rather than save democracy in America.

Eisenhower's difficulties were a sign of new stresses on American society. The great majority of Americans were not about to give up the benefits of the prosperous consumer economy, but many people worried whether consumerism and Modern Republicanism were enough to meet the challenges of the cold war world.

Conclusion

Along with the cold war, the triumph of consumerism dramatically affected the United States in the 1950s. The booming consumer economy gave Gene Ferkauf and other Americans a new sense of security and affluence during the unsettling confrontation with Communism. Breaking with the past, they moved to the suburbs, had record numbers of children, bought televisions at E. J. Korvettes, and defined life as the pursuit of material pleasures. Consumerism helped promote homogeneity and conformity in American society and spurred the victory of Dwight Eisenhower and his moderate approach to government. For a moment, perhaps, it seemed as if America had achieved stability and harmony in a dangerous cold war world, but that feeling did not last. At the close of the 1950s, many Americans wanted more for themselves and their country. They questioned whether the consumer society could provide prosperity, democracy, and security for all its citizens. The next decade would give them an unsettling answer.

Further Readings

Stephen E. Ambrose, *Eisenhower: Soldier and President* (2007). Readable biography.

David L. Anderson, *Trapped by Success: The Eisenhower Administration and Vietnam, 1953–1961* (1993). Examines the American decision to support South Vietnam after the French withdrawal.

Michael T. Bertrand, *Race, Rock, and Elvis* (2000). The impact of Elvis Presley on southern race relations.

Lizabeth Cohen, *A Consumers' Republic: The Politics of Mass Consumption in Postwar America* (2003). Connects consumerism to broader political trends.

Karal Ann Marling, *As Seen on TV: The Visual Culture of Everyday Life in the 1950s* (1996). Engaging studies of consumer culture.

Joanne Meyerowitz, ed., *Not June Cleaver: Women and Gender in Postwar America, 1945–1960* (1994). An important set of revisionist essays on women after World War II.

Adam Rome, *The Bulldozer in the Countryside: Suburban Sprawl and the Rise of American Environmentalism* (2001). Revealing study of the emergence of environmental consciousness.

Kathryn C. Statler and Andrew L. Johns, eds., *The Eisenhower Administration, the Third World, and the Globalization of the Cold War* (2006). Useful range of essays on key aspects of foreign policy.

Who, What?

William J. Levitt 895
Alfred Kinsey 899
Dwight Eisenhower 905
Richard Nixon 906

John Foster Dulles 907
Martin Luther King Jr. 917
Rosa Parks 917
Dynamic obsolescence 898

Modern Republicanism 906
Massive retaliation 907
Domino theory 911

Review Questions

1. How did the consumer society of the 1950s differ from the modern culture of the 1920s?

>> Timeline >>

▼ **1947**
Levittown suburban development
Announcement of Truman Doctrine

▼ **1948**
First McDonald's fast-food restaurant
Alfred Kinsey, *Sexual Behavior in the Human Male*

▼ **1950**
Diners Club credit card

▼ **1951**
UNIVAC 1 computer

▼ **1952**
Dwight D. Eisenhower elected president

▼ **1953**
First suburban E. J. Korvettes store
Korean cease-fire

▼ **1954**
"Baby boom" birthrate over 4 million per year
Supreme Court school desegregation decision, *Brown v. Board of Education, Topeka, Kansas*
Army-McCarthy hearings
Creation of divided Vietnam in Geneva peace talks

▼ **1955**
Formation of AFL-CIO

2. Compare and contrast Modern Republicanism with the New Era and other Republican domestic policy programs of the 1920s to 1940s. Was Modern Republicanism a break with the party's past?

3. Why did the civil rights movement make progress in the 1950s?

4. What was Eisenhower and Dulles's strategy for fighting the cold war? Was it successful?

5. Why did social-class differences decrease after World War II? Did class still matter?

6. On balance, did the domestic and international events of the 1950s leave Americans more or less well-off than before? Did the decade make American democracy stronger?

Websites

The Digital Documents and Photographs Project of the Dwight D. Eisenhower Presidential Library & Museum (http://www.eisenhower.archives.gov/index.html) has digitized many documents and photographs dealing with key issues of Eisenhower's administration.

The Digital Library of Georgia (http://dlg.galileo.usg.edu/?Welcome), with plenty of civil rights materials, cartoons, photographs, and other items from the 1950s, is a particularly good example of the digital resources of state libraries and historical societies.

The Literature & Culture of the American 1950s, University of Pennsylvania (http://www.writing.upenn.edu/~afilreis/50s/home.html), has a broad, idiosyncratic collection of texts.

The Prelinger Archives (http://www.archive.org/details/prelinger) is a treasure trove of newsreels, commercials, and other films from the 1950s and other decades.

Television News of the Civil Rights Era, 1950–1970, University of Virginia (http://www.vcdh.virginia.edu/civilrightstv/), offers streaming video footage of speeches, interviews, Klan rallies, desegregation, and other events, mainly in Virginia.

For further review materials and resource information, please visit www.oup.com/us/ofthepeople

▼ **1955–56**
Montgomery, Alabama, bus boycott

▼ **1956**
National System of Defense Highways Act
William H. Whyte Jr., *The Organization Man*
Suez crisis
Reelection of President Eisenhower

▼ **1957**
Eisenhower Doctrine
School desegregation crisis, Little Rock, Arkansas

Jack Kerouac, *On the Road*
Soviet *Sputnik* satellite launch

▼ **1958**
National Defense Education Act
TV quiz show scandals

▼ **1959**
Alaska and Hawaii statehood
Nixon-Khrushchev "Kitchen Debate" in Moscow

▼ **1960**
President Eisenhower's Commission on National Goals
Soviet downing of U.S. U-2 spy plane
John F. Kennedy elected president

▼ **1961**
Eisenhower's farewell address on "military-industrial complex"

▼ **1965**
U.S. escalation of Vietnam War

Common Threads

>> How did the prosperity of the 1950s shape the politics of the 1960s?

>> What was the impact of the civil rights movement on other groups?

>> How did the new liberalism, the new conservatism, and the New Left define democracy?

>> How did anti-Communism shape U.S. foreign policy?

>> How would desires for rights and worries about limited resources continue to shape American society beyond the 1960s?

The Rise and Fall of the New Liberalism 1960–1968

>> Lt. Fred Downs

On the night of January 10, 1968, Second Lieutenant Fred Downs of the U.S. Army looked up at the stars over the coast of South Vietnam. Only 23, he was thousands of miles from the Indiana farm where he had grown up. His job now was to lead a platoon of American soldiers in the war to protect anti-Communist South Vietnam from Viet Cong insurgents and the North Vietnamese army. Downs faced his duty with absolute confidence. "I knew we would never be beaten," he declared.

Still, the months in Vietnam had tested Downs severely. The hot sun "cooked" him by day, the rain drenched him by night, and leeches sucked his blood. He worried about stepping on land mines and booby traps. He worried whether he could trust the South Vietnamese. He worried whether his country was fighting the war the right way. Too often, the Americans' advanced weapons didn't work: frighteningly, his M16 rifle jammed in the middle of a fight. Downs was wounded four times, but he put aside his worries and kept fighting.

Much of the time, Lt. Downs and his men went out hunting for the enemy on "search and destroy" missions. To his frustration, the Viet Cong and the North Vietnamese were hard to find. When he did get close to them, the result was a "deadly game of hide and seek." Downs shot and killed Viet Cong and North Vietnamese soldiers with his rifle. He stabbed a soldier to death in the throat with a bayonet. He killed women. He watched his own men die.

Despite all his experiences, Downs never lost his confidence. "My men thought I was invulnerable," he reported. "I did too." On the night of January 10 he saw "no clouds on my horizon." "Nothing would happen to me," he believed.

Fred Downs's story mirrored the experience of his country in the 1960s. With growing confidence in its wealth, power, and wisdom, the United States cast aside the cautious politics of the 1950s and began bold new projects at home and abroad. Across the political spectrum, Americans offered new solutions for the problems of consumer society, civil rights, and the cold war. Increasingly the nation turned to a vigorous liberalism that pledged to confront Communism abroad and reform life at home. To save South Vietnam, the federal government sent Lt. Downs and hundreds of thousands of other soldiers around the world. To create a "Great Society" in the United States, the government tried to wipe out poverty, heal race relations, protect consumers and the environment, and improve education and health care.

By 1968, these efforts had torn the nation apart. As the 1960s ended, the confidence that sustained Fred Downs and his country would be gone. ●

New Ideas, New Leaders

The popular discontents at the close of the 1950s created an opportunity for new ideas and new leaders in the 1960s. Buoyed by the nation's power and prosperity, Americans faced the new decade with a sense of both urgency and optimism. From right to left, activists, intellectuals, and politicians offered conflicting solutions for America's domestic and international problems.

> As a **social system** we seek the establishment of a democracy of individual participation, governed by two central aims: that the individual share in those social decisions determining the quality and direction of his life; that society be organized to encourage independence in men and provide the media for their common participation.
>
> THE PORT HURON STATEMENT, 1962

Grassroots Activism for Civil Rights

By 1960, a new generation of African Americans was impatient with the slow, "deliberate speed" of the desegregation ordered by the Supreme Court in *Brown v. Board of Education* (see Chapter 27). Young blacks were ready to go beyond court cases and boycotts and try new tactics. In 1960, grassroots activists, committed to peaceful civil disobedience, spurred a wave of sit-ins and the formation of a new civil rights organization.

The sit-ins began in Greensboro, North Carolina. On February 1, four black male students from North Carolina Agricultural and Technical College politely insisted on being served at the whites-only lunch counter of the local Woolworth store. When the white waitress refused their order, the students, who would become known as the Greensboro Four, stayed all afternoon. Returning the next day with about thirty male and female colleagues, the four were again denied service. Soon hundreds of African American students from North Carolina A & T and other campuses, along with some white students, were besieging lunch counters. Under pressure, Woolworth and other large stores allowed their lunch counters to serve African Americans. "I felt," concluded Franklin McCain, one of the Greensboro Four, "as though I had gained my manhood."

The new tactic spread quickly across the South and North. There were wade-ins at whites-only beaches, kneel-ins at whites-only churches, and even paint-ins at whites-only art galleries. The demonstrations forced reluctant whites to open up lunch counters and other facilities to black patrons. The demonstrations also helped produce a new organization, the Student Nonviolent Coordinating Committee (SNCC). The SNCC (pronounced "Snick") brought together white and black young people, influenced by "Judaic-Christian traditions" and eager to create "a social order permeated by love."

Energizing the civil rights movements, the sit-ins demonstrated that ordinary people could successfully confront the powerful. This example of grassroots activism inspired Americans to confront other problems as well.

The Greensboro Sit-Ins, February 2, 1960 African American college students at the whites-only lunch counter of Woolworth on the second day of protest in Greensboro, North Carolina. The first two students from the left, Joseph McNeill and Franklin McCain, had helped start the sit-ins the day before.

The New Liberalism

Out of power during the 1950s, liberal intellectuals and politicians, mostly Democrats, had been forced to reconsider their ideas and plans. By the 1960s, the liberals were offering a fresh agenda that responded to the civil rights movement, consumerism, and the cold war confrontation with Communism.

A powerful faith in economic growth drove the new liberalism. To meet its domestic and international challenges, the United States, liberals believed, had to expand its economy more rapidly. As one liberal economist observed, growth would provide "the resources needed to achieve great societies at home and grand designs abroad." By manipulating its budget, the federal government could keep the economy growing. The right amount of taxes and expenditures would ensure full employment, strong consumer demand, and a rising gross national product.

Growth alone would not make America great, the liberals cautioned. A society devoted mainly to piling up personal wealth and spending it on consumer goods was fundamentally flawed. Economic growth had to be used to create a better, more satisfying life for all Americans. Because the private sector could not solve pressing national problems, the federal government had to step in to deal actively with poverty, racial inequality, pollution, housing, education, world Communism, and other problems.

Like the liberals of the 1930s and 1940s (see Chapter 24), 1960s liberals believed in employing government to correct problems created or ignored by the private sector. Nevertheless, the new liberalism differed from the old in important ways. New Dealers had worried most of all about restoring prosperity in the Great Depression; the new liberals almost took prosperity for granted. They were sure that the economy could pay for a host of reforms. The old liberals had feared that big business and class conflict posed dangers for the United States. Their successors generally saw racial divisions as the country's greatest domestic problem.

The New Conservatism

Conservatives had been out of power even longer than the liberals. In the 1930s, Herbert Hoover's failure to halt the Great Depression had discredited the conservative faith in minimalist government; then Hitler's aggression had undercut the conservative belief in isolationism. In 1950, critic Lionel Trilling could declare that America had no conservative ideas, only a liberal intellectual tradition.

By then, conservative ideas had already begun a quiet resurgence. In 1951, conservative intellectual William F. Buckley's book *God and Man at Yale* attacked his alma mater for its liberalism and denial of individualism. Two years later, theorist Russell Kirk published *The Conservative Mind* to prove that there was in fact a conservative tradition in America. In 1955, Buckley and Kirk founded the magazine *National Review* to serve as a forum for conservative ideas, including the rejection of isolationism in favor of staunch anti-Communism.

Conservatives soon had a new political hero in outspoken Senator Barry Goldwater of Arizona. With a western belief in individual freedom and fear of federal power, Goldwater was a blunt opponent of New Deal liberalism. A major general in the air force reserve, he was also a staunch advocate of a more aggressive stance toward Communism.

By 1960, the growing conservative movement had its own younger generation of activists. That year, the Young Americans for Freedom gathered at Buckley's estate in Sharon, Connecticut, to adopt a manifesto. The Sharon Statement called for government to protect individual liberty by preserving economic freedom and maintaining a strong national defense.

The New Left

At the opposite end of the political spectrum, another young group, inspired by civil rights activism and troubled by student life on campus, rejected both conservatism and liberalism. By the early 1960s many students felt confined and oppressed in overcrowded and impersonal colleges and universities. These schools ordered students' lives through parietal rules that governed eating in dining halls, drinking alcohol, keeping cars on campus, and socializing in dorm rooms. Female students were subject to particularly strict rules, including curfews.

Conservative Hero Senator Barry Goldwater Campaigns for President, 1964 "Y.A.F." stands for Young Americans for Freedom, the collegiate activists who helped advance the conservative agenda in the 1960s.

Some of these youth created the New Left, a radical movement that attempted to build a more democratic nation. The key organization of the New Left was Students for a Democratic Society (SDS), which emerged in 1960 to produce "radical alternatives to the inadequate society of today." During its national convention at Port Huron, Michigan, in 1962, SDS approved an "Agenda for a New Generation" that laid out its developing vision. An answer to the Sharon Statement, the Port Huron Statement argued that American society denied people real choice and real power in their lives. The answer, SDS claimed, was "participatory democracy." The members of SDS did not believe that liberalism would promote real democracy in America. SDS did not expect much help from the old left of socialists and Communists, with their Marxist faith in the revolutionary power of the working class. Instead, the Port Huron Statement looked to students to lead the way by fighting for control of their schools. The message began to resonate: SDS membership rose from 2,500 to 10,000 in late 1965.

The Presidential Election of 1960

As so often in American history, new ideas didn't immediately transform mainstream politics. Fought out in the political center, the presidential election of 1960 offered a choice between a vaguely liberal Democratic future and a moderate Republican status quo. The Democratic nominee, Senator John F. Kennedy of Massachusetts, was open to the liberals' agenda and shared their optimism. Only 42 when he announced his candidacy, Kennedy was youthful, energetic, and charismatic. Although he had compiled an undistinguished record in Congress, he promoted a sense of expectation. The candidate exuded, said one of his speechwriters, "the promise, almost limitless in dimensions, of enormous possibilities yet to come."

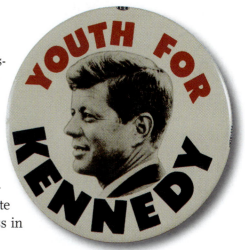

The ideas of the New Left resonated throughout the 1960s. Here a crowd estimated at 3,500 gathers outside an administration building at the University of California, Berkeley for a protest sponsored by the Free Speech Movement, led by Mario Savio (center), January 1965.

Kennedy gave voice to that promise during the campaign. Americans, he explained, stood "on the edge of a New Frontier—the frontier of the 1960s—a frontier of unknown opportunities and paths, a frontier of unfulfilled hopes and threats." The United States needed to foster economic growth, rebuild slums, end poverty, improve education for the young, and enhance retirement for the old.

In contrast, Kennedy's Republican opponent, Vice President Richard Nixon of California, represented the cautious Eisenhower administration that favored balanced budgets, limited government, and qualified acceptance of New Deal programs. Nixon embraced neither the bold programs and dynamic economic growth of the new liberalism nor the soaring individualism and strident anti-Communism of the new conservatives.

Despite Kennedy's stirring rhetoric and apparent triumph in televised debates, the election was the closest in history. Kennedy managed to keep much of the Democratic New Deal coalition of liberals, workers, and African Americans together, but he won by less than 120,000 votes (see Map 28–1). However narrowly, the voters had turned to a Democrat, influenced by liberal ideas, who was eager to explore the New Frontier.

Candidate (Party)	Electoral Vote (%)	Popular Vote (%)
Kennedy (Democratic)	303 (56%)	34,226,731 (49.7%)
Nixon (Republican)	219 (41%)	34,108,157 (49.6%)
Minor parties	15 (3%)*	501,643 (0.7%)

*15 electoral votes went to segregationist Democrat Harry F. Byrd

Map 28–1   The Presidential Election, 1960 Democrat John F. Kennedy's clear margin in the electoral vote belies just how narrowly he outpolled Republican Richard M. Nixon in the popular vote.

The New Frontier

Style and Substance

From the first moments of his presidency, Kennedy voiced the confident liberal faith in America's unlimited power and responsibility. "Let every nation know," he declared in his inaugural address in January 1961, "that we shall pay any price, bear any burden, meet any hardship, support any friend, oppose any foe to assure the survival and the success of liberty. This much we pledge—and more." Kennedy's extravagant promise perfectly captured the optimistic spirit of the early 1960s.

So did the president's space program. The exploration of space, the ultimate frontier, seemed like an ideal occupation for confident Americans in the 1960s. Moreover, the space race allowed Kennedy to reject cautious Eisenhower policies and confront the Soviet challenge. In April 1961 the Soviet Union sent up the first astronaut to orbit Earth. The next month, NASA managed only to launch astronaut Alan Shepard for a brief, suborbital flight. Once again Americans feared "that the wave of the future is Russian."

> The 1930s taught us a clear lesson: aggressive conduct, if allowed to go unchecked and unchallenged, ultimately leads to war. This nation is opposed to war. . . . We will not prematurely or unnecessarily risk the costs of worldwide nuclear war in which even the fruits of victory would be ashes in our mouth; but neither will we shrink from that risk at any time it must be faced.
>
> JOHN F. KENNEDY,
> Address on the Cuban Missile Crisis, October 22, 1962

The Kennedy administration responded with dramatic rhetoric and the abundant resources of the growth economy. Insistent on "beating the Soviets," the president boldly pledged to land "a man on the moon before the decade is out." Apollo, the moon project, got under way with 60,000 workers and billions of dollars. Meanwhile, in February 1962 astronaut John Glenn became the first American to orbit Earth. That year the United States launched Telstar, the first sophisticated communications satellite. In all, the space program mixed practical achievements such as Telstar with less practical, more symbolic gestures such as manned space flights.

That mixture of style and substance reflected the Kennedy administration as a whole. The president maintained a dynamic, energetic image, but his administration, hampered by a weak electoral mandate, did not venture too far out onto the liberal New Frontier.

For liberals, the persistence of poverty amid prosperity stood as a chief failure of the consumer society and an embarrassment for the United States around the world. Liberals argued that the poor needed help from the federal government to become productive workers and contribute to economic growth. Increasing the productivity of the poor was not a simple matter, however. Liberals contended that the battle against poverty should include improved housing, education, health, and job opportunities, as well as job training.

Kennedy supported some modest antipoverty measures. In 1961 he signed into law the Area Redevelopment Act to help revive depressed areas. He also signed the

Omnibus Housing Act to clear slum housing and bring urban renewal to inner cities. But these measures were not enough to wipe out poverty.

Civil Rights

Grassroots activism for civil rights posed a critical challenge for the Kennedy administration. In one place after another, attempts to break down segregation and promote African American voting met with resistance.

After the Supreme Court outlawed the segregation of interstate bus terminals, a small group of African American and white "Freedom Riders" traveled south on buses to test the decision in the spring of 1961. The Freedom Riders met with beatings from white citizens and harassment from local authorities. Only then did the Kennedy administration send federal marshals to protect them.

White resistance proved effective, especially if there were no federal marshals around. In 1961, when SNCC started a voter-registration drive in Mississippi, white people struck back. SNCC workers were beaten and shot. When SNCC tried to register black voters in the small city of Albany, Georgia, members of the Albany Movement, as it was called, were beaten and arrested. Martin Luther King Jr., leader of the Southern Christian Leadership Conference (SCLC) and veteran of the Montgomery bus boycott of 1955–1956, came to Albany and got arrested, too, but segregation still ruled in the city.

SNCC activists resented the lack of presidential support. Kennedy found himself caught in a bind. Like earlier cold war presidents, he understood that racial inequal-

Hosing Down Civil Rights Demonstrators, Birmingham, Alabama, May 1963 Shocking pictures such as this one earned international sympathy for the civil rights movement.

ity damaged the United States' image abroad, but the president also knew that the civil rights issue could split the Democratic Party.

The defiance of southern whites gradually pushed Kennedy toward action. In 1962 the governor of Mississippi, Ross Barnett, disregarded a federal court order by preventing a black student from enrolling at the University of Mississippi. When federal marshals escorted the student, James Meredith, to school, white students pelted them with rocks and Molotov cocktails. After the rioting killed two people and wounded more than one hundred marshals, Kennedy called in federal troops to stop the violence and allow Meredith to enroll.

Two confrontations in Alabama forced the president's hand in 1963. In April, Martin Luther King Jr. and the SCLC tried to end segregation in the southern steelmaking center Birmingham, perhaps the most segregated city in America. The city's public safety commissioner, Eugene "Bull" Connor, was a stereotypical racist white southern law-enforcement officer. To win a badly needed victory, King and local allies planned to boycott department stores and overwhelm the jails with arrested protestors. In the next days, Connor's officers arrested demonstrators by the hundreds. Ignoring a judge's injunction against further protests, King ended up in solitary confinement. In a powerful statement, "Letter from Birmingham Jail," King rejected further patience: "We must come to see . . . that 'justice too long delayed is justice denied.'" Out on bail, King pushed harder with the SCLC for justice, with demonstrations by thousands of young African American students.

Goaded by the new protests, "Bull" Connor turned fire hoses on young demonstrators, set dogs on them, and hit them with clubs. Shocking pictures of the

"I Have a Dream" Martin Luther King, Jr. at the Lincoln Memorial, Washington, DC, August 28, 1963.

scenes, shown around the world, increased the pressure on the white leadership of Birmingham and on President Kennedy. Mediators from Kennedy's Justice Department arranged for a deal in which the SCLC gave up the demonstrations, and local businesses gave up segregation and promised to hire African Americans. However, soon thereafter the Ku Klux Klan marched outside the city, and bombs went off at the home of King's brother and at SCLC headquarters. In response, African Americans rioted in the streets of Birmingham. Kennedy was forced to send federal troops to keep the peace.

A second confrontation in Alabama drew the president still deeper into the civil rights struggle. The state's segregationist governor, George Wallace, defied federal officials and tried to stop two black students from enrolling at the University of Alabama. In an eloquent televised address, Kennedy finally admitted that there was "a moral crisis" and called for sweeping civil rights legislation.

Two months later, on August 28, a march on Washington brought together a crowd of nearly 200,000 people, including 50,000 whites, at the Lincoln Memorial to commemorate the 100th anniversary of the Emancipation Proclamation and to demand "jobs and freedom." Whites and African Americans, workers and students, singers and preachers joined hands to sing the stirring civil rights anthem, "We Shall Overcome." Martin Luther King Jr. moved the nation with his vision of racial harmony. "I have a dream," he said, "that one day . . . little black boys and black girls will be able to join with little white boys and white girls as sisters and brothers." King looked forward to "that day when . . . black men and white men, Jews and Gentiles, Protestants and Catholics, will be able to join hands and sing . . . 'Free at last! Free at last! Thank God Almighty, we are free at last!'"

Kennedy's address and the March on Washington marked a turning point. The surging grassroots movement for racial equality had created broad-based support for civil rights and finally forced the federal government to act.

Flexible Response and the Third World

More confident about the economy than President Eisenhower had been, Kennedy believed the nation could afford to spend more money on the military. He also abandoned the doctrine of massive retaliation, Eisenhower's threat to use nuclear weapons against any Soviet aggression. Kennedy and his advisers preferred flexible response, a strategy that enabled the president to choose different military options, not just nuclear weapons, in dealing with the Soviets. While spending generously on nuclear weapons, the Kennedy administration built up the country's conventional ground forces and special forces—the highly trained troops, known as Green Berets, who could fight in guerilla wars. Flexible response better prepared the United States for challenges around the world.

Kennedy was more willing than Eisenhower to intervene in the affairs of the third world. This was partly a reflection of Kennedy's characteristic confidence about American power and partly a response to Soviet actions. In January 1961 Nikita Khrushchev announced Soviet support for "wars of national liberation," insurgencies against established governments in Asia, Africa, and Latin America. In reply, Kennedy encouraged democracy and prosperity in developing countries.

To counter the appeal of Communism, his administration supported modernization for Africa, Asia, and Latin America; that is, policy makers wanted these continents to develop capitalist, democratic, independent, and anti-Communist regimes along the lines of the United States. In 1961, the Kennedy administration created the Peace Corps to send thousands of young volunteers to promote literacy, public health, and agriculture around the world. The Peace Corps reflected not only the idealism and anti-Communism of the Kennedy years but also many Americans' arrogant sense of superiority. Not surprisingly, the organization was not always welcomed by the people it was supposed to help. To promote the modernization of Latin America, Kennedy announced the formation of the Alliance for Progress in 1961. Over the next eight years, this venture provided $20 billion for housing, health, education, and economic development for poorer countries in the Western Hemisphere.

The Kennedy administration sometimes helped to thwart third world independence and democracy in the name of anti-Communism. In some cases, the United States intervened in the domestic affairs of supposedly independent countries. In the Republic of the Congo, the CIA engineered the election of an anti-Communist leader. The CIA secretly tried to manipulate elections in Chile as well. The United States also backed antidemocratic, but anti-Communist, regimes in Argentina, Guatemala, Haiti, and Honduras.

Similarly, Kennedy wanted to bring down Fidel Castro, whose successful Cuban Revolution was an example for the rest of Latin America. Taking office, the president inherited a plan from the Eisenhower administration for a CIA-directed invasion of the island by anti-Communist Cuban exiles. To conceal U.S. responsibility, Kennedy canceled U.S. flights that would have protected the invaders. As a result, nearly all 1,500 exiles who landed at the Bay of Pigs in April 1961 were killed or captured by Castro's troops. Embarrassed, Kennedy turned to the CIA, which launched "Operation Mongoose," an unsuccessful secret campaign to kill or depose Castro. The Cuban leader, aware of the American plot, declared himself a Communist and turned to the Soviets for help.

Two Confrontations with the Soviets

Kennedy faced two direct confrontations with the Soviet Union. In 1961, Khrushchev threatened to stop Western traffic into West Berlin, which was surrounded by Soviet-dominated East Germany. In response, Kennedy called up reserve troops, asked Congress to increase defense spending, and hinted at a preemptive nuclear strike against the Soviets. Khrushchev backed down, but the East German government built a barbed-wire-and-concrete fence between East Berlin and West Berlin. By halting the embarrassing flight of East Germans to freedom in West Berlin, the so-called Berlin Wall defused the crisis and became a symbol of cold war Europe, a visible "iron curtain" that separated Communists and non-Communists.

In 1962 Kennedy entered a more dangerous confrontation with the Soviet Union. On October 15 photos from an American spy plane showed that the Soviets were building launch sites in Cuba for nuclear missiles that could strike the United States. In tense secret meetings, Kennedy and his advisers debated how to force the Soviet Union to withdraw the missiles. On October 22, he put ships in place to intercept Soviet vessels bound for Cuba. That night, a somber Kennedy told a television audience about the Russian missiles and demanded their removal. Fearing a nuclear war, Americans waited for the Soviets' response. Khrushchev,

The Tension of the Cuban Missile Crisis Customers in a store watch President John F. Kennedy address the nation, October 22, 1962.

unable to confront the United States in its own hemisphere, backed down. The Soviets withdrew the missiles in exchange for the removal of obsolete American missiles from Turkey.

The Cuban Missile Crisis both eased and intensified the cold war. Faced with a nuclear conflict, neither side found the prospect appealing. To ensure Soviet and American leaders could communicate in a crisis, a teletype "hotline" was installed between the White House and the Kremlin. In 1963 the two powers also approved a Limited Test Ban Treaty halting aboveground tests of nuclear weapons. On the other hand, the Cuban crisis made both the Soviets and the Americans more determined to stand firm against each other.

Kennedy and Vietnam

Kennedy inherited a deteriorating situation in South Vietnam in 1961. Ngo Dinh Diem's anti-Communist government faced increasing attacks from the Viet Cong guerillas determined to overthrow his regime. Diem also faced the Viet Cong's new political organization, the National Liberation Front, which was trying to mobilize his Communist and non-Communist opponents. In addition, he faced the continuing hostility of Ho Chi Minh's Communist government in North Vietnam, which was secretly sending soldiers and supplies into South Vietnam.

Like Eisenhower, Kennedy tried to shore up the Diem government by providing advice and financial aid. Further, Kennedy sent American advisers, including the Special Forces, to teach the South Vietnamese army how to stop the Viet Cong insurgency. Before Kennedy took office, there were 900 American troops filling non-combat roles in South Vietnam. At his death, there were more than 16,000.

Despite all this support, Diem's regime spiraled downward. His army could not stop the Viet Cong. A cold, unpopular ruler, he alienated his own people. In 1963 Americans were shocked by pictures of South Vietnamese Buddhists burning themselves to death with gasoline as a protest against the government. Losing confidence in Diem, the Kennedy administration did nothing to stop a military coup that resulted in the murder of the South Vietnamese leader at the beginning of November.

What Kennedy would have done in Vietnam will never be known. On a trip to Dallas, Texas, on November 22, 1963, the president was shot while riding in an open limousine at 12:33 p.m. Two bullets tore through Kennedy's throat and skull, and doctors pronounced him dead half an hour later. That afternoon, police arrested Lee Harvey Oswald for the shooting. A quiet former marine, Oswald had spent time in the Soviet Union. Two days later, as police transferred him from a jail, he was shot and killed by Jack Ruby, the troubled owner of a local nightclub.

Americans were shocked and numbed by the assassination and its aftermath. Some could only believe the assassination was the product of a dark conspiracy, but there was never proof of such a plot. The presidency of John Kennedy, little more than 1,000 days long, left a sad sense of unfulfilled promise. To many Americans, Kennedy's White House seemed like Camelot, the royal seat of the mythical English King Arthur who led the Knights of the Round Table before his tragic death in battle. The reality of the New Frontier was less magical. Kennedy gave voice to the new liberalism, but he seldom translated liberal ideas into action. In later years, some Americans wanted to believe that Kennedy, if he had lived, would have kept the United States from escalating the Vietnam War. Yet there was no compelling evidence that the president intended to withdraw American troops. Instead, Kennedy's commitment only made it more difficult for his successor to pull the United States out of Vietnam.

The Great Society

After Kennedy's death, Lyndon Johnson and the Democratic-controlled Congress carried out most of the liberal agenda. A flood of new laws addressed poverty, race relations, consumer and environmental protection, education, and health care. At the same time, the liberal majority on the Supreme Court afforded new protections for individual rights. By the mid-1960s, the principles of the new liberalism, turned into law, were transforming American government and society.

Lyndon Johnson's Mandate

In background and personality, the new president, Lyndon Johnson, seemed far different from his slain predecessor. Born to modest circumstances in rural Texas, he had made his own fortune, largely through political connections.

> The Great Society rests on abundance and liberty for all. It demands an end to poverty and racial injustice, to which we are totally committed in our time. But that is just the beginning. The Great Society is a place where every child can find knowledge to enrich his mind and to enlarge his talents. It is a place where leisure is a welcome chance to build and reflect, not a feared cause of boredom and restlessness. It is a place where the city of man serves not only the needs of the body and the demands of commerce but the desire for beauty and the hunger for community.
>
> LYNDON JOHNSON,
> Commencement Address, University of Michigan, May 22, 1964

He was never an eloquent public speaker or a charismatic figure. But he was an especially effective legislator who knew how to bully and cajole Senate colleagues into making a deal.

Despite obvious differences in style and background, there were fundamental similarities between Johnson and Kennedy. Both were products of the Democratic Party that had engineered the New Deal, won World War II, and fought the cold war. Both shared the liberals' expansive sense of American might. "Hell, we're the richest country in the world, the most powerful," Johnson declared. "We can do it all."

Taking office, Johnson stressed continuity with his predecessor. Yet the situation had changed. Kennedy's martyrdom left Americans more willing to accept political innovation. Rather than discourage people, his death seemed to inspire them.

The presidential election of 1964 strengthened Johnson's mandate. The contest offered voters an unusually clear choice between competing solutions for America. Influenced by the new liberalism, Johnson stood for activist government, growth economics, and civil rights. His Republican opponent, Barry Goldwater, stood unequivocally for the new conservatism. "We have gotten where we are," he declared, "not because of government, but in spite of government."

It was not much of a contest. Democrats portrayed Goldwater as a dangerous radical who would gut popular programs and perhaps start a war. Johnson, in contrast, was supposed to be a statesman and a man of peace. He won 61.1 percent of the popular vote, 44 states, and 486 electoral votes. Moreover, the Democrats increased their majorities in the House and Senate. It was a greater victory than Johnson's hero, Franklin Roosevelt, had ever enjoyed.

"Success Without Squalor"

With his mandate, Johnson moved to enact a legislative program that would rival Roosevelt's New Deal. At the University of Michigan in May, 1964, he had called for the creation of the "Great Society"—"a society of success without squalor, beauty without barrenness, works of genius without the wretchedness of poverty." To create that society, Johnson turned to the ideas of the new liberalism. His administration pushed through new laws that aimed to wipe out poverty, end segregation, and enhance the quality of life for all Americans.

Johnson, like many Americans, was disturbed by the persistence of poverty in the consumer society: by the standards of the day, nearly one in five Americans was poor. Declaring "unconditional war on poverty," the Johnson administration won congressional approval of the Economic Opportunity Act of 1964, which created an independent federal agency, the Office of Economic Opportunity (OEO), to spend nearly $1 billion on antipoverty programs. The OEO managed Volunteers in Service to America (VISTA), whose workers taught literacy and other skills in impoverished areas. It ran the Job Corps, which taught necessary job skills to poor youth, and implemented Community Action Programs (CAPs), which encouraged the poor to organize themselves in American cities. By supporting the "maximum feasible participation" of the poor, the CAPs, unlike other poverty programs, had the potential to redistribute power away from local officials.

In 1965 and 1966 Congress continued the war on several fronts. It established an expanded food stamp program and created Head Start, which provided early schooling, meals, and medical exams for impoverished preschool-aged children. To protect the rights of the poor, the Legal Services Program brought lawyers into slums. To improve urban life, the Model Cities Program targeted 63 cities for slum clearance and redevelopment. Congress also created the Department of Housing and Urban Development in 1965 and the Transportation Department in 1966 partly to help manage antipoverty programs.

The War on Poverty President Lyndon Johnson, hat in hand, talks with a family of poor sharecroppers in Nash County, North Carolina, May 1964.

To improve the quality of life, Congress used the fruits of economic growth to furnish security, opportunity, and cultural enrichment. The Great Society took a major step toward national health insurance when Congress created Medicare in 1965. This program provided the elderly with insurance coverage for doctors' bills, surgery, and hospitalization. At the same time, Congress created Medicaid, a program that helped the states provide medical care to the nonworking poor.

The Johnson administration confronted the growing issue of consumer protection. In 1965, Ralph Nader, an intense young lawyer, published a disturbing book, *Unsafe at Any Speed,* charging that car manufacturers cared more about style and sales than about safety. American cars lacked safety features, such as seat belts, that could save lives. Moreover, Nader reported, executives at General Motors had ignored safety defects in the Chevrolet Corvair. Faced with these revelations, General Motors seemed to confirm its arrogance by trying to discredit Nader rather than promising immediately to improve the Corvair. In response, Congress passed the National Traffic and Motor Vehicle Safety Act of 1966, which set the first federal safety standards for automobiles, and the Highway Safety Act, which required states to establish highway safety programs.

The president and Congress adopted the new liberals' belief in using the federal government to support education at all levels. The Elementary and Secondary School Act of 1965 channeled $1.3 billion into school districts around the country.

The Higher Education Act of 1965 encouraged youth to attend college by offering federally insured educational loans.

The Great Society included programs for cultural enrichment. In 1965 Congress established the National Endowment for the Arts to fund the visual and performing arts, and the National Endowment for the Humanities to support scholarly research. The Public Broadcasting Act of 1967 established a nonprofit corporation to support educational and cultural programming. Before long, the Corporation for Public Broadcasting would be giving money for such commercial-free television shows as *Sesame Street*.

Protection of the environment was a natural issue for liberals to address. In the 1960s Americans had become further sensitized to the ecological threat that the consumer economy posed to the countryside because of the best-selling book *Silent Spring* (1962), which emphasized the dangerous power that human beings held over the natural world. The author, marine biologist Rachel Carson, warned that environmental contamination from pesticides, like nuclear weapons, threatened human survival. Here was a problem, created by the booming consumer economy, that government could solve.

During Johnson's presidency, more than 300 pieces of legislation led to the expenditure of more than $12 billion on environmental programs. In 1963 the Clean Air Act encouraged state and local governments to set up pollution-control programs. Two years later, amendments established the first pollution-emission standards for automobiles. The Air Quality Act of 1967 further strengthened federal authority to deal with air pollution. Meanwhile, the Water Quality Act of 1965 and the Clean Waters Restoration Act of 1966 enabled states and the federal government to fight water pollution. The Wilderness Act of 1964 responded to environmentalists' calls for a system of wilderness lands protected from development. Johnson's wife, Lady Bird, campaigned to limit outdoor advertising and contribute to the beautification of the nation's highways.

Preserving Personal Freedom

The new liberalism contained a paradox: liberals wanted both to enhance the power of the federal government and to expand individual rights. Their concern for individual rights was apparent in their support for civil rights for African Americans and in a series of decisions by the Supreme Court, led by Chief Justice Earl Warren.

Several rulings by the Court protected the freedom to speak out and to live free from undue governmental interference. In *New York Times v. Sullivan* in 1964, the justices encouraged free speech by making it more difficult for public figures to sue news media for libel. In addition, two decisions protected the rights of people accused of crimes. In 1963 the Court ruled in *Gideon v. Wainwright* that governments had to provide lawyers to poor felony defendants. Three years later, *Miranda v. Arizona* required police to inform individuals of their rights when they were arrested, including the right to remain silent and the right to an attorney.

The Warren Court also protected sexual and religious freedom. In 1965 in *Griswold v. Connecticut* the Court threw out a state law that banned the use of contraceptives. Affirming individuals' right to privacy, the justices in effect kept government out of the nation's bedrooms. In 1963 the Court acted to prohibit mandatory prayer in the nation's public schools. *School District of Abington Township v. Schempp* prohibited state and local governments from requiring public school students to say the Lord's Prayer or read the Bible.

The Supreme Court's rulings were controversial. Some people charged that the Court was "driving God out" of the classroom. Others believed that the Court had gone too far to protect the rights of alleged criminals. Some conservatives demanded the impeachment of Chief Justice Warren. Through its rulings, the liberal majority on the Court substantially increased individual freedom, but few people had yet thought much about the tension between expanding both individual rights and government power.

Much of the liberal agenda had been accomplished by 1967. The Great Society's programs added up to a major change in American democracy. Government claimed more authority than ever to manage many Americans' daily lives. The Great Society brought a massive expansion of the size, cost, and power of the federal government (see Table 28–1).

That expansion would be controversial for years to come. Some Great Society measures—Medicare in particular—proved to be enormously expensive. Conservatives did not welcome an enlarged federal government, and some corporations resented the government's regulation of business in the name of consumer protection. Despite these concerns, the various attempts to improve the quality of life represented some of the major accomplishments of the new liberalism. The War on Poverty was at least a partial success. Mainly because of the ongoing economic boom, the percentage of people living in poverty decreased to 13 percent by 1970. But that meant that 25 million Americans were still poor. Moreover, poverty was unevenly distributed. About a third of African Americans and a quarter of Americans of Spanish origin were impoverished as the 1970s began. Still, the liberal War on Poverty made a significant, enduring difference in American life.

The Death of Jim Crow

As Johnson became president, the battle for civil rights became still more intense. In the 10 weeks after the Birmingham confrontation, 758 demonstrations led to 14,733 arrests across the United States. When a bomb killed four African American girls in a Baptist church in Birmingham in September, African American rioters burned stores and destroyed cars, and the police killed two more children.

The violence continued the following year: CORE, SNCC, SCLC, and the NAACP had created the Council of Federated Organizations (COFO) to press for African American voting rights in Mississippi. Robert Moses, an African American schoolteacher, led the COFO crusade uniting young African American and

 Table 28–1 Expanding the Federal Government, 1955–1970

Year	Civilian Employees (thous.)	Total Spending (millions)	Defense (millions)	Space (millions)	Health (millions)	Education and Manpower (millions)
1955	2,397	$68,509	$40,245	$74	$271	$573
1960	2,399	$92,223	$45,908	$401	$756	$1,060
1965	2,528	$118,430	$49,578	$5,091	$1,704	$1,284
1970	2,982	$196,588	$80,295	$3,749	$12,907	$1,289

Source: *Historical Statistics of the United States* (1976), II, 1102, 1116.

AMERICAN LANDSCAPE

>> "The Long Cool Summer" of Greenville, Mississippi

The dramatic pictures of brave marchers, menacing dogs, ominous police, and murdered activists can make the civil rights movement seem like a continuously violent confrontation. But civil rights, like much social change, was also a more quiet process, a slow dance in which blacks and whites gradually, haltingly created and accepted a new, more democratic order. That was the case in Greenville, Mississippi, in the "Freedom Summer" of 1964, when civil rights workers fanned out across the state to ensure the voting rights of African Americans. While there was turbulence and violence in much of the state, Greenville witnessed what the local newspaper, the *Delta Democrat-Times,* described as "The Long Cool Summer."

Like the rest of Mississippi, Greenville, a city of 41,000 in the state's rich cotton-growing delta, was segregated. Although African Americans made up half the city's population, they faced second-class social and economic status. "I don't like it," a young black man declared, "when the white man works an easy job for $25 a day and I work a mean one for $3." African Americans lived with second-class political status, too: thanks to state-imposed literacy requirements and poll taxes, black voters had long been effectively disfranchised. Few African Americans were registered to vote in Greenville; the city had no black elected officials.

The Council of Federated Organizations (COFO), a coalition of leading civil rights groups, intended to change that with the voting-rights drive known as Freedom Sum-mer. In the fall of 1963, COFO organizers visited the city to plan their campaign. In the spring of 1964, white and black activists moved into Greenville. The arrival of these outsiders, mostly in their 20s, touched off a wave of speculation and anxiety among the city's whites. The enactment of the federal Civil Rights Act of 1964, banning segregation, intensified fears of demonstrations, confrontations, and bloodshed. "There are many of us . . . who are today dismayed by the attitude, actions and statements of some of the young men and women who are temporarily within the state," declared the *Democrat-Times.* "At times it would appear that nothing less than a calculated attempt to provoke wholesale violence is their aim."

Despite these fears, local officials urged "patience and self-control." In fact, COFO's strategy focused, not on demonstrations, but on voter registration. "If you can't vote you have no power." COFO presented voting as an "alternative to violence," Fred Anderson, an African American official of the Student Nonviolent Coordinating Committee, told local blacks. "If you get the vote you don't have to shoot a gun," a COFO leader insisted. "You can pull a trigger with a vote and kill off a politician." To help encourage black activism, COFO set up two summer "freedom schools" in Greenville. "Mississippi schools are poisoning your kids' minds," Anderson explained.

In July, COFO began to bring African Americans to the county courthouse to register to vote. The first day, 100 took the preliminary registration test; the turnout was so large that 35 would-be voters were still outside when the office closed for the day. The next day, another 45 began the registration process. And so the COFO drive went on. "There was no sustained violence, no bombings, no riots, no murders and no unruly mass demonstrations," the *Democrat-Times* reported. "[R]owdies of both races never felt free to follow the course tolerated in other state communities."

Why were the African Americans of Greenville able to begin reclaiming their democratic rights with so little upheaval? Certainly, the nonconfrontational tactics of COFO made a difference. The city's growth and relative prosperity probably made whites more secure about sharing power. At least some whites accepted that Amer-

ican democracy demanded the registration of African Americans. "This is their undeniable right," the *Democrat-Times* conceded, "and what they seek is entirely within the American political pattern." The paper also pointed out that southern whites faced "inevitable changes" because of the federal government and the national civil rights movement; for many whites, it probably seemed pointless to disrupt the quiet lines of would-be black voters.

There was one final, ironic explanation for The Long Cool Summer of Greenville. As the editor of the *Democrat-Times* noted, most of the city's whites didn't care enough to exercise their right to vote. The paper suggested that Greenville also needed a voting drive for whites, "to make our democratic republic more truly democratic." Paradoxically, blacks won the vote in Greenville because whites cared so little about their own rights. ●

white activists to register black voters and start "Freedom Schools" for African American children. The effort, known as Freedom Summer, met hostility from whites. Two white activists, Michael Schwerner and Andrew Goodman, and one African American activist, James Chaney, were found, shot to death, near Philadelphia, Mississippi. Eventually a white deputy sheriff, a local Klan leader, and five other whites were convicted of "violating the rights" of Chaney, Goodman, and Schwerner. The violence continued in Mississippi throughout Freedom Summer. Homes and churches were burned, and three more COFO workers were killed.

Lyndon Johnson could not escape the events in Mississippi. In the summer of 1964, the Mississippi Freedom Democratic Party (MFDP) sent a full delegation to the Democratic National Convention in Atlantic City, New Jersey. The MFDP delegates, including the eloquent Fannie Lou Hamer, hoped at least to share Mississippi's convention seats with the whites-only Democratic Party delegation. Hamer, the daughter of sharecroppers, told the Credentials Committee how she had been jailed and beaten for trying to register African American voters. Afraid of alienating white southerners, Johnson tried to stop the publicity and offered the delegates two seats in the convention. "We didn't come all this way for no two seats," Hamer retorted. The MFDP delegation went away empty-handed.

Johnson and the Democratic Party were clearly not ready to share power with African American activists, but they were ready to end legalized segregation. In July, Congress adopted the Civil Rights Act, which outlawed racial discrimination in public places. The measure also set up an Equal Employment Opportunity Commission (EEOC) to stop discrimination in hiring and promotion. Even the schools gradually became integrated. In 1964 hardly any African American students attended integrated schools; by 1972 nearly half of African American children attended integrated schools.

However, across the South, most African Americans still could not vote. In January 1965 the SCLC and SNCC tried to force the voting-rights issue with protests in Selma, Alabama. Predictably, the demonstrations produced violent opposition and helpful publicity. The sight of state troopers using tear gas, cattle prods, and clubs on peaceful marchers built support for voting rights.

Seizing the moment, Johnson called for the end of disfranchisement, and Congress passed the Voting Rights Act of 1965. This powerful measure forced

"VOTE" Marching for African-American voting rights, Alabama, 1965.

southern states to give up literacy tests used to disfranchise black voters and empowered federal officials to make sure that African Americans could register to vote. In three years, Mississippi saw African American registration increase from 6 percent to 44 percent of eligible voters.

Together with the Civil Rights Act of 1964, the Voting Rights Act transformed the South. These twin achievements of the civil rights movement and the Great Society effectively doomed Jim Crow and laid a foundation for African American political power. However, the struggle for racial equality was far from over

The American War in Vietnam

The war in Vietnam was the decisive event for the new liberalism and the nation in the 1960s. American participation in the conflict reflected the liberals' determined anti-Communism and their boundless sense of power and responsibility. Driven by these beliefs, Johnson made the fateful decision to send American troops into battle in 1965. When the war did not go according to plan, Americans divided passionately over the conflict, and the economy faltered. By the end of 1967 the war was destroying the Great Society.

Johnson's Decision for War

Kennedy's assassination made little difference for American defense and foreign policies. Johnson, too, was a committed cold warrior with an optimistic view of American power. He kept flexible response in place and was equally willing to undermine the independence of third world countries. In 1965, Johnson sent 22,000 American troops to the Dominican Republic to stop an increasingly violent struggle for political power. The president violated the sovereignty of this Caribbean nation without obtaining evidence of a Communist threat and without consulting Latin American countries as required by treaty.

At first, Johnson followed Kennedy's policy in Vietnam. The new president believed in the domino theory, the idea that the fall of one country to Communism would lead to the fall of others. Like many Americans who had witnessed the rise of Adolf Hitler in the 1930s, Johnson thought it was a mistake to tolerate any aggression. The president also felt he could not turn his back on commitments made by Kennedy, Eisenhower, and Truman. As one weak government followed another, Johnson sent more aid and advisers to South Vietnam and stepped up covert action against the North.

This secret activity helped Johnson get congressional approval to act more aggressively. On August 2, 1964, a U.S. destroyer, the *Maddox,* was cruising a few miles off the coast of North Vietnam in the Gulf of Tonkin, in order to monitor communications. When three North Vietnamese torpedo boats unsuccessfully attacked the *Maddox,* the American ship sank two of the boats and damaged a third. Two days later the *Maddox,* along with a second U.S. destroyer, fired at a nonexistent North Vietnamese attack. Johnson ordered retaliatory strikes from U.S. aircraft carriers and asked Congress for the power to protect American military personnel. With only two dissenting votes, Congress approved what became known as the Tonkin Gulf Resolution, which gave the president the authority, without a declaration of war, to use military force to safeguard South Vietnam. Even though Johnson knew there had been no real threat to the United States, he had misled Congress to obtain a "blank check" to fight in Southeast Asia.

He soon cashed it. After American soldiers were killed in a Viet Cong attack on a U.S. base in February 1965, Johnson authorized air strikes against North Vietnam itself. In March the United States began Operation Rolling Thunder, a series of bombing raids on military targets in North Vietnam.

When the raids failed to deter the North Vietnamese and Viet Cong, Johnson had a disagreeable but clear choice. If he wanted to save both South Vietnam and his reputation, he had to commit American ground troops to battle; otherwise, he would be blamed for the loss of South Vietnam to Communism. In July 1965, Johnson gave the order to send 180,000 soldiers to fight in South Vietnam without a declaration of war.

Johnson's decision was the ultimate expression of the new liberalism. The president went to war not only because he opposed Communism, but also because he had faith in American wealth and wisdom. Johnson believed that the United States could transform a weak, divided South Vietnam into a strong, united, modern nation. Even though he was cautious about going to war, Johnson could not accept that the United States might lose. Moreover, he believed that the United States could afford to fight a war abroad and still build the Great Society at home. It was a fateful choice.

Fighting a Limited War

Johnson and his advisers believed the United States did not need all its power to save South Vietnam (see Map 28–2). Unlike World War II, America would not attack civilian targets, use nuclear weapons, and demand "unconditional surrender." Instead of another total war, Vietnam was to be a limited war in which the U.S. forces, led by General William Westmoreland, would use conventional weapons against military targets. The goal was not to take over territory but rather to kill enough enemy soldiers to persuade the North Vietnamese and the Viet Cong to give up. Relying on America's superior technology, Westmoreland expected the United States to prevail by the end of 1967.

Westmoreland's strategy turned out to be poorly suited to the realities of Vietnam. As Fred Downs discovered, the North Vietnamese and the Viet Cong usually escaped by hiding in tunnels, fleeing through the jungle, fighting mainly at night, or retreating into Cambodia, Laos, and North Vietnam. Their strategy was to live long enough for a frustrated U.S. military to leave South Vietnam.

American troops fought well. Yet at the close of 1967, too many North Vietnamese and Viet Cong were still alive and committed to the overthrow of South Vietnam. Meanwhile, the United States had lost many troops: 9,000 died in 1967 alone. Even though there were now half a million troops in Westmoreland's command, he had not won the war on schedule. He had not lost the war, either. But the United States was running out of time to win (see Table 28–2).

The War at Home

The war in Vietnam had a divisive impact back home. An impassioned antiwar movement, led by SDS and other student radicals, emerged to condemn American policy. For the New Left, the war confirmed their analysis of America's ills. Communism in Southeast Asia, they believed, did not pose a real threat to the United States. But the misguided cold war had led liberals to support an antidemocratic regime. The war

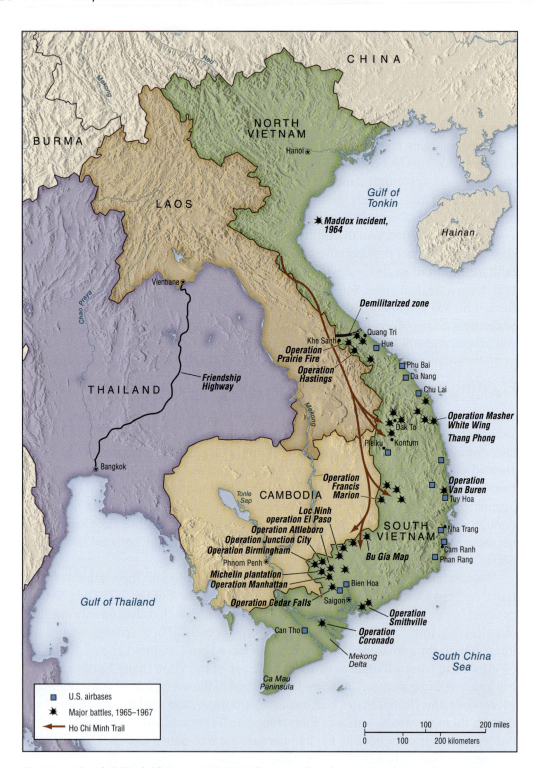

Map 28–2 America's War in Vietnam, 1965–1968 The many military bases suggest how much power the United States had to commit to South Vietnam; the many major battles show how hard American troops had to fight to protect the South Vietnamese regime from the Viet Cong and from the North Vietnamese soldiers who traveled the Ho Chi Minh Trail.

Table 28–2 The Escalating War in Vietnam, 1960–1968

Year	U.S. Troops	U.S. Battle Deaths	S. Vietnamese Battle Deaths	N. Vietnamese and Viet Cong Battle Deaths (estimated)
1961	3,164	11	(three-year	12,000
1962	11,326	31	total =	21,000
1963	16,263	78	13,985	21,000
1964	23,310	147	7,457	17,000
1965	184,000	1,369	11,403	35,382
1966	385,000	5,008	11,953	55,524
1967	486,000	9,378	12,716	88,104
1968	536,000	14,589	27,915	181,149

Sources: Michael Clodfelter, *Vietnam in Military Statistics*, 46, 57, 209 and 258; Fox Butterfield, ed., *Vietnam War Almanac*, 50, 54, 57, 64, 102, 132, 158, 192; Shelby Stanton, ed., *Vietnam Order of Battle*, 333.

also revealed how undemocratic America had become. Johnson, the New Left pointed out, had ignored the Constitution by sending troops into battle without a declaration of war. In addition, the selective service law was forcing a repugnant choice on young men: they could either fight this illegal war or obtain student deferments to stay in school and prepare for empty lives as corporate employees in the consumer society.

A growing number of liberals and Democrats shared at least some of the radicals' analysis. These "doves" acknowledged that the United States was backing an antidemocratic government in a brutal and apparently unnecessary war. The conflict appeared to be a civil war among Vietnamese rather than some plot to expand Soviet or Chinese influence at the cost of the United States. Meanwhile, the war had

The Toll of War A South Vietnamese refugee, displaced by American bombing.

shattered many liberals' and Democrats' overconfident view of the Great Society. The United States, confessed Senator J. William Fulbright of Arkansas in 1966, was a "sick society" suffering from an "arrogance of power." The nation apparently could not solve major problems as readily as the liberals had believed a few years earlier.

Some African Americans viewed the conflict as a painful illustration of American racism. A disproportionate number of poor African Americans, unable to go to college and avoid the draft, were being sent to kill nonwhites abroad on behalf of a racist United States. First SNCC and then Martin Luther King Jr. condemned the war. Refusing to be drafted, boxer Muhammad Ali was sentenced to jail and stripped of his championship in 1967.

The growing opposition to the war produced large and angry demonstrations. In 1965 students and faculty staged "teach-ins" at college campuses to explore and question American policy in Vietnam. In April, 20,000 people gathered at the Washington Monument to protest the war. Some young men risked jail by returning or burning their draft cards. On campuses, students protested the presence of recruiters trying to hire workers for defense contractors. In October 1967 the National Mobilization Committee, known as the "Mobe," staged Stop the Draft Week. As part of the protest, radicals in Oakland, California, tried to shut down an army draft induction center, fought with police, and briefly took over a 25-square-

Stop the Draft Week Protestors and police in front of an induction center, Oakland, California, October 1967.

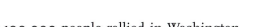

block area of the city. Meanwhile, nearly 100,000 people rallied in Washington, DC, to protest the war.

Despite the protests, most Americans supported the war. To many people, the demonstrators were unpatriotic. "America—Love It or Leave It," read a popular bumper sticker. "Hawks," mostly conservative Republicans and Democrats, wanted Johnson to fight harder. Nevertheless, by October 1967 support for the war had fallen to 58 percent, in one public opinion poll, and only 28 percent of the people approved of Johnson's conduct of the war.

Bad economic news contributed to the public mood. Massive government spending for the war and the Great Society had overstimulated the economy. With jobs plentiful, strong consumer demand drove up prices, which in turn put upward pressure on wages. Anxious about inflation, the Federal Reserve contracted the money supply, making it harder for businesses to get loans. When interest rates reached their highest levels since the 1920s, there were fears of a financial panic. Despite liberal economic policies, the United States had not created perpetual prosperity after all.

By the end of 1967 the war had put enormous stress on the Great Society. It undermined liberals' commitment to anti-Communism and their confidence in American power and wisdom. By dividing the nation, the conflict also undermined support for the Great Society. By weakening the economy, furthermore, the Vietnam War made it harder to pay for the Great Society. The United States could not, as Johnson believed, "do it all." The new liberalism had reached its crisis.

The Great Society Comes Apart

Liberals attained power in the early 1960s because their agenda responded to popular discontent with the consumer society, but even as Congress enacted that agenda, many Americans were expressing new dissatisfactions that liberalism could not accommodate. The Black Power movement, the youth rebellion, and a reborn women's movement exposed the limits of the liberal vision. In 1968 the strain of new demands, the Vietnam War, and economic realities tore apart the Great Society and destroyed the fortunes of Lyndon Johnson, the Democratic Party, and the new liberalism.

The Emergence of Black Power

For many African Americans, the Great Society's response to racial inequality was too slow and too weak. Even as the civil rights movement reached its climax, a wave of more than 300 race riots from 1964 to

> [T]he world is all messed up. The nation is sick. Trouble is in the land. Confusion all around. . . . But I know, somehow, that only when it is dark enough, can you see the stars. And I see God working in this period of the twentieth century in a way that men, in some strange way, are responding—something is happening in our world. The masses of people are rising up. And wherever they are assembled today . . . the cry is always the same— "We want to be free."
>
> MARTIN LUTHER KING JR.,
> last speech, Memphis, Tennessee, April 3, 1968

1969 dramatized the gap between the promise of the Great Society and the reality of life in black America. When a white policeman shot a 15-year-old African American in the Harlem district of New York in July 1964, angry African Americans burned and looted buildings. In August 1965 friction between white police and African American citizens touched off a riot in the Watts section of Los Angeles, where 40 percent of the mostly African American population lived in poverty. In five days more than 1,000 fires burned, and 34 people died. The wave of riots peaked in Detroit, in July 1967, when 43 people died before U.S. Army paratroopers stopped the violence (see Map 28–3).

To many onlookers, the riots were, in the words of an official report on Watts, "senseless," but the disturbances flowed from the real frustrations of African Americans. Despite the civil rights movement's successful challenge to legalized segregation in the South, African Americans still lived with poverty and discrimination all across the country. Northern cities, the center of the riots, had been largely ignored by Martin Luther King Jr. and other civil rights leaders. The riots signaled that the civil rights movement and the new liberalism, for all their accomplishments, had not addressed some of the most difficult problems of racial inequality.

For years King and other activists had relied on nonviolent demonstrations and ties to white liberals to achieve integration, but that approach proved ineffective in the North. In 1965, King confronted "the Negro's repellent slum life" in Chicago by joining marches protesting the de facto segregation of the city's educational sys-

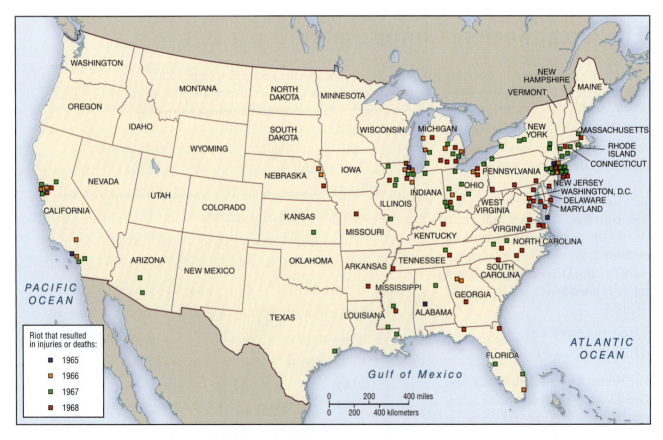

Map 28–3   Race Riots, 1965–1968 The clusters of riots in the Northeast, Midwest, and California emphasize that race was not just a southern issue in the 1960s. *Mark C. Carnes et al.,* Mapping America's Past *(New York: Henry Holt and Co., 1996), p. 217.*

tem. King faced the determined opposition of the city's Democratic political boss, Mayor Richard Daley. Reluctant to challenge the powerful mayor, the Johnson administration would not give King real support. In 1966, King returned to lead the "Chicago Movement" to wipe out slums and win access to better housing in white neighborhoods. "Go back to Africa," white demonstrators chanted. Daley accepted a compromise on fair housing but repudiated it as soon as King left town. Under the leadership of 24-year-old Jesse Jackson, Operation Breadbasket threatened demonstrations and boycotts against businesses that refused to hire African Americans. The project produced few results; King's nonviolent tactics had failed.

African Americans already had the example of a different approach to the problem of black-white relations. The Nation of Islam believed that whites were devils and African Americans were God's chosen people. The Black Muslims, as they were known, preached separation of the races and the self-reliance of African Americans. One of the Muslims' most powerful preachers was Malcolm X, a former pimp, drug pusher, and convict who angrily rejected integration and nonviolence. "If someone puts a hand on you," he said, "send him to the cemetery." Malcolm X moderated his view of whites before being gunned down, apparently by Muslims, in 1965. But he was best known for his militant call "for the freedom of the 22 million Afro-Americans by any means necessary."

By the mid-1960s, many African Americans were willing to follow at least some of Malcolm X's example. Rejecting the longtime goal of integration, they now emphasized maintaining and celebrating a separate African American identity. Now, many African Americans declared that "Black is beautiful." In asserting their distinctive identity, some African Americans accentuated their African heritage. They wore African robes and dashikis, explored African language and art, and observed the seven-day holiday Kwanzaa, based on an African harvest festival. Instead of working with white liberals and depending on the federal government, some African American activists insisted blacks needed to create their own institutions. In 1966, SNCC ousted its white members.

In rejecting nonviolence and integration, a number of African American activists adopted a more militant stance. "What we gonna start saying now is Black Power!" Stokely Carmichael told a rally in Mississippi. The new slogan had different meanings for different people. The most radical interpretation came from the Black Panthers, who were first organized in Oakland, California, by Huey P. Newton and Bobby Seale. Dressed in black clothes and black berets, the Panthers armed themselves to protect their neighborhoods from white police. Newton, admiringly described by an associate as "the baddest motherfucker ever to step foot inside of history," went to jail after a shootout with police. The Panthers also founded schools and promoted peaceful community activism, but they were best known in the media for their aura of violent militance.

Black Panther Organizers Huey Newton and Bobby Seale

Particularly because of the violent image of the Panthers, many people, African American and white, were hostile to the new slogan. For King and his allies, Black Power all too obviously meant repudiation of nonviolent integration. For many whites, Black Power stirred fears of violence. For white leaders like Richard Daley, Black Power meant giving up political authority to African Americans. For Lyndon Johnson, Black Power obviously meant a rejection of his Great Society.

The Youth Rebellion

The anti–Vietnam War movement was part of a broader rebellion against adult authority and expectations. The battle began at the University of California at Berkeley in 1964. That fall, the university's administration banned political speaking and organizing at the one street corner where it had been allowed. When a civil rights activist was arrested for defying the ban in October, hundreds of students sat down around the police cars, trapping the officers for 32 hours. After the standoff, students created the Free Speech Movement (FSM) to pursue greater student involvement in the educational process. When the university refused to accept that demand, students took over the main administration building. Speaking that day, the student leader Mario Savio reflected the ideas of the New Left. "We have an autocracy which runs this university," he exclaimed. "[W]e're a bunch of raw material[s] that . . . don't mean to end up being bought by some clients of the University, be they the government, be they industry, be they organized labor, be they anyone! We're human beings!" The administration eventually succumbed to faculty protests and a student boycott of classes and agreed to new rules on free speech.

Americans had never seen anything quite like the Berkeley protests. Here were privileged students, on their way to comfortable middle-class lives, condemning society, storming a building, and being dragged off by the police. Many people were infuriated; some younger Americans were inspired.

As campus activism flourished, young people were also creating the rebellious lifestyle that became known as the counterculture. Less politically oriented than the New Left, the counterculture challenged conventional social values. By the mid-1960s, many younger Americans were condemning conformity, careerism, materialism, and sexual repression as they groped toward an alternative lifestyle.

The counterculture rested on the enjoyment of rock music, drugs, and sexual freedom. Beginning in 1964, the sudden popularity of the Beatles, the Rolling Stones, and other British rock groups brought back a rebellious note to rock and roll. The Beatles' irreverent attitude toward authority, symbolized by their long hair, helped create "Beatlemania" in the United States. Young Americans loved the Beatles' first movie, *A Hard Day's Night*, in 1964, because, a student wrote, "all the dreary old adults are mocked and brushed aside."

Rock also became more socially and politically conscious in the 1960s. Bob Dylan, Simon and Garfunkel, and other musicians rooted in folk music sang about racism, nuclear weapons, and other issues.

Rock music often sang of the virtues of drugs and sex, two more elements of the counterculture. The use of marijuana, the hallucinogen LSD, and other drugs increased during the 1960s. The counterculture saw drugs, most of them illegal, as a way of flouting adult convention and escaping everyday reality for a more liberated consciousness.

Sex offered a similar mix of pleasure and defiance. On campuses across the country, students demanded greater freedom, including the repeal of the parietal rules that restricted the mixing of male and female students in dorms. By the end of the decade, students were living together before marriage, to the consternation of college authorities and other adults.

Many young people hoped that the counterculture would weave sex, drugs, and rock into a new lifestyle. Novelist Ken Kesey joined with his followers, the Merry Pranksters, to set up a commune, complete with "Screw Shack," outside San Francisco. The Merry Pranksters used drugs to synchronize with the cosmos and attain a state of ecstasy. By 1965 Kesey had created the "acid test," which fused drugs, rock, and light shows into a multimedia experience. The acid test helped establish the popularity of "acid rock," the "San Francisco sound" of Jefferson Airplane and the Grateful Dead.

The purest form of the countercultural lifestyle was created by the hippies, who appeared in the mid-1960s. Hippie culture centered in the Haight-Ashbury section of San Francisco. Rejecting materialism and consumerism, hippies celebrated free expression and free love. They wanted to replace capitalism, competition, and aggression with cooperation and community. One group of hippies, the Diggers, gave away clothes and food and staged the first "Human Be-In" at Golden Gate Park "to shower the country with waves of ecstasy and purification."

The youth rebellion was easy to exaggerate. There were not many full-time hippies. The countercultural lifestyle quickly became conformist consumerism, as young Americans flocked to buy the right clothes and records.

The counterculture also had roots in the orthodox culture it attacked. By the close of the 1950s, adults themselves had become ambivalent about consumerism, conventional morality, and institutional authority. Sexual freedom for youth was encouraged partly by the greater sexual openness of mainstream culture, the Supreme Court's *Griswold* decision, and the introduction of the oral contraceptive ("the pill") in 1960. Americans chafed at the authority of religious denominations. The pop art paintings of Andy Warhol and Roy Lichtenstein, the productions of the Living Theater, the essays of Susan Sontag, and the novels of Thomas Pynchon broke with formal, artistic conventions.

Nevertheless, the counterculture was a disruptive force in 1960s America. Like the Black Panthers, hippies deeply influenced young people and adults. The counterculture encouraged Americans to question conventional values and authority and to seek a freer way of life.

The Rebirth of the Women's Movement

By the 1960s American women were reacting against the difficult social roles enforced on them after World War II. More women than ever went to college, but they were not expected to pursue long-term careers. More women than ever worked outside the home, but they were still expected to devote themselves to home and family. Women also had to put up with the continuing double standard of sexual behavior, which granted men more freedom to seek sexual gratification outside of marriage. By the start of the new decade, educated middle-class women, in particular, questioned their second-class status. In part, they were inspired by the example of the civil rights movement.

Two best-selling books reflected these women's complaints. In *The Feminine Mystique* (1963), journalist Betty Friedan described "the problem that has no name," the growing frustration of educated, middle-class wives and mothers who had subordinated their own aspirations to the needs of men. Meanwhile, journalist Helen Gurley Brown rejected unequal sexual opportunities in her book, *Sex and the Single Girl* (1962). Brown did not challenge male sexual ethics, just as Friedan did not challenge male careerism. Instead, like Friedan, Brown wanted equal opportunity for women, both in and out of marriage. She explained, coyly, that "nice, single girls do."

The complaints of Friedan, Brown, and other women received attention but little action from men. In 1961 Kennedy appointed the Presidential Commission on the Status of Women, chaired by Eleanor Roosevelt. The commission's cautious report, *American Women*, documented gender discrimination but reaffirmed women's domestic role. In 1963 Congress passed the Equal Pay Act, which mandated the same pay for men and women who did the same work, but the measure, full of loopholes, had little impact on women's comparatively low earnings. A year later, Title VII, a provision slipped into the Civil Rights Act of 1964, prohibited employers from discriminating on the basis of sex in hiring and compensating workers. Yet the Equal Employment Opportunity Commission (EEOC) did little to enforce the law.

Male inaction pushed women to organize. In 1966 Betty Friedan and a handful of other women, angry at the EEOC, formed the National Organization for Women (NOW). Although frustrated with the Great Society, Friedan and the founders of NOW expressed essentially liberal values. They saw NOW as "a civil rights organization," and wrote a "Bill of Rights" for women that focused on government action to provide rights and opportunities. NOW also demanded access to contraception and abortion.

NOW's platform was too radical for many women and not radical enough for others. Some younger women, particularly activists in the civil rights movement and the New Left, wanted more than liberal solutions to their problems. By the fall of 1967, activists were forming new groups dedicated to "women's liberation." Influenced by the New Left, radical feminists blamed the capitalist system for the oppression of women, but a growing number of radicals saw men as the problem. Like African Americans in the Black Power movement, radical women talked less about rights and more about power. Their slogan was "Sisterhood Is Powerful!" Like the Black Power movement and the New Left, radical feminists rejected collaboration with male liberal politicians.

Few in number, radical feminists nevertheless commanded public attention. In September 1968, New York Radical Women organized a protest against the annual Miss America pageant in Atlantic City, New Jersey. The pageant, they said, was an act of "thought control" intended "to make women oppressed and men oppressors; to enslave us all the more in high-heeled, low-status roles." The protestors threw bras, girdles, makeup, and other "women-garbage" into a "Freedom Trash Can." Then they crowned a sheep "Miss America."

Not surprisingly, men and many women were generally uncomfortable with radical feminism. Onlookers at the Miss America protest called the women "lesbians" and "screwy, frustrated women."

Conservative Backlash

The rebellions against the Great Society strengthened the conservative movement. Just two years after humiliating defeat in the presidential election of 1964, conservative figures won new national prominence. Two politicians in particular became focal points for many Americans' resentment against feminism, civil rights and black power, the counterculture and the antiwar movement, and the new liberalism.

George Wallace, former governor of Alabama, increasingly combined his hostility to civil rights and federal power with a populist appeal to working-class and middle-class whites. In 1964, he ran for the Democratic presidential nomination calling for "law and order." Encouraged by his success in northern primaries that year, Wallace prepared to mount an independent campaign aimed at the "average man—your taxi driver, your steel and textile worker" in 1968. Now he played on anger over the youth rebellion and the antiwar movement, as well as the civil rights movement. "If I ever get to be President and any of these demonstrators lay down in front of my car," Wallace vowed, "it'll be the last car they ever lay down in front of." Wallace's independent campaign loomed as a threat to the two major parties.

Meanwhile, former actor Ronald Reagan became a major conservative force in the Republican Party. A lifelong liberal Democrat, the amiable Reagan had moved to the right and supported Barry Goldwater in 1964. Two years later, Reagan ran for governor of California vowing to "clean up the mess at Berkeley," with all its "Beatniks, radicals and filthy speech advocates" and its "sexual orgies so vile I cannot describe them." He opposed high taxes, Medicaid, and other liberal activism. Condemning the antiwar movement, Reagan also favored escalation of the U.S. war effort in Vietnam.

1968: A Tumultuous Year

In 1968 the stresses and strains of the Great Society came together to produce the most tumultuous year in the United States since World War II. In January, the Viet Cong and North Vietnamese launched bold, sometimes suicidal attacks all over South Vietnam on the first day of Tet, the Vietnamese New Year. Although U.S. and South Vietnamese forces inflicted punishing losses on the attackers, the Tet Offensive shocked Americans. If the United States was winning the war, how could the North Vietnamese and the Viet Cong have struck so daringly? Many Americans who had supported the decision to send troops into South Vietnam now began to believe the war was unwinnable.

The Tet Offensive doomed Johnson's increasingly troubled administration. The president needed to send reinforcements to Vietnam, but he knew public opinion would oppose the move. As it was, he could not even pay for more troops. The economy would not support both the war and the Great Society any longer. The political situation was bad, too. On March 12 Senator Eugene McCarthy of Minnesota, an antiwar candidate with little money and seemingly no chance of success, nearly beat Johnson in New Hampshire's Democratic primary. Four days later, Senator Robert Kennedy of New York, the younger brother of John Kennedy, announced his own candidacy for the Democratic nomination. The charismatic Kennedy, opposed to

>> International Student Protest, 1968

The unrest had built on campus almost from the moment it opened in 1964. Many students hated the sterile, modern buildings, erected in the midst of a big-city slum. The students also chafed at the many rules: no cooking in the dorms; no changes to the furniture; no males in females' rooms. The campus represented, one student critic complained, "an assembly-line conception of educational organization." As the student body grew from 2,000 to more than 12,000 by the fall of 1967, the Vietnam War escalated half a world away. When six local leaders of the antiwar movement were arrested, radical students rushed into the university administration building and occupied the dean's office. "Professors," they wrote on the walls, "you are past it and so is your culture!"

The protest took place, not in the United States, but on the Nanterre campus of the University of Paris. The student movement of the 1960s was, in fact, a global phenomenon. In Europe, Asia, and Latin America as well as the United States, mostly middle-class students criticized the authority of universities and governments, demanded more freedom, and condemned the Vietnam War. The wave of protest surged and reached its crest in the spring of 1968. In Western Europe, there were vast student demonstrations, strikes, and confrontations with police. Even in authoritarian, pro-Soviet Eastern Europe, students protested against universities and police. In Japan, students protested the Vietnam War. In Brazil, students confronted their universities' rigid governance and the nation's repressive military regime.

There were significant differences among these protest movements. In the United States, the New Left rejected the Old Left and did not see organized labor as an ally. In Western Europe, students were influenced by socialism and eager to make common cause with workers and unions. In France, the result was a general strike of students and workers unlike anything seen in the United States. While American protestors seldom criticized the Soviet Union, East European students condemned their own Communist governments and the USSR.

Nevertheless, important commonalities united the international student movements of the 1960s. They generally had common origins in youthful uneasiness about the cold war and the repressiveness of modern, bureaucratized society dominated by big organizations. The movements reflected a powerful yearning for free-

dom and free expression. The simultaneity of these largely separate national protests was a product of rapid communication in this age of satellites and television: students learned quickly what was going on elsewhere around the globe. The rise of student movements was a reminder, too, of the global influence of the United States: America's war in Vietnam angered students abroad; America's student movement set the example for protest around the world.

Finally, the international student protests produced a common reaction—a frightened backlash from educators, police and military, and politicians. Tear gas, water hoses, and clubs were common sights in 1968. As in the United States, the result of protest was often the triumph of conservatism and the status quo. In France, the movement that began with Nanterre ended in the reelection of President Charles de Gaulle. The harshest backlash came in Czechoslovakia: the Soviets invaded, killed and wounded more than 700, and ended any loosening of authority. But in the long run, the international student movements also signaled a persisting, even growing, demand for freedom and democracy in the face of great organizations and worldwide superpower competition. ●

the war, would be a formidable opponent for the president. Besieged by the war, the economy, and the presidential campaign, Johnson went on television the night of March 31. He announced that he had ordered a halt to the bombing of much of North Vietnam and indicated his willingness to talk peace with the North Vietnamese. Then Johnson, drained by events, announced that he would not run again for president.

Johnson painfully accepted new limits to the Great Society. Congressional leaders forced him to agree to spending cuts for Great Society programs. Despite liberal pressure, Johnson did not have the money or the clout for new welfare programs, new initiatives to improve race relations, or even the space program, that symbol of great liberal dreams. The president continued the Apollo program but abandoned other space projects. The Great Society was coming back down to earth.

Meanwhile, the United States was torn by upheaval and violence. In the first six months of 1968, students carried out demonstrations at 101 colleges and universities. On April 4, a white man assassinated Martin Luther King Jr. in Memphis, Tennessee, where he had gone to support striking African American and white sanitation workers. King's assassination set off riots in more than 100 cities. Forty-one African Americans and five whites died. African Americans "have had all they can stand," two black psychologists wrote.

The violence soon spread to the presidential campaign. After winning the California Democratic primary on the evening of June 5, Robert Kennedy was shot in a Los Angeles hotel by Sirhan Sirhan, a troubled Palestinian. Kennedy's death the next

The Anguish of Vietnam President Lyndon Johnson listens to a tape-recorded report on the state of the American effort in South Vietnam, 1968.

The Funeral Procession of Martin Luther King, Jr., Atlanta, Georgia, April 9, 1968 The widowed Coretta Scott King, center, walks with her family.

morning left Eugene McCarthy to contest the Democratic presidential nomination with Vice President Hubert Humphrey of Minnesota, who still supported the American war effort in Vietnam. Humphrey won the nomination at the Democratic convention in Chicago in August, but the party was deeply divided. Outside the convention hall, Mayor Daley's police battled in the streets with antiwar demonstrators.

The Republican Party nominated Richard Nixon, the man who lost to John Kennedy in 1960. A critic of the Great Society, Nixon promised to end the Vietnam War and unify the country. Like the more conservative Reagan and Wallace, Nixon tried to exploit the nation's social divisions with promises to speak for "the forgotten Americans, the nonshouters, the nondemonstrators." Wallace, meanwhile, appealed even more bluntly to frustrated middle- and working-class whites.

Unlike 1960, Nixon won this time. Although Humphrey made it close by repudiating Johnson's Vietnam policy, the vice president could not overcome the troubles of the Great Society. Nixon attracted 43.4 percent of the popular vote to Humphrey's 42.7 percent and Wallace's 13.5 percent. Running strongly in every region of the country, Nixon piled up 301 electoral votes. Although the Democrats retained control of the House and Senate, the party's eight-year hold on the White House had been broken.

Conclusion

The upheavals of 1968 marked the end of illusions about limitless American power. John Kennedy's confident nation—able to "pay any price, bear any burden, meet any hardship, support any friend, oppose any foe"—had vanished. By 1968 the

American economy could no longer "pay any price." The United States could not successfully support its friends in South Vietnam. The government could not create the Great Society. Instead, the nation was deeply divided by generation, race, and gender. The assassinations of Robert Kennedy and Martin Luther King Jr. dramatized the breakdown of democracy.

The year 1968 was tumultuous for Lt. Fred Downs, too. On the morning of January 11, he walked through a gate and stepped on a mine. The explosion threw him into the air, ripped through his eardrums, tore away pieces of his legs and hips, mutilated his right hand, laid bare the bones of his right arm, and blew off his left arm at the elbow. Horrified, Downs looked at his wounds. "I felt," he recalled, "the total defeat of my life."

Back in the United States, Downs had to deal with the loss of his arm, his confidence, and his plans. At a military hospital, he had to learn how to use a prosthetic arm and to accept the breakup of his marriage. He also had to learn how to deal with a divided, angry America. On the street, a man pointed to the hook sticking out of Downs's left sleeve. "Get that in Vietnam?" the man asked. Downs said he had. "Serves you right," the man snapped, and walked away. The United States, like that man, would have a difficult time coming to terms with the events of the 1960s.

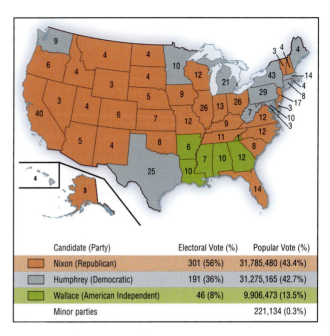

Map 28–4   The Presidential Election, 1968 Like the 1960 election, this was another close contest with widespread consequences. But this time, former vice president Richard M. Nixon was the winner.

Further Readings

Terry H. Anderson, *The Movement and the Sixties* (1995), offers a sweeping chronicle of the varieties of protest in the 1960s. Robert Cohen and Reginald E. Zelnik, eds. *The Free Speech Movement: Reflections on Berkeley in the 1960s* (2002). Perspectives on this key moment of emerging student radicalism.

Robert Dallek, *An Unfinished Life: John F. Kennedy, 1917–1963* (2003). Carefully researched, balanced treatment.

Gareth Davies, *From Opportunity to Entitlement: The Transformation and Decline of Great Society Liberalism* (1999). How Lyndon Johnson's program went wrong.

Betty Friedan, *The Feminine Mystique* (1963). Pioneering liberal-feminist exploration of the plight of middle-class women.

George C. Herring, *America's Longest War: The United States and Vietnam, 1950–1975*, 4th ed. (2001). A balanced overview of the war.

Mark Kurlansky, *1968: The Year That Rocked the World* (2003). A readable survey of global unrest.

Howell Raines, *My Soul Is Rested: Movement Days in the Deep South Remembered* (1977). A moving collection of interviews that vividly re-create the struggle against segregation.

Who, What?

Review Questions

1. How did the new liberalism differ from the liberalism of the New Deal and the Fair Deal? How did the new conservatism differ from the old?

2. Compare and contrast the New Frontier and the Great Society. Did their goals differ?

3. Why was the civil rights movement able to attain its major goals by the mid-1960s?

>> Timeline >>

▼ **1955–56**
Montgomery, Alabama, bus boycott

▼ **1957**
Soviet *Sputnik* satellite launch

▼ **1960**
Greensboro, North Carolina, lunch-counter sit-ins
Sharon Statement

John F. Kennedy elected president

▼ **1961**
First U.S. suborbital space flight, by Alan Shepard
Freedom Rides

▼ **1962**
Port Huron Statement

Integration of University of Mississippi
Cuban Missile Crisis

▼ **1963**
Birmingham, Alabama, civil rights protests
Civil rights march on Washington, DC
Assassination of John F. Kennedy

▼ **1964**
Civil Rights Act of 1964

4. How did the United States fight the cold war in the 1960s? Was America winning by the end of the decade?

5. Compare liberal and radical feminism. Were these movements incompatible with each other?

6. Compare the Black Power movement, the New Left, and the counterculture. Did any of these want radical change for the United States?

Websites

Free Speech Movement Digital Archive, from the Bancroft Library of the University of California (http://bancroft.berkeley.edu/FSM/), offers a wealth of documents and other resources for studying student activism on the Berkeley campus.

The Lyndon Baines Johnson Library and Museum website (http://www.lbjlib.utexas.edu/) includes many primary sources, including speeches, photographs, oral histories, national-security documents, audio, and video.

The National Security Archive of George Washington University (http://www.gwu.edu/~nsarchiv/) features excellent collections on the Cuban Missile and Berlin crises.

The Vietnam Center and Archive website, maintained by Texas Tech University (http://vietnam.ttu.edu/index.php), includes many oral histories of the war.

The online Voices of Civil Rights exhibit of the Library of Congress (http://www.loc.gov/exhibits/civilrights/) includes words and images of the African American, Chicano, and Native American struggles of the 1960s.

For further review materials and resource information, please visit www.oup.com/us/ofthepeople

Lyndon Johnson's "War on Poverty"
Free Speech Movement
Tonkin Gulf incidents
Lyndon Johnson's landslide election as
    president

▼ 1965
U.S. escalation of Vietnam War
Voting Rights Act of 1965

Water Quality Act
Watts race riot

▼ 1966
National Organization for Women (NOW)

▼ 1967
Air Quality Act
Stop the Draft Week

▼ 1968
Tet Offensive in Vietnam
Assassinations of Martin Luther King Jr. and
    Robert F. Kennedy
Richard Nixon elected president

▼ 1975
Surrender of South Vietnam to North Vietnam

Common Threads

>> How did economic problems continue to shape American life from the 1960s to the 1970s?

>> Why did liberalism continue to influence politics in the 1970s?

>> How did a sense of limits drive Richard Nixon's foreign and domestic policies?

>> Did American society become more democratic in the 1970s?

>> What were the ways the Vietnam syndrome would affect the United States after the 1970s?

Living with Less
1968–1980

>> "Fighting Shirley Chisholm"

At the end of the 1960s, Shirley Chisholm, an African American congresswoman from Brooklyn, New York, worried about her country. Amid the upheaval of the Great Society, the United States "sometimes seemed to be poised on the brink of racial and class war." Blacks, women, the poor, and the young demanded change, but the political system refused to meet their needs. "Our representative democracy is not working," Chisholm declared. "It is ruled by a small group of old men."

It was not in Chisholm's nature to give in. Born to working-class West Indian parents in Brooklyn, she had pushed her way to a master's degree and a career as an educator. Running as "Fighting Shirley Chisholm," she won election to Congress from her poor, predominantly black and Puerto Rican district in 1968. In January 1972, she became the first black and first female candidate for the Democratic presidential nomination. "You've never had anyone looking like me running for President," Chisholm declared. "Other kinds of people can steer the ship of state besides white men."

Chisholm's campaign continued the 1960s battle for rights. Chisholm wanted to create a coalition of African Americans, women, and the young "to get their share of the American dream and participate in the decision-making process that governs our lives."

Chisholm campaigned hard in several primaries. But with little money and organization, she had little chance. Chisholm had to fight for equal time on television. Black male politicians withheld their support. Black voters wondered whether an African American could really win. Her female and black supporters squabbled. The Chisholm campaign ended in defeat in California.

Chisholm's daring presidential candidacy enhanced her reputation. In November, she won reelection to Congress with a huge majority. But she was worn down. "I am tired," she admitted. "I am tired of fighting, fighting, fighting all the time." Still, Chisholm did not regret her presidential bid. "I ran for the Presidency in order to crack a little more of the ice which has congealed to nearly immobilize our political system and demoralize people," she explained. "I ran for the Presidency, despite hopeless odds, to demonstrate sheer will and refusal to accept the status quo."

Chisholm's failed campaign was part of a collision between Americans' aspirations for equality and new political, economic, and cultural realities. As the struggle for rights and opportunities expanded in the 1970s, the nation's economy and global influence continued to weaken. Without enough oil and industrial jobs, the United States no longer seemed a land of unlimited possibilities. Americans worried whether the nation could afford to meet everyone's needs in an age of dwindling resources. As a magazine concluded, the American people were "Learning to Live with Less."

The result was not the "racial and class war" that Chisholm feared. But neither did the liberal Great Society give way to a stable new order dominated by one party or ideology. Instead, workers, employers, politicians, and families struggled with the consequences of limited resources and power. While Americans puzzled over the relationship between the economy and government and between the nation and the world, the political system broke down in scandal and failure. ●

A New Crisis: Economic Decline

During the social, political, and military crises of the 1960s, Americans had largely taken the economy for granted. Prosperous and growing, the United States seemed destined to remain the world's preeminent economic power. But the economy had faltered as the Great Society came apart. By the 1970s, it was in crisis. The failings of business, government, and economists, a shortage of oil, intensifying foreign competition, and the multinational strategies of giant corporations combined to weaken the foundations of prosperity. By the end of the 1970s, the United States seemed to be in economic decline.

Weakness at Home

There were signs of economic weakness almost everywhere in the 1970s. Although the economy continued to grow, corporate profits and workers' productivity fell off. Unemployment increased; inflation, which usually dropped when unemployment rose, also increased. At best, the economy seemed stagnant. The unprecedented combination of high unemployment and high inflation led to the coining of a new word—stagflation—to describe the nation's economic predicament (see Table 29–1).

Corporations were partially responsible for the weak state of the economy. Corporate leaders had tended to maximize short-term profits at the cost of the long-term health of their companies. Some companies had not plowed enough of their earnings back into research, development, and new equipment. As a result, some American products seemed less innovative and reliable. Detroit's automobiles, so attractive and advanced in the 1950s, now struck consumers as unglamorous, inefficient, and poorly made. Ford's new Pinto sedan had to be recalled because its fuel tank was prone to explode.

Long an emblem of security and stability, corporations themselves appeared as vulnerable as the Pinto. In 1970, the Penn Central Railroad became the largest corporation in American history to go bankrupt. That year, only massive federal aid saved Lockheed Aircraft from going under as well.

The federal government also played a part in the nation's economic predicament. Massive federal spending had stimulated the economy from the 1940s to the 1960s but did not have the same effect in the 1970s. Some analysts claimed that Washington had diverted too much of the nation's talent and resources from the private sector to military projects during the cold war. In addition, the government's huge expenditures for the Vietnam War promoted inflation.

Economists did not give federal policy makers much help. In the 1960s, liberal economists had been confident that they understood the secret of maintaining prosperity. The novel problem of stagflation left them baffled. "The rules of economics," admitted the chairman of the Federal Reserve, "are not working quite the way they used to."

Table 29–1 Stagflation in the 1970s

Year	Inflation % Change	Unemployment % Change	Combined* % Change
1970	5.9	4.9	10.8
1971	4.3	5.9	10.2
1972	3.3	5.6	8.9
1973	6.2	4.9	11.1
1974	11.0	5.6	16.6
1975	9.1	8.5	17.6
1976	5.8	7.7	13.5
1977	6.5	7.1	13.6
1978	7.7	6.1	13.8
1979	11.3	5.8	17.1
1980	13.5	7.1	20.6

*"Combined" means annual percentage changes of inflation and unemployment.

Source: *Statistical Abstract of the United States*, 1984, pp. 375–76, 463; tables 624–25, 760. (1971 inflation data from *Statistical Abstract*, 1973, p. 348, table 569.)

The Energy Crisis

An emerging energy crisis intensified economic problems. By 1974, the nation had to import over a third of its oil from foreign countries, particularly from the Middle East. The energy needs of the United States and other western countries empowered the Organization of the Petroleum Exporting Countries (OPEC), a group of third world nations that had joined together to get higher prices for their oil. In October 1973, war broke out between Israel and a coalition of Arab nations including Egypt and Syria. Arab members of OPEC refused to send petroleum to the United States and other nations that supported Israel in the conflict. OPEC soon raised oil prices nearly 400 percent.

The effect of the oil shortage spread well beyond gas stations. In some states, truck drivers blockaded highways to protest the high cost of fuel and low speed limits. Lack of fuel grounded some airline flights. Heating oil for homes and businesses was also in short supply. Communities opened shelters for people who could not afford to heat their homes. Although the Arabs ended the oil embargo in March 1974, the underlying energy problem remained.

The Energy Crisis Motorists crowd around an open gas station, New York City, December 1973.

Competition Abroad

Weakened by trouble at home, the United States was all the more vulnerable to increasingly tough competition from abroad. Thanks to American aid after World War II, Japan and Western European countries now had efficient, up-to-date industries. By the 1970s, these nations rivaled the United States, not only abroad, but even in the American market.

The rise of Japan was the most dramatic of these developments. For decades, Americans had derided Japanese goods. Yet by the 1970s, Japan's modern factories turned out high-quality products. Japanese televisions and other electronic goods filled American homes. Japanese cars—small, well made, and fuel efficient—attracted American buyers worried about the high price of gas.

Because of such competition, the United States fell back in the global economic race. In 1950, the nation had accounted for 40 percent of the value of all the goods and services produced around the world. By 1970 that figure was down to 23 percent. By the end of the 1970s, the United States imported more manufactured goods than it exported.

The Multinationals

Multinational corporations—firms with factories and other operations in several nations—played a key role in the economic crisis. Taking advantage of new technologies and lower trade barriers, corporations in the United States and Western Europe had moved aggressively into global markets after World War II. All told, multinationals accounted for about 15 percent of the world's annual gross product. The biggest multinationals had annual sales larger than the annual product of some countries.

AMERICA AND THE WORLD

>> Carl Gerstacker's Dream

In February 1972, Carl A. Gerstacker, chairman of the multinational Dow Chemical Company, confessed his secret fantasy to an audience of executives, economists, and policy makers at a White House conference. "I have long dreamed of buying an island owned by no nation," Gerstacker revealed. But this sober executive did not plan to escape to his island and enjoy a life of solitary primitive leisure. Instead, Gerstacker wanted to take Dow Chemical along. "If we were located on such truly neutral ground," he explained, "we could then really operate in the United States as U.S. citizens, in Japan as Japanese citizens and in Brazil as Brazilians rather than being governed in prime by the laws of the United States." The multinational would effectively be on its own, free to do as it pleased without interference from the U.S. government.

Gerstacker's audience probably did not wonder whether he had been working too hard lately. By the 1970s, the leaders of American multinationals felt surprisingly few ties to their home country. "We are not an American company," a U.S. oil executive told a congressional committee. Explaining why most of his company's top executives came from foreign countries, an executive vice president of Bendix responded that "nationality is unimportant." So unattached to the United States or any other country, multinational leaders did not believe their companies should let patriotism interfere with business. "It is not proper for an international corporation to put the welfare of any country in which it does business above that of any other," a spokesman for Dow's competitor, Union Carbide, sanctimoniously observed. As Carl Gerstacker concluded, giant corporations were becoming not so much multinational or international as "anational" and "nationless."

Multinational leaders seemed to prefer a world with no nations at all. Eager to create a unified global economy, these executives felt that governments only got in the way. They imposed tariffs on exports and imports, regulated and limited trade, taxed profits, dictated working conditions, nationalized resources, and started wars. "The world's political structures are completely obsolete," fumed Jacques Maisonrouge, a French-born senior vice president of IBM. "They have not changed in at least a hundred years and are woefully out of tune with technological progress." Nation-states represented the past; multinationals, creating new technologies and serving the planet, represented the future. José Béjarano, vice president of the Latin American division of Xerox, declared, "The multinational corporation today is a force that can serve global needs of mankind far better than the medieval concept of nation states." Of course, the heads of the multinationals conveniently forgot how often their firms had turned to the U.S. government for diplomatic and military support when other nations had threatened their investments over the decades.

Few Americans shared the antinational vision of men like Béjarano. Around the world, the United States and other nation-states, fueled by the intense patriotism of their citizens, were not about to disappear—or leave the multinationals alone. As Gerstacker acknowledged, U.S. tax laws made it impossible for Dow Chemical to move its headquarters to his island paradise. For all their impact on the world around them, the multinational executives were ahead of their time. But they could fantasize. With the fervent certainty of a prophet in a crowd of unbelievers, John J. Powers, president of the drug company Pfizer, insisted a unified global economy "is no idealistic pipe dream but a hard-headed prediction." Time would tell. ●

U.S. firms made up the majority of the largest multinationals in the 1970s. As Americans struggled, U.S. multinationals still earned large profits because their overseas units were often more profitable than their domestic operations. Not surprisingly, these American firms rapidly expanded abroad. In 1957, just 9 percent of American investments went abroad; by 1972, the figure had reached 25 percent.

The multinationals' most controversial foreign investment was the transfer of manufacturing from the United States to nations with lower wages and less restrictive labor laws. As corporations shifted production to plants just over the Mexican border or to facilities in Asia, American plants closed with stunning job losses. The combination of overseas production and foreign competition was devastating. In 1954, U.S. companies had made 75 percent of the world's televisions. Twenty years later, U.S. companies produced less than 25 percent—and almost all of that production took place in Mexico and overseas.

Responding to critics, multinational executives argued that investment abroad increased jobs and prosperity in the United States. Capital invested in Mexico and Asia came back home, the executives insisted, as dividends to stockholders and tax payments to the government. It was unclear whether the multinationals or their critics were right.

The Impact of Decline

Economic decline began to reshape life in the United States in the 1970s. It seemed as if the Industrial Revolution was being reversed. As factories closed, Americans witnessed the deindustrialization of their country. Huge steel plants, the symbol of American industrial might, stood empty. These developments intensified the trend, first evident in the 1950s, toward a service-centered economy. In the 1970s, most new jobs were in the sales and retail sectors. The United States, a union official lamented, was turning into "a nation of hamburger stands."

For workers, the consequences of deindustrialization were demoralizing. Heavy industry had been the stronghold of the labor movement. Organized labor lost members, power, and influence. By the late 1970s, less than one in four workers belonged to a union.

The shift away from unionized industrial jobs eroded workers' incomes. After rising from the 1950s into the 1960s, workers' spendable income began to drop. To keep up, more and more women took full-time jobs outside the home: the percentage of women in the workforce, 36 percent in 1960, rose to 50 percent in 1980—the highest level in American history to that time. Many Americans could not find work, however. As the huge baby boom generation came of age, the economy did not produce enough jobs. The unemployment rate, which had dipped as low as 2.8 percent in 1969, jumped up to a high of 9 percent only six years later.

Economic decline accelerated the transformation of America's regions. The energy crisis and deindustrialization sped up the shift of people and power from north to south and east to west (see Map 29–1). With its cold, snowy winters, the North was especially vulnerable to the oil embargo and higher energy prices. America's Snowbelt now seemed a less attractive place to live and do business. In the 1970s, the sight of empty, decaying factories made the Northeast and the Midwest America's "Rustbelt."

AMERICAN LANDSCAPE

>> Youngstown, Ohio

For more than 75 years, workers made steel in the open-hearth furnaces at the Campbell Works of the Youngstown Sheet and Tube Company. Opened just after the start of the twentieth century, the huge mill was one of the plants that gave the community of Youngstown, in northeast Ohio, its reputation as a "Steel City." In exchange for hard labor, the Campbell Works also gave generations of Youngstown's workers a chance for prosperity. "Youngstown," a resident observed, "was a place in which the American Dream seemed to have come true for many working-class families."

The dream came to a sudden end in 1977. By then, the mill was an inefficient "antique" that made steel more slowly and expensively than new mills. On September 19 the parent company of Youngstown Sheet and Tube, Lykes Corporation, announced it was closing down the Campbell Works and transferring some production to a new facility in Illinois. As many as 5,000 workers would lose their jobs. Once a symbol of American industrial might, the Campbell Works had instantly become a symbol of deindustrialization and decline on that "Black Monday" in 1977.

The announcement of the shutdown stunned the mill's employees. To many, it was like another Pearl Harbor. Some workers realized right away that their way of life was gone. On the way home, they threw their hard hats and work boots into the Mahoning River.

Although many workers hoped that the Campbell Works could be saved, the Lykes Corporation refused to reopen the mill. The company claimed that the low price of foreign steel, especially from Japan, and the high cost of U.S. environmental regulations made it impossible to operate the mill at a profit. A coalition of workers and churches tried to buy the mill, but their plan fell through. Congress and President Jimmy Carter, believing the Campbell Works was too inefficient to save, refused to help. Carter, an angry worker grumbled, "ought to run for president of Japan."

In the end, there was no way to save the Campbell Works. The workers lost their jobs, and much more. They felt cut off from their past and their future. "Our fathers worked here and our grandfathers worked here," said a union official. "Now I face the prospect of this turning into a ghost town." The optimistic future of the American Dream had disappeared. "They used to tell us: 'Get out of high school, get a job in a mill and you're fixed for life,'" said a steelworker. "Now I know better."

Facing such bleak prospects, a quarter of the labor force at Campbell Works moved away from Youngstown. Many of them went to the booming Sunbelt. About half of the workers stayed on in Youngstown and found new jobs. Many of those jobs did not pay nearly as well as work at Youngstown Sheet and Tube. The remaining quarter of the workforce also stayed on but found no work at all.

Other Youngstown residents also suffered because of the closing of the Campbell Works. Business dropped in the taverns where steelworkers had gone for a drink after the job. Other stores missed the steelworkers' patronage. "It will kill our business," a Youngstown store owner lamented.

The shutdown at Youngstown Sheet and Tube was just the beginning of deindustrialization in Youngstown. By 1980, the "Steel City" was dotted with the decaying hulks of empty mills. Other communities feared they would be next. "There are going to be a few more Youngstowns before it's over," an economist predicted. ●

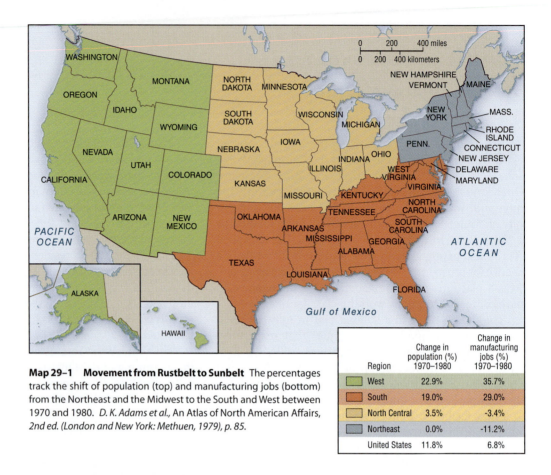

Map 29–1   Movement from Rustbelt to Sunbelt   The percentages track the shift of population (top) and manufacturing jobs (bottom) from the Northeast and the Midwest to the South and West between 1970 and 1980. *D. K. Adams et al., An Atlas of North American Affairs, 2nd ed. (London and New York: Methuen, 1979), p. 85.*

Region	Change in population (%) 1970–1980	Change in manufacturing jobs (%) 1970–1980
West	22.9%	35.7%
South	19.0%	29.0%
North Central	3.5%	-3.4%
Northeast	0.0%	-11.2%
United States	11.8%	6.8%

Fleeing deindustrialization, many northerners migrated south to the band of states ranging from Florida to California. As the Sunbelt boomed, farms turned into suburbs, and cities such as Orlando, Houston, Phoenix, and San Diego exploded in size. If anything, Texas and the southwestern states, rich in oil and natural gas reserves, profited from the energy crisis. The Sunbelt was home to new high-technology businesses: aerospace firms, electronics companies, and defense contractors. The Sunbelt was also at the cutting edge of the service economy, with its emphasis on leisure and consumption. More retirees moved to Florida than to any other state. Tourists flocked to the original Disneyland in California and the new Disney World in Florida. They gambled their money in Las Vegas.

> ## All I want is my damn job back.
>
> MARY FARMER KINNEY,
> a laid-off African American autoworker in Hamtramck, Michigan, 1979.

Confronting Decline: Nixon's Strategy

Richard Nixon was the first president to confront the decline of America's prosperity and power. He recognized that the failure of the war in Vietnam marked the end of America's cold war pretensions. He accepted, too, that the American economy had weakened. Despite his long opposition to Communism and the New Deal, Nixon was a pragmatist, open to new realities and approaches as he coped with the nation's problems.

A New Foreign Policy

The president and his national security advisor, Henry Kissinger, still regarded Communism as a menace and saw the cold war rivalry between the United States and the Soviet Union as the defining reality of the modern world. However, Nixon and Kissinger understood that the relative decline of American power dictated a new approach to the cold war.

> . . I think of what happened to Greece and Rome . . . great civilizations of the past, as they have become wealthy, as they lost their will to live, to improve, they then have become subject to the decadence which eventually destroys a civilization. The United States is now reaching that period.
>
> RICHARD NIXON,
> 1971

The twin pillars of the new foreign policy were the Nixon Doctrine and détente. In July 1969, the president announced that the United States "cannot—and will not—conceive all the plans, design all the programs, execute all the decisions and undertake all the defense of the free nations of the world." America would continue to provide a nuclear umbrella, but its allies would have to defend themselves against insurgencies and invasions. This Nixon Doctrine amounted to a repudiation of the Truman Doctrine, the 1947 promise "to support free peoples who are resisting attempted subjugation by armed minorities or by outside pressures" (see Chapter 26).

The United States also pursued a new relationship with the Soviet Union and the People's Republic of China. Nixon and Kissinger wanted to lessen the cost of America's rivalry with these two Communist nuclear powers. Separate agreements with the Soviet Union and China would, the American leaders hoped, keep those two nations from combining forces against the United States. Nixon and Kissinger therefore worked to establish détente, the relaxation of tensions.

At the start of Nixon's presidency, the United States had not recognized the legitimacy of the People's Republic of China. Instead, America supported the Communists' bitter foes, the Nationalist Chinese regime on Taiwan. In February 1972, Nixon became the first American president to go to mainland China. He gave the Chinese leaders what they most wanted—a promise that the United States would eventually withdraw its troops from Taiwan. The two sides also made clear that they opposed any Soviet attempt to dominate Asia.

Nixon's trip brought American policy in line with the reality of the 1970s and underscored the gradual ending of anti-Communist hysteria back home in America. As Nixon intended, the trip also left the Soviets with the frightening possibility of a Chinese-American alliance.

Architects of Détente President Richard Nixon and his National Security Advisor, Henry Kissinger, 1972.

Nixon did not want a confrontation with the Soviets, the only power that could destroy America with nuclear weapons. The United States no longer had clear military superiority. Instead, the president sought détente. Above all, he wanted the Soviets to agree to limit their long-range or strategic nuclear arsenals. The Soviets also wished to reduce the expense and danger of the cold war and to counter Nixon's overture to the Chinese. Moreover, they badly needed American grain to help feed their own people.

Under these circumstances, the two sides began talks on the Strategic Arms Limitation Treaty (SALT I) in 1969. In May 1972, three months after his trip to China, Nixon became the first American president to travel to Moscow, where he signed the SALT treaty, limiting for five years the number of each nation's nuclear missiles. An Anti–Ballistic Missile (ABM) treaty sharply limited the number of defensive missiles that the two sides could deploy. Although they did not stop the arms race, the ABM and SALT treaties symbolized the American and Soviet agreement that "there is no alternative to . . . peaceful coexistence."

Ending the Vietnam War

The Nixon administration sought better relations with the Soviet Union and the People's Republic of China in part to help end the Vietnam War. Nixon and Kissinger hoped the Soviets and the Chinese would pressure the North Vietnamese to accept a peace agreement. The president needed such an agreement. Nixon knew the United States could not win the Vietnam War. Meanwhile, the ongoing conflict divided the American people and undermined American prestige and power around the world. But Nixon did not want the United States to look weak.

Détente at the Great Wall of China, 1972 President Nixon, with his wife Pat, became the first American president to visit mainland China.

To appease public opinion, Nixon began to bring American soldiers home in 1969. Without those soldiers, he had a hard time persuading North Vietnam to accept the continued existence of South Vietnam. The president attempted to resolve this dilemma with a policy known as "Vietnamization," or encouraging the South Vietnamese to take over their own defense. However, the South Vietnamese military alone could not beat back the Communists.

Accordingly, Nixon turned to U.S. airpower to support South Vietnamese troops and intimidate the North Vietnamese. In March 1969, he authorized B-52 raids on North Vietnamese sanctuaries in Cambodia. Because bombing this neutral country might outrage American and world opinion, the president kept the raids secret. However, the Cambodian operation did not force North Vietnam to make peace. Secret negotiations between Henry Kissinger and North Vietnamese diplomats also went nowhere.

Meanwhile, Nixon's actions angered many Americans. News of the secret bombings leaked out. In October, millions of Americans participated in Moratorium Day, a dramatic break from business as usual, to protest the war. In November, more than 250,000 people staged a "March Against Death" in Washington. That month, Americans learned about one of the most troubling episodes of the war. On March 16, 1968, United States soldiers had shot and killed between 200 and 500 unarmed South Vietnamese women, children, and old men in the hamlet of My Lai. This atrocity led to the 1970 court-martial and eventual conviction of Lieutenant William Calley Jr. for mass murder.

Demonstrations and public opinion did not stop the president from using violence to force a peace agreement. When General Lon Nol, the new pro-American leader of Cambodia, appealed for United States aid to stop a Communist insurgency, a joint United States–South Vietnamese force invaded Cambodia to look for North Vietnamese troops in April 1970. The Cambodian invasion produced turmoil in the United States. Students demonstrated on campuses across the country. On May 4, National Guard troops fired at an unarmed crowd of protestors at Kent State University in Ohio. Four students died. Ten days later, state police killed two African American students at Jackson State College in Mississippi. These deaths intensified the outrage over the invasion of Cambodia. Students went out on strike at about 450 campuses.

Some Americans, angered by the demonstrating college students, mobilized in support of the president and the war. In New York City, construction workers attacked student demonstrators. "The country is virtually on the edge of a spiritual—and perhaps physical—breakdown," New York's mayor lamented. "For the first time in a century, we are not sure there is a future for America."

The Vietnam War Comes to Cambodia Cambodian landscape devastated by the 1969 bombings that President Nixon tried to keep secret.

As American troop withdrawals continued, the war and the peace negotiations dragged on. Meanwhile, the *New York Times* began publishing the so-called Pentagon Papers, a secret government history of the American involvement in Vietnam. The documents, which made clear that the Johnson administration had misled the American people, further undermined support for the war. The Nixon administration tried unsuccessfully to persuade the Supreme Court to block publication of the papers.

Unable to stop the publication of the Pentagon Papers or secure a peace agreement, Nixon stepped up efforts to pressure North Vietnam into a settlement. When the North Vietnamese army swept across the border into South Vietnam in March 1972, the president struck back with Operation Linebacker, an aerial attack against North Vietnam. When negotiations stalled again, the president intensified the air raids in December. On January 27, 1973, negotiators signed a peace agreement in Paris. For the United States, at least, the Vietnam War was over.

Nixon had promised "peace with honor" in Vietnam. But the agreement did not guarantee the survival of our South Vietnamese ally. The cease-fire came at a heavy cost. Twenty thousand Americans and more than six hundred thousand North and South Vietnamese soldiers had died since Nixon took office in 1969. The number of civilian casualties will never be known. Nixon had ended U.S. participation in the Vietnam War, but the president's critics asked whether four more years of fighting had really been necessary when the result was such a flawed peace agreement.

Chile and the Middle East

Détente, a practical accommodation with Soviet power, did not mean that the Nixon administration accepted the rise of potentially hostile regimes around the world. To stop the spread of socialism and Communism, Nixon, like the presidents before him, was willing to subvert a democratically elected government and tolerate an authoritarian substitute. In 1970, he ordered the CIA to block the election of Salvador Allende, a Marxist, as president of Chile. Allende was elected anyway. "I don't see why we need to stand by and watch a country go communist due to the irresponsibility of its own people," Kissinger fumed. "The issues are much too important for the Chilean voters to be left to decide for themselves." The CIA then helped destabilize Allende's regime by aiding right-wing parties, driving up the price of bread, and encouraging demonstrations. When a military coup deposed Allende in 1973, the United States denied responsibility and offered financial assistance to the new military dictator, General Augusto Pinochet.

In the Middle East, the Nixon administration also displayed both its continuing hostility to Communism and its inability to shape events decisively. During the Six-Day War in 1967, Israel had defeated Egyptian and Syrian forces and occupied territory belonging to Egypt, Syria, and Jordan. Seeking revenge, Egypt and Syria attacked Israel in October 1973, on Yom Kippur, the holiest day of the Jewish calendar. When the United States sent critical supplies to Israel, Arab countries responded with the oil embargo. Meanwhile, the Soviets supplied the Arabs and pressed for a role in the region. Determined to keep out the Soviet Union, Nixon put American nuclear forces on alert. Kissinger mediated between the combatants, who agreed to pull back their troops in January 1974. Although the embargo ended, American weakness was obvious. Supporting Israel, the United States still needed the Arabs' oil. Nixon and Kissinger held back the Soviet Union, but they could not bring peace to the Middle East.

Taming Big Government

The problem of decline, imaginatively addressed in Nixon's foreign policy, proved more difficult to handle at home. Nixon took office with the conventional Republican domestic goals of taming big government. He wanted the federal government to balance its budget and shed some of its power.

So, Nixon's administration cut spending for some programs, including defense. The fate of the space program epitomized the new budgetary realities. On July 20, 1969, a lunar landing module touched down on the moon. As astronaut Neil Armstrong set foot on the surface, he proclaimed, "That's one small step for man, one giant leap for mankind." The United States had beaten the Soviets to the moon. This triumph suggested that there was still no limit to what Americans could do.

There were, however, firm limits to what the space program could do. The administration slashed NASA's budget.

In 1969, the president called for a New Federalism, in which Washington would return "a greater share of control to state and local governments and to the people." Three years later, the administration persuaded Congress to pass a revenue-sharing plan that allowed state and local governments to spend funds collected by the federal government.

Despite his commitment to Republican ideology, Nixon took the same pragmatic approach to domestic problems that he did to foreign affairs. Although the president pushed for the New Federalism, he left popular New Deal and Great Society programs largely intact. Despite his budget cuts, the government kept spending vast amounts of money. By 1971, the cost of big government, combined with the unsettled economy, had produced a huge, un-Republican budget deficit.

The president did try to reform the federal welfare system put in place by the New Deal. Like many Republican conservatives, Nixon believed that welfare made the federal bureaucracy too large and the poor too dependent. During the president's first term, his administration tried to replace the largest federal welfare program, Aid to Families with Dependent Children, with a controversial system inspired by presidential aide Daniel Patrick Moynihan, a Harvard sociologist. Moynihan's Family Assistance Plan would have provided poor families with a guaranteed minimum annual income, but it also would have required the heads of poor households to accept any jobs available. Opposed by both liberals and conservatives, the program failed to pass Congress.

Meanwhile, the Nixon administration went along with several liberal initiatives that expanded the government's regulatory powers. By the end of the 1960s, many Americans worried that corporations did not protect workers, consumers, or the environment. A grassroots environmental movement grew rapidly, particularly on college campuses. On April 22, 1970, tens of millions of Americans celebrated the first Earth Day. Echoing anti–Vietnam War activism, they staged teach-ins, demonstrations, and cleanup campaigns. "If you care about this mess," one marcher's sign read, "why not stop it?" After this great initial turnout, Earth Day became an annual event.

Liberals in Congress responded to popular opinion by establishing three new federal regulatory agencies: the Environmental Protection Agency (EPA), the Occupational Safety and Health Administration (OSHA), and the Consumer Product Safety Commission. These agencies considerably enhanced the government's power over corporations, as did a series of measures to safeguard coastlines and endangered species and to limit the use of pesticides, the strip-mining of coal, and the pollution of air and water.

The Grassroots Environmental Movement Organizing the first Earth Day, April 22, 1970.

An Uncertain Economic Policy

Nixon, like most Republicans, believed government should not interfere much in the economy. But high inflation, rising unemployment, and falling corporate profits tested the president's commitment to Republican orthodoxy. He was unable to persuade business to control price increases and organized labor to limit wage demands.

Meanwhile, the U.S. dollar was in crisis. Since the Bretton Woods conference during World War II (see Chapter 25), many other nations had tied the value of their own currencies to the dollar. The value of the dollar, in turn, had been supported by the U.S. commitment to give an ounce of gold in return for 35 dollars. The U.S. commitment to the gold standard had stabilized the international financial system and helped spur worldwide economic development for more than two decades. But by the 1970s, the United States' weakening economy had undermined the dollar: strong European economies had too many dollars and too little confidence in the United States, and the U.S. government didn't have enough gold. If other countries demanded gold for their dollars, Washington would be unable to pay and panic would follow.

Confronting inflation, monetary crisis, and economic weakness, Nixon announced his New Economic Policy in August 1971. To prevent the breakdown of the monetary system, the president took the United States off the gold standard by ending the exchange of gold for dollars. To strengthen U.S. producers against foreign competitors, Nixon lowered the value of the dollar and slapped new tariffs on imports; as a result, American goods would sell more cheaply abroad and foreign goods would cost more in the United States. To slow inflation, the president authorized a freeze on wages and prices.

The New Economic Policy did strengthen the international monetary system and help U.S. producers. But wage and price controls did not solve the underlying economic problems that caused inflation. The ongoing cost of the Vietnam War, along with the Arab oil embargo, continued to drive up prices. Deindustrialization continued, too. Nixon and his advisers had no domestic counterpart to détente.

Refusing to Settle for Less: Struggles for Rights

Despite the troubled economy, many Americans, like Shirley Chisholm, refused to settle for less. In the late 1960s and 1970s, African Americans and women continued their struggles for the rights that they had long been denied. Their example inspired other disadvantaged groups to demand recognition. Mexican Americans, Native Americans, and gays and lesbians organized and demonstrated for their causes. But other Americans, worried about preserving their own advantages in an era of limited resources, were often unwilling to support these new demands for rights and opportunities. At times, the result was almost the "racial and class war" that Chisholm dreaded.

African Americans' Struggle for Racial Justice

As the civil rights struggle continued, attention focused on two relatively new and controversial means of promoting racial equality—affirmative action and mandatory school busing. First ordered by the Johnson administration, affirmative action required businesses, universities, and other institutions receiving federal money to provide opportunities for women and nonwhites. Supporters viewed the policy as a way to make up for past and present discrimination. Opponents argued that affirmative action was itself a form of discrimination reducing opportunities for whites, particularly white men.

Somewhat surprisingly, Nixon, despite his commitment to limited government, generally supported affirmative action. His administration developed the Philadelphia Plan, which encouraged the construction industry to meet targets for hiring minority workers. In 1978, the Supreme Court offered qualified support for affirmative action with its decision in *Regents of the University of California v. Allan Bakke*. The justices ruled that the medical school of the University of California at Davis could not deny admission to Bakke, a white applicant who had better grades and test scores than some minority applicants accepted by the institution. While the court barred schools from using fixed admissions quotas for different racial groups, it did allow educational institutions to use race as an admissions criterion. By the end of the 1970s, affirmative action had become an important means of increasing diversity in schools and other institutions.

School busing was more controversial than affirmative action. By the late 1960s, the Supreme Court had become impatient with delays in integrating the nation's schools. Even in the North, where there had been no de jure or legal segregation, there was still extensive de facto segregation. In *Swann v. Charlotte-Mecklenburg Board of Education* in 1971, the court upheld the mandatory busing of thousands of children to desegregate schools in the Charlotte, North Carolina, area. But many Americans opposed busing, because they did not want integration or did not want children taken out of neighborhood schools.

Protesting Mandatory Busing White demonstrators, some dressed in colonial costume, march against court-ordered school busing in Boston in September 1970.

Nixon sided with the opponents of busing. Privately ordering his aides to enforce busing less vigorously, the president publicly called for a "moratorium" on new busing plans. Some communities implemented busing peacefully. Others faced protest and turmoil. In 1974, a federal court ordered busing in Boston. When the white-dominated local school committee refused to comply, a federal judge imposed a busing plan on the community. Working-class and lower-middle-class whites formed Restore Our Alienated Rights (ROAR) and other organizations to protest plans to bus students between the predominantly African American neighborhood of Roxbury and the largely Irish American neighborhood of South Boston. In "Southie," whites taunted and injured black students. Although violence spread and continued through the fall, the busing plan went into effect. With busing and affirmative action, the civil rights movement seemed to have reached its limits: many Americans were unwilling to go any further to ensure racial equality.

Women's Liberation

By the 1970s, the movement for women's liberation was flourishing. Many women were coming together in "consciousness-raising" groups to discuss a broad range of issues in their lives. To commemorate the 50th anniversary of the ratification of the women's suffrage amendment to the Constitution, thousands marched in the Women's Strike for Equality on August 26, 1970.

The women's liberation movement, like the struggle for African American equality, was diverse. Liberal feminist groups, such as the National Organization for Women (NOW), concentrated on equal public opportunities for women. Radical feminists focused on a broader range of private and public issues. Oppression, they insisted, took place in the bedroom and the kitchen as well as the school and the workplace. Some radical feminists, influenced by the New Left, blamed women's plight on the inequalities of capitalism; others traced the oppression of women to men. Cultural feminists insisted that women's culture was different from and superior to male culture. They felt that women should create their own separate institutions rather than seek formal equality with men. Some lesbian feminists took this separatist logic one step further to argue that women should avoid heterosexual relationships.

Linking the private and personal with the public and political, the women's movement necessarily fought on many fronts. More women who married decided to keep their maiden names rather than adopt their husbands' surnames. Rather than identifying themselves by their marital status, many women abandoned the forms of address "Miss" or "Mrs." for "Ms." Women's liberation made its mark on the media. In 1972, Gloria Steinem began to publish the feminist magazine *Ms.* On television, popular sitcoms portrayed independent women. Some feminists condemned the availability of pornography, which, they argued, incited violence against women.

In the 1970s, feminists focused especially on three public issues—access to abortion, equal treatment in schools and workplaces, and passage of the equal rights amendment (ERA) to the Constitution. Long effectively outlawed, abortions were generally unavailable or unsafe. In *Roe v. Wade* in 1973, the Supreme Court ruled a Texas antiabortion law unconstitutional on the grounds that it violated the "right to privacy" guaranteed by the Ninth and Fourteenth Amendments. With this decision, abortion began to become legal and widely available.

Like the civil rights movement, the women's movement demanded equal treatment in schools and workplaces. Women filed many complaints against discrimination by employers. At first reluctant, the Nixon administration moved to open up government employment to women and to press colleges and businesses to end discriminatory practices. In 1972, Congress approved Title IX of the Higher Education Act, which required schools and universities receiving federal funds to give equal opportunities to women and men in admissions, athletics, and other programs.

The women's movement also continued the longtime struggle to enact the ERA. "Equality of rights under the law," the amendment read, "shall not be denied or abridged by the United States or by any State on account of sex." In 1972 Congress passed the ERA. If 38 states had ratified the amendment within 7 years, it would have become law. But after 28 states had ratified within a year, the ERA met heavy opposition. To male critics, feminists were a "small band of braless bubbleheads" who suffered from "defeminization." Some women feared that equal rights would end their femininity and their protected legal status. Conservative activist Phyllis Schlafly organized an effective campaign against the ERA. Although more states ratified the amendment, some rescinded their votes and the ERA never became law.

The ERA's defeat underscored the challenges that the women's movement faced. Women still did not have full equality in American society. Nevertheless, women had more control over their bodies, more access to education, and more opportunity in the workplace.

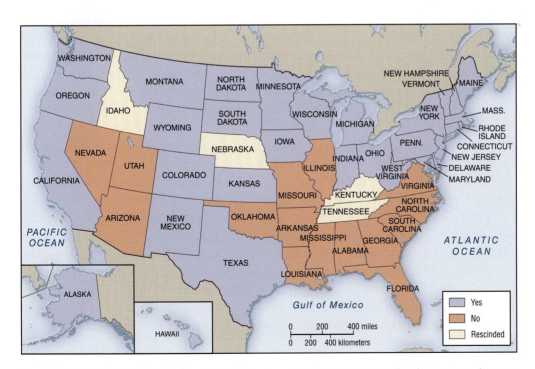

Map 29–2   The Equal Rights Amendment (ERA) Despite substantial support in state legislatures across the country, the ERA faced crippling opposition in the mountain West and the South.

Mexican Americans and "Brown Power"

In the 1960s and 1970s, Mexican Americans, the second-largest racial minority in the United States, developed a new self-consciousness. Proudly identifying themselves as Chicanos, Mexican Americans organized to protest poverty and discrimination.

Despite federal efforts to keep out Mexican immigrants, the Mexican American population grew rapidly. By 1980, at least 7 million Americans claimed Mexican heritage. The great majority lived in Arizona, California, Colorado, New Mexico, and Texas. By the 1970s, most Mexican Americans lived in urban areas. More than 1 million lived in Los Angeles. Holding an increasing percentage of skilled and white-collar jobs, Mexican Americans nevertheless earned substantially less as a group than did Anglos (white Americans of non-Hispanic descent). One in four Mexican American families lived in poverty in the mid-1970s.

Mexican Americans faced racism and discrimination. The media stereotyped them as lazy and shifty. Schools in their neighborhoods were underfunded. In some California schools, Mexican American children could not eat with Anglo children. California and Texas law prohibited teaching in Spanish.

Although Mexican Americans were not legally prevented from voting, gerrymandering diluted their political power. Despite its large Mexican American population, Los Angeles had no Hispanic representative on the city council at the end of the 1960s. The justice system often treated Mexican Americans unfairly.

The combination of poverty and discrimination marked Mexican American life. In cities, many Mexican Americans were crowded into *barrios,* run-down neighborhoods. In the countryside, many lived without hot water or toilets. Infant mortality was high, and life expectancy was low. Nationwide, almost half of the Mexican American population was functionally illiterate.

Encouraged by the civil rights movement, Mexican Americans protested against poverty and injustice for migrant farm workers. In the fertile San Joaquin Valley of California, the Mexican Americans who labored for powerful fruit growers earned as little as 10¢ an hour and lived in miserable conditions. César Chávez, a former migrant worker influenced by Martin Luther King Jr.'s nonviolent creed, helped them organize what became the United Farm Workers of America. In 1965 this union went on strike. The growers, accusing Chávez of Communist ties, called for police, strikebreakers, intimidation, and violence. Chávez's nonviolent tactics, which included a 25-day hunger strike in 1968, gradually appealed to liberals and other Americans. Chávez also initiated a successful nationwide consumer boycott against grapes. Under this pressure, the grape growers began to settle with the union.

While Chávez turned for inspiration to Martin Luther King Jr., other Mexican Americans responded to the nationalism of the Black Power movement. In New Mexico, Reies López "Tiger" Tijerina, a former preacher, favored separatism over integration and nationalism over assimilation. He created the Alianza Federal de Mercedes (Federal Alliance of Land Grants) to take back land that the United States had supposedly stolen from Mexicans. In 1967, Tijerina's raid on a courthouse and other militant acts earned him a jail sentence and a reputation as the Robin Hood of New Mexico.

Mexican American activism flourished in the late 1960s. In East Los Angeles, the Brown Berets, a paramilitary group, showed the influence of the Black Panthers.

In California in 1969, college students began the Movimiento Estudiantil Chicano de Aztlán (Chicano Student Movement of Aztlán). The organization was known by its initials, MEChA, which spelled the word for "match" in the Spanish dialect of Mexican Americans. MEChA was meant to be the match that would kindle social change for Chicanos. In Crystal City, Texas, a boycott of Anglo businesses led to the formation of La Raza Unida ("The Unified Race"), a political party that won control of the local school board in 1970. Thousands of students marked September 16, 1969, Mexican Independence Day, with a boycott of high schools.

All these protests and organizations reflected a strong sense of pride and a powerful desire to preserve the Mexican American heritage. Reflecting a strong, assertive sense of group identity, activists more frequently referred to Mexican Americans as "Chicanos." The term had uncertain origins, but its connection to group pride was obvious. "A Chicano," declared reporter Rubén Salazar, "is a Mexican-American with a non-Anglo image of himself." Chicano activists wanted bilingual education and Mexican American studies in the schools, and equal opportunity and affirmative action in schools and workplaces. Most fundamentally, Mexican American activism reflected the desire for empowerment, for what some called "Brown Power."

On the whole, white Americans paid less attention to Chicano activism than they did to African Americans' struggles. But Mexican American activists made some important gains. On the national level, Congress prohibited state bans on teaching in Spanish.

Asian American Activism

Asian Americans also pressed for rights and recognition as the 1960s ended. Like Mexican Americans, they confronted a history of discrimination in the United States. They, too, had to contend with denigrating stereotypes and hurtful epithets.

The small size of the Asian American population limited organization and protest, but the Immigration Act of 1965 had made possible increased Asian migration to the United States. From the 1960s through the 1970s, the war in Southeast Asia, political conditions in the Philippines, and economic opportunity spurred waves of Asian immigration. By 1980 America was home to more than 3 million Asian immigrants, including 812,000 Chinese, 781,000 Filipinos, and 716,000 Japanese. Overall, there were 3.7 million Americans of Asian descent. The majority lived in the Pacific states and in cities.

Asian American activism followed the pattern of other minority movements. By the late 1960s, Asian Americans were demonstrating a new ethnic self-consciousness and pride. Many Asian Americans saw themselves not only as Chinese or Japanese, inheritors of a particular national and ethnic heritage, but as members of a broader, pan-Asian group.

In 1968, the Asian American Political Alliance (AAPA) emerged on the campus of the University of California at Berkeley to unite Chinese, Japanese, and Filipino students. Asian Americans pushed for Asian-studies programs on college campuses. By the end of the 1970s, a number of colleges and universities had responded to Asian American students' demands for courses and programs.

Asian American activism spread beyond campuses. In 1974 protests forced the hiring of Chinese American workers to help build the Confucius Plaza complex in

New York City's Chinatown. In San Francisco, activists brought suit against the public school system on behalf of 1,800 Chinese pupils. In *Lau v. Nichols* in 1974, the Supreme Court declared that school systems had to provide bilingual instruction for non-English-speaking students.

In the 1970s, Japanese groups demanded compensation for the U.S. government's internment of Japanese Americans during World War II. In 1976 Washington did rescind Executive Order 9066, the 1942 presidential directive that allowed internment to occur. But the federal government did not make a more comprehensive settlement until 1988.

Asian Americans, like Chicanos, made only limited gains by 1980. However, Asian Americans had developed a new consciousness and new organizations; they had also forced real change at the local and national levels.

The Struggle for Native American Rights

After many years of decline and stagnation, the Indian population had grown rapidly since World War II (see Map 29–3). By 1970, there were nearly 800,000 Native Americans, half of whom lived on reservations. Native Americans were divided into about 175 tribes and other groups, but, like Mexican Americans and African Americans, they were united by poor living conditions and persistent discrimination. Native Americans had the lowest average family income of any ethnic group. Reservations had especially high unemployment rates. Many Indian children attended substandard schools.

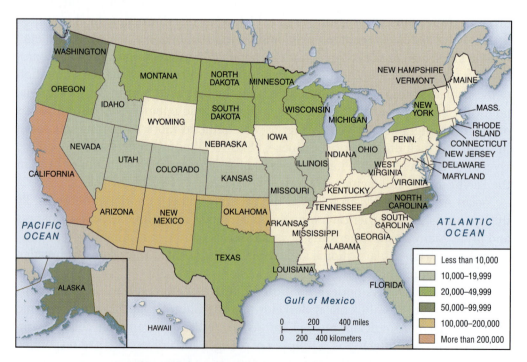

Map 29–3 Native American Population, 1980 After rapid growth in the years following World War II, the Native American population remained largest west of the Mississippi River and, above all, across the Southwest. But there were substantial numbers of Native Americans in every region. *Data from* Statistical Abstract of the United States, 1973 *(Washington: U.S. Bureau of the Census, 1973), p. 348; and* Statistical Abstract of the United States, 1984 *(Washington: U.S. Bureau of the Census, 1984), pp. 375–376, 463, 760.*

Native American life was shaped by the Indians' unique relationship with the federal government. Many resented the Bureau of Indian Affairs (BIA), which had long patronized and exploited tribes. Like African American and Mexican American separatists, some Native Americans began to see themselves as a nation apart. Calling themselves "prisoners of war," these Native Americans struck an aggressive stance, expressed in such slogans as "Custer Had It Coming" and "Red Power."

Beginning in the 1960s, a Native American movement emerged to protest federal policy, combat stereotypes, unite tribes, and perpetuate their cultures. Native Americans called for an end to employment discrimination and to the sale of Indian lands and resources to corporations. Activists staged "hunt-ins" and "fish-ins" to protest lost hunting and fishing rights. Native Americans also condemned the use of Indian symbols by schools and sports teams and demanded Indian-centered school curricula.

Some Indians favored more radical action. Copying the Black Panthers, a group of red-beret-clad Native Americans in Minneapolis, Minnesota, formed an "Indian Patrol" to defend against the police. The patrol evolved into the American Indian Movement (AIM), which spread to other cities. In 1969, AIM activists occupied the abandoned federal prison on Alcatraz Island in San Francisco Bay and told the authorities to leave. The occupiers unsuccessfully offered the government "$24 in glass beads and cloth" for the prison, which they planned to convert into a Native American museum and center. In 1972 and 1973, AIM took over BIA headquarters in Washington and the BIA office in Wounded Knee, South Dakota, where federal troops had massacred Indians in 1890.

The Native American rights movement made few gains in a society worried about limited resources and an uncertain future. Through the Indian Self-Determination Act of 1975, the federal government did allow Native Americans more independence on the reservations. Still, Native Americans themselves were divided about their relationship to the government. Many tribal leaders wanted to continue selling off their lands through the BIA, but AIM assailed Native Americans who accepted the BIA's authority. Despite such divisions, the movement had forced American society to confront the inequitable treatment of Indians more directly than at any time since the Great Depression.

Homosexuals and Gay Power

Singled out for persecution in the McCarthy era, most homosexual men and women had learned to conceal their sexual identity in public. Mainstream American culture mercilessly ridiculed homosexuals as "faggots," "queers," and "dykes." The medical profession treated homosexuality as an illness. In the late 1960s, that began to change.

A catalyst for change was the struggle of women, racial minorities, and students. Another was a police raid on the Stonewall Inn, a gay bar in New York City's Greenwich Village, in June 1969. Such raids were commonplace, but this time, to the surprise of the police, gay men resisted. The next night, the police beat and arrested gay protestors, who yelled, "Gay Power!"

Stonewall became a rallying cry for gay activism. The Gay Liberation Front, the Student Homophile League, and other organizations appeared. Activists picketed companies that discriminated against gays, and homosexuals socialized more openly. On the first anniversary of Stonewall, 10,000 gay men and lesbians paraded down New York's Sixth Avenue. "Two, four, six, eight!" marchers chanted. "Gay is just as good as straight!" The gay movement began to have an effect on mainstream culture. In 1974, the American Psychiatric Association decided that homosexuality was not a "mental disorder" and that homosexuals deserved equal rights.

The emerging movements for gay, Native American, and Chicano rights, along with the ongoing crusades of women and African Americans, made a deep impact on the 1970s. American society could not escape demands for equal rights and opportunities for all people. Women, gays, African Americans, Native Americans, and Chicanos did not win full equality, but these groups made important gains despite the troubled economic climate of the 1970s.

Backlash: From Radical Action to Conservative Reaction

By the close of the 1960s, American society reverberated with demands to end the war in Vietnam and allow equal rights at home. Some activists believed the United States would indeed be torn apart and remade by the "racial and class war" that Shirley Chisholm feared; but the revolution never came. Radical movements squabbled and fell apart. Many Americans abandoned activism for their own private concerns; others angrily rejected protest movements. Encouraging this backlash, President Nixon won reelection in 1972.

"The Movement" and the "Me-Decade"

Many activists believed that the struggles of women and minorities, along with student protests and the antiwar movement, were creating a single coalition, known simply as "the Movement." At the close of the 1960s, it sometimes seemed as if the Movement might truly take shape. In August 1969, an astonishing crowd of nearly half a million mostly young people gathered for a music festival on a dairy farm near Woodstock in upstate New York. For three days, they created a temporary utopia dedicated to love and other countercultural values and vocally opposed to the Vietnam War. What activist Abbie Hoffman called the "Woodstock Nation" briefly symbolized the possibility of a true mass-based coalition for radical change.

Nevertheless, the Movement stalled. "We had the dream and we are losing it," lamented the activist Julius Lester the year of Woodstock. The different protest groups never merged, and they were often hostile to each other. Black activists, for instance, criticized white activists for neglecting poverty and other working-class problems.

> We are letting the people of America know that we will not sit still for this government to take away our basic parental rights. We will fight, and we will never, never quit. Our enemies can go straight to hell.
>
> STATE SENATOR WILLIAM BULGER
> addressing an antibusing rally, Boston, 1975

The "Woodstock Nation," August 1969 Perhaps half a million people created a huge temporary community celebrating countercultural values.

In addition, key groups within the Movement fell apart. Plagued by internal divisions, SDS held its last convention in 1969. The violent Weathermen called for "Days of Rage" in the "pig city" of Chicago in October 1969, but only a few hundred protestors showed up. Transient radical groups bombed or burned corporate headquarters and other "establishment" targets but succeeded only in giving the New Left and the Movement a bad name. The FBI secretly penetrated Black Panther chapters and worked to discredit the organization. Panther leaders fled the country, went to jail, or died at the hands of police. Radical feminist groups also declined as women's liberation increasingly focused on liberal demands, such as the ERA.

Some protest movements lost their targets. After the widespread demonstrations of 1970, the antiwar movement declined as the United States pulled out of Vietnam. The student movement declined as young people lost some of their grievances. Around the country, colleges and universities eased parietal rules and other regulations. In 1971, the states completed ratification of the Twenty-sixth Amendment to the Constitution, which lowered the voting age to 18.

The revolution also failed to materialize because many people turned away from activism and political engagement. Some were disillusioned by the failure of the Great Society and the duplicity of the Johnson and Nixon administrations. Others were disappointed by the limited accomplishments of radicalism. Still others found themselves caught up in therapeutic and religious movements, as Americans focused on their inner needs rather than on political change.

The 1970s, announced the writer Tom Wolfe, were the "Me-Decade." Wolfe and other observers believed Americans had become self-absorbed and narcissistic. The cause, explained the historian and social critic Christopher Lasch, was the crisis of capitalism in "an age of diminishing expectations." The fears about the self-absorbed Me-Decade were as exaggerated as the hopes for the revolutionary Movement. People did not stop hoping and working for change, but in a time of economic decline and political disappointment, many Americans felt they could not afford the expansive liberal dreams of the 1960s. They had to look out for themselves.

The Plight of the White Ethnics

The "new American revolution" was a victim of anger as well as apathy. Most lower-middle-class and working-class whites rejected the Movement. They decried radical feminism and resented the students and protestors who had avoided fighting in Vietnam. They also increasingly rejected the new liberalism of the 1960s. Feeling threatened by urban renewal projects, welfare spending, and court-ordered busing, many whites believed the Great Society did too little for them and too much for minorities and young radicals. Most of all, the white working and middle classes feared the consequences of economic decline. In a decade of deindustrialization, they faced the loss of their jobs and their standard of living. "I work my ass off," said an ironworker. "But I can't make it."

The media painted an unflattering portrait of these Americans as frustrated racists and reactionaries. In reality, they were not all so racist and forlorn. They took renewed pride in the ethnic heritage that set them apart from other Americans. "White ethnics" were self-consciously German American or Irish American, like the opponents of busing in Boston. They were "PIGS"—Poles, Italians, Greeks, and Slovaks.

The white ethnics used their heritage to affirm an alternative set of values—their own counterculture. For them, ethnicity meant a commitment to family, neighborhood, and religion in place of the individualistic American dream and the centralizing federal government. In response, some colleges and universities created ethnic-studies programs. In 1972, Congress passed the Ethnic Heritage Studies Act to "legitimatize ethnicity" and promote the study of immigrant cultures. Most important, the white ethnics formed a large potential voting bloc, attractive to politicians.

Television's View of the White Ethnic The popular 1970s comedy *All in the Family* derided its main character, the conservative Archie Bunker, who was upset with his feminist daughter, his liberal son-in-law, and all the social change around him.

The Republican Counterattack

Nixon tried to combine the white ethnics and white southerners in a Republican counterattack against radicalism, liberalism, and the Democratic Party. The president condemned protestors and demonstrations. "Anarchy," the president declared, "this is the way civilizations begin to die." The Nixon administration used more than words against protestors. The president ordered IRS investigations to harass liberal and antiwar figures. He used the FBI to infiltrate and disrupt the Black Power movement, the Brown Berets, and the New Left. He even made illegal domestic use of the CIA to obstruct the antiwar movement.

To oppose the forces of disruption, Nixon called for support from "the great silent majority of my fellow Americans." With his "southern strategy," the president reached out to Sunbelt voters by opposing busing, rapid integration, crime, and radicalism. He also tried to create a more conservative, less activist Supreme Court. In 1969, he named the cautious Warren Burger to succeed Earl Warren as chief justice. To fill another vacancy on the court, Nixon nominated first a conservative South Carolina judge, Clement Haynsworth, who had angered civil rights and union leaders, and then Judge G. Harrold Carswell of Florida, a former avowed white supremacist. Both nominations failed, but the president had sent an unmistakable message to the "silent majority" and to white southerners.

The counterattack paid off in the 1972 presidential election. The Republican ticket of Nixon and Vice President Spiro Agnew benefited from some unforeseen occurrences. More than any other politician, George Wallace, the segregationist governor of Alabama, rivaled Nixon's appeal to the "silent majority." But Wallace's campaign for the Democratic nomination came to an end when a would-be assassin's bullet paralyzed him from the waist down. In addition, the Democratic vice-presidential nominee, Senator Thomas Eagleton of Missouri, had to withdraw over revelations about his treatment for depression.

Nixon did not really need good luck in 1972. The Democrats chose a strongly liberal senator, George McGovern of South Dakota, for president. McGovern's eventual running mate was another unabashed liberal, Sargent Shriver, a brother-in-law of the Kennedys. The Democratic ticket—which endorsed busing and affirmative action and opposed the Vietnam War—alienated white ethnics, white southerners, and organized labor.

Carrying 49 out of 50 states, Nixon easily won reelection in November 1972. With nearly 61 percent of the popular vote, the president scored almost as big a triumph as Lyndon Johnson in 1964, but Nixon's victory was deceptive. The Republican counterattack had not produced a partisan political realignment: the Democrats still controlled both houses of Congress.

Nevertheless, the 1972 election was a sign that the traditional Democratic coalition was breaking up. More broadly, Nixon's triumph, along with the failure of the Movement, the rise of the white ethnics, and the self-absorption of the Me-Decade, showed that the glory days of liberalism and radicalism were over.

Political Crisis: Three Troubled Presidencies

Nixon's triumph turned out to be his undoing. The discovery of illegal activities in the president's campaign led to the revelation of other improprieties and, finally, to his resignation. Nixon's successors, Gerald Ford and Jimmy Carter, could not master the problems of a divided nation discovering the limits of its power. Unable to handle the conflicting issues of rights and economic decline, the three troubled presidencies of the 1970s intensified the sense of national crisis. The decade ended with Americans wondering whether their democracy still worked.

Watergate: The Fall of Richard Nixon

Nixon's fall began when five men were caught breaking into the offices of the Democratic National Committee in the Watergate complex in Washington, DC, just before

2:00 A.M. on June 17, 1972. The five burglars had ties to Nixon's campaign organization, the Committee to Re-Elect the President (CREEP). They were attempting to repair an electronic eavesdropping device that had been previously planted in the Democrats' headquarters.

At first, Watergate had no impact on the president. He won reelection easily, but gradually, a disturbing story emerged. Two reporters for the *Washington Post,* Bob Woodward and Carl Bernstein, revealed payments linking the five burglars to CREEP and to Nixon's White House staff. The burglars went on trial with two former CIA agents, who had directed the break-in for CREEP. Faced with heavy sentences in March 1973, the burglars admitted that "higher-ups" had planned the break-in and orchestrated a cover-up. One of those higher-ups, Nixon's presidential counsel John Dean, revealed his role in the Watergate affair to a grand jury. By the end of April, the president had to accept the resignations of his most trusted aides, H. R. "Bob" Haldeman and John Ehrlichman. To emphasize his commitment to justice, Nixon named a special federal prosecutor, Archibald Cox, to investigate Watergate.

> America is not over the hill as a people. But tomorrow is not going to get better in the way that people in 1955 would say that tomorrow would be better. That's gone.
>
> FRANZ HELDNER,
> a college art teacher, New Orleans, 1975

In the end, the president was trapped by his own words. A Senate committee, chaired by Sam Ervin of North Carolina, began hearings on Watergate in May 1973. Testifying before the committee, a White House aide revealed that a secret taping system routinely recorded conversations in the president's Oval Office. Claiming "executive privilege," Nixon refused to turn over tapes of his conversations after the break-in. When Archibald Cox continued to press for the tapes, Nixon ordered him fired on Saturday, October 20, 1973. Attorney General Elliot Richardson and a top aide refused to carry out the order and resigned. A third official finally discharged Cox. Nixon's "Saturday Night Massacre" set off a storm of public anger. Nixon had to name a new special prosecutor, Leon Jaworski. The Democratic-controlled House of Representatives began to explore articles of impeachment against the president. "I am not a crook," Nixon insisted.

By 1974, it became clear that the Nixon administration had engaged in a shocking range of improper and illegal behavior. Infuriated by news leaks in 1969, Henry Kissinger had ordered wiretaps on the phones of newspaper reporters and his own staff. Two years later, the White House had created the "Plumbers," a bumbling group of operatives to combat leaks, including the release of the Pentagon Papers. Anxious to win in 1972, Nixon's men had also engaged in dirty tricks to sabotage Democratic presidential aspirants. Nixon's personal lawyer had collected illegal political contributions, "laundered" the money to hide its source, and then transferred it to CREEP.

Nixon himself had ordered the secret and illegal bombing of Cambodia. He had impounded (i.e., refused to spend) money appropriated by Congress for programs he disliked. He had secretly approved the use of federal agencies to hurt "political enemies."

As a result of the Watergate break-in and other scandals, many of Nixon's associates had to leave office. No fewer than 26, including former attorney general John Mitchell, went to jail. Vice President Spiro Agnew was found to have accepted bribes as the governor of Maryland in the 1960s. In October 1973 Agnew accepted a plea bargain deal and resigned as vice president. He was replaced by Republican Congressman Gerald R. Ford of Michigan.

Under growing pressure to release his tapes, Nixon tried to get away with publishing selected edited transcripts. Revealing a vulgar, rambling, and inarticulate president, the transcripts only fed public disillusionment. In July 1974 the House Judiciary Committee voted to recommend to the full House of Representatives three articles of impeachment—obstruction of justice, abuse of power, and defiance of subpoenas.

Nixon still wanted to fight the charges, but the Supreme Court ruled unanimously that he had to turn over his tapes to the special prosecutor. The tapes showed that Nixon himself had participated in the cover-up of Watergate as early as June 23, 1972. The president had conspired to obstruct justice and had lied repeatedly to the American people. Almost certain to be impeached, the president agreed to resign rather than face a trial in the Senate. On August 9, 1974, Nixon left office in disgrace. "My fellow Americans, our long national nightmare is over," the new president, Gerald Ford, declared. "Our constitution works."

Gerald Ford and a Skeptical Nation

At first, Gerald Ford was a welcome relief for a nation stunned by the misdeeds of Richard Nixon. Modest and good-humored, the new president seemed unlikely to abuse the authority of the White House. But Ford also seemed stumbling and unimaginative in the face of the nation's declining prosperity and power. Moreover, his administration had no popular mandate. Ford was the first unelected vice president to succeed to the presidency. His vice president, former New York governor Nelson Rockefeller, had not been elected either.

Ford had to govern a nation that had grown skeptical about politicians. Johnson's deceitful conduct of the Vietnam War and Nixon's scandals raised fears that the presidency had grown too powerful. To reestablish its authority, Congress passed the War Powers Act of 1973, which allowed the president to send

Putting a Brave Face on Scandal Forced to resign from office because of Watergate, Richard Nixon gives a victory sign as he prepares to fly away from the White House, August 1974.

troops to hostile situations overseas for no more than 60 days without obtaining congressional consent. In 1975 Congress conducted hearings on the secret operations of the CIA. Amid revelations about the agency's improper roles in domestic spying and the assassination of foreign leaders, the House and Senate created permanent committees to oversee the agency. Ford had to ban the use of assassination in American foreign policy.

Soon after taking office, Ford himself fed public skepticism about the presidency by offering Nixon a full pardon for all crimes committed as president. Ford's popularity dropped immediately and his presidency never fully recovered.

Ford's handling of economic issues did not make up for the pardon. A moderate Republican, the president did not want the federal government to take too active a role in managing the economy. But like Nixon, he could not stop some liberal initiatives. Congress, reflecting popular concern about corporations and the environment, strengthened the regulatory power of the Federal Trade Commission and extended the 1970 Clean Air Act.

Ford had no solutions for deindustrialization and stagflation. Believing inflation was the most serious problem, Ford did little to stop rising unemployment, which topped 9 percent. His anti-inflation program, known as WIN for "Whip Inflation Now," mainly encouraged Americans to control price increases voluntarily. Ford wore a WIN button on his lapel, but inflation continued.

In foreign affairs, the president had to accept limits on American power. Despite the 1973 cease-fire agreement, the fighting continued in Vietnam. Ford promised to protect South Vietnam, but Congress cut the administration's requests for monetary aid to the Saigon government. Sending American armed forces back to South Vietnam was out of the question. When North Vietnamese troops invaded early in 1975, panicked civilians fled southward and Congress refused to provide any more aid. As Saigon was overrun, the last Americans evacuated in helicopters. Thousands of loyal South Vietnamese fled with them, but many more were left behind. For more than 20 years, the United States had worked to preserve an independent, anti-Communist South Vietnam. Yet, on April 30, 1975, South Vietnam surrendered. There was nothing Ford could do to prevent the final, ignominious failure of America's Vietnam policy.

The president could also do nothing to save the pro-American government of Cambodia from Communist insurgents, the Khmer Rouge, earlier in April 1975. Ford did act the next month when the Khmer Rouge captured an American merchant ship, the *Mayaguez,* off Cambodia. At the cost of 41 deaths, United States marines rescued the 39-man crew. Despite the rescue, the United States no longer wielded much power in Southeast Asia.

The policy of détente with the Soviet Union was supposed to help America cope with its limited power, but détente was clearly in trouble during the Ford administration. The United States and the Soviets failed to agree to a second Strategic Arms Limitation Treaty (SALT II). American critics of détente, including Democratic Senator Henry Jackson of Washington, claimed that the policy sapped American defenses and overlooked human rights violations by the Soviets. In

1974, Jackson added an amendment to a trade bill linking commerce to freedom for Soviet Jews to emigrate. The Jackson-Vanik Amendment helped sour the Soviets on détente. In turn, Ford further alienated American conservatives when he traveled to Helsinki, Finland, in 1975 to sign an agreement accepting the post–World War II boundaries of European nations.

Ford's troubles were reflected at the polls. The Democrats made large gains in the congressional elections in 1974. Two years later, Ford won the Republican nomination for president, replacing Rockefeller with a more conservative vice-presidential nominee, Senator Robert Dole of Kansas. The Democrats' presidential choice was a far cry from the liberal George McGovern. Former Georgia governor Jimmy Carter ran as a moderate who promised efficiency rather than new reforms.

With low turnout at the polls, Carter took 50.1 percent of the vote to Ford's 48 percent. The Democrats won a majority in the Electoral College by carrying much of the industrial Northeast and taking back almost all the South from the Republicans. The outcome was less an endorsement of Carter than a rejection of Ford, who became the first sitting president to lose an election since Herbert Hoover during the Great Depression in 1932.

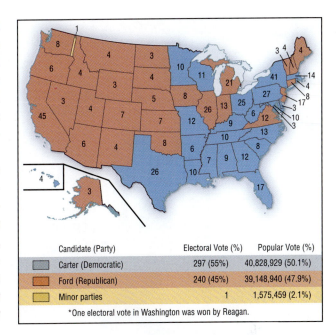

Candidate (Party)	Electoral Vote (%)	Popular Vote (%)
Carter (Democratic)	297 (55%)	40,828,929 (50.1%)
Ford (Republican)	240 (45%)	39,148,940 (47.9%)
Minor parties	1	1,575,459 (2.1%)

*One electoral vote in Washington was won by Reagan.

Map 29–4 The Presidential Election, 1976 Jimmy Carter managed to reestablish the Democratic Party's appeal to white southerners.

"Why Not the Best?": Jimmy Carter

As he took office in 1977, Jimmy Carter seemed capable and efficient. A graduate of the Naval Academy, he had served as an engineer in the navy's nuclear submarine program and successfully managed his family's peanut farm before entering politics. Carter's commitment to perfectionism was captured in the title of his autobiography, *Why Not the Best?*

Carter responded more energetically and imaginatively than Ford to the nation's problems. But Carter came to be seen as a weak, uncertain leader. More important, he faced the same intractable problems that had bedeviled Ford.

Like his predecessor, Carter had trouble putting to rest the recent past. The president met angry criticism when he pardoned most American men who had resisted the draft during the Vietnam War, offending many veterans and conservatives

Carter also had to contend with increasing popular resentment of government. Many Americans believed that government regulation and taxation had gotten out of hand. When the Endangered Species Act of 1973 forced a halt to the construction of a Tennessee dam because it threatened the survival of the snail darter, a small local fish, it seemed as if the federal government worried more about fish than about people's need for electricity and recreation.

The West was the stronghold of antigovernment sentiment in the 1970s. Assailing the bureaucrats in Washington, DC, the Sagebrush Rebellion demanded state control over federal lands in the West. Businessmen in the West also wanted Washington to

President Jimmy Carter Wearing a beige wool cardigan instead of a suit jacket, the new President asks Americans to conserve energy, February 2, 1977.

allow more exploitation of oil, forests, and other resources on federal lands. Meanwhile, California became the center of an antitax movement in 1978. Angered by high taxes and government spending in their communities, California voters passed Proposition 13, which sharply reduced property taxes.

As always, antigovernment sentiment was inconsistent. Many of the same people who attacked taxes and regulation expected aid and benefits from Washington. When the giant automaker Chrysler faced bankruptcy in 1979, the government had to save the company with a $1.5 billion loan guarantee. When Carter moved to cancel federal water projects in the West in 1977, he encountered a storm of protest from the heart of the Sagebrush Rebellion.

Carter was most successful when he moved to limit government. By the 1970s, some economists were advocating deregulation of businesses as a way to lower costs, increase competition, and improve services. In 1978, the government removed price controls on the airline industry. In the short run the move lowered fares, but in the long run it drove some airlines out of business.

Deregulation was a sign of a changing balance of political power. Big business, under attack since the 1960s, now lobbied effectively against regulation, organized labor, and taxes. Liberals, meanwhile, had lost influence. As a result, Congress never created the Consumer Protection Agency advocated by consumer activists. Legislation to make labor organization easier also failed. In 1978, Congress watered down the Humphrey-Hawkins Bill, which reasserted the government's responsibility to ensure full employment. When Carter tried to raise taxes on business, Congress instead cut taxes on capital gains and added more loopholes to the tax law.

Carter attempted, with mixed results, to adjust the economy to the realities of living with less. His program of voluntary wage and price controls did not stop soaring inflation. After fuel shortages forced some schools and businesses to close in the harsh winter of 1976/1977, Carter addressed the energy crisis. The president told Americans that "the energy shortage is permanent" and urged them to conserve. His energy plan included establishment of the Department of Energy, taxes on gas-guzzling automobiles and large consumers of oil, tax incentives to stimulate production of oil and gas, and development of nuclear power. But conservatives thought the program expanded government authority. Liberals and environmentalists objected to its support for nuclear power and oil-company profits. The final plan, passed in 1978, was considerably weakened, but it did encourage conservation.

Nuclear power, a key part of Carter's energy plan, soon lost much of its appeal. In March 1979 a nuclear reactor at Three Mile Island, Pennsylvania, nearly suffered a catastrophic meltdown. As 100,000 frightened residents fled their homes, the reactor had to be permanently closed. Around the country, utilities scrapped plans for new nuclear power plants.

Three Mile Island fed broader anxieties about the environmental damage caused by industrial capitalism. Americans wondered whether their neighborhoods would suffer the fate of Love Canal, near Niagara Falls, New York. There, hazardous waste buried by a chemical company caused so many cases of cancer, miscarriages, and other health problems that residents had to move away. Despite business concerns about regulation, Washington created a "superfund" of $1.6 billion to clean up hazardous-waste sites. The Carter administration also took control of 100 million acres of Alaska to prevent damage from economic development.

At first, Carter had more success with foreign policy than with domestic affairs. Continuing Nixon's de-escalation of the cold war, Carter announced that "we are now free of the inordinate fear of Communism." The president did not abandon Nixon's emphasis on détente with the Soviet Union, but he focused on supporting human rights and democracy and building harmony around the world. In 1978, Carter won Senate approval of a treaty yielding ownership of the Panama Canal to Panama at the end of the century. The treaty signaled a new and more respectful approach to Central and Latin America.

In 1978, Carter also mediated the first peace agreement between Israel and an Arab nation. Bringing together Israeli and Egyptian leaders at the Camp David presidential retreat, Carter helped forge a framework for peace that led to Israel's withdrawal from the Sinai Peninsula and the signing of an Israeli-Egyptian treaty. The agreement did not settle the fate of the Israeli-occupied Golan Heights and Gaza Strip or the future of the Palestinian people, but it did establish a basis for future negotiations in a region torn by conflict for centuries.

Carter viewed a commitment to human rights and democracy abroad as a way of recapturing the international respect that the United States had lost during the Vietnam War. In practice, however, his administration did not speak out consistently against the violation of rights around the world. Instead, Carter was supportive of authoritarian American allies such as the rulers of Iran and the Philippines who clearly abused human rights in their own countries.

Carter's foreign policy suffered from the eventual collapse of détente. The president did reach agreement with the Soviets on the SALT II treaty, but the Senate was reluctant to ratify the agreement. Then, in December 1979, the Soviet Union invaded its southern neighbor, Afghanistan. In response, Carter withdrew the SALT II treaty, stopped grain shipments to the Soviet Union, forbade American athletes to compete in the 1980 Olympics in Moscow, and increased American military spending. These moves had no effect on the Soviet invasion, but détente was obviously over, and the direction of American foreign policy had become unclear.

By 1979, Carter was a deeply unpopular president. He had not stabilized the economy or set out a coherent foreign policy. After pondering the situation at the Camp David retreat for 11 days in July, the president came back to tell a television audience that the nation was suffering a "crisis of spirit." The president offered a number of proposals to deal with the energy crisis, but he spoke most strongly to the state of the nation. "All the legislation in the world can't fix what's wrong with America," Carter maintained. "What is lacking is confidence and a sense of community." The speech only seemed to alienate more Americans.

Carter became still more embattled when the Shah of Iran was overthrown by the followers of an Islamic leader, the Ayatollah Ruholla Khomeini, early in 1979. The Shah had long received lavish aid from the United States. Now, the Iranian revolutionaries, eager to restore traditional Islamic values, condemned America for imposing the Shah and modern culture on their nation. In the wake of the revolution, oil prices rose. Once again, Americans had to contend with gas lines, and inflation spread through the economy.

The situation worsened when Khomeini condemned the United States for allowing the Shah to receive medical treatment in New York. On November 4, students loyal to Khomeini overran the United States embassy in Teheran, the Iranian capital, and took 60 Americans hostage. Carter froze Iranian assets in the United States, but he could not compel the release of the hostages. As days passed, the United States seemed helpless. In the spring of 1980, the frustrated president ordered a secret military mission to rescue the hostages. On April 24, eight American helicopters headed for a desert rendezvous with six transport planes carrying troops and supplies. When two helicopters broke down and an-

Disaster in the Iranian Desert, April 1980 The wreckage of this Army helicopter, part of the failed attempt to free American hostages in Iran, symbolizes the weakness of the United States at the start of the 1980s.

other became lost, the mission had to be aborted. An accident left eight soldiers dead. The hostages remained in captivity. The limits of American power seemed more obvious than ever.

Conclusion

As the 1970s ended, Shirley Chisholm was still deeply worried about her nation. Noting the many problems of the United States, the congresswoman concluded "there was a real crisis . . . in this country. . . . Government was being conducted by crisis." The mixture of economic decline and aspirations for rights and opportunity had proved too much to handle. To Chisholm, the nation even seemed to be undoing the changes of the liberal 1960s. "Lots happened in the '60s," she noted sadly. "What's happening today? Every gain has been eroded." As always, Chisholm refused to give in to pessimism. "I will continue to do what I'm doing—fighting, fighting, fighting," she vowed, "because I realize that this country is moving to the right." As the 1980s would reveal, Chisholm was correct about the direction of the United States. After the political uncertainty of the 1970s, the nation would finally deal with economic decline and the other challenges of the decade by embracing a new conservatism. The future lay to the right.

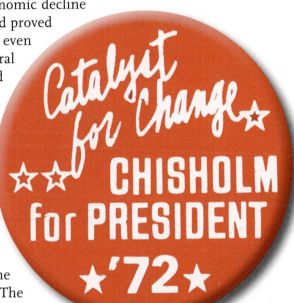

Further Readings

Beth L. Bailey and David Farber, eds., *America in the Seventies* (2004). A collection of scholarly essays.

Jefferson Cowie and Joseph Heathcott, eds., *Beyond the Ruins: The Meanings of Deindustrialization* (2003). Case studies of economic decline.

Robert Dallek, *Nixon and Kissinger: Partners in Power* (2007). A joint study of the architects of détente.

Ronald P. Formisano, *Boston Against Busing: Race, Class, and Ethnicity in the 1960s and 1970s* (1991). Neatly analyzes the white resistance to school desegregation.

Ignacio Garcia, *Chicanismo: The Forging of a Militant Ethos Among Mexican Americans* (2000). Offers a balanced account of the emerging Chicano rights movement.

Eric Marcus, *Making History: The Struggle for Lesbian and Gay Equal Rights* (2002). Moving, candid oral histories that personalize the gay and lesbian liberation movement.

Rick Pearlstein, *Nixonland: The Rise of a President and the Fracturing of America* (2008). An opinionated account of the dominant political figure of the 1970s.

Bruce J. Schulman, *The Seventies: The Great Shift in American Culture, Society and Politics* (2001). Provides an overview of the period.

Who, What?

Richard Nixon 968

Henry Kissinger 969

César Chávez 978

Gerald Ford 987

Jimmy Carter 989

Multinationals 964

Deindustrialization 966

Détente 969

Affirmative action 974

Busing 974

Roe v. Wade 976

Watergate 985

Review Questions

1. How did economic decline affect the lives of Americans?

2. Why was President Nixon's strategy for ending the Vietnam War so controversial?

3. Discuss the foreign policies of the Nixon administration, including détente and the Nixon Doctrine. How did these policies mark a departure from previous American approaches to the cold war?

4. How did the demands of the African American civil rights movement change from the 1960s to the 1970s?

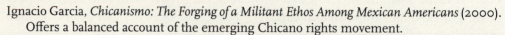

>> Timeline >>

▼ 1965
Decision to send U.S. troops into battle in South Vietnam

▼ 1968
Assassinations of Martin Luther King Jr. and Robert F. Kennedy
Election of Richard Nixon

▼ 1969
Secret bombing of Cambodia
Stonewall Riot in New York's Greenwich Village

Apollo 11 moon landing
Nixon Doctrine

▼ 1970
First Earth Day
Invasion of Cambodia

▼ 1971
United States off gold standard
Ratification of Twenty-sixth Amendment, lowering voting age to 18
Supreme Court busing decision, *Swann v. Charlotte-Mecklenburg Board of Education*

▼ 1972
President Nixon's trips to the People's Republic of China and the Soviet Union
Strategic Arms Limitation Treaty (SALT I) and Anti–Ballistic Missile (ABM) Treaty
Congressional passage of equal rights amendment
Watergate burglary
Reelection of President Nixon

▼ 1973
Peace agreement to end Vietnam War
Supreme Court ruling to legalize abortion, *Roe v. Wade*

5. Discuss the Republican counterattack of the late 1960s and early 1970s. How did Nixon and his party take advantage of discontent?

6. Analyze the troubled presidencies of Nixon, Ford, and Carter. Did these leaders create their own problems, or did they face impossible situations?

Websites

The Jimmy Carter Library and Museum (http://www.jimmycarterlibrary.org/documents/) includes documents, photographs, and the diary of an American hostage in Iran.

The Electronic Reading Room of the Federal Bureau of Investigation (http://foia.fbi.gov/room.htm) features files the FBI maintained on gay activists, the Weathermen, and the Watergate affair.

Nixontapes.org (http://www.nixontapes.org/) offers the most complete collection of the secret Oval Office recordings that brought down a presidency.

Oyez (http://www.oyez.org/) is a growing, comprehensive guide to the history of the Supreme Court, featuring audiotapes of such modern cases as *Roe v. Wade*.

The scanned and transcribed materials of Documents from the Women's Liberation Movement, Duke University Library (http://scriptorium.lib.duke.edu/wlm/), make an excellent guide to the varieties of feminism in the 1960s and 1970s.

The Center for Working-Class Studies at Youngstown State University (http://www.centerforworkingclassstudies.org/) features online resources including documents, photos, and poetry about Youngstown, "Steel City U.S.A."

For further review materials and resource information, please visit www.oup.com/us/ofthepeople

▼ **1973–74**
OPEC oil embargo

▼ **1974**
Boston busing struggle
Resignation of President Nixon

▼ **1975**
Surrender of South Vietnam to North Vietnam
Helsinki Agreement

▼ **1976**
Announcement of the "Me-Decade" by Tom Wolfe
Jimmy Carter elected president

▼ **1977**
Carter's energy plan

▼ **1978**
Camp David peace accords
Supreme Court affirmative action decision, *Regents of the University of California v. Allan Bakke*

▼ **1979**
Accident at Three Mile Island nuclear power plant

▼ **1979–81**
Iranian hostage crisis

▼ **1980**
Ronald Reagan elected president

Common Threads

>> How did Ronald Reagan's approach to economic decline differ from his predecessor Jimmy Carter's?

>> How did conservatism's emphasis on personal responsibility shape the economic and social policies of the Reagan administration?

>> Why was religion so important to the Reagan Revolution?

>> How would the emergence of microcomputing shape the economy beyond the 1980s?

The Triumph of Conservatism 1980–1991

>> Linda Chavez

"On Election Day 1980," Linda Chavez recalled, "I did something I had never imagined I could do: I voted for a Republican for president." A lifelong Democrat, she rejected her party's nominee, incumbent Jimmy Carter, and pulled the lever instead for the conservative GOP candidate, Ronald Reagan.

As Chavez admitted, she made "an unlikely conservative." The daughter of an Anglo mother and a Mexican American father, Chavez had grown up in the Mexican American neighborhoods of Albuquerque, New Mexico, and Denver, Colorado. Her father, like most Mexican Americans, was a Democrat. Chavez herself was drawn to the party and its causes. As a girl in the early 1960s, she joined the civil rights organization CORE and demonstrated against racial discrimination outside a Denver Woolworth store. As a young woman, Chavez had gone to work for the Democratic National Committee, a liberal Democratic congressman, two liberal teachers unions, and the Carter administration.

Despite her partisan commitments, Chavez had been quietly changing. As an undergraduate at the University of Colorado at Boulder in the late 1960s, Chavez discovered that she did not have to settle for her parents' working-class existence. "For the first time," she said, "I realized that I could control my own destiny." Chavez also felt that the university's affirmative action programs shortchanged Mexican Americans by admitting unqualified students, allowing them to flounder academically, teaching them to blame their problems on racism, and then leaving them to drop out.

From those realizations, Chavez gradually developed a new political outlook in the 1970s. She believed that individuals should take responsibility for their lives. "[T]hinking of yourself as a victim and hating those that have oppressed you doesn't get you anywhere," Chavez concluded. She rejected affirmative action programs, race-based hiring quotas, busing, and bilingual education as misguided liberal attempts to create equality in America.

Meanwhile, her stint in the Carter administration left her skeptical about another liberal article of faith. "The federal government was not at all what I expected," Chavez confessed. "Nothing—and almost no one—worked." She was troubled, too, that Carter and the Democrats did not support anti-Communism and a strong defense.

In some ways, Chavez felt that she was not the one who had changed. "Hispanics tend to be fairly traditional," she insisted, "somewhat conservative on social issues, and very patriotic and prodefense." It was her party that had changed by adopting controversial solutions to racial and gender inequality and by abandoning its longtime commitment to the containment of Communism. In 1976, Chavez stayed home rather than vote for Carter. By 1980, she was ready to vote for Reagan, another longtime Democrat who felt that his party had changed.

In one respect, Linda Chavez was an unusual figure: there were hardly any prominent Mexican American conservatives, male or female. But her transformation from liberal Democrat to conservative Republican typified a basic change of the 1980s. Still coming to terms with economic and political decline, a new majority of Americans, including businesspeople, evangelical Christians, and "Reagan Democrats" like Chavez, turned toward a conservative vision of the country. Rejecting the pessimism of the 1970s, these Americans wanted to believe that individual and national success were still possible. The new conservative majority was more open to materialism and to a government that left people free to succeed or fail.

continued

>> **AMERICAN PORTRAIT** *continued*

The trend toward conservatism had wide-ranging consequences. Eager to restore old social, economic, and political values, Reagan set out to recast the United States by cutting taxes, reducing government regulation, and diminishing union power to restore economic growth. The president also embraced a conservative social agenda including attacks on affirmative action and abortion. Abroad, he carried out a foreign policy dedicated to confronting Communism. Despite scandals, setbacks, and compromises, Reagan and the new conservatism arrested fears of America's decline and altered the nation's politics and culture for a generation. ●

Creating a Conservative Majority

In the 1970s and 1980s, the conservative movement continued its rise to power. The New Right drew strength from the transformation of the economy, the changing reputation of big business, and the growth of evangelical Christianity. The power of the conservative coalition became clear in the 1980 presidential election, when voters sent Ronald Reagan to the White House.

The New Economy

Conservatism benefited from the gradual emergence of a postindustrial, computer-centered economy. As deindustrialization continued, technological change pointed the way to national economic revival. Along with other innovations, semiconductors—transistorized integrated circuits attached to small silicon crystals—allowed manufacturers to shrink the computer. By the late 1970s they could put the power of an old, room-sized mainframe computer into a box that would fit on a desktop. In 1981, the computing giant IBM introduced its first personal computer, or PC. By the end of the 1980s, Americans were buying 7 million PCs a year (see Figure 30–1).

Computers seemed to promise a way out of national economic decline. The microcomputer bolstered older companies such as IBM and created new firms such as Apple and Dell; it enriched new entrepreneurs such as Steve Jobs, a founder of Apple, and Bill Gates, a founder of the software firm Microsoft. Whereas Asian manufacturers built most consumer-electronics products, American companies dominated computer hardware and software.

The growth of the computer industry inspired utopian dreams of a high-technology society built on the production of knowledge rather than things. Promoting literacy and education, the computer would lift up the poor and disadvantaged. Unlike the old industrial economy, the computerized economy would cut down on pollution and the consumption of raw materials. By enabling people to work at home, the microcomputer would eliminate commuting and relieve urban congestion.

The vitality and promise of the computer-driven economy helped conservatism. The traditional faith of conservatives in capitalist free enterprise, unaided by government, seemed to be confirmed by the appearance of new industries, new companies, and new jobs. Correspondingly, there was seemingly less need for the government intervention in the economy that liberals preferred.

The emergence of the new economy also benefited conservatism by stimulating the continued flow of people, jobs, and political power from the North and East to the South and West. Computing did revive parts of the Rustbelt. In Massachusetts, a string of computer companies sprang up around Boston along Route 128 to replace the textile mills and shoe factories that had long since left the state. But computing more visibly benefited the Sunbelt, the birthplace of the new conservatism in the 1950s and 1960s. Dell's headquarters were in Texas. Apple was one of many computer firms clustered in Silicon Valley outside San Francisco. Rustbelt industrial cities such as Pittsburgh and Detroit lost population, while some Sunbelt counties more than doubled in population. The shifting regional

> We see our lives as boundless. . . . Yes, we read about high interest rates and an economy that may hamper our success. But we don't think of that as meaning us.
>
> MARK SANDERS,
> a junior at the University of
> Texas at Austin, 1984

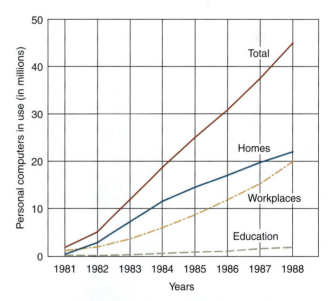

Figure 30–1 The Rise of the Personal Computer The rapid rise in the number of microcomputers in use in homes, workplaces, and schools in the 1980s inspired hopes that the nation's economic decline had ended. *Statistical Abstract of the United States, 1989 (Washington, D.C.: U.S. Bureau of the Census, 1990), p. 743; Statistical Abstract, 1993 (Washington, D.C.: U.S. Bureau of the Census, 1994), p. 761.*

A Revolution on a Desktop In 1981, the new IBM PC or personal computer conveniently offered the power of an old room-filling mainframe computer.

balance had direct political consequences. Reapportionment in 1980 gave more congressional seats and electoral votes to the relatively conservative states of the Sunbelt.

The Rehabilitation of Business

While the 1980s pointed to a utopian future, the decade also recalled the cutthroat capitalism of the turn of the twentieth century. A wave of corporate takeovers and mergers swept across the economy. Aggressive investment bankers and entrepreneurs such as Michael Milken and Ivan Boesky used a variety of techniques, such as junk bonds—high-risk, high-paying securities—to finance takeovers. Executives took golden parachutes, huge payments for selling their companies and losing their jobs. Enormous deals merged some of the largest American corporations. In 1985 General Electric bought RCA for $6 billion. In 1986 alone there were more than 4,000 mergers worth a total of $190 billion. The biggest deal of all came in 1988 when RJR Nabisco was sold for $25 billion and the company's President and CEO received a $53 million golden parachute.

The takeover wave, along with the growth of the computer industry, helped rehabilitate business and its values, which had been assailed in the 1960s and 1970s. Although some observers criticized the concentration of so much economic power, others saw the takeovers as a sign of economic vitality. They argued that the mergers created larger, more efficient companies able to compete more successfully. These observers praised takeover artists as models of entrepreneurial energy and creativity. The media enthusiastically reported the achievements and opinions of Milken, Boesky, Jobs, and Gates. *Dallas, Dynasty,* and other popular television shows wallowed happily in the fictional sagas of wealthy, freewheeling businessmen and their families. Business was more respectable than at any time since the 1950s.

So was materialism. Business figures helped legitimize the pursuit and enjoyment of wealth. "Everybody should be a little greedy," Boesky advised. "You shouldn't feel guilty." There was renewed interest in lavish living. "Thank goodness it's back," gushed the *New York Times,* "that lovely whipped cream of a word—luxury."

Michael Milken One of the aggressive leaders of the corporate takeover movement of the 1980s, his tactics, including the use of junk bonds, soon landed him in jail.

The baby boom generation reflected the new appeal of business values. Abandoning social action, former 1960s radicals such as Yippie (Youth Independent Party) leader Jerry Rubin took up business careers. By 1983 the media were talking about the emergence of yuppies, young urban professionals in their 20s and 30s. Uninterested in reform, these optimistic, self-centered baby boomers were supposedly eager to make lots of money and then spend it on BMW cars, Perrier water, and other consumer playthings. Although the transition from idealistic Yippies to radical yuppies was exaggerated, the yuppie stereotype underscored how much Americans aspired to a more conservative, money-centered way of life.

The Rise of the Religious Right

At the same time American culture celebrated materialism, many Americans still turned to spirituality to find meaning in their lives. Their choice of denominations reinforced the trend to conservatism. Such mainline Protestant denominations as the United Methodist Church, the Episcopal Church, and the Presbyterian Church, USA, had attracted a declining share of the nation's church members since at least 1940. Meanwhile, evangelical churches boomed (see Map 30–1). By the 1980s, the Southern Baptist Convention was the largest American Protestant denomination.

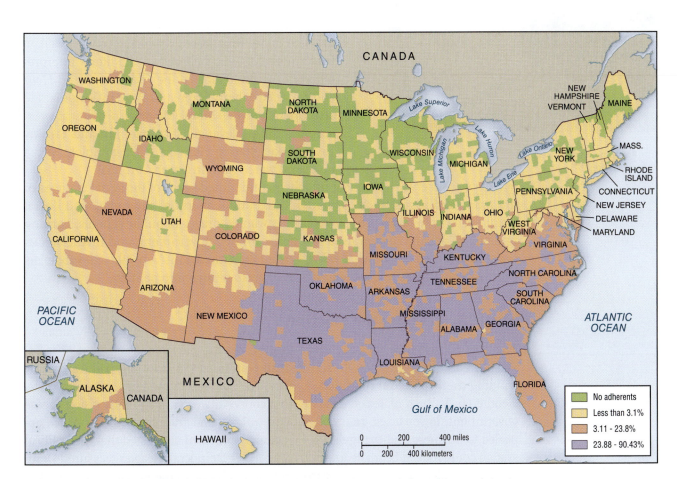

Map 30–1   The Growth of Evangelical Christianity The Southern Baptist Convention's share of the population, by county, reveals its gradual spread beyond its traditional base in the South by 1990. *Peter L Halvorson and William M. Newman,* Atlas of Religious Change in America, 1952–1990 *(Cincinnati, Ohio: Glenmary Research Center, 1994), p. 120.*

The Reverend Jerry Falwell Falwell (left), fundamentalist and leader of the religious right.

Such smaller evangelical bodies as the Assemblies of God and the Church of God more than doubled in size from the 1960s to the 1980s.

The changing balance between mainline and evangelical churches had social and political consequences. The mainline denominations often took moderate or liberal positions on such social issues as civil rights and abortion, but the evangelical churches were much more likely to support conservative positions. Troubled by social change and emboldened by their own growth, evangelicals wanted to spread a conservative message across American culture and politics.

The emergence of "televangelists" was the most obvious result of this impulse. From 1978 to 1989 the number of Christian television ministries grew from 25 to 336. In addition to their own television shows, the most successful televangelists had their own networks, colleges, political groups, and even an amusement park. Pat Robertson, a born-again Baptist from Virginia, hosted *The 700 Club* and ran the Christian Broadcast Network. Jerry Falwell, a fundamentalist who believed in the literal interpretation of the Bible, hosted the *Old Time Gospel Hour* and founded Liberty Baptist College in Virginia. He also organized the Moral Majority, a political pressure group. A televangelist couple, Jim and Tammy Faye Bakker, started Heritage USA, complete with a hotel and water park, in South Carolina.

Deeply conservative, the televangelists condemned many of the social changes of the 1960s and 1970s, such as women's liberation, abortion, gay rights, and liberal Great Society programs. The broadcasters wanted prayer in public schools. Earning millions of dollars, they praised low taxes, limited government, and financial success. Determined to win what Falwell called the "war against sin," the televangelists were the spearheads of a religious right ready to plunge into politics.

The 1980 Presidential Election

The new conservative majority came together in the presidential election of 1980. Former California governor Ronald Reagan continued his stunning political rise by winning the Republican nomination. Although he chose a moderate running mate, George H. W. Bush of Texas, Reagan ran a conservative campaign. His vision of less government, lower taxes, renewed military might, and traditional social values appealed to business and evangelicals. His genial optimism suggested that the political system could indeed be made to work. As a former Democrat, Reagan reassured Democrats and independents that they too could find a home in the Republican Party.

Meanwhile, the Democratic nominee, incumbent president Jimmy Carter, struggled with the double burdens of a weak economy and the ongoing hostage crisis in

Iran. His moderate and sometimes conservative policies had alienated liberal Democrats. His poor economic record had alienated the party's white ethnics. Moderate Republican congressman John Anderson of Illinois, who ran as an independent, drew more voters away from Carter than from Reagan. Meanwhile, the Republican nominee focused relentlessly on the continuing decline of American fortunes during Carter's presidency. In the last presidential debate before election day, Reagan told the audience, "I think . . . it might be well if you would ask yourself, are you better off than you were four years ago?"

Americans answered that question by giving Reagan the presidency. The Republican nominee carried all but four states and the District of Columbia (see Map 30–2). Reagan managed only 50.7 percent of the popular vote, but his tally, combined with Anderson's 6.6 percent, suggested the extent of popular disaffection with Carter and the Democratic Party. Although the Democrats held on to the House of Representatives, Republicans took control of the Senate for the first time since 1962. Sixteen years after Barry Goldwater's conservative candidacy had ended in a crushing defeat, the nation had turned sharply to the right.

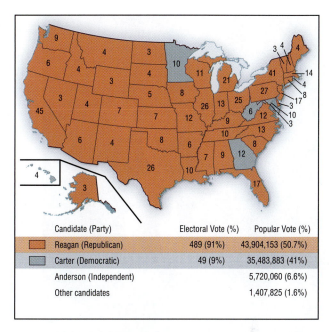

Candidate (Party)	Electoral Vote (%)	Popular Vote (%)
Reagan (Republican)	489 (91%)	43,904,153 (50.7%)
Carter (Democratic)	49 (9%)	35,483,883 (41%)
Anderson (Independent)		5,720,060 (6.6%)
Other candidates		1,407,825 (1.6%)

Map 30–2   The Presidential Election, 1980 As in other elections, a narrow victory in the popular vote translated into a landslide in the electoral college.

The Reagan Revolution at Home

Ronald Reagan shaped American life more decisively than any president since Franklin Roosevelt. Reagan's style—folksy and optimistic—made him popular, but the Reagan years were more than a triumph of style. With some justice, his supporters believed that the president spurred a "Reagan Revolution," a sweeping conservative transformation of American economic and political life.

The Reagan Style

The Reagan Revolution was partly a matter of style. Despite the frustrations of the 1960s and 1970s, Reagan exuded optimism. Rather than teach Americans how to live with less, he embraced luxury. Reagan's presidency signaled a confident, even opulent, new era. On inauguration day, as if to mark the belated end of the frustrating 1970s, the Iranian government finally released its American hostages. In his inaugural address, Reagan firmly rejected pessimism about the nation's future. "We are not," the new president declared, "doomed to an inevitable decline." That night, he and his wife Nancy danced at a series of lavish balls. The Reagan inaugural cost five times more than Jimmy Carter's had four years earlier.

Even while the Reagans continued their lavish lifestyle in the White House, the president retained a popular, common touch.

> **In this present crisis, government is not the solution of our problem.**
>
> RONALD REAGAN,
> inaugural address,
> January 1981

The Return of Confident Luxury Newly-inaugurated President Ronald Reagan dances with his wife Nancy at a ball, January 1981.

After his career in movies and television, he knew how to speak simply and effectively to the American people. Although the president did not always absorb the details of issues, he became known as the "Great Communicator."

Reagan also appeared to enjoy and master his job. After the troubled presidencies of the 1970s, Reagan made the presidency seem manageable again. Even though he took office as America's oldest president at the age of 69, he projected an image of vigor and energy.

The president even managed to survive an assassination attempt. On March 30, 1981, John W. Hinckley, a troubled young loner, shot and wounded Reagan, his press secretary, and a policeman. Reagan's chest wound was more serious than his spokesmen admitted, but the president met the situation with good humor. "Honey," he told his wife, "I forgot to duck." The president's popularity soared.

Shrinking Government

More than just a master of style, Reagan offered a clear conservative alternative to the liberal policies of the New Deal and the Great Society. Above all, he denied that a large, activist federal government could deal with the challenges of American life in the 1980s. Accordingly, Reagan wanted to shrink the government's size and reduce its power.

The president's efforts to shrink the federal government met with mixed success. In his 1982 State of the Union address, Reagan, like the previous Republican president, Richard Nixon, endorsed the New Federalism, a plan to transfer federal programs and tax revenues to the states. Reagan insisted the New Federalism would promote efficiency and economic growth, but governors worried that their states would be saddled with expensive responsibilities. In the end, the federal government transferred only a few programs.

Reagan also created a commission, headed by business executive J. Peter Grace, to explore ways the federal government could save money. The Grace Commission claimed that Washington could save more than $400 billion over three years, partly by making it more difficult for Americans to qualify for welfare, pension, and other benefits. Congress was unwilling to make such reforms. The commission also called for the line-item veto, which would allow a president to reject particular spending programs in Congress's annual budget without having to veto the entire budget bill. Congress was not ready to give Reagan so much new power.

The president had more success when he attacked social welfare programs. Like many other conservatives, Reagan condemned antipoverty programs as a waste of federal resources that sapped the work ethic and the morals of the poor. Reagan and his followers believed that the nation thrived when workers had to succeed or fail on their own. He wanted reductions in food stamps, school meal programs, and aid to cities. In response, Congress cut appropriations for urban public housing and eliminated job training for the unemployed.

Reagan found it nearly impossible to touch Medicare and Social Security, two expensive and popular programs that benefited most Americans. The Social Security system proved especially difficult to cut. By the 1980s there was growing concern that workers' Social Security payments would eventually not be enough to cover the cost of benefits to retirees. After a long struggle, Congress produced the Social Security Reform Act of 1983, which raised the minimum age for full benefits from 65 to 67 and made retirees pay taxes on some benefits. The measure did little to reduce the total cost of the program. By 1984, Reagan was promising not to cut Social Security.

Although expenditures for welfare programs continued to rise, the Reagan administration managed to slow the growth of such spending. Benefits did not expand dramatically; there were no costly new programs. As expenditures for national defense grew, welfare outlays fell from 28 percent of the federal budget in 1980 to 22 percent by 1987. Reagan did not reduce the federal government overall, but he did succeed in shrinking the relative size of some parts of it that he disliked.

Reaganomics

For Reagan and his followers, shrinking the government also meant decreasing Washington's role in the economy. True to conservative ideology, they argued that the nation prospered most when government left Americans free to manage their own businesses and keep their own earnings. The Reagan administration worked to lower taxes, deregulate business, and cut federal support for unions.

"Reaganomics" drew on a new theory known as supply-side economics. Beginning in the 1970s, economist Arthur Laffer had offered an alternative to the liberal, Keynesian economics that had guided federal policy since the New Deal. While Keynesians believed that increased consumer demand would spur economic growth, Laffer contended that an increased supply of goods and services was the key to growth. He rejected the Keynesian prescription for raising government spending to put more money in the hands of consumers. To promote prosperity, he believed government should cut, rather than hike, taxes. By leaving more money in the hands of businesses, government would allow them to invest in more production of goods and services. The increase in supply would stimulate prosperity and increase, rather than decrease, tax revenues.

Supply-side economics was controversial. To liberal critics it seemed to be an excuse to let the rich keep more of their money. Even some Republicans doubted that a tax cut would produce more tax revenues. But the supply-side approach fit neatly with conservative dislike for high taxes and big, active government.

Following supply-side principles, Reagan asked a joint session of Congress in 1981 to cut taxes dramatically. Impressed by Reagan's popularity and the electorate's increasing conservatism, the Democratic-controlled House joined the Republican-dominated Senate to pass the Economic Recovery Act of 1981 (also known as the Kemp-Roth Bill). An important victory for Reagan, this measure cut federal income taxes 5 percent the first year and then 10 percent in each of the next two years. It especially benefited the wealthy by making the tax structure less progressive and by reducing the tax rate on the highest individual incomes and on large gifts and estates.

Like other conservatives, Reagan believed that federal rules and requirements hamstrung American business and prevented economic growth. Accordingly, his administration stepped up the campaign for deregulation begun by Jimmy Carter. The government cut the budgets of such key regulatory agencies as the Environmental Protection Agency and the Occupational Safety and Health Administration. The Reagan administration also made sure that government officials did not strictly enforce regulatory rules and laws. Further, the administration deregulated the telephone industry. In 1982 the government broke up the giant American Telephone and Telegraph Company into smaller regional companies and allowed new firms such as Sprint and MCI to compete for AT&T's long-distance business.

Reagan moved to lift environmental restrictions on American businesses. His administration made it easier for timber and mining companies to exploit wilderness areas and allowed oil companies to drill off the Pacific coast. The administration also opposed environmentalists' demands for laws to protect against acid rain—air pollution, caused by industrial emissions, that harmed lakes, forests, and crops, especially in the Northeast and Canada.

Reaganomics also meant weakening organized labor, already suffering from deindustrialization. Ironically, Reagan, once the head of the Screen Actors Guild, was the first former union official to serve as president. Like most conservatives, Reagan believed that unions obstructed business and limited the freedom of individual workers. He believed as well that the federal government had done too much to encourage organized labor since the New Deal.

Reagan made probusiness appointments to the National Labor Relations Board. More important, he took a strong antiunion stance during a strike by the Professional Air Traffic Controllers Organization (PATCO) in 1981. Despite a law forbidding strikes by federal workers, PATCO walked out to protest unsafe conditions in the air traffic control system. Reagan fired the striking controllers, refused to hire them back, and replaced them with nonunion workers. The president's action encouraged business to take a hard line with employees. By the end of the 1980s, the union movement was weaker than at any time since the Great Depression.

Reaganomics did not quite have the effect that its supporters anticipated. In the short run, Reagan's measures did not prevent a sharp recession, which began in the fall of 1981. As the Federal Reserve Bank fought inflation by raising interest rates, the economy slowed, and unemployment increased. Reaganomics also increased the federal budget deficit. The supply-side theory that tax cuts would boost tax revenues and balance the budget proved incorrect.

By the spring of 1984, the recession had ended. Thanks largely to the Federal Reserve's monetary policy, the high inflation of the 1970s was over. The economy began a long period of growth and higher employment, and Reagan's supporters gave the president credit. His critics charged that the deficit rather than Reaganomics had produced the boom and that the deficit would ultimately hurt the economy. In the mid-1980s, however, Reaganomics appeared to be a success. Certainly "stagflation," the combination of stagnant economic growth and high inflation that plagued the 1970s, was over.

Organized Labor Confronts the Reagan Revolution These and other striking members of the Professional Air Traffic Controllers Organization would soon be fired by President Ronald Reagan in 1981.

The 1984 Presidential Election

The changing impact of Reaganomics shaped national politics. In the depths of the recession, the Republicans lost 26 House seats in the midterm congressional elections of 1982. But with the return of prosperity, the president was easily renominated in 1984. Reagan ran against a liberal Democratic nominee, former vice president Walter Mondale of Minnesota. The Democrat, confronting a popular incumbent, made bold moves. Mondale chose the first female vice-presidential nominee of a major party, Representative Geraldine Ferraro of New York. To prove his honesty and openness, Mondale made the politically foolish announcement that he would raise taxes as president. The Democrat was also saddled with the disappointing record of the Carter administration and the alienation of white working- and middle-class Democrats.

Reagan ran an optimistic campaign emphasizing the renewal of America. "It's morning again in America," a Reagan campaign commercial announced. "Life is better, America is back," another commercial declared. "And people have a sense of pride they never felt they'd feel again." Mondale would jeopardize all that, the Reagan campaign charged, with tax increases and favors to such "special interests" as labor unions, feminists, and civil rights activists.

Election day revealed both the strength and the weakness of the Reagan Revolution. The contest was a personal triumph for the president. With his conservative message, Reagan polled 58.8 percent of the popular vote and lost only the District of Columbia and Mondale's home state of Minnesota. Reagan's big vote did not translate into a sweeping victory for his party. Holding on to the Senate, the Republicans failed to win a majority in the House of Representatives.

The Reagan Revolution Abroad

Reagan's foreign policy, like his domestic policy, rested on old conservative values. The president rejected the main diplomatic approaches of the 1970s—Richard Nixon's détente with the Soviet Union and Jimmy Carter's support for international human rights. Instead, the Reagan Revolution revived the strident anti-Communism of the 1940s and 1950s. The president moved to restore the nation's military and economic power in order to challenge the Soviet Union and stop Communism in the Western Hemisphere. Communism, however, had little to do with such difficult international issues as conflict in the Middle East, terrorism, and economic relations with Japan and developing nations. Nevertheless, the Reagan Revolution abroad plainly refocused American policy on the cold war confrontation with Communism.

Restoring American Power

After losing the Vietnam War, the United States had cut back its armed forces and become reluctant to risk military confrontations abroad. Reagan set out to restore American power in the 1980s—and the will to use it.

Like most conservatives, the president did not believe that cutting government spending should include cutting the armed forces. Under Reagan, the nation's defense spending more than doubled, from $134 billion in 1980 to more than $300 billion by 1989. Reagan's administration built up all branches of the armed services and ordered development of controversial weapons systems. Construction of the B-1 strategic jet bomber, stopped by Jimmy Carter, resumed. Reagan began development of the B-2 Stealth bomber, an innovative plane that could evade detection by enemy radar. He won congressional approval for the MX Peacekeeper, a nuclear missile with multiple warheads. He also persuaded Congress to authorize work on the neutron bomb, a nuclear weapon that could spread lethal radiation over a half-mile radius.

As he pursued his military buildup, Reagan faced a growing mass movement against nuclear weapons. In both Europe and the United States, millions of people, frightened by the horror of nuclear war, called for a halt to the introduction of new nuclear arms. In June 1982, a crowd of 700,000 gathered in New York's Central Park to demand a nuclear freeze. The National Conference of Catholic Bishops supported the freeze and declared nuclear war immoral. But Reagan rejected the movement as naive and Communist-infiltrated. The best way to ensure peace, he believed, was to keep developing weapons.

The military buildup was a matter of changing attitudes as well as increasing weapons and budgets. In the wake of the Vietnam War, many Americans were reluctant to endorse U.S. intervention abroad. They feared that the nation might become entrapped in another costly, losing, possibly immoral battle overseas. This "Vietnam syndrome" threatened the Reagan administration's foreign policy. The president could not afford to let other countries think the United States would not back up its words with action. Accordingly, Reagan used his speeches to stir up patriotic emotion. The president also tried to persuade Americans that the Vietnam War had been "a just cause," well worth supporting.

Some of the 700,000 Demonstrators at the Nuclear Freeze Rally in New York City's Central Park, June 1982 For a time, the movement to halt new nuclear weapons challenged President Reagan's plans for an arms buildup.

By the mid-1980s, Reagan had succeeded in restoring much of America's military power. It remained to be seen, however, whether Americans were willing to use that power abroad.

Confronting the "Evil Empire"

The main purpose of the military buildup was to contain the Soviet Union. Suspicion of the Soviets and their Communist ideology was the heart of Reagan's diplomacy. In the early 1980s, Reagan called the USSR the "evil empire" and insisted that the Soviet Union and its Communist allies were doomed by failing economies and unpopular regimes. Communist ideology, Reagan declared, would end up "on the ash heap of history."

Reagan avoided cooperation with the Soviet Union and held no summit meetings during his first term. The Reagan administration openly supported the mujahedeen, the Afghan rebels who were resisting the Soviets. More important, the president avoided arms-control agreements with the Soviets during his first term. Instead, he used the American military buildup to pressure the USSR. Reagan refused to submit the second Strategic Arms Limitation Treaty, signed by Jimmy Carter, to the Senate for ratification. In response to the United States' deployment of new intermediate-range nuclear missiles in Western Europe, the Soviets walked out of arms-control talks in 1983.

That year, Reagan put even more pressure on the USSR when he announced plans for the Strategic Defense Initiative (SDI), a space-based missile-defense

The Dream of President Reagan's "Star Wars" An artist's illustration of how the Reagan administration's Strategic Defense Initiative would knock Communist missiles out of the sky.

system that would use lasers and other advanced technology to shoot down nuclear missiles launched at the United States. Although funded by Congress, SDI was a long way from reality in 1983. Critics, convinced SDI was science fiction, called the plan "Star Wars," after the epic space movie.

The American initiative doubly threatened the Soviets. SDI seemingly made the USSR vulnerable to attack. Since the 1950s, the Americans and the Soviets had relied on the theory of *mutual assured destruction* as a deterrent to war: since a nuclear war would destroy both sides, the theory ran, there was no incentive for either nation to start one. Now SDI raised the possibility that the United States could survive a nuclear attack and therefore might be willing to start a war with the Soviets. To avoid this threat, the Soviets would need to develop their own SDI. There was the second threat: the USSR would have to divert scarce resources and perhaps weaken their economy in order to compete with the United States.

While the United States pressed the Soviets, Reagan clearly wanted to avoid open confrontation with the major Communist powers. In 1983, a Soviet fighter plane shot down an unarmed Korean airliner, killing all 269 passengers and crew. Although a U.S. congressman was one of the victims, Reagan responded with restraint. A year later, Reagan traded visits with the premier of the People's Republic of China and encouraged cultural exchanges, economic cooperation, and a nuclear-weapons agreement.

The Reagan Doctrine in the Third World

The Reagan administration also changed American foreign policy toward the third world. Reagan, along with other conservatives, had been impatient with the Carter administration's attempts to promote human rights abroad. The United States, conservatives believed, needed to back anti-Communist, pro-American governments, whether or not they respected human rights. Jeane J. Kirkpatrick, who became Reagan's ambassador to the United Nations, called for a distinction between totalitarian regimes hostile to the U.S. and authoritarian governments friendly to American interests. Critics claimed that this distinction was meaningless and insisted that the nation should not support antidemocratic governments. The administration adopted Kirkpatrick's view, which became known as the Reagan Doctrine.

During the president's first term, his administration applied the Reagan Doctrine aggressively in Central America and the Caribbean (see Map 30–3). Determined to keep Communism out of the Western Hemisphere, the United States opposed the

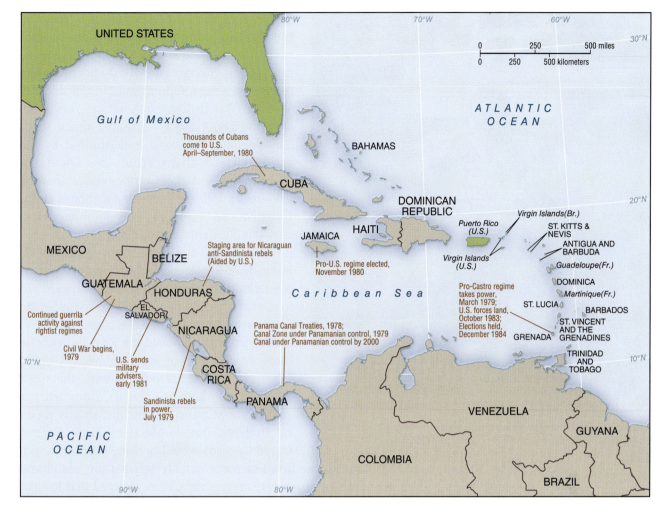

Map 30–3   The Reagan Doctrine in Central America and the Caribbean Events that shaped Reagan's anti-Communist initiative in the Western Hemisphere.

Marxist Sandinista government of Nicaragua and supported the repressive anti-Communist government of neighboring El Salvador.

The Sandinistas had come to power in the late 1970s by overthrowing the dictatorship of Anastasio Somoza with the encouragement of the Carter administration. The Reagan administration believed the Sandinistas were too friendly to the Soviet Union and to leftist rebels in El Salvador. Reagan halted aid to Nicaragua in April 1981 and directed the CIA to train, arm, and supply the Contra rebels, who opposed the Sandinistas. Many of the Contras had ties to the oppressive Somoza government, but Reagan praised them as "freedom fighters" and "the moral equivalent of our Founding Fathers."

Meanwhile, the president strongly backed the right-wing military government of El Salvador, which was locked in a deadly civil war with pro-Sandinista and pro-Cuban rebels. Ultimately, some 75,000 people died in the conflict. Employing infamous "death squads," the military government engaged in kidnapping, torture, and murder. Nevertheless, Reagan did not want this brutal, undemocratic regime to fall. El Salvador, the president explained, was "a textbook case of indirect armed aggression by Communist powers."

Reagan's Central American Policy The president holds up a T-shirt summing up his approach to the region: "STOP COMMUNISM CENTRAL AMERICA."

Despite such anti-Communist rhetoric, the Reagan administration could not persuade Congress to support its Central American policy. Congressional Democrats, like many Americans, did not want to risk another Vietnam War in Central America. They were skeptical about the Communist threat to El Salvador and Nicaragua and troubled by the antidemocratic character of the Salvadoran government and the Contra rebels. In 1983 Congress approved Reagan's Caribbean Basin Initiative, an economic development package, but Reagan did not get the military aid he wanted for the Salvadoran government. Instead, in September 1982 Congress passed the Boland Amendment, which restricted aid to the Contras and banned efforts to topple the Sandinista regime.

The president applied the Reagan Doctrine more successfully in the Caribbean. On October 25, 1983, U.S. troops invaded the small West Indian island of Grenada, supposedly to protect about 1,000 Americans, mostly medical students, from a Marxist regime. Reagan feared Grenada would become a Cuban or Soviet base close to U.S. shores. The invading force quickly secured the island and replaced the government with a pro-American regime. Critics charged that Reagan had undermined the sovereignty of another state in order to win an easy military victory. For the president's supporters, the invasion was a welcome demonstration of the Reagan Doctrine and an antidote to the Vietnam syndrome.

The president also implemented the Reagan Doctrine in Africa. With its commitment to human rights, the Carter administration had condemned the long-standing policy of *apartheid*—racial separation—pursued by the white government of South Africa. Reagan, despite America's own struggle with racial segregation, would not take a similarly strong stance. Rather than impose economic sanctions on the South African regime, the president endorsed a mild policy of diplomatic discussions known as "constructive engagement" while South Africa suffered violence and near civil war. Reagan held back because his administration viewed the South African regime as a vital ally in the struggle against Communism in southern Africa. During the 1980s, the United States supported South African military intervention in Angola, Mozambique, and Namibia against groups aided by Cuba and the Soviet Union. More than a million people died in these conflicts.

The Middle East and Terrorism

The Reagan Doctrine was not much help in dealing with the Middle East and the growing problem of terrorism. Communism and the Soviet Union, the focus of Reagan's foreign policy, had little impact on Middle Eastern issues in the 1980s.

As before, the United States wanted to ensure its supply of oil and to support its longtime ally, Israel. There was no new Arab oil embargo during the Reagan years, but the administration could not bring peace to the Middle East or end the threat of terrorism.

Reagan found it difficult to build on the Camp David Accords between Israel and Egypt, which were supposed to lead to self-government for the Palestinian Arabs who lived in the Israeli-occupied West Bank and Gaza Strip. However, Israel and the Palestine Liberation Organization (PLO), the official representative of the Palestinians, remained at odds. The PLO continued to threaten Israel from bases in neighboring Lebanon. In the spring of 1982, the Israelis invaded Lebanon, which was already convulsed by a civil war between Muslims and Christians.

To end the Israeli invasion and stabilize Lebanon, the United States sent marines to join an international peacekeeping force. On October 23, 1983, a terrorist killed 241 Americans by driving a truck bomb into marine headquarters at Beirut. The attack shocked Americans and marked a low point of Reagan's administration. The president did not retaliate. He did not want to reward terrorism by removing U.S. troops from Lebanon. Nevertheless, he pulled out the soldiers in 1984, even though there was still no peace in Lebanon and no agreement between the Israelis and the PLO.

The attack on the marine headquarters illustrated the growing threat of terrorism against the United States and its allies. Reagan vowed to make terrorists "pay for their actions," but terrorism proved hard to stop. Acts of terrorism by Palestinians and Libyans drew quick American reprisals in the 1980s. After Palestinians murdered an American passenger on a cruise ship in the Mediterranean in 1985, U.S. planes forced down the Egyptian airliner carrying the escaping terrorists. The Reagan administration believed that Muammar Qaddafi, leader of the North African nation of Libya, supported terrorism. In 1982 U.S. Navy fighter planes shot down two Libyan fighters off the Libyan coast. After American soldiers died in a terrorist bombing in West Germany in 1986, U.S. jets bombed several targets in Libya, among them the military barracks and headquarters including Qaddafi's personal residence. Among the 40 or so dead was one of the Libyan leader's daughters. Qaddafi, whom Reagan called "the mad dog of the Middle East," seemed to become less critical of the United States, but the threat of terrorism did not go away.

Reagan also acted to safeguard America's oil supply. During a war between Iran and Iraq, the United States sent navy ships to protect oil tankers in the Persian Gulf. As in Lebanon, American intervention was costly. In May 1987 Iraqi missiles struck the U.S. destroyer *Stark*, killing 37 of its crew. The Reagan administration, unwilling to help Iran, accepted Iraq's apology. In July 1988, the U.S.

The Threat of Terrorism U.S. Marines carry a survivor from the rubble of marine headquarters in Beirut, Lebanon, after a truck bomb explosion in October 1983.

missile cruiser *Vincennes* accidentally shot down an Iranian airliner, killing 290 passengers. An American apology did little to quell Iranian anger, but the Iran-Iraq war soon ended, and with it the threat to America's oil supply.

The United States and the World Economy

Middle Eastern oil was only one of the economic factors shaping Reagan's foreign policy. The president had to deal with strains on the world economy. Like twentieth-century presidents before him, Reagan believed strongly that free trade would boost national economies around the world. He believed, too, that his conservative formula of tax cuts, lower government spending, and less government regulation would benefit other nations. But after years of relative economic decline, the United States could not always impose its will on other nations.

Reagan did successfully force his views on debt-ridden, relatively weak third world countries. By the end of the 1980s, the developing nations owed foreign banks more than $1.2 trillion in loan payments. Mexico was more than $100 billion in debt. American banks stood to lose heavily if Mexico and other nations defaulted on loans. American producers stood to lose, too, if these countries could not afford to buy U.S. goods. The Reagan administration nevertheless refused to protect American banks from loan defaults, instead forcing debtor countries to adopt freer trade, deregulation of business, and government austerity programs in return for new loans.

The Reagan administration had much less power to dictate trade policy with Japan. As Japanese exports flowed into the United States, Americans increasingly resented Japan's domination of the Japanese home market. Congress, believing the Japanese discriminated against American goods, pushed for retaliation. Japan placed voluntary quotas on its export of steel and automobiles to the United States. Although the Reagan administration devalued the dollar to make American goods cheaper, the trade imbalance continued. In 1988 the president signed the Omnibus Trade and Competitiveness Act, which allowed the government to place high tariffs on Japanese goods if Japan continued to discriminate against American goods. However, as long as Americans wanted to buy Japanese products, retaliation was unlikely. By 1989 a Japanese car, the Honda Accord, had become the biggest-selling model in the United States for the first time.

Many of those Accords had been made in the United States. Even as the Reagan administration struggled to open up Japanese markets for American goods, Japanese firms greatly increased their direct investment in the United States. Honda, for instance, built a new factory in Marysville, Ohio, to produce Accords for the American market. As Japanese companies built or took over other manufacturing facilities, many Americans wondered whether the global expansion of trade was really beneficial to their country after all.

The Battle over Conservative Social Values

For all of Ronald Reagan's success in the early 1980s, the new conservatism met with considerable opposition. The conservatives' social values were especially controversial. Eager to combat the legacies of the 1960s, many conservatives, like Linda Chavez, wanted to restore supposedly traditional values and practices. The conservative agenda collided head-on with one of the chief legacies of the 1960s—disadvantaged groups'

AMERICA AND THE WORLD

>> Japanese Management, American Workers

Until the 1980s, American workers had generally missed one of the quintessential experiences of globalization—management by foreigners. For decades, it was the workers of other countries who found themselves adapting to foreign managerial techniques, often those of U.S. multinational companies and their American executives. But with the weakening of American industry and the rebuilding of the Japanese and West European economies, expansive foreign firms began to set up operations in the United States in the 1970s and 1980s.

Japanese firms rushed to invest. By 1988, more than 300,000 American workers labored for Japanese companies in the United States. The most publicized Japanese ventures came in the auto industry, long dominated by U.S. manufacturers and their pioneering mass production techniques. In the 1980s, leading Japanese auto manufacturers set up factories in such places as Marysville, Ohio, Smyrna, Tennessee, and Fremont, California. In these and other facilities, Japanese companies set about teaching Americans new ways to work.

The Japanese approach emphasized the importance of the group over the individual. Japanese managers urged their American workers to see the company as a harmonious family whose members had the same interests. To foster harmony, the Japanese eliminated reserved parking spaces and dining rooms for management and time clocks for labor. At the Nissan plant in Smyrna, managers and workers wore the same blue uniform. The Japanese also tried to improve communication with workers and draw them into decision making. To empower workers and increase efficiency, Japanese companies often gave workers the means to stop production to eliminate a problem—something U.S. firms seldom did.

Japanese companies tried to make factory life more pleasant. Plants were clean and efficient. At the Nissan factory in Smyrna, workers had basketball hoops and Ping-Pong tables close to their stations for use during breaks. But the Japanese companies also banned smoking and radios. More important, management pushed workers to speed up production. Japanese companies also wanted workers to be flexible enough to do different jobs in a plant.

Some workers enthusiastically accepted the new approach. "I love it," gushed Nancy Nicholson, a laid-off factory worker who found a job in a Japanese plant in Virginia. "They make you feel like a part of a family." Workers appreciated that Japanese managers put in long hours and seemed devoted to efficiency and quality.

Laboring harder than before, many American workers were not quite so enthusiastic. They felt that the Japanese were hostile to unions, African Americans, and women. Some American managers charged that their Japanese employers would not promote them to top jobs. But most employees were glad to have a well-paying job that might last. "This plant is our survival," explained a union representative at the General Motors–Toyota plant in Fremont.

Japanese executives had some criticisms of their own. They felt that American workers needed too many instructions and too much motivation to do a job. Still individualistic, the Americans were not "team players" ready to confess mistakes or perform work outside their job description. "Americans are too sensitive about fairness," complained Kosuke Ikebuchi, after his years in the United States. Japanese veterans of the United States generally concluded their American subordinates were less productive than Japanese workers.

Despite such criticism, the Japanese companies seemed successful in the United States in the 1980s. Typically, Japanese-run units showed gains in productivity and quality. At the General Motors–Toyota plant in Fremont, workers turned out a car in 20 hours compared to 28 hours at another GM plant. Moreover, that car was more likely to satisfy buyers than the typical product of American-run companies. ●

> I bought feminism, and a lot of other things. It didn't work in any way, in my marriage or in child rearing. I'm talking about anarchy.
>
> ～～～
> NADA JAGERSON,
> a conservative Christian activist from San Bernardino, California, 1985

demands for equal rights and opportunities. Moreover, many Americans were unwilling to abandon the social changes of the last generation. Faced with such opposition, conservatives failed to achieve much of their vision for American society.

Attacking the Legacy of the 1960s

The new conservatism was driven by a desire to undo the liberal and radical legacies of the 1960s. Conservatives blamed federal courts for much of the social change in the United States over the last generation. In the 1960s and 1970s liberal justices with an activist conception of the courts' role had supported defendants' rights, civil rights, affirmative action, busing, and abortion while rejecting such conservative causes as school prayer.

Determined to take control of the courts, Reagan appointed many staunch, relatively young conservatives to the federal bench and the Supreme Court. In 1981 Sandra Day O'Connor, a fairly conservative judge from Arizona, became the Court's first woman justice. When Chief Justice Warren Burger retired, Reagan replaced him with conservative William Rehnquist. With the appointments of two more conservatives, Antonin Scalia and Anthony Kennedy, the Supreme Court seemed ready to turn away from liberalism.

It did not quite work out that way. In the 1980s the Court followed conservative views in limiting the rights of defendants. Ruling in *United States v. Leon* and *Nix v. Williams* in 1984, the justices made it easier for prosecutors to use evidence improperly obtained by police. However, on a variety of other issues, the court took a moderate stance. In *Wallace v. Jaffree* in 1985, the Court disappointed evangelical Christians and other advocates of school prayer by invalidating an Alabama law that allowed schools to devote a minute each day to voluntary prayer or meditation.

Prayer was just one element of conservatives' broad plan to reform public education. They believed that the federal government had played too large a role in the schools since the 1960s. Parents, meanwhile, had too little say in the education of their children. Conservative educational reformers preferred to use market forces rather than government power to reform the schools. They wanted to dismantle the federal Department of Education. In addition, they wanted the government to enable parents to choose the best schools—public or private—for their children, with federally funded vouchers or tax credits to help pay for the choice.

Because many Americans were worried about the quality of the schools, conservatives had a golden opportunity. In 1983 a federal study, *A Nation at Risk,* documented American students' shortcomings, especially in math and science. Despite such revelations, Congress refused to adopt the voucher system or to abolish the Department of Education.

Drug use was another issue that conservatives traced to the 1960s. In the early 1980s, drugs again became a

The First Woman Supreme Court Justice Sandra Day O'Connor, with President Reagan, who had nominated her to the court, 1981.

major public concern with the spread of crack, a cheap but addictive form of cocaine. The sale and use of crack, especially in the cities, led to crime and violence. In 1986 the president and his wife, Nancy, announced a "national crusade" for a "drug-free" America. Their campaign encouraged young people to "Just Say No" to drugs, implemented drug testing for federal employees, and imposed mandatory minimum sentences for some drug use. The "war on drugs" was controversial. Critics ridiculed the "Just Say No" slogan as naive and ineffective. They also condemned new federal and state sentencing laws, which put millions in jail, as unfair to African Americans and expensive to taxpayers. Despite the new penalties and expenditures, drug use did not decrease appreciably.

Women's Rights and Abortion

One of the chief legacies of the 1960s was the women's rights movement. The new conservatism condemned feminism and lamented the changing role of women in America. Many conservatives, especially evangelical leaders, blamed feminists and liberal government for encouraging women to abandon their traditional family role for paid jobs. The conservative movement was especially determined to halt federal initiatives, such as affirmative action programs and the equal rights amendment (ERA), that used government power to protect women's rights (see Chapter 29).

The conservative agenda on women's rights met with mixed results. The campaign for the ERA, already lagging in the 1970s, ended unsuccessfully, but affirmative action programs, designed to promote the hiring of women, continued. So did women's push into the workplace and public life as more and more American families needed two incomes. By 1983 women made up half of the paid workforce. As their economic role expanded, American women received more recognition from the political system. Ironically, Reagan himself gave women new public prominence by choosing Jeane J. Kirkpatrick and Sandra Day O'Connor for important offices.

Women still did not enjoy equality in America. They were generally paid less than men doing the same sort of work, and they had less opportunity to break through the glass ceiling and win managerial jobs. Moreover, commentators had begun to note the feminization of poverty. Unmarried or divorced women, many with children, made up an increasing percentage of the poor. This suffering and inequality, liberals and feminists argued, disproved the conservative claim that women did not need special protection.

For many conservatives, the right to abortion, guaranteed by the Supreme Court in *Roe v. Wade* in 1974, was the most troubling sign of the changed status of women. A growing Right to Life movement passionately denounced abortion as the murder of the unborn, practiced by selfish women who rejected motherhood and family.

Conservatives failed to narrow abortion rights significantly in the 1980s. Reagan successfully urged Congress to stop the use of federal funds to pay for abortions, but a constitutional amendment outlawing abortion stalled in the Senate. In 1983 and 1986, the Supreme Court made rulings that upheld *Roe v. Wade*.

Gays and the AIDS Crisis

The gay rights movement was another legacy of the 1960s that troubled many conservatives. Evangelical leaders such as Jerry Falwell condemned homosexuality on

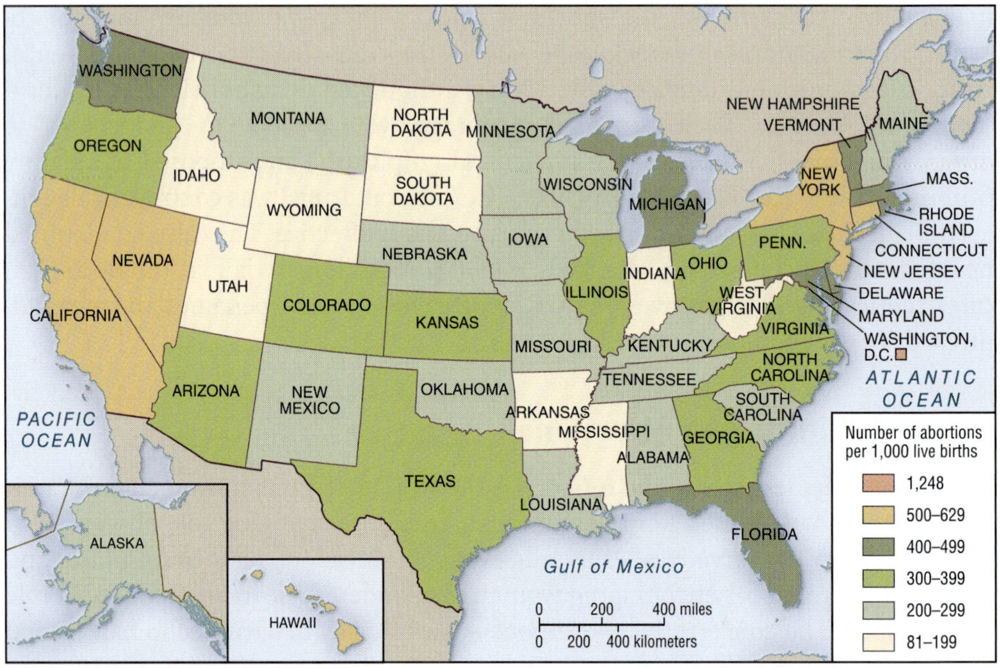

Map 30–4   Abortion in the 1980s The rate of abortions across the United States 14 years after the Supreme Court's decision legalizing abortion in *Roe v. Wade. Timothy H. Fast and Cathy Carroll Fast,* The Women's Atlas of the United States, *rev. ed. (1995), p. 166.*

religious grounds. Some people believed that the public acceptance of equal rights for gay men and women would promote immorality and corrupt children. In 1977 Anita Bryant, a former Miss America, launched a national crusade, Save Our Children, to protest the passage of a gay rights ordinance in Dade County, Florida, where Miami is located. Voters soon repealed the measure. In San Francisco in 1978, Harvey Milk, the first avowedly gay member of the city's board of supervisors, was assassinated, along with the mayor, by a former supervisor. Many gays were shocked when the assassin received only a short jail sentence.

Despite such opposition, the gay rights movement made progress in the 1980s. By the end of the decade, most states had repealed sodomy laws that criminalized gay sex. In 1982 Wisconsin became the first state to pass a law protecting the rights of gay men and women. At the federal level, however, a majority of the U.S. Supreme Court dismissed a gay man's right to sexual privacy as "facetious" in *Bowers v. Hardwick* in 1986.

The battle over gay rights took place against a tragic backdrop. In 1981 the Centers for Disease Control began reporting cases of acquired immune deficiency syndrome (AIDS), a disease that destroyed the body's immune system and left it unable to fight off infections and rare cancers. By the mid-1980s, researchers had traced AIDS to different forms of the human immunodeficiency virus (HIV) that were transmitted in semen and blood. But no cure had been found. By 1990 there were nearly 100,000 recorded deaths from the AIDS epidemic in the United States (see Figure 30–2).

Because 75 percent of the first victims were gay men, Americans initially considered AIDS a homosexual disease. Some people, including evangelical leaders, believed this "gay cancer" was God's punishment for the alleged sin of homosexuality. As soon became clear, however, AIDS could also be transmitted by heterosexual

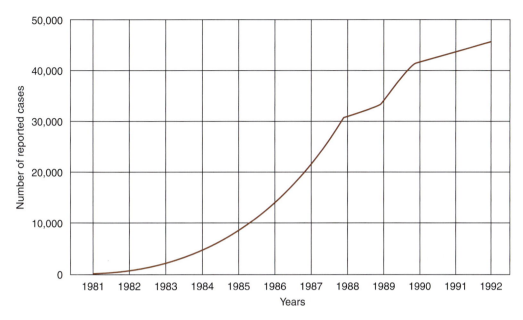

Figure 30–2   The Rapid Rise of AIDS Statistical Abstract of the United States, 1989, p. 111; Statistical Abstract, 1993, p. 203.

intercourse, by intravenous drug use that involved sharing needles, and by tainted blood transfusions.

Public understanding of AIDS and HIV gradually increased. Nevertheless, the specter of "gay cancer" promoted homophobia and slowed the public response to the disease. Gay activists pushed for government action. The AIDS Coalition to Unleash Power, known as ACT UP, and other organizations staged demonstrations and acts of civil disobedience to focus attention on the crisis. Nevertheless, the Reagan administration did not fund research on AIDS for several years. Meanwhile, the disease continued to spread.

The AIDS epidemic complicated the struggle over gay rights. For some Americans, the disease reinforced the conservative condemnation of homosexuality. For others, the suffering of AIDS victims engendered sympathy and compassion. As the 1980s ended, the conservative backlash against gay rights had not succeeded, but the AIDS epidemic continued.

African Americans and Racial Inequality

Conservatives were uneasy with still another legacy of the 1960s, the expansion of African American civil rights and benefits

"How Many More Must Die?" Gay rights advocates protest President Bush's AIDS policies in the Maine town where he was vacationing in September 1991.

guaranteed by the federal government. The New Right believed that the liberal policies of the Great Society hurt, rather than helped, black people. Conservatives maintained that individual initiative, and not government action, would promote racial equality. In keeping with these ideas, President Reagan opposed renewal of the Voting Rights Act and condemned busing and affirmative action. The president, like many Republicans, opposed the creation of a national holiday marking the birthday of Martin Luther King Jr.

The conservatives' tough stance came at a difficult time in the struggle for racial equality. Compared with the 1950s and 1960s, African Americans' crusade for justice and opportunity generally slowed in the 1970s and 1980s. Despite legal equality, African Americans faced persisting racism and discrimination. Disproportionately clustered in manual occupations, African Americans were particularly hurt by the deindustrialization and economic decline of the 1970s and 1980s. After years of improvement, African Americans' economic status relative to whites stagnated or declined during the Reagan era. African Americans still made less money than whites did for comparable work and had much less chance to attain managerial positions.

Economic hardship and persistent discrimination did not affect all African Americans equally. In the 1980s the African American middle class continued to thrive. Among college-educated Americans, the incomes of black men rose faster than those of whites into the mid-1980s. Middle-class African Americans could afford to move to better housing, often in suburbs and integrated areas. Meanwhile, working-class African Americans found their wages stagnating or falling compared with those of white workers. In the 1970s and 1980s, poverty rates rose faster among African Americans than among whites. The feminization of poverty hit black families particularly hard. In 1985, 75 percent of poor African American children lived in families headed by a single female. Observers feared that there was now a permanent African American underclass living segregated in inner-city neighborhoods with poor schools and widespread crime.

As in the past, African American culture, driven by the distinctiveness of the black experience, proved dynamic and controversial. In the poverty and decay of the Bronx in New York City in the 1970s, young African Americans had begun to create a powerful new music, rap. Reflecting the diversity of the city's culture, pioneering rap artists such as Kool Herc, Afrika Bambaataa, and Grandmaster Flash drew on Caribbean musical practices and the popular dance music disco, as well as on African American linguistic and musical traditions. Rap typically featured spoken lyrics over a driving percussive "break" beat, often sampled from recordings of

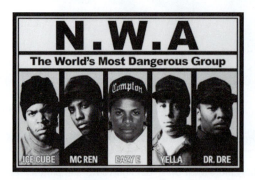

other music. The new sound was part of a loose African American cultural movement known as hip-hop, which included graffiti art and break dancing.

Rap was the first new musical form to rival the impact of jazz in the 1920s and rock and roll in the 1950s. Spreading rapidly around the country, rap crossed boundaries of race, class, and nation to appeal to middle-class, white, and eventually international audiences. Commercially successful, rap was also controversial for its often blunt, unblushing look at ghetto life. The subgenre of gangsta rap, with its first-person celebrations of gang life, violence, and misogyny in such tracks as N.W.A.'s "Fuck tha Police," proved particularly provocative to conservatives and other Americans. In the meantime, rap deeply influenced other genres of music—yet another instance of the powerful impact of African Americans on American culture.

African Americans also mobilized to fight for equality and opportunity. Across the nation, the number of African American elected officials increased markedly. The Reverend Jesse Jackson, a protégé of Martin Luther King Jr., won wide attention. Preaching self-esteem and economic self-help for African Americans, Jackson was the leader of Operation PUSH—People United to Save Humanity. In 1984 Jackson challenged Walter Mondale for the Democratic presidential nomination. His campaign suggested how far American society had come in accepting African American political participation.

African American activism made it difficult for Reagan and other conservatives to undo the civil rights revolution, as did the persistence of discrimination and inequality. Most Americans seemed to accept that some federal action was essential to redress the imbalance between races in America. Despite Reagan's opposition, in 1982 Congress voted to extend the Voting Rights Act for 25 years. In 1983 the Supreme Court ruled overwhelmingly against Bob Jones University, an evangelical institution that attempted to retain its tax-exempt status even though it prohibited interracial dating and engaged in other forms of racial discrimination. The court also rejected the Reagan administration's bid to set aside local affirmative action programs. In other decisions, the justices limited affirmative action somewhat, but this important liberal program survived the Reagan administration.

The battles over the rights of African Americans, gays, and women underscored the limits of conservatism. Many Americans were not ready to undo the social and cultural legacies of the 1960s. New cultural expressions, such as rap, clashed with conservative values. The result was a stalemate. Disadvantaged groups made relatively little political progress in the 1980s, but conservatives also made little progress in their social and cultural agenda.

"The Decade of the Hispanic"

After the upheavals of the 1960s and 1970s, the Hispanic experience in the United States took on a quieter, more confident tone in the 1980s. Hispanics were not a homogeneous group but a diverse population defined by geographical, cultural, and even linguistic differences. In New York City, Puerto Ricans predominated; in South Florida, Cubans; and in the long arc from South Texas to Southern California, Mexican Americans. The census of 1980 revealed that Hispanics were the nation's fastest-growing minority group. The birthrate for Hispanic women was 75 percent higher than the national average. Most immigrants to the United States were Hispanic. Looking ahead, demographers predicted that Hispanics would outnumber African Americans and become the nation's largest minority group within a generation.

These population numbers shaped the outlook of both Hispanics and the rest of American society. There was a new sense in the 1980s that the Hispanics mattered,

>> San Antonio

In the 1980s, tourists still came to San Antonio, Texas, to glimpse the past. Strolling the Paseo del Rio, the sunken, tree-lined River Walk along the San Antonio River, they visited the chain of Roman Catholic missions erected by the colonizing Spanish in the eighteenth century. The tourists usually stopped at the most famous of the old mission buildings, the Alamo, where a Texian and Tejano garrison died fighting the Mexican army in 1836.

Some hundred and fifty years later, San Antonio had also become a place to see the future. By the 1980s, Hispanics, concentrated on the West Side, made up a majority of the city's population. Home to nearly a million people, San Antonio was the largest Hispanic-majority city in the nation. Here was a glimpse, perhaps, of how the United States would develop in the years to come.

In San Antonio, the increase in the Mexican American population translated into political power. For decades, the city's Anglo business elite had controlled the community. But by the 1970s, the emerging Hispanic majority threatened to sweep away Anglo domination. COPS—Citizens Organized for Public Service—practiced a divisive, confrontational politics on behalf of Mexican Americans who lacked quality housing, education, and job opportunities. COPS animated Mexican American voters and shook the Anglo elite. Then, in 1977, the federal government used the federal Voting Rights Act to destroy a critical instrument of elite power, at-large elections for city council. San Antonio had chosen council members in citywide contests that virtually guaranteed victory for white candidates. Now the city had to adopt single-member council districts, which meant that the barrios on the West Side could elect candidates of their own. Five of the eleven positions went that year to Chicanos, who allied with a black councilman to create a majority.

The results were disappointing: confrontational politics brought few gains for Chicanos. Then, the Democrats nominated a young councilman, Henry Cisneros, for mayor in 1981. An urban planner from the West Side, Cisneros argued that Mexican Americans would not flourish unless business also flourished in San Antonio. His campaign appealed successfully both to the barrios of the West Side and to the Anglo neighborhoods of the North Side. On election day, Cisneros became the first Mexican American mayor of San Antonio since 1842. At a victory party, Cisneros embodied the artful culture balance that spurred Chicano power in San Antonio: dressed in a Ralph Lauren business suit, the mayor happily broke a traditional piñata.

Reelected three times, Cisneros aggressively pursued his economic vision for San Antonio. Here, again, the city offered a glimpse of the future for the United States. San Antonio's fragile economy had depended on tourism and U.S. military bases. Now Cisneros wanted to create a "no-smokestack" economy of high-technology firms. As Advanced Micro Devices, Control Data, and other corporations invested in San Antonio, electronics plants sprang up along Interstate Loop 410 on the city's North Side. As Cisneros pushed to expand tourism, Sea World opened and a $200 million shopping plaza came to the River Walk.

With his term coming to an end, Cisneros designated 1988 "The Year of Emergence," when the nation would have to take note of San Antonio's redevelopment. "This is a city that has had to learn to accommodate different points of view," he maintained. Others were not so sure. San Antonio was still a poor city, above the national average in unemployment and below it in income. Proud of Cisneros, Mexican Americans still lived less well than whites. To some, Cisneros's accommodation of business had shortchanged the West Side. The community, warned the president of COPS, wanted "development, not exploitation." Only time would tell who was right. San Antonio gave glimpses of the future, not the whole picture. ●

that they could not be ignored. "We are," a Hispanic Roman Catholic priest confidently declared, "the future."

In this consumer society, the growing importance of the Hispanic population could be measured in goods and services. Hispanic culture affected the nation's foodways. From the 1970s into the 1980s, more and more Americans discovered "Tex-Mex," the distinctive cuisine of the Tejanos, the Mexican Americans of South Texas. Consumers flocked to Tex-Mex restaurants to enjoy enchiladas and tamales covered with chili, refried beans, and Spanish rice, all with plenty of cheese and salsa. By the 1990s, salsa had passed catsup as the best-selling condiment in the United States.

Meanwhile, American business, recognizing the size of the Hispanic market, moved to attract Spanish-speaking consumers. The Coors brewery enthusiastically declared the 1980s "The Decade of the Hispanic." By 1983, Coors and other companies could advertise their products in the growing Spanish-language media, including newspapers, magazines, and 67 television stations.

For politicians, the 1980s were also "The Decade of the Hispanic." The Republican Party, long unable to attract a majority of African Americans, hoped that overwhelmingly Roman Catholic Hispanic voters, like Linda Chavez, would respond to the new conservatism's emphasis on values, family, and religion. Thanks to Reagan's anti-Communism, Republicans did attract Cuban Americans, so many of whom were refugees from the regime of Fidel Castro. However, most Hispanics, including Mexican Americans, emphasized economic issues over foreign policy and cultural appeals. Mainly working class, the Hispanic population continued to grapple with poverty and struggle for educational and economic opportunity in the United States. In these circumstances, the majority, unlike Linda Chavez, preferred the more activist economic and educational policies of the Democrats.

The increasing importance of Hispanic voters helped temper the response to another critical number in American political life—the perhaps 3 million illegal immigrants who had slipped across the border from Mexico into the United States. The Immigration Reform and Control Act of 1986, known as the Simpson-Mazzoli Act, imposed harsher penalties on Americans who knowingly brought illegal aliens into the country and hired them. But the measure also reflected the sentiments of Mexican Americans and other Americans by offering amnesty to illegal aliens who had arrived since 1981.

From Scandal to Triumph

The stalemate over social values was not the only sign that there were limits to conservatism in the 1980s. Scandals plagued business and religious figures who had helped create the conservative climate of the decade. Policy setbacks, economic woes, and scandals plagued the Reagan administration. For a time, the conservatives' triumph was in doubt, but then the cold war began to come to an end.

Business and Religious Scandals

By the mid-1980s the new conservatism was suffering a series of business and religious scandals. In 1986 Ivan Boesky, the swaggering Wall Street deal maker, was indicted for insider trading, the illegal use of secret financial information. Rather than go to trial, he agreed to give up stock trading, inform on other lawbreakers, spend two years in jail, and pay a $100 million fine. In 1987 Michael Milken, the junk bond king, was indicted on fraud and racketeering charges. His eventual plea bargain agreement included a 10-year jail sentence and a stunning $600 million fine, the largest judgment against an individual in American history.

Such scandals provoked second thoughts about the celebration of business and materialism. Critics pointed out that Boesky's and Milken's business methods had hurt the economy by saddling corporations with a great deal of debt and little cash to pay for it. Lavish lifestyles no longer seemed quite so attractive.

Scandal touched religion as well as commerce. Leading televangelists were caught in embarrassing predicaments. In 1987 Americans learned that Jim Bakker had defrauded investors in Heritage USA and paid hush money to hide an adulterous liaison with a church secretary. The scandal hurt the reputation of Jerry Falwell, who had taken over Bakker's organization. In 1988 Falwell resigned from his own Moral Majority. That same year, televangelist Jimmy Swaggart admitted that he "had sinned" with prostitutes.

> At its best, the Reagan Presidency provided a tonic of self-confidence that helped to restore vigor to the national economy and psyche; at its worst, it fostered greed, chauvinism and intolerance.
>
> R. W. APPLE,
> 1989

Political Scandals

The Reagan administration had its own scandals. Before the end of the president's first term, more than 20 officials of the EPA resigned or were fired over charges of favoritism toward lobbyists and polluters. In 1985 Secretary of Labor Raymond Donovan resigned after becoming the first cabinet officer ever indicted. In 1988 Reagan's friend and attorney general, Edwin Meese III, resigned amid questions about his role in the corrupt awarding of government contracts to a defense firm. To critics, the administration's "sleaze factor" stemmed from the president's contemptuous conservative attitude toward government and his eagerness to please business.

In his second term, Reagan faced much more damaging accusations. In October 1986, Sandinista soldiers in Nicaragua shot down a transport plane attempting to supply the Contra rebels. It soon became clear that the plane had been part of a secret effort by the Reagan administration to violate the Boland Amendment's ban on aid to the Contras. Then, a Lebanese magazine reported that the United States had traded arms to Iran. Despite denials from the president, the government had sold arms to win the release of American hostages held by terrorists in Lebanon. The Reagan administration had broken the president's pledge not to negotiate with terrorists and had violated a ban on arms sales to Iran. Americans soon learned that the arms deal and the Nicaraguan plane crash were connected. Government officials had illegally used proceeds from the arms sale to pay for supplying the Contras.

The scandal that became known as the Iran-Contra affair had the potential to drive Reagan from office. If the president had ordered or known about the arms deal and the supply effort, he might have faced impeachment. The Reagan administration underwent three separate investigations. These inquiries made clear that the president was probably deeply involved in the Iran-Contra affair, but none turned up enough evidence to impeach him.

Nevertheless, the Iran-Contra affair badly damaged Reagan's reputation. Several of his associates left office and faced jail sentences. Former national security adviser Robert "Bud" McFarlane pleaded guilty to withholding information from Congress. His successor, Rear Admiral John Poindexter, was allowed to resign. Poindexter's charismatic aide, Marine Lieutenant Colonel Oliver North, had to be fired. Meanwhile, the director of the CIA, William Casey, died in 1987, the day after testimony implicated him in the effort to aid the Contras. Much of the public concluded that the president must have known about his associates' dealings; his popularity dropped.

Setbacks for the Conservative Agenda

Against this backdrop of scandal, conservatives faced a series of policy setbacks. The Democratic-controlled House of Representatives was less cooperative during Reagan's second term. Democrats became even more combative after winning majorities in both the House and Senate in the congressional elections of 1986.

Accordingly, Reagan had to compromise more often with Congress. In 1985 the president called for a Second American Revolution, a comprehensive overhaul of the income tax system. But the Tax Reform Act that Congress passed in 1986 did not lower and simplify income taxes nearly as much as the president had wanted.

Reagan also met outright defeat in Congress. In 1988, a coalition of Democrats and Republicans passed a bill compelling large companies to give workers 60 days' notice of plant closings and layoffs. Reagan opposed this liberal, prolabor measure, but he allowed the bill to become law without his signature.

The president faced repeated defeat on environmental policy. During the 1980s there was growing concern about environmental hazards. In December 1984 the subsidiary of a U.S. corporation accidentally allowed toxic gas to escape from a pesticide plant in Bhopal, India. The emission killed more than 2,500 people and injured 200,000. In April 1986 an explosion and fire allowed radioactive material to escape a nuclear power plant at Chernobyl in the Soviet Union. The accident killed more than 30 people, injured more than 200, exposed countless others to radioactivity, and caused extensive environmental damage.

In this alarming context, Reagan's conservative hostility to environmentalism was no longer so appealing. The president had to accept the extension of the federal Superfund program to clean up hazardous waste in the United States in 1986. The next year, Congress overrode his veto of a bill renewing the Water Quality Control Act. In 1988 the Reagan administration signed an international agreement placing limits on emissions linked to acid rain.

A Vulnerable Economy

Even the economy, the centerpiece of the Reagan Revolution, became a problem during the president's second term. During the 1980s the gap between rich and poor widened sharply. While the average family income, after taxes, of the highest-paid tenth of Americans rose 27 percent from 1977 to 1988, the average family

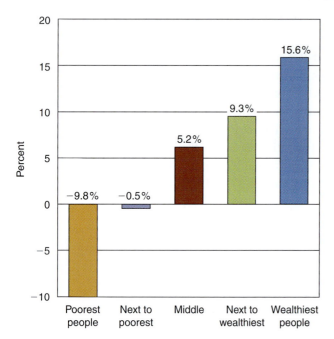

Figure 30–3 Changes in Families' Real Income, 1980–1990 The Reagan Revolution had very different consequences for rich and poor. *Copyright © 1989 by the New York Times Co. Reprinted by Permission.*

income of the poorest tenth fell 11 percent (see Figure 30–3). In the 1980s only the rich earned more and kept more. Other Americans faced economic stagnation or decline.

The falling incomes of the poorest Americans ensured the persistence of poverty. Twenty-nine million Americans lived below the poverty line in 1980. Ten years later, that figure had grown to almost thirty-seven million. Despite Reaganomics, the United States had one of the highest poverty rates among industrialized nations.

One of the most visible consequences of poverty was homelessness. In the 1980s the number of homeless Americans increased markedly. The sight of men and women sleeping on sidewalks, their belongings in shopping carts, was common during the Reagan years.

Homelessness, poverty, and inequality produced a spirited debate in the 1980s. Democrats and liberals blamed these problems on Reaganomics. The president, they charged, had done nothing to stop the erosion of high-paying factory jobs. His welfare, housing, and job-training cuts hurt the poor, while his tax cuts and deregulation helped the rich. In response, conservatives and Republicans maintained that activist, liberal government had hurt manufacturing and weakened the economy. Moreover, welfare programs caused poverty by destroying poor people's work ethic and making them dependent on handouts.

Not surprisingly, neither side persuaded the other. In reality, both liberal and conservative policies had produced flawed economic results. Lyndon Johnson's spending for the Great Society, along with the cost of the Vietnam War, had begun to undermine the economy in the 1960s. His antipoverty programs had been less effective than liberals wanted to admit, but the Reagan Revolution had offered no solution to poverty, either. Reaganomics did not reinvigorate manufacturing or substantially boost middle-class incomes.

There were other signs of economic vulnerability by the mid-1980s. Despite the promises of Reaganomics, the federal budget deficit did not disappear. Instead, between 1981 and 1986, as the government cut taxes and increased defense spending, the deficit soared from $79 billion to $221 billion—a staggering new record.

Like poverty and inequality, the deficit was controversial. Some economists believed the deficit was a sign of great economic weakness; others believed it did not matter. Democrats and liberals blamed Reagan for the budgetary red ink. Reagan's supporters blamed Congress for failing to cut the budget.

In fact both the president and Congress were to blame. Neither Republicans nor Democrats wanted to reduce such popular benefits as Medicare and Social Security. Congress enacted the Balanced Budget and Emergency Deficit Control Act of 1985, known as the Gramm-Rudman Act, which promised automatic cuts to balance the budget by 1990. The next year, a Supreme Court ruling critically weakened the measure. The deficit remained high during Reagan's last years in office, and the national debt—the total amount owed by the federal government to its creditors—reached $2.6 trillion.

Along with this burgeoning debt, the Reagan years produced a growing international trade deficit. In 1980 the annual value of imports was $25.4 billion greater than the value of the nation's exports. By 1986 that gap had grown to $145.1 billion. American business was still not able to compete with foreign producers in the 1980s. Consumers at home and abroad found foreign goods more attractive than ever. Reaganomics had not solved the problem of America's relative decline in the world economy.

Doubts about Reagan's economic policy increased when the stock market plummeted unexpectedly on Monday, October 19, 1987, losing 508 points, or 23 percent of its value. It was the biggest one-day decline since "Black Tuesday" in October 1929. The market drop reflected underlying economic problems including the federal budget deficit, the trade deficit, and deindustrialization, plus lax regulation of Wall Street by the Reagan administration. The crash seemed to be a mortal blow to the Reagan Revolution. "What crashed was more than just the market," a journalist concluded. "It was the Reagan Illusion: the idea that there could be a defense buildup and tax cuts without a price, that the country could live beyond its means indefinitely."

Reagan's Comeback

Beset by scandals and economic troubles, Reagan began a comeback. He showed a remarkable ability to withstand scandal and defeat. Opponents dubbed him the "Teflon president" because nothing seemed to stick to him. That was a tribute to Reagan's political skills as well as many Americans' real affection for him. After a series of disappointing presidencies, Americans seemed unwilling to let Reagan fail.

The economy also helped the president. Notwithstanding Americans' fears, the stock market crash did not lead to depression or recession. The market soon recovered and the economy continued to grow.

Reagan's comeback was probably helped most of all by the transformation of the Soviet Union. By the mid-1980s the Soviets suffered from a weakening economy, an unpopular war in Afghanistan, and a costly arms race. At this critical juncture, Mikhail Gorbachev became General Secretary of the Communist Party. The dynamic and charismatic Gorbachev signaled a new era with a series of stunning reforms. At home, he called for restructuring the economy (*perestroika*) and tolerating more open discussion (*glasnost*). Abroad, he sought an easing of tensions with the United States and the West.

Gorbachev's reforms gave the U.S. government a politically popular opportunity to thaw cold war tensions. Reagan met with the Soviet leader in a series of positive summits beginning in Geneva, Switzerland, in November 1985. Visiting West Berlin in June 1987, the president challenged Gorbachev to "tear down" the Berlin Wall. Meanwhile, it became apparent that the Soviets were, in fact, changing their foreign policy, as they withdrew their troops from Afghanistan and eased their control over Eastern Europe.

The United States and the Soviets also made striking progress on arms control. In December 1987 Reagan and Gorbachev signed the Intermediate-Range Nuclear Forces Treaty (INF), promising to destroy more than 2,500 intermediate-range nuclear missiles. For the first time, the two powers had agreed to give up a weapon altogether.

The INF treaty signaled a permanent easing of tensions. The cold war, so intense just a few years earlier, suddenly ended. Asked in 1988 about calling the USSR the "evil empire," Reagan replied, "I was talking about another time, another era." Reagan's presidency ended in 1989; a year later, the United States and the Soviet Union agreed to end production of chemical weapons and reduce existing stockpiles. In 1991, the two nations signed the START (Strategic Arms Reduction Talks) Treaty, which called for each side to reduce its arsenals of nuclear weapons as much as 30 percent.

Meanwhile, the Soviet Union weakened. In 1989, Gorbachev could do nothing to stop the collapse of its repressive allies in Eastern Europe. Hard-line Communist regimes toppled in Bulgaria, Czechoslovakia, Hungary, Poland, and Rumania. Most dramatically, a new East German government agreed in November to allow travel through the Berlin Wall, which had symbolized the cold war division of Europe. As jubilant Berliners dismantled the wall, it epitomized the collapse of Communism. Accepting the transition to democracy, the Soviets withdrew their troops from Eastern Europe.

Powerless to stop its allies from abandoning Communism, the Soviet leadership soon could not save itself. Despite Gorbachev's attempts to improve life in the Soviet Union, many people were unhappy with the low standard of living, Communist repression, and the unpopular war in Afghanistan. Estonia, Latvia, Lithuania, and other republics chafed under Russia's domination of the USSR. In 1990 Russia itself chose a charismatic president, Boris Yeltsin, who quit the Communist Party, supported independence for the republics, and challenged Gorbachev. The next year, Gorbachev had to resign as party leader and president of the Soviet Union. The Soviet parliament suspended the Communist Party. As one republic after another declared its independence, the USSR ceased to exist.

With the collapse of the Soviet Union, the United States and its allies had won the cold war. Conservatives insisted that Reagan's defense buildup had pushed the Soviets into a military and economic race they could not win and so had forced them to surrender. Democrats maintained that the buildup and the president's harsh rhetoric had actually slowed the thaw in U.S.-Soviet relations. America won the cold war, they argued, because of its long-term strength and strategy. With typical modesty, Reagan himself seemed to agree with the Democrats in a speech at Fulton, Missouri, where Winston Churchill had decried the iron curtain and the onset of the cold war in 1946. "The road to a free Europe that began there in Fulton led," Reagan observed, "to the Truman Doctrine and the Marshall Plan, to NATO and the Berlin Airlift, through nine American presidencies and more than four decades of military preparedness."

Meanwhile, Americans did not celebrate very much as the Berlin Wall came down and the Soviet Union collapsed. The cold war had cost a great deal in money and lives. Many Americans wondered whether Communism had posed a mortal danger to the United States in the first place.

The Fall of the Berlin Wall On November 11, 1989, a man helps dismantle the barrier that divided East and West Berlin and symbolized the division between communism and the west during the cold war.

Conclusion

Reagan left office with the highest popularity rating of any president since the beginning of modern polling in the 1930s. His comeback culminated the triumph of the new conservatism. Americans would debate the nature of that triumph for years to come. The nation did not embrace much of the conservative social agenda. The Reagan Revolution did not solve such basic economic problems as poverty. It even worsened some problems, such as inequality and the budget deficit.

Nevertheless, the conservative triumph was real. Reagan successfully combated the sense of national decline that had pervaded America in the 1970s. His presidency reinvigorated faith in capitalist innovation, minimal government, and American military power. At the end of the 1980s, business values and evangelical religion claimed a more prominent place in American culture.

The accomplishments of the new conservatism, as Reagan's troubled second term indicated, were fragile. The nation's economic revival was shaky, as was the revival of its spirit. Americans were still worried about the future. "I think," a businessman concluded, "the '90s are going to be much trickier than the 1980s."

Further Readings

Connie Bruck, *The Predators' Ball: The Inside Story of Drexel Burnham and the Rise of the Junk Bond Raiders* (1989). A vivid account of the controversial business practices of the 1980s.

Lou Cannon, *Ronald Reagan: A Life in Politics* (2004). A journalistic two-volume biography offering perhaps the best insight into Reagan and his remarkable career.

Paul Freiberger and Michael Swaine, *Fire in the Valley: The Making of the Personal Computer* (2000). Anecdotal account of a critical development in the creation of a new economy.

William Martin, *With God on Our Side: The Rise of the Religious Right in America* (2005). Places the evangelical movement of the 1980s in long-term context.

Gil Troy, *Morning in America: How Ronald Reagan Invented the 1980s* (2005). A scholarly survey of society during the Reagan Revolution.

Sean Wilentz, *The Age of Reagan: A History, 1974–2008* (2008). A sweeping account of the conservative ascendancy.

Who, What?

Ivan Boesky 1000

Yuppies 1001

Rev. Jerry Falwell 1002

Ronald Reagan 1002

Sandra Day O'Connor 1016

Mikhail Gorbachev 1027

Religious right 1001

Reaganomics 1005

Reagan Doctrine 1010

Review Questions

1. What were the main values and goals of the new conservatism in the 1980s? What role did business and religion play in shaping the conservative movement?

2. What was the Reagan Revolution in domestic policy? How did Reagan's domestic programs reflect conservative values?

>> Timeline >>

▼ **1973–74**
OPEC oil embargo

▼ **1979–1981**
Iranian hostage crisis

▼ **1980**
Ronald Reagan elected president

▼ **1981**
IBM personal computer

Air traffic controllers' strike
Economic Recovery Act

▼ **1982**
Nuclear freeze rally in New York City
Boland Amendment

▼ **1983**
Strategic Defense Initiative
U.S. invasion of Grenada
Terrorist attack on U.S. Marines in Lebanon

▼ **1984**
Reelection of Ronald Reagan

3. Describe the aims of Reagan's foreign policy. How did his goals differ from those of earlier presidents during the cold war?

4. What groups resisted the conservative social agenda in the 1980s? Did the desire for equal rights and opportunities conflict with conservatism?

5. What factors limited the triumph of the new conservatism? Did conservatives really succeed in the 1980s?

6. How did the conservatism of the 1980s differ from earlier forms of conservatism in the twentieth century?

Websites

Hartford Institute for Religion Research (http://hirr.hartsem.edu/) offers many resources for the study of religion in the 1980s, as well as other eras.

The Living Room Candidate (http://www.livingroomcandidate.org/) is a fascinating collection of presidential campaign commercials from 1972 to the present, including Reagan's from 1980 and 1984.

Making the Macintosh: Technology and Culture in Silicon Valley, Stanford University (http://library.stanford.edu/mac/index.html), explores the early history of the path-breaking Apple computer.

The Public Papers of President Ronald W. Reagan, Ronald Reagan Presidential Library (http://www.reagan.utexas.edu/archives/speeches/publicpapers.html), is a searchable collection of all the public statements of the "Great Communicator" as president.

For further review materials and resource information, please visit www.oup.com/us/ofthepeople

▼ **1985**
General Electric purchase of RCA
Gramm-Rudman Act

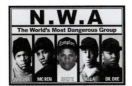

▼ **1986**
U.S. bombing of Libya
Tax Reform Act
Revelation of Iran-Contra affair

▼ **1987**
Stock market crash
Intermediate-Range Nuclear Forces Treaty

▼ **1988**
Omnibus Trade and Competitiveness Act

▼ **1991**
Collapse of the Soviet Union

31

WAL★MART SUPERCENTER
沃尔玛购物广场

Common Threads

>> What were some of the most pervasive consequences of technological change in the last decades of the 1900s? Where and when did these changes begin? How did they unfold?

>> How did the new conservatism of the 1980s continue to impact American politics and culture?

>> Did the African American civil rights movement extend its influence beyond the twentieth century?

>> What were the main uncertainties of a post–cold war, postindustrial, postfeminist, post–civil rights society?

" **H**ello world," smiled 20-year-old Stanford undergraduate Tiger Woods as he became a professional golfer in 1996. A talented prodigy ready to take on the world, Woods was a distinctive product of global forces. His father, Earl, was part African American, Native American, and Chinese. A U.S. Army officer, the elder Woods had met Kultida Punsawad in Thailand during the Vietnam War. Kultida, part Thai, Chinese, and Dutch, had become Earl's wife and Tiger's mother.

Tiger quickly succeeded. In 1997, he became the youngest player to win the prestigious Masters tournament at the Augusta National Golf Club. Setting record after record, Woods became the greatest golfer and the best-paid athlete of his generation.

Observers interpreted Woods's success as a triumph for African Americans. Golf was a notoriously segregated sport; blacks had long been denied admission to elite clubs such as Augusta. Woods's Masters victory, the first for a nonwhite, seemed like one more milestone in the struggle for African American civil rights.

Woods himself fed that perception. "[E]ven though I'm mathematically Asian," he said, "if you have one drop of black blood in the United States, you're black." But Woods also defined himself as the sum of all his parents' racial identities. The golfer was, he said in 1997, "Cablinasian"—a mixture of Caucasian, black, Indian, and Asian. "As proud as I am of Tiger Woods, I realize I have to share him," said a veteran African American civil rights activist. "He is part of a new reality. [P]eople are going to have to get comfortable with it."

Many observers welcomed Woods as an emblem of a more diverse nation. "He is more than just one race, he is many races," said a radio talk show host. "And that's what makes us Americans, because we're the melting pot. We're kind of mutts." The African American television personality Oprah Winfrey dubbed Woods "America's son."

Yet sometimes he did not seem American. Representing the nation in the Ryder Cup, Woods, who also had Thai citizenship, felt that he was "playing for the United Nations, not the United States." His parents held up their multiracial son as a transnational man with a globalizing mission. "He can hold everyone together," his mother said. "He is the Universal Child." "[H]e's qualified through his ethnicity to accomplish miracles," Earl Woods agreed. "He's the bridge between the East and the West." Tiger's transnational image became even stronger when he married a Swedish model in 2004.

As the world drew together in new ways, Woods's racial and national identities made him an ideal figure—"a one-man symbol of globalization in the twenty-first century." American, Asian, and European multinational corporations paid him lavishly to reach the expanding global marketplace. Woods's greeting "Hello World" was the slogan of his Nike marketing campaign. Playing a game invented in Scotland, the American traveled the world to promote golf courses, credit cards, computer video games, watches, coffee, automobiles, jet planes, laser eye surgery, and corporate consulting, technology, and international job outsourcing.

Despite his transnational image, Woods's activities sometimes seemed to serve U.S. values and interests. In the Philippines in 1998, he promoted a golf community built on land taken from thousands of peasants. "Tiger Woods should be barred from entering the country and from propagating golf," the peasants' lawyer insisted. "We have globalization, we have privatization, we have land conversion, all of these are just complete manifestations of U.S.-dictated policies."

Distinctive as he was, Tiger Woods epitomized forces changing the United States. As his endorsements reflected, an emerging information economy still manufactured

continued

automobiles but leaned towards computing, medical services, and leisure. Like Woods, with his ties to multinationals, jet travel, and outsourcing, the new economy was increasingly globalized. The multiracial golfer, who embraced his mother's Buddhism, also reflected a new social and cultural diversity in America.

While Woods profited handsomely in a changing world, the United States struggled with the consequences of the information economy, globalization, and diversity. Although conservatism continued to shape American democracy, conservatives had less success shaping social and cultural change. America's place in a globalizing world was uncertain, particularly after a devastating terrorist attack in September 2001 and then a stunning stock market collapse in September 2008. Americans lived, as the commission investigating the attack put it, in "a nation transformed." But the exact nature of that transformation still remained unclear as the new president—as transnational as Tiger Woods—prepared to take office amid a national crisis. ●

OUTLINE

The Age of Globalization

By the end of the twentieth century, Americans increasingly felt enmeshed in global forces. That had always been the case, of course. Throughout its history, the nation had been defined by its relationship to the world; the cold war had been one more phase in this relationship. But Americans' global connection entered a new, more self-conscious phase beginning in the 1980s. During the decade, the term "globalization" first came into use to describe the web of technological, economic, military, political, and cultural developments binding people and nations ever more tightly together. The cold war's end, technological advances, the spread of multinationals and other organizations, the creation of transnational economic alliances, and a new wave of immigration all drew the United States deeper into globalization.

The Cold War and Globalization

For two generations, the cold war had both facilitated and hindered globalization. In some ways, the confrontation between the United States and the Soviet Union linked the world more closely together. Each power had forged a host of ties to other nations. To hold off Communism, the United States had established regional military alliances around the world. To rebuild Western European and Asian economies, America had lowered trade barriers and created the World Bank and the International Monetary Fund.

Still, the cold war inhibited globalization, too. The United States and the Soviet Union had largely avoided trading with each other. Each power had discouraged its allies from ties with the other side.

The collapse of the Soviet Union in 1991 opened the way to further globalization. Key international mechanisms such as the World Bank and the United Nations remained in place. But now nations and companies could forge new ties more freely across the old cold war divide.

> **Globalization is not just a trend, not just a phenomenon, not just an economic fad. It is the international system that has replaced the cold-war system.**
>
> THOMAS L. FRIEDMAN, 1999

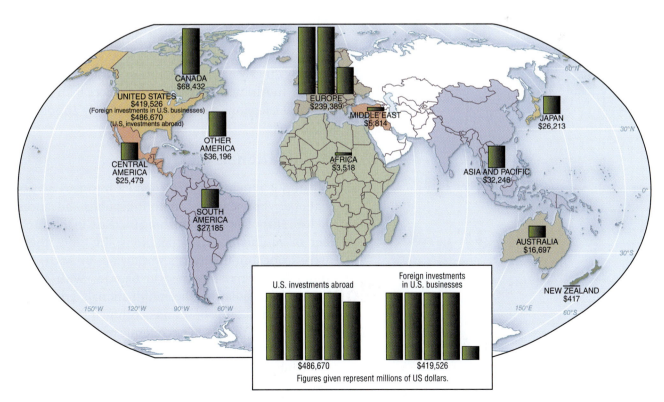

Map 31–1   The Globalization of the U.S. Economy In 1992, the large value of U.S. investment in other regions around the world was nearly equaled by the value of foreign investments in the United States.

New Communications Technologies

New communications technologies were especially important in speeding up the global flow of news, ideas, and money. The Internet, another product of the cold war, emerged from a Department of Defense search in the 1960s for a means of maintaining communications in the event of a nuclear attack on America. Aided by the development of the telephone modem and fiber-optic cable, the Internet spread quickly through universities, across America, and around the world in the 1990s and 2000s. At first, people used the Internet to send and receive electronic messages, but by the middle of the 1990s, computer users also explored the World Wide Web, a rapidly expanding segment of the Internet that blended text, graphics, audio, and video. The new "information superhighway" of the Web and the Internet enabled people to do research, create and exhibit art, listen to music, share photographs and films, and buy and sell online. By 2000, some 304 million people from more than 40 nations were using the global information superhighway.

Communications satellites also played a critical role in globalization. Following the U.S. deployment of Telstar and other satellites in the 1960s, Canada, Japan, and several other nations had launched their own. In the 1990s, the ready availability of global satellite communications revolutionized the news business. Cable News Network (CNN), founded in 1979 by the flamboyant American entrepreneur Ted Turner, used satellite uplinks to provide live televised coverage of news events around the world. Turner wanted CNN to be a "positive force in the world, to tie the world together." The huge success of CNN inspired the creation of satellite news organizations in other countries.

Improvements in telephony further facilitated globalization. Mobile and cellular telephones spread especially quickly in many countries outside the United States. In Africa, there were already more than 15 million cell telephone subscribers in the early 2000s.

The Birth of the Internet Sketched in 1969, this crude diagram of the first four nodes of the Advanced Research Projects Agency Network (ARPANET) would lead to the explosive growth of the Internet in the 1990s and 2000s.

Multinationals and NGOs

Making it much easier to conduct business across national boundaries, communications advances helped stimulate an astonishing increase in the number of multinational corporations. In 1990, there were 3,000 multinationals worldwide. By 2003, the number had mushroomed to 63,000. With some 821,000 subsidiaries, the multinationals employed about 90 million people and accounted for perhaps one-fourth of the world's economic output.

Long a leader in the creation of multinationals, the United States was still home to many of the largest and wealthiest firms. By 2003, Wal-Mart was Mexico's largest employer, with 100,000 workers. But America now faced intense competition from

Overcoming the Boundary Between Capitalism and Communism United States retail giant Wal-Mart opens another store in the People's Republic of China, 2006.

Japan, Europe, and other nations. In 1962, nearly 60 percent of the top 500 multinationals were American; by 1999, the percentage had declined to 36.

Along with multinational business companies, private nongovernmental organizations—NGOs—also fostered globalization. Some NGOs, such as the International Red Cross, dated back to the nineteenth century. The World Economic Forum, which brought elite businessmen, politicians, and intellectuals together each year in Davos, Switzerland, was a product of the 1970s. So were the environmentalist Greenpeace and the humanitarian Doctors Without Borders. By the 2000s, there were more than 10,000 NGOs worldwide.

Expanding Trade

After international peace, the most basic necessity for globalization was the easy movement of goods, services, and capital across national boundaries. In the 1990s and 2000s, the United States and other nations, eager to support their multinational corporations and seize their share of the global market, moved aggressively to remove barriers to trade and investment. With the end of the cold war, America established economic relationships with the former republics of the USSR, the Eastern European countries of the Soviet bloc, the Socialist Republic of Vietnam, and the People's Republic of China. By 1996, Wal-Mart had a store in Beijing. Meanwhile, McDonald's had opened restaurants in Russia and several Eastern European nations.

To spur international trade and investment, nations also created regional economic alliances. Typically, these took the form of agreements in which member states guaranteed one another trading and investment privileges and lowered or

Making Economic Policy in a Global Age World leaders, including President George W. Bush (sixth from left, front row), meet in Washington, DC, in the midst of a developing economic crisis, November 2008.

abolished tariffs on imports and exports. In 1991, the member states of the European Economic Community, a pioneering regional trade alliance, signed the Maastricht Treaty drawing their economies together in a single vast unit, the European Union (EU), with its own currency, the euro. With a mere 6.4 percent of global population, the EU produced a third of the world's goods and more than a third of its trade.

The 1990s also witnessed the transformation of the international General Agreement on Tariffs and Trade (GATT). Another U.S. cold war creation, GATT had drawn together more than 100 nations. Its efforts to liberalize trade through agreements known as "rounds" culminated in 1993 when the Uruguay Round produced a dramatic victory for free-trade policies. The Uruguay Round also led to the rebirth of GATT as a new, more powerful global body, the World Trade Organization (WTO), whose decisions would be binding on member nations. The U.S. Senate approved American participation in the WTO, which opened in Geneva, Switzerland, in 1995.

Moving People

The movement of human beings was critical to globalization. Thanks to regional economic agreements and the end of the cold war, people could cross national borders more easily to provide needed labor. The United States remained a major destination. Between 1990 and 1994 alone, 4.5 million immigrants came to the United States. By 2000 the immigrant population had reached 26.3 million, about 11 percent of the national total population, the largest percentage since before World War II.

Short-term travel also facilitated globalization by exposing people to other nations and cultures. Low-cost jet flights and improved living standards enabled

AMERICA AND THE WORLD

....

>> Globalization's Final Frontier

Pervasive on earth, globalization also reached into space. Like the United States and the Soviet Union during the cold war, more and more of the world's nations translated their hopes, ambitions, and fears into space programs. Like America, other countries found satellites an indispensable part of globalization: they were critical to communications and information-gathering, and, accordingly, essential to building economies, spying on enemies, and positioning soldiers. A secure military foothold in space might even assure survival on earth. As a result, outer space became globalization's final frontier.

Dozens of countries had space programs by the 2000s. Most of these nations had to use the facilities of a relative handful of nations with the sophisticated technology needed to launch satellites. Reflecting the gradual economic and political integration of Europe, 13 Western European nations, including France, Germany, and the United Kingdom, had formed the European Space Agency in 1975. By the end of the twentieth century, ESA was using the Ariane launch vehicle to send satellites and probes into space. By then, too, India, Israel, and Japan were launching satellites, and Brazil was attempting to develop a launch capability.

The People's Republic of China had the most ambitious of the newer space programs. Despite its still-developing economy and limited investment in science, the PRC was determined to rival the United States not only in the exploration of space but perhaps also in the development of space-based military capabilities. The Chinese space program had launched satellites in the 1970s, developed the commercially successful Changzheng ("Long March") launch vehicle in the 1980s, and then begun a manned space program in the 1990s. In October 2003, the PRC became the third nation to put a man in space when the vehicle Shenzhou ("Sacred Vessel"), based on old Soviet technology, successfully carried an astronaut on a 21-hour flight. "This gives China a seat at the table," a European admitted.

Meanwhile, the original, cold war space powers struggled. The Russians, inheriting the remnants of the Soviet space program in the 1990s, could barely afford to keep it going. Their space station, Mir, was chronically unsafe. Desperate for money, the Russians auctioned memorabilia from past space voyages and signed up wealthy civilians as the first space tourists.

For most Americans, space no longer seemed exciting or important. Now that the Soviet Union was gone, NASA faced even leaner budgets. In February 2003, the shocking explosion of the space shuttle *Columbia*—the second tragic destruction of a shuttle—left Americans unsure about the safety and value of the space program.

As on earth, the United States pursued friendly collaboration with other countries. After partnering with the Soviets on space flights in the 1970s, the American

continued

崇尚科学　破除迷信

>> **AMERICA AND THE WORLD** *continued*

space program joined Canada, Japan, Russia, and other nations in an often troubled effort to build the International Space Station in the 1990s.

The United States also unilaterally pursued its own interests in space. In the 2000s, President George W. Bush, like Ronald Reagan before him, favored the development of a space-based system to defend the United States against missile attack. Warily eying the PRC, policy makers feared an assault on American satellites and potential space weaponry. "The U.S. is an attractive candidate for a 'Space Pearl Harbor,'" a national committee warned in 2000. The globalization of space, like the globalization of the world, was both exhilarating and frightening. ●

Americans and others to vacation and study around the world. By the 1990s, tourism was possibly the largest single global industry. Study abroad increased nearly 10 percent a year.

The Politics of a New Economy

Globalization combined with ongoing technological change to create a new, information-centered American economy. This transformation produced a record economic boom in the 1990s; it also produced new insecurity and inequality. Faced with this situation, the political system offered generally conservative solutions emphasizing individual responsibility and limited government at the beginning of the new century. Despite unrest over immigration and trade, American leaders remained firmly committed to globalization.

> [A]ll of us know that the problem with the new global economy is that it is both more rewarding and more destructive.
>
> PRESIDENT BILL CLINTON, June 1999

The Information Economy

As deindustrialization continued, the nature of the postindustrial economy became clearer at the close of the twentieth century. By the 1990s, factories employed fewer production workers than in 1955; meanwhile, the service sector accounted for about 70 percent of the nation's economic activity. The rise of services using sophisticated communications, computing, and biotechnology encouraged the belief that the creation, organization, and distribution of information would define the twenty-first-century economy.

In the 1990s and 2000s, innovations in electronics continued to transform communications. More and more Americans carried pagers and cellular telephones. High-speed fiber-optic cables and satellite dishes expanded the power and reach of telephone and television systems. These developments spurred the spread of computing. By 1999 more than half of the nation's households had at least one computer. The development of computing and communications also spurred the hope that Americans would process information instead of raw materials, and produce knowledge instead of steel.

Advances in genetics and medical technology further sparked hopes for an information-centered economy. In the last decades of the twentieth century, scientists had made rapid advances in understanding animal and human genomes.

Corporations soon began applying this genetic knowledge to agriculture, medicine, and other fields. The result was biotechnology—the use of organisms and their products to alter human health and the environment. By the end of the 1990s, about one-third of the U.S. corn, cotton, and soybean crops were products of genetic engineering. By then, too, the U.S. Food and Drug Administration had approved more than 125 genetically engineered drugs for the treatment of cancer and other diseases.

Computing played a key role in the development of biotechnology. Drawing on computers and statistical techniques, researchers pioneered bioinformatics, the application of information science and technology to biological problems. Computers also drove the rapid development of medical technologies, including magnetic resonance imaging and computed tomography.

The Promise of Biotechnology President Bush touts the merits of bio-engineered fuel for automobiles.

A Second Economic Revolution?

In fundamental respects, the information and industrial economies were quite different. Manual, blue-collar labor tended the machines of smokestack America; white-collar, well-educated labor tended the computers of information America. The industrial economy had eaten up fossil fuels, minerals, and other exhaustible resources and produced substantial pollution; the information economy promised less damage to the earth.

In some ways, however, the rise of the information economy repeated the Industrial Revolution. As in the late 1800s and early 1900s, technological change pushed new corporations to the forefront of American capitalism: software firms such as Microsoft and Oracle; hardware firms such as Dell and Intel; e-commerce pioneers such as Amazon.com and eBay; and the search engine giant Google.

Like the Industrial Revolution, the information revolution spurred a wave of corporate consolidation. The ABC television network, already merged with Capital Cities Communications in the 1980s, was taken over by Walt Disney in 1995. That year, media giant Time Warner, the product of a merger in 1989, bought out Turner Broadcasting. Then, in a sign of the growing importance of the Internet, Time Warner merged with Internet service provider America Online in 2000.

The information revolution also paralleled the Industrial Revolution by producing a new, hugely wealthy elite. The most famous of this new group of multibillionaires was Bill Gates, the cofounder of Microsoft, who became the richest American since John D. Rockefeller, the cofounder of Standard Oil, nearly a century before.

Just as the appearance of trains, planes, and machines stimulated the imagination of artists and intellectuals in the nineteenth and twentieth centuries, so did the appearance of computers at the end of the twentieth century and the beginning of the twenty-first. Digital technology made it easier than ever before to copy and manipulate text, images, and sounds, a development that encouraged collage and undermined linear narratives. More broadly, some thinkers believed a new, postmodern culture was replacing the modern culture inspired by industrialism. Hard to define, the postmodern culture embraced a more skeptical view of accepted truths and dominant ideologies.

Despite the parallels between the industrial and information revolutions, the information economy was still immature. Machine tools, railroads, and electricity had greatly boosted workers' productivity in the industrial era. Computers, the Internet, and biotechnology had yet to do the same in the 2000s. Moreover, most service positions required little education, used limited technology, and paid less than the best blue-collar jobs of the old industrial economy. By the 2000s, the biggest employer in America was neither a software company nor a car manufacturer, but rather a low-wage retail store, Wal-Mart.

Boom and Insecurity

For most of the 1990s, globalization and the information revolution seemed to benefit the economy overall. The productivity of American workers and the vitality of the service sector produced economic growth for nearly the entire decade, a record. Because of global competition, corporate cost cutting, and low oil prices, inflation was negligible. Interest rates were low; unemployment rose early in the decade but then dropped off to record lows. Driven by excitement about information-related companies, the stock market reached one record high after another. After passing 3,000 for the first time ever in 1991, the Dow Jones industrial average soared past 11,000 in 1999. As memories of the 1987 market crash faded, many Americans no longer felt the need to live with less. Symbolically, Congress repealed the federal 55-mile-per-hour speed limit for interstate highways in 1995, and big gas-guzzling sport-utility vehicles became popular.

Despite new SUVs, speed limits, and stock records, many Americans faced new economic challenges in the 1990s and 2000s. Employers, confronting global competition, reduced their labor forces aggressively. Traditionally, white-collar workers had enjoyed more job security than blue-collar workers. But corporate downsizing now affected both groups. In the 2000s, American multinationals outsourced white- as well as blue-collar jobs overseas. Even positions in computing and customer service migrated to the United Kingdom, the Philippines, and India, where English was spoken and wages were lower. Outsourcing jolted Americans who believed that college degrees and corporate employment guaranteed middle-class status. "This has been a very nasty journey," admitted an unemployed stockbroker. "You mourn your lifestyle. You mourn your identity."

The increasing costs of health care also troubled Americans. By the 1990s, the United States was spending a greater proportion of its

A cartoonist lampoons life in the age of outsourcing: no American seems to be doing the work anymore.

gross domestic product on health care than were other developed nations. Nevertheless, 43 million Americans did not have health insurance in 2003. The United States, almost alone among developed nations, had no national health insurance plan for its citizens. As employers cut costs, they decreased medical benefits for employees. The need for costly medical care would only increase as Americans' life expectancy continued to rise and the huge baby boom generation aged.

Americans feared, too, that they could not afford retirement. With the aging of the baby boom generation, there were more Americans over 65 and eligible for Social Security benefits than ever before (see Map 31–2). Many people believed there would not be enough money to pay the baby boomers' pensions in the twenty-first century. Private employers, meanwhile, reduced pension benefits for many retirees.

The Return of Inequality

The insecurities of many working- and middle-class Americans reflected a trend toward economic inequality. Allowing for inflation, the average weekly earnings of American workers in 1998 were less than in 1970. The decline of manufacturing meant the loss of relatively high-paying jobs. Employers were determined to hold down the growth of wages and salaries in the 1990s. Workers, facing the threats of downsizing and outsourcing, were reluctant to demand big wage increases, as were labor unions, which continued to have difficulty persuading workers to organize.

To stay even, Americans borrowed and worked more than before. Many families now had both parents in the paid workforce. In 1960, only a fifth of women with children under six held paying jobs; in 1995, two-thirds of such women worked for pay. Partly because many Americans now held two and even three jobs, people put in much more time at work. In 1960, Americans worked less—1,795 hours a year—

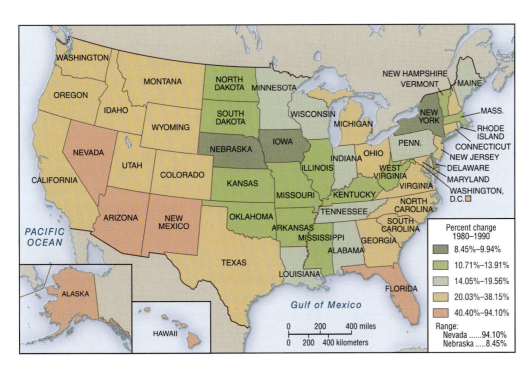

Map 31–2   Aging in America The increase in the percentage of the U.S. population aged 65 and over from 1980 to 1990 helped fuel worries about health care and Social Security.

than their counterparts in Britain, France, Germany, and Japan. By 1997–1998, they worked more—1,966 hours a year. Not surprisingly, more Americans told pollsters that they felt rushed.

Meanwhile, the wealthy fared exceptionally well in the transition to a globalized information economy. By 1949, the richest 1 percent of American households had seen its share of the nation's wealth dwindle to 20 percent. By 1997, the top 1 percent's share had zoomed up to 40 percent, nearly back to the record heights of the 1920s. In 2000, the richest 400 Americans had an average annual income of $174,000,000, almost quadruple their earnings only eight years earlier.

Several factors spurred the rebirth of great fortunes. The boom of the 1990s, fed by the information revolution, rewarded Bill Gates and other wealthy men and women with vast profits on their stocks and bonds. Tax cuts allowed the rich to keep more of their wealth. A change in public attitudes also benefited the rich. In the 1990s, observers noted the emergence of a "winner-take-all" culture in which it was acceptable for those at the top of companies and professions to earn far more money than ordinary workers.

At the start of the new century, the United States, the richest country in the world, was also the country with the largest gap between rich and poor. Many observers wondered whether strong social class differences, which had decreased in the mid-twentieth century, would once again define the nation and limit democracy.

The Power of Conservatism

Faced with troubling economic change, Americans had relatively little faith in the political system after the upheavals of the 1960s and 1970s. In 1994 only 19 percent of the people felt they could trust government. Politicians, Americans believed, were out of touch with ordinary citizens. Partly as a result, most voters did not favor a return to liberalism, with its faith in activist government. Instead, politics seldom strayed far from the conservative trail blazed by the Reagan Revolution of the 1980s. Nevertheless, national politics was closely, intensely contested.

In 1988, Reagan's vice president, George H. W. Bush of Texas, easily defeated the rather colorless liberal Democratic nominee, Governor Michael Dukakis of Massachusetts, to become the nation's 41st president. But the Republicans' hopes of continuing the conservative Reagan Revolution faded as voters left the Democrats in control of both the House and Senate. Squabbling with Congress, Bush vetoed 40 bills and even closed down the government briefly rather than accept the new budget authorization needed to fund federal operations. Yet Bush also made compromises that alienated conservatives. He supported new environmental controls and federal funding for education. In order to cut the federal budget deficit, he broke his firm campaign pledge not to raise taxes.

Running a tired campaign for reelection in 1992, Bush faced a surprisingly strong third-party challenge from the pugnacious Texas billionaire businessman, H. Ross Perot, who promised to balance the budget and end the "gridlock" in Washington. But it was Governor Bill Clinton of Arkansas, a moderate "New Democrat," who seemed to embody the best chance for change. Bush's broken tax promise and a weak economy doomed his campaign. Winning the presidency with only 43 percent of the popular vote, Clinton had a chance to partner with the Democratic-controlled Congress to push government back toward liberalism. But when the president proposed a liberal solution to the nation's health care crisis in 1993, Congress rejected the plan as too expensive and too intrusive in doctors' business and patients' lives. A year later, the Democrats lost control of Congress.

Fighting for his political future, Clinton catered to moderates and conservatives. "The era of big government is over," he declared. Through budget cuts and tax increases, he managed to end the budget deficit. The president accepted a bill limiting the federal government's authority to impose costly regulations and requirements, known as unfunded mandates, on the states. In 1996, he signed a welfare bill that significantly reduced federal support for the poor, especially children. To discourage dependence on government handouts, the bill limited welfare recipients to five years of assistance over their lifetime and required heads of households on welfare to find work within two years. Many Democrats and liberals angrily claimed that the president had embraced the conservative ideology of individual responsibility and betrayed the poor.

To keep the economy booming, Clinton blended liberal and conservative financial policies. In 1995, the White House and Congress pleased liberals by revising the Credit Reinvestment Act, originally passed during the Carter administration in 1977, to encourage banks to offer "subprime" mortgages—home loans to low-income Americans who would not traditionally qualify for such financing. Clinton also endorsed the conservative goal of easing federal regulation of the financial industry. In 1999, the president signed the Financial Services Modernization Act (also known as the Gramm-Leach-Bliley Act), which effectively repealed the Glass-Steagall Act of 1933, a New Deal measure preventing institutions from engaging in insurance and investment banking along with commercial banking. Now commercial banks, investment banks, and insurance companies would be free to compete for one another's business. Democrats went along with the new financial act in part because Republicans agreed to revise the Credit Reinvestment Act again to make it easier for low-income Americans to get the credit to buy houses. In the short run, subprime mortgages and deregulation helped sustain both the economic boom and President Clinton. But in little more than a decade, these actions would become much more controversial.

Thanks to his move to the right and the continuing economic boom, Clinton easily beat the Republican presidential nominee, longtime senator Bob Dole of Nebraska, in 1996. But Clinton's second term nearly collapsed in scandal over his real estate dealings and his adulterous affairs. In 1998, the House of Representatives voted two articles of impeachment charging the president with perjury and obstruction of justice. Only the second president to go on trial in the Senate, Clinton remained popular nonetheless. Most Americans seemed willing to separate the private and public lives of the president and wanted to keep him in office, particularly when his policies seemed to bring prosperity. Reflecting popular opinion, the Senate voted to acquit Clinton on both articles of impeachment.

Although Clinton had charted a moderate course between liberalism and conservatism, his scandal-ridden presidency did not guarantee Democratic success. In one of the closest elections in history, his vice president, Al Gore of Tennessee, lost to Governor George W. Bush of Texas, the son of the first President Bush, in 2000. Although Gore won the popular ballot by 550,000 votes, Bush appeared to capture a narrow majority of the Electoral College on election night. But it took the intervention of the Supreme Court to halt a controversial recount of Florida's vote and thereby make him the 43rd president.

The Disputed Presidential Election of 2000 A judge tries to decide how to count a voter's ballot in Broward County in the crucial state of Florida.

Influenced by Reagan's success, the younger Bush was more conservative than his father. In his first term, "Bush 43" pushed successfully for tax cuts to stimulate the economy. Reflecting conservative opposition to government intervention, his administration weakened regulatory oversight of the financial industry. But Bush also accepted a quintessentially liberal initiative, an expensive drug benefit program for retired Americans.

In 2004, Bush faced another liberal Democrat, Senator John Kerry of Massachusetts, who tried to capitalize on worries over outsourcing and economic change. Yet Bush prevailed with 50.7 percent of the popular vote and a solid electoral majority. Buoyed by his victory, the president vowed to spend his "political capital" on conservative initiatives, including a reform of the Social Security system. His plans went nowhere, particularly after the Democrats won control of both houses of Congress in 2006. Thanks to Bush's tax cuts, drug plan, and military expenditures, the federal government ran a budget deficit again—another disappointment to conservatives, who yearned for smaller, less expensive government.

Contesting Globalization

Divided over many issues, Republican and Democratic leaders generally agreed with big businessmen that globalization represented a triumph for American institutions and values, including capitalism, free trade, and democracy. Even though the United States faced tough international economic competition, American political and corporate elites thought the nation was still better off than in a divided world without free trade. Some multinational executives did not see their interests as completely identical with those of the government. "I'm an internationalist first and a nationalist second," Ted Turner declared. But multinationals still depended on a powerful U.S. government to protect their investments around the globe.

In contrast, many middle- and working-class Americans did question whether globalization made their lives better. In the mid-1990s, the presence of between 2 and 4 million illegal migrants from Mexico angered many American citizens, particularly in Texas and California. Their argument was familiar: these illegal aliens drove down wages and took jobs from native-born Americans who paid higher taxes to provide the tax-evading migrants with education, health care, and welfare benefits. Supposedly, Spanish would rival English, immigrant cultures would dilute Anglo culture, and whites would lose political power. In response to such fears in 1994, California voters passed Proposition 187, a referendum denying illegal aliens access to public education and other benefits. Two years later, Congress appropriated more resources to stop the flow of illegal immigrants.

The anti-immigrant movement did not get much further than that. Business generally welcomed immigration because it provided needed workers. Calculating the rapid growth of the Hispanic population, political leaders thought twice about antagonizing an increasingly powerful group of voters. Many native-born Americans, themselves the descendants of immigrants, believed immigration would help the economy and invigorate the dominant culture.

Three Presidents From left, George H. W. Bush ("Bush 41"), his son, George W. Bush ("Bush 43"), and 42nd president Bill Clinton.

International trade provoked a more complex battle. The U.S. government, faced with the rapid-fire appearance of regional economic alliances, moved to create its own economic bloc. In 1992, the United States joined with Canada and Mexico to announce the North American Free Trade Agreement (NAFTA), which established the world's largest and richest low-tariff trading zone, to promote commerce among the three countries. Fearing more lost jobs at home, organized labor opposed the agreement. So did many environmentalists, who believed corporations would get around U.S. environmental laws by moving factory operations to Mexico. Third-party candidate H. Ross Perot capitalized on popular opposition to NAFTA. But the leadership of both major parties favored the agreement. In 1993, the Senate ratified NAFTA.

Opposition to globalization flared again at a meeting of the WTO in Seattle, Washington, in 1999. Labor unions, environmentalists, consumer activists, women's groups, and other organizations staged parades, meetings, and street theater. Demonstrators charged that the WTO served corporations and developed nations, damaged the environment, allowed AIDS to spread, and destroyed indigenous cultures. "The allegedly inevitable force of globalization has met the immovable object of grass-roots democracy," exulted one of the protestors. Fears of protest and terrorism led to cancellation of the WTO meetings scheduled for 2001.

Combating Illegal Immigration A U.S. Border Patrol agent takes down the details of a group of illegal immigrants from Mexico arrested in the Altar Valley, Arizona, in 2008.

Nevertheless, globalization was hard to contest. It would take more than isolated protests to alter the impact of new technologies; change the behavior of multinationals, trade blocs, and governments; and divert, let alone halt, the worldwide movement of people, ideas, goods, and capital in the twenty-first century.

A Changing People

Globalization was one of several forces reshaping American society and culture at the turn of the twenty-first century. As Latinos became the largest "minority" group, the United States headed rapidly toward the time when people of color, rather than whites, would make up a majority of the nation's population. As the experience of African Americans underscored, race and rights remained divisive issues. Concern about rights also spurred "culture wars" over family and sexual values and the status of women and homosexuals. In general, these struggles moved American society in a liberal rather than a conservative direction: the changing population became more tolerant of diversity and more willing to extend rights to disadvantaged groups.

A Diverse Society of Color

The racial and ethnic composition of the United States changed rapidly at the turn of the twenty-first century. In 2001, Americans of Hispanic or Latino origin outnumbered African Americans and became the largest minority group. Thanks to a strong job market, the Hispanic and Latino population had spread well beyond its traditional concentrations in south Florida and the rim of states from Texas to California. Mexican immigrants, for instance, came to stay in a host of small Midwestern towns and cities where semiskilled and unskilled jobs paid 10 and 15 times more than jobs in Mexico. At the edge of Kendallville, Indiana, a billboard beckoned to new Mexican arrivals, "Estamos Occupando"—We are hiring. By 2004, nonwhites made up one-quarter of the population. Americans of Hispanic or Latino origin, both white and nonwhite, numbered about 40 million—almost 14 percent of the nation's population. Expecting the number of Hispanics and Asians to triple in the next 50 years, the Census Bureau predicted that the United States would become a diverse society of color, with a nonwhite majority.

> White men are an endangered species. I absolutely believe that, . . . what with affirmative action and everything.
>
> HELEN CHENOWETH,
> Republican congresswoman,
> Idaho, January, 1996

As the population changed, the concept of race became more complicated. Many Americans had thought of race as largely a divide between black and white. But the growth of the Hispanic or Latino population confounded this simple division. Latinos and Latinas were conscious of their own distinctive histories. "White means mostly privilege and black means overcoming obstacles, a history of civil rights," explained Patria Rodriguez in 2003. "As a Latina, I can't try to claim one of these."

Like Tiger Woods, many Americans felt that mixed racial background was a basic and distinctive part of their identity. In response, the Census Bureau let people choose more than one race to describe themselves in 2000. Hispanics, epitomizing the complications of race, were allowed to identify themselves both as Hispanic and as members of any race. "It's a reminder," said a population expert, "that we will

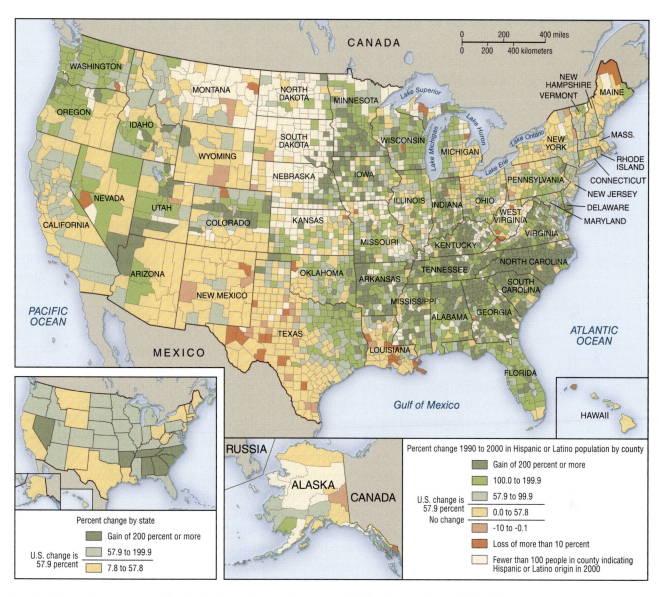

Map 31–3   The Growing Population of Americans of Hispanic or Latino Origin: Percent Change, 1990–2000
Thanks to a strong job market nationwide, the Hispanic and Latino population increased dramatically across the country. *Data Sources: U.S. Census Bureau, Census 2000 Redistricting Data (PL 94-171) Summary File and 1990 Census.*

increasingly, as Americans, need to find new ways of categorizing people and talking about their differences."

African Americans in the Post–Civil Rights Era

As Americans thought about the future, the African American experience was a reminder that issues of race and rights remained volatile and unresolved. By the 2000s, half a century after *Brown v. Board of Education,* southern schools were largely desegregated. But thanks to white flight from inner cities, northern schools were in many cases more segregated than ever. Despite continuing inequities, African Americans had made notable gains since *Brown.* In 1957, only 18 percent of black adults had graduated from high school. By 2002, 79 percent had graduated.

Yet the African American graduation rate lagged 10 percentage points behind the rate for whites.

African Americans had also made notable economic and political gains. The black middle class continued to grow at the turn of the century. But high rates of unemployment and imprisonment meant that only about six of every ten African American men were in the paid workforce in 2002. Despite the wealth and fame of talk show host and entrepreneur Oprah Winfrey, relatively few African Americans ranked among the wealthiest people in the United States. The number of high-profile African American public officials did grow at the turn of the century. By 1992, there were already more than 10,000 black officeholders nationwide. In 2001, Colin Powell became the first African American secretary of state, and Condoleezza Rice became the first African American (and female) national security advisor. Four years later, Rice became secretary of state.

These and other firsts did not mean the end of racial injustice and conflict in the United States. In 1991, white police in Los Angeles stopped a black motorist, Rodney King, for drunk driving and then savagely beat him. Despite a videotape of the beating, an all-white jury acquitted four of the policemen of all charges in the affair on April 29, 1992. The stunning verdict set off a riot in the predominantly African American community of South Central Los Angeles, including the Watts section that had been the center of rioting in 1965. Three days of violence left 51 people dead, 1,800 injured, and nearly 3,700 buildings burned. In the aftermath, Americans debated whether the legal system offered justice to African Americans, while liberals and conservatives blamed each other for the poverty and despair of many black communities. Eventually a federal court convicted two of the police for depriving King of his civil rights and another court awarded him $3.8 million in damages. But no one had concrete solutions for the problems of South Central Los Angeles.

Despite the riots, the federal government took few new steps to deal with racial inequality. In an age of popular pessimism about government, relatively few Americans believed that liberal programs, even on the scale of the Great Society of the 1960s, could secure equal conditions for African Americans.

At the same time, Americans did not want to undo the achievements of the past. Despite conservative opposition to affirmative action, this means of promoting equal opportunity in education and employment remained legal. In *Gratz v. Bollinger* in 2003, the Supreme Court, reflecting popular uneasiness with racial quotas and statistical formulas for diversity, struck down a "mechanical" point system used by the University of Michigan automatically to advantage minority applicants to its undergraduate program. But in *Grutter v. Bollinger*, the court endorsed Michigan's affirmative action program for law school admissions.

Culture Wars

Concerns about rights also drove a cluster of controversies, known as "culture wars," centering on changes in the family, marriage, gender, and sexuality. By the turn of the century, the ongoing transformation of the American family had become unmistakable. In the 1950s, two out of three families had a parent staying at home full-time; in 2000, with so many mothers in the workforce, less than one family in four had a stay-at-home parent. The supposedly "traditional" nuclear family of father, mother, and children no longer predominated in American households. Married couples with children, 40 percent of all households as late as 1970, made up only 25 percent by 1996 (see Table 31–1). That year, 27 percent of families with children contained one parent, usually a mother, rather than two.

A number of factors led to these changes. Americans were marrying later, having fewer children, and having them later in life. The divorce rate doubled from 1960 to 1990. In the 1990s about half of all marriages were ending in divorce. As women's wages gradually rose, more women could afford to live alone or to head families by themselves.

Many conservatives and Republicans blamed these developments on the nation's alleged moral decline. In their view, the counterculture of the 1960s, liberals, the media, feminists, and gays had undermined the nation's "family values." "It is a cultural war, as critical to the kind of nation we will one day be as was the cold war itself," thundered the conservative commentator Patrick Buchanan in a speech to the Republican National Convention in 1992.

To defend the family, some conservatives argued that single mothers should receive fewer welfare benefits and that divorce should be made more difficult. In response, liberals claimed that the family was not dying but simply adapting to change as it always had. The different forms of the family, like social diversity in general, could be viewed as a good thing.

Whatever the merits of the liberal argument, conservatives found the battle for "family values" almost impossible to win. In 1992, George H. W. Bush's vice president, Dan Quayle, attacked the TV sitcom *Murphy Brown* for its positive portrayal of a career woman's decision to have a child out of wedlock. The show stayed on the air; Quayle and Bush lost their reelection bid. A decade later, a Federal Communications Commission crackdown on graphic and ostensibly obscene radio "shock jocks" such as Howard Stern led some radio networks and stations to drop controversial programming, but the business continued pretty much as before and Stern drew more listeners than ever. Hollywood movies and television programs continued to become more explicit.

Women in the Postfeminist Era

As the *Murphy Brown* controversy suggested, women, so often a focal point for fears about social change, were at the center of the culture wars. Women's position in American society had changed dramatically since the 1960s. The percentage of adult

 Table 31–1 The Changing American Family, 1960–2006*

Year	Households	Families	Married-Couple Families	Single-Parent Families	One-Person Households
1960	52,799	44,905	23,358	3,332	6,917
1970	63,401	51,456	25,541	3,271	10,851
1980	80,776	58,426	24,961	6,061	18,296
1990	93,347	66,090	24,537	7,752	22,999
1996	99,627	69,594	24,920	9,284	24,900

Source: U.S. Census Bureau website, http://www.census.gov/population/socdemo/hhfam/rep86/96hh4.txt, http://www.bls.census.gov/population/socdemoc/hhfam/rep96/96hh1.txt and /96fml.txt.

*Numbers given in thousands.

women in the workforce rose, as did the percentage of women in high-paying white-collar jobs. Women were more visible in politics. After the 1992 elections, a record 53 women held seats in Congress. Bill Clinton selected and the Senate confirmed the first female attorney general, Janet Reno, in 1993, and the first female secretary of state, Madeleine Albright, in 1997.

Yet there was a sense of stagnation in the new century. In 2002, women earned on average 77.5 percent as much as men—little better than 10 years before. Women were still more likely than men to live in poverty. Bill Clinton's adulterous affairs dramatized women's insistence that men "just don't get it" about relationships between the sexes. Nearly half of women believed the women's movement had made their lives better, but the movement was now less visible and less vocal. Just as the 2000s were part of the "post–civil rights era," so they were part of the "postfeminist era."

Still, conservatives could not turn back the clock. Forced to raise troops without a draft, the military, one of the last and most intensely masculine preserves, needed female volunteers. In 1994, the Department of Defense rescinded the "Risk Rule" that kept women out of units in which they could be harmed or captured. As more women entered the military, the armed services repeatedly had to deal with charges of harassment. In 2000, the army even admitted that its highest-ranking woman general had been sexually harassed by a male general.

Conservatives also tried to limit women's access to abortion. At the grassroots level, the Right to Life movement picketed abortion clinics and tried to discourage pregnant women from having abortions. Some radicals resorted to violence, including the murder of clinic workers. Meanwhile, both presidents Bush opposed abortion and named antiabortion judges to the federal courts.

In spite of the protests and political maneuvers, the right and practice of abortion continued in the new century. In *Planned Parenthood v. Casey* in 1992, the Supreme Court narrowly voted to uphold much of a Pennsylvania law limiting access to abortions. But the Court also declared that a woman's right to choose an abortion was "a component of liberty we cannot renounce." As president, Clinton chose proabortion justices and vetoed antiabortion legislation.

Winning Gay and Lesbian Rights

Homosexuality was yet one more front in the culture wars. Although most Americans believed businesses should not discriminate on the basis of sexual preference, a majority in the 1990s still believed that homosexuality was morally wrong. Every year, there were hundreds of documented instances of violence against gays and lesbians.

As homosexuals pressed for equal rights, evangelical Christians and conservatives fought back. In 1992 Colorado voters passed a state referendum forbidding communities to pass laws protecting gay rights, but the state supreme court declared the referendum unconstitutional. In 1996, Congress passed the Defense of Marriage Act, which denied federal benefits to same-sex couples and allowed states to refuse to recognize same-sex marriages from other states.

The military was another battle zone. Officially barred from serving, homosexuals had long concealed their sexual orientation in order to remain in the military. Then, in 1992, a federal court ordered the navy to reinstate an openly gay petty officer who had been discharged. Campaigning for president that year,

Clinton promised to lift the ban on gays in the armed services. But in the White House, he compromised by instituting a "don't ask, don't tell" policy. The military would no longer ask recruits whether they were gay, and gays and lesbians would continue to conceal their sexual orientation.

Nevertheless, the tide seemed to turn. As AIDS spread more slowly among the gay population and heterosexuals contracted the disease, Americans were less likely to consider it "gay cancer" or God's punishment of homosexuals. Meanwhile, gays became a more accepted presence in society. More television shows positively depicted homosexuality. Openly gay men and women served in Congress. Many businesses, including Disney-

The Spread of Same-Sex Marriage In June 2008, a ruling by the California State Supreme Court allowed same-sex couples, including this one, to marry.

land, welcomed gay customers. Leading corporations, including Ford and General Motors, began providing benefits to the partners of gay employees.

In the new century, Americans, especially younger ones, increasingly accepted the legitimacy of gay relationships. In *Lawrence v. Texas* in 2003, the U.S. Supreme Court struck down state antisodomy laws and effectively legalized gay sexual behavior. Invoking gays' "right to liberty," the majority declared, "The state cannot demean their existence or control their destiny by making their private sexual conduct a crime."

After *Lawrence,* there was new support for legalizing same-sex marriage. In 2004, the mayor of San Francisco, flouting state law, issued marriage licenses to same-sex couples. Strongly liberal Massachusetts became the first state to legalize same-sex marriages, and couples flocked to be married. Despite the support of conservatives and George W. Bush, a constitutional amendment banning gay marriage failed to pass that year. In 2008, the California Supreme Court overturned a state ban on same-sex marriage. But in November, a majority of California voters passed a referendum imposing a ban. The struggle over gay rights would continue.

The various battles over family values did little to alter the direction of social change in the United States. After a decade of the culture wars, Americans seemed willing to balance conservative economic policy with more liberal social values.

America in the Post–Cold War World

With the end of the cold war, America's role in the world, so plainly fixed for nearly half a century, suddenly became unclear. In 1991, the American-led victory in the Persian Gulf War suggested that the United States might serve as an active international police officer in a "New World Order." Nevertheless, Americans remained reluctant about intervention in crises abroad in the 1990s. But then the terrorist attacks of September 11, 2001, forced the United States into an ongoing global war on terror.

The New World Order

As the cold war ended, some Republicans called for a less internationalist foreign policy. Echoing conservatives of the 1940s and 1950s, they insisted that the United States should no longer provide financial aid and military protection to other countries. American soldiers, they felt, should risk their lives to protect the United States, not other countries. In contrast, a broad range of internationalists in both the Democratic and Republican parties believed the United States could protect itself and advance its political and economic interests only by remaining active in world affairs.

> You guys want to start a fight in my backyard, I got something for you.
>
> STAFF SGT. DAVID SAFSTROM, 82nd Airborne Division, on how he felt after 9/11

The most powerful internationalist was President George H. W. Bush. A naval aviator in World War II, the elder Bush believed that American isolationism had encouraged fascist aggression and world war in the 1930s and 1940s. So, Bush argued, the United States had to maintain its overseas commitments. With the help of other powerful countries, America should use foreign aid, military strength, NATO, and the United Nations to maintain a stable international system, a "New World Order." Bush wanted "a world in which democracy is the norm, in which private enterprise, free trade, and prosperity enrich every nation—a world in which the rule of law prevails." Much like Woodrow Wilson and Harry Truman before him, Bush mixed idealism and self-interest: a free world would be good both for other nations and for the United States. But only American power and leadership could preserve that world.

The New World Order was a broad, vague concept. Internationalists had a hard time explaining just what overseas commitments America needed to make. Critics noted a tension between Bush's call for order and his support for democracy. Was the United States supposed to protect antidemocratic countries in the name of international stability?

There was also a tension between Bush's commitment to international cooperation and the long-standing tendency for the United States to act alone in its own hemisphere. While the president spoke of the New World Order, he intervened unilaterally in the Central American nation of Panama in 1989. Bush had grown frustrated with General Manuel Noriega, the Panamanian leader who engaged in drug sales to the United States and other illegal activities. After Noriega thwarted democratic elections, Bush dispatched American troops, who captured Noriega and sent him to the United States for prosecution on drug charges in 1989. Bush's unilateral action, condemned by other Latin American countries, contradicted his rhetoric about international collaboration in the post–cold war world.

Finally, the New World Order, like the containment of Communism, could be expensive in lives and money. It was unclear whether Americans, mindful of the costs of the Vietnam War, would endorse armed intervention abroad. With the end of the cold war, many people also wanted a "peace dividend" of savings on foreign aid and military expenditures that could be spent on domestic needs.

The Persian Gulf War

The test of the New World Order came soon enough. On August 2, 1990, Iraq, led by President Saddam Hussein, overran Kuwait, its oil-rich but defenseless neighbor to the south. Entrenched in Kuwait, Iraq threatened its much larger western neighbor, oil-producing Saudi Arabia. Hussein's actions clearly jeopardized America's oil supply and its Saudi Arabian ally. The Kuwaiti invasion also obviously challenged Bush's calls for a stable global system of free and free-trading nations.

Comparing Hussein to Adolf Hitler, Bush created an international coalition opposing Iraq. By the end of 1990 over half a million U.S. troops had joined with forces from 36 nations in Operation Desert Shield to protect Saudi Arabia (see Map 31–4). Meanwhile, the Bush administration persuaded the United Nations to authorize military action if the Iraqis did not withdraw by January 15, 1991. The president also obtained congressional approval for the use of force.

When Hussein refused to pull back by the deadline, Operation Desert Shield became Operation Desert Storm. As television audiences around the world watched live CNN coverage, coalition missiles and planes struck Iraq on the night of January 17. Unable to contest the coalition's air power, Hussein launched Scud missile attacks against America's ally, Israel, hundreds of miles away. The missiles did little damage and failed to provoke Israeli retaliation that might have split the coalition. Instead, ground forces led by U.S. General Norman Schwarzkopf swept into Kuwait, devastated the Iraqi army, and pushed into Iraq in just 100 hours. Fearing accusations of cruelty, Bush called a halt before the invasion reached the Iraqi capital of Baghdad and toppled Hussein.

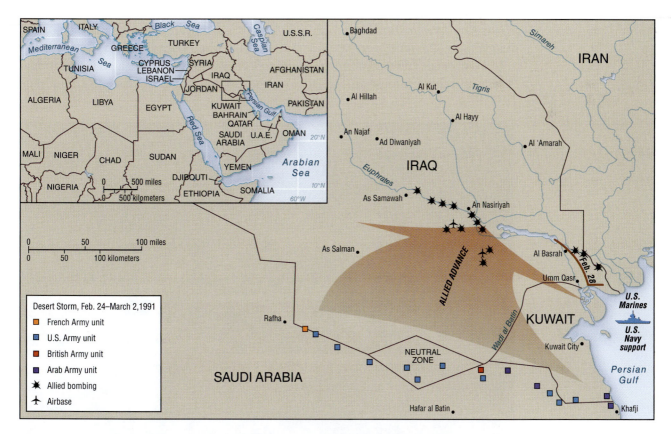

Map 31–4   The Persian Gulf War Operation Desert Storm, the allied attack on the forces of Iraq, tested President George H. W. Bush's vision of a "New World Order" in the oil-rich heart of the Middle East. *Mark C. Carnes et al,* Mapping America's Past *(New York: Henry Holt and Co., 1996), p. 267;* Hammond Atlas of the Twentieth Century *(New York: Times Books, 1996), p. 166.*

The Persian Gulf War seemed like a great victory for the United States and the New World Order. American technology appeared to work perfectly. Coalition forces suffered only about 220 battle deaths while killing thousands of Iraqis. American leadership and American power had halted aggression and restored freedom abroad. As Bush's popularity soared, the New World Order seemed like a practical reality.

Americans' euphoria did not last. Studies showed that U.S. weapons had not worked quite so well. As many as a quarter of Gulf War veterans suffered major health problems caused by exposure to chemical pesticides and, ironically, ingestion of pills intended to protect them from Iraqi chemical weapons. Despite the devastation of his forces, Saddam Hussein held on to power and ruthlessly repressed the Shiite and Kurdish populations. Despite the massive war effort, he would remain a threat to his neighbors and to American interests into the new century. The goals of the New World Order had not been fully achieved after all.

Retreating from the New World Order

In the years after the Persian Gulf War, the United States retreated from Bush's vision. Unwilling to maintain cold war spending levels, the nation cut troops, closed bases, and canceled weapons, including Reagan's Strategic Defense Initiative. The Central Intelligence Agency and other intelligence operations struggled with tight budgets, low morale, and public criticism. The federal government's foreign aid budget also stagnated.

As U.S. power diminished, the Vietnam syndrome returned: Americans were reluctant to intervene overseas when the nation had no critical military or economic interest at stake. In 1992, a civil war among local warlords complicated international efforts to relieve famine in Somalia, on the eastern horn of Africa. As hundreds

The Power Behind the "New World Order" American soldiers on a sophisticated M1 A1 Abrams tank, in the surreal glow of Kuwaiti oil fields burned by retreating Iraqi forces in March 1991.

of thousands of Somalis died, President Bush ordered 1,800 marines to serve in a United Nations force protecting the relief efforts. After Clinton took office in 1993, a warlord's forces massacred 32 U.S. troops in the capital city, Mogadishu. Clinton temporarily increased American forces in Somalia, but only on the condition that they all would be withdrawn in 1994. The chastened president directed that future U.S. involvement in peacekeeping operations would require a threat to international peace and security, or a benefit to "U.S. interests."

The United States showed a similar reluctance to intervene in the violence following the collapse of Communist rule in Yugoslavia. As this Eastern European country broke apart in the early 1990s, three ethnic groups—Serbs, Croats, and Muslim Slavs—fought a bitter civil war in the newly independent province of Bosnia-Herzegovina. The remnants of the old Yugoslavia, under the harsh leadership of Slobodan Milosevic, aided the Serbs in carrying out "ethnic cleansing," the forcible expulsion of Muslims and Croats from their homes. Faced with the worst mass brutality in Europe since World War II, Bush and Clinton were unwilling to risk American lives. Under intense pressure to stop the slaughter, Clinton allowed U.S. planes and missiles, operating in conjunction with NATO, to attack Serb forces in 1994. Backed by this devastating assault, the United States brokered a peace agreement in 1995. Clinton committed 20,000 troops to a peacekeeping force, even though most Americans opposed the move.

Yugoslavia posed a challenge again when the Milosevic regime attacked ethnic Albanians in the region of Kosovo. Humiliated by its inability to negotiate an end to the suffering in Kosovo, the Clinton administration finally supported a NATO air offensive against the Yugoslavian government in March 1999. The 78-day war that ended in June killed 2,000–5,000 people, badly damaged Yugoslavia's infrastructure, and forced Milosevic to accept a multinational peacekeeping force. NATO suffered no casualties, because Clinton and other leaders were unwilling to risk them. There was no longer any talk about a U.S.-led New World Order.

Al Qaeda and 9/11

As Americans shied away from international commitment, a mortal threat to the United States took shape. In February 1993 an explosive-laden truck blew up in an underground garage beneath the twin towers of New York City's giant office complex, the World Trade Center. Six people were killed and more than a thousand injured in the first major international terrorist incident inside the United States. Investigators traced the attack to followers of a radical Islamist spiritual leader from Egypt, Sheikh Omar Abdel-Rahman, who lived in New Jersey. Rahman and over a dozen associates were convicted for the bombing and other plots.

Surprisingly, most Americans paid little attention to terrorism in the aftermath of the attack. U.S. authorities generally ignored the plotters' connections to a terrorist organization, Al Qaeda, led by a wealthy Saudi Arabian exile, Osama bin Laden. A veteran of the resistance to the Soviet invasion of Afghanistan, bin Laden had gradually made Al Qaeda—Arabic for "base" or "foundation"—into an anti-Western movement dedicated to restoring the supposedly lost glory of Islam. The terrorist financier particularly hated the United States, for its support of Israel and its military presence in the Middle East.

Operating out of Sudan and then Afghanistan, Al Qaeda supported Muslim fighters in Bosnia and warlords in Somalia. In 1995 and 1996, the organization was

Osama bin Laden The terrorist leader sits for an interview at a secret location two months after the 9/11 attacks.

involved in deadly terrorist attacks on U.S. soldiers in Saudi Arabia. In 1996, bin Laden declared jihad—holy war—on the United States.

Although Clinton declared terrorism "the enemy of our generation," Americans paid little attention. Al Qaeda attacks continued. In 1998, almost simultaneous truck bombs at U.S. embassies in Kenya and Tanzania killed at least 224, including 12 Americans, and wounded 5,000. Blaming bin Laden, the Clinton administration unsuccessfully authorized his assassination and launched missile attacks on Al Qaeda facilities in Sudan and Afghanistan. In 2000, Al Qaeda members slammed an explosive-laden motorboat into the side of the U.S. destroyer *Cole* in the Yemeni port of Aden. Although 17 American sailors died, the president and his advisers did not retaliate against bin Laden (Map 31–5) .

Despite warnings, Clinton's successor, George W. Bush, paid little attention to Al Qaeda. Then, on the morning of September 11, 2001, the most ambitious Al Qaeda plot took place in a clear blue, morning sky. Nineteen Middle Eastern members of bin Laden's organization successfully passed through security at East Coast airports and boarded four passenger jets. In flight, the terrorists, brandishing box cutters and Mace or pepper spray, overwhelmed flight attendants and passengers, killed or wounded the pilots, took the controls, and redirected the flights. At 8:46 A.M., American 11 sped into the North Tower of the World Trade Center; 17 minutes later, United 175 hit the Trade Center's South Tower. At 9:37, American 77 struck the west wall of the Pentagon, outside Washington, DC. Aboard United 93, apparently headed toward Washington, too, there were sounds of struggle, a voice shouted, "Allah is the Greatest," and the jet crashed into an empty field in Shanksville, Pennsylvania, at 10:03. By then, the North Tower of the World Trade Center had collapsed in a cloud of smoke and debris. The South Tower followed at 10:28.

All told, the tragedy, which became known as "9/11," killed the 19 hijackers, 40 people in the crash at Shanksville, 184 at the Pentagon, and 2,751 at the World Trade Center. More Americans died on 9/11 than had died in the Japanese attack at Pearl Harbor on December 7, 1941. Only the Civil War battles of Antietam on September 17, 1862, and Cold Harbor on June 3, 1864, had been deadlier days in the nation's history. America's place in the post–cold war world had suddenly come into focus. "Terrorism against our nation will not stand," Bush vowed. A decade after the end of the cold war, the United States had begun the war on terror.

The War on Terror

In the days after 9/11, stunned Americans felt that the attacks had "changed everything." Much of national life stayed the same, but the catastrophe did funda-

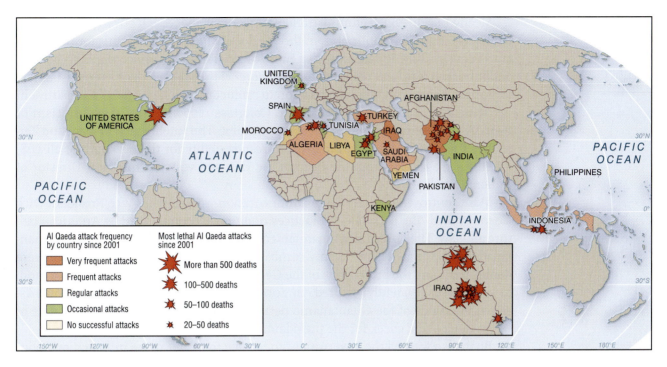

Map 31-5   The Global Reach of Al Qaeda

mentally reshape American foreign and security policy. Vowing privately on 9/11 "to kick some ass," President Bush declared publicly that evening, "We will make no distinction between the terrorists who committed these acts and those who harbor them." The United States demanded that the Taliban regime in Afghanistan, which protected bin Laden, turn over the terrorist. When the Taliban refused, Bush promised they would "pay the price." In October, U.S. and other NATO forces attacked Afghanistan. After American and British air strikes against Al Qaeda and Taliban targets, U.S., British, and Australian troops invaded the country to hunt down bin Laden, destroy his training camps, and drive out the Taliban.

Afghanistan, weak and impoverished, fell quickly, as the Taliban surrendered the capital, Kabul, in November and fled their stronghold Kandahar in December. Yet bin Laden and many of his men escaped in the remote, rugged, mountainous terrain to continue their fight along the border with Pakistan. So U.S. and NATO forces remained to protect the fragile new government and keep hunting bin Laden.

New York, September 11, 2001 As the North Tower of the World Trade Center burns in the background after being hit by a hijacked jet airliner, a second hijacked plane roars toward a fiery collision with the South Tower. Within hours, both towers would collapse, killing thousands.

Meanwhile, the Bush administration reorganized the federal government to combat terror. Within a month of 9/11, the president chose the first Director of Homeland Security, Tom Ridge, and gave him responsibility for protecting U.S. borders and infrastructure, and responding to emergencies in the event of a terrorist strike. In 2002, Congress elevated the position to cabinet rank and created the Department of Homeland Security. Two years later, Congress responded to harsh criticism of the CIA and FBI for failing to detect the 9/11 plot. The Intelligence Reform and Terrorism Prevention Act of 2004 stripped responsibility for the oversight of all U.S. intelligence agencies from the head of the CIA and vested it in a new Director of National Intelligence.

More controversially, the Bush administration worked what Vice President Dick Cheney called "the dark side"—practices traditionally condemned by American culture and law. The government maintained a controversial detention center at Guantánamo Bay, Cuba, where "enemy combatants" captured in the war on terror were denied trials and the protections of the Geneva Convention for prisoners of war and, in some cases, evidently tortured. In 2006 and 2008, the U.S. Supreme Court asserted the rights of the Guantánamo detainees and reminded Bush that "a state of war is not a blank check for the president."

Bush also wanted the government to be able to gather more information about its own citizens. In October, 2001, Congress hastily passed the USA Patriot Act—an acronym for the "Uniting and Strengthening America by Providing Appropriate Tools Required to Intercept and Obstruct Terrorism Act of 2001." This measure made it easier for the federal government to spy on Americans. The Patriot Act also allowed the attorney general to imprison indefinitely, without trial, noncitizens considered threats to national security.

Opponents condemned the Patriot Act as an unlawful and unequaled deprivation of civil liberties. In 2004, a federal judge declared part of the measure an unconstitutional infringement on First Amendment rights. Despite the controversy, the Bush administration pushed successfully for renewal and expansion of the act.

Bush also reconsidered the use of American military power. In the past, presidents had rejected preemptive, peacetime attacks on other nations. But Bush believed that terrorism presented "a threat without precedent." As 9/11 demonstrated, enemies did not need "great armies and great industrial capabilities to endanger the American people and our nation." So the president threatened to strike before a war began and even before a threat emerged in the first place. Bush further broke with cold war presidents, including his father, by calling for the United States to act alone when necessary rather than through alliances and the United Nations.

The Bush Doctrine of preemption and unilateral action risked isolating the United States in the world and making it seem selfish, dangerous, and illegitimate. Yet Bush, confident of American power and virtue, was willing to go it alone. "That's OK with me," he said. "We are America."

The Iraq War

The president knew where to apply his new doctrine. It was not enough to go after terrorist organizations, Bush said in his State of the Union address in January 2002. The United States must also "prevent regimes that sponsor terror from threatening America or our friends and allies with weapons of mass destruction."

>> Gitmo, "The Least Worst Place"

From the camera eye of a satellite miles above, Guantánamo Bay stood out from the rest of eastern Cuba. The inlet was a horseshoe of brown and grey terrain amid the lush green of the island and the bright blue of the Atlantic. To the administration of George W. Bush, Guantánamo Bay was a grey area, too: one of the few places on earth that was American and yet not American, a drab anomaly perfect for one of the most controversial phases of the war on terror.

Guantánamo Bay, some 520 miles from Miami, Florida, had been an anomaly for more than a century. After the Spanish-American War of 1898, the U.S. government had taken the spot for a naval base: the inlet made a perfect harbor; the hills blocked off the rest of the island. The Cuban-American Treaty of 1903, modified in 1934, effectively gave America perpetual control over the base. For the bargain price of less than $4,000 a year, the United States could keep the facility until both Washington and Cuba agreed to end the arrangement.

Even when Fidel Castro came to power in 1959, the U.S. base remained at Guantánamo Bay, like a capitalist shard stuck in the side of the new Communist regime. Castro objected to the base and refused to cash all but one of America's annual checks, but he did not try to drive out the United States either. So Guantánamo Bay, or "Gitmo," as Americans called it, remained the oldest U.S. overseas naval base and the only one in a Communist country.

Nevertheless, Gitmo became less and less valuable over the years. As the cold war ended and the United States closed down many military bases, there was no real need for a naval installation so close to the U.S. mainland. The number of American military personnel assigned to Gitmo dwindled.

Then the war on terror began. The Bush administration needed to put captured Taliban fighters and other "enemy combatants" somewhere safe. It was too risky to leave detainees in unstable Afghanistan or Iraq; but it was also too risky to bring them to the United States, where courts, Congress, and public opinion could interfere in their imprisonment. So, the Bush administration looked, in the words of Secretary of Defense Donald Rumsfeld, for "the least worst place" to hold those captured in the war on terror.

Rumsfeld and his colleagues found it at Guantánamo Bay. The U.S. military controlled the base, but U.S. civil law did not apply. Gitmo, with its grey, pebbly beaches, was the perfect grey area for an administration determined to find its way around the law to prosecute the war on terror. Before 2001 was over, detainees began to arrive from Afghanistan. By the end of 2008, some 775 people had been incarcerated at Gitmo. To accommodate them, the U.S. government built up the base. There were soon no fewer than seven separate prison facilities; one of them, known only as "Camp 7," remained secret. Thousands of American personnel streamed in to run Gitmo.

For a time, the base provided the Bush administration with just the freedom it wanted and needed. CIA, FBI, and military interrogators, apparently copying Chinese Communist techniques from the 1950s, tortured some prisoners. According to detainees, their captors used sleep deprivation and beatings; they also mocked detainees' religious practices by defacing the Qur'an or flushing it down the toilet. Deprived of the

continued

>> **AMERICAN LANDSCAPE** *continued*

rights of captured military prisoners under the Geneva Convention, the detainees were also deprived of the right to trial—a feature of justice back in the United States. These conditions took a heavy toll on the prisoners: an unknown number committed suicide.

As details of life at Gitmo leaked out, critics of the Bush administration denied that the base was any sort of grey area at all. They argued that the laws of the United States should apply to the prisoners at the base: they deserved the protections of the Geneva Convention and the right to trial. More broadly, they saw Gitmo as proof that the war on terror, like other wars, had eroded due process, human rights, and other features of democracy, all in the name of battling for democracy. Even the lord chancellor of the United Kingdom—a U.S. ally—called the base a "shocking affront to democracy" in 2006.

Even though the U.S. Supreme Court seemed to agree, in its rulings of 2006 and 2008, Gitmo remained open—a swath of grey amid all the green and blue. ●

The Fall of Saddam Hussein As the coalition invasion overthrew the Iraqi regime, jubilant Iraqis pulled down statues of Saddam Hussein, like this one, in the spring of 2003.

The president identified Iran, Iraq, and North Korea as an "an axis of evil," potentially able to arm terrorists with nuclear, chemical, or biological weapons to threaten the United States directly.

Iraq was the focus of Bush's attention. In recent years, Saddam Hussein had plotted the assassination of the president's father and seemingly resumed attempts to gain weapons of mass destruction (WMD). In the Bush administration's view, a U.S. missile strike and United Nations economic sanctions and weapons inspections had not deterred Hussein, who had forced the inspectors to withdraw in 1998. After 9/11, Bush shared the view of key advisors that Hussein still had WMD and supported Al Qaeda. Further, some administration members argued that the replacement of Hussein with a democratic regime would encourage the spread of democracy around the Middle East and make Israel safer.

As the Bush administration moved toward confrontation with Iraq, nearly all of America's European allies, as well as Russia, China, and Middle Eastern countries, opposed a unilateral U.S. war. The United States did assemble a "coalition of the willing," but it was far smaller than the coalition assembled by the president's father 12 years earlier. Only Great Britain, Australia, and Poland joined the U.S. in committing troops.

On the night of March 19, 2003, Operation Iraqi Freedom began with a hail of Tomahawk cruise missiles aimed at Baghdad in an unsuccessful attempt to kill Hussein. To the surprise of many observers, the rest of the attack went almost flawlessly. On March 21, some 1,300 bombs and missiles rained down on Baghdad in a display of "shock and awe" meant to demoralize the Iraqi leadership. Meanwhile, coalition ground forces moved into Iraq, with the British striking south to seize the port city of Basra and the United States moving east to occupy Baghdad. American technology, particularly highly accurate missiles and smart bombs, worked quite well. The Iraqi army offered little resistance, as many of its soldiers simply disappeared into the civilian population. Hussein disappeared, too. By mid-April, his statues were toppling.

Swift and short, the war with Iraq seemed to be everything that the Bush administration had hoped. Only 138 U.S. soldiers had died. Standing before a huge banner declaring "Mission Accomplished" aboard an aircraft carrier on May 1, the president jubilantly announced, "Major combat operations in Iraq have ended." The United States seemed well on the way to winning the war on terror and reshaping the Middle East.

America in Crisis

By the 2000s, a new America, "a nation transformed," seemed to have taken shape. The twenty-first-century United States was a globalized, information-based, diverse nation, socially liberal and politically conservative. But the transformation of America was far from over. The costly war on terror dragged on without victory in either Afghanistan or Iraq. In 2008, financial catastrophe, gradually developing for several years, engulfed the economy. Along with the strain of the war on terror, the frightening economic downturn created a national crisis. Long-standing monuments of American capitalism teetered on the brink of collapse. So did the conservative policies that had shaped American governance for nearly two generations. Against this troubling backdrop, Americans used the presidential election to point their country in a new direction.

Iraq and Afghanistan in Turmoil

The jubilant announcement of "Mission Accomplished" soon gave way to sober realities in Iraq during 2003. There was looting in many communities. Despite an intensive search, no weapons of mass destruction could be found. It was difficult to restart the economy and train new Iraqi police and defense forces. Rather than embrace their liberators, many Iraqis resented the Americans. Worst of all, a violent insurgency, perhaps orchestrated by Saddam Hussein, tried to destabilize Iraq and drive out the United States.

Although U.S. forces captured Hussein in December 2003, the conflict went badly. Unable to prove that Hussein's regime had had ties to Al Qaeda before 9/11, the Bush administration faced charges of fighting an expensive, needless war and weakening the hunt for bin Laden in Afghanistan. Bush was further embarrassed by the brutal execution of Hussein and revelations of the humiliation and torture of Iraqis at a U.S. prison in Abu Ghraib. Although the Bush administration handed over sovereignty to a new Iraqi government, chosen by the United States, in 2004, more than 100,000 American troops remained.

Those forces now confronted "Al Qaeda in Iraq," a new terrorist group pledging allegiance to bin Laden, and also a sectarian civil war between Shiites and Sunnis. The insurgents' use of IEDs—improvised explosive devices—took a heavy toll on American troops. By the end of 2006, 3,000 U.S. soldiers had died and Iraq remained in turmoil.

Facing failure, the Bush administration responded with a controversial "surge," a temporary increase in troop strength to 130,000, in 2007. By mid-2008, the surge, along with changes in Iraqi politics, succeeded in decreasing the violence. But more than 4,000 U.S. soldiers and uncounted Iraqis had died, the Iraqi economy still struggled, and the Iraqi government was not truly democratic. American public opinion had largely turned against the war.

Meanwhile, the conflict in Afghanistan had worsened. As the United States focused resources and attention on Iraq, the Taliban, aided by foreign fighters, had gradually regained strength and the pro–United States government had lost power. Osama bin Laden remained at large, most likely somewhere along the mountainous border with Pakistan. Calling the situation "precarious and urgent," U.S. military leaders admitted they did not have enough troops to commit to Afghanistan. But the United States did prosecute the war more aggressively by striking into Pakistan. The American death toll climbed to a record of more than 100 in 2007 and passed 100 again in 2008. By then, over 600 U.S. soldiers had died since 2001 in what was becoming one of America's longest wars. Uncounted thousands of Afghans had died as well.

In addition to lives and money, the wars in Afghanistan and Iraq cost the United States popularity and influence around the globe. Sympathetic to Americans in the months after 9/11, many people no longer supported U.S. military action in the Middle East. The tragic toll of civilian deaths and the use of torture proved particularly costly for America's standing in the world. Critics argued that the U.S. government's callous mistreatment of Middle Easterners was winning converts for Al Qaeda and terrorism. At the same time, as the situation in Afghanistan underscored, the United States had seriously depleted its military power. When Russia invaded neighboring Georgia, a U.S. ally, in the summer of 2008, there was nothing the Bush administration could do to change the course of events. The United States no longer seemed like an unstoppable superpower or an unflagging champion of democracy.

The Economy in Jeopardy

In retrospect, the economic boom of the 1990s and 2000s looked a lot like the boom of the 1920s. In both periods, optimistic American consumers, buoyed by good times, borrowed money and bought houses and cars. Investors borrowed money, too, to buy stocks. All that buying spurred the economy and drove the stock market to record heights. But eventually all that borrowing reached its limits: new credit ran out, and many Americans found themselves unable to meet their debts. In both periods, too, business leaders and government officials paid too little attention to dangerous financial practices until it was too late.

Inflating the Housing Bubble In 2002, President George W. Bush encourages mortgage lenders to make it easier for Americans to buy homes.

By the early 2000s, the housing industry was developing a classic "bubble," an inflation of prices based on air and delusion, not reality. As Americans—some of them aided by subprime mortgages—bought houses in record numbers, the nation began to believe that homes were great investments whose value would just keep on increasing. Acting on this belief, some people bought houses they could not really afford and many people used houses as collateral for loans. In the process, banks made loans they should not have made. Moreover, financial institutions intentionally or unintentionally obscured the reality of bad mortgage loans by folding those loans into complex, risky new financial instruments, known as Collateralized Debt Obligations (CDOs), that they sold around the world. As a result, firms in the United States and abroad were vulnerable to trouble in housing but did not understand the danger.

The trouble began in 2005, when U.S. house prices stagnated and then began to fall the next year. As the housing bubble burst, many home owners discovered they were not as wealthy as they thought they were. Some of them, particularly those with subprime loans, had trouble making their payments; foreclosures—banks' repossession of homes for unpaid mortgages—began to increase. The consequences rippled outward: the home-construction industry suffered; it became harder for consumers to get credit.

The most dramatic consequences befell financial institutions. In the spring of 2008, the New York investment bank Bear Stearns, deeply involved in subprime mortgage loans and other risky practices, nearly collapsed despite help from the federal government. Only a takeover by banking giant JPMorgan Chase saved the

Crash Distraught traders at the Chicago Mercantile Exchange watch the stock market plunge, October 2008.

firm from bankruptcy. In the summer, the nation's largest mortgage lender, IndyMac Bank, failed; in line with New Deal legislation, the federal government stepped in to guarantee depositors' money. Then, Washington had to take over two key private corporations that bought and sold mortgages from banks—the Federal National Mortgage Association, known as "Fannie Mae," and the Federal Home Loan Mortgage Corporation, known as "Freddie Mac."

As these events unfolded, other developments joined to threaten not only the United States but the global economy as well. The cause of globalized free trade suffered when the World Trade Organization's round of trade talks held in Doha, Qatar, collapsed in failure. Oil prices, driven by rising demand from the rapidly growing economies of China and India, surged to record levels. High oil prices drove up the price of other goods, including food, and spurred inflation. Rising oil prices also hurt the auto industry, particularly the Big Three U.S. automakers—Chrysler, Ford, and General Motors—whose gas-guzzling SUVs became suddenly hard to sell. Although felt worldwide, these events particularly hurt the United States, which saw the value of the dollar decline around the globe. All these developments eroded the confidence of American consumers, particularly those who had run up big balances on their credit cards. The Dow Jones Industrial Average, which had reached a record high over 14,000 in October 2007, had declined into the 11,000s in early September 2008.

Despite these ominous trends, most people were still unprepared when disaster struck in mid-September. In a matter of days, the U.S. financial industry nearly collapsed: Lehman Brothers, another investment firm caught up in the subprime debacle, went bankrupt—the most valuable American corporation ever to fail; the Bank of America bought Merrill Lynch, still another near-bankrupt victim of dubious mortgage and other financial practices; and AIG, an insurance giant heavily involved in CDOs, headed toward collapse as well until the Federal Reserve effectively bought the company.

Meanwhile, U.S. and foreign stock markets buckled. The Dow Jones lost more than 4 percent of its value on September 15, and then another 4 percent two days later. As government officials and financial leaders around the world scrambled to save banks, keep the financial system operating, and prop up the stock markets, Americans worried whether the world faced a repeat of the great crash of 1929. At the end of the month, a panicked Congress approved the Emergency Economic Stabilization Act of 2008, an extraordinary financial package, worth as much as $700 billion, to try to bail out the U.S. financial industry, ensure the availability of credit to borrowers, and save the nation from depression.

The Presidential Election of 2008

As the economy reeled, Americans went about choosing the 44th president of the United States. Even before the financial meltdown, the election was proving a milestone in American history. Democratic senator Hillary Clinton of New York, the wife of Bill Clinton, seemed likely to become the first woman major-party presidential candidate. But Clinton's campaign, which emphasized her "experience" and her original support for the Iraq War, met unexpectedly tough resistance from the younger, first-term senator Barack Obama of Illinois. The son of a black Kenyan father and a white American mother, Obama, like Tiger Woods, evoked a more diverse, globalized nation. In contrast to Clinton, he ran on a platform of "change" for America and an end to the Iraq War. Narrowly defeating Clinton in an epic primary battle, Obama became the first African American major-party presidential nominee.

Obama's Republican opponent, Senator John McCain of Arizona, seemed much more a candidate of the status quo. The second-oldest major-party nominee in American history, the 72-year-old McCain was a generation older than the 47-year-old Obama. But the Republican, drawing attention away from his support of Bush administration policies, presented himself as a tough-minded, independent "maverick" with the courage to chart a new political course. The surprise selection of Alaska's reform governor Sarah Palin as the second female major-party candidate for the vice presidency underscored McCain's commitment to change.

The intensification of the economic crisis in October mortally wounded the Republican cause. Saddled with the unpopular wars and weak economy of the Bush administration, McCain seemed old and uncertain. Meanwhile, many voters were impressed by Obama's cool performance during the crisis, including his three televised debates with McCain. On election day in November, a majority of the electorate did what had seemed unthinkable even after the civil rights movement of the 1960s: they made an African American the president of the United States. Moreover, Obama won a clear victory, with 52.8 percent of the popular vote, the highest percentage in 20 years, and 365 electoral votes. Americans had seemingly given the Democrat his mandate for "change."

He would need it. Even before the celebration of Obama's history-making victory ended, the economic crisis deepened. In mid-November, the stock market lurched down again, dropping below the 8,000 mark. Despite the Emergency Economic Stabilization Act, financial institutions were still in peril and loans were still scarce. With the collapse of vehicle sales, the Big Three domestic automakers, so long the backbone of the American economy, headed toward bankruptcy. Unemployment rose and consumer spending fell. As the world economy slowed, oil prices did come down and inflation abated.

"Change We Can Believe In" Democratic nominee Barack Obama campaigns for the presidency in 2008.

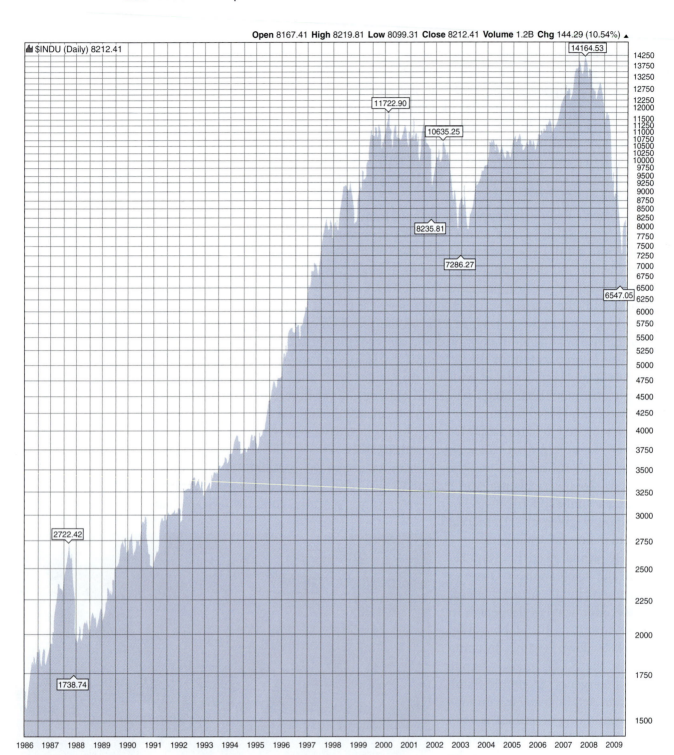

Open 8167.41 **High** 8219.81 **Low** 8099.31 **Close** 8212.41 **Volume** 1.2B **Chg** 144.29 (10.54%) ▲

Figure 31–1 Dow Jones Industrial Average, 1986 to 2008 *Source: $INDU (Dow Jones Industrial Average) INDX, May 1, 2009. ©StockCharts.com.*

But now economists began to worry about the chances for deflation, the kind of long-term catastrophic decline in prices that intensified the Great Depression.

Conclusion

Whatever the outcome of the great crisis of 2008, the United States had reached the end of one era and the beginning of another. In the generation from the triumphal end of the cold war to the fearful collapse of the economic boom, the United States had effectively completed its long-term transformation into a globalized, information-based, racially diverse nation. The crisis seemed unlikely to change that basic reality. If anything, the demise or restructuring of old industrial giants such as General Motors would only reinforce the postindustrial identity of the United States.

Much else was already changing. The conservatism that had shaped American politics and government since the age of Ronald Reagan in the 1980s was in retreat. In the midst of the economic meltdown in the fall of 2008, the government and the people had spurned conservative ideology and accepted the kinds of dramatic government intervention reminiscent of the liberal New Deal of the 1930s and Great Society of the 1960s. The American people had turned as well to a president who called for change and embodied the social transformation of a globalized nation.

Much else about America's identity had become uncertain. Amid worldwide economic crisis, the nature of global ties could change. As the United States struggled with declining economic and military power and the war on terror, the nation's relationship to the world was at another crossroads. As Americans grappled with the prospect of economic recession or even depression, their attitude toward social and cultural diversity could change.

And so the American people prepared to move forward. "America, we have come so far. We have seen so much," Obama declared the night of his election. "But there's so much more to do."

Further Readings

Rajiv Chandresekaran, *Imperial Life in the Emerald City: Inside Iraq's Green Zone* (2006). A sensitive study of the U.S. occupation of Iraq in 2003–2004.

Steve Coll, *The Bin Ladens: An Arabian Family in the American Century* (2008). Engaging investigation of the origins of Al Qaeda's leader.

Stephanie Coontz, *The Way We Really Are: Coming to Terms with America's Changing Families* (1997). Details strains on family life.

Alfred A. Eckes Jr. and Thomas W. Zeiler, *Globalization and the American Century* (2003). Places the different aspects of globalization in long-term perspective.

National Commission on Terrorist Attacks Upon the United States, *The 9/11 Commission Report*, "Authorized Edition" (2004). This politically important document gains much of its power from its detailed, evenhanded unraveling of the events leading to the September 11 attack.

Kevin Phillips, *Wealth and Democracy: A Political History of the American Rich* (2002). A political scientist's passionate exploration of economic inequality and its political consequences.

Who, What?

>> Timeline >>

▼ 1987
Intermediate-Range Nuclear Forces Treaty

▼ 1988
George H. W. Bush elected president

▼ 1989
Collapse of Communist regimes in Eastern Europe
Invasion of Panama

▼ 1990
Partial shutdown of federal government

▼ 1991
Persian Gulf War
Collapse of the Soviet Union
Dow Jones Industrial Average over 3,000 for first time

▼ 1992
Los Angeles riot after first Rodney King verdict
U.S. troops sent to Somalia
Bill Clinton elected president

▼ 1993
Terrorist truck bombing of World Trade Center, New York City

Ratification of North American Free Trade Agreement (NAFTA)

▼ 1994
End of "Risk Rule" for women soldiers

▼ 1995
Peace treaty in Bosnia-Herzegovina civil war
Opening of World Trade Organization

▼ 1996
Federal welfare reform
First Wal-Mart in People's Republic of China
Reelection of Bill Clinton as president

Review Questions

1. What set apart the globalization of the 1990s and 2000s from earlier linkages between the United States and the world?

2. What were the main features of the postindustrial political economy? Why were Americans anxious about the economy even though it was relatively strong?

3. Why did conservatives enjoy mixed political success in the 1990s and 2000s?

4. How did the foreign and security policies of the two presidents Bush differ? Which was more successful?

5. Did globalization, the information economy, and struggles for rights make it easier or harder for ordinary Americans to control their lives?

For further review materials and resource information, please visit www.oup.com/us/ofthepeople

---

▼ 1998
Terrorist truck bombings of U.S. embassies in Kenya and Tanzania

▼ 1999
Acquittal of Bill Clinton in Senate impeachment trial
NATO air war against Yugoslavia
Dow Jones Industrial Average over 10,000 for first time

▼ 2000
Terrorist attack on destroyer *Cole*

▼ 2001
George W. Bush declared president
9/11 attacks
Invasion of Afghanistan

▼ 2002
Creation of Department of Homeland Security

▼ 2003
U.S. Supreme Court gay rights ruling, *Lawrence v. Texas*
"Operation Iraqi Freedom," Coalition invasion of Iraq

▼ 2004
George W. Bush reelected

▼ 2007
U.S. military "surge" in Iraq

▼ 2008
Collapse of Doha world trade talks
U.S. financial crisis
Barack Obama elected president

Appendix A

Historical Documents

The Declaration of Independence

When in the course of human events, it becomes necessary for one people to dissolve the political bands which have connected them with another, and to assume, among the powers of the earth, the separate and equal station to which the Laws of Nature and of Nature's God entitle them, a decent respect to the opinions of mankind requires that they should declare the causes which impel them to the separation.

We hold these truths to be self-evident, that all men are created equal, that they are endowed by their Creator with certain unalienable Rights, that among these are life, liberty and the pursuit of happiness. That to secure these rights, governments are instituted among men, deriving their just powers from the consent of the governed; that whenever any form of government becomes destructive of these ends, it is the right of the people to alter or to abolish it, and to institute new Government, laying its foundation on such principles and organizing its powers in such form, as to them shall seem most likely to effect their safety and happiness. Prudence, indeed, will dictate that Governments long established should not be changed for light and transient causes; and, accordingly, all experience hath shown, that mankind are more disposed to suffer, while evils are sufferable, than to right themselves by abolishing the forms to which they are accustomed. But when a long train of abuses and usurpations, pursuing invariably the same object evinces a design to reduce them under absolute despotism, it is their right, it is their duty, to throw off such government, and to provide new guards for their future security. Such has been the patient sufferance of these colonies; and such is now the necessity which constrains them to alter their former systems of government. The history of the present King of Great Britain is a history of repeated injuries and usurpations, all having in direct object the establishment of an absolute tyranny over these States. To prove this, let facts be submitted to a candid world:

He has refused his assent to laws, the most wholesome and necessary for the public good.

He has forbidden his governors to pass laws of immediate and pressing importance, unless suspended in their operation till his assent should be obtained; and, when so suspended, he has utterly neglected to attend to them.

He has refused to pass other laws for the accommodation of large districts of people, unless those people would relinquish the right of representation in the legislature, a right inestimable to them and formidable to tyrants only.

He has called together legislative bodies at places unusual, uncomfortable, and distant from the depository of their public records, for the sole purpose of fatiguing them into compliance with his measures.

He has dissolved representative houses repeatedly, for opposing with manly firmness his invasions on the rights of the people.

He has refused for a long time, after such dissolutions, to cause others to be elected; whereby the legislative powers, incapable of annihilation, have returned to the People at large for their exercise; the State remaining in the mean time exposed to all the dangers of invasion from without, and convulsions within.

He has endeavored to prevent the population of these States; for that purpose obstructing the laws for naturalization of foreigners; refusing to pass others to encourage their migrations hither, and raising the conditions of new appropriations of lands.

He has obstructed the administration of justice, by refusing his assent to laws for establishing judiciary powers.

He has made judges dependent on his will alone, for the tenure of their offices, and the amount and payment of their salaries.

He has erected a multitude of new offices, and sent hither swarms of officers to harass our people, and eat out their substance.

He has kept among us, in times of peace, standing armies without the consent of our legislatures.

He has affected to render the Military independent of, and superior to, the civil power.

He has combined with others to subject us to a jurisdiction foreign to our constitution and unacknowledged by our laws; giving his assent to their acts of pretended legislation:

For quartering large bodies of armed troops among us;

For protecting them, by a mock trial, from punishment for any murders which they should commit on the inhabitants of these States;

For cutting off our trade with all parts of the world;

For imposing taxes on us without our Consent;

For depriving us, in many cases, of the benefits of Trial by Jury;

For transporting us beyond Seas to be tried for pretended offences;

For abolishing the free System of English Laws in a neighbouring Province, establishing therein an Arbitrary government, and enlarging its Boundaries so as to render it at once an example and fit instrument for introducing the same absolute rule into these colonies;

For taking away our charters, abolishing our most valuable laws, and altering fundamentally the forms of our governments;

For suspending our own legislatures, and declaring themselves invested with power to legislate for us in all cases whatsoever.

He has abdicated government here, by declaring us out of his protection and waging war against us.

He has plundered our seas, ravaged our coasts, burnt our towns, and destroyed the lives of our people.

He is at this time transporting large armies of foreign mercenaries to complete the works of death, desolation and tyranny, already begun with circumstances of cruelty and perfidy scarcely paralleled in the most barbarous ages, and totally unworthy the head of a civilized nation.

He has constrained our fellow citizens taken captive on the high seas to bear arms against their country, to become the executioners of their friends and brethren, or to fall themselves by their hands.

He has excited domestic insurrections amongst us, and has endeavored to bring on the inhabitants of our frontiers, the merciless Indian savages, whose known rule of warfare, is an undistinguished destruction of all ages, sexes and conditions.

In every stage of these oppressions we have petitioned for redress in the most humble terms; our repeated petitions have been answered only by repeated injury. A prince whose character is thus marked by every act which may define a tyrant, is unfit to be the ruler of a free people.

Nor have we been wanting in attentions to our British brethren. We have warned them from time to time of attempts by their legislature to extend an unwarrantable jurisdiction over us. We have reminded them of the circumstances of our emigration and settlement here. We have appealed to their native justice and magnanimity, and we have conjured them by the ties of our common kindred to disavow these usurpations, which, would inevitably interrupt our connections and correspondence. They, too, have been deaf to the voice of justice and of consanguinity. We must, therefore, acquiesce in the necessity, which denounces our separation, and hold them, as we hold the rest of mankind, enemies in war, in peace friends.

We, therefore, the representatives of the United States of America, in general Congress, assembled, appealing to the Supreme Judge of the world for the rectitude of our intentions, do, in the name, and by the authority of the good people of these colonies, solemnly publish and declare, that these united colonies are, and of right ought to be free and independent states; that they are absolved from all allegiance to the British Crown, and that all political connection between them and the state of Great Britain, is and ought to be totally dissolved; and that, as free and independent states, they have full power to levy war, conclude peace, contract alliances, establish commerce, and to do all other acts and things which independent states may of right do. And for the support of this declaration, with a firm reliance on the protection of Divine Providence, we mutually pledge to each other our lives, our fortunes and our sacred honor.

The Constitution of the United States of America

We the People of the United States, in Order to form a more perfect Union, establish Justice, insure domestic Tranquility, provide for the common defence, promote the general Welfare, and secure the Blessings of Liberty to ourselves and our Posterity, do ordain and establish this Constitution for the United States of America.

Article I

Section 1

All legislative Powers herein granted shall be vested in a Congress of the United States, which shall consist of a Senate and House of Representatives.

Section 2

The House of Representatives shall be composed of Members chosen every second Year by the People of the several States, and the Electors in each State shall have the Qualifications requisite for Electors of the most numerous Branch of the State Legislature.

No Person shall be a Representative who shall not have attained to the Age of twenty five Years, and been seven Years a Citizen of the United States, and who shall not, when elected, be an Inhabitant of that State in which he shall be chosen.

Representatives and direct Taxes shall be apportioned among the several States which may be included within this Union, according to their respective Numbers, which shall be determined by adding to the whole Number of free Persons, including those bound to Service for a Term of Years, and excluding Indians not taxed, three fifths of all other Persons. The actual Enumeration shall be made within three Years after the first Meeting of the Congress of the United States, and within every subsequent Term of ten Years, in such Manner as they shall by Law direct. The Number of Representatives shall not exceed one for every thirty Thousand, but each State shall have at Least one Representative; and until such enumeration shall be made, the State of New Hampshire shall be entitled to choose three, Massachusetts eight, Rhode-Island and Providence Plantations one, Connecticut five, New York six, New Jersey four, Pennsylvania eight, Delaware one, Maryland six, Virginia ten, North Carolina five, South Carolina five, and Georgia three.

When vacancies happen in the Representation from any State, the Executive Authority thereof shall issue Writs of Election to fill such Vacancies.

The House of Representatives shall choose their Speaker and other Officers; and shall have the sole Power of Impeachment.

Section 3

The Senate of the United States shall be composed of two Senators from each State, chosen by the Legislature thereof for six Years; and each Senator shall have one Vote.

Immediately after they shall be assembled in Consequence of the first Election, they shall be divided as equally as may be into three Classes. The Seats of the Senators of the first Class shall be vacated at the Expiration of the second Year, of the second Class at the Expiration of the fourth Year, and of the third Class at the Expiration of the sixth Year, so that one third may be chosen every second Year; and if Vacancies happen by Resignation, or otherwise, during the Recess of the Legislature of any State, the Executive thereof may make temporary Appointments until the next Meeting of the Legislature, which shall then fill such Vacancies.

No Person shall be a Senator who shall not have attained to the Age of thirty Years, and been nine Years a Citizen of the United States, and who shall not, when elected, be an Inhabitant of that State for which he shall be chosen.

The Vice President of the United States shall be President of the Senate, but shall have no Vote, unless they be equally divided.

The Senate shall choose their other Officers, and also a President pro tempore, in the Absence of the Vice President, or when he shall exercise the Office of President of the United States.

The Senate shall have the sole Power to try all Impeachments. When sitting for that Purpose, they shall be on Oath or Affirmation. When the President of the United States is tried, the Chief Justice shall preside: And no Person shall be convicted without the Concurrence of two thirds of the Members present.

Judgment in Cases of Impeachment shall not extend further than to removal from Office, and disqualification to hold and enjoy any Office of honor, Trust or Profit under the United States: but the Party convicted shall nevertheless be liable and subject to Indictment, Trial, Judgment and Punishment, according to Law.

Section 4

The Times, Places and Manner of holding Elections for Senators and Representatives, shall be prescribed in each State by the Legislature thereof; but the Congress may at any time by Law make or alter such Regulations, except as to the Places of chusing Senators.

The Congress shall assemble at least once in every Year, and such Meeting shall be on the first Monday in December, unless they shall by Law appoint a different Day.

Section 5

Each House shall be the Judge of the Elections, Returns and Qualifications of its own Members, and a Majority of each shall constitute a Quorum to do Business; but a smaller Number may adjourn from day to day, and may be authorized to compel the Attendance of absent Members, in such Manner, and under such Penalties as each House may provide.

Each House may determine the Rules of its Proceedings, punish its Members for disorderly Behaviour, and, with the Concurrence of two thirds, expel a Member.

Each House shall keep a Journal of its Proceedings, and from time to time publish the same, excepting such Parts as may in their Judgment require Secrecy; and the Yeas and Nays of the Members of either House on any question shall, at the Desire of one fifth of those Present, be entered on the Journal.

Neither House, during the Session of Congress, shall, without the Consent of the other, adjourn for more than three days, nor to any other Place than that in which the two Houses shall be sitting.

Section 6

The Senators and Representatives shall receive a Compensation for their Services, to be ascertained by Law, and paid out of the Treasury of the United States. They shall in all Cases, except Treason, Felony and Breach of the Peace, be privileged from Arrest during their Attendance at the Session of their respective Houses, and in going to and returning from the same; and for any Speech or Debate in either House, they shall not be questioned in any other Place.

No Senator or Representative shall, during the Time for which he was elected, be appointed to any civil Office under the Authority of the United States, which shall have been created, or the Emoluments whereof shall have been increased during such time; and no Person holding any Office under the United States, shall be a Member of either House during his Continuance in Office.

Section 7

All Bills for raising Revenue shall originate in the House of Representatives; but the Senate may propose or concur with Amendments as on other Bills.

Every Bill which shall have passed the House of Representatives and the Senate, shall, before it become a Law, be presented to the President of the United States: If he approve he shall sign it, but if not he shall return it, with his Objections to that House in which it shall have originated, who shall enter the Objections at large on their Journal, and proceed to reconsider it. If after such Reconsideration two thirds of that House shall agree to pass the Bill, it shall be sent, together with the Objections, to the other House, by which it shall likewise be reconsidered, and if approved by two thirds of that House, it shall become a Law. But in all such Cases the Votes of both Houses shall be determined by yeas and Nays, and the Names of the Persons voting for and against the Bill shall be entered on the Journal of each House respectively. If any Bill shall not be returned by the President within ten Days (Sundays excepted) after it shall have been presented to him, the Same shall be a Law, in like Manner as if he had signed it, unless the Congress by their Adjournment prevent its Return, in which Case it shall not be a Law.

Every Order, Resolution, or Vote to which the Concurrence of the Senate and House of Representatives may be necessary (except on a question of Adjournment) shall be presented to the President of the United States; and before the Same shall take Effect, shall be approved by him, or being disapproved by him, shall be repassed by two thirds of the Senate and House of Representatives, according to the Rules and Limitations prescribed in the Case of a Bill.

Section 8

The Congress shall have Power

To lay and collect Taxes, Duties, Imposts and Excises, to pay the Debts and provide for the common Defence and general Welfare of the United States; but all Duties, Imposts and Excises shall be uniform throughout the United States;

To borrow Money on the credit of the United States;

To regulate Commerce with foreign Nations, and among the several States, and with the Indian Tribes;

To establish an uniform Rule of Naturalization, and uniform Laws on the subject of Bankruptcies throughout the United States;

To coin Money, regulate the Value thereof, and of foreign Coin, and fix the Standard of Weights and Measures;

To provide for the Punishment of counterfeiting the Securities and current Coin of the United States;

To establish Post Offices and post Roads;

To promote the Progress of Science and useful Arts, by securing for limited Times to Authors and Inventors the exclusive Right to their respective Writings and Discoveries;

To constitute Tribunals inferior to the supreme Court;

To define and punish Piracies and Felonies committed on the high Seas, and Offences against the Law of Nations;

To declare War, grant Letters of Marque and Reprisal, and make Rules concerning Captures on Land and Water;

To raise and support Armies, but no Appropriation of Money to that Use shall be for a longer Term than two Years;

To provide and maintain a Navy;

To make Rules for the Government and Regulation of the land and naval Forces;

To provide for calling forth the Militia to execute the Laws of the Union, suppress Insurrections and repel Invasions;

To provide for organizing, arming, and disciplining the Militia, and for governing such Part of them as may be employed in the Service of the United States, re-

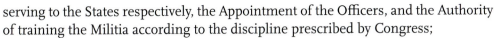

serving to the States respectively, the Appointment of the Officers, and the Authority of training the Militia according to the discipline prescribed by Congress;

To exercise exclusive Legislation in all Cases whatsoever, over such District (not exceeding ten Miles square) as may, by Cession of particular States, and the Acceptance of Congress, become the Seat of the Government of the United States, and to exercise like Authority over all Places purchased by the Consent of the Legislature of the State in which the Same shall be, for the Erection of Forts, Magazines, Arsenals, dock-Yards, and other needful Buildings;—And

To make all Laws which shall be necessary and proper for carrying into Execution the foregoing Powers, and all other Powers vested by this Constitution in the Government of the United States, or in any Department or Officer thereof.

Section 9

The Migration or Importation of such Persons as any of the States now existing shall think proper to admit, shall not be prohibited by the Congress prior to the Year one thousand eight hundred and eight, but a Tax or duty may be imposed on such Importation, not exceeding ten dollars for each Person.

The Privilege of the Writ of Habeas Corpus shall not be suspended, unless when in Cases of Rebellion or Invasion the public Safety may require it.

No Bill of Attainder or ex post facto Law shall be passed.

No Capitation, or other direct, Tax shall be laid, unless in Proportion to the Census or enumeration herein before directed to be taken.

No Tax or Duty shall be laid on Articles exported from any State.

No Preference shall be given by any Regulation of Commerce or Revenue to the Ports of one State over those of another; nor shall Vessels bound to, or from, one State, be obliged to enter, clear, or pay Duties in another.

No Money shall be drawn from the Treasury, but in Consequence of Appropriations made by Law; and a regular Statement and Account of the Receipts and Expenditures of all public Money shall be published from time to time.

No Title of Nobility shall be granted by the United States: And no Person holding any Office of Profit or Trust under them, shall, without the Consent of the Congress, accept of any present, Emolument, Office, or Title, of any kind whatever, from any King, Prince, or foreign State.

Section 10

No State shall enter into any Treaty, Alliance, or Confederation; grant Letters of Marque and Reprisal; coin Money; emit Bills of Credit; make any Thing but gold and silver Coin a Tender in Payment of Debts; pass any Bill of Attainder, ex post facto Law, or Law impairing the Obligation of Contracts, or grant any Title of Nobility.

No State shall, without the Consent of the Congress, lay any Imposts or Duties on Imports or Exports, except what may be absolutely necessary for executing it's inspection Laws: and the net Produce of all Duties and Imposts, laid by any State on Imports or Exports, shall be for the Use of the Treasury of the United States; and all such Laws shall be subject to the Revision and Control of the Congress.

No State shall, without the Consent of Congress, lay any Duty of Tonnage, keep Troops, or Ships of War in time of Peace, enter into any Agreement or Compact with another State, or with a foreign Power, or engage in War, unless actually invaded, or in such imminent Danger as will not admit of delay.

Article II

Section 1

The executive Power shall be vested in a President of the United States of America. He shall hold his Office during the Term of four Years, and, together with the Vice President, chosen for the same Term, be elected, as follows:

Each State shall appoint, in such Manner as the Legislature thereof may direct, a Number of Electors, equal to the whole Number of Senators and Representatives to which the State may be entitled in the Congress: but no Senator or Representative, or Person holding an Office of Trust or Profit under the United States, shall be appointed an Elector.

The Electors shall meet in their respective States, and vote by Ballot for two Persons, of whom one at least shall not be an Inhabitant of the same State with themselves. And they shall make a List of all the Persons voted for, and of the Number of Votes for each; which List they shall sign and certify, and transmit sealed to the Seat of the Government of the United States, directed to the President of the Senate. The President of the Senate shall, in the Presence of the Senate and House of Representatives, open all the Certificates, and the Votes shall then be counted. The Person having the greatest Number of Votes shall be the President, if such Number be a Majority of the whole Number of Electors appointed; and if there be more than one who have such Majority, and have an equal Number of Votes, then the House of Representatives shall immediately choose by Ballot one of them for President; and if no Person have a Majority, then from the five highest on the List the said House shall in like Manner choose the President. But in choosing the President, the Votes shall be taken by States, the Representation from each State having one Vote; A quorum for this purpose shall consist of a Member or Members from two thirds of the States, and a Majority of all the States shall be necessary to a Choice. In every Case, after the Choice of the President, the Person having the greatest Number of Votes of the Electors shall be the Vice President. But if there should remain two or more who have equal Votes, the Senate shall choose from them by Ballot the Vice President.

The Congress may determine the Time of choosing the Electors, and the Day on which they shall give their Votes; which Day shall be the same throughout the United States.

No Person except a natural born Citizen, or a Citizen of the United States, at the time of the Adoption of this Constitution, shall be eligible to the Office of President; neither shall any Person be eligible to that Office who shall not have attained to the Age of thirty five Years, and been fourteen Years a Resident within the United States.

In Case of the Removal of the President from Office, or of his Death, Resignation, or Inability to discharge the Powers and Duties of the said Office, the Same shall devolve on the Vice President, and the Congress may by Law provide for the Case of Removal, Death, Resignation or Inability, both of the President and Vice President, declaring what Officer shall then act as President, and such Officer shall act accordingly, until the Disability be removed, or a President shall be elected.

The President shall, at stated Times, receive for his Services, a Compensation, which shall neither be increased nor diminished during the Period for which he shall have been elected, and he shall not receive within that Period any other Emolument from the United States, or any of them.

Before he enter on the Execution of his Office, he shall take the following Oath or Affirmation:—"I do solemnly swear (or affirm) that I will faithfully execute the Office of President of the United States, and will to the best of my Ability, preserve, protect and defend the Constitution of the United States."

Section 2

The President shall be Commander in Chief of the Army and Navy of the United States, and of the Militia of the several States, when called into the actual Service of the United States; he may require the Opinion, in writing, of the principal Officer in each of the executive Departments, upon any Subject relating to the Duties of their respective Offices, and he shall have Power to grant Reprieves and Pardons for Offences against the United States, except in Cases of Impeachment.

He shall have Power, by and with the Advice and Consent of the Senate, to make Treaties, provided two thirds of the Senators present concur; and he shall nominate, and by and with the Advice and Consent of the Senate, shall appoint Ambassadors, other public Ministers and Consuls, Judges of the supreme Court, and all other Officers of the United States, whose Appointments are not herein otherwise provided for, and which shall be established by Law: but the Congress may by Law vest the Appointment of such inferior Officers, as they think proper, in the President alone, in the Courts of Law, or in the Heads of Departments.

The President shall have Power to fill up all Vacancies that may happen during the Recess of the Senate, by granting Commissions which shall expire at the End of their next Session.

Section 3

He shall from time to time give to the Congress Information of the State of the Union, and recommend to their Consideration such Measures as he shall judge necessary and expedient; he may, on extraordinary Occasions, convene both Houses, or either of them, and in Case of Disagreement between them, with Respect to the Time of Adjournment, he may adjourn them to such Time as he shall think proper; he shall receive Ambassadors and other public Ministers; he shall take Care that the Laws be faithfully executed, and shall Commission all the Officers of the United States.

Section 4

The President, Vice President and all civil Officers of the United States, shall be removed from Office on Impeachment for, and Conviction of, Treason, Bribery, or other high Crimes and Misdemeanors.

Article III

Section 1

The judicial Power of the United States shall be vested in one supreme Court, and in such inferior Courts as the Congress may from time to time ordain and establish. The Judges, both of the supreme and inferior Courts, shall hold their Offices during good Behaviour, and shall, at stated Times, receive for their Services a Compensation, which shall not be diminished during their Continuance in Office.

Section 2

The judicial Power shall extend to all Cases, in Law and Equity, arising under this Constitution, the Laws of the United States, and Treaties made, or which shall be made, under their Authority;—to all Cases affecting Ambassadors, other public Ministers and Consuls;—to all Cases of admiralty and maritime Jurisdiction;—to Controversies to which the United States shall be a Party;—to Controversies between two or more States;—between a State and Citizens of another State;—between Citizens of different States;—between Citizens of the same State claiming Lands under Grants of different States, and between a State, or the Citizens thereof, and foreign States, Citizens or Subjects.

In all Cases affecting Ambassadors, other public Ministers and Consuls, and those in which a State shall be Party, the supreme Court shall have original Jurisdiction. In all the other Cases before mentioned, the supreme Court shall have appellate Jurisdiction, both as to Law and Fact, with such Exceptions, and under such Regulations as the Congress shall make.

The Trial of all Crimes, except in Cases of Impeachment, shall be by Jury; and such Trial shall be held in the State where the said Crimes shall have been committed; but when not committed within any State, the Trial shall be at such Place or Places as the Congress may by Law have directed.

Section 3

Treason against the United States, shall consist only in levying War against them, or in adhering to their Enemies, giving them Aid and Comfort. No Person shall be convicted of Treason unless on the Testimony of two Witnesses to the same overt Act, or on Confession in open Court.

The Congress shall have Power to declare the Punishment of Treason, but no Attainder of Treason shall work Corruption of Blood, or Forfeiture except during the Life of the Person attainted.

Article IV

Section 1

Full Faith and Credit shall be given in each State to the public Acts, Records, and judicial Proceedings of every other State. And the Congress may by general Laws prescribe the Manner in which such Acts, Records and Proceedings shall be proved, and the Effect thereof.

Section 2

The Citizens of each State shall be entitled to all Privileges and Immunities of Citizens in the several States.

A Person charged in any State with Treason, Felony, or other Crime, who shall flee from Justice, and be found in another State, shall on Demand of the executive Authority of the State from which he fled, be delivered up, to be removed to the State having Jurisdiction of the Crime.

No Person held to Service or Labour in one State, under the Laws thereof, escaping into another, shall, in Consequence of any Law or Regulation therein, be discharged from such Service or Labour, but shall be delivered up on Claim of the Party to whom such Service or Labour may be due.

Section 3

New States may be admitted by the Congress into this Union; but no new State shall be formed or erected within the Jurisdiction of any other State; nor any State be formed by the Junction of two or more States, or Parts of States, without the Consent of the Legislatures of the States concerned as well as of the Congress.

The Congress shall have Power to dispose of and make all needful Rules and Regulations respecting the Territory or other Property belonging to the United States; and nothing in this Constitution shall be so construed as to Prejudice any Claims of the United States, or of any particular State.

Section 4

The United States shall guarantee to every State in this Union a Republican Form of Government, and shall protect each of them against Invasion; and on Application of the Legislature, or of the Executive (when the Legislature cannot be convened), against domestic Violence.

Article V

The Congress, whenever two thirds of both Houses shall deem it necessary, shall propose Amendments to this Constitution, or, on the Application of the Legislatures of two thirds of the several States, shall call a Convention for proposing Amendments, which, in either Case, shall be valid to all Intents and Purposes, as Part of this Constitution, when ratified by the Legislatures of three fourths of the several States, or by Conventions in three fourths thereof, as the one or the other Mode of Ratification may be proposed by the Congress; Provided that no Amendment which may be made prior to the Year One thousand eight hundred and eight shall in any Manner affect the first and fourth Clauses in the Ninth Section of the first Article; and that no State, without its Consent, shall be deprived of its equal Suffrage in the Senate.

Article VI

All Debts contracted and Engagements entered into, before the Adoption of this Constitution, shall be as valid against the United States under this Constitution, as under the Confederation.

This Constitution, and the Laws of the United States which shall be made in Pursuance thereof; and all Treaties made, or which shall be made, under the Authority of the United States, shall be the supreme Law of the Land; and the Judges in every State shall be bound thereby, any Thing in the Constitution or Laws of any State to the Contrary notwithstanding.

The Senators and Representatives before mentioned, and the Members of the several State Legislatures, and all executive and judicial Officers, both of the United States and of the several States, shall be bound by Oath or Affirmation, to support this Constitution; but no religious Test shall ever be required as a Qualification to any Office or public Trust under the United States.

Article VII

The Ratification of the Conventions of nine States, shall be sufficient for the Establishment of this Constitution between the States so ratifying the Same.

The Word, "the," being interlined between the seventh and eighth Lines of the first Page, the Word "Thirty" being partly written on an Erazure in the fifteenth Line of the first Page, The Words "is tried" being interlined between the thirty second and thirty third Lines of the first Page and the Word "the" being interlined between the forty third and forty fourth Lines of the second Page.

Attest William Jackson Secretary

Done in Convention by the Unanimous Consent of the States present the Seventeenth Day of September in the Year of our Lord one thousand seven hundred and Eighty seven and of the Independence of the United States of America the Twelfth In witness whereof We have hereunto subscribed our Names,

G°. Washington
Presidt and deputy from Virginia

Delaware
Geo: Read
Gunning Bedford jun
John Dickinson
Richard Bassett
Jaco: Broom

Maryland
James McHenry
Dan of St Thos. Jenifer
Danl. Carroll

Virginia
John Blair
James Madison Jr.

North Carolina
Wm. Blount
Richd. Dobbs Spaight
Hu Williamson

South Carolina
J. Rutledge
Charles Cotesworth Pinckney
Charles Pinckney
Pierce Butler

Georgia
William Few
Abr Baldwin

New Hampshire
John Langdon
Nicholas Gilman

Massachusetts
Nathaniel Gorham
Rufus King

Connecticut
Wm. Saml. Johnson
Roger Sherman

New York
Alexander Hamilton

New Jersey
Wil: Livingston
David Brearley
Wm. Paterson
Jona: Dayton

Pennsylvania
B Franklin
Thomas Mifflin
Robt. Morris
Geo. Clymer
Thos. FitzSimons
Jared Ingersoll
James Wilson
Gouv Morris

Articles

In addition to, and Amendment of the Constitution of the United States of America, proposed by Congress, and ratified by the Legislatures of the several States, pursuant to the fifth Article of the original Constitution.

(The first ten amendments to the U.S. Constitution were ratified December 15, 1791, and form what is known as the "Bill of Rights.")

AMENDMENT I

Congress shall make no law respecting an establishment of religion, or prohibiting the free exercise thereof; or abridging the freedom of speech, or of the press; or the right of the people peaceably to assemble, and to petition the Government for a redress of grievances.

AMENDMENT II
A well regulated Militia, being necessary to the security of a free State, the right of the people to keep and bear Arms, shall not be infringed.

AMENDMENT III
No Soldier shall, in time of peace be quartered in any house, without the consent of the Owner, nor in time of war, but in a manner to be prescribed by law.

AMENDMENT IV
The right of the people to be secure in their persons, houses, papers, and effects, against unreasonable searches and seizures, shall not be violated, and no Warrants shall issue, but upon probable cause, supported by Oath or affirmation, and particularly describing the place to be searched, and the persons or things to be seized.

AMENDMENT V
No person shall be held to answer for a capital, or otherwise infamous crime, unless on a presentment or indictment of a Grand Jury, except in cases arising in the land or naval forces, or in the Militia, when in actual service in time of War or public danger; nor shall any person be subject for the same offence to be twice put in jeopardy of life or limb; nor shall be compelled in any criminal case to be a witness against himself, nor be deprived of life, liberty, or property, without due process of law; nor shall private property be taken for public use, without just compensation.

AMENDMENT VI
In all criminal prosecutions, the accused shall enjoy the right to a speedy and public trial, by an impartial jury of the State and district wherein the crime shall have been committed, which district shall have been previously ascertained by law, and to be informed of the nature and cause of the accusation; to be confronted with the witnesses against him; to have compulsory process for obtaining witnesses in his favor, and to have the Assistance of Counsel for his defence.

AMENDMENT VII
In Suits at common law, where the value in controversy shall exceed twenty dollars, the right of trial by jury shall be preserved, and no fact tried by a jury, shall be otherwise re-examined in any Court of the United States, than according to the rules of the common law.

AMENDMENT VIII
Excessive bail shall not be required, nor excessive fines imposed, nor cruel and unusual punishments inflicted.

AMENDMENT IX
The enumeration in the Constitution, of certain rights, shall not be construed to deny or disparage others retained by the people.

AMENDMENT X
The powers not delegated to the United States by the Constitution, nor prohibited by it to the States, are reserved to the States respectively, or to the people.

AMENDMENT XI

Passed by Congress March 4, 1794. Ratified February 7, 1795.

Note: Article III, Section 2, of the Constitution was modified by Amendment XI.

The Judicial power of the United States shall not be construed to extend to any suit in law or equity, commenced or prosecuted against one of the United States by Citizens of another State, or by Citizens or Subjects of any Foreign State.

AMENDMENT XII

Passed by Congress December 9, 1803. Ratified June 15, 1804.

Note: A portion of Article II, Section 1, of the Constitution was superceded by the Twelfth Amendment.

The Electors shall meet in their respective states and vote by ballot for President and Vice-President, one of whom, at least, shall not be an inhabitant of the same state with themselves; they shall name in their ballots the person voted for as President, and in distinct ballots the person voted for as Vice-President, and they shall make distinct lists of all persons voted for as President, and of all persons voted for as Vice-President, and of the number of votes for each, which lists they shall sign and certify, and transmit sealed to the seat of the government of the United States, directed to the President of the Senate;—the President of the Senate shall, in the presence of the Senate and House of Representatives, open all the certificates and the votes shall then be counted;—The person having the greatest number of votes for President, shall be the President, if such number be a majority of the whole number of Electors appointed; and if no person have such majority, then from the persons having the highest numbers not exceeding three on the list of those voted for as President, the House of Representatives shall choose immediately, by ballot, the President. But in choosing the President, the votes shall be taken by states, the representation from each state having one vote; a quorum for this purpose shall consist of a member or members from two-thirds of the states, and a majority of all the states shall be necessary to a choice. [And if the House of Representatives shall not choose a President whenever the right of choice shall devolve upon them, before the fourth day of March next following, then the Vice-President shall act as President, as in case of the death or other constitutional disability of the President.—]* The person having the greatest number of votes as Vice-President, shall be the Vice-President, if such number be a majority of the whole number of Electors appointed, and if no person have a majority, then from the two highest numbers on the list, the Senate shall choose the Vice-President; a quorum for the purpose shall consist of two-thirds of the whole number of Senators, and a majority of the whole number shall be necessary to a choice. But no person constitutionally ineligible to the office of President shall be eligible to that of Vice-President of the United States.

*Superceded by Section 3 of the Twentieth Amendment.

AMENDMENT XIII

Passed by Congress January 31, 1865. Ratified December 6, 1865.

Note: A portion of Article IV, Section 2, of the Constitution was superceded by the Thirteenth Amendment.

Section 1.

Neither slavery nor involuntary servitude, except as a punishment for crime whereof the party shall have been duly convicted, shall exist within the United States, or any place subject to their jurisdiction.

Section 2.

Congress shall have power to enforce this article by appropriate legislation.

AMENDMENT XIV
Passed by Congress June 13, 1866. Ratified July 9, 1868.

Note: Article I, Section 2, of the Constitution was modified by Section 2 of the Fourteenth Amendment.

Section 1

All persons born or naturalized in the United States, and subject to the jurisdiction thereof, are citizens of the United States and of the State wherein they reside. No State shall make or enforce any law which shall abridge the privileges or immunities of citizens of the United States; nor shall any State deprive any person of life, liberty, or property, without due process of law; nor deny to any person within its jurisdiction the equal protection of the laws.

Section 2

Representatives shall be apportioned among the several States according to their respective numbers, counting the whole number of persons in each State, excluding Indians not taxed. But when the right to vote at any election for the choice of electors for President and Vice-President of the United States, Representatives in Congress, the Executive and Judicial officers of a State, or the members of the Legislature thereof, is denied to any of the male inhabitants of such State, being twenty-one years of age,* and citizens of the United States, or in any way abridged, except for participation in rebellion, or other crime, the basis of representation therein shall be reduced in the proportion which the number of such male citizens shall bear to the whole number of male citizens twenty-one years of age in such State.

Section 3

No person shall be a Senator or Representative in Congress, or elector of President and Vice-President, or hold any office, civil or military, under the United States, or under any State, who, having previously taken an oath, as a member of Congress, or as an officer of the United States, or as a member of any State legislature, or as an executive or judicial officer of any State, to support the Constitution of the United States, shall have engaged in insurrection or rebellion against the same, or given aid or comfort to the enemies thereof. But Congress may by a vote of two-thirds of each House, remove such disability.

Section 4

The validity of the public debt of the United States, authorized by law, including debts incurred for payment of pensions and bounties for services in suppressing insurrection or rebellion, shall not be questioned. But neither the United States nor any State shall assume or pay any debt or obligation incurred in aid of insurrection or rebellion against the United States, or any claim for the loss or emancipation of any slave; but all such debts, obligations and claims shall be held illegal and void.

Section 5

The Congress shall have the power to enforce, by appropriate legislation, the provisions of this article.

*Changed by Section 1 of the Twenty-sixth Amendment.

AMENDMENT XV
Passed by Congress February 26, 1869. Ratified February 3, 1870.

Section 1.

The right of citizens of the United States to vote shall not be denied or abridged by the United States or by any State on account of race, color, or previous condition of servitude.

Section 2

The Congress shall have the power to enforce this article by appropriate legislation.

AMENDMENT XVI
Passed by Congress July 2, 1909. Ratified February 3, 1913.

Note: Article I, Section 9, of the Constitution was modified by Amendment XVI.

The Congress shall have power to lay and collect taxes on incomes, from whatever source derived, without apportionment among the several States, and without regard to any census or enumeration.

AMENDMENT XVII
Passed by Congress May 13, 1912. Ratified April 8, 1913.

Note: Article I, Section 3, of the Constitution was modified by the Seventeenth Amendment.

The Senate of the United States shall be composed of two Senators from each State, elected by the people thereof, for six years; and each Senator shall have one vote. The electors in each State shall have the qualifications requisite for electors of the most numerous branch of the State legislatures.

When vacancies happen in the representation of any State in the Senate, the executive authority of such State shall issue writs of election to fill such vacancies: *Provided,* That the legislature of any State may empower the executive thereof to make temporary appointments until the people fill the vacancies by election as the legislature may direct.

This amendment shall not be so construed as to affect the election or term of any Senator chosen before it becomes valid as part of the Constitution.

AMENDMENT XVIII
Passed by Congress December 18, 1917. Ratified January 16, 1919. Repealed by Amendment XXI.

Section 1

After one year from the ratification of this article the manufacture, sale, or transportation of intoxicating liquors within, the importation thereof into, or the exportation thereof from the United States and all territory subject to the jurisdiction thereof for beverage purposes is hereby prohibited.

Section 2

The Congress and the several States shall have concurrent power to enforce this article by appropriate legislation.

Section 3

This article shall be inoperative unless it shall have been ratified as an amendment to the Constitution by the legislatures of the several States, as provided in the Constitution, within seven years from the date of the submission hereof to the States by the Congress.

AMENDMENT XIX
Passed by Congress June 4, 1919. Ratified August 18, 1920.

The right of citizens of the United States to vote shall not be denied or abridged by the United States or by any State on account of sex.

Congress shall have power to enforce this article by appropriate legislation.

AMENDMENT XX
Passed by Congress March 2, 1932. Ratified January 23, 1933.

Note: Article I, Section 4, of the Constitution was modified by Section 2 of this amendment. In addition, a portion of the Twelfth Amendment was superceded by Section 3.

Section 1

The terms of the President and the Vice President shall end at noon on the 20th day of January, and the terms of Senators and Representatives at noon on the 3d day of January, of the years in which such terms would have ended if this article had not been ratified; and the terms of their successors shall then begin.

Section 2

The Congress shall assemble at least once in every year, and such meeting shall begin at noon on the 3d day of January, unless they shall by law appoint a different day.

Section 3

If, at the time fixed for the beginning of the term of the President, the President elect shall have died, the Vice President elect shall become President. If a President shall not have been chosen before the time fixed for the beginning of his term, or if the President elect shall have failed to qualify, then the Vice President elect shall act as President until a President shall have qualified; and the Congress may by law provide for the case wherein neither a President elect nor a Vice President shall have qualified, declaring who shall then act as President, or the manner in which one who is to act shall be selected, and such person shall act accordingly until a President or Vice President shall have qualified.

Section 4

The Congress may by law provide for the case of the death of any of the persons from whom the House of Representatives may choose a President whenever the right of choice shall have devolved upon them, and for the case of the death of any of the persons from whom the Senate may choose a Vice President whenever the right of choice shall have devolved upon them.

Section 5

Sections 1 and 2 shall take effect on the 15th day of October following the ratification of this article.

Section 6

This article shall be inoperative unless it shall have been ratified as an amendment to the Constitution by the legislatures of three-fourths of the several States within seven years from the date of its submission.

AMENDMENT XXI
Passed by Congress February 20, 1933. Ratified December 5, 1933.

Section 1

The eighteenth article of amendment to the Constitution of the United States is hereby repealed.

Section 2

The transportation or importation into any State, Territory, or Possession of the United States for delivery or use therein of intoxicating liquors, in violation of the laws thereof, is hereby prohibited.

Section 3

This article shall be inoperative unless it shall have been ratified as an amendment to the Constitution by conventions in the several States, as provided in the Constitution, within seven years from the date of the submission hereof to the States by the Congress.

AMENDMENT XXII
Passed by Congress March 21, 1947. Ratified February 27, 1951.

Section 1

No person shall be elected to the office of the President more than twice, and no person who has held the office of President, or acted as President, for more than two years of a term to which some other person was elected President shall be elected to the office of President more than once. But this Article shall not apply to any person holding the office of President when this Article was proposed by Congress, and shall not prevent any person who may be holding the office of President, or acting as President, during the term within which this Article becomes operative from holding the office of President or acting as President during the remainder of such term.

Section 2

This article shall be inoperative unless it shall have been ratified as an amendment to the Constitution by the legislatures of three-fourths of the several States within seven years from the date of its submission to the States by the Congress.

AMENDMENT XXIII
Passed by Congress June 16, 1960. Ratified March 29, 1961.

Section 1

The District constituting the seat of Government of the United States shall appoint in such manner as Congress may direct:

A number of electors of President and Vice President equal to the whole number of Senators and Representatives in Congress to which the District would be entitled if it were a State, but in no event more than the least populous State; they shall be in addition to those appointed by the States, but they shall be considered, for the purposes of the election of President and Vice President, to be electors appointed by a State; and they shall meet in the District and perform such duties as provided by the twelfth article of amendment.

Section 2

The Congress shall have power to enforce this article by appropriate legislation.

AMENDMENT XXIV
Passed by Congress August 27, 1962. Ratified January 23, 1964.

Section 1

The right of citizens of the United States to vote in any primary or other election for President or Vice President, for electors for President or Vice President, or for Senator or Representative in Congress, shall not be denied or abridged by the United States or any State by reason of failure to pay poll tax or other tax.

Section 2

The Congress shall have power to enforce this article by appropriate legislation.

AMENDMENT XXV
Passed by Congress July 6, 1965. Ratified February 10, 1967.

Note: Article II, Section 1, of the Constitution was affected by the Twenty-fifth Amendment.

Section 1

In case of the removal of the President from office or of his death or resignation, the Vice President shall become President.

Section 2

Whenever there is a vacancy in the office of the Vice President, the President shall nominate a Vice President who shall take office upon confirmation by a majority vote of both Houses of Congress.

Section 3

Whenever the President transmits to the President pro tempore of the Senate and the Speaker of the House of Representatives his written declaration that he is unable to discharge the powers and duties of his office, and until he transmits to them a written declaration to the contrary, such powers and duties shall be discharged by the Vice President as Acting President.

Section 4

Whenever the Vice President and a majority of either the principal officers of the executive departments or of such other body as Congress may by law provide, transmit to the President pro tempore of the Senate and the Speaker of the House of Representatives their written declaration that the President is unable to discharge the powers and duties of his office, the Vice President shall immediately assume the powers and duties of the office as Acting President.

Thereafter, when the President transmits to the President pro tempore of the Senate and the Speaker of the House of Representatives his written declaration that no inability exists, he shall resume the powers and duties of his office unless the Vice President and a majority of either the principal officers of the executive department or of such other body as Congress may by law provide, transmit within four days to the President pro tempore of the Senate and the Speaker of the House of Representatives their written declaration that the President is unable to discharge the powers and duties of his office. Thereupon Congress shall decide the issue, assembling within forty-eight hours for that purpose if not in session. If the Congress, within twenty-one days after receipt of the latter written declaration, or, if Congress is not in session, within twenty-one days after Congress is required to assemble, determines by two-thirds vote of both Houses that the President is unable to discharge the powers and duties of his office, the Vice President shall continue to discharge the same as Acting President; otherwise, the President shall resume the powers and duties of his office.

AMENDMENT XXVI
Passed by Congress March 23, 1971. Ratified July 1, 1971.

Note: Amendment XIV, Section 2, of the Constitution was modified by Section 1 of the Twenty-sixth Amendment.

Section 1

The right of citizens of the United States, who are eighteen years of age or older, to vote shall not be denied or abridged by the United States or by any State on account of age.

Section 2

The Congress shall have power to enforce this article by appropriate legislation.

AMENDMENT XXVII
Originally proposed Sept. 25, 1789. Ratified May 7, 1992.

No law, varying the compensation for the services of the Senators and Representatives, shall take effect, until an election of representatives shall have intervened.

Lincoln's Gettysburg Address

Four score and seven years ago our fathers brought forth on this continent, a new nation, conceived in Liberty, and dedicated to the proposition that all men are created equal.

Now we are engaged in a great civil war, testing whether that nation, or any nation so conceived and so dedicated, can long endure. We are met on a great battlefield of that war. We have come to dedicate a portion of that field, as a final resting place for those who here gave their lives that that nation might live. It is altogether fitting and proper that we should do this.

But, in a larger sense, we can not dedicate—we can not consecrate—we can not hallow—this ground. The brave men, living and dead, who struggled here, have consecrated it, far above our poor power to add or detract. The world will little note, nor long remember what we say here, but it can never forget what they did here. It is for us the living, rather, to be dedicated here to the unfinished work which they who fought here have thus far so nobly advanced. It is rather for us to be here dedicated to the great task remaining before us—that from these honored dead we take increased devotion to that cause for which they gave the last full measure of devotion—that we here highly resolve that these dead shall not have died in vain—that this nation, under God, shall have a new birth of freedom—and that government of the people, by the people, for the people, shall not perish from the earth.

Appendix B

Historical Facts and Data

U.S. Presidents and Vice Presidents

 Table App B–1 Presidents and Vice Presidents

	President	Vice President	Political Party	Term
1	George Washington	John Adams	No Party Designation	1789–1797
2	John Adams	Thomas Jefferson	Federalist	1797–1801
3	Thomas Jefferson	Aaron Burr George Clinton	Democratic Republican	1801–1809
4	James Madison	George Clinton Elbridge Gerry	Democratic Republican	1809–1817
5	James Monroe	Daniel D. Tompkins	Democratic Republican	1817–1825
6	John Quincy Adams	John C. Calhoun	Democratic Republican	1825–1829
7	Andrew Jackson	John C. Calhoun Martin Van Buren	Democratic	1829–1837
8	Martin Van Buren	Richard M. Johnson	Democratic	1837–1841
9	William Henry Harrison	John Tyler	Whig	1841
10	John Tyler	None	Whig	1841–1845
11	James Knox Polk	George M. Dallas	Democratic	1845–1849
12	Zachary Taylor	Millard Fillmore	Whig	1849–1850
13	Millard Fillmore	None	Whig	1850–1853
14	Franklin Pierce	William R. King	Democratic	1853–1857
15	James Buchanan	John C. Breckinridge	Democratic	1857–1861
16	Abraham Lincoln	Hannibal Hamlin Andrew Johnson	Union	1861–1865
17	Andrew Johnson	None	Union	1865–1869
18	Ulysses Simpson Grant	Schuyler Colfax Henry Wilson	Republican	1869–1877
19	Rutherford Birchard Hayes	William A. Wheeler	Republican	1877–1881
20	James Abram Garfield	Chester Alan Arthur	Republican	1881
21	Chester Alan Arthur	None	Republican	1881–1885
22	Stephen Grover Cleveland	Thomas Hendricks	Democratic	1885–1889
23	Benjamin Harrison	Levi P. Morton	Republican	1889–1893
24	Stephen Grover Cleveland	Adlai E. Stevenson	Democratic	1893–1897
25	William McKinley	Garret A. Hobart Theodore Roosevelt	Republican	1897–1901
26	Theodore Roosevelt	Charles W. Fairbanks	Republican	1901–1909
27	William Howard Taft	James S. Sherman	Republican	1909–1913
28	Woodrow Wilson	Thomas R. Marshall	Democratic	1913–1921

continued

Table App B–1 Presidents and Vice Presidents (cont.)

	President	Vice President	Political Party	Term
29	Warren Gamaliel Harding	Calvin Coolidge	Republican	1921–1923
30	Calvin Coolidge	Charles G. Dawes	Republican	1923–1929
31	Herbert Clark Hoover	Charles Curtis	Republican	1929–1933
32	Franklin Delano Roosevelt	John Nance Garner Henry A. Wallace Harry S. Truman	Democratic	1933–1945
33	Harry S. Truman	Alben W. Barkley	Democratic	1945–1953
34	Dwight David Eisenhower	Richard Milhous Nixon	Republican	1953–1961
35	John Fitzgerald Kennedy	Lyndon Baines Johnson	Democratic	1961–1963
36	Lyndon Baines Johnson	Hubert Horatio Humphrey	Democratic	1963–1969
37	Richard Milhous Nixon	Spiro T. Agnew Gerald Rudolph Ford	Republican	1969–1974
38	Gerald Rudolph Ford	Nelson Rockefeller	Republican	1974–1977
39	James Earl Carter Jr.	Walter Mondale	Democratic	1977–1981
40	Ronald Wilson Reagan	George Herbert Walker Bush	Republican	1981–1989
41	George Herbert Walker Bush	J. Danforth Quayle	Republican	1989–1993
42	William Jefferson Clinton	Albert Gore Jr.	Democratic	1993–2001
43	George Walker Bush	Richard Cheney	Republican	2001–2008
44	Barack Hussein Obama	Joseph Biden	Democratic	2008–

Admission of States into the Union

 Table App B–2 Admission of States into the Union

	State	Date of Admission		State	Date of Admission
1	Delaware	December 7, 1787	26	Michigan	January 26, 1837
2	Pennsylvania	December 12, 1787	27	Florida	March 3, 1845
3	New Jersey	December 18, 1787	28	Texas	December 29, 1845
4	Georgia	January 2, 1788	29	Iowa	December 28, 1846
5	Connecticut	January 9, 1788	30	Wisconsin	May 29, 1848
6	Massachusetts	February 6, 1788	31	California	September 9, 1850
7	Maryland	April 28, 1788	32	Minnesota	May 11, 1858
8	South Carolina	May 23, 1788	33	Oregon	February 14, 1859
9	New Hampshire	June 21, 1788	34	Kansas	January 29, 1861
10	Virginia	June 25, 1788	35	West Virginia	June 20, 1863
11	New York	July 26, 1788	36	Nevada	October 31, 1864
12	North Carolina	November 21, 1789	37	Nebraska	March 1, 1867
13	Rhode Island	May 29, 1790	38	Colorado	August 1, 1876
14	Vermont	March 4, 1791	39	North Dakota	November 2, 1889
15	Kentucky	June 1, 1792	40	South Dakota	November 2, 1889
16	Tennessee	June 1, 1796	41	Montana	November 8, 1889
17	Ohio	March 1, 1803	42	Washington	November 11, 1889
18	Louisiana	April 30, 1812	43	Idaho	July 3, 1890
19	Indiana	December 11, 1816	44	Wyoming	July 10, 1890
20	Mississippi	December 10, 1817	45	Utah	January 4, 1896
21	Illinois	December 3, 1818	46	Oklahoma	November 16, 1907
22	Alabama	December 14, 1819	47	New Mexico	January 6, 1912
23	Maine	March 15, 1820	48	Arizona	February 14, 1912
24	Missouri	August 10, 1821	49	Alaska	January 3, 1959
25	Arkansas	June 15, 1836	50	Hawaii	August 21, 1959

Glossary

Antinomianism   The belief that moral law was not binding on true Christians. The opposite of Arminianism, antinomianism held that good works would not count in the afterlife. Justification, or entrance to heaven, was by faith alone. See Calvinism.

Arminianism   Religious doctrine developed by the Dutch theologian Jacobus Arminius that argued that men and women had free will and suggested that hence they would earn their way into heaven by good works.

Armistice   A cessation of hostilities by agreement among the opposing sides; a cease-fire.

Associationalism   President Herbert Hoover's preferred method of responding to the Depression. Rather than have the government directly involve itself in the economy, Hoover hoped to use the government to encourage associations of businessmen to cooperate voluntarily to meet the crisis.

Autarky   At the height of the world depression, industrial powers sought to isolate their economies within self-contained spheres, generally governed by national (or imperial) economic planning. Japan's Co-Prosperity Sphere, the Soviet Union, and the British Empire each comprised a more or less closed economic unit.

Benevolent Empire   The loosely affiliated network of charitable reform associations that emerged (especially in urban areas) in response to the widespread revivalism of the early nineteenth century.

Berdache   In Indian societies, a man who dressed and adopted the mannerisms of women and had sex only with other men. In Native American culture, the *berdache,* half man and half woman, symbolized cosmic harmony.

Budget deficit   The failure of tax revenues to pay for annual federal spending on military, welfare, and other programs. The resulting budget deficits forced Washington to borrow money to cover its costs. The growing budget deficits were controversial, in part because the government's borrowing increased both its long-term debt and the amount of money it had to spend each year to pay for the interest on loans.

Busing   The controversial court-ordered practice of sending children by bus to public schools outside their neighborhoods in order to promote racial integration in the schools.

Calvinism   Religious doctrine developed by the theologian John Calvin that argued that God alone determines who will receive salvation and, hence, men and women cannot earn their own salvation or even be certain about their final destinies.

Carpetbagger   A derogatory term referring to northern whites who moved to the South after the Civil War. Stereotyped as corrupt and unprincipled, "carpetbaggers" were in fact a diverse group motivated by a variety of interests and beliefs.

Charter colony   Settlement established by a trading company or other group of private entrepreneurs who received from the king a grant of land and the right to govern it. The charter colonies included Virginia, Plymouth, Massachusetts Bay, Rhode Island, and Connecticut.

City busting   As late as the 1930s, President Roosevelt and most Americans regarded attacking civilians from the air as an atrocity, but during World War II cities became a primary target for U.S. warplanes. The inaccuracy of bombing, combined with racism and the belief that Japanese and German actions justified retaliation, led American air commanders to follow a policy of systematically destroying urban areas, particularly in Japan.

Communist   Member of the Communist Party or follower of the doctrines of Karl Marx. The term (or accusation) was applied more broadly in the twentieth century to brand labor unionists, progressives, civil rights workers, and other reformers as agents of a foreign ideology.

Communitarians   Individuals who supported and/or took up residence in separate communities created to embody improved plans of social, religious, and/or economic life.

Commutation   The controversial policy of allowing potential draftees to pay for a replacement to serve in the army. The policy was adopted by both the Union and Confederate governments during the Civil War, and in both cases opposition to commutation was so intense that the policy was abandoned.

Consent   One of the key principles of liberalism, which held that people could not be subject to laws to which they had not given their consent. This principle is reflected in both the Declaration of Independence and the preamble to the Constitution, which begins with the famous words "We the people of the United States, in order to form a more perfect union."

Constitutionalism   A loose body of thought that developed in Britain and the colonies and was used by the colonists to justify the Revolution by claiming that it was in accord with the principles of the British Constitution. Constitutionalism had two main elements. One was the rule of law, and the other the principle of *consent,* that one cannot be subject to laws or taxation except by duly elected representatives. Both were rights that had been won through struggle with the monarch. Constitutionalism also refers to the tendency in American politics, particularly in the early nineteenth century, to transpose all political questions into constitutional ones.

Consumer revolution   A slow and steady increase over the course of the eighteenth century in the demand for, and purchase of, consumer goods. The consumer revolution of the eighteenth century was closely related to the Industrial Revolution.

Consumerism   An ideology that defined the purchase of goods and services as both an expression of individual identity and essential to the national economy. Increasingly powerful by the 1920s and dominant by the 1950s, consumerism urged people to find happiness in the pursuit of leisure and pleasure more than in the work ethic.

Containment   The basic U.S. strategy for fighting the cold war. As used by diplomat George Kennan in a 1947 magazine essay, "containment" referred to the combination of diplomatic, economic, and military programs necessary to hold back Soviet expansionism after World War II.

Contraband of war   In its general sense, contraband of war was property seized from an enemy. But early in the Civil War the term was applied to slaves running to Union lines as a way of preventing owners from reclaiming them. The policy effectively nullified the fugitive slave clause of the U.S. Constitution. It was a first critical step in a process that would lead to a federal emancipation policy the following year.

Cooperationists   Those southerners who opposed immediate secession after the election of Abraham Lincoln in 1860. Cooperationists argued instead that secessionists should wait to see if the new president was willing to "cooperate" with the South's demands.

Copperhead   A northerner who sympathized with the South during the Civil War.

Deindustrialization   The reverse of industrialization, as factory shutdowns decreased the size of the manufacturing sector. Plant closings began to plague the American economy in the 1970s, prompting fears that the nation would lose its industrial base.

Democratic Republicans   One of the two parties to make up the first American party system. Following the fiscal and political views of Jefferson and Madison, Democratic Republicans generally advocated a weak federal government and opposed federal intervention in the economy of the nation.

Détente   This French term for the relaxation of tensions was used to describe the central foreign policy innovation of the Nixon administration—a new, less confrontational relationship with Communism. In addition to opening a dialogue with the People's Republic of China, Nixon sought a more stable, less confrontational relationship with the Soviet Union.

Diffusion   The controversial theory that the problem of slavery would be resolved if the slave economy was allowed to expand, or "diffuse," into the western territories. Southerners developed this theory as early as the 1800s in response to northerners who hoped to restrict slavery's expansion.

Disfranchisement The act of depriving a person or group of voting rights. In the nineteenth century the right to vote was popularly known as the franchise. The Fourteenth Amendment of the Constitution affirmed the right of adult male citizens to vote, but state-imposed restrictions and taxes deprived large numbers of Americans—particularly African Americans—of the vote from the 1890s until the passage of the Voting Rights Act of 1964.

Domestic patriarchy The practice of defining the family by the husband and father, and wives and children as his domestic dependents. Upon marriage a wife's property became her husband's, and children owed obedience and labor to the family until they reached adulthood. In combination with an exclusive male suffrage, domestic patriarchy described the political as well as the social system that prevailed among free Americans until the twentieth century.

Downsizing American corporations' layoffs of both blue- and white-collar workers in an attempt to become more efficient and competitive. Downsizing was one of the factors that made Americans uneasy about the economy in the 1990s, despite the impressive surge in the stock market.

Dust Bowl Across much of the Great Plains, decades of wasteful farming practices combined with several years of drought in the early 1930s to produce a series of massive dust storms that blew the topsoil across hundreds of miles. The area in Texas and Oklahoma affected by these storms became known as the Dust Bowl.

E-commerce Short for "electronic commerce," this was the term for the Internet-based buying and selling that was one of the key hopes for the computer-driven postindustrial economy. The promise of e-commerce was still unfulfilled by the start of the twenty-first century.

Encomienda A system of labor developed by the Spanish in the New World in which Spanish settlers (*encomenderos*) compelled groups of Native Americans to work for them. The *encomendero* owned neither the land nor the Indians who worked for him, but had the unlimited right to compel a particular group of Indians to work for him. This system was unique to the New World; nothing precisely like it had existed in Europe or elsewhere.

"Establishment" The elite of mainly Ivy League–educated, Anglo-Saxon, Protestant, male, liberal northeasterners that supposedly dominated Wall Street and Washington after World War II. The Establishment's support for corporations, activist government, and containment engendered hostility from opposite poles of the political spectrum—from conservatives and Republicans like Richard Nixon at one end and from the New Left and the Movement at the other. Although many of the post–World War II leaders of the United States did tend to share common origins and ideologies, this elite was never as powerful, self-conscious, or unified as its opponents believed.

Eugenics The practice of attempting to solve social problems through the control of human reproduction. Drawing on the authority of evolutionary biology, eugenists enjoyed considerable influence in the United States, especially on issues of corrections and public health, from the turn of the century through World War II. Applications of this pseudoscience included the identification of "born" criminals by physical characteristics and "better baby" contests at county fairs.

Federalists One of the two political parties to make up the first American party system. Following the fiscal and political policies proposed by Alexander Hamilton, Federalists generally advocated the importance of a strong federal government, including federal intervention in the economy of the new nation.

Feminism An ideology insisting on the fundamental equality of women and men. The feminists of the 1960s differed over how to achieve that equality: while liberal feminists mostly demanded equal rights for women in the workplace and in politics, radical feminists more thoroughly condemned the capitalist system and male oppression and demanded equality in both private and public life.

Feudalism A social and political system that developed in Europe in the Middle Ages under which powerful lords offered less powerful noblemen protection in return for their loyalty. Feudalism also included the economic system of *manorialism,* under which dependent serfs worked on the manors controlled by those lords.

Fire-eaters Militant southerners who pushed for secession in the 1850s.

Flexible response The defense doctrine of the Kennedy and Johnson administrations. Abandoning the Eisenhower administration's heavy emphasis on nuclear weapons, flexible response stressed the buildup of the nation's conventional and special forces so that the president had a range of military options in response to Communist aggression.

Front Early twentieth-century mechanized wars were fought along a battle line or "front" separating opposing sides. By World War II, tactical innovations—blitzkrieg, parachute troops, gliders, and amphibious landings—complicated warfare by breaking through, disrupting, or bypassing the front. The front thus became a more fluid boundary than the fortified trench lines of World War I. The term also acquired a political meaning, particularly for labor and the left. A coalition of parties supporting (or opposing) an agreed-upon line could be called a "popular front."

Gentility A term without precise meaning that represented all that was polite, civilized, refined, and fashionable. It was everything that vulgarity was not. Because the term had no precise meaning, it was always subject to negotiation, striving, and anxiety as Americans, beginning in the eighteenth century, tried to show others that they were genteel through their manners, their appearance, and their styles of life.

Glass ceiling The invisible barrier of discrimination that prevented female white-collar workers from rising to top executive positions in corporations.

Greenbackers Those who advocated currency inflation by keeping the type of money printed during the Civil War, known as "greenbacks," in circulation.

Gridlock The political traffic jam that tied up the federal government in the late 1980s and the 1990s. Gridlock developed from the inability of either major party to control both the presidency and Congress for any extended period of time. More fundamentally, gridlock reflected the inability of any party or president to win a popular mandate for a bold legislative program.

Horizontal integration More commonly known as "monopoly." An industry was "horizontally integrated" when a single company took control of virtually the entire market for a specific product. John D. Rockefeller's Standard Oil came close to doing this.

Humanism A Renaissance intellectual movement that focused on the intellectual and artistic achievements of humankind. Under the patronage of Queen Isabel, Spain became a center of European humanism.

Immediatism The variant antislavery sentiment that demanded immediate (as opposed to gradual) personal and federal action against the institution of slavery. This approach was most closely associated with William Lloyd Garrison and is dated from the publication of Garrison's newspaper, *The Liberator,* in January 1831.

Imperialism A process of extending dominion over territories beyond the national boundaries of a state. In the eighteenth century, Britain extended imperial control over North America through settlement, but in the 1890s, imperial influence was generally exercised through indirect rule. Subject peoples generally retained some local autonomy while the imperial power controlled commerce and defense. Few Americans went to the Philippines as settlers, but many passed through as tourists, missionaries, traders, and soldiers.

Individualism The social and political philosophy celebrating the central importance of the individual human being in society. Insisting on the rights of the individual in relationship to the group, individualism was one of the intellectual bases of capitalism and democracy. The resurgent individualism of the 1920s, with its emphasis on each American's freedom and fulfillment, was a critical element of the decade's emergent consumerism and Republican dominance.

Industrious revolution Beginning in the late seventeenth century in western Europe and extending to the North American colonies in the eighteenth century, a fundamental change in the way people worked, as they worked harder and organized their households to produce goods that could be sold, so they could have money to pay for the new consumer goods they wanted.

Initiative, recall, and referendum   First proposed by the People's Party's Omaha Platform (1892), along with the direct election of senators and the secret ballot, as measures to subject corporate capitalism to democratic controls. Progressives, chiefly in western and midwestern states, favored them as a check on the power of state officials. The *initiative* allows legislation to be proposed by petition. The *recall* allows voters to remove public officials, and the *referendum* places new laws or constitutional amendments on the ballot for the direct approval of the voters.

Interest group   An association whose members organize to exert political pressure on officials or the public. Unlike political parties, whose platforms and slates cover nearly every issue and office, an interest group focuses on a narrower list of concerns reflecting the shared outlook of its members. With the decline of popular politics around the turn of the twentieth century, business, religious, agricultural, women's, professional, neighborhood, and reform associations created a new form of political participation.

Isolationist   Between World War I and World War II, the United States refused to join the League of Nations, scaled back its military commitments abroad, and sought to maintain its independence of action in foreign affairs. These policies were called isolationist, although some historians prefer the term "independent internationalist," in recognition of the United States' continuing global influence. In the late 1930s, isolationists favored policies aimed at distancing the United States from European affairs and building a national defense based on air power and hemispheric security.

Joint-stock company   A form of business organization that was a forerunner to the modern corporation. The joint-stock company was used to raise both capital and labor for New World ventures. Shareholders contributed either capital or their labor for a period of years.

Judicial nationalism   The use of the judiciary to assert the primacy of the national government over state and local government and the legal principle of contract over principles of local custom.

Keynesian economics   The theory, named after the English economist John Maynard Keynes, that advocated the use of "countercyclical" fiscal policy. This meant that during good times the government should pay down the debt, so that during bad times, it could afford to stimulate the economy with deficit spending.

Liberalism   A body of political thought that traces its origins to John Locke and whose chief principles are consent, freedom of conscience, and property. Liberalism held that people could not be governed except by their own consent and that the purpose of government was to protect people as well as their property.

Linked economic development   A form of economic development that ties together a variety of enterprises so that development in one stimulates development in others, for example, those that provide raw materials, parts, or transportation.

Manifest destiny   A term first coined in 1845 by journalist John O'Sullivan to express the belief, widespread among antebellum Americans, that the United States was destined to expand across the North American continent to the Pacific and had an irrefutable right to the lands absorbed in this expansion. This belief was frequently justified on the grounds of claims to political and racial superiority.

Market revolution   The term used to designate the period of the early nineteenth century, roughly 1815–1830, during which internal dependence on cash markets and wages became widespread.

Mass production   A system of efficient, high-volume manufacturing based on division of labor into repetitive tasks, simplification, and standardization of parts, increasing use of specialized machinery, and careful supervision. Emerging since the nineteenth century, mass production reached a critical stage of development with Henry Ford's introduction of the moving assembly line at his Highland Park automobile factory. Mass production drove the prosperity of the 1920s and helped make consumerism possible.

Massive resistance   The rallying cry of southern segregationists who pledged to oppose the integration of the schools ordered by the Supreme Court in *Brown v. Board of Education* in 1954. The tactics of massive resistance included legislation, demonstrations, and violence.

Massive retaliation   The defense doctrine of the Eisenhower administration which promised "instant, massive retaliation" with nuclear weapons in response to Soviet aggression.

McCarthyism   The hunt for Communist subversion in the United States in the first years of the cold war. Democrats, in particular, used the term, a reference to the sometimes disreputable tactics of Republican Senator Joseph R. McCarthy of Wisconsin, in order to question the legitimacy of the conservative anti-Communist crusade.

Mercantilism   An economic theory developed in early-modern Europe to explain and guide the growth of European nation-states. Its goal was to strengthen the state by making the economy serve its interests. According to the theory of mercantilism, the world's wealth, measured in gold and silver, was fixed; that is, it could never be increased. As a result, each nation's chief economic objective must be to secure as much of the world's wealth as possible. One nation's gain was necessarily another's loss. Colonies played an important part in the theory of mercantilism. Their role was to serve as sources of raw materials and as markets for manufactured goods for the mother country alone.

Middle ground   The region between European and Indian settlements in North America that was neither fully European nor fully Indian, but rather a new world created out of two different traditions. The middle ground came into being every time Europeans and Indians met, needed each other, and could not (or would not) achieve what they wanted through use of force.

Millennialism   A strain of Protestant belief that holds that history will end with the thousand-year reign of Christ (the millennium). Some Americans saw the Great Awakening, the French and Indian War, and the Revolution as signs that the millennium was about to begin in America, and this belief infused Revolutionary thought with an element of optimism. Millennialism was also one aspect of a broad drive for social perfection in nineteenth-century America.

Modernization   The process by which developing countries in the third world were to become more like the United States—i.e., capitalist, independent, and anti-Communist. Confidence about the prospects for modernization was one of the cornerstones of liberal foreign policy in the 1960s.

Moral suasion   The strategy of using persuasion (as opposed to legal coercion) to convince individuals to alter their behavior. In the antebellum years, moral suasion generally implied an appeal to religious values.

Mutual aid societies   Organizations through which people of relatively meager means pooled their resources for emergencies. Usually, individuals paid small amounts in dues and were able to borrow large amounts in times of need. In the early nineteenth century, mutual aid societies were especially common among workers in free African American communities.

National Republicans   Over the first 20 years of the nineteenth century, the Republican Party gradually abandoned its Jeffersonian animosity toward an activist federal government and industrial development and became a strong proponent of both of these positions. Embodied in the American system, these new views were fully captured in the party's designation of itself as National Republicans by 1824.

Nativism   A bias against anyone not born in the United States and in favor of native-born Americans. This attitude assumes the superior culture and political virtue of white Americans of Anglo-Saxon descent, or of individuals assumed to have that lineage. During the period 1820–1850, Irish immigrants became the particular targets of nativist attitudes.

New Left   The radical student movement that emerged in opposition to the new liberalism in the 1960s. The New Left condemned the cold war and corporate power and called for the creation of a true "participatory democracy" in the United States. Placing its faith in the radical potential of young, middle-class students, the New Left differed from the "old left" of the late nineteenth and early twentieth centuries, which believed workers would lead the way to socialism.

Patriotism   Love of country. Ways of declaring and displaying national devotion underwent a change from the nineteenth to the twentieth centuries. Whereas politicians were once unblushingly called patriotic, after World War I the title was appropriated to describe the sacrifices of war veterans. Patriotic spectacle in the form of public oration and electoral rallies gave way to military-style commemorations of Armistice Day and the nation's martial heritage.

Political virtue   In the political thought of the early republic, the personal qualities required in citizens if the republic was to survive.

Polygyny   Taking more than one wife. Indian tribes such as the Huron practiced polygyny, and hence they did not object when French traders who already had wives in Europe took Indian women as additional wives.

Popular sovereignty   A solution to the slavery controversy espoused by leading northern Democrats in the 1850s. It held that the inhabitants of western territories should be free to decide for themselves whether or not they wanted to have slavery. In principle, popular sovereignty would prevent Congress from either enforcing or restricting slavery's expansion into the western territories.

Postindustrial economy   The service- and computer-based economy that was succeeding the industrial economy, which had been dominated by manufacturing, at the end of the twentieth century.

Principle of judicial review   The principle of law that recognizes in the judiciary the power to review and rule on the constitutionality of laws. First established in *Marbury v. Madison* (1803) under Chief Justice John Marshall.

Producers ideology   The belief that all those who lived by producing goods shared a common political identity in opposition to those who lived off financial speculation, rent, or interest.

Proprietary colony   Colony established by a royal grant to an individual or family. The proprietary colonies included Maryland, New York, New Jersey, Pennsylvania, and the Carolinas.

Public opinion   Not quite democracy or consent, public opinion was a way of understanding the influence of the citizenry on political calculations. It emerged in the eighteenth century, when it was defined as a crucial source of a government's legitimacy. It was associated with the emergence of a press and a literate public free to discuss, and to question, government policy. In the twentieth century, Freudian psychology and the new mass media encouraged a view of the public as both fickle and powerful. Whereas the popular will (a nineteenth-century concept) was steady and rooted in national traditions, public opinion was variable and based on attitudes that could be aroused or manipulated by advertising.

Realism   A major artistic movement of the late nineteenth century that embraced writers, painters, critics, and photographers. Realists strove to avoid sentimentality and to depict life "realistically."

Reconversion   The economic and social transition from the war effort to peacetime. Americans feared that reconversion might bring a return to the depression conditions of the 1930s.

Re-export trade   Marine trade between two foreign ports, with an intermediate stop in a port of the ship's home nation. United States shippers commonly engaged in the re-export trade during the European wars of the late eighteenth and early nineteenth centuries, when England and France tried to prevent each other from shipping or receiving goods. United States shippers claimed that the intermediate stop in the United States made their cargoes neutral.

Republicanism   A set of doctrines rooted in classical antiquity that held that power is always grasping and dangerous and presents a threat to liberty. Republicanism supplied constitutionalism with a motive by explaining how a balanced constitution could be transformed into a tyranny as grasping men used their power to encroach on the liberty of citizens. In addition, republicanism held that people achieved fulfillment only through participation in public life, as citizens in a republic. Republicanism required the individual to display *virtue* by sacrificing his (or her) private interest for the good of the republic.

Requerimiento **(the Requirement)** A document issued by the Spanish Crown in 1513 in order to clarify the legal bases for the enslavement of hostile Indians. Each *conquistador* was required to read a copy of the *Requerimiento* to each group of Indians he encountered. The *Requerimiento* promised friendship to all Indians who accepted Christianity, but threatened war and enslavement for all those who resisted.

Safety-valve theory An argument commonly made in the nineteenth century that the abundance of western land spared the United States from the social upheavals common to capitalist societies in Europe. In theory, as long as eastern workers had the option of migrating west and becoming independent farmers, they could not be subject to European levels of exploitation. Thus the West was said to provide a "safety-valve" against the pressures caused by capitalist development.

Scalawag A derogatory term referring to southern whites who sympathized with the Republicans during Reconstruction.

Second-wave feminism The reborn women's movement of the 1960s and 1970s that reinterpreted the first wave of nineteenth- and early twentieth-century feminists' insistence on civil rights and called for full economic, reproductive, and political equality.

Separation of powers One of the chief innovations of the Constitution and a distinguishing mark of the American form of democracy, in which the executive, legislative, and judicial branches of government are separated so that they can check and balance each other.

Slave power In the 1850s northern Republicans explained the continued economic and political strength of slavery by claiming that a "slave power" had taken control of the federal government and used its authority to keep slavery alive artificially.

Slave society A society in which slavery is central to the economy and political structure, in contrast to a *society with slaves,* in which the presence of slaves does not alter the fundamental structures of the society.

Slavery A system of extreme social inequality distinguished by the definition of a human being as property, or chattel, and thus, in principle, totally subordinated to the slave owner.

Social Darwinism Darwin's theory of natural selection transferred from biological evolution to human history. Social Darwinists argued that some individuals and groups, particularly racial groups, were better able to survive in the "race of life."

Stagflation The unusual combination of stagnant growth and high inflation that plagued the American economy in the 1970s.

Strict constructionism The view that the Constitution has a fixed, explicit meaning which can be altered only through formal amendment. Loose constructionism is the view that the Constitution is a broad framework within which various interpretations and applications are possible without formal amendment.

Suburbanization The spread of suburban housing developments and, more broadly, of the suburban ideal.

Supply-side economics The controversial theory, associated with economist Arthur Laffer, that drove "Reaganomics," the conservative economic policy of the Reagan administration. In contrast to liberal economic theory, supply-side economics emphasized that producers—the "supply side" of the economic equation—drove economic growth, rather than consumers—the "demand side." To encourage producers to invest more in new production, Laffer and other supply-siders called for massive tax cuts.

Tariff A tax on goods moving across an international boundary. Because the Constitution allows tariffs only on imports, as a political issue the tariff question has chiefly concerned the protection of domestic manufacturing from foreign competition. Industries producing mainly for American consumers have preferred a higher tariff, while farmers and industries aimed at global markets have typically favored reduced tariffs. Prior to the Civil War, the tariff was a symbol of diverging political economies in North and South. The North advocated high tariffs to protect growing domestic manufacturing ("protective tariffs"), and the South opposed high tariffs on the grounds that they increased the cost of imported manufactured goods.

Taylorism   A method for maximizing industrial efficiency by systematically reducing the time and motion involved in each step of the production process. The "scientific" system was designed by Frederick Taylor and explained in his book *The Principles of Scientific Management* (1911).

Universalism   Enlightenment belief that all people are by their nature essentially the same.

Vertical integration   The practice of taking control of every aspect of the production, distribution, and sale of a commodity. For example, Andrew Carnegie vertically integrated his steel operations by purchasing the mines that produced the ore, the railroads that carried the ore to the steel mills, the mills themselves, and the distribution system that carried the finished steel to consumers.

Virtual representation   British doctrine that said that all Britons, even those who did not vote, were represented by Parliament, if not "actually," by representatives they had chosen, then "virtually," because each member of parliament was supposed to act on behalf of the entire realm, not only his constituents or even those who had voted for him.

Voluntarism   A style of political activism that took place largely outside of electoral politics. Voluntarism emerged in the nineteenth century, particularly among those Americans who were not allowed to vote. Thus women formed voluntary associations that pressed for social and political reforms, even though women were excluded from electoral politics.

Waltham system   Named after the system used in early textile mills in Waltham, Massachusetts, the term refers to the practice of bringing all elements of production together in a single factory setting with the application of non-human-powered machinery.

Watergate   The name of the Washington, DC, office and condominium complex where five men with ties to the presidential campaign of Richard Nixon were caught breaking into the headquarters of the Democratic National Committee in June 1972. "Watergate" became the catchall term for the wide range of illegal practices of Nixon and his followers that were uncovered in the aftermath of the break-in.

Whig Party   The political party founded by Henry Clay in the mid-1830s. The name derived from the seventeenth- and eighteenth-century British antimonarchical position and was intended to suggest that the Jacksonian Democrats (and Jackson in particular) sought despotic powers. In many ways the heirs of National Republicans, the Whigs supported economic expansion, but they also believed in a strong federal government to control the dynamism of the market. The Whig Party attracted many moral reformers.

Whitewater   With its echo of Richard Nixon's "Watergate" scandals in the 1970s, "Whitewater" became the catchall term for the scandals that plagued Bill Clinton's presidency in the 1990s. The term came from the name of a real estate development company in Arkansas. Clinton and his wife Hillary supposedly had corrupt dealings with the Whitewater Development Corporation in the 1970s and 1980s that they purportedly attempted to cover up in the 1990s.

Women's rights movement   The antebellum organizing efforts of women on their own behalf, in the attempt to secure a broad range of social, civic, and political rights. This movement is generally dated from the convention of Seneca Falls in 1848. Only after the Civil War would women's rights activism begin to confine its efforts to suffrage.

Photo Credits

Chapter 1: Benson Latin American Collection, University of Texas, Austin, 2, 32; The London Art Archive/Alamy, 3; The Granger Collection, 7; Cahokia Mounds State Historic Site. Photo by Art Grossman, 8; Courtesy of the Trustees of the British Museum, 15; J. Dallet/ agefotostock, 16; Image copyright ©The Metropolitan Museum of Art/ Art Resource, NY, 17; Pierpont Morgan Library/ Art Resource, NY, 20; The Granger Collection, 29; Newberry Library, Chicago/Superstock, 31; The Granger Collection, 33; The Granger Collection, 34; National Museum, Damascus, Syria/Gianni Dagli Orti/The Art Archive, 35.

Chapter 2: Service Historique de la Marine, Vincennes, France/The Bridgeman Art Library, 38, 61; The Bridgeman Art Library, 39; National Anthropological Library, Smithsonian Institution, 43; University of Pennsylvania Museum, object NA9143, image #12972, 47; Wolfgang Kaehler, 48; Pilgrim Hall Museum, Plymouth, MA, 56; The Bridgeman Art Library, 58; Courtesy of the Trustees of The British Museum 59; Service Historique de la Marine, Vincennes, France/ The Bridgeman Art Library, 62; The British Museum/The Art Archive, 63; The Gilcrease Museum, Tulsa OK, 65.

Chapter 3: The Granger Collection, 68, 98; Borough of King's Lynn and West Norfolk, 69; Preservation Virginia, 71; University of Oxford/Ashmolean Museum of Art and Archaeology, 74; Marilyn Angel Wynn/ Nativestock.com, 75; Ira Block/National Geographic Stock/Getty Images, 75; Private Collection/Getty Images, 76; Pierre Dan, Histoire de Barbarie et de ses Corsaires, Paris, 1637, 80; Courtesy of Lester Walker, 92.

Chapter 4: Pennsylvania Academy of the Fine Arts, Philadelphia/The Bridgeman Art Library, 102, 110; Illustration by Walter Rane, 103; Private Collection/ The Bridgeman Art Library, 105; Museum of the City of New York/ The Bridgeman Art Library, 108; Collection of the New-York Historical Society, neg#81885d, 109; North Carolina State Archives, Division of Archives and History, 111; Plymouth County Commissioners, Plymouth Court House, Plymouth, MA/Dublin Seminar for New England Folklife, Concord, MA, 120; North Wind Picture Archives, 121; Springfield Library, Springfield, MA, 126; Museum of the City of New York/The Bridgeman Art Library, 127; ©President and Fellows Harvard University, Peabody Museum, 99-12-10/53121, 132; Kevin Fleming/Corbis, 134; Giraudon/The

Bridgeman Art Library, 136; Chuck Place/ Place Photography, 137.

Chapter 5: Private Collection/The Bridgeman Art Library, 140, 154; Private Collection/ The Bridgeman Art Library, 141; Stowage of the British Slave Ship Brooks under the Regulated Slave Trade Act of 1788/Library of Congress, 147; The Granger Collection, 149; © Royal Geographical Society, 156; Virginia Historical Society, 157; Gibbes Museum, Gift of Mr. Joseph E. Jenkins ©Image Gibbes Museum of Art/Carolina Art Association, 1968.005.0001, 159; Library Company of Philadelphia, 160; Collection of the New-York Historical Society, neg#81577d, 155; Museum of Fine Arts, Boston. Bequest of Buckminster Brown, MD, 95.1359, 162; American Antiquarian Society, 173.

Chapter 6: The Granger Collection, 176, 204; Owned by Kate S. Rowland/Mrs. John Carrere; photography courtesy of Barbara M. Jones/ Mrs. Warner E. Jones. Frontispiece from A Narrative of the Captivity of Mrs. Johnson (Bowie, Md.: Heritage Books, Inc., 1990), 177; Courtesy of Dartmouth College Library, Rauner Specials Collections Library, 177; Washington University, St. Louis, MO/The Bridgeman Art Library, 184; The Granger Collection, 185; Albany Institute of History and Art, Purchase, 1993.44, 186; Hulton Archive/Getty Images, 187; Hulton Archive/Getty Images, 191; The Granger Collection, 193; Vereinigte Ostindische Compagnie bond, 194; The Granger Collection, 198; The Granger Collection, 200; The Manhattan Rare Book Company, 202; MPI/Gerry Images, 206; Division of Military History, National Museum of American History/Smithsonian Institution, 209.

Chapter 7: Reunion des Musees Nationaux/Art Resource, NY, 212, 231; The Granger Collection, 213; Bettmann/Corbis, 218; Library of Congress, 219; Yale University Art Gallery/Art Resource, NY, 221; James Nesterwitz/Alamy Images, 222; Division of Military History, National Museum of American History/Smithsonian Institution, 223; Erich Lessing/Art Resource, NY, 225; The Granger Collection, 226; American Numismatic Association, 235; The Granger Collection, 238; National Gallery of Canada, Ottawa, 242; The Granger Collection, 248; The Colonial Williamsburg Foundation, 251.

Chapter 8: The Granger Collection, 254, 259; Library Company of Philadelphia, 255; The Colonial Williamsburg Foundation.

Gift of the Lasser Family, 256; The Granger Collection, 261; Edward Lawler, Jr., 264; American Antiquarian Society, 266; Maritime Museum of the Atlantic, 272; The Granger Collection, 281; The Granger Collection, 286; The Granger Collection, 287.

Chapter 9: Collection of the New-York Historical Society/The Bridgeman Art Library, 290, 301; The Granger Collection, 291; General Records of the U. S. government, National Archives, 295; American Antiquarian Society, 297; Peter Harholdt/Corbis, 305; Central Library Birmingham, West Midlands, UK/The Bridgeman Art Library, 308; The Granger Collection, 310; American Museum of Textile History, 311; National Portrait Gallery, Smithsonian Institution/Art Resource, NY, 317; The Granger Collection, 320; Franklin Institute, Philadelphia, PA, 323.

Chapter 10: Chicago History Museum/The Bridgeman Art Library, 328, 249; National Portrait Gallery, Smithsonian Institution/Art Resource, NY, 329; Chicago History Museum/ The Bridgeman Art Library, 333; Rare Books and Special Collections, Cornell University, 333; The Granger Collection, 334; Duke University Rare Book, Manuscript and Special Collections Library, 335; Dinodia Images/Alamy, 338; Image ©The Metropolitan Museum of art, New York/Art Resource, NY, 339; Collection of the New-York Historical Society, acc. 1953.251, 340; Wilberforce House, Hull City Museums and Art Galleries, UK/ The Bridgeman Art Library, 341; Library of Virginia, 342; Chicago History Museum/The Bridgeman Art Library, 344; The Granger Collection, 355; Photographs and Prints Division, Schomburg Center for Research in Black Culture, The New York Public Library, Astor, Lenox and Tilden Foundations, 358.

Chapter 11: St. Louis Art Museum/The Bridgeman Art Library, 362, 368; Bentley Historical Library, University of Michigan, 363; The Granger Collection, 366; The Granger Collection, 372; The Granger Collection, 373; Department of Political History, National Museum of American History, Smithsonian Institution, 378; picturehistory.com, 379; Library of Congress, 382; Bettmann/Corbis, 384; Woolrac Museum, Oklahoma/The Bridgeman Art Library, 386; The Granger Collection, 388; American Numismatic Association, 391.

Chapter 12: Geoffrey Clements/Corbis, 398, 409; The Granger Collection, 399; The Granger Collection, 402; Denver Public

Index

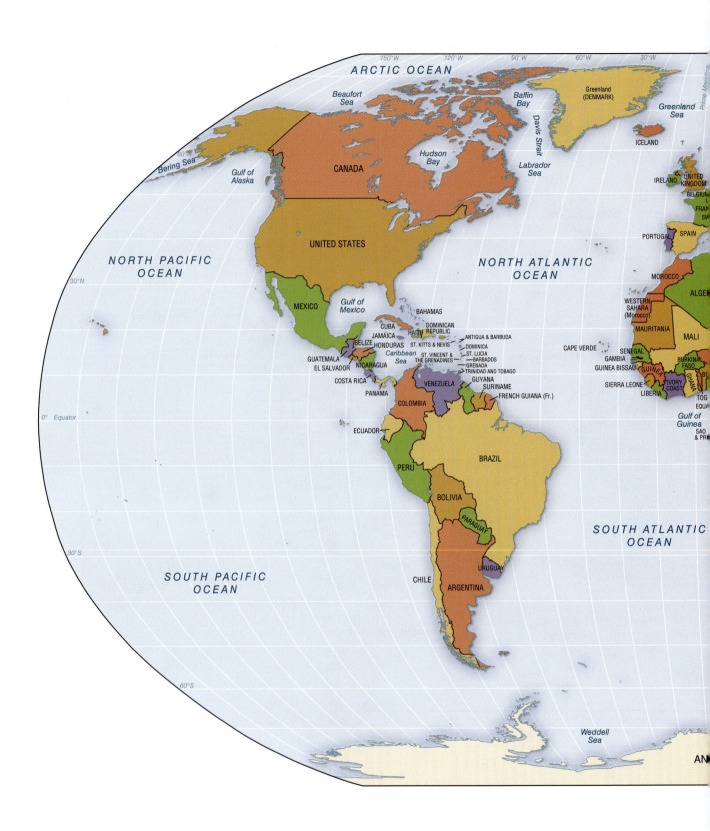

ARCTIC OCEAN

Beaufort
Sea

Baffin
Bay

Greenland
(DENMARK)

Greenland
Sea

ICELAND

Bering Sea

60°N

Gulf of
Alaska

CANADA

Hudson
Bay

Davis Strait

Labrador
Sea

IRELAND

UNITED
KINGDOM

BELGIUM

**NORTH PACIFIC
OCEAN**

UNITED STATES

**NORTH ATLANTIC
OCEAN**

FRANCE
SW

PORTUGAL

SPAIN

30°N

MEXICO

Gulf of
Mexico

BAHAMAS

MOROCCO

WESTERN
SAHARA
(Morocco)

ALGE

CUBA

DOMINICAN
REPUBLIC

JAMAICA

HAITI

ANTIGUA & BARBUDA

BELIZE

HONDURAS

ST. KITTS & NEVIS

DOMINICA

ST. LUCIA

CAPE VERDE

MAURITANIA

MALI

GUATEMALA

NICARAGUA

Caribbean
Sea

BARBADOS

GRENADA

SENEGAL

GAMBIA

BURKINA
FASO

EL SALVADOR

TRINIDAD AND TOBAGO

GUINEA BISSAU

GUINEA

COSTA RICA

ST. VINCENT &
THE GRENADINES

GUYANA

SIERRA LEONE

IVORY
COAST

GHANA

PANAMA

VENEZUELA

SURINAME

LIBERIA

TOG

0° Equator

COLOMBIA

FRENCH GUIANA (Fr.)

EQUA

ECUADOR

Gulf of
Guinea

SAO
& PR

BRAZIL

PERU

BOLIVIA

PARAGUAY

**SOUTH ATLANTIC
OCEAN**

30°S

**SOUTH PACIFIC
OCEAN**

URUGUAY

CHILE

ARGENTINA

60°S

Weddell
Sea

AN